DATE DUE

MAY 0 6 2009

FIGHTING FAMINE IN NORTH CHINA

Fighting Famine in North China

State, Market, and Environmental Decline,

1690s–1990s

LILLIAN M. LI

Stanford University Press
Stanford, California 2007

Stanford University Press
Stanford, California

Printed in the United States of America on acid-free, archival-quality paper

Library of Congress Cataloging-in-Publication Data

Li, Lillian M.
    Fighting famine in North China : state, market, and environmental
decline, 1690s–1990s / Lillian M. Li.
        p.   cm.
    Includes bibliographical references and index.
    ISBN 978-0-8047-5304-3 (cloth : alk. paper)
        1. Famines—China—History.   2. Disaster relief—China—History.
3. China—Economic conditions—History.   4. Hebei Sheng (China)—
Economic conditions—History.   I. Title.
HC430.F3L35   2007
363.80951'1—dc22   2006037715

Typeset by James P. Brommer in 10/13 Garamond

For Stephen

CONTENTS

TABLES

FIGURES

MAPS AND PHOTOGRAPHS

xv

ACKNOWLEDGMENTS

I BECAME INTERESTED in the subject of famine in Chinese history because of its human importance, and because of the intellectual challenges it poses. It raises critically important historical questions about the relationship of the state, economy, and environment. Or perhaps I remembered my mother's admonishing me to eat *every grain of rice* in the bowl because my sisters and brothers in China must be hungry. Whatever the conscious or subconscious motives, when I first became involved in this project, I never dreamt that it would become almost a lifetime employment. I have been fortunate to have been given the opportunity to pursue this subject at length. As Chinese history has taught, to engage in scholarship is a precious privilege that also confers a great responsibility. My endeavors have depended on the kindness of an international community of scholars and the support of academic institutions that have provided the resources to undertake a such a long-term project.

For generous support I am grateful to the Fairbank Center for East Asian Research at Harvard, the American Council of Learned Societies, the Social Science Research Council, the National Endowment for the Humanities, the Bunting Institute, the Committee on Scholarly Communication with the People's Republic of China, the Woodrow Wilson International Center for Scholars, and the Institute for Advanced Study. Swarthmore College has provided both time and support for research including the Mary Albertson Faculty Fellowship.

The National Palace Museum in Taipei and the First Historical Archives in Beijing provided access to the archives of the Qing period, including the grain price data that are a key part of this study. Historian Ju Deyuan and archivist Wang Daorui were especially helpful in Beijing.

Beijing Agricultural University, now the China Agricultural University, served as my host institution in 1989 and later. I am especially grateful to Shi Yuanchun, then president of the university, and Professors Li Yunzhu, Dong Kaichen, Ke Bingsheng, and others for sharing their expertise about agriculture in North China and for facilitating visits to Quzhou, Wei, and Linzhang counties. They also provided introductions to the Ministry of Water Conservancy and Hydroelectric Power's Scientific Research Institute in Beijing, and also to the Hebei Province Water Conservancy Office, Hebei Province Agricultural Office, Hebei Province Meteorological Bureau, Hebei Province Grain Bureau, the Hebei Agriculture and Forestry Institute, and the Hebei Academy of

Social Sciences in Shijiazhuang. I am grateful to the many experts and scholars who welcomed me and took the time to brief me on their work and their experiences. I also visited Nanjing Agricultural University, where Professors Song Zhanqing and Cao Xingsui were most helpful.

The Hai River Water Conservancy Commission, Ministry of Water Conservancy and Hydro-electrical Power, arranged an extended tour of water conservancy sites in Hebei in 1989, including the Xidayang Dam; Baiyang Lake; Anxin, Wen'an, and Baodai counties; and the Yongding River. Vice Chief Engineer Wu Zhongjian was an incomparable teacher and gracious guide, sharing with me his vast knowledge of the region.

Zhang Peiyuan, Deputy Director of the Institute of Geography of the Chinese Academy of Sciences, has most generously shared data on rainfall and precipitation on which several key analyses in this book depend.

In Beijing, Professor Wu Chengming gave me the benefit of his insights. Han Guanghui and Wu Jianyong provided guidance in the study of Beijing's history. At the Tianjin Academy of Social Sciences, Liu Haiyan provided access to materials from the Republican period. After the manuscript for this book was completed, I had the opportunity to meet Professor Xia Mingfang and his research group on famine history at the Institute for Qing History at People's University, and to learn about the new work that is currently being done on this topic.

I am grateful for the wisdom and knowledge that valued scholar-friends have imparted over the years. Pierre-Étienne Will's work has provided an important foundation for understanding famine relief in the Qing, and I greatly value the knowledge of sources and the critical perspective that he has generously shared over the years. Thomas Rawski has challenged economic historians to be better economists, and has been my economics guru and coach. Susan Naquin has constantly shared with me sources and insights about North China and Qing history. Alison Dray-Novey's knowledge of Beijing history and sources made Chapter 5 possible. James Lee generously shared with me the grain price data from Fengtian, numerous other sources and references, as well as his enthusiasm for quantitative history. Peter Perdue provided a method for solar-lunar conversion of the price data, and valuable perspectives on our mutual interests. Robert Marks shared theories and methodology regarding price studies.

Other scholars and friends have provided important references, shared their unpublished materials, or read sections of draft manuscript: Beatrice Bartlett, Richard Bohr, Pamela Crossley, Helen Dunstan, Mark Elliott, Linda Grove, Marta Hansen, Charles Hayford, Martin Heijdra, Manbun Kwan, Philip Kuhn, Jean Oi, Charles Peterson, Evelyn Rawski, William Rowe, Paul Smith, Richard von Glahn, Tyrene White, R. Bin Wong, and Yunxiang Yan.

At Swarthmore College, economist Frederic Pryor and mathematician-statistician Gudmund Iversen have been wise and patient consultants on quantitative methods and on numerous occasions reviewed various parts of the price studies. Other members of the Economics Department, including Stephen O'Connell and F. M. Scherer, have been most helpful. Asian Studies colleagues—notably Tyrene White, Haili Kong, and Alan Berkowitz—have shared expertise of various types. History Department colleagues have provided a supportive environment for research as well as teaching. In addition, Keith Head, Oliver Richard, Yi Yang, and Mark Tong served as research assistants when they were students. Theresa Brown and Douglas Willen have lent valuable technical support.

The quantitative analysis in this book was completed by Scott Hodges, whose work is found in Chapters 4, 7, 8, and 9. His special contributions are indicated in the Notes and Appendices.

Yan Ke undertook the research in local gazetteers at the Library of Congress. Chen Chia-hsiu assisted me in the Taipei archives. Ren Yunlan located materials in Tianjin.

The maps in the book were created by Geoffrey Compton using the Chinese Historical Geographic Information Service (CHGIS), Version 1.0: 1820 Qing Dynasty (Cambridge, MA: Harvard Yenching Institute, April 2002). Merrick Lex Berman provided guidance in the use of this source.

Librarians Timothy Connor (Harvard-Yenching Library), Nancy Hearst (Fairbank Center, Harvard University), Martin Heijdra (Gest Library, Princeton University), and Mi Chu Wiens (Library of Congress) have been unfailing scholarly consultants.

Chapter 5 was previously published in the *Journal of Asian Studies*, and Chapter 7 in the *Journal of Economic History*. I particularly thank the editors of the latter for their help (and for awarding me the Arthur H. Cole Prize of the Economic History Association). A portion of Chapter 10 was published in a special issue of *Chengshi yanjiu.*

I have presented research for this book to various academic gatherings over the years. I would particularly like to acknowledge the formative experience gained at the Workshop on Food and Famine in Chinese History at Harvard in 1980. A selection of papers, with an introductory essay by me, was published in the *Journal of Asian Studies* (August 1982). The Workshop and Conference on Economic Methods for Chinese Historical Research (1987 in Honolulu; 1988 in Oracle, Arizona) were also rich in ideas and energy. Papers were published in *Chinese History in Economic Perspective* edited by Thomas Rawski and myself (1992). The Second Conference on Modern Chinese Economic History held by the Academia Sinica in Taipei (1989) was most stimulating. Presentations at California Institute of Technology (1998), Cornell University (1999), and the Tianjin Academy of Social Sciences (2001) provided useful feedback.

Muriel Bell of Stanford University Press has made a lasting contribution to the field of Asian studies through her sponsorship of notable scholarly publications. I thank her for including this book among them.

I owe special thanks to members of my family who have contributed directly and indirectly to this project. When it was in its first stage, my father, Zen Zuh Li, used his literary skills to decipher tough passages for me, and he continued to take an interest in the work. My third sister Li Yunzhu and brother-in-law Shi Yuanchun always welcomed me to their home in Beijing, and their contributions to agricultural science in North China were an inspiration to me. My third brother, Li Yisheng, used to joke that he was my "representative-in-China" because of the numerous times he cheerfully took care of me. My second sister, Ellen Li, has been the head of the New York-New Jersey branch of the family.

Above all, I express my gratitude to my husband, Stephen Dale, whose own historical scholarship sets a high standard and whose understanding, encouragement, and devotion have meant so much.

FIGHTING FAMINE IN NORTH CHINA

Introduction

IN THE 1920S when China was called "the Land of Famine" by an American relief worker, the phrase immediately gained currency, not only internationally but with the Chinese public as well.[1] It seemed to capture exactly the situation of China—a land where floods and droughts occurred ceaselessly, where famines of huge dimensions followed one after the other, and where poverty and hunger seemed ever present. From the mid-nineteenth century onward, the disasters had been deadlier and more frequent. The Yellow River, called "China's Sorrow," shifted its course in the 1850s, causing great hardship. Man-made disasters such as the Taiping and other rebellions of mid-century wreaked great physical destruction and exacted a human toll probably in excess of 20 million. An extensive drought in northern China in the 1870s may have cost 9 to 13 million lives. Toward the end of the nineteenth century and the first half of the twentieth, the man-made catastrophes of rebellion, revolution, and war alternated with the natural disasters of flood, drought, and locusts. The plight of China attracted international sympathy and assistance, and both Chinese and foreigners wondered if China would ever cease being the land of famine.

Of course China had not always seemed poor and backward to the West. For Marco Polo and other travelers, China had been the land of riches—displaying an abundance unknown in the Europe of the thirteenth century.[2] When Jesuits such as Matteo Ricci arrived in China in the late sixteenth and seventeenth centuries, it was Chinese learning that they admired, and in the eighteenth century French *philosophes* such as Voltaire found China's scholar-bureaucrat system a model of enlightened government. Indeed the view of China as a prosperous and cultured civilization was well grounded in the historical reality of most of the thirteenth to eighteenth centuries, with the notable exception of periods of transition from one dynastic regime to another. From the Southern Song period through the Ming dynasty, the twelfth through sixteenth centuries, the development of Chinese culture—literature, arts, and scholarship—was supported by a bureaucracy selected by civil service examinations. The development of commerce and science proceeded concurrently. In the Qing period, under the Manchu rulers, the boundaries of the empire were extended to include not just the provinces within the Great Wall but also Mongolia, Xinjiang, Tibet, Taiwan, as well as Manchuria itself.

Yet even during the periods of prosperity and expansion, the occurrence or possibility of famine in some part of the empire never disappeared, and the responsibility to avert it was part of the political ideology. China in ancient or premodern history may or may not have experienced more famine than any other empire or territory of comparable size—it would be impossible to determine this—but the consciousness of famine played an important ideological role in the formation of state policy and shaping of state goals. No other civilization has had such a continuous tradition of thinking about famine, and no other nation's modern history has been so influenced by hunger and famine. It is in this sense that China could be called the land of famine.

The legendary origins of the Chinese state emphasize the control over nature achieved by the ancient sage emperors, Yao, Shun, and Yu. The latter tamed the so-called nine rivers (dragons) of mythical prehistoric China and founded the Xia dynasty. These legends embody the Confucian notion that nature is dangerous and must be controlled by a meritorious ruler. The concept of the Mandate of Heaven, articulated by the Confucian follower Mencius in the third century B.C., stated clearly that weak and incompetent rulers would inevitably lose the mandate, which would in turn be claimed by a new dynasty. Indeed Yu showed his moral legitimacy when his predecessor had not prevented a great flood from taking place, and his achievement is immortalized in the slogan "Yu the Great controls the waters" [*Da Yu zhishui*].³ Likewise the last Xia dynasty ruler allowed a drought to rage for several years, but Tang was able to assume moral leadership and credit for stopping the crisis, and he established the next dynasty, the Shang.⁴ According to the theory of the dynastic cycle, strong early emperors would encourage the tilling of fields and nourish the people, but they would be followed by weak emperors who would allow natural calamities to take their tolls, and eventually righteous rebellions against unjust rule would develop. Earthquakes and floods were natural portents of the imminent demise of the dynasty. All the more reason why rulers should strive to prevent their occurrence whenever possible, or at least minimize their effect.

The ancient texts clearly articulated the principle that famines were not caused by nature, but by the negligence of the rulers. Xunzi, another of Confucius's important disciples, wrote:

> If the Way is cultivated [followed] without deviation, then Nature cannot cause misfortune. Therefore flood and drought cannot cause a famine, extreme cold or heat cannot cause illness, and evil spiritual beings cannot cause misfortune. . . . [But] if people violate the Way and act foolishly, then Nature cannot give them good fortune. There will be famine before flood or drought approaches. . . . This cannot be blamed on Heaven; this is how the Way works. Therefore one who understands the distinctive functions of Heaven and man may be called a perfect man.

Thus, Xunzi firmly believed in man's ability to control nature. "Therefore to neglect human effort and admire Heaven is to miss the nature of things."⁵

Many of the important principles and instruments of famine prevention originated in the ancient times. The concept of the ever-normal granary, for example, is attributed to Mencius and may have had even earlier origins.⁶ The officials were to establish such granaries, buying grain when the price was low and selling it when the price was high, thus keeping grain prices low and stable. Such grain stocks could also be distributed as famine relief. The sage ruler was to help tame the rivers by sponsoring river control projects. He also had the responsibility for maintaining agricultural productivity. If floods occurred, it was because the rivers had not been properly controlled. If droughts occurred, their effects could be alleviated by irrigation and their human suffering stemmed by famine relief. A natural calamity (*tianzai*) might cause a harvest failure (*huang* or *zaihuang*), but the harvest failure did not necessarily result in a famine or "great hunger" (*ji, daji,* or *jihuang*). The purpose of imperial or official intervention was first to prevent the occurrence of famine, but secondly, if famine occurred, to take measures to restore agricultural production.

Over the course of imperial China's long history, such principles were honored more in the breach than the practice, but it seems important to recognize that the principles did endure, and they shaped expectations of imperial and bureaucratic responsibility. Under Legalist influence, the basic administrative measures to deal with famine were codified in the first imperial dynasty, the Qin (221–206 B.C.).[7] By the Song period (960–1279 A.D.), famine relief was one of the several areas designated by the great scholar officials as needing reform and renewed attention. Not only rulers and officials should mind these institutions, but local elites—scholars, landlords, and other notables—should also sponsor famine relief, granaries, and charitable works. By the late Ming period (1368–1644), traditions of philanthropic works were well established in many localities, particularly in the more prosperous areas of southern and central China, such as the Lower Yangzi valley.

The importance attached to *huangzheng*—the administration of official disaster relief—can be seen in the late imperial historical records, where the chronology of disasters, the methods of agriculture, the building of granaries, and the maintenance of river control were all detailed.[8] Local gazetteers also devoted large sections to these topics. In addition, especially from the fourteenth century onward, there were numerous agricultural manuals, famine relief treatises, essays on river control, and other compilations—all bearing eloquent testimony of the importance of famine prevention and relief in the administrative agenda.

Famines of catastrophic proportions characterized the later part of the Ming dynasty during the mid-sixteenth and early seventeenth centuries, compounding, or perhaps causing, widespread rebellions.[9] When the new Manchu rulers assumed the throne in 1644, they needed to transform their tribal and military style of governance to take into account a large agrarian economy. For the great emperor Kangxi, who reigned for more than sixty years (1662–1722), the south was a source of agricultural abundance and human talent that he needed to understand and command. He and his successors, Yongzheng (1723–35) and Qianlong (1736–95), and their top advisors, drew on the traditional ideas and experience about political economy to develop the institutions and techniques of agricultural support, grain storage, river conservancy, and famine relief to a degree of efficiency never before known in Chinese history. Because these efforts were recorded in great detail, it is possible to study the ways in which imperial policy actually affected economic life. (This has been especially so since the Qing archives were opened for scholarly use in the late 1970s.) In the eighteenth century, China experienced a level of peace and prosperity that was unprecedented, even as territorial conquest and diplomacy extended the boundaries of the empire.

Although these triumphs could be understood as the high point of the Qing dynastic cycle, there were other historical developments, barely perceived at the time, that can now be seen as unprecedented and not cyclical in nature. The first of these was a great surge in population, which is usually estimated to have doubled from 150 million people in 1700 to 300 million in 1800.[10] By mid-nineteenth century, population size was probably about 430 million. In the late nineteenth century through the first half of the twentieth, the rates of increase slowed, most likely due to the high mortality from military and other disasters. Nevertheless, by 1950, the population was close to 600 million. During the second half of the twentieth century, under the People's Republic of China, population more than doubled. By the turn of the twenty-first century, it was about 1.2 billion. The reasons for these rates of growth, as well as their exact magnitude, are not completely understood, but their impact on the history of the twentieth century is indisputable.

Environmental decline was another important trend. The human impact on the forests, soils, and rivers of China was a centuries-old historical process, but by the eighteenth century, the ef-

fects of human encroachment on land, forest, and water resources was becoming evident to officials and local elites of many parts of China. Increasing population size demanded greater agricultural productivity from these diminished natural resources, thus vastly compounding the task of
"feeding the people." The containment of waterways through levees and dikes, necessitated by
denser land settlement, increased the possibility of damage in times of heavy downpours. In the
second half of the twentieth century, industrial and urban needs have further depleted land and
water resources, and chemical pollutants have threatened air quality as well as soil and water.

Increased population pressure on the land in the late Qing period created an even greater need
for bureaucratic interventions—such as more investment in river control or greater emergency
grain reserves—just at a point when the dynasty's capability was much diminished by internal decay—in the form of weak emperors, corrupt bureaucracy, and rebellions. At the same time, a more
visible threat emerged in the form of Western imperialism in the nineteenth century—in all its
military, economic, and cultural aspects—further reducing the possibility of imperial leadership
just when it was most needed.

In the early twentieth century, promising new opportunities for commercial development and
industrialization were undercut by the lack of a strong central government as well as foreign aggression. The political instability brought about by warlords, Japanese invasion, and Communist
insurgency made hunger and rural poverty even more visible problems. Although forced to retreat
to the northwest, Communist forces dramatically expanded their control over most of northern
China and large parts of central China by appealing to the rural villagers' genuine grievances over
their material hardships and channeling them into social and political action. Although the reasons for the ultimate victory of the Chinese Communist Party continue to be hotly debated, there
can be no question that hunger and poverty were the fundamental issues addressed by Mao's rural
strategy; without those issues, the revolution would have taken a very different path. Widespread
devastation from internal warfare and Japanese invasion made more profound the already familiar problem of rural immiseration. A large portion of the urban middle class and intellectuals, although relatively sheltered from poverty, also became convinced that China's rural problems urgently needed to be addressed.

In the second half of the twentieth century, under the People's Republic of China, the need to
feed a rapidly expanding population played a key role in the shifts in party policy concerning land
distribution and the organization of production. From land reform through collectivization and
finally decollectivization, the need to provide food self-sufficiency became increasingly acute as the
population size doubled. Faced with severe limitations of land and other resources, the party first
emphasized the rationing of land and grain, as well as other redistributive methods, and later the
collectivization of agriculture, which gave the state further control over scarce resources. The Great
Leap Forward essentially shifted the emphasis from redistributive mechanisms to grandiose and
fantastic schemes for rapidly increasing production. The resulting famine caused the death of at
least 30 million people, the greatest famine in world history, and one that was almost entirely
man-made. It is one of history's most deeply ironic tragedies that a government that came to
power on the basis of its promise to address the issue of hunger only succeeded in making it a
more central and urgent issue.

In the 1960s and 1970s, the renewed emphasis on subsistence and regional self-sufficiency was
expressed in the slogan "Taking grain as the key link." After Mao's death in 1976, the party's emphasis shifted to economic reform that included decollectivization of agriculture, incentives for investment in industries, opening up to foreign trade and investment. Yet this radical reshaping of

"socialism with Chinese characteristics" did not displace a type of food fundamentalism that had been so deeply engrained in the Chinese experience. In the same decades that the market economy was liberalized, population control policies, enacted in order to support economic growth, were the opposite of liberal. The strict enforcement of the one-child policy—with its often tragic personal outcomes such as late-term abortions and infanticide—represented the latest form of state intervention in the population-food equation.

In the 1990s, the success of economic reforms seemed to have brought security to most urban and rural Chinese, to the extent that obesity, not malnutrition, became a problem among spoiled city children who were called "little emperors." Yet food self-sufficiency remained a sensitive issue for the leadership and for technocrats. In 1989, on the eve of the fortieth anniversary of the establishment of the People's Republic of China, and just months after the Tiananmen demonstrations and shootings, the *People's Daily* proclaimed, "Our country's accomplishment in disaster relief work receives the attention of the world: Socialism has sent running 'China the land of famine.'"[11] At other times, however, it was convenient to invoke China's still-precarious population-land situation. In interviews during his 1997 visit to the United States Jiang Zemin pointed out that China had the task of feeding 22 percent of the world's population on only 7 percent of its arable land; therefore, political dissent and democratization had to take second place.[12]

The importance of famine in shaping Chinese history of the last few centuries can be contrasted with the European experience. Mortality crises were not unknown in Europe of the Middle Ages and later, but they were not considered regular and inevitable occurrences. Europeans were unprepared for the great famine in northern Europe from 1315–22 because there had been no bad weather since the twelfth century, and there would not again be weather-related crises until the sixteenth century. Famine was experienced not as a periodic phenomenon, but as a catastrophic event that must be a form of divine punishment for human sins.[13] The sense of retribution was even greater during the Black Death, the plague that tormented Europe just a few decades later and that exacted a great mortality.[14] The religious interpretation of such events is not surprising given the central role of the church in medieval society and the weakness of the state. Charitable relief of suffering was also the undertaking of the churches, not the secular authorities.

Although Europe experienced many mortality crises in the sixteenth century, historians now emphasize that the link between nutritional status and mortality was probably indirect, and infectious disease probably played a more pivotal role. High mortality was not a necessary outcome of food scarcity as measured by high food prices.[15] The eventual disappearance of the plague is given greater credit for ending mortality crises in Europe than improvements in agriculture or economic developments.[16] The links between poor harvests (as measured by high food prices) and mortality were weakening in the seventeenth century, and they were severed by the eighteenth century.[17] After the 1740s, "subsistence crises no longer produced major mortality peaks." Europe's "last subsistence crisis" took place in 1816–17. Due partly to weather and partly to the disruptions of warfare, this crisis affected most of Europe, and its effects were felt elsewhere in the "western world."[18] In the end, state intervention helped to relieve the crisis, not religious charity. Various governments, such as those of France, the Netherlands, and Prussia, took advantage of large quantities of grain that could be supplied from the United States and Russia. They did not distribute the grain as relief, but sold it at below-market prices.[19] Such forms of intervention resembled the methods of below-market price sales known in China. After this, large-scale food shortages in Europe due to harvest or other crises did not necessarily result in major increases in mortality, it is argued.[20] The Irish potato famine of 1840s did result in high rates of mortality, but it was restricted to Ireland. Although crop failure was the direct cause, the famine has always been controversial, blamed on factors ranging from backward Irish farming techniques to failures in British policy.[21]

The difference between the role of famines in Europe and China was not simply that one developed beyond self-subsistence and mortality crises two or three centuries earlier than the other, but that from earliest times, there were different cultural and social meanings associated with the phenomenon. In China, the control of famine was a responsibility of the ruler; hence, it played a role in the ideological foundations of the Chinese state. Indeed the very fact of the continuity, albeit not unbroken, of a centralized state in "China" since the Qin-Han empires in the third century B.C. forms a fundamental difference with "Europe," when the kingdoms and principalities that fragmented after the Roman Empire were never brought back together into a single state. Not coincidentally, state formation in nineteenth-century Europe coincided with the disappearance of subsistence crises. In the premodern period, there were only a few major mortality crises that affected all of "Europe" at the same time, and almost none that affected all of China at the same time. Yet in the Chinese empire in the Ming and the Qing periods, a famine in one region was considered the central government's responsibility and required intervention, at least theoretically. In Europe, no single state was charged with the responsibility for conditions beyond its borders even when many states were affected at the same time.

In Europe from the late seventeenth century, public demonstrations over food were a frequent phenomenon. The mob protests over bread prices in revolutionary Paris are the best known, and Marie Antoinette's "Let them eat cake" symbolized the disregard of the French monarchs for the welfare of the people. The grain blockages, price riots, and other forms of protest in France, England, and elsewhere were caused by fear of hunger and dearth, but they developed in the period in which subsistence conditions were improving, and crises were actually decreasing. They were expressions of a popular sense of food entitlement as European states tried to assert greater control over grain markets. "State-making, the maintenance of public order and control of food supply therefore depended on each other intimately."[22] In China the very same concerns prevailed, but these centuries did not witness any fundamental institutional innovation, similar to European state-building; indeed, the traditional state was stronger than ever in this period. Because the relationship between the "state" and the "people" was differently construed, food did not become the subject of political struggle until the twentieth century. There were some food riots in China, but they tended to be small in scale and to have food supply as their focus, not political change.[23] The best-documented grain blockages occurred in the more commercialized regions of China, where local residents protested the export of local grain supplies that would raise prices. Food riots almost never occurred in Zhili, a grain-deficient region. In Beijing—in striking contrast to Paris, and also to Edo (Tokyo) in the same period—the poor never rioted over food.

Throughout its late imperial period, from the tenth century onward, Chinese civilization was unique in world history for its stable form of government, based to a large extent on a bureaucracy chosen by scholarly merit. Its high culture and material riches were admired in the West. In the Qing period, the empire was greatly expanded through territorial conquest. These historic achievements would make it absurd to identify China as "the land of famine." Yet without understanding this darker aspect of China's history, we cannot understand the transition from the glorious eighteenth century to the deeply tragic twentieth century.

This book is about the struggle against hunger and famine in North China throughout three centuries, from the late seventeenth century until the end of the twentieth century. It is North China that has been most regularly visited by droughts and floods, particularly in recent centuries.

Although North China was predominantly a dry region, it was nevertheless vulnerable to flooding because of the seasonal concentration of rain and the increasing siltation of the Yellow River and other rivers. In the late nineteenth century, after the Yellow River changed course, Westerners dubbed it "China's Sorrow." Unlike South China where rice is abundant, agriculture in North China traditionally consisted of dry-land crops like wheat, millet, and sorghum. In more recent times, cotton and corn have been extensively cultivated.

This book focuses on one important region within North China, the Hai River Basin, which comprises the present-day province of Hebei and adjacent parts of Inner Mongolia, Shanxi, Shandong, and Henan, as well as the independent municipalities of Beijing and Tianjin. During the Qing period, it was equivalent to the metropolitan province of Zhili, including the capital area of Beijing and some peripheral parts of Shandong and Shanxi. Because most of this physiographically defined region is contained within one province, it is, as a practical matter, more suitable for research purposes than a region less clearly bounded in administrative terms.

As a drainage basin, the Hai River system shared many of the characteristics of the larger and better-known Yellow River system. Although extending only a few miles from Tianjin to the ocean, the Hai River in the Qing period and in the first half of the twentieth century formed the single outlet for the entire system of rivers and streams in the region. Because of increasing siltation and excessive engineering combined with periodic neglect, the propensity of these rivers to overflow posed a grave and persistent challenge for officials charged with river conservancy. The environmental decline and agricultural limitations of the Hai River Basin were balanced in part by the region's political centrality. Because Beijing was located in its center, Zhili Province received direct economic benefits from tribute grain from central and southern China transported via the Grand Canal, as well the benefit of close bureaucratic attention to its rivers and crops. In modern times, the city of Tianjin has served as a major port and as a commercial and industrial center.

North China, or Huabei as it is known today, has many cultural and historical identities. It has long been considered the "cradle of Chinese civilization" because the early states of Xia, Shang, and Zhou originated there. Centuries later, as the south became fully settled and rivaled the north culturally and economically, different social patterns developed in the Lower Yangzi valley and elsewhere in the south, ones in which powerful lineages and elites, supported by wealth from fertile land, played a larger role in informal local governance. In the north, by contrast, a less productive agricultural economy resulted in a more austere way of life that did not support strong local elite activism, and the state played a larger role in maintaining local functions such as river control.

This north-south binary had other dimensions. The north was more connected to the Central Asian steppe, the homeland of the Mongol and Manchu rulers. The south often meant the coastal south, more exposed to overseas commerce and influence, first with Southeast Asia and later with the West. By the late Qing, the northern orientation certainly implied traditionalism and conservatism; the general Zuo Zongtang prevailed in his determination to secure Qing territorial control in the northwest, which permitted Xinjiang to be fully incorporated as a province. By contrast, Li Hongzhang's suggestion to build a modern navy to defend against the new threats from the West and Japan received far less support at the court. In the 1988, a daring television documentary, "The River Elegy," made by the dissident Su Xiaokang, found a large and sympathetic audience in China. It invoked the dualistic images of yellow river (and the yellow earth) and blue ocean to represent traditionalism and enlightenment, respectively. The message was not subtle; China's Communist leaders, like the yellow emperors before them, were not open to the new ideas and thinking from the blue ocean.[24]

After 1949, the recent experience of the Chinese Communist leaders in North China greatly influenced their goals and methods for the rest of China. The "Yan'an model" was based on the experience of the party not only in the poor northwest, but on the extreme poverty and hardship that prevailed in all the base areas they controlled in the north. The Yan'an experience was imposed on all China, even when it was more appropriate for the conditions of the north. Many now see this as a fundamental error that led to much unnecessary hardship. Yet this issue leads back to fundamental geopolitical and cultural unity that has endured despite regional disparities and the essentializing north-south binary. There may be a North China or South China economy, or even cultural predilection, but there has been one Chinese political entity that has prevailed. It is far more appropriate to call North China, rather than South China, "the land of famine." The fact of political unity, however, has meant that the hardships of the north affected the entire country and had to be addressed by it. Although this book focuses on one well-defined region, the issues it raises and their consequences have significance for all of China.

The term "famine" is used in this book to refer to hunger and food scarcity in the broadest sense, as well as subsistence crises that were catastrophic in scale and resulted in elevated levels of mortality.[25] Usually their cause was a harvest failure resulting from natural causes such as flood or drought. In studies of famines in other societies, the term famine is sometimes defined more precisely. John Post states, "The term 'subsistence crisis' refers primarily to the demographic and economic consequences of doubled or tripled cereal prices and, while the effects are due more to the high cost than to the absolute shortage of food, the conditions may range from dearth and scarcity to actual famine, with deaths from starvation."[26] It is the latter result, "deaths from starvation," that constitutes the essential part of the conventional understanding of famine. One definition employs the term "true famine" to distinguish between those situations where there is an absolute shortage of food and those created by economic scarcities. "True famine is shortage of total food so extreme and protracted as to result in widespread persisting hunger, notable emaciation in many of the affected population, and a considerable elevation of community death rate attributable in part to deaths from starvation."[27] The 1885 *Famine Relief Code* of the Bombay Presidency distinguished between scarcity and the economic effects of scarcity. The latter was "when in consequence of the failure of the harvest of over a large area the price of food is raised and the usual employment of labour for wages is diminished in such a degree that the poorer classes will perish from starvation unless Government intervenes with measures of relief."[28]

Increasingly the major famines of the twentieth century were caused more by "man-made" factors than by natural catastrophe. The Ukraine famine of 1930s, the Bengal famine of 1943, the Ethiopian famines of the 1970s, and the North Korean famine of the 1990s—in addition to Great Leap Forward famine in China—all originated as arguably weather-related crises that were turned into major tragedies by wartime situations or government neglect or grievously bad policy. Other recent mortality crises, such as in Cambodia and in Rwanda, have resulted almost entirely from violence and warfare, not from bad harvests. In *Poverty and Famines: An Essay on Entitlement and Deprivation*, Amartya Sen views famines as failures of entitlement and not the result of food shortages. His case studies include Bengal, Ethiopia, the Sahel, and Bangladesh.

In speaking of China, the English term "famine" must be applied very generally because the most commonly used Chinese terms that correspond to famine—such as *tianzai, zaihuang*—actually focus on harvest failures, assumed to be weather-related, rather than mortality as the outcome. In the local records, as explained below in Chapter 1, disasters are usually described in terms of natural phenomena, either drought or excess rain—*han, shui, lao*—and very rarely described in terms of social outcomes—hunger, starvation, or mortality—*ji, daji,* or *jihuang.* In the Qing period, official records of harvests, grain prices, rainfall, granary stocks, and the like were carefully kept, but no one counted or recorded the numbers of deaths from disasters. To some extent, this may mean that high excess mortality was not always the outcome of floods and droughts because it is certainly true that excess deaths are *sometimes* found in the records. Yet, more fundamentally, it signifies that in the agrarian economy of China what really mattered was the harvest and anything that affected it.

Although it is human welfare and human suffering that underlie all the historical processes discussed in this book, it is the state that has the central role. The imperial, bureaucratic, and local leaders are the agents of change. This is in part due to the official origins of the sources upon which this study relies. But it is a premise of this book that the state was actually the most important player in this historical drama, and that the Chinese assumptions about the rulers' responsibility for preventing disasters should be taken seriously, if not literally. The state in the high Qing made possible dense population settlement in North China by investing in river conservancy and grain transport; such measures allowed the population to expand and live more securely. The Qing state was not necessarily suppressing market activities to intervene in the economy. In fact, the state often used merchants and markets to achieve adequate supplies and price stability. Nor was the state waging "a war against nature."[29] These polarities—state versus people, state versus market, and state versus nature—reflect a modernist perspective; they do not recognize the benefits of state intervention in the early modern context. Yet it must be acknowledged that rapid population growth, underdeveloped markets, and environmental decline were the unintended consequences of a relatively large state role both in the high Qing and under the People's Republic of China (PRC).

The issues of population, land, and famine are Malthusian in nature, but this book does not assume a Malthusian outcome. Thomas R. Malthus thought that when population growth outstripped available land, the outcome would be famine. "Famine seems to be the last, the most dreadful resource of nature."[30] Although Malthus's predictions were proven by historical evidence to be wrong, the notion of the inevitability of famine as a result of population pressure on land remains difficult to dispel. Most of the Chinese historical experience belies historical inevitability and instead shows the importance of human decisions and actions. Yet, without a doubt, famines in particular, and hunger and poverty in general, have been fundamentally important in the history of China—particularly during the last two centuries. This view is contrary to recent trends in Western scholarship that have dismissed the importance of famines, either by denying their existence, or by treating them as an "exogenous" events, outside the normal processes of economic development. Two demographic historians have written, "Famines were relatively few and had a very limited impact. . . . Overall there is no evidence of increases in mortality or in the frequency and intensity of mortality crises during the last 300 years. . . . Despite a sustained population increase from 225 million in 1750 to almost 600 million in 1950 and to over 1.2 billion today, the threat of overpopulation appears to have been a myth."[31] Writing about the 1930s, an economic historian dismissed famines as "random disturbances."[32]

The topic of this book sets it somewhat apart from recent American and European scholarship on Ming and Qing socioeconomic history, which emphasizes the mature growth of Chinese agriculture and commerce, the development of a more affluent and influential merchant class, and the proactive policies of the Qing state in agriculture, river control, and famine relief.[33] These scholars tend to emphasize the role of rationality and efficiency in guiding the decisions of individuals as well as statesmen. Others in this group have pointed to the ways in which the Chinese economy was as advanced as that of Europe prior to 1800 or even 1850, for example in the standard of living, or in the demographic trends.[34] This new scholarship has fundamentally changed the view of the past. The late imperial Chinese state has been cast in a more favorable light. Merchants and commerce have been given a more progressive look, helping to work against the older essentialist view that traditionally China was hostile to science and entrepreneurship. The late imperial period has been given its due as a period of accomplishment. Eurocentrism has been dealt a blow.[35]

Much of this book shares and draws from these perspectives and, indeed, largely concurs with them. By concentrating on the more prosperous, and arguably more glorious, eighteenth century, however, most of these writers have largely ignored its darker outcomes in the nineteenth and twentieth. By considering a longer period of three centuries, this book hopes to trace some of the twisted threads of historical change and examine how the land of prosperity become the land of famine. The "high Qing" period did not inevitably lead to the "low" nineteenth and twentieth centuries, but at the same time there were tendencies set in motion, consequences suffered and poorly understood, choices made then and later—all of which are better understood in *la longue durée*.

Although Western historians have turned away from the study of hunger and poverty in Chinese history, scholars in China have recently returned to this subject in great numbers.[36] Most of the recent publications were supported by government research grants; in the 1980s and 1990s party leaders were concerned about the recurrence of famines and were interested in the historical background.[37] This academic trend was preceded by officially sponsored compilations of archival and other documents concerning the history of weather, disasters, and rivers. In the 1970s and 1980s researchers from the Ministry of Water Conservancy and Electrical Power were among the most active in using the Qing-dynasty documents of the First Historical Archives in Beijing. Their purpose was to understand long-term historical trends in climate in order to predict future trends. At the same time their compilations, together with new gazetteers published by various other national and provincial agencies, have also benefited historians.[38]

The sources for this book are derived from the enormous corpus of published and archival documents of the Qing court and bureaucracy. Essays and collections of documents on river conservancy, agriculture, famine relief, and related topics supplement the official record. The early twentieth-century local gazetteers, social surveys, and reports are rich resources. For the second half of the twentieth century, which is in the memory of those alive today, recently published data on agriculture and food helps to confirm and illuminate widely shared experiences that are not yet in the conventional historical record.

This book also makes use of a unique set of grain-price data from the Qing archives. (The origin and nature of these data are described in Appendix 2.) Collected by local and provincial officials, the grain prices formed a way to forecast and measure impending harvest crises, and they provided the basis for determining the degree of damage suffered by different localities within a disaster area. Although price data were collected from all over the empire, they were the most complete and probably the most accurate for Zhili Province because of its proximity to the capital. As a source for economic history, the price data are invaluable for establishing long-term economic trends in China for the eighteenth and nineteenth centuries, measuring the degree of market integration, as well as providing a quantitative basis for case studies of particular subsistence crises. Although grain prices have been used in European economic history since the Middle Ages, no European price series can match these Chinese grain price data for their length, continuity, and quality.

The twelve chapters of this book proceed both chronologically and topically. After describing the geographic and climatic characteristics of the Hai River Basin, Chapter 1 examines the historical record of climate, natural disasters, and famines, emphasizing the constant interaction between natural forces and human experience. Chapter 2 traces the efforts by Qing emperors and their high officials to control the rivers in Zhili through ambitious engineering projects. With each new emperor a new "reign cycle" commenced, characterized by bold ambitions at the outset and decaying environmental conditions by the end. When emperors acted as engineers, they had to work through a complex bureaucracy, which became even more difficult to manage than the rivers. Chapter 3 analyzes the agricultural system in Zhili during the Qing period and later. Focusing on the functions of different grain crops in the seasonal cycle, the chapter also considers whether the standard of living declined from the eighteenth to the twentieth century as the population increased.

Chapter 4 employs the grain price data from 1738 to 1911 to learn about the long-term, secular movement of prices, which are the foundation for understanding economic trends. The quantitative analysis measures the impact of natural disasters on grain prices and concludes that the price effects of rainfall and drought were *in the aggregate* less severe than the literary or documentary record leads one to believe.

The next three chapters provide some explanations for why the price of grain was not determined solely by the local weather and harvest. Chapter 5 shows that the presence of Beijing at its center benefited the region rather than draining resources from it. Tribute grain from central and southern China was intended for the provisioning of the capital, but it also found its way into the wider market. The measures that the state took to guard the food security of the capital also served to stabilize the grain supply of the entire region. Chapter 6 shows that the state granaries also supplemented the local harvest, but the cost in both financial resources and bureaucratic corruption proved too high to sustain the system adequately in the nineteenth century. Using both grain price analysis and documentary sources, Chapter 7 discovers that the market integration achieved in the high Qing declined in the nineteenth century as transport routes decayed. As in Chapter 5, the relationship between state and market is the focus.

The next two chapters look at particular famines in the eighteenth and nineteenth centuries respectively through the lens of famine relief. Chapter 8 reviews the various famine relief techniques during the period that Pierre-Étienne Will has called "the golden age of famine relief," and then uses price data to measure the effectiveness of these techniques. Chapter 9 sees that the partial breakdown of the high Qing model did not affect the fundamental assumptions and approaches toward relief even as crises became more severe and frequent, and the larger historical context was changing.

Chapter 10 examines famine relief during the early twentieth century, when China became the "the land of famine." International relief workers subjected Chinese social and economic life to close scrutiny while providing some new approaches to famine relief. While famine seemed to reach its most desperate proportions in this period, the development of railroads, treaty ports, migration to Manchuria, agricultural commercialization, and industrialization have seemed to some historians evidence of important structural changes in the economy. Chapter 11 evaluates these new trends against the background of chronic famine described in Chapter 10.

Chapter 12 looks at the second half of the twentieth century, dominated by the Chinese Communist Party's leadership. Inheriting a problem of intense population pressure on diminished natural resources, the party intensified the techniques of economic intervention already practiced in prototypical form in late imperial times, controlling the distribution of scarce resources down to the household level. Having failed to raise per capita grain production in the 1950s, the party and people fell victim to the delusion of a great leap forward in agriculture. After China suffered the worst man-made famine in history, the party leaders resorted to a form of food fundamentalism that placed grain production above all else. Even after repudiating that policy, and turning to a market economy, at the end of the twentieth century the party continued to exercise strong control of the grain market.

The book concludes with some reflections on how three centuries of fighting famine resulted in short-term successes as well as long-term failures and other unintended consequences. Both famine and fighting famine have determined the destiny of North China—and hence of China as a whole—all the way to the end of the twentieth century.

CHAPTER ONE

"Heaven, Earth, and Man" in North China

IN THE ANCIENT CHINESE VIEW, Heaven, Earth, and Man were expected to achieve a perfect harmony. In the historical experience of North China, however, nature presented itself as a hostile force to be tamed, neither harmonious nor benign. Rivers that changed course and easily flooded and climate that could sometimes bring drought or flood in the same year were the greatest threats, but locusts, earthquakes, and pestilence also posed dangers. The view of North China as "the Land of Famine" is based on its more recent historical experience—especially since the late nineteenth century—but is consistent with the legends of the sage river-tamers of the ancient past. In both ancient and modern tales, imperial will conquers natural forces that are turbulent, unpredictable, and dangerous.

North China had not always presented such an inhospitable natural environment. Bronze-age North China was warmer in temperature and possibly more abundant in rainfall. "Much of the north China plain seems to have been marshy and the hills thickly forested; bamboo grew near the Yellow river." Animal life included not only domestic animals such as dogs, pigs, and cattle, but also elephants and rhinoceros.[1] In ancient times, North China was richly watered by numerous rivers and lakes, but over the centuries, through human settlement and agricultural cultivation, as well as deliberate engineering, the ecological balance of this vast area has dramatically changed. To some extent, this has been the universal experience of human settlement of the earth, but as one of the oldest continuously settled regions of the world, North China perhaps embodies the process of environmental decline most intensely. Chinese environmental scientists claim that "the physical features of the Huang-Huai-Hai plain of northeastern China have been altered profoundly by human activity over a much longer span of time than have those of almost any other region of earth."[2]

The Chinese view of the cosmos and nature has historically contained contradictory impulses. Heaven, or *Tian*, was seen to dominate all existence, yet rulers and subjects could act to modify their behavior in accordance with Heaven. Natural disasters reflected cosmic disharmony, but Confucians saw that they were brought on by human failures. Heaven, Earth, and Man were engaged in dynamic interaction where Earth and Man were not the passive victims of an unpredictable Heaven. Since serious natural disasters were portents of the loss of the Mandate of Heaven, rulers were to take steps to prevent floods from occuring by building canals and reclaiming land, by diking rivers and dredging riverbeds, and by storing grain for hard times. If Nature could not be completely controlled, its worst effects could at least be prevented or minimized. Throughout Chinese history the ambitious measures taken to control the rivers and to provide irrigation for agriculture have been motivated by the Confucian impulse for taming nature.

North China was the original and principal location for imperial intervention into the environment. The Yellow River, the Huai River, and the tributaries of the Hai River have all been subject to intense engineering. The Zheng Guo Canal of Shaanxi Province, dating from 246 B.C., became the basis of an elaborate irrigation system for the Wei River valley that was periodically rebuilt throughout the imperial period.[3] The Grand Canal, first built by the Sui emperors in the seventh century and rebuilt by the Yuan in the thirteenth century, was imperial China's most ambitious engineering project. It served to bring abundant supplies of grain from the south to provision the northern capitals, first Loyang and then Beijing; in so doing, it provided the only significant commercial link between North and South China.

The daily agricultural activities of millions of cultivators over the centuries have changed the natural environment as profoundly as the actions of rulers have. In South China the introduction of early ripening rice, multiple annual crops, and elaborate terracing and irrigation of fields all transformed the natural landscape at least from the Song dynasty onward. The encroachment of population on land caused the disappearance of lakes and other surface water in many regions.[4] Although the process has received less attention, the natural environment of North China has also been profoundly transformed by human agricultural activity over the centuries. Historically the North China plain has been one of the most agriculturally productive regions of China, although its natural resources could not compare with those of the south. In the past, wheat, millet, and sorghum were the major crops, but in modern times, corn and cotton have played an increasing role. In recent years, North China has accounted for about one-quarter of China's grain production, as well as roughly 60 percent of its raw cotton.[5]

From a global perspective, "China was, from about 650 A.D. to 1800, almost always the most ecologically resilient and resourceful state on earth," in the words of an environmental historian.[6] If the ability of people to be agriculturally productive despite land and water limitations is the measure of resilience, then North China, like China in general, should be considered resilient. The population of the Zhili-Hebei region—the subject of this book—tripled between 1750 and 1953, and doubled again between 1953 and 1999 despite the experience of natural disasters and challenges. (See Tables 3.1 in Chapter 3 and 12.1 in Chapter 12.) Although never entirely self-sufficient in grain until recent years, North China has been agriculturally productive despite poor soil conditions and uncertain weather. However, such "resilience"—which might also be called survival—has been accomplished with mounting ecological costs. Population density has led to deforestation, which has contributed to increased silting, which in turn accelerated the tendency of rivers in this area to overflow and change their course. Population pressure led to encroachment on river banks and lakes, causing the disappearance or shrinkage of lakes and ponds. Diking and channeling of rivers denied them their normal floodplains, making the rivers more dangerous when they did overflow. Waterlogging, common to a large portion of the North China plain, results from poor drainage and damages crops. In the second half of the twentieth century, the expansion of irrigation—particularly in the form of tube-wells—lowered the water table and increased the degree of salinization and alkalinization of the soil, resulting in further environmental degradation and posing technological challenges. Industrial and urban demand for water has created a mounting crisis in the north, which has been addressed principally by diversion of water from the Luan River south to Tianjin and by the planned diversion of Yangzi River waters north to Beijing and Tianjin.

Natural disasters and human behavior have thus been even more closely related than Xunzi could have envisioned. The philosopher saw that human effort could prevent flood or drought from causing a famine. But as history has unfolded, human efforts to control nature may have prevented disasters in the short run, but they increased the likelihood, or severity, of human disasters in the long run. The higher the stakes, the more ambitious each successive stage of human intervention has been, and the greater the risks. In North China, and most areas of the modern world, however, ecological balance—the harmony of Heaven, Earth and Man—can never truly be regained.

History of the Hai River System

In ancient times, the rivers that now comprise the Hai River system were part of the Yellow River system. The Yellow River originally flowed out to the ocean near present-day Tianjin, but in the period between the Warring States and the Western Han (300–200 B.C.), it began to shift in a more southerly direction, while the smaller rivers in the northern part of this region continued to flow to the ocean near Tianjin. By the late Western Han and early Eastern Han, the Hai River Basin could be defined as a separate river system.[7] It has remained a discrete system ever since then although the mouth of the Yellow River today is north of Shandong peninsula.

The earliest known irrigation canal in this region is associated with the Warring States (475–221 B.C.) general Ximen Bao, who around 422 B.C. directed the construction of twelve canals using the Zhang River waters for irrigation and channeled it from its southeasterly course toward the northeast.[8] According to legend, when Ximen Bao arrived at the district of Ye, now Linzhang County in Hebei, he learned that many people had fled because they feared their daughters might be chosen to be sacrificed to the god of the Zhang River in order to appease him and prevent the river from flooding the next year. Ximen Bao exposed the superstition by throwing the witch who presided over the annual ceremony into the river, followed by the corrupt officials who used the ceremony to exact heavy taxes from the local residents. The local people realized they had been deceived, and Ximen Bao proceeded to build canals that irrigated the fields on both banks of the river, allowing bumper harvests to take place and securing his reputation as a river-tamer.[9]

Around the period of Three Kingdoms (220–280 A.D.), the famous general Cao Cao undertook substantial engineering projects to alter the flow of rivers in this area for the purpose of military transport. A dried-up tributary, the Baigou, formerly part of the Yellow River drainage, was directed toward a separate northerly channel in 204 A.D. In 206 and later, other canals were built that provided a north-south link between tributaries that flowed west to east. One of the most important of these was the Pinglu canal that linked the Qinghe-Baigou River to Tianjin and thence to the ocean. In addition, other channels were cut to the ocean. Thus, the rivers of the Hebei plain became linked together through a system of canals. This was the true origin of the Hai River system, in the view of some historical geographers. In subsequent years, the unification of North China encouraged the further development of water conservancy, and more canals were built.[10]

The construction of the Grand Canal under Sui dynasty (589–618 A.D.) further contributed to the gradual separation of the Hai River system from the Yellow River system. Although the Sui Grand Canal had as its objective the link between the Lower Yangzi valley and the capital at Loyang on the Yellow River in Henan, the Sui sponsored the building of another canal, named the

Yongqi qu, to connect Loyang with Tianjin. This link helped stabilize the Hebei plain region and encouraged its economic and political development. This was further supported by the construction of *dianpo*, or catchment basins, and dikes. At the same time, the concentration of rivers at Tianjin increased the risk of flooding in that area.[11]

The construction of the Yuan-dynasty Grand Canal to link the Lower Yangzi region to the new imperial capital at Beijing was the next major step in the development of the Hai River system. Although some old hydraulic construction, such as the Yongji qu, could be utilized, the challenges were more formidable in this period because in 1194 the Yellow River had shifted its course to flow south of the Shandong peninsula—where it remained until 1855. Thus the Grand Canal was built to work against the resistance of water flowing downstream in both the Yangzi and Yellow River segments. In the northern section, from Xuzhou via Linqing to Tongzhou and Beijing, the normal flow of the rivers toward Tianjin and to the ocean beyond was reinforced by the new Grand Canal. But difficult shifts in elevation presented additional challenges to boats traveling the canal. The last section from Zhigu, an older designation for the Hai River, via Tongzhou to Beijing was so difficult that during the Ming it was abandoned in favor of land transport, but in the Qing, water routes were maintained to Tongzhou, just at the outskirts of Beijing.[12] Although the Yuan and early Ming courts also used sea transport to bring grain from the south, the use of the Grand Canal for grain tribute became more important during the Ming dynasty and reinforced the need to contain the rivers along its route. The Zhang, Wei, and Daqing rivers were all channeled into the Grand Canal, prevented from following their own natural paths to the sea—although the Ming did build or rebuild a number of diversionary channels with dikes to the sea.[13] The basic configuration of the rivers today has its origin in the Ming-Qing periods.

During the Ming and Qing periods, five major rivers all found their way to the ocean via the Hai River at Tianjin. (See Map 1.1.)

(1) The Bei River flowed southward to Tianjin; the section from Tongzhou to Tianjin had been used in the construction of the northern extension of the Grand Canal to Beijing, known as the Bei Yunhe, or northern Grand Canal. Its main branch was formed from the Chao and Bai rivers.[14]

(2) The Yongding River flowed from the Taihang mountains in a southeasterly direction, skirting Beijing on the south (today it crosses the Beijing-Hankou rail line at Lugou Bridge (Lugouqiao, known to Westerners as the Marco Polo Bridge) before joining the Hai River at Tianjin. The Sang'gan River was one of its important tributaries, as well as one of its ancient names. Heavily silted, the Yongding was historically subject to frequent shifting, so much so that in the Yuan it was dubbed the "Little Yellow River," and later the Wuding, or "Never-Stable River," but ever since the Kangxi dike construction project of 1698, it has maintained its general pathway and has been called the Yongding, or "Eternally Stable River." Its other names included the Xiao Qing River ("Little Qing River"), the Hun River ("Turbulent River"), or the Lugou River. In 1738, further dike construction stabilized the river pathways. Between 1698 and 1938, so much silt accumulated in the Sanjiao dian, the swamp-lake formed by the two large north-south dikes, that its bed was raised by three to six meters above ground level. (Its approximate location is indicated on Map 1.1.) Between 1939 and 1943, the Yongding River broke out of its northern dike, flooding the swampy areas, forming the route that it follows today.[15]

(3) The Daqing River was formed by many smaller tributaries—principally the Juma, Tang, and Zhulong rivers—and flows eastward from the Taihang mountains into the Hai River. These tributaries were also historically unstable, shifting their beds and sometimes aligning with the Yongding system, and at other times flowing more to the south. Not until the Yongding River was

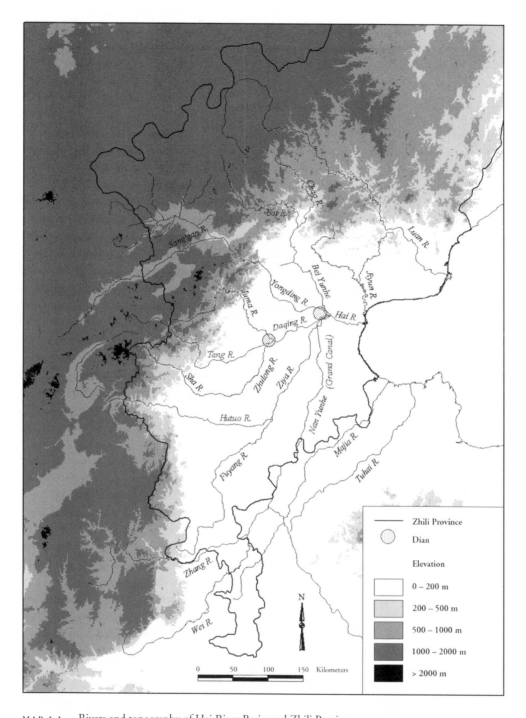

Zhili Province

Dian

Elevation

0 – 200 m

200 – 500 m

500 – 1000 m

1000 – 2000 m

> 2000 m

0   50   100   150   Kilometers

MAP 1.1.   Rivers and topography of Hai River Basin and Zhili Province

NOTE: Unless otherwise indicated, maps were created from Chinese Historical Geographic Information Service (CHGIS), Version 1.0: 1820 Qing Dynasty (Cambridge, MA: Harvard Yenching Institute, Apr. 2002) by Geoffrey Compton.

finally brought under control in the eighteenth century (after 1738) did the Daqing River become stabilized as a separate river system.[16]

(4) The Ziya River was formed by several tributaries, principally the Hutuo and the Fuyang rivers. The latter had previously, before the fifteenth century, been part of the Zhang River, but between the fifteenth and seventeenth centuries, it shifted and finally separated completely. In 1706, the latter river shifted southward into the Wei River, while the Fuyang and Hutuo rivers joined together and flowed into the Ziya. The Hutuo and Ziya were repaired many times in the Qing, and after 1763, the lower reaches of the Hutuo finally became the principal channel of the Ziya River. In 1868 the Hutuo broke loose and again flowed northward, but in 1871 a large north-south dike was built along its course, and 1881 the Hutuo was brought back into the Ziya.[17] Today, the Hutuo and Fuyang still flow into the Ziya, which converges with the Hai River at Tianjin, but in addition, a drainage canal called the New Ziya River has been constructed directly to its own outlet on the Bo hai. (See Map 12.1 in Chapter 12.)

(5) The Nan Yunhe, or southern Grand Canal, was fed by many tributaries, including the Wei and were Zhang rivers. Historically the rivers in this area had been part of the Yellow River system, and they were heavily influenced by canal-building from the time of Cao Cao in the third century. The Zhang River was particularly unstable, constantly changing its course. Although it was needed to supply water to the Nan Yunhe, after the mid-Ming it typically split into three branches, one of which joined with the Fuyang River and was called the Xin Zhang he (New Zhang River). After 1698, three tributaries flowed into the Nan Yunhe, but one flowed north to join the Ziya Rver. The Wei and Zhang cut across the leg of Zhili Province from Henan into Shandong. After 1706, because the Wei River was weak in its flow, the Zhang was principally diverted to the Grand Canal at Guantao and became basically integrated into the Nan Yunhe system.[18] In the Qing period, the Zhang and Wei rivers converged and joined the Grand Canal at the city of Linqing in Shandong. Today the two rivers are called the Zhang-Wei River.

These river systems and subsystems are characterized by being wider at their sources and narrower at their mouths, a phenomenon that increases the tendency for the waters to crest.[19] The heavy degree of siltation is their most fundamental characteristic. The accelerating rate of siltation during recent centuries, combined with shallow riverbeds and inadequate drainage, has resulted in riverbeds that are level with the ground, or above ground level, similar to the lower reaches of the Yellow River. The Yongding, Zhang, and Hutuo rivers are the chief examples. The Yongding River was conspicuously silted and unstable. By the Yuan period, its problem of siltation was second only to that of the Yellow River, and it was especially prone to shifting its bed. According to one estimate, its pathway could shift by as many as seventy kilometers from north to south. Even after the various Qing construction projects siltation continued unabated, and riverbeds rose higher and higher until they were above the ground. Other rivers—such as the Chao-Bai and Daqing—were heavily silted, but their beds were still level with the ground, or lower than ground level. The latter was originally not too silted, and because of effective engineering in the Qing period, such as the building of the Thousand-Li Dike, it never became an above-ground-level river. The Nan Yunhe depended on the Wei River, which was also vulnerable to silting but usually maintained through engineering efforts.[20]

Human intervention was certainly responsible in large measure for the behavior of the river system. Siltation was, and is, due to deforestation and overexploitation of the land. In addition, intense engineering from Han times onward contributed to the vulnerability of the rivers to flooding. Especially from the time of the construction of the first Grand Canal in the Sui Dynasty, the various large and small rivers were channeled into the Grand Canal and its major tributaries, thus increasing the possibility of flooding. In the Han period there were many channels and outlets to the Bo hai, but after the Tang period, for the most part, rivers were directed into the Hai River near Tianjin, although the Tang did cut many diversionary canals, *jianhe* (also translated as distributaries), to the ocean, as well as build collection basins to hold water overflow, the tendency for flooding increased.[21] The Yuan Grand Canal, which constituted the capital's main link with the south, was the dominant geopolitical factor in this region from its construction to the late nineteenth century. It too cut off the natural outlets of many rivers that had previously flowed into the Bo Hai and, instead, forced them to drain into the Grand Canal, leaving the Hai River as the only outlet to the ocean. In the Republican era, Western engineers and Chinese administrators alike attributed the flooding problem to human interference in past eras.[22] In the Mao era, the official line was that the Grand Canal represented a sacrifice of northern Chinese agrarian interests to the need to provision the court and officials; by directing the rivers to the Grand Canal, the irrigation needs of peasants in the Wei River region were neglected.[23] Although the highly political interpretation may seem outdated, the ecological impact of such engineering is not exaggerated.[24]

Under the People's Republic of China, the problem of shifting rivers, waterlogging, and low yields were intensely addressed through numerous engineering projects. To deal with flooding and waterlogging, numerous diversion channels were cut to the sea to allow for proper drainage. Along the Yongding and Zhang-Wei rivers that were historically so silted and unstable, dredging and deepening of the channels, along with construction of dikes and diversion channels, were designed to contain cresting waters. Twenty-nine major reservoirs/dams in the mountains, and 1,900 medium and small reservoirs downstream, were built to retain water and control the delivery of water when it is needed for irrigation. Thirty-two detention basins (also called detention depressions, *wa*; or shallow lakes, *dian*) were maintained in the middle and lower reaches of the rivers to contain overflows in the summer season, necessary because the rivers are so short in length. The Baiyang dian (Baiyang Lake) in the Daqing River system is a project for flood control that has also been developed for tourism and production of fish, reeds, and other enterprises.[25]

Surface water has also diminished over the centuries, and the retention of water upstream since 1949 has accelerated this process. Scientists cite the example of Nanyuan, a royal hunting ground for the Manchu court on the outskirts of Beijing, which once had numerous springs and swamps, but now has been reclaimed as farmland with no surface water at all. Of the three lakes—the Xi dian, Dong dian, and Sanjiao dian—considered important for the coordination of drainage in the central part of the province only the Xi dian, renamed the Baiyang dian, still remains important; the Sanjiao dian has disappeared, and the Dong dian is not represented on recent maps. Even the surface area of the Baiyang Lake, however, has been reduced by 400 sq. km during the last twenty-five years or so despite the attention it has received as a coordinated water-management project.[26]

Today, standing at the Yongding River, either at the Lugou Bridge in Beijing, or downstream at Lanfang not far from Tianjin, it is difficult to imagine that water had ever flowed abundantly and caused such trouble. Indeed, the bed of this river, and most others in the region, is completely dry during most of the year and cannot be readily recognized as a river in most places. Scarce rainfall, seasonally concentrated, is retained upstream in the large reservoirs whenever possible and is released only when needed for irrigation. The riverbeds are used by farmers for planting winter crops since the soil is relatively fertile. Such is the conclusion of a long process of environmental change over the centuries.

The Hai River Basin of North China

The designation of this region as the Hai River Basin is a relatively recent development that reflects the administrative divisions of the Ministry of Water Conservancy of the People's Republic of China. The Hai River Commission, established in 1980 at Tianjin, is one of six river commissions under the ministry, together with those for the Yellow (Huang), Yangzi, Huai, Pearl (Zhu), and Liao (Song) rivers. Unlike these other rivers, the Hai River is neither great nor famous; in conversation it is easily confused with the far better known Huai River Basin to the south. The term *Haihe liuyu*, or the Hai River Basin, is not usually recognized by Chinese living outside the region, but is commonly used by officials, agricultural specialists, engineers, and technicians.

The Hai River Basin is defined by the rivers that flow east from the Taihang and Yan mountain ranges, converge near Tianjin, and find their major outlet to the ocean through the short and narrow river known as the Hai he, or "Ocean River." (See Map 1.2.) The rivers in the Hai River Basin today include the Jiyun, Chao-Bai, Bei Yunhe, Yongding, Daqing, Ziya, Zhang-Wei, Nan Yunhe, Tuhai, and Majia. In the 1980s, the boundaries of the basin on the north were extended to include the Luan River, which has been diverted toward Tianjin municipality. The Luan system includes other small rivers in the eastern part of Hebei. The entire Hai River Basin covers a catchment area of 317,900 square kilometers, containing 166 million mu of cultivated land. This includes the province of Hebei, the municipalities of Beijing and Tianjin, the northern sections of Henan and Shandong, the eastern section of Shanxi, and parts of Liaoning Province and the Inner Mongolian Autonomous Region. Its population in 1989 was about 105 million.[27]

The choice of a river drainage basin as an appropriate unit of study conforms to G. William Skinner's definition of China's macroregions by drainage basins. His North China macroregion, however, covers several of the smaller river systems of the north and corresponds more generally to the larger Huang-Huai-Hai agricultural region than to the Hai or any single river basin. "North China includes the lower basin of the Yellow River plus the drainage areas of the Huai, the Wei, and the host of smaller rivers that cross the North China plain."[28]

Most of the documentary sources used in this study center on the Qing-dynasty province of Zhili, which corresponds to the dominant portion of today's Hai River Basin and was fundamentally equivalent to the present-day province of Hebei and the independent municipalities of Beijing and Tianjin. Zhili differed from today's Hebei by including to the northwest the large military district of Koubei Santing, which today has been largely incorporated into Inner Mongolia Autonomous Region. To the northeast, Zhili included the large area of Chengde Prefecture, which contained the summertime imperial capital of Chengde (also called Rehe); the eastern section of Chengde Prefecture today belongs to the province of Liaoning. Also, the southern section of Zhili included a leg or boot, shaped somewhat like Italy, that effectively formed a corridor between Henan and Shandong provinces. Today those districts of the former Daming Prefecture are part of either Henan or Shandong. These adjacent portions of Inner Mongolia, Liaoning, Shanxi, Henan, and Shandong provinces that are now part of the Hai River Basin are included in the discussion or analysis when possible, but for all practical purposes this book focuses on the administratively defined Zhili Province, or Hebei Province including Beijing and Tianjin, which correspond fairly well to the drainage basin. (See Appendix 1 and Map A.1 for prefectures and counties of Zhili during the Qing period.)

The Hai River Basin forms one part of the larger agricultural region known today as the Huang-Huai-Hai region that includes all three river basins. Topographically, climatically, and in other ways, these three river basins share much in common. In research and planning, agricultural

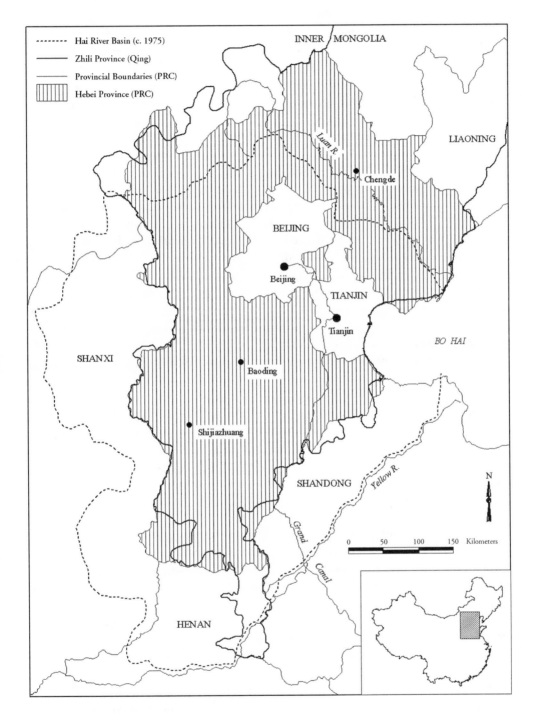

INNER MONGOLIA

LIAONING

Luan R.

• Chengde

BEIJING

● Beijing

TIANJIN

● Tianjin

SHANXI

BO HAI

• Baoding

• Shijiazhuang

SHANDONG

Yellow R.

N

0   50   100   150   Kilometers

Grand

Canal

HENAN

MAP 1.2.   Hai River Basin, Hebei, and Zhili

specialists have focused on the plains sector of the region (Huang-Huai-Hai *pingyuan*), which is commonly known in English as the North China plain, but it incorporates several distinct subregions with varying soil, topography, and climate.

The most distinctive feature of the topography of the North China plain in general, and the Hai River Basin in particular, is that the plains region lies mostly below 100 meters, and the mountains rise steeply from the plains—so the region is bifurcated into plains and mountains. The Hai River Basin subsection itself incorporates several distinct agricultural zones. Map 1.3 pictures the zones within Hebei Province.[29]

(I) The highland plateau area in the northwest that is linked to Inner Mongolia. This comprises semiarid steppe, or pasture land, and is not in itself mountainous although at high elevation. It is a dominantly pastoral area with little agriculture.

(II) The Yanshan mountain area in the north and northeast, which is truly mountainous and relatively moist and humid, but also encompasses some low mountain and basin areas suitable for agriculture. Forestry and animal husbandry were once particularly abundant, and some agriculture, with fruits and grains, is practiced here today. Chengde, Tangshan, and Qinhuangdao are the principal urban centers. The upper reaches of the Luan, Chao-Bai, and Jiyun rivers are found in this area.

(III) The catchment basin in the Zhangjiakou (Kalgan) area to the northwest. The Yongding River and its tributaries originate here. Because of uneven rainfall and poor soil, this region's agricultural production has been limited to millet, beans, and other drought-resistant crops. Some fruit trees are raised here, and there is forestry and pastoralism. Soil erosion is a major problem.

(IV) The Taihang mountains to the west. Some agriculture (fruits and grains) is practiced in the valleys, on the eastern side of the range, but neither forest nor green cover are so good as in the Yanshan mountain range. Some cotton and peanuts are grown. On the western side of the range some forestry and livestock raising are practiced. Soil erosion is also a problem here.

(V) The Yanshan foothills and plains. The area stretching from the northern section of Tianjin municipality eastward to Tangshan in the area north of the Bo hai is considered a separate agricultural district by geographers. It also extends westward into Beijing municipality. At present this is the most densely populated and industrialized portion of Hebei Province and provides vegetables, meat, and eggs for the urban population.

(VI) The Taihang foothills and plains. The piedmont zone (*shanqian*, lit., "in front of the mountains") at the foot of the Taihang range bordering both sides of the Beijing-Hankou rail line and including the key cities of Baoding and Shijiazhuang. This includes the best agricultural land, with plentiful surface and ground water sources. In the 1980s 70 to 80 percent of the land was irrigated. No alkalinization problem exists. Wheat, corn, and cotton are cultivated in abundance, as well as other grain and oil crops. Animal husbandry is also successful here.

(VII) The low plain region stretching from the piedmont region eastward, including the centers of Tianjin, Cangzhou, Handan, and Xingtai, occupies the southeast of the province. It includes sixty-two counties and accounts for 40 percent of the cultivated acreage of Hebei Province.[30] This region is characterized by low-lying land where river streams do not flow easily. Both surface and ground water are scarce. Waterlogging, with its associated problems of soil alkalinization and salinization, has historically been a problem. This area was the most vulnerable to flooding of all varieties. It is also vulnerable to droughts. Cotton and grain crops are grown here. This part of Hebei is also known today as the Heilonggang District.[31]

(VIII) The salt districts on the north and south Bo hai coast. Salt production and fishing are the principal industries here.

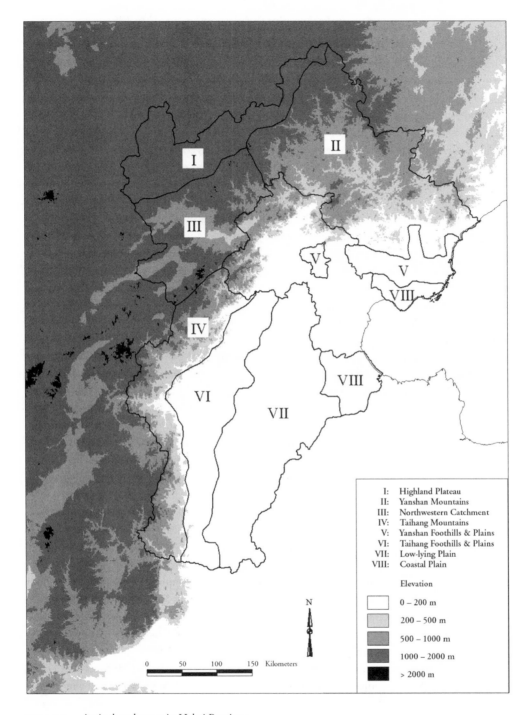

I:	Highland Plateau
II:	Yanshan Mountains
III:	Northwestern Catchment
IV:	Taihang Mountains
V:	Yanshan Foothills & Plains
VI:	Taihang Foothills & Plains
VII:	Low-lying Plain
VIII:	Coastal Plain

Elevation

0 – 200 m
200 – 500 m
500 – 1000 m
1000 – 2000 m
> 2000 m

N

0   50   100   150   Kilometers

MAP 1.3.   Agricultural zones in Hebei Province

SOURCE: Adapted from *Hebei sheng zonghe nongye quhua*, ed. Hebei sheng zonghe nongye quhua committee, map facing p. 124.

NOTE: This publication excludes information about the independent municipalities of Beijing and Tianjin.

Climate of the Hai River Basin

The Hai River Basin is characterized by its marked intraregional topographic differences and diverse agricultural conditions in addition to an unstable river system.[32] Climate, however, has always been the least predictable of the natural factors in the Hai River Basin, interacting with topography, soil, and rivers to produce the highly variable and uncertain environment for agriculture. Scarce rainfall, seasonally concentrated, results in wide annual variation in rainfall, highly uneven seasonal variation, and significant intraregional variation in agricultural conditions.

As in North China generally, the shortage of rainfall was and remains the major limiting factor, ranging between 500–900 mm a year on average. But the Hai River Basin receives far less than the average for the Huang-Huai-Hai plain as a whole—400–600 mm a year. In the 1980s, 560 mm was the annual average, significantly less than the estimated annual averages in the last two centuries.[33] By contrast, the fertile Lower Yangzi River region of China receives more than 1,000 mm per year, and the Pearl River (Zhujiang) region of South China receives more than 1,400 mm per year.[34]

Like eastern China in general, the North China plain experiences both winter and summer monsoon climate. During the winter and spring the prevailing wind from the Siberian northwest carries little moisture and much cold. In the summer and fall, the subtropical high pressure sweeps from the Pacific Ocean in the southeast, carrying warm and humid air. "Variations in the movement of these two high pressure systems from year to year causes a great variation in annual rainfall. For example, at Beijing . . . , the variation between different years is more than 50 percent."[35] As early as the 1930s, the eminent climate historian and geographer, Zhu Kezhen, wrote that the variability of annual rainfall in North China and the frequency of natural disasters was unmatched among the world's densely populated regions, and it was no wonder that China was called the "land of famine."[36]

Because of these two weather systems, rainfall is concentrated in the summer months, while the winter and spring tend to be dry. In the North China plain, about 60 percent of the rainfall occurs in the summer months, but in the Hai River Basin the concentration is even greater, with 70–80 percent falling in the summer months, June–September.[37] (See Table 1.1.)

The seasonal variation is the most important yet most unpredictable factor in influencing cropping patterns. Rain must fall at the right time to have favorable harvests. Winter wheat requires rainfall from April to May, although inadquate rainfall in the current year may be compensated for by water stored from the previous summer and winter. Climatologists have found a positive correlation between precipitation from September through May and the winter wheat harvest in the Beijing area from 1736 until the 1950s. After the 1950s, the expansion of irrigation weakened the direct link between rainfall and harvest size.[38]

Spring drought, *chunhan*, can also make it impossible to sow spring crops. Unless there is at least 20 mm of rainfall in each ten-day period (*xun*) in April and May, seeds cannot be sown. In the Hai River Basin, represented by localities such as Beijing, Shijiazhuang, Handan, and Hengshui, the average ten-day rainfall in April and May is only 10 mm; thus by the end of May there is a 50 percent probability of not being able to sow seeds.[39] This is why irrigation has been so critical to agriculture in this area.

Drought in the early summer, June, can delay the bud formation of cotton, the harvesting of winter wheat, and heading of spring crops (corn, sorghum, and millet). Midsummer drought, from July to August (less than 300 mm in July–August, or less than 100 mm in August), can delay the growth of corn and soybean and make the buds and bolls of cotton fall. The frequency of

TABLE 1.1

The Seasonal Distribution of Rainfall in the Hai River Basin, 1961–1980

(millimeters)

Place	*Annual*	*Dec.–Feb.*	*Mar.–May*	*June–Sept.*	*Oct.–Dec.*
Beijing	644.2	13.0 (2%)	61.1 (9%)	539.6 (84%)	30.5 (5%)
Shijiazhuang	549.9	15.5 (3%)	70.2 (13%)	415.7 (76%)	48.5 (9%)
Quzhou	545.4	15.8 (3%)	60.3 (11%)	409.0 (75%)	60.3 (11%)

SOURCE: *Huang Huai Hai diqu nongye qihou ziyuan kaifa liyong*, 33.

midsummer drought in the North China plain in general, including Heilonggang, is about 30–40 percent.[40] The northern sector of the plain also experiences fall drought. In the Heilonggang region by itself, the probability of spring drought (*chunhan*) is 70–83 percent, early summer drought (*chuxiahan*) 60–65 percent, summer drought (*fuhan*) 52–55 percent, and fall drought (*qiuhan*) 77–83 percent.[41]

Floods, on the other hand, are frequent in the summer months (*xialao*); *lao* is defined as rainfall exceeding 100 mm in June, or exceeding 400 mm in July and August. It can cause cotton to fail, does damage to the corn, and creates difficulty in sowing. It is especially severe in the low-lying areas where water cannot drain off fast enough.[42] *Lao* or *li* are also the terms for waterlogging. Frequently the summer storms called *baoyu* can be sudden and contribute to flash flooding because the riverbeds are so silted that they cannot contain the sudden rise in water level.[43] Although the low-lying plain receives less rainfall than the mountain and piedmont areas, it does receive water from upstream. Such water is called *keshui*, or guest water, and in times of sudden downpour, it can pose a great danger resulting in a great flood, or *hongshui*. These turbulent floods are distinct from the more commonly experienced waterlogging in the low-lying region.

Within these parameters, the experience of different zones within the region varies greatly. Beijing, for example, has more abundant rainfall than other places in the region and a greater certainty of summer rains, but the seasonal distribution of rainfall is not even. Its annual variation is great, and it is thus fairly vulnerable to drought and flood disasters.[44] By contrast, rainstorms in Handan, in the south, tend to be sudden and also continuous. One season of flood often leads to another; one year of drought is followed by a second. There are also mixed combinations such as summer drought and fall flood, or summer flood and fall drought.[45] As seen in Map 1.4, several subregions experience different average levels of precipitation. In the Yanshan mountain area, annual precipitation exceeds 750 mm. Along the coast and in the Taihang mountain district, annual rainfall is 650–750 mm. In the plains areas, with the exception of a few localities, the yearly average is 550–650 mm. The low-lying, waterlogged center of the province receives only 450–550 mm a year. In the plateau area north of Zhangjiakou, rainfall does not reach 450 mm.[46]

Uneven rainfall and topographical features affect cropping choices of the subregions. Millet, sorghum, and sweet potato are the most drought resistant, while peanut, sesame, and cotton are not so well adapted. Soybean, wheat, corn, and rape are the least drought resistant.[47] Sorghum is also flood resistant because as its Chinese name, *gaoliang*, suggests, it grows tall in the field. In the Qing period, millet and sorghum were the staple crops all over the region, while wheat was cultivated in limited quantity probably in the piedmont and southern sector of Zhili that today is part of Henan Province. Because of scarce rainfall, cotton and corn, known to this region since the

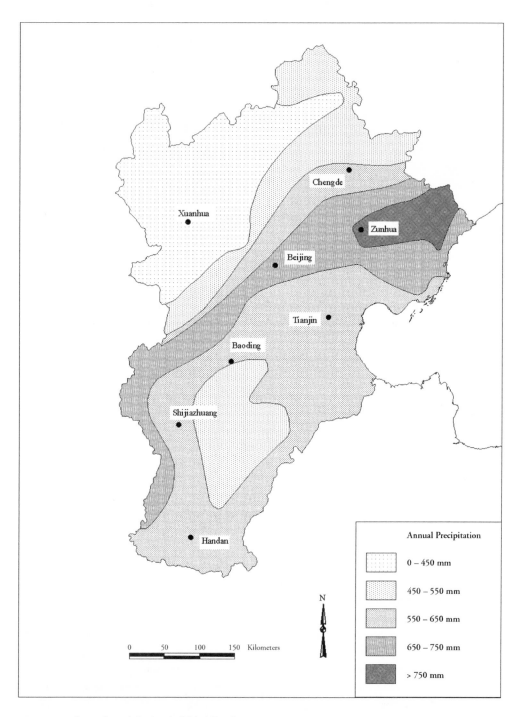

Annual Precipitation	
	0 – 450 mm
	450 – 550 mm
	550 – 650 mm
	650 – 750 mm
	> 750 mm

MAP 1.4. Annual precipitation in Hebei Province

SOURCE: Adapted from *Hebei sheng zonghe nongye quhua*, ed. Hebei sheng zonghe nongye quhua committee, Map facing p. 20.

sixteenth century at least, were not extensively grown until the twentieth century although the extent of cotton cultivation in Qing times is controversial. Although the greater amount of rain in the piedmont still accounts for higher yields in that region, since 1949 the extension of irrigation and use of chemical fertilizers has allowed the dramatic expansion of wheat, cotton, and corn production. All three crops are found in all districts of the region except zones I, II, III, and the northern part of IV, but with variations. (See Map 1.3.) Wheat is grown principally in the mountains and piedmont, and partly in the low-lying plains of the region (zones IV, VI, and VII). Corn is grown in some parts of the mountain and piedmont regions, but not so much in the lowest areas along the southeast boundary of Hebei and along the coast. Cotton, the major commercial crop, is cultivated more in the low-lying areas than the other two crops.[48] In Heilonggang, and northern Shandong, cotton is much more adaptable to climatic uncertainty than grain crops, particularly wheat.[49]

Historical Climate

Seasonal and annual fluctuations in rainfall and other aspects of weather were the most important factor in harvests and, hence, the lives of peasants. Climate was also subject to long-term variations—both secular trends and cyclical patterns—which have been of great interest to scientists as well as historians. North China undoubtedly experienced a warmer climate in the early Zhou dynasty (1100 B.C.), for example, than it does at present; the documentary evidence of bamboos in the Yellow River valley suggests this. After the Tang dynasty, plum trees apparently disappeared from the north, although they had been frequently mentioned before that time. The tenth to fourteenth centuries are believed to have been colder than before.[50] In the seventeeth century, all of China experienced a cooling trend similar to, and almost contemporary with, that of the Little Ice Age in Europe, which is said to have occurred roughly from 1550 to 1700. Some Chinese historians have suggested that China's seventeenth-century political turmoil might have been related to this climatic shift.[51]

The sources for climate history fall into three or four principal categories. Documentary and literary/anecdotal sources record harvests, disasters, flowering, and other events. Dynastic and local histories also chronicle the occurrence of natural disasters such as floods, droughts, typhoons, and earthquakes. Phenological evidence allows estimations of the occurrence of frosts and so on. Instrument readings began with the Jesuits in the eighteenth century, but they were not continuous. In the mid-nineteenth century H. Fritsche, a meteorologist sent by the Russian Academy of Sciences to Beijing to study climate, published observations for 1841–55, 1860–61, and 1869–74.[52] Only after 1911 did the new Chinese government establish meteorological stations for the systematic observation of weather in various other locations in the country.

Because of its centrality, Beijing has the best continuous record of climate conditions. In addition to the early instrument readings, the observations of rainfall taken by the Qing court from 1724 to 1902 have been preserved by the Central Meteorological Bureau.[53] Although they record the days of rainfall rather than measuring amounts, these data have enabled scholars to reconstruct a continuous record of Beijing precipitation for the period 1724–1979. In the 1970s, scholars from the Institute of Geography of the Chinese Academy of Sciences began a project to transcribe other rain and snowfall records (*qingyu lu* and *yuxue fencun*) found in the vast collection of Qing-dynasty memorials held at the First Historical Archives in Beijing. These data are particularly full for Beijing and have allowed Zhang Peiyuan, Gong Gaofa, and other climatologists to reconstruct a more accurate picture of climate patterns since the early eighteenth century.

Based on these and other sources the Beijing Meteorological Station derived a pattern of droughts and floods in Beijing during the last 500 years. Using rainfall data for June–September only, investigators rated each year in one of five categories: flood, partial flood, normal, partial drought, or drought, with "normal" being defined as the range of 465–625 mm of rainfall for these four months. Generally they found fairly regular weather cycles or waves of about eighty years. Using the more reliable information for the period since the 1730s, this study identified dry or below average rainfall for the period 1728–69, wet or above average for 1770–1825, below average for 1826–70, and above average for 1871–94. In the twentieth century there was a dry period from 1895–1948, while 1949–64 was a wet period.[54]

Using the record of rainfall collected from the Qing archives and looking at no-rain days for April–October of 1724–1979, Feng Liwen of the Institute of Geography of the Chinese Academy of Social Sciences found roughly the same periodicity. The dry periods were 1724–63, 1814–63, and 1924–43; the wet periods were 1764–1813, 1864–1923, and 1944–79. However, the probability of two consecutive seasons of dry weather was less than 10 percent, and the probability of three consecutive seasons (spring–summer–autumn) was less than 3.4 percent.[55]

Another team under Duan Yunhuai achieved roughly the same results. They identified the dry periods as 1728–78, 1813–40, 1857–69, 1963–80, and the early 1980s; the wet periods were 1779–1812, 1870–97, and 1948–62.[56] Wang Shao-wu and colleagues had similar results using different materials and looking only at summer rainfall all over China and in Beijing. They too identified a clear eighty-year cycle, which they attribute to an eighty-year cycle of solar activity. They also observed that the amplitude between lowest and highest rainfall increased in the Qing period, but declined after 1949.[57] Using rainfall between September and May, during the winter wheat-growing season, Gong Gaofa and colleagues also found similar long-term swings.[58] A recent publication, *Beijing shuihan zaihai*, also gives similar results for 1724–1990, showing dry periods in 1728–77, 1812–39, 1857–70, 1926–48, and 1980–89; wet periods in 1724–27, 1778–1811, 1840–56, 1871–1901, 1911–15, and 1949–59; and periods of oscillation as 1902–10, 1916–25, and 1960–79.[59]

Although these studies vary somewhat in methodology, their periodization of wet and dry periods fundamentally concur because they draw from the same basic estimated data of historical climate. The mid-eighteenth century was a dry period; the late eighteenth to the first two decades of the nineteenth century was fundamentally a wet period; the mid-nineteenth century was dry; and the last two or three decades of the century were quite wet. The early twentieth century witnessed a mixed weather pattern, but the period from 1926–48 was generally dry. In the PRC period, in Hebei the period from 1949 to 1964 was a wet period, and the period from 1965 through the 1980s was a dry period.[60] Using rainfall measured at Beijing as the standard, the decade from 1949–59 generally experienced above average rainfall; the 1960–79 was a period of oscillation; while the 1980s was particularly dry.[61]

Figure 1.1 presents the annual rainfall at Beijing from 1725–1912, based on the *qingyu lu* and *yuxue fencun* archival data reconstructed by the Institute of Geography (also described in Appendix 2). The graphed data shows less extreme periodic trends than the studies cited above, most of which were based on the older Central Meteorological Station records. One reason for this is that the simulation methods used to fill in missing data may have underestimated the magnitude of some of the floods. Nevertheless, the ten-year moving average also reveals that the mid-eighteenth century was relatively dry, while the early nineteenth century was relatively wet, much of the mid-nineteenth century was very dry, and the third quarter of the century was very wet. Zhang Peiyuan and his colleagues have also found that winter precipitation declined after the mid-nineteenth

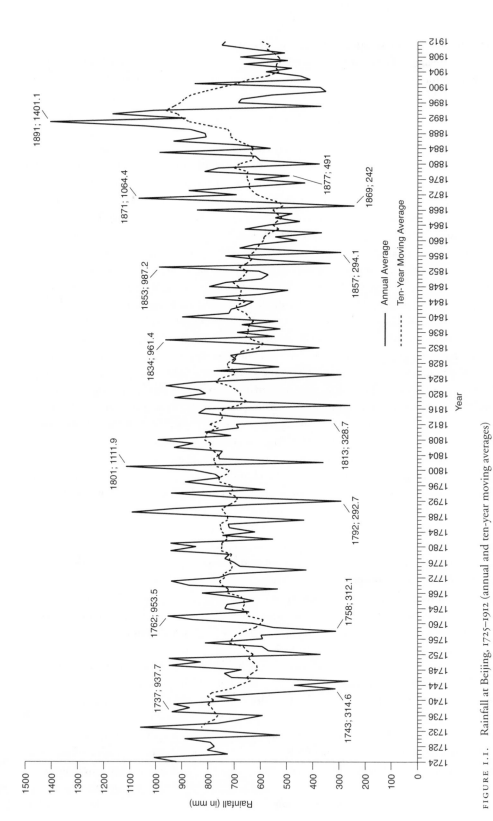

FIGURE 1.1. Rainfall at Beijing, 1725–1912 (annual and ten-year moving averages)

NOTE: All figures, unless otherwise noted, are based on grain price and other data explained in text and Appendix 2.

century, as did the harvest ratings, but they are uncertain whether this was a fundamental shift in climate or a change in the reporting system. We have calculated that 712 mm was the average annual rainfall from 1738–1850, while 653 mm was the annual average from 1851–1911.[62]

Floods, Droughts, and Disasters

The pattern of little and uneven rainfall has resulted in frequent droughts and floods in the Hai River Basin, as well as the rest of North China, that are abundantly chronicled in the historical record, namely, the standard dynastic histories and chronicles, prefectural and county gazetteers, and offical documents. Unlike the harvest and rainfall reports, the typical gazetteer descriptions of floods and droughts used descriptive terms in a subjective way. A drought could be a dry period, *gan*, or it could be an excessively deficient period, *han*, or even worse, *dahan*, a big drought. A severe drought that reaches crisis proportions was, and is, a *hanzai*. Terms for flood are more complex. Often, records will simply say *shui* (water), *dashui* ("big water"), or *shuizai* (a flood crisis). Today, Chinese officials, technical experts, and farmers use the terms *lao* or *li*, which mean a local flood, or waterlogging, arising from local rainfall. A large flood arising from either local rain or from "guest waters" upstream is called *hongshui*. Neither *hong* nor *lao* necessarily results in the overflowing of the banks of a river, which is described as *juekou* or *fanlan*.

These natural disasters may lead to a harvest failure, or *huang*. Although *huang* is assumed to have severe human or social impact, only in the worst cases do the records specify hunger and starvation. *Jihuang* describes a subsistence crisis that is accompanied by hunger and is the closest equivalent to the English term "famine." Sometimes the term *ji*, "hunger" or "starvation," is used simply by itself, occasionally *daji*, "big hunger." These terms occur far less often than those for flood and drought, and they suggest a more critical situation, a *zaihuang*. The use of such terms in local records was entirely at the discretion of the compilers or authors and was not scientific in any way. We cannot assume that a particular flood or drought did not result in deaths from starvation, but we cannot be certain of the extent to which it did. During a natural disaster the focus was not on famine mortality, but on the extent of crop loss and physical damage.

While droughts and floods of various sorts were the disasters most frequently chronicled in these sources, other disasters included epidemic (*yi*), hail (*bao*), locusts (*huang*), earthquakes (*zhen*), and parching heat (*shu*). The traditional records not only provide ample evidence of the regularity and frequency of such events but also reflect their importance for the bureaucracy and local communities. The provincial gazetteer, *Jifu tongzhi*, has a vast section on famine relief that compiles information from many local gazetteers.[63] For the entire period of the Qing covered by the gazetteer, up to the late nineteenth century, there is scarcely a year during which a disaster did not occur in at least one part of the province and often several events occurred in the same year.

Three recent compilations on floods and droughts have reorganized the information from these records so that they might be used for the study of historical climate. The first, *Zhongguo jin wubainian hanlao fenbu tuji* (1981), is compiled by the Central Meteorological Bureau based on the transcription of floods and droughts over the past 500 years found in local gazetteers from all over China and from other histories. It assembles this information on yearly maps of precipitation. The second and more useful compilation by the Hebei Province Meteorological Station, *Haihe liuyu lidai ziran zaihai shiliao* (1985), presents excerpts about local flood and drought culled from local gazetteers and other sources arranged year by year. It does not attempt quantification. The third and most useful volume, *Haihe Luanhe honglao dang'an shiliao* (1981), edited by the Hai

River Commission, presents extracts from memorials found in the Qing archives concerning local flood conditions each year; it does not cover droughts. It is mostly useful for its qualitative material, but tables and lists provide some basis for quantification.

Table 1.2 presents the major floods and droughts that took place in the Hai River Basin, including Zhili Province (known as Jifu, or the capital area), during the Qing period. From these sources, one can make several observations about the timing and frequency of major disasters. During the Shunzhi and Kangxi reigns, there were regular disasters, mostly of medium size, with the rare exception of the extensive drought in 1691–92. Droughts and floods were sometimes listed as causing hunger (*ji*), but not nearly so often as in the late Ming. During the relatively prosperous early and mid-eighteenth century, the periodic floods and droughts were not usually accompanied by reports of hunger or starvation. In only a few of the worst crises, such as the 1743–44 drought or the 1761 flood, was grave starvation and high mortality mentioned. In the 1780s and 90s, toward the end of the Qianlong reign, however, disasters were sometimes, but not always, noted with mentions of hunger, even cannibalism, and high mortality.

Following the serious floods of the 1790s, the great flood of 1801 proved a crisis to test the will of the new Jiaqing emperor. Although he oversaw a massive relief effort, that flood was only one of a close succession of floods that followed in the 1800s, 1810s, and 1820s, all very wet decades to be sure. As if on cue, the Daoguang reign was initiated by a cholera epidemic in 1821 and huge floods in 1822–23. The period 1830–34 was also troubled, first with an earthquake in 1830, drought accompanied by flood in 1832, and a megaflood in 1834. The rest of the 1830s witnessed hunger and distress in some part of the region in every year. The decade of the 1850s was accompanied by natural disasters that were compounded by the human disasters of the Taiping Rebellion and conflicts with the Western powers. The Tongzhi reign began with an epidemic, not a flood, but in 1871–73, there was a succession of floods in the capital area. In 1876–79 all of North China including Zhili experienced a devastating drought famine. The final decades of the century were beset with almost yearly problems of flooding, as well as political disturbance caused by the Boxer Uprising and foreign military presence in the capital area. Disease was also more frequently mentioned in the records of these late decades.

These natural crises seemed to occur periodically and regularly, particularly in the case of floods. One can observe that a large flood usually occurred once a decade. This is particularly noticeable for the seventeenth and eighteenth centuries. Also observable is the phenomenon of successive years of flood and/or drought; the large crises always tended to be multiyear events. There was also a distinct "reign cycle" whereby a new reign was generally accompanied by an extraordinarily large flood. This was true of the Kangxi, Yongzheng, Qianlong, Jiaqing, Daoguang, and Tongzhi reigns, but the Guangxu reign started with an extremely serious drought. This pattern can be seen as the legacy of decay and neglect of river conservancy at the end of the previous reign, and in part it served as a "wake-up call," prompting each new emperor to devote some attention to the rivers. Overall dynastic decline can also be observed in the increasing frequency of large-scale floods at the end of the dynasty that can be related to imperial neglect. Pierre-Étienne Will has described this phenomenon as a "hydraulic cycle."[64] For the Qing period, floods certainly increased dramatically at the end of the era. From 1870, flooding was almost a yearly occurrence in Zhili.[65]

Yet from a broader historical perspective, the deterioration of the river system by the end of the Qing was not simply part of a cyclical process; it was also the culmination of centuries of secular, long-term, environmental decline. Before Tang Dynasty (618–907) at least, the Yongding River was navigable. Only after Liao (947–1125) did silt start to be a problem and dikes built. In the

TABLE I.2

Major Natural Crises in the Hai River Basin During the Qing Period

Year	Reign Year	Type	Location/Extent/Description
1668	KX 7	Flood	50 xian (counties)
1680	KX 19	Drought	big drought (*da han*), hunger (*ji*), epidemic (*yi*), and migration
1691–92	KX 30–31	Drought	more than 70 xian
1696	KX 35	Flood	32 xian
1703	KX 42	Flood	26 xian
1721–22	KX 60–61	Drought	42 xian
1725	YZ 3	Flood	72 xian
1737–39	QL 2–4	Flood	87, 96, 72 xian
1743–44	QL 8–9	Drought	27 xian, very devastating, especially in 16 xian
1747	QL 12	Flood	63 xian
1750	QL 15	Flood	75 xian
1759	QL 24	Drought	many perished
1761–62	QL 26–27	Flood	70–115 xian, many deaths
1771	QL 36	Flood	74 xian
1780	QL 45	Flood	61 xian
			entire decade of 1780s saw much hunger; instances of cannibalism cited
1790	QL 55	Flood	61 xian
1794	QL 59	Flood	121 xian, high mortality
1801	JQ 6	Flood	160 xian
			entire decade of 1800s a succession of floods; also 1810s, 1820s
1813	JQ 18	Drought	southern prefectures, very serious, high mortality
1821	DG 1	Cholera	many deaths
1822–23	DG 2–3	Flood	120, 139 xian, high mortality
1830	DG 10	Earthquake	
1832	DG 12	Drought	
1834	DG 14	Flood	101 xian, followed by years of hunger
1859	XF 9	Drought	migration, deaths
1862	TZ 1	Epidemic	
1871–73	TZ 10–12	Flood	more than 70 xian
1876–77	GX 2–3	Drought	all of North China
			1880s and 1890s, almost yearly minor and major floods
1890	GX 16	Flood	112 xian, disease
1894	GX 20	Flood	117 xian
1899–1900	GX 25–26	Drought	"natural disaster and human calamity (*tianzai renhuo*)," Boxer Uprising coincided with drought

SOURCES: *Jifu tongzhi* 1884, juan 108–110; Wang Shulin, table 4, 168; *Zhongguo jin wubainian hanlao fenbu tuji*; *Haihe liuyu lidai ziran zaihai shiliao*; and *Haihe Luanhe honglao dang'an shiliao*.

Ming Dynasty (1368–1644), the river flooded twenty-nine times; on four of those occasions, Beijing was affected. There were much diking along the river, with stone being used for the first time.[66] Floods increased in Ming Wanli period (1573–1620) and into the Qing period; generally speaking, they were more dangerous than they had previously been.[67] According to one count, during the 268 years of the Qing, the Beijing area experienced drought in 161 years, flood in 129 years, famine in 30 years, and various other disasters.[68]

Zhu Kezhen, the climate historian, believed that the number of floods in Zhili had increased significantly in the past 300 years compared to earlier times. With population increase, there was more pressure on land, more cultivation in low-lying areas, and possibly more victims in times of disaster. Before there was such dense settlement, excess rain was not necessarily experienced as disaster. The Tianjin area had a population of about 400,000 in the Yuan, about 1.2 million in the late Ming, about 2 million in the Guangxu period, and 2.3 million in the 1920s.[69] In nearby Wen'an County, local residents in the 1920s were certain that the chronic flooding experienced in this low-lying area had been unknown a hundred years earlier.[70]

The number of disasters, their intensity, and their impact were not always directly proportional to the amount of precipitation. Although the rainfall data represented in Figure 1.1 is partly derived from historical chronologies, there is by no means a perfect corrrespondence between rainfall and experienced disaster. (Even less is there a strong correlation between amounts of rainfall and the economic impact as measured by grain prices.) In the eighteenth century there were some floods or droughts of notable proportion that did not receive as much mention in the historical records as other disasters of similar proportion. In 1743–44 there was a drought caused by a rainfall about 40 percent short of normal. Prices rose a moderate amount above their normal level, but were kept in check by relief grain supplies sent from other provinces. Two years later, in 1745–46, there was a similar deficit of rain, but little measurable price effect in millet.[71] In 1759–60, there was a major drought in northern China; its center was more in the northwest than in the Zhili region, but still many perished and grain prices soared. Yet, curiously, it is seldom mentioned in the *Jifu tongzhi* and in the local gazetteers, and it did not seem to receive much official attention in Zhili. Prices were higher in the 1813 drought than they were in 1817, when even less rain fell. In the late nineteenth century, the frequent and large-scale inundations were not always proportional to the amounts of rainfall because the deterioration of the river systems made any sudden and large rainfall a catastrophic event. In the Republican period, this was even more apparent. In the huge flood of 1917 only 415 mm fell in Tianjin, and less than 800 mm of rain fell in Beijing, far less than what fell in the great 1801 flood and less than the amounts during the 1890s floods, and certainly not an amount that should have been considered disastrous.

Several factors may help to account for the lack of perfect correspondence. It is the Beijing rainfall data that is used here, and Beijing tends to have more rain than other parts of the region. Moreover, a flood could often occur in one locality, but be absent from an adjacent community. The same amount of rain in two localities with different local diking and management situations could have different impacts. Floods could result from waters upstream and not from local rainfall. Moreover, multiple events could occur in the same year, such as spring drought–fall flood, or other combinations, but these are difficult to distinguish in a standard chronicle of events. In the agricultural statistics collected in China today, a distinction is made between the acreage subject to disaster each year (*shouzai mianji*) and the area where disaster actually results (*chengzai mianji*).[72]

Moreover, floods and droughts operated in very distinct ways. Drought is generally a more geographically widespread phenomenon, not contained in one locality. A major drought could usually be anticipated because it was the cumulative effect of several months, seasons, and even years of dry conditions. Although it could not be prevented by human intervention, its consequences could be mitigated by grain storage and famine relief, as in 1743–44. It was possible for officials to plan for relief in advance, but the major droughts in the Hai River Basin during the past three centuries—in 1759–60, 1813, 1876–77, 1900, and 1920—had far more serious human consequences than the major floods. In Kangxi reign, the Zhili governor-general Li Guangdi had observed that in the north drought was 80 percent of the problem, while flood was 20 percent.[73] This was so despite the greater bureaucratic attention paid to flood prevention and relief and the more frequent references to flooding. In the late nineteenth century floods became more frequent and disruptive than before, but it was still true that severe drought was more harmful, and recovery required a longer period. A deficit of rainfall was responsible for low productivity in North China, not excess rainfall, which was rarer and could produce positive benefits under certain circumstances.

Major floods may have been less predictable than major droughts, and when they occurred, there was physical destruction of houses and fields and dislocation of the population. However, floods were more directly affected by human engineering, which could either contribute to, or prevent, their occurrence. Smaller-scale floods could be more locally contained, depending on the terrain and the degree of local preparation. Eighteenth-century official Wang Fengsheng said, "Famine caused by flooding stretches like a thread, famine caused by drought spreads like a sheet."[74]

Floods, moreover, were sometimes regarded as beneficial to crops. In low-lying localities, there were some fields called *yishui yimai* land, or "one flood, one wheat crop," because the land that had been inundated in the late summer and fall left the soil very fertile for the planting of winter wheat, which would grow abundantly by the time of its harvest next spring. The seventeenth-century scholar and agricultural expert Xu Guangqi helped promote this positive attitude toward flooding. The eighteenth-century Zhili governor-general Fang Guancheng observed the local practice of taking advantage of the summer floods for winter wheat. In the twentieth century, John Lossing Buck, the American agricultural expert, saw the same phenomenon in the 1920s: "In North China some of the low land, which is often spoken of as 'lake land' because it is flooded and becomes a lake in the summer time, is only free from water during the season that wheat can be grown."[75]

The Local Records and Social Consequences of Disasters

Local gazetteers usually list crises, but generally only major events. The criteria by which crises were determined to be noteworthy were certainly not consistent or self-apparent. The social consequences of such disasters are described less frequently than one might expect. In the Qing gazetteers, hunger and mortality are explicitly mentioned only infrequently. The fact that many people fled is occasionally mentioned: *liuwang shencong*. The fact that people died is mentioned very rarely: *ren si shenduo*. Mention of cannibalism is even rarer: *ren xiang shi* ("people ate each other").

The gazetteer of Xincheng County on the waterlogged plain in Baoding Prefecture records the following years in which the terms for hunger, *ji* or *daji*, or mention of mortality, occurs: 1654–56 (flood); 1668 (death by drowning); 1725 (rain); 1762–63 (rain); 1773 (sunstroke deaths); 1799 (locusts, big hunger); 1801 (big flood); 1813 (rain, hail); 1817; 1821 (epidemic, not hunger); 1823; 1832; 1878 (epidemic, deaths plus hunger); and 1892.[76] These years of suffering roughly correspond to the provincewide list, but there were many other years when flood or drought affected the county, but not to the extent of creating hunger or famine mortality.

In Xingtai County, in the relatively better piedmont section of Shunde Prefecture, there is mention of cannibalism in the Ming, but for the Qing, in 1742, many people died of heat. In 1760 there was great hunger in the spring and people died. In 1791–92, there were crop failures and people died. There was great hunger in 1801 and again in 1804 and 1806. Not again for half a century was hunger mentioned, in 1857, 1877, and 1880.[77] In Pingxiang County in the same prefecture, there was big hunger in 1708–9 and 1792–93. In 1812–13, poor people sold their children. In 1846 there was big hunger.[78]

In Xinhe County in Jizhou, a very poor area, hunger was listed for 1721 and 1723. For 1757, 1791, and 1794, there were big floods, but no hunger is mentioned. Similarly in 1799 and 1802, there were floods and in 1813 drought, but no hunger is mentioned. In 1822–24, there were floods. In 1857, 1859, and 1866, there was great hunger due to droughts. In 1859, people all fled. In 1878 there were corpses on the road in spring and summer, but there was a good fall harvest. In 1900 and the occurrence of the Boxer Uprising during a prolonged drought was described as "natural disaster and human calamity" (*tianzai renhuo*).[79]

In comparison with the records of Ming dynasty, the Qing records contain few heart-wrenching stories of famine victims. The rare references to mortality and suffering in the Qing records are different from records of the Ming, and even the early Qing, which routinely described in highly dramatic terms personal and local tragedies related to famines and epidemics. The local gazetteers of the region recorded yearly for the last decades of the Ming the occurrence of hunger or "big hunger," *ji* or *daji*, and many examples of cannibalism, *ren xiang shi*.[80] Another expression, *yizi er shi*, "exchange your sons and eat them," often accompanies such descriptions. (This latter intends to express the repugnance at resorting to the eating of one's own child.) Such tragedies were the result of widespread epidemics in the late Ming, as well as natural disasters and rebellions.[81] There were some spectacularly horrible famines in the mid-sixteenth century.[82] A considerable literature on famine and famine relief was produced, including the *Jiuhuang bencao*, written by Zhou Dingwang, an encyclopedia of plants that could be used as famine foods.[83] The information contained in this work was considered important enough to be included in a substantial section of Xu Guangqi's famous agricultural encyclopedia *Nongzheng quanshu*, also compiled in the late Ming.[84] Illustrated accounts of famine in Henan in the 1590s provide some of the most gruesome views of the human tragedies that resulted.[85]

The 1675 edition of the gazetteer of Xianghe County in Shuntian Prefecture records that in 1639, just at the end of the Ming reign, there was a major famine. Grain prices were sky-high. People ate bark and grass, and died. People also resorted to cannibalism. Famine refugees from Shandong Province came carrying their children and died on the road. Their barely dead bodies were preyed upon by others, who cut off flesh. In 1655, a huge flood resulted in food and resource scarcity; this was followed by severe winter snow and frost. In one village there was a young couple named Guo who had a little girl of four *sui*. To save themselves from starvation, the wife was sold for 1,000 or 2,000 cash (*qian*), but the husband was so overcome with grief when his wife left that he clung to his daughter and cried for three or four days without stopping. When neighbors discovered him, they saw that he and the girl had died, with the money still at the side of the bed.[86]

Does the infrequency of such stories for most of the Qing period, especially compared with the Ming and Republican periods, suggest that high mortality was actually averted? During the eighteenth century, only a few of the worst crises, such as the 1743–44 drought, or the 1761 flood were accompanied by mention of grave starvation and high mortality. By the 1780s and 1790s, however, disasters were sometimes, but not always, noted with mentions of hunger, even cannibalism, and high mortality. In the early nineteenth century, mortality was mentioned in some crises, but not until the great North China drought of the 1870s were dreadful stories of starvation a significant part of the local records. Could this mean that while there were an increasing number of natural disasters in the Qing, their human and social consequences were less severe than in the Ming? Or does this mean that Qing historical sources simply fail to mention the human consequences of famine? Although it is difficult to prove a negative, there is considerable evidence to support the first view. In the Qing period some of the extreme economic and social consequences of floods and droughts were mitigated by the generous use of famine prevention and relief measures, such as grain transfers from other provinces, grain storage and distributions, soup kitchens, tax remissions, and the like.

Starvation, migration, cannibalism, and high excess mortality were among the visible outcomes of "famine"—extreme subsistence crises that resulted from harvest failures, which in turn usually had "natural" causes. Although large-scale, regionwide disasters occurred periodically, the year-to-year experience of local communities and peasant households included the more numerous and frequent smaller-scale disasters that did not necessarily result in visible famine mortality, but were the basis for constant uncertainty about each year's harvest. When rainfall was so scarce even in good years, the margin between an adequate harvest and deficient harvest was narrow. Uncertainty due to climatic variability led to low agricultural productivity, locking most peasants into a low-level subsistence standard of living. The economic consequence of a small negative event, such as a poor harvest or loss of one crop, could spell difficult social consequences, such as incurring debts, the sale of property, begging, the sale of wife or children, or infanticide. Such events were sometimes so "normal" that it is hard to classify them as outcomes of a particular crisis rather than those of persistent scarcity and dearth. Such "normal" events are even more difficult to measure quantitatively than crisis events.

High mortality and low life expectancy were the rule for North China's population. Malnutrition and disease were the main causes, but these were difficult to quantify before the twentieth century.[87] Infanticide, particularly female infanticide, for example, was undoubtedly a well-known practice. Although almost never documented, infanticide was probably practiced as an act of desperation in economically impoverished circumstances that did not necessarily have to reach the level of "famine." Thus it is difficult to say whether infanticide should be considered only a crisis-driven action, or whether it should be considered "normal."[88] In Jingxing County's gazetteer, the practice of female infanticide was seen as an evil old custom that should be extirpated, but unfortunately it seemed to be increasing during the early twentieth century, extending even to the killing of boy babies. Such an observation reflects the Republican-period social reformist perspective and is not found in earlier editions.[89] Infanticide was one means by which the high fertility rates in China were undercut by high "normal" mortality, not even the high "excess" mortality associated with famines. ("Excess mortality" is a demographic term that refers to mortality in excess of normal rates.) It is one of several examples of the impossibility of defining "famine" formally as a subsistence crisis that results in high excess mortality, and distinguishing it as an abnormal event. The line between "famine"—*zaihuang* or *jihuang*—and everyday, year-to-year subsistence and hunger was thin indeed.

Conclusion

Throughout centuries of human habitation, the river systems, the terrain, and the climatic patterns of the Hai River Basin formed a natural environment that made agricultural production vulnerable to year-to-year uncertainty and periodic large-scale harvest failures. For the millions of farmers who have toiled in this region, as well as agricultural researchers and state planners, the weather was, and still is, the single most important variable in their year-to-year output, although in recent decades the extent of direct impact has been reduced.[90]

For historians, knowledge of climatic history forms an essential context for understanding the agrarian economy of China past and present. Yet we must eschew a simple historical reductionism. What is important about the climate of the past or present is not that it directly causes particular political, economic, or social results, but rather the way in which politics, economy, and society have adapted to the weather and other environmental challenges. Since the excitement caused by the work of Ferdinand Braudel, chronicler of the history of the Mediterranean world, and H. H. Lamb, the eminent climate historian—both of whom saw the direct impact of climatic forces on European history—scholars of Europe have become more skeptical about seeing large causal connections between the climate and history. Although it is tempting to attribute the population decline, epidemics, warfare, and falling yields of Europe's seventeenth-century crisis to a "Little Ice Age," or to imply that years of poor harvests impelled American colonists to revolution, such broad-brushed explanations seem too crude to explain the difference between responses in England or France to the same climate patterns, for example.[91] Likewise, the fact that rainfall in North China increased during the late eighteenth and early nineteenth centuries hardly seems a sufficient explanation, for example, of the complex politics of the Heshen period of the late Qianlong reign.

Understanding the environment helps us to understand the context in which the agrarian economy developed, but it does not by itself explain how history has evolved. The response of state, society, and individuals is not predictable by statistics on rainfall. The unstable climate and unfavorable environment of North China formed a challenge to state and society to develop coping strategies. These responses and strategies in turn affected the environment, yielding short-term advantages and cushioning the impact of natural disasters, but producing unintended consequences that increased vulnerability in the long run. The repeated efforts to control the rivers, when successful, facilitated more stable farming and allowed the land to support a denser population. But channeling and diking the rivers hastened the process of silting, which in turn increased the likelihood of flooding. The denser population settlement meant that more people would be victimized when floods and droughts occurred; it also meant that the population-to-land ratio increased, making it more challenging to meet the fundamental requirements of subsistence.

CHAPTER TWO

Managing the Rivers:
Emperors as Engineers

THE QING EMPERORS devoted an extraordinary amount of attention and resources to the management of the rivers in Jifu, "the capital region." Although less central and smaller in scale than the Yellow River, the Zhili rivers demanded attention because of their proximity to the capital and their close relationship to the Grand Canal. The most ambitious of the emperors sought to emulate the Great Yu conquering the waters, but, working in consultation with their top advisors, they also found themselves in the role of engineers. This historic process followed a "hydraulic cycle" that resembled the classic dynastic cycle.[1] The early emperors invested prodigious effort and resources into river management, while the later emperors were increasingly unable to do so. There was also a "reign cycle" evident in the history of imperial river management. In each reign period—starting with Kangxi and ending with Guangxu—a large flood, usually at the beginning of the reign, caused the new emperor to launch a major river conservancy campaign. The initial event served as both a wake-up call and an opportunity for the new emperor to show his merit and his concern for the people. A major river construction campaign required large sums of money and also provided an opportunity to shake up the bureaucracy. By the end of the reign, however, neglect again set in, and inevitably more frequent flooding occurred, setting the stage for the cycle to begin anew.

There were some exceptions to the normal pattern. In the Kangxi reign, the major flood occurred not at the beginning, but at the midpoint, in the 1690s. For the Yongzheng, Qianlong, Jiaqing, and Daoguang reigns, however, the pattern is striking. Especially large floods in 1725, 1737, 1801, 1822, all close to the start of these reigns, galvanized emperor and bureaucracy into major relief campaigns followed by large-scale hydraulic reconstruction. (See Table 2.1.) In the Qianlong period, which lasted sixty years, there was a minor cycle in midreign, around 1759–62, when major floods and droughts inspired Fang Guancheng, an energetic and experienced provincial official trusted by the emperor, to undertake major river control and famine relief projects. In the late nineteenth century, we can see the same pattern if we substitute the first year of Li Hongzhang's rule as governor-general of Zhili in 1870, the ninth year of the Tongzhi reign, for the beginning of a reign period. Especially large floods occurred in 1871–73. Although limited in the resources he could bring to the deteriorating situation, Li Hongzhang followed precedents by trying to organ-

TABLE 2.1

Major Construction Projects in Zhili, 1698–1824

Reign	Year	Project	Cost (taels)
Kangxi	1698	Yongding River	30,000
	1700–01	Yongding River	52,000
Yongzheng	1726–30	Rice irrigation	
	1726	Comprehensive plan, including Thousand-Li Dike	
Qianlong	1739	Various projects	
	1744–47	Comprehensive plan	700,000 (900,000 budgeted)
	1762–63	Comprehensive plan, including Thousand-Li Dike and Hai River	200,000 shi grain tribute, and 526,000 taels for construction
Jiaqing	1801–02	Comprehensive plan	971,000
	1806	Comprehensive plan, including Thousand-Li Dike	400,000 (600,000 budgeted) of which 270,000 on dike
	1810	Tang River between Xi dian and Dong dian	1,000,000
Daoguang	1822–23	Relief and rivers	1,800,000
	1824	Comprehensive	1,200,000 needed (550,000 to be raised from contributions)
		Thousand-Li Dike	370,000 granted

SOURCE: See text.

ize a limited solution of the Zhili river crisis and also by reviving famine relief procedures from the early nineteenth century. Only the mid-nineteenth-century reign of Xianfeng was a full exception to this reign pattern; there was no ability to launch campaigns given the crises of the Taiping Rebellion and foreign imperialism, and it was also a relatively dry period.

The management of water was generally known as *shuili*, lit., "water benefits." The control of rivers, *hegong*, lit., "river works," was one aspect of *shuili* and emphasized flood prevention, particularly that of the Yellow River. It usually involved the official sponsorship of hydraulic construction, such as dikes or levees (*di*), sluice gates (*shuimen, zha*), weirs and dams (*ba*), or canals (*qu*).[2] It often involved maintenance activities such as dredging, scouring, and annual repairs. On the Yellow River, the Grand Canal, and the major rivers in Zhili, the cost of such river work was usually borne by the central government, not local authorities, although the labor was usually recruited, and sometimes paid for, locally. The other, equally important, aspect of water management in China was regulating its use for agriculture; this was *shuili* in its narrower sense. *Shuili* might involve lakes and streams as well as rivers, and its principal purpose was irrigation. In specific terms, *shuili* might involve engineering projects such as drainage and reclamation of land, diversion of waterways, the creation of irrigation channels, polders, and rice fields—usually undertaken through local initiatives. For the wet-rice cultivation of central and southern China that had been intensively practiced since the Song period, *shuili* was both motive and method. Only with the sophisticated techniques of dams, bridges, wheels, and pumps was the transformation of the landscape of the south into terraced rice paddies accomplished.

Shuili and *hegong* balanced the interests of state, community, and landowner rather differently. *Hegong* required larger-scale organization and greater costs; it often pitted the interests of upstream and downstream communities against each other, but the interests of the state had the highest priority. *Shuili* for irrigation, on the other hand, could be accomplished on a smaller scale, sometimes within a single community. The state's priorities did not necessarily conflict with those of the community; more prominent were the conflicts of interests and competition for resources among local residents. In Hunan and Zhejiang, two regions that have been the subject of recent books, the state often intervened on the side of the local community's collective interest in having its water resources protected, and against the predatory encroachment of individuals trying to reclaim lakes for agricultural use.[3] In Zhili, the control of rivers was the paramount concern, but since the rivers were connected to lakes, wetlands, or swamps, there were aspects of *shuili* involved. Although irrigation was not widely used in North China, on several occasions, emperors and bureaucrats were convinced that the irrigation techniques of the south could and should be applied to the capital region.

The extraordinary degree of imperial and bureaucratic attention paid to the Zhili rivers, sometimes more rhetorical than real, is reflected in numerous collections of documents and essays pertaining to the subject. Rivers, especially the Yellow River, generally form a substantial section of the traditional histories and documentary collections. Zhili rivers also merit an entire section of the provincial gazetteer, *Jifu tongzhi*. Other collections focus exclusively on the Zhili rivers and represent only the tip of a huge documentary iceberg. Stored in the vast collections of the First Historical Archives in Beijing and the Palace Museum in Taipei are thousands of edicts and memorials pertaining to the year-by-year, month-by-month, and sometimes even the day-to-day, routine management of rivers in Zhili, not to mention the Yellow River and Grand Canal. They record length of dikes repaired, volume of silt removed, bales of straw or reeds secured, and their various costs. Representing almost every period, the sheer volume of this collection is evidence of the importance of river control as a bureaucratic function. For Zhili, the greatest concentration of documents is in the early and mid-Qianlong period, and the Jiaqing period. Documents are sparse for the mid-nineteenth century and then become more numerous in the 1870s and 1880s, following the career of Li Hongzhang.

While traditional dynastic history celebrates the leadership of emperors in river control, in the twentieth century both Western and Chinese observers have been critical of hydraulic imperialism. In his theory of "hydraulic despotism," Karl Wittfogel theorized that great ancient civilizations such as China, India, Egypt, and Mesopotamia had become authoritarian, or despotic, *because of* the need to recruit masses of laborers to tame their unruly rivers.[4] Mao-era Chinese scholarship also condemned the imperial agenda in the Hai River Basin, but from a Marxist perspective.[5] More recently Chinese scholars have turned away from these political agendas and, instead, emphasized environmental deterioration as the cause of natural crises.[6]

The emperors did make a difference. Even though they were not ideally qualified to be engineers, their political resolve was necessary for anything to be done. Yet imperial power, even at its height, had limitations. Whether they were motivated by a desire "to protect the livelihood of the people," or by a narrow concern for the food security of the capital, emperors met obstacles and resistance to their ambitions. The large sums of money spent for river projects, as well as for famine relief, invited corruption, and the numbers of officials, subofficials, and functionaries required to execute and maintain them meant that supervising the personnel became a challenge as great as controlling the rivers. Equally frustrating in the later reigns was the environmental decline that was the unforeseen consequence of the earlier engineering successes. Dynastic hagiography and the Wittfogelian critique were alike in overestimating the long-term efficacy of imperial authority.

Kangxi and the Yongding River

In the management of Zhili's rivers, as in almost all aspects of Qing history, both the history and legend accord the great Kangxi emperor the pride of leadership. In 1698, in the thirty-seventh year of his reign, he commemorated the completion of a major dike by renaming the river that was causing so much trouble in the capital region, the Yongding, or "Eternally Stable River." Since that time all accounts of river control in this region begin here. They also speak of the emperor's compassion for the local people when he saw them eating grass after a major flood.[7]

Life in North China in the mid- to late seventeenth century was, by all accounts, harsh and tumultuous. In the last years of the Ming period, Jifu had been beset with dreadful hunger and social unrest, largely the consequence of rebellion and conquest, but also resulting from epidemic, locusts, and drought. For the first four decades of the Qing, hunger, poverty, and banditry were prevalent. The spring of 1653 saw serious drought followed by summer flood. In 1668 there was a flood affecting fifty counties.[8] The year 1689 witnessed severe drought throughout much of the region, which was followed by a more extensive drought in 1691–92.[9] But for the most part, large-scale flooding was not a major problem in the first decades of the Qing, and there was little attention to river matters in Zhili.

Instead, after the Manchu conquest of North China, the first two emperors had been unavoidably concerned with the settlement of banner forces in the capital area and with the process of appropriation of former Ming estates for the use of bannermen in the capital area. Both Shunzhi and Kangxi seem to have recognized the hardships of peasant life and the unpredictability of the natural conditions in the capital region. In 1655–57, in recommending tax remissions and other relief for Jifu residents, Shunzhi specified that half should be given to bannermen and half to the poor (Han) people of the region. He knew that local people were bitter about the confiscation of their lands, and that in addition they were subjected to flood and drought in successive years and had very few resources to fall back on. "Jifu's territory is the root of the universe, and we must nurture it and its people carefully," he declared.[10] Kangxi, like his father, expressed his concern for the welfare of Jifu residents displaced by banner lands.[11] He paid special attention also to the problem of banditry that threatened the security of the people of the region, as well as the hunger and social disorder caused by an epidemic in 1681.[12] To demonstrate his sympathy for the impoverished lives of peasants in this region, he often granted tax remissions. On one such occasion, in 1689, he wrote, "The life of the small people is bitter," and only the rich households could afford to buy [grain] cheap and sell high; the rest had no recourse in times of disaster.[13]

Starting in the 1690s, in the middle of his reign, however, the frequent small breaks in the Yongding River became more critical, posing a potential danger to the capital and attracting the direct attention of the Kangxi emperor. As silting increased, the left bank of the river, which skirted the city wall of Beijing at Lugou Bridge, was in constant danger of overflowing and threatening the city itself. While the Yongding River was not a central problem of the empire, as the Yellow River was, its critical location posed a problem impossible to ignore. In the previous decade, Kangxi had been heavily involved in the Yellow River conservancy and the Grand Canal. He considered the control of the Yellow River and the grain transport system extremely critical to the empire, and he personally selected the officials to mastermind the major engineering projects. One of the purposes of his six imperial tours of the south between 1684 and 1707 was to observe personally the operation of the Grand Canal.[14]

The emperor may have been emboldened by successes in the Yellow River conservancy to apply some of its lessons to the Yongding River. Some of the officials who came to play a large role in the Yongding conservancy had been prominent in the management of the Grand Canal and Yellow River. Yu Chenglong, who served as governor in Zhili and played a major role in the Yongding River matters, was one. He had advocated deepening the riverbed in the lower reaches of the river, but he had been opposed by Jin Fu, the major force in the Yellow River conservancy during the 1680s; the two were rivals who were alternately in favor until Jin Fu's death in 1692. Wang Xinming, a river official who eventually succeeded Jin Fu, later served in Zhili.[15]

In the last thirty years of his reign, Kangxi sponsored seven major dike construction projects on the Yongding River.[16] Although the first project, building a new dike to protect Gu'an and Yongqing counties downstream from Beijing, took place in 1692, the first major construction was in 1698.[17] After the river overflowed its banks and threatened Bazhou, Xin'an, and surrounding localities, the emperor personally went to inspect the area and saw the flooded fields and the homeless and hungry people eating grass. He ordered Yu Chenglong, now Zhili governor, to inspect the area, make a map, and draw up a plan for him to study. He resolved to dredge the river and build a new dike. Especially interesting is that the emperor explicitly forbade the use of the ordinary people (*baixing*) in river work because their labor was needed for farming; instead he ordered able-bodied young bannermen to prepare tools and be given money and provisions to do the work.[18]

This was the first time any diking or dredging had been done in the middle and lower reaches of the Yongding River, although in previous dynasties stone dikes had been constructed in its upper reaches, north of Lugou Bridge. The project was on a large scale, affecting seven counties and 139 qing of land and costing 30,000 taels.[19] Dikes on both banks were greatly extended below the Lugou Bridge, for a distance of 82 li on the south bank, and 102 li on the north bank. In addition, 145 li of river was dredged.[20] The emperor was well informed about the problem of siltation and the rapidly rising riverbeds.[21] The work, begun in the fourth month and completed in the seventh month, was considered a triumph of imperial acumen. At Yu Chenglong's suggestion, Kangxi changed the name of the river to "Yongding" and ordered the construction of a river god temple with a commemorative plaque.[22]

In the next year, however, especially heavy rains caused the dikes to collapse in many places. The emperor went personally to inspect the dikes, where he observed the silting there and the flooded fields south of the Lugou Bridge. He observed how the water needed to be deep and run fast to scour the river of silt. Two days later he went again to a place in Yongqing, and, grasping a *Baoweiqiang* (for Ximen Bao) instrument, he personally measured the silt below the ice and found it had risen seven to eight feet. He ordered the digging of another channel that would make the south bank into the north bank, allowing some water to drain into swamps and the rest to flow out to the ocean at Tianjin.[23] The water would be channeled between two long levees and would flow rapidly. Work began in 1700, with the emperor taking a personal interest in the engineering and the personnel, and was completed in a year and a half at a cost of 52,000 taels. The south bank was extended 70 li, for a total of 179 li, and the north bank for more than 70 li, for a total of 180 li, and from that time, the middle and lower reaches of the Yongding River were entirely protected by levees.[24]

The Kangxi emperor regarded the taming of the Yongding River as a test of his leadership and the character of the bureaucracy. He saw that control of the river was dependent on his personal example and also on the ability of the high and low officials. For him control of the rivers and control of the bureaucracy were closely related. "If the officials are not clear [*qing*], then it harms the people. If the water is not clear [*qing*], that, too, is of no benefit to the people. All the muddiness [*zhuo*] in the world is like this. As for officials that are not clear, I have a method to correct them. As for water that is not clear, I have a policy to manage it."[25] The emperor proudly assumed the role of engineer, boasting of his own technological know-how. In 1700, he wrote, "When I went to inspect the Yongding River, I saw that the river workers did not have much knowledge. The various river officials felt enlightened and were very happy when I pointed out many details to them. In general, those who have the responsibility for river work are diligent and honest and will soon achieve results. When this work is completed, the Yellow River repairs can follow this example." When he took a small boat into the Langcheng district, where the riverbed was completely silted and raised up, and demanded some answers, the high officials were too frightened to come forward.[26]

Kangxi continued to be attentive to every detail and seemed to know the character and ability of even the lower-level personnel. The Zhili governor-general kept an eye on the river officials and regularly reported to the emperor on their conduct. When he reported that several functionaries were absent from the river site and faulted their supervising official, a subdistrict magistrate, for negligence, the emperor commented that this did not surprise him: "I have long had a deep knowledge of that person. He was, to begin with, nothing but an ordinary type."[27] On at least one occasion, he also asked both high and low officials to contribute money for river construction.[28]

The administration of the Yongding River was institutionalized in 1698, with separate officials under the direction of the Zhili governor to supervise the north and south banks. Each bank had eight separate patrols with thirty-six staff who would daily supervise the patrolling of the river by a force of 2,000 river soldiers.[29] In 1698, the total for urgent repairs (*qiangxiu*) and annual repairs (*suixiu*) was 30–40,000 taels a year, which was considered generous. Officials could memorialize anytime for additional funds of 70–80,000 taels for construction.[30] In 1704 new procedures and military patrols for river surveillance were put in place. Local prefectural and district officials were required to cooperate in river surveillance. Secret reports of breaches in the river were to be made within two or three days and attended to immediately.[31]

From 1701–22, no major crises occurred, and the river did not shift again. There were, however, four more repairs, with large expenditures in KX 49, 55, 59, and 60. In his later years, Kangxi no longer personally went to the river, but he continued to express his concern that river work get done promptly. If the dikes ruptured, he admonished, the harm to people would be great.[32] Historian Ding Jinjun praised the Kangxi emperor's accomplishment in controlling the river, which did not shift again during his reign. Kangxi showed his concern for the people by ordering soldiers under bannermen and bondservants, as well as hired laborers, to work on the river. Even if he asked for contributions or local taxes, most of this work was financed by the central government and did not exploit the people.[33] Ding's view is at least partly supported by the memorials of Governor Zhao Hongxie, who was in constant communication with the emperor about the various rivers, especially the Yongding. In 1706 he noted that in several key points *yaodi* ("distant dikes") had been consolidated with the main dikes (the big dike). The *yaodi* were the responsibility of the local officials, but sometimes the funds were inadequate and needed to be supplemented by official funds.[34] In other places, rich households that had built weirs, or *ba*, had been asked to contribute to the cost, but in 1715, given the severity of flood damage that year, Zhao pointed out that the wealthy households could not be expected to provide all the manpower or costs by themselves.[35] Elsewhere in the empire, construction was supposed to be funded by local communities, but it is clear that the central government assumed many of the costs in Zhili.[36]

Yongzheng, Prince Yi, and a Comprehensive Plan

The Kangxi emperor was the great empire-builder and exemplary ruler, whose reign lasted sixty-one years; the Yongzheng emperor, his son and successor, was the formidable institution-builder, who in a relatively short, thirteen-year reign, left a lasting legacy. In 1725, the third year of his reign, extensive floods in Zhili captured the new emperor's attention and caused him to put Zhili river control high on his ambitious administrative agenda. Heavy summer rains reached most parts of the region, affecting seventy or more counties. In the especially low-lying Tianjin area, water stayed on the land like a "vast ocean," *yipian wangyang*. Fields were ruined and private dikes (*mindi*) were toppled in thirty-two places. The Nan Yunhe was breached in thirteen places. Close to Beijing, roads and bridges were washed out, and in the sixth and seventh month, floodwaters reached even into the capital.[37] The emperor must surely have been impressed with the vulnerability of the region to excessive rainfall.[38] A total of seventy-four counties were affected in this year, and the next year all taxes were forgiven.[39] Some local records describe this year as one of *dahuang* (a big crop failure) or *daji* (big famine).[40]

In the seventh month, the Yongzheng emperor enjoined his high officials to make a comprehensive plan for river conservancy in the Zhili region, and the next month he replaced Li Weijun with Li Fu as governor-general of Zhili charged with the task of overseeing the problem. In addition he appointed Zhu Shi and others experienced with river conservancy to posts in Zhili.[41] And finally, in the eleventh month, he authorized his most trusted brother, Prince Yi (Yi Qinwang, or Yinxiang), to work with Zhu Shi in a thorough investigation of Zhili's rivers and to produce a plan within one month![42] The emperor had a fairly clear view of the difficulties in Zhili. "Zhili's land is low-lying and water does not drain off." He ordered Zhu Shi and Prince Yi to undertake a comprehensive investigation of Zhili's *shuili*—not just its *hegong*—with the assumption that there were "benefits," or positive aspects, of Zhili's water that could be harnessed for productive use. He hoped for a multifaceted plan that would provide a permanent solution to Zhili's flood problems and bring *yilao yongyi*, or "eternal ease after one effort."[43]

Prince Yi's comprehensive report to the emperor stressed the need to manage the complex network of rivers, channels, and swamps in the core of the capital region. He wrote that in the Tianjin region there were three sources of water: the Bai River, which flowed south; the Wei River, which flowed northward; and the "Dian he," which flowed eastward.[44] In this period "Dian he" was the name of a river, probably the section of river connecting the Dong dian, Eastern Lake, at the confluence of the Yongding, Ziya, and Qing rivers, with the Bei Yunhe.[45] (See Map 2.1.) Prince Yi said that the Dian was composed of the waters from the swamps and ponds between the Bai and Wei rivers, and the Dong dian in particular was the key to drainage in the area, but the rivers draining into it had become silted. To solve Zhili's river problems, one should start from these *dian*, or swamps. But most central to Prince Yi's vision was that these accumulated waters could be used for the irrigation of fields that could be planted with rice.[46] *Xinhe*, or diversionary canals, should be dug to divert the water to the ocean.[47] With considerable hyperbole, he said that "Jifu's soil is the most fertile in the empire."[48] If rice cultivation and irrigation could be launched in Zhili, eternal ease would be achieved after this one big effort, *yilao yongyi*, and the needs of the people's livelihood could be met.[49]

The emperor approved the project and gave Prince Yi total authority to manage it. Starting the next year, 1726, Prince Yi divided the capital area into four regions, each with a staff directly appointed by himself. Over the next few years until his death in 1730, he supervised the digging of canals and ditches and had rice planted in about 5,351 qing. Of these, about 65 percent was state managed (*guoying*) and 35 percent privately undertaken (*minying*). These rice fields were spread over approximately forty counties in the province; the densest concentration was in the low-lying swampy areas just west and south of the capital, including Wen'an, Xin'an, and Anxiu counties, but they extended as far south and west as Zhengding and Xingtai.[50]

By all accounts this was an astonishing accomplishment achieved in four short years. The rice was intended to provide a buffer for the state, perhaps reducing its dependency on grain tribute from the south, but it was also designed to benefit the farmers of the region. However, the officials knew that the local people preferred wheat and millet for their own diet; so the government had a plan to buy the rice they produced, and the farmers were to use the proceeds to purchase their own food. Yields were up to 3–4 shi per mu, according to one local claim.[51]

Although the rice project (*shuili yingtian*) was associated with Prince Yi, this was not the first time that the idea of rice cultivation was promoted for the north, nor was it to be the last time. In the Ming period, well-known agricultural authorities such as Xu Guangqi in his *Nongzheng quanshu* advocated the growing of rice in the north. During the Wanli period, the official Xu Zhenming was a spirited advocate of rice cultivation for North China. Petitioning the emperor, he said that the people in the north feared water because of the danger of floods, but they had not studied *shuili* and learned to take advantage of water. Rice cultivation in the north would relieve the southeast of the burden of feeding the north and, in addition, save the state the cost of grain transport, which was double the cost of the grain itself. Xu Zhenming also argued that rice cultivation would help to reduce the burden of military conscription in the north, which it disproportionately bore, while the south had the burden of grain transport. If the north could be self-sufficient in grain, he reasoned that its military conscription could also be lightened. For his ideas, Xu Zhenming received severe criticism and was banished to Lu he, where he wrote his famous essay "Lushui ketan."[52]

After Prince Yi's death, rice cultivation continued in some localities, but on a much smaller scale. At the end of Yongzheng's reign, the new emperor decreed that the responsibility for rice cultivation should pass to local officials, but be supervised by higher officials.[53] Still, where it continued, it was substantially subsidized by the government and was controversial. Although Prince Yi is best remembered for the rice irrigation scheme, his river conservancy plan included other more enduring features.[54] In 1726 Prince Yi reported also on the completion of work on the major rivers in Zhili: the Bai and Wei rivers, the Yongding River, and the so-called Thousand-Li Dike, which followed the Daqing River north of Baoding and Wen'an counties, near the confluence of the Ziya River, not far from Nan Yunhe and Jinghai County. This long dike would protect the fields and productive marshlands of ten counties.[55] In addition the southern dike on the Yongding River was extended another 44 li to Wuqing County, the northern dike another 74 li, and dredging was extended another 74 li to the swamps, the Sanjiao dian in particular, near Tianjin where water could drain out to the ocean.[56] The entire south dike, now 196 li, and north dike, now 230 li, were still divided into eight sections, under the supervision of the southern and northern bank managers, later consolidated into one post.[57]

The Dong dian, or Eastern Lake, was another major focus of the overall plan. (A *dian* is a shallow lake or swamp.) "The Dong dian controls the water of the entire province, and the only exit

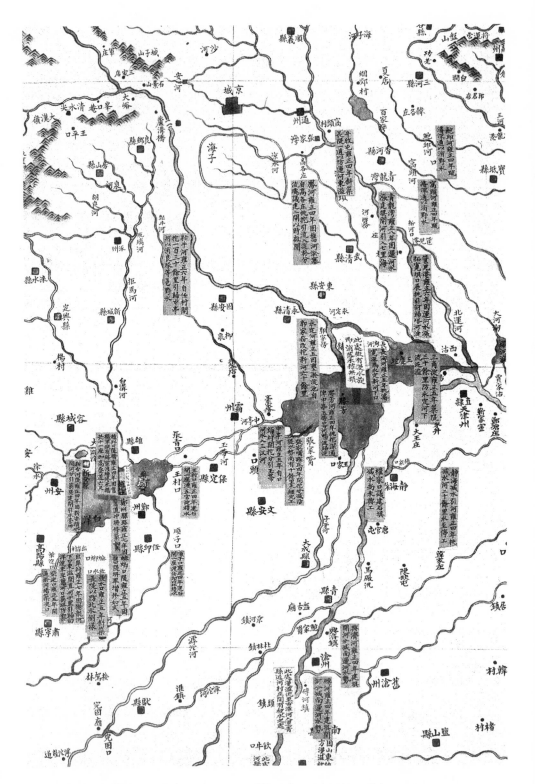

MAP 2.1A. Yongzheng map with major projects. View of central portion of river system.
The Xi dian is on the left, linked to the Dong dian (also called Sanjiao dian) on the right.

SOURCE: First Historical Archives, Neiwufu yutu, Number 104.

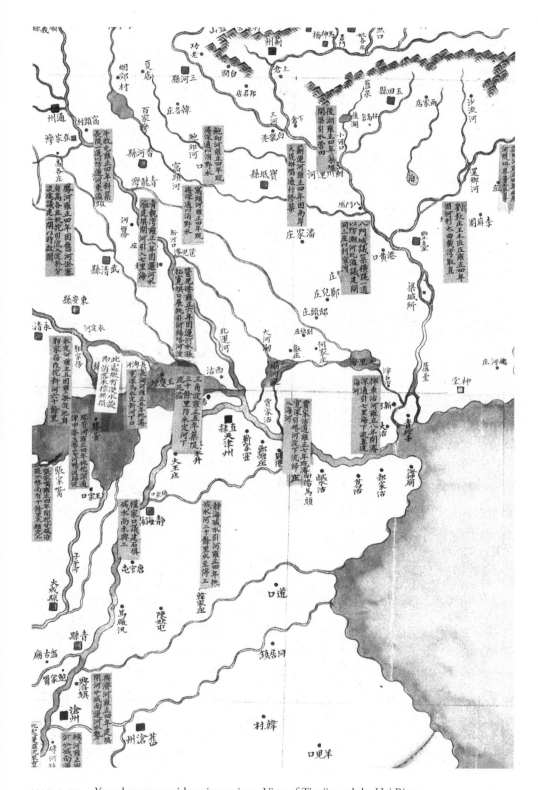

MAP 2.1B.   Yongzheng map with major projects. View of Tianjin and the Hai River.

for the water is the Dian he."[58] Whenever the Dian he was dredged and its dikes strengthened, the laborers were chosen from among local residents within the dike to undertake the work of flood control, and "the people were all happy to comply." They were a convenient source of labor and equipment because "the people of the *dian* have boats for their work. One boat of 1 zhang, 2 feet, 5 inches, could support three people, and three men's labor could dig 3 fang of mud a day. In one month, they could use ten days for dredging and twenty days for their own livelihood." Local laborers would not need to be compensated by wages and food (because they had their own means of livelihood).[59]

The concept of a bold and comprehensive plan characterized river management in the Yongzheng emperor's brief reign. Map 2.1 reproduces a portion of a provincial map, drawn probably in the eighth year (1730) or later, that meticulously lays out the entire river system with labels designating the engineering projects that had been completed or were about to be undertaken. The ambition of controlling Zhili's unstable natural environment not only by *hegong*, but also through *shuili*, would often be admired in later reigns but never actually realized again until the second half of the twentieth century, when irrigation and coordinated water management were achieved on a wide scale.

During the Yongzheng and early Qianlong periods, the basic empirewide structure of river administration was put into place; thereafter only minor adjustments were made. Previously, in the Shunzhi period, there had been a director-general of river conservancy, who held jurisdiction over Zhili, Shandong, Henan, Jiangnan, and Zhejiang, and resided at Jining (Shandong), but in 1731, the Zhili river system was placed under a separate director and deputy director, located at Tianjin, with jurisdiction over Zhili rivers, including the Yongding River administrators and other second-tier officials. In the first year of Qianlong, 1736, the deputy official was abolished, and in 1749, finally all river authority in Zhili was vested directly in the governor-general.[60]

The Zhili system formed the northern section of the three-part empirewide system of river authority. While the Zhili governor-general was responsible for the northern sector, the eastern sector became the responsibility of the Hedong hedao zongdu, often known as the director-general of the Yellow River and Grand Canal Conservancy, with headquarters in Jining, Shandong Province. This post was handled jointly by the Henan and Shandong governors. The southern sector became the responsibility of the governor-general of Liang Jiang (Jiangxi, Jiangsu, and Anhui).[61] Thus by the mid-eighteenth century, there were two bureaucracies responsible for the Yellow River, with more than 400 officials under their control, in addition to two military river commands, with 20,000 men under their jurisdiction. In the view of later historians, as well as earlier bureaucrats, such proliferation of bureaucracy and fragmentation of authority only served to hinder efficient river conservancy efforts.[62]

Although the highest authority for Zhili rivers was vested in the governor-general, the secondary positions became increasingly fragmented with authority for the Yongding River, for example, divided into sections.[63] In 1726 the position of Yongding River *daotai* was created to replace the north and south bank directors created in 1698. Responsible to the Zhili governor-general, the *daotai* oversaw a staff of more than fifty minor officials responsible for different sections of the river. Most were concurrently responsible to military officials.[64] The regulation of the Yongding River had a militaristic aspect, with sections of the river patrolled by various teams on a regular schedule. In the Jiaqing period, there were eighteen patrols, *xun*, along the river, with the guards supposedly recruited from the local area.[65]

The annual schedule of duties also followed the annual agricultural cycle. The character for *xun* was the same as that for seasonal floods. In the spring there were the *lingxun*. All dredging should be finished by the *maixun*, or the wheat harvest—before labor was needed for agriculture, and before the rain that usually fell five days on either side of the ripening of wheat. For the *fuqiu daxun*, the big floods expected in the late summer, the governor-general was expected to move to the flood area to oversee the work, but after 1807, he delegated the responsibility to a deputy.[66] For routine work, the Yongding River and the north and south Grand Canal were patrolled by river soldiers, whose duties also included dredging and digging dirt for repairs, following precedents already set in Jiangnan and Henan.[67] In 1726 and again in 1731 the budget for annual repairs was adjusted, but the precedent of a routine budget for *suixiu*, annual repairs, and *qiangxiu*, urgent repairs, was followed. *Daxiu*, or major repairs, needed special appropriations.[68]

The ambitious plans of Yongzheng and his deputies sometimes—we cannot really say how often—met with local resistance of various sorts. After the Hutuo River flooded in 1730, a rare event, local residents protested when the Qinghe circuit intendant proposed building an embankment to protect them against future floods. Two thousand workers were put on the job but protested against the hard work. Furthermore, the people of Shulu County felt that the floodwaters helped to enrich the soil and gave them a doubly good wheat harvest the next spring.[69] In 1734 Governor-general Li Wei similarly found after an inspection of the flooding of the Yongqing xian city that people were not willing to be moved away from the river partly because the flooded land was fertile and would produce an abundant wheat harvest the next year.[70] Yongqing was a rather special case because the county was bisected by the Yongding River, and the xian city wall itself was an embankment against floodwaters. Other protests seemed to be more purely labor disputes. For example, one near the Grand Canal, when some laborers blocked the way of the river intendant, overturned boats, seized goods, and so forth.[71]

Like his father, the Yongzheng emperor recognized the importance of bureaucratic honesty and experience in conducting large-scale water conservancy projects. Fortunately, he had his trusted brother. The emperor had said that he would spare no expense to benefit the people's livelihood and save them from floods; Prince Yi would manage the projects capably, and he would understand the emperor's intention and love the people, and the personnel would work hard. However, those functionaries who violated the trust and stole money would be apprehended and punished according to precedent.[72] With his brother's illness, and later death, in 1730, the emperor admonished Grand Secretary Zhu Shi, who had assisted Prince Yi, to watch strictly over river functionaries so there would be no malfeasance.[73]

The emperor, whose succession to the throne had been accompanied by scandal and rumor, was always sensitive to reports of strange natural events that could be interpreted as portents of dynastic demise.[74] In 1734, the year before his death, he dwelt at length on the repeatedly bizarre weather in Xuanhua Prefecture, to the northwest of the capital. In that year there had first been drought, and then in the seventh month there was hail "with stones the size of fists or chicken eggs" that destroyed all the crops. The emperor said that in the past he had seen such events as omens that caused him to reflect on his own behavior. "Ever since I have assumed the throne, each time there has been a flood or drought disaster, I immediately become fearful and alarmed, and I have reflected on the failings in my governance and have reverentially examined my behavior in order to reform it. I have not been willing to lay blame on the officials or people." But since the weather had been perfect everywhere else, surely such weather was not a sign of his shortcomings, but those of the people of Xuanhua? "It appears obvious that Heaven has repeatedly sent portents as a warning to the people of Xuanhua. If the officials and people of those places see these events as random events of nature and do not tremble with fear and think about their shortcomings, it means that they do not respect and fear Heaven, and are just inferior people."[75] This emperor thus rearranged the balance between Heaven, Earth, and Man, and in effect used the bad weather to threaten the people and officials before *they* could threaten his rule.

Qianlong and Routinization

Although only a decade or more had elapsed since the major river conservancy efforts of the Yongzheng reign, extensive floods marked the start of the next reign. In the summer of 1737, for a period of about ten days in the sixth lunar month, it rained day and night, toppling dikes in the Tianjin area and obstructing local travel. Except for *gaoliang* shoots that had been planted early on high ground, all the other maturing crops on low-lying ground were completely destroyed. Local reports showed that the extent of disaster varied greatly according to the elevation of the locality. The counties of Baodi, Ninghe, Gu'an, Yongqing, Dong'an, and elsewhere all received some disaster relief. The problem was not simply local rainfall but also the run-off from rain in the mountains of Shanxi, which affected the area of the Zhulong, Zhang, and Fuyang rivers in the southern part of Zhili.[76]

The following summer, an even more serious disaster occurred: it poured continuously for almost a month during the sixth and seventh lunar month. The rain came down "in sheets" (*lianmian*). In the low-lying counties all the crops, including *gaoliang*, were destroyed. Districts in the Tianjin County were declared 8th or 9th degree disasters (10 being the most severe); 394 villages were affected, of which 141 were heavily damaged, with 6,839 households having 20,200 people.[77] In Baoding and Hejian prefectures, the water drained off slowly, and in the fall the ground was still waterlogged. A contributing factor was that some villages had built weirs to contain water for irrigation, but during times of excessive water, these weirs blocked the needed drainage and caused water to flood the fields.[78] Reports in the ninth month showed extremely mixed conditions, with some districts having achieved only 10, 20, or 30 percent of normal harvest.[79] The heavily affected areas were found in the central prefectures of Shuntian, Baoding, Hejian, and Tianjin, while the southern and western prefectures of Daming, Guangping, and Zhengding were not affected. A grave concern was that some areas would not be able to plant winter wheat and would not have a wheat harvest next spring to offset the losses from the fall.[80]

In the twelfth month, the governor-general reported that 105,339 qing of land had been affected by the disaster, including 503,400 households having 1,574,800 adults and children.[81] One hundred thousand qing of land, or 10 million mu, would have represented at least 10 percent of the arable land of Zhili, which could not have exceeded 100 million mu in the early eighteenth century.[82] Substantial tax relief was given in this crisis.[83] Early the next year, in the third month of 1739, Tianjin officials requested a month's additional relief; although 50–60 percent of the fields had dried out, other places still had four to five feet of water on the ground.[84] In the fifth month, the governor-general reported that 900,000 taels of taxes had been forgiven.[85]

The crises of 1737 and 1738 demanded decisive and dramatic action, but early efforts at repairing damage to the river works were uncoordinated and troubled by bureaucratic disputes. Unlike his grandfather, who turned to Yu Chenglong, or his father, who relied on Prince Yi, the Qianlong emperor did not at first seem to find a river expert whom he could trust. From the fall of 1737 until the spring of 1739, many opinions were expressed about how to handle the Zhili river situation, but no consensus emerged about the right course of action. Oertai, Li Wei, Gu Cong, and other top officials had originally agreed on a plan that promised a "once-and-for-all" solution (*yilao yongyi*), but later Gu Cong seemed to back off. The emperor expressed dissatisfaction with these officials and was looking for an even more comprehensive plan.[86] Responsibility for river work was a risky business for which many officials were unprepared. There was much vacillation, finger-pointing, and back-biting.[87] By the end of 1738, the river commissioner had been dismissed, the incumbent governor-general had died, and the emperor was looking to a new governor-general to take the lead—Sun Jiagan, a metropolitan official of formidable credentials.[88]

Sun Jiagan and the top river official, Gu Cong, were ordered to devise a comprehensive plan to address this disastrous situation. The two were assisted by Chen Hongmou, who was serving as river intendant at Tianjin and Hejian.[89] In their report, Sun and his colleagues paid special attention to the situation in the Tianjin region, observing how after one year of heavy rain, the swampy lands would take several years to dry out. This problem was compounded by the fact that the salt water would back up into the swamps. They also emphasized the problems at the confluence of the rivers near Tianjin, particularly the functions of the Dong dian and the Xi dian.[90] They observed that the current crisis arose partly from recent engineering efforts. Originally neither the Yongding nor the Ziya River had levees; mud and water would drain off into fields. Since the long dikes had been built and the water contained, the various swamps had become more silted. Since the exits from the swamps were also blocked up, the consequence was that silt had raised the riverbeds. When the pressure on the diversionary canals became too great and the embankments were too weak they would collapse, causing the fields to flood.[91] Encroachment by farmers on river embankments, canals, and swamps also contributed to waterlogging and siltation. They concluded that the Yongding River levees needed to be raised since they were only two to three feet higher than the riverbed. In Hejian and Baoding prefectures this problem was especially serious.[92]

After extensive surveying, Sun submitted in the eighth month of 1739 a plan for dredging of the major rivers and dike construction at 523 locations in ninety-three counties; he received imperial approval for this in the ninth month.[93] He recommended that 40 percent of the work be assumed by the people (*minli*), 30 percent by work relief, and the remaining 30 percent paid with regular dike repair funds.[94] He also requested additional personnel to assist him. The cost of relief this year and last had been burdensome for the government, he said. One-third of the work had already been completed; he hoped the rest could be speedily done during the winter and completed by the fourth or fifth month of the next year.[95] The work was actually completed in the ninth month of 1740.

The early Qianlong-period water conservancy plans downplayed the role of *shuili* for rice cultivation while not dismissing it completely. Sun Jiagan reported that his predecessor Li Wei had previously requested permission to temporarily suspend the subsidies to rice irrigation because the harvest had been poor. Previously the rice grown in Zhili had been purchased and transported by the state, setting aside more than 100,000 taels, and this had been considered a savings over the grain tribute from the south. But this spring, he said, only the fields on high ground had produced a harvest; the low-lying areas were waterlogged. It would be difficult to carry out official purchases on a wide scale without raising prices and causing hardship. So Sun requested suspending purchases for another year. The government, he argued, would save money, while the people would benefit from lower prices.[96]

Labor discontent was another issue. Qianlong said that he had heard of disturbances in Hejian Prefecture where the river functionaries had been inflexible in demanding labor from the locals. In the past, labor was usually recruited off-season or in an intercalary month. During the busy farming season, however, one out of three adult males would be drafted, but the others would be left alone to tend to their farm work. In this period, the universal call for labor might lead to unrest. If food and wages were siphoned off (*kouke*), or not handled according to the regulations, then the locals would be angry. Because the local officials regarded this as the business of the river functionaries and did not interfere, the "small people" had no one to complain to. "I have heard rumors about these things," said the emperor, ordering Sun Jiagan to investigate the matter.[97] In the ninth month, Sun reported that investigation showed that the distribution of rations had been decided by the river officials in consultation with local officials, and that there had been no *kouke*.[98] Appropriate supervision of labor and the management of functionaries were serious problems that needed to be addressed. In 1739 Sun and his colleagues recommended that special officials be appointed to supervise those engineering projects that were complex, large in scale, requiring centralized management that local officials could not provide.[99]

Despite the completion of so much repair work so quickly, Sun Jiagan and Gu Cong had vacillated about how to handle the Yongding River, and whether they should open up the mouth of the river, or wait until all the dredging had been done. The emperor thought they were too changeable in their opinions, did not trust their judgment, and dismissed them.[100] It was clear that despite the numerous projects that they had overseen, many problems remained. In the ninth month of 1740, Gao Bin, who had served as Jiangnan river commissioner, assumed the position of Zhili governor-general. In the tenth month it was deemed that some rivers needed to be widened. The Xi dian and the Baigou and other rivers were too constrained by their levees.[101] In the eighth month of 1741, the emperor decided that the management of the Zhili river system should be centralized in the hands of the governor-general, and he retained Gao Bin in that position.[102]

Gao Bin, however, was much in demand elsewhere and was considered too busy to devote himself entirely to river work; he was succeeded in the governor-general's position by Liu Yuyi, but he still played an advisory role.[103] During 1744–47 under their joint leadership, additional conservancy projects were started. This followed on the devastating drought of 1743–44 that principally affected Hejian and Tianjin prefectures.[104] After touring more than thirty counties in Tianjin, Baoding, and Zhengding prefectures, the two jointly submitted a comprehensive plan that involved twelve major work sites along the Yongding River and in the Baoding and Zhengding regions. These projects would require a total of 443,510 taels in labor costs to be apportioned locally if possible and 473,400 taels in materials, for a total of more than 900,000 taels; they requested that 500,000 taels immediately be set aside from the treasury for this work.[105] Careful rules were laid out for the handling of these funds; any amount above 30,000 taels would require specially deputed officials. Detailed accounts of money, labor, and materials had to be kept.[106] Common workers would receive daily wage rations of six fen; supervisors at various levels received more.[107]

These projects were successfully carried out over the next two to three years.[108] In 1747, the emperor's edict announced the completion of the work. The cost of river conservancy between 1744–47 was reported as only 700,000 taels—200,000 taels less than budgeted. Detailed reports had been submitted, and meticulous accounts had been kept. The emperor expressed appreciation for Gao Bin and Liu Yuyi's overall supervision of the project, and for the results that had been achieved at present, but he said that the two officials should consult with the Grand Council about whatever might arise in the future. Unlike those before him, the Qianlong emperor expressed no optimism about a permanent solutions or quick fixes, and he did not use rhetoric about "once-and-for-all" solutions.[109]

For the next fifteen years or so, no serious disasters struck the Zhili region until the extensive floods of 1761–62.[110] Some villages were rated ninth- or tenth-degree disaster cases, and several months of general famine relief were given.[111] Occurring relatively soon after the last big conservancy campaigns, and not at the beginning of the reign, these floods confirmed the emperor's doubts about the finality of any engineering project. Extensive river work was undertaken all over the province from 1762–64 but was concentrated in the area of the Thousand-Li Dike and along the Hai River. Dredging and repair jobs were undertaken in Tianjin and other low-lying areas.[112] This time the statesman in charge of rivers was the incumbent governor-general Fang Guancheng, who had previously served as circuit intendant, provincial judge, and financial commissioner in Zhili. He had established a reputation during the 1743–44 drought, and his account of the famine relief campaign, *Zhenji*, served as a primer for famine relief elsewhere in the empire.[113] He subsequently served as Zhili governor-general for nineteen years 1749–55, 1755–68—an unusually long continuous period of service for a provincial official.[114] With deep knowledge of the environment and economy of the Zhili region, Fang Guancheng enjoyed the confidence of the Qianlong emperor, who had finally found a trusted advisor. Fang Guancheng regarded the river conservancy problems of the 1760s not just as an engineering project, but as an administrative challenge requiring vast expenditures of money and labor, as well as delicate negotiations with local authorities and communities.

Fang's good reputation helped to put to rest another attempt to revive rice cultivation. In the fall of 1762, a Board of Works minister criticized Fang for failing to take advantage of the abundant water that had accumulated to restore the rice fields that had been abandoned.[115] In a responding edict, the emperor definitively sided with Fang Guancheng against the revival of rice-cultivation schemes. The situation of excess water, he said, was temporary. The north was basically dry and the land relatively unproductive. North and South China were fundamentally different and should be treated differently. "The development of rice fields in the capital region had been tried repeatedly in the past, but in the end was without concrete results. From this we can see that [north and south] cannot be forcibly made the same."[116] The emperor emphatically stated that the rice-irrigation project in Zhili had never worked.[117] Fang concurred by citing several examples of local experiments that had failed. Planting millet and sorghum was much more convenient for the people, he emphasized.[118] From this time, rice cultivation became very minor in Zhili; after 1765, rice or *daomi*, was not included in the grain price reporting system in Zhili.[119]

Fang's approach to Zhili's water conservancy stressed not simply the identification of needy sites, but also comprehensive planning that took finances and labor into account, matching resources with needs. From the third month of 1762 Fang asserted that the cost of the work would be considerable, and that *minli*, or people's labor, could not be relied on entirely since people from many localities were already exhausted by the disaster. He requested the emperor to follow the precedent of labor relief (*yigong daizhen*) and approve a program of payment according to amounts of earth dug up.[120] For each fang of earth (1 fang = 10 ft x 10 ft x 1 ft), a worker would receive 1 sheng of husked grain (*mi*), 8 wen cash, and 8 wen pickled vegetable.[121] He requested, and received, 200,000 shi of tribute grain from the Tongzhou granary for this purpose. The next month he submitted a list of projects and estimated that since 4,624,391 fang of earth should be dug, he would require, according to the formula stated earlier, 46,243 shi of *mi* and 46,243 taels. The grain would be drawn from the Tongzhou granary, with additional stocks from Shandong grain tribute. The money would be taken from the provincial treasuries of "the three provinces"— presumably Zhili, Shandong, and Henan.[122]

Throughout this reconstruction campaign, Fang repeatedly emphasized the importance of having grain and money with which to pay for labor relief, and he called upon grain tribute and additional shipments of grain from Fengtian and Henan for this purpose. By the fall of 1763, on top of the 200,000 taels that had been set aside for river work in the Tianjin area, the cost of emergency river construction amounted to an additional 326,058 taels.[123] The list of projects covered by the latter extended all over the province including the Dong dian and Xi dian, the Ziya and other rivers and many small tributaries. The projects covered by the former funds included work on the Hai River and the low-lying areas near Tianjin such as Wen'an. Unlike the earlier campaigns, these projects were numerous and scattered, and they did not involve a specific strategy or have a particular focus; reconstruction or repair seemed to be the goal.

In 1764, Fang proposed to divert Fengtian grain from the Northern Granary at Tianjin to pay for river construction. There were 30,000 workers spread over a big distance, and Fang feared that they would not be able to buy grain cheaply during the *qinghuang bujie* lean season. He calculated that 1.5 million fang of earth needed to be dug. Each day each worker would dig one fang of dirt and consume one sheng of *mi*. At 100 sheng per shi, 15,000 shi of grain would be needed. Fang proposed that the 19,000 shi of millet that had been purchased the previous year from Fengtian be used. Including the cost of transport, each shi of grain cost 1.40 taels, more or less. The market price of millet was now up to about 2 taels per shi. If the government sold reduced-price (*pingtiao*) grain to the workers at 1.70 per shi, they would benefit considerably, and the market price might also come down. In this case he apparently meant that laborers would be compensated not through labor relief, but benefited through reduced prices.[124]

Labor costs for river construction were an empirewide concern. A Shandong censor memorialized that heavy labor on dikes and canals could take place during the winter when it would not interfere with agricultural activity.[125] The grand secretaries and Board of Works approved the suggestion, and ordered each governor to put this system into effect. Each winter during the slack season, local elders should convene to decide what river work needed to be done. Labor should be contributed by households according to their wealth or the amount of land they owned. Henan had been ordered to try this out. Although the empire had ceased to require corvée labor, the emperor pointed out that digging canals was definitely beneficial to agriculture.[126] Fang Guancheng was ordered to read this proposal and apply it to Zhili. Fang concurred, pointing out the similarities between Henan and Zhili. In recent years many canals had been constructed in Hejian and Baoding prefectures, so the water receded more quickly than before. But conditions in the province varied, he cautioned, and in some localities *minli* was not up to the task, and government granary grain was still needed to support labor costs.[127]

An additional problem was the encroachment by the expanding population on the fertile lands within dikes and near the rivers. Many households had settled and cultivated the land within the Yongding River dikes. It was the policy to pay people to move, but the emperor noticed that there were many people, and even entire villages, living on the river. In 1753 he had ordered Fang Guancheng to look into the situation.[128] Fang reported that although the residents of several villages in the counties of Yongqing, Bazhou, Dong'an, and Wuqing had been persuaded to move, there were still families and villages that refused.[129] In the following year more households were evacuated from flood-endangered areas. In one case the suggestion was to reward each household with one shi of unhusked grain from the granaries; in another, he suggested payment of two ounces of silver to each household to enable 259 households in seventeen villages to move out.[130]

Pursuing the same matter in 1766, Fang found that some households in these counties did not wish to move and had petitioned officials to remain. Since they had resided in there for many years and the Yongding River had not changed course in this area, Fang recommended that their requests be granted.[131] People in this area had previously regarded water as a threat, but now they competed for its benefits. He also pointed out that since lands within the dikes were considered official land, *guandi*, they had not been taxed regularly. In times of flood, however, the residents had no basis for requesting tax relief. He recommended that they be taxed in good years and that the tax be forgiven in the flood years.[132] In an edict of 1772, the emperor discussed this issue of encroachment on lakes near dikes in Zhili and elsewhere: when the water receded, the people immediately planted the land, which was quite fertile, but the larger number of settlers were more vulnerable in the next flood. This problem was not unique to Zhili; it also persisted in the West Lake district of Zhejiang.[133] In 1782 in discussing the problem of the Yellow River, the emperor talked of the need to build weirs and dikes to protect the villages. It would be impossible, however, to move all those who were already settled; they should not be forced to move. Besides, there was not sufficient room in the neighboring villages to resettle people. This was a problem reported by the governors of many provinces including Henan, Shandong, Jiangnan, and Zhili.[134]

Although Fang Guancheng generally enjoyed the emperor's confidence, even he was not immune from serious criticism by censors, who were widely employed by the emperor to check on other officials. Fang had ordered that the sluice gates on the Hai River be closed because he was afraid sea water would back up, but censors criticized this decision for causing delay in draining the floodwater off the fields and hence a delay in sowing grain. The emperor found that the criticism of Fang lacked real merit and generally supported his efforts, saying that Fang was highly experienced and would send for more help if necessary.[135] Shortly afterward, the emperor had occasion to reprimand Fang about a case of extortion in transport for labor relief grain. Two local functionaries had taken advantage of boat rentals for transporting grain to extort money from boat owners, and they were punished. The emperor said that Fang Guancheng should have kept a stricter watch over such personnel, and that he should try to reflect on his shortcomings and improve his work.[136] Fang replied that he was anxious that the culprits be punished, explaining that local functionaries had been ordered to rent boats to transship the 119,000 shi of millet from Fengtian and 70,000 shi from Henan (that had arrived by sea) to granaries in the interior, but instead they had confiscated boats or had taken a cut of the rentals.[137]

One censor also advocated the appointment of a special river czar because it seemed that the Zhili governor-general was too busy to manage the rivers in addition to his other administrative duties. The emperor rejected this proposal, reaffirming the importance of centralizing control in the hands of the governor-general. Authority for rivers should be kept from local officials. In case of special river projects, the governor-general could depute high-ranking officials to oversee the work at any time; there was no need for regular, separate, and specialized river officials. For the present he deputed Grand Secretary Agui to Zhili to look into the situation.[138] In reaffirming the importance of the governor-general in river management, the Qianlong emperor was not only expressing his continued support of Fang but also acknowledging the need for close surveillance of the many subordinate officials and functionaries who were likely to take advantage of the large sums of money and grain that were involved in river work.

Routinization of river management seemed to provide ample opportunity for financial peculation, as well as neglect of river control. Some documents from 1778 and 1782 provide a window into the problem. They revealed deep concerns about corruption, but, at the same time, they maintained at least the appearance of attention to detail in reporting, surveillance, and even micromanagement. In 1778, Zhou Yuanli, the governor-general, was required to report on the overspending of the budget for urgent repairs on the Yongding River, the Nan Yunhe, and Bei Yunhe. By the regulations established in 1775, each year 10,000 taels were to be set aside for urgent repairs on the Yongding River and 6,000 taels each for the Nan Yunhe and Bei Yunhe, and additional funds could be requested if that amount was insufficient. In 1778, the actual amounts spent were 12,892, 5,415, and 13,686 taels *in excess of* the budgeted amounts.[139] There was concern that the "urgent" budget was used to disguise graft. In 1782 the Board of Works required the acting governor-general Yinglian to conduct an inquiry. They suspected that river officials must be trying to profit illicitly and invoked such details as the fact that large sums had been requested even when there had been a dry year. He dispatched various circuit intendants to the Yongding River, Nan Yunhe, and Bei Yunhe to inspect each section personally. They found no fraud, except in Bei Yunhe where there was evidence of cheating in the crescent-shaped dikes. They recommended that the Bei Yunhe's expenses be handled under the category of *suixiu*, or regular annual repairs. The category of "anticipating urgent repairs" (*yuban qiangxiu*) should be eliminated because it invited excess and falsification. And the category "urgent hanging of willows and reeds" (*qiang gua xiliu*) should be limited to 1,000 taels, to eliminate the opportunity to cheat.[140]

Although such a case gives the appearance of effective disciplining of the lower bureaucracy, in fact it disguises the general deterioration of standards in the late Qianlong period, when the court and bureaucracy were dominated by Heshen, the imperial bodyguard who had gained the emperor's favor, amassed a vast personal fortune, and tyrannized the bureaucracy. We know from the 1801–2 crisis that 1785 was considered an approximate turning point because river officials after 1785 were held financially responsible for the deterioration of the river system.

Jiaqing: Heroic Hydraulics

In 1796 the Qianlong emperor abdicated after sixty years on the throne so that his reign would not exceed in length that of his grandfather, the Kangxi emperor. Although the new Jiaqing emperor was already thirty-six years old and well prepared to assume power, it was not until his father's death in 1799 that he was able to act on his own initiative. One of his first acts was to order the arrest and execution of Heshen and to clear the court of his influence and reestablish the dynasty on a firmer footing.[141] With the bureaucracy in considerable disarray, the White Lotus rebellion in the north, west, and northwest, and constant problems with the management of the Yellow River and Grand Canal, Jiaqing faced considerable challenges with great probity and determination. Although these problems loomed larger, the Zhili river system also received careful attention from him; in fact, it demanded immediate attention because massive flooding in 1801—the sixth year of his reign—threatened the Imperial City itself.

The 1801 flood was the result of torrential rains in the sixth lunar month, which caused the Yongding River to break its dikes. Initially the area around the Lugou Bridge was the most seriously flooded. Later, as other waterways such as the Bei, Tang, and Hutuo rivers, and the Grand Canal also overflowed, the flood area became quite extensive. The Imperial City's moats overflowed and the Imperial Stables were also affected. The Summer Palace, Yuanmingyuan, was also flooded. As the rains continued throughout the month, Tianjin was also inundated. The Hai River water backed up, and waters did not subside until the eighth month. Some ships in the harbor were damaged, and many tribute vessels were prevented from returning to southern ports. The salt production and commerce in this region was also severely affected—with fields in 88 counties damaged or washed away, and close to half a million bags of salt were lost to water damage. Flooding was reported from neighboring Shanxi Province and as far north as Rehe (Chengde). The source of flood-water was not just direct rainfall but also runoff from mountains and hills to the north and west.[142] Ninety-nine out of 122 counties (zhou or xian) reported damage in the seventh month. By the tenth month, however, out of 131 counties reporting, only 74 were still in need of relief. After a difficult winter, by the third month of 1802, only 43 out of 128 counties were still in need.[143] So unusually rapid was this flood that it was described years later as *yizhang*, or "a strange rising of the water."[144]

The Jiaqing emperor regarded this crisis as a personal challenge and directly involved himself in every aspect of the flood control and famine relief campaign. This was an opportunity for the emperor to demonstrate his administrative skills and also to tighten his control over the metropolitan bureaucracy. The entire effort was conducted in the style of a campaign—both military and political in nature. At the conclusion of the crisis, he ordered the compilation of documents to commemorate this effort, *Xinyou gongzhen jishi*.[145] Here is evidence of the almost daily attention of the emperor to even the smallest details of the relief and reconstruction effort, as well the detailed reports of local conditions.[146] The new emperor was aware of the precedents set in previous reigns. Both he and his top officials frequently invoked the methods of Fang Guancheng in both famine relief and river conservancy.[147]

The emperor managed the flood and famine relief operation by closely controlling his officials. Once again, the Zhili governor-general was the key figure, powerful yet vulnerable. The incumbent at the time of the flood was Jiang Sheng, who was dismissed by the emperor on 6/9 for failing to alert the court to the potential seriousness of the flood.[148] The provincial treasurer Tongxing was reprimanded for laxity in reporting the impending the crisis.[149] Lesser incumbents were also dismissed for inadequate reporting, including the director of the Yongding River conservancy.[150] Xiong Mei was temporarily appointed governor-general until Chen Dawen, a trusted official, assumed office from the seventh month until the sixth month of the following year, when Xiong Mei took over again on a temporary basis.[151] Ming'an, commander of the Beijing gendarmerie, served as the emperor's trusted advisor and trouble-shooter.[152] Two other Manchu officers, Nayanbao, vice president of the Board of War, and Baning'a, who was director of the Imperial Armory, were charged with the responsibility for river conservancy work. While giving them great responsibilities, the emperor also supervised them closely. For example, in the eighth month, he reprimanded them both for abusing their privileges by returning too often to the capital, on the pretext of business, to visit their families, and he ordered them to remain at the river sites.[153] On the other hand, the emperor seemed just as anxious to reward good work as to punish the slightest hint of unscrupulous behavior—for later in the fall he promoted Nayanbao to imperial bodyguard and Baning'a to minister of the imperial household.[154] He allowed Xiong Mei to ride horseback in the Forbidden City after charges that Xiong Mei had made excessive demands on local communities when he made his tours of inspection were found to be groundless.[155]

The emperor also kept close check on lesser officials and, where possible, enforced the principle of collective responsibility. Initially, for example, he had appointed four teams of officials to survey the four main districts into which he had divided the flood area, and he was quick to follow up on their work.[156] The south team had done good work and was to be rewarded, the west team was to be punished for negligence, the east team should be severely punished for disobeying instructions, and the north team was neither rewarded nor punished.[157] Even minor cases of malfeasance were reported to the emperor.[158]

Officials were responsible for executing their duties and exercising moral probity, but they were also held financially accountable for their official functions. For example, Yanjian, the newly appointed governor-general in the seventh month of 1802, offered to contribute 100,000 taels, the equivalent of two years' salary for flood relief.[159] More importantly, when river conservancy work was completed, the emperor decided that expenses should be apportioned in accordance with the principle of *xiaoliu peisi*: 60 percent of the total cost should be assumed by the central government, while 40 percent should be the responsibility of those officials since 1785 who had neglected river conservancy in Zhili to the extent that the present flood could occur. The 388,527 taels, which represented about 40 percent of the total cost of 971,220 taels, should be levied according to prescribed proportions: 30 percent to the former governors-general, 30 percent to directors of river conservancy, 20 percent to other provincial officials, and 20 percent to minor officials. Those officials who had died were excused from paying.[160] This was one of several ways in which officials who had formerly been associated with Heshen were punished for negligence of their duties and misappropriation of public funds.[161]

During the 1801 crisis the corruption and incompetence that had become pervasive and had been encouraged by bureaucratic fragmentation of river conservancy duties seemed to be overcome by the emperor's intense personal interest in all the details of reconstruction. He gave orders that the repairing of dikes should start immediately, but that the digging of drainage canals should wait until the lower reaches of the river could be dredged.[162] When Nayanbao and Baning'a reported that the stonework and earthwork had been completed by 50,000 laborers under their direction, the emperor sent his trusted deputy Ming'an to check the accuracy of their report.[163] The first phase of work was completed by the fall, and the local magistrates in the relevant localities were instructed by Chen Dawen to make preparations for next spring's work. But when Chen Dawen reported that the harvest would average 50 percent over normal, the emperor ridiculed him, saying this was merely a whitewash.[164] Work resumed on 2/10, with the emperor impatient at its slow pace, and was completed on 3/30.[165]

Throughout the crisis, the emperor and his officials projected an air of confidence in their ability to deal with the flood problem. This reflected not only the emperor's "can-do" attitude but also a collective "party line" that the river system of Zhili, particularly the Yongding River, was controllable by human effort. In the short run, at least, this attitude was confirmed by reality, for the rains of the following summer, 1802, did not result in further flooding, apparent evidence of the success of the imperial flood control effort.[166] In addition to the 1 million taels spent on river work, 2 million taels were spent in this campaign for relief. These sums far exceeded the amounts spent in even the largest campaigns of the eighteenth century.[167] The years 1801–2 marked the last comprehensive famine relief and river conservancy campaign in Zhili in the Qing.

Yet in the larger context, this major campaign appears no more than a brief holding action. There were no floods between 1803–5, but in almost every subsequent year of the Jiaqing reign, between 1806–20, there was flooding of significant proportions including 54 counties in 1808, 74 counties in 1816, 85 in 1819, and 67 in 1820, the final year of the reign.[168] The record of the last decade indicates considerable human suffering and widespread hunger.[169]

The cost of river work as well as relief was a great drain on the coffers. Overwhelmingly the costs were borne by the central government, but to a greater extent than had been customary, there were attempts to ask others to share the financial burden. From the start, there were some merchant and gentry contributions.[170] Precedents for using such contributions in Yangzi provinces, or in Henan, were cited to promote a similar effort in the north.[171] Liang-Huai salt merchants "contributed" 1 million taels for relief in Beijing, but only half had been delivered as of the ninth month.[172] After the 1801 crisis, however, the emperor no longer permitted the large-scale use of contributions for river work in Zhili. This was in great contrast to the considerable compulsory, or forced, contributions from officials and degree-holders that were required for river work on the Yellow River and the Yangzi River. In 1806 large "contributions" were required of all metropolitan and provincial officials above a certain rank and degree-holders for work on these rivers.[173] In the same year, the emperor rejected a proposal by high-ranking metropolitan officials to use 400,000 taels from Changlu district salt taxes. The emperor argued that the Changlu salt merchants had only recently received assistance from the government when the salt costs had been raised. Since this had been intended to boost their business, they now should not be asked to make a contribution to river work. The cost of river conservancy should be paid through the regular government funds. However, the ministers of the Board of Revenue responded by arguing that since the Changlu salt merchants had not forwarded their taxes for the last year or two, and they were more than 1.1 million taels in arrears, they could be asked to make a contribution of 400,000 taels for river conservancy as a form of restitution.[174]

The central government expenditures on Zhili rivers in 1806 were still very high. More than 600,000 taels was set aside for work on Zhili rivers. By the end of the year, when work was suspended due to the onset of cold weather, more than 400,000 had already been spent. A total of 270,000 taels had been spent on the Thousand-Li Dike area and its swamps, including paths, bridges, and gates. Another 43,000 had been spent dredging the Daqing River, and yet another 20,000 on dredging sections of the Ziya River. An additional 69,000 was spent on other projects. The memorialists pointed out that there would be other unanticipated expenses, and this was definitely *not* a case of a "once-and-for-all" plan. The remaining 190,000 would be reserved for other contingencies, such as dredging the Bei Yunhe.[175] Two years later, the reports said that the dike work had been completed, and 200,000 taels still remained—suggesting either false reporting or a lack of progress.[176]

Following the example of Fang Guancheng, the Jiaqing officials invoked the concept of labor relief to pay for the necessary labor, on the one hand, and also provide relief to the needy, on the other. It seems to have been the general principle that labor relief was paid at half of the rate for labor used on government dikes, but the actual rates varied.[177] Even so, this was a large expense for the government, while providing barely a subsistence income for the laborers. During the fall of 1801 and again next spring when work resumed, labor relief was used. The emperor worried about the 50,000 laborers at the river sites—50 percent were not locals. He worried about how these workers would be dispersed over the winter and how to gather them again next spring. Chen Dawen said the workers were paid enough wages that they would have funds to get them through the winter.[178]

The next spring Nayanbao and Baning'a reported that many famine victims had gathered in the vicinity of Lugou Bridge, outside the capital, looking for relief, and labor relief would help them a great deal. Last fall, they said, there were up to 50,000 men working on the Yongding River; many disaster victims took advantage of labor relief. Although the numbers of refugees at Lugou Bridge had increased, they were peaceful. About 4,000 per day were going to the soup kitchens within the city. Officials were ordered to provide food relief as well as labor relief.[179] By 3/6 there were 30,000 workers on the Yongding River, as well as more than 1,000 soldiers to patrol the worksites.[180] Labor relief continued to be used in the spring. Chen Dawen estimated that 422,670 fang of earth was needed for both banks of the Nan Yunhe. According to labor relief regulations, for each fang of dirt, one fen of silver (nominally = 10 cash or wen) and one sheng of mi were given. In this case, the estimated needs were 4,226 taels and 4,226 shi of grain. The funds were to be taken from the provincial treasury and leftover grain from Tianjin's Northern Granary and from grain purchased from neighboring provinces for below-price sales.[181]

In the central area of Zhili, attempts to pass the responsibility for dike repairs to local communities did not work well. In 1808, there was a proposal to ask villages along the Thousand-Li Dike to select dike administrators, *dizhang*, to take responsibility for maintaining sections of the dike, one per 100–200 zhang in critical stretches, and one per 700–800 zhang in routine stretches (1 zhang = 10 Chinese feet). According to the reports received by emperor's specially deputed ministers, it had always been the responsibility of the people to repair the long dikes; the extraordinary damage done in 1801 required that the state do a larger share. However, Wen Chenghui disputed this, saying that it had never been the custom to ask the public to take responsibility for dike repairs.[182] Later the same month, another memorial from Wen Chenghui revealed the extent of the failure to recruit *dizhang*. Although there had been an order to start appointing *dizhang*, he said, there had yet been no results. No one wanted to serve as *dizhang*, just as no one wanted to serve as the *baozhang* (in the *baojia* system of mutual security). An alternative proposal to appoint gentry members to manage dike repairs on a five-year rotation had also been disregarded by these communities. In response to the emperor's query about the reason for this, Wen Chenghui reported that the villages within ten li of the Thousand-Li Dike had no gentry members (*shenshi*) at all. If the people select an earnest person to be *dizhang*, there would be no need to have a gentry member. But if the emperor was concerned, they could appoint gentry from the neighboring areas; for every five to ten *dizhang*, one wise gentry member should be appointed to inspect the work. Each year before and after the *daxun* (big flood), they would go to inspect the river. Functionaries would not be allowed to interfere. If the functionaries and the officials did not take their work seriously, they would be punished.[183]

Although local communities in the Zhili region often took the initiative to build and maintain small dikes, they could not possibly undertake the responsibility for the long dikes along the Yongding, Ziya, and Daqing rivers, which required central direction and financing. This situation was almost the reverse of that in central and southern China, where it was a question of lakes that provided opportunities for reclamation and polders. There, the *dizhang* system apparently worked well in the Ming and early Qing because there were communal interests in maintaining the dikes, which were round dikes that enclosed polders in contrast with the long dikes along the northern rivers. In the eighteenth century polder communities around Dongting Lake in Hunan Province resisted the attempts of officials to regulate and limit the *dizhang* system.[184] In the Xiang Lake region of Zhejiang, in the Ming dynasty, the lake dikes were divided into sections each managed by a township through locally selected dike administrators. The maintenance of the dikes was supposed to be chiefly a local responsibility, but there is little evidence of what actually happened.[185] In the Qing period, three important local families had been appointed overseers of the lake. This might appear to be evidence of local self-responsibility, but it could also have allowed these families to take unfair advantage of the economic benefits offered by the lakes.[186]

Despite the attention to river work and the substantial sums of money that were expended in the early part of the reign, there were no new approaches or initiatives during the Jiaqing reign toward resolving Zhili's mounting problems. The efforts were directed at repairing and maintaining dikes, gates, and bridges that had been previously constructed. The rules and precedents from the Qianlong era were modified or expanded. The annual budget for routine annual repairs (*suixiu*) on the Yongding River, for example, was doubled from 10,000 per year to 20,000 taels per year, and with miscellaneous other items, it actually amounted to 34,000 a year. The allocation for the urgent repairs (*qiangxiu*) was raised from 24,000 to 27,000 taels. The Bei Yunhe and Nan Yunhe regular and urgent budgets were also raised.[187] The amounts for the other rivers were also increased slightly. In fact, the annual budgets were constantly supplemented by extraordinary dispensations for the emergencies that occurred almost annually. Dredging along the Zhang and Wei rivers in the south was to be done every spring and fall at a cost of more than 8,000 taels per year; the cost was to be supported by Caozhou County and the Changlu salt merchants.[188]

The emperor reaffirmed the authority of the Zhili governor-general to control the entire river system, resisting any suggestions for fragmentation of authority. An edict of 1807 endorsed the practice established in 1749 of giving control of the rivers to the Zhili governor-general. There was no need for a separate post of Zhili river commissioner, it said. In recent years at the time of the summer and fall floods the governor-general had resided at the river work site(s) and conducted his other business by post. Those who wished to see him needed to go to the work site. This was a good idea for a while; during the 1801 crisis the governor-general could not reach the work sites, and as a result, important communications got mixed up. Now, however, the requirement to live at the work sites, sometimes for several months, got in the way of the conduct of other business, and the emperor recommended that it be rescinded.[189]

Despite Jiaqing's strict handling of his subordinates, it appears that corruption in the Zhili provincial and local bureaucracy remained a serious problem after the 1801 crisis. Large deficits in the provincial treasury—amounting to more than 2 million taels that had been uncovered in 1799, when Jiaqing began to take control, were still not cleared up years later. In 1805, in a sweeping review of Zhili officials, the emperor angrily said that he was utterly dismayed when he read the reports of this figure; despite numerous calls for a thorough investigation, nothing much had been done. In fact he had not received any reports since 1799. When Yanjian assumed the office of Zhili governor-general, instead of making an investigation, he had been good at covering up the matter, and the officials protected each other. When the lower functionaries saw this, they felt free not only to avoid making up the past fiscal deficits but also to engage in corrupt practices such as buying land and doing business, amusing themselves with women and entertainments, making contributions to buy office for their sons, and so forth. Although there was a deficit of more than 110,000 taels in the Yizhou treasury, the governor-general pretended to know nothing about it. "Yanjian has received great imperial favor, and yet he has never given serious attention to finances. Instead he gives protection to evil functionaries, and has maintained the deficit of 2 million taels. Where is his conscience?" The emperor ordered lowering of rank and transfer for Yanjian but treated him leniently because of his reliability in handling some of the tasks of reconstruction. In addition to Yanjian, all the other Zhili governors-general and provincial treasurers since 1799 came under scrutiny. The emperor ordered the incumbent governor-general Qiu Xingjian to conduct a thorough investigation of local finances and to try to get restitution of deficiencies and punishment of guilty officials.[190]

In the next few years, numerous other cases of bureaucratic corruption and malfeasance in Zhili were investigated.[191] Although they pertained to general administration and famine relief rather than river conservancy, these cases also cast some doubt on how effective the 1801 effort had been in achieving an improvement in the river system. If the emperor himself could not get satisfaction about vast deficits in the provincial treasury despite the extent to which he had directly intervened in personnel matters after 1799, and a network of "cover-ups" persisted, it suggests the great likelihood of misappropriation of at least some of the vast sums that had been allocated for river work in 1801–2.

The emperor continued to pay attention to the Zhili rivers, but he was concerned about expenses, both real and fabricated. In 1808 he toured the Thousand-Li Dike and deemed the dike repairs to have been well done. He emphasized the importance of routine annual as well as urgent dike maintenance. In the past, he said, there were ample funds to finance river work, but now it was important to attend to repairs and maintenance of the dike so that people's fields would be protected and imperial funds saved.[192] In 1810, Wen Chenghui requested the appropriation of 1 million taels for construction and dredging in the area between the Xi dian and Dong dian along the Tang River. Due to silting and blockage upstream, the fields in these counties over 200 li were constantly under water and requiring tax remissions. The emperor said it would be difficult to grant such a sum until the major construction projects on rivers in the south were completed. Zhili river construction was of great importance, but the emperor's edict to the Grand Council admonished that the empire's expenditures should not be misused and urged it to consider overall exactly how much was needed for Zhili's rivers and how many years it would take to complete the work.[193] After the serious banditry in Zhili and the rebel attack on the Forbidden City in 1813, the main focus of imperial and bureaucratic attention turned to pacification of the rebels and reconstruction of production in the regions damaged by the bandits. In 1820, the last year of the Jiaqing reign, the governor-general, Fang Shouchou, revealed that very little, if any, attention had been paid to the Yongding River dikes since 1801.[194]

The approach to river conservancy in the Jiaqing reign emphasized control over regulations and finance, fighting a valiant battle against an overwhelming tide of environmental, bureaucratic, and financial obstacles. The emperor and his top officials did not engage in theoretical discourse about rivers and pondering long-term—*yilao yongyi*—solutions. Nor did they engage in wishful thinking about expanding *shuili* for the sake of rice cultivation in Zhili.[195] Only once did the emperor seem to express an interest in a wider perspective; in 1802 Chen Yi's essay on Zhili rivers was copied for the emperor's attention. Chen Yi was a native of Wen'an, the district that was the center of destruction during 1801, who had been an articulate and prolific essayist on Zhili's rivers when he served in office in the Yongzheng period.[196] In addition to the documentary record of the 1801 relief effort, *Xinyou gongzhen jishi*, the emperor ordered the publication of *Jifu shuili anlanzhi* (Gazetteer of the pacification of Zhili's water conservancy), an encyclopedic compendium about Zhili's rivers. Compiled in 1808, it contains descriptions of each of twenty-three rivers in Zhili, their engineering sites, regulations about their supervisory officials and functionaries, budgets for repairs, and lists of temples along each river. The emperor enjoined his river officials to use this work as a reference.

Daoguang: Earnest Efforts

The Daoguang reign began with two major disasters. In 1821 a massive cholera epidemic spread through Zhili, resulting in high mortality.[197] And then in 1822–23 a great flood affected 104 counties, 92 of which needed relief.[198] The Daoguang emperor was conscious of the precedents in famine relief set by his father and grandfather. Even in 1801, he said, his father had generously given aid to the people and did not resort to burdening the villages and people (through labor and other demands) or asking for loans or contributions. Moreover, the land tax burden on Zhili had always been light, and tax remissions and famine relief had been granted whenever there was a disaster. In the current crisis, the emperor proclaimed, "I feel your pain, and have not spared any funds for relief." Rejecting the suggestions of governor-general Jiang Youxian, he declared that there was no need to ask for private contributions, to transfer money from military funds, to ask local officials for contributions, or to request the suspension of the autumn hunt at Rehe. Even his father in 1802 had resumed the autumn hunt without affecting the villages in the disaster area. He angrily denounced these suggestions as muddle-headed and wondered if this was not asking for a temporary measure in the expectation that it would become the regular practice?[199] Earlier the emperor had refused the suggestion of a censor to use flood victims for labor before they had received any food relief, saying it would be a disgrace to ask starving people to work for nothing.[200]

Despite the note of bravado, this relief and reconstruction effort was not so well organized or effective as that of 1801–2, and funding it was a major problem. The relief effort took place in the context of considerable social unrest and bureaucratic muddle. The governor-general reported that, generally speaking, the management of the famine relief had not been good.[201] Unlike his father or grandfather, the Daoguang emperor did not seem to have a high official, or a team of officials, to entrust with the planning and execution of the needed river work. Cheng Hanzhang, vice minister of the Board of Works, was deputed to survey the situation together with the Zhili governor-general, Jiang Youxian, but the emperor did not seem to trust them. It appears that the survey and recommendations were undertaken during 1824, even as emergency repairs were being made in many places. Although the heavily silted rivers demanded swift action, Cheng and Jiang's reports were preoccupied with how to finance the operations, while the emperor's responses reflected his anxiety about the probable misappropriation of the very considerable sums that were needed.

The region of the Daqing River between the Xi dian and Dong dian was frequently inundated and its drainage was blocked because the Yongding River, which was its outlet to the ocean, was heavily silted. Cheng and Jiang's plan called for dredging of the rivers and constructing diversionary canals to help drain the water from this area and also a series of locks to direct the flow. When this was questioned by censors who wondered if work should not first be done upstream to contain the water rather than downstream, invoking a precedent of Sun Jiagan of the Qianlong reign, the emperor sided with the current proposal to concentrate first on the downstream area, but he cautioned Cheng and Jiang to get the big picture back in focus.[202] For dredging and other work to open up the silted Zhang and Wei rivers, Governor-general Jiang proposed that the various costs of materials and labor be borne by the local communities, in return for which they would be forgiven their tax obligations. Laborers from the Nan Yunhe should be hired because the local people were not accustomed to doing this kind of work. The costs were to be assumed by Changlu salt merchants, and in the future they were to take the responsibility for dredging without any official management. Since most of the Wei River was within Henan Province, work there would commence at the same time and be finished before the summer rains.[203] Cheng Hanzhang had memorialized that Zhili's rivers were complicated and expensive to regulate. Except for the Yongding River, which was maintained by the government, Zhili's many other rivers, he said, should be the responsibility of the local communities. He designated three important sites as having priority. The emperor said he could raise the money, but "Were these three important sites the same as what the Jiang Youxian, the governor-general, had designated as critical areas?"[204] The language of this edict and others in this period suggests a lack of coordination among responsible officials and absence of an overall plan. Here, as in the previous year, the emperor enjoined the governor-general and river officials not to make excuses but to work together.[205]

Cheng Hanzhang and Jiang Youxian finally recommended work at nine sites—including the harbor at Tianjin, the Dong and Xi dian, and the lower reaches of the Yongding River—that would cost 1.2 million taels.[206] They proposed raising 400,000 from Guangdong, Jiangxi, and

Zhejiang provinces, another 400,000 from Shandong, Henan, and Shanxi, and other amounts to be raised elswhere.[207] In response to the Board of Revenue's report that there were insufficient funds for river work in Zhili, an imperial edict ordered 550,000 taels to be raised through diversions from the Changlu salt treasury of 200,000, with additional amounts from the land tax revenues of other provinces. Zhili's river construction costs were a "troublesome burden," said the emperor, but he did not begrudge the expenditures because he grieved about the suffering of the people. These appropriated funds must, however, be guarded carefully to see that there was no waste or fraud. It should not be like the recent experience of fixing the dikes along the Bei Yunhe one year, only for them to topple the next. "Unscrupulous officials and functionaries should be strictly punished."[208]

The emperor revealed his suspicions and doubts in almost every edict on the subject. When there was a dispute about whether to build a sluice gate near the mouth of the Yongding River and whether it would endanger adjacent communities, he enjoined the top officials to stop squabbling over what to do.[209] When the Board of Works' team headed by Cheng Hanzhang estimated that work on the Thousand-Li Dike—which was everywhere in disrepair and frequently breached—would require 370,000 taels, the emperor granted the request, but he also cautioned the high officials to guard carefully against misuse of the funds.[210] Again and again, these officials bemoaned the costs of government dikes that were more and more "troublesome."[211]

The high cost of river work in the face of diminished resources was not the only problem. River management had fundamentally broken down because intrabureaucratic controls had failed. Large appropriations for relief and reconstruction provided golden opportunities for abuse. Lower functionaries took advantage of the crisis situation to make harsh and often illegal demands on peasants in localities. Zhili was beset with cases of misappropriation or extortion by messengers or runners of local resources, such as coal, or more often carts and horses, or else demanding silver as commutation. This type of dividing the spoils must be strictly punished, the emperor enjoined.[212] Pervasive corruption, particularly among lower-level functionaries, was probably of greater concern to the emperor than the flood victims because no effective relief could be achieved without upright officials.[213] The demands on localities increased the social unrest and banditry in the countryside that was so characteristic of the mid-nineteenth century. Despite all this, the bureaucratic routines of river management continued during the Daoguang period, with budgets for annual repairs and emergency repairs raised somewhat, and reports submitted on a regular basis.[214]

Although serious, the Zhili floods were not the center of attention in the early Daoguang period since these years were marked by natural disaster and famines in many parts of China.[215] Most urgent, however, was the mounting crisis of the Yellow River and Grand Canal. Increased silting and serious disrepair of the major Grand Canal dikes at the point where the Grand Canal crosses the Yellow River required the use of transfer shipping—transferring grain shipments to small light boats that were actually hauled by trackers overland—and for one year, 1826, the use of sea transport for part of the annual tribute. The emperor was totally focused on this crisis and managed it "from afar" on a daily basis. Although the crisis of the Yellow River and the inability of the central government to deal with it effectively have often been taken as a sign of dynastic decline, Jane Leonard has argued that the emperor's ability to surmount this crisis showed "the state's organizational capacity in the early nineteenth century," and that "it was capable of moving quickly and flexibly at the emperor's direction."[216] Randall Dodgen points out that there was no major flooding in the Yellow River until 1841 and agrees that the Daoguang emperor did deal with the issues energetically and responsibly, but the environmental and technical problems were essentially intractable.[217]

The Grand Canal crisis was truly a national crisis, not a regional event. The geopolitical balance of the empire since the late sixth century rested on the concept of the need for the south to support the north through large surpluses of grain. The political hegemony of the north rested on the economic wealth of the south. Yet over time the grain tribute's political significance became more important than its economic benefit. In fact, as many critics pointed out, the cost of maintaining the Grand Canal and shipping rice from the Yangzi region greatly exceeded the original cost of the grain itself. Fang Guancheng had estimated in 1759 that the transport costs of tribute grain amounted to 6 or 7 taels per shi.[218] Sea transport was used, but it was always controversial.[219] The grain tribute system was not only geopolitically important, but hundreds of bureaucrats and subbureaucrats, as well as thousands of boatmen, had deeply entrenched interests in its survival.

The Grand Canal and Yellow River crisis impacted directly on the river situation in Zhili. The eventual shift of the Yellow River in 1852–55 from its bed south of Shandong peninsula, which it had followed since the twelfth-thirteenth centuries, to an outlet north of Shandong, placed greater pressure on the Zhang-Wei River system in Zhili and diverted more of their water from irrigation to the Grand Canal. In 1825 and 1826 this shift was already anticipated by the river experts and affected Zhili in two ways. First, the best river experts, including Yanjian, who had considerable experience in Zhili under both Jiaqing and Daoguang, were assigned to the Grand Canal crisis. Qishan, later to be Zhili governor-general, was also key to the management of the 1825 Grand Canal crisis. Second, the grain tribute and empirewide geopolitical issues formed the context for the theoretical thinking and writing about river conservancy in Zhili. Since the original raison d'être of the Grand Canal was to supply grain to the capital, those who questioned or opposed the grain tribute system were quick to point out that investment in Zhili's water conservancy, particularly to develop rice paddies, would provide a more cost-efficient solution to the challenge of feeding the capital area than maintaining the costly grain tribute.

In this context it is not surprising that the Daoguang period saw a revival of interest in rice cultivation in the capital region. Again and again Confucian statecraft experts could not see why all the unwanted floodwater in Zhili's swampy regions could not be directed toward the development of rice fields, thus solving two problems at the same time—a prospect that was irresistible to armchair hydraulic experts.[220] Important collections of essays and documents on Zhili rivers were published in the early years, perhaps in response to an imperial decree. *Jifu shuili si'an* (1823; Four cases of water conservancy in the capital region) showcased the rice irrigation experiment of Prince Yi as its first case. *Jifu hedao shuili congshu* (1824; Collected essays of rivers and water conservancy in the capital area), edited by Wu Bangqing, gave great prominence to the famous late Ming essay on rice irrigation by Xu Zhenming and to Prince Yi's experiment. The Daoguang emperor, like his father, urged his top river officials to read the work of Chen Yi of the Yongzheng period, "Zhili hequ zhi," which is reprinted in this collection.[221] In addition to these collections, the famous compendium of statecraft memorials, *Huangchao jingshi wenbian* (1826), contained a large section of essays on the Zhili river problem, including essays by Chen Hongmou, Gao Bin, and Chen Yi.

In his preface to Xu Zhenming's essay, "Lushui ketan," Wu Bangqing recognized that those who spoke of *shuili* wanted to conserve water (*liu shui*), while those who wanted to eliminate disasters wanted to expel water (*pai shui*). He also underscored Xu Zhenming's point that the cost of shipping 4.6 million shi of grain from the south could be saved; if 10,000 or more qing were planted to rice, with a yield of 2 shi per mu, you could get 2 million shi.[222] There were three essential differences between rivers in the south and rivers in the north, Wu observed. In the south the rivers were clear; in the north they were turbulent. Clear water flowed swiftly; muddy water meandered and changed routes. The water in the north was fierce, while the soil was loose; when the loose soil met the fierce water, there could not be much benefit for very long. Finally, the rivers of the north originated in the northwest and carried heavy sand and stones that caused silting downstream. Clearly, *shuili* could not be practiced in the vicinity of the Yongding, Hutuo, Bei Yunhe, and Nan Yunhe rivers, but there were many other Zhili locations where *shuili* was possible: Fuhe, Shahe, Baiquan in Xingtai and Daming, and Xiaoming River in Zhengding, and so forth.[223]

Jifu shuiliyi (1877; Opinions about Jifu's water conservancy) is a collection of similar essays compiled by Lin Zexu and published posthumously. More famous for his role in opium suppression, Lin Zexu had considerable experience early in his career in river conservancy and flood relief, especially in Jiangsu. In 1850, the year of his death, in response to the Daoguang emperor's request, Lin submitted twelve proposals in this book citing documents and essays from previous eras about the possibility of extending rice cultivation in North China. He cited figures saying that 1 mu of land could yield 5 shi of unhusked grain, or 2.5 mu of husked grain. With 20,000 qing Zhili could produce enough husked grain to offset 4 million shi of grain tribute; 6,000 qing was enough to produce 1.5 million shi. In this way the burdensome costs and corruption of the grain tribute system could be avoided.[224]

Fin-de-siècle Floods

The middle decades of the nineteenth century were marked by the crises of the Taiping and other rebellions, as well as the invasion and looting of Beijing by Western forces. For the capital, and the metropolitan region in general, these military and diplomatic crises overwhelmed the normal bureaucratic routines. The documentary record of these decades is sparse—perhaps due to the governmental crisis and inattention to the routine domestic matters, or to archival dysfunctions. When the court's attention shifted to coastal defense matters, the inland water routes of North China were left to decay.[225] The shift of the Yellow River and the gradual abandonment of the Grand Canal and grain tribute also meant that the Zhili river system was no longer so high on the imperial agenda. Concern for the security of Tianjin drew attention, but little action, to protect the constantly flooded villages in the adjacent counties.[226]

In 1870 Li Hongzhang—the most powerful Chinese statesman of the second half of the nineteenth century—was appointed governor-general of Zhili as well as imperial commissioner with responsibility for the northern ports. Li was based at Tianjin, not at the provincial capital at Baoding. With these appointments, as well as that of grand secretary, Li became the most important Chinese official in the metropolitan region, using his position to influence both domestic and foreign affairs until the end of the century. Although his role in national and foreign affairs far overshadowed his role as governor-general, flood control and famine relief were among Li's most important concerns in provincial administration.[227] Indeed, with Li Hongzhang another reign/rain cycle began; the early 1870s saw heavy rainfall in the Zhili region, with serious flooding in 1871–73. In 1871 the amount of rain that fell was probably more than 1,000 mm, almost equal to 1801 (see Figure 1.1 in Chapter 1). Li Hongzhang met this crisis, and others in the next two decades, by soliciting contributions from gentry of South China mainly for relief efforts and immediate needs, not for river control. Li Hongzhang was well informed about the extensive damage and disrepair to Zhili's water system but realistic about the limits of the state's capacity to do any fundamental engineering.

In 1881, in response to court injunction that it was his responsibility to do something about

Zhili's river control problem, Li wrote a long memorial with a comprehensive analysis of the situation in historical perspective. All acknowledged that the current situation was grave for the people, he said. Droughts and floods followed closely upon each other, and some comprehensive reconstruction effort was urgently needed, but there were fundamental limitations to the state's financial resources. He said that all the efforts before the Qing, with the possible exception of one project in the Northern Song, had not really had many concrete results. But the population had expanded and encroached on the land, leaving less ground for rivers and streams to find outlets. *Altogether in the Qing—during the Kangxi, Yongzheng, and Qianlong eras—more than 10 million taels of public and private funds had been spent on river construction, and yet catastrophes could not be prevented.* For example in YZ 4 (1726) a big project was completed, and yet, the very next year the Yongding and other rivers overflowed. Also because of lack of rain, the wet fields from rice project had to be converted back to dry fields. In QL 27 (1762) the emperor definitively said that rice irrigation was inappropriate. In the subsequent reigns since Qianlong, the military expenses had been great, so there had not been large construction projects. Even the annual repair budgets had been reduced. "On each of the five major rivers—Yongding, Daqing, Hutuo, Nanyun, and Beiyun—and on their sixty or more tributaries, there is not one old lock, weir, dike, or embankment that is not damaged. As for diversionary canals, there is not one that is not blocked up. As a result, the silt on the riverbeds in the main body of water is getting ever higher." This had been a problem ever since the Yongzheng period, but now the bed of the Yongding River had risen above the level of the fields outside the dikes by several zhang.[228]

In addition, the Dong dian and Xi dian, which had both been important for draining off excess water, were either silted up or claimed by peasants as farmland over the last hundred or more years, he wrote in another memorial. In fact, today the richer and larger farm families work this land and have holdings of tens of mu, he said. Originally the Dong dian was a large body of water measuring 145 li from east to west and 60–70 li from north to south. It was the catchment basin for the Daqing River. But after years of silting and encroachment, it was only one-third of its previous size; at that rate it would eventually disappear.[229] Consequently the drainage of all the rivers was channeled into the Hai River at Tianjin, which often was not able to contain the water, or in the cold weather, the ocean waves would back up the channel. The situation since TZ 10 (1871) was so bad that the land in Shuntian, Baoding, Tianjin, and Hejian was subject to especially disastrous flooding.

Of all the urgent river problems, Li regarded the dredging of the Hai and Yongding rivers as the most critical. He saw that the Yongding River needed to be dredged for a length of 200 li by one or two feet of silt, or else he feared it would break out of its dike and shift southward, and its southern dike would in effect become its northern dike. But this would be tremendously costly, and there was no known technology that could accomplish this, and nowhere to put the dirt. On the other hand, allowing the river to shift would harm the farmers in a wide area. Reviewing the needs of the other rivers and the Dong dian and Xi dian, Li observed that he could not in good conscience ask the throne for the sufficient funds (knowing of its desperate financial straits), but he also could not sit by and watch the people suffer. So all he could do was authorize the dredging of a few miles here and there, focusing on the Wen'an area this year, while trying to raise funds. Unlike the previous eras, Li said they could only take stock and make repairs; there was no way to plan large projects. For the present he would put the dredging of the 200 li of the Yongding River as his first priority. If this were like the Kangxi or Yongzheng periods, the state could authorize a million taels for repairs with no difficulty, but for the present crisis, they were forced to depend exclusively on contributions from the officials and gentry of the southeastern provinces since there were no provincial funds available.[230]

The continued deterioration of Zhili's rivers, compounded by unusually heavy precipitation, produced seemingly endless catastrophes for the region. From 1890 to 1895, there was excessive rain in almost every year. According to meteorological records, in 1890, 1,043 mm of rain fell in the Beijing area, and in 1891, 1,401 mm—exceeding even the record of 1801, when 1,112 mm of rain fell. Following an average rainfall in 1892, the next two years, 1893 and 1894, also saw rain in excess of 1,000 mm in each year. (See Figure 1.1 in Chapter 1.)

In 1890, all the rivers were affected and overflowed their banks, creating a lake about two zhang deep over an area of several hundred li. Many people and animals drowned.[231] People fled to Tianjin by the tens of thousands. Low-lying areas were all affected, and there was little hope for a fall harvest. The governor-general predicted that prices would soar.[232] Western missionaries active in North China famine relief, such as Arthur H. Smith, also described the flood region covering the southeastern part of Zhili and a large part of Shandong as "like a lake." Villages were inundated and crops destroyed.[233] C. A. Stanley, another missionary, estimated that 400 sq. miles in Zhili were inundated. "The area is a vast sea—of which the limit cannot be seen. . . . There is no prospect of water flowing out for more than a year."[234]

These floods were far more serious than the periodic waterlogging of earlier eras. The next year, 1891, Stanley described the strange topography of the land in the low-lying region in Xian County (in Hejian Prefecture on the Ziya River):

> This entire tract of country, between the upper and lower West rivers, and containing forty seven villages, was flooded, much to a depth of ten or twelve feet. Many of the villages are built on land raised eleven feet, or more, high. The villagers had to scrape together all available land and form a dyke around the edge of this elevated land, which was a foot or more below the level of the water. They had to keep bailing the water that soaked through the dyke, and continually watching the dyke itself to prevent their mud houses from being melted down. Had a strong wind arisen during the time when the waters were so high, many of the villages would have been washed away. . . . It was well over six weeks before the tract as a whole was free from water, and much of the lowest ground was even then, in October, covered with water, or was soft mud that could not be planted.[235]

Local Initiatives

The relative weakness of gentry leadership in the Zhili area—relative to South China and relative to the central government—was characteristic of North China generally. After the mid-nineteenth century, however, there was a distinct trend toward greater local leadership and involvement in many activities. Some localities began to take a greater initiative in river control than had been customary. Even so, these efforts were unsuccessful in addressing the overwhelming problems.

The history of Wen'an County's water conservancy projects illustrates the relationship of bureaucratic leadership to local control. Without a doubt, Wen'an was the most critically affected county in the entire Hai River Basin; its location at the confluence of many rivers, together with its low-lying topography—it was referred to as the Wen'an wa (Wen'an Swamp)—made it the most central and conspicuous disaster area, particularly after the 1801 flood. According to its 1922 gazetteer, the county was situated at the crossroads of sixty-six rivers and yet derived only harm and no benefit from them. The locality was completely dependent on the techniques of water management. At the confluence of the Daqing and Ziya rivers, Wen'an was the site of the critical sections of the Thousand-Li Dike. To the southwest, it was affected by the Zhulong River, and to the north, the Yongding River. To the west was the Xi dian, and in the northeast corner of the county was the Dong dian, with the Daqing River connecting the two.[236] There were six dikes that critically affected the safety of Wen'an. In addition to the Thousand-Li Dike were the "remote dikes" to the west, which were the responsibility of the locality, and four other dikes along the Zhulong, Ziya, and new Hutuo (Hutuo xinhe) rivers that needed to be guarded.[237] So the burden of the local people was very great, and during the late summer and fall floods when the rivers rose, the local folks would call to each other and run to the dikes to stand guard all night.[238] Although it was the most chronically depressed location in Zhili's flood zone, and had always been vulnerable to waterlogging and flooding, it was *only in the last hundred years* that crises had struck regularly, according to local chroniclers.[239] It was during the later floods that this area was described by foreign observers as a vast lake.

The major dikes had been constructed with government funds starting from the late Ming period. The first recorded instance of government-sponsored dike construction was in 1561, followed by major construction in 1583 and later, involving Bazhou, Xiong, Baoding, and Dacheng counties as well as Wen'an, which shared the responsibility for the labor, but it was not until Yongzheng period that this region got major attention with the construction of the Thousand-Li Dike.[240] In the early Qianlong reconstruction, Wen'an received major government funding for dike construction, and again in 1771, after a major flood, substantial official funds were allocated for repairs.[241] In the Jiaqing period the government continued to support dike repairs in this area, especially after the megaflood of 1801, but also in 1812, when there was major construction after successive years of damage to the dikes.[242]

From the Daoguang period, government support was not provided, and after the 1822–23 floods for the first time the gazetteer referred to the local people and sometimes "gentry" contributing funds for repairs. In 1830 and 1836, the local *taotai* contributed funds. In 1852 another dike was breached, and a local police official worked with the local people and gentry to repair it, saving the fall crops. Again in 1865, another local official called on the gentry and people to contribute funds for repairs. Again, in 1868, the distant dike was destroyed, and the local gentry repeatedly had it repaired at great cost to themselves. Finally in 1871, the great northern dike was breached and submerged under several feet of water. Flood victims fled their villages, leaving the old and weak to fend for themselves.[243]

Because of the withdrawal of government funds and the collapse of local support, in 1873 and 1875 Li Hongzhang stepped in to sponsor the repair of the Thousand-Li Dike and other dikes in the area. He did this again in 1882 when the Ziya and Hutuo rivers overflowed.[244] From the 1890s on, the gazetteer records various local initiatives to protect the dike in the absence of any public support. In 1904, the local gentry took out a loan to repair the gaps in the dikes and managed to save half the harvest.[245] In subsequent years they drew up a schedule of repair obligations for each village.[246] In 1912, the first year of the republic, the Dike Works Society was established, with Dacheng County agreeing to provide 60 percent of the financing, and Wen'an 40 percent, but they found their funds to be insufficient and requested help from the province. Starting in 1917, the district received help from the Chinese Christian clergy and church.[247]

This chronicle of Wen'an epitomizes the stages in the history of river management in Zhili, especially since the early Qing period. First, from the early eighteenth through early nineteenth centuries, there were substantial central government investments in engineering projects. Second, in the nineteenth century, provincial officials raised funds from extraprovincial sources, and later, local officials tried to raise funds and support from the local elites and people. Third, in the late nineteenth century, local leaders and people tried to organize their own support but ultimately looked to the provincial government for funds. Finally, in the Republican period, the region accepted some financial support from Chinese and foreign missionary sources, as well as provincial and national governments. Although there is evidence of greater local community initiative in the late Qing, it is clear that local resources could not meet the needs, and in any case localities could not deal with river management individually. Strong central leadership was necessary to compel cooperation among neighboring localities.[248]

In the 1870s and 1880s, Li Hongzhang, with his formidable fund-raising abilities, took the lead in promoting local initiatives, but he himself was pessimistic about the river system. In Xincheng County at the confluence of the Daqing River and the Xi dian and Dong dian, the body of the river was so crooked that it could not contain the water without overflowing. During the Guangxu period Li Hongzhang had used dredgers to open up a diversionary canal that had first been dug in 1745, and built a lock to help control the water. A local leader named Wang Xi said that because the soil was loose like sand, this was an effort in vain, and sure enough, the next year the waters rose so high that the lock was washed away. In 1886 Li Hongzhang personally toured the river and ordered Wang Xi to measure the land and topography and devise a new plan. The old lock was reconstructed as a stone weir, which was higher by several feet than the river. In essence two channels were created to even out the current. For the next ten years or so there were no more accidents, but after Wang Xi there was no one else to manage repairs, the weir was allowed to deteriorate, and the diversionary canal became silted and impassable.[249]

Other counties had similar experiences. Yongqing County in Shuntian Prefecture, in the lower reaches of the Yongding River, was in a situation similar to Wen'an's. Each time the river flooded, the county became a lake, and the city walls were endangered. Since the Daoguang period, the gentry and merchants would attempt raise money for dike and city wall repairs but had difficulty sustaining this effort.[250]

In localities that could sustain rice cultivation, the incentive for local cooperation was greater. Wangdu County in Baoding Prefecture seemed to support rice cultivation to an unusual extent.[251] Originally banner land, the district was low-lying and fed by many rivers, which it called the Nine Dragons Springs. From the late Ming period, local leaders and people joined in an effort to dredge the waterways and create rice fields. In the Kangxi period, leaders of five villages contributed funds to repair the stone dikes but also petitioned the governor-general to underwrite the repairs, saying the people's resources were enough to support only three days' effort. Apparently the fate of these rice fields was not secure; in 1727, as part of Prince Yi's project, twelve qing and 50 mu of rice fields were created, but these were converted back to dry fields later.[252] The record is not entirely clear, but along the banks of one river, rice was cultivated, perhaps continuously, until sixty days of heavy rainfall in the early Daoguang period finally filled in all the ditches and canals and raised the level of the ground so that the rice fields were transformed into dry fields.[253] In the Qianlong era the county focused more on the repairs of protective dikes, *hegong*, rather than *shuili*. The gazetteer records the initiative in 1738 of Mr. Shen, probably the magistrate, in dredging 40 li of the Dragon Spring River and constructing three stone locks to control the water. At the time, the local people resented the labor, but after thirty years they were grateful because there had been no disasters.[254] In 1771, there was another local effort to reconstruct the dikes, using labor relief and borrowing 1,200 shi grain from the local granaries. By then the ditches and canals had silted up, and "nine years out of every ten there was waterlogging [*shinian jiulao*]."[255]

Officials like Hu Jitang in the early Jiaqing period, who had a South China perspective, expected that the localities would assume a greater responsibility for managing rivers. However, there were many fundamental reasons why this could not happen in Zhili, and, indeed, in North China generally. The lower standard of living in the north could not support local elites in the manner of the south. The lesser productivity of the land, combined with the great annual and seasonal fluctuations in weather, did not provide the prospect of good returns on investments in infrastructure. Local leadership was generally weak, and the role of the state generally strong, for good reasons. Indeed, even in regions of the empire where there were better-endowed elites, the relative shares of responsibility for hydraulics that should be assumed by the state and local communities were the source of unending tension and ambiguity. At times, the state wished to encourage local and indeed private initiative and financing of waterworks, while, at other times, the state acted as an intermediary between competing local forces.[256]

Emperors, Bureaucrats, and Ecology

To commemorate the hydraulic achievements of the emperors, numerous temples and shrines were erected along the major rivers. Variously called Longwang miao (Dragon King temples), or Heshen miao (River God temples), and sometimes designated as Huiji miao or ci (imperially sponsored temple or shrine), these temples provided a sacred space where ceremonies could be performed to pray to the deities to be spared from flood, but in the capital region they also served as highly visible reminders of imperial and, sometimes, bureaucratic merit. "Shrines and temples are for the purpose of proclaiming merit," stated the *Jifu shuili anlanzhi*, the Jiaqing compendium, which records numerous shrines and temples for each of the Zhili rivers, often with the name of the officials, usually local magistrates or sometimes river officials, who were responsible.[257]

The Yongding River, the focus of imperial attention, had the largest number of temples with imperial sponsorship, or at the least, high official sponsorship. The most famous were the North and South Huiji Heshen miao in Beijing's Wanping County. The South, or Nan Huiji Heshen miao, had its origins in the Jin, Yuan, and Ming periods and was located south of the Lugou Bridge. It was rebuilt in 1698 and repaired in 1750. Yu Chenglong, Kangxi's trusted river consultant who suggested the renaming of the river, contributed land for the purpose. The northern temple was built in 1729–30, also in Wanping, 40 li to the south of Shijing shan, in the upper reaches of the Yongding River.[258] Various other temples along the Yongding River, located in Gu'an or Yongqing County, were heavily supported by official contributions. For example, we learn that in 1751, Governor-general Fang Guancheng deputed a magistrate to supervise repairs on a temple on the south bank at the third station, and he contributed one qing of riverbank land for its support. Rituals were performed annually, and the civil and military officers who contributed funds to support the temple had their names inscribed on the back of a stone tablet.[259]

The other major rivers in Zhili were also protected by temples and shrines, many of them officially sponsored. The Hutuo River, for example, had Longwang miao, Heshen ci, Da Yu miao (temple to the great Yu), and other types of temples; a great many had late Ming origins and were fixed up in the Kangxi period by a local magistrate.[260] The Jiaqing emperor's river officials commissioned a strikingly beautiful and clear map showing numerous small and large temples along each river and another map showing the location of commemorative stone tablets along the rivers.[261]

These monuments commemorated the imperial role in river management. River conservancy succeeded when emperors took personal interest and direct responsibility for engineering. The experience of the Kangxi, Yongzheng, and Qianlong reigns shows that the emperor's leadership was vital. The Yellow River and Grand Canal were the most urgent. The southern tours of Qianlong had as an immediate objective the display of imperial concern for river control.[262] But imperial ambition alone was not enough. The emperor could not work without the bureaucracy. He empowered his top advisors to deal with the problems in a comprehensive way. Greatest responsibility was given to high official advisors, but official responsibility for the rivers in the north carried with it great risks as well. The Qianlong emperor's immediate distrust of his early Zhili officials, their vacillation, and his interference made the stakes in engineering decisions very high. Gao Bin, governor-general in 1741, was an exemplary official with impeccable banner credentials and extensive experience in river work. After his term in Zhili, he served as director-general of the Grand Canal and Yellow River conservancy from 1748–53, but he was held responsible for damage caused in heavy flooding and was dismissed.[263] Even Fang Guancheng, renowned for famine relief and river conservancy, became the target of censorial criticism in the 1760s. Failures in river work were attributed to the erroneous policies of particular individuals, and river work was one source of bureaucratic and factional disputes. When the Jiaqing emperor held individual officials financially responsible for past mistakes, his objective was to clean up the bureaucracy as much as it was to restore the rivers to stability.

Unlike the Yellow River conservancy, the problems of Zhili's waterways were not subject to deep ideological disputes, with the exception of the rice project.[264] However, many high and low officials called on to undertake river work had no expertise or experience, and may not have been familiar with the region. Officials were trained to be generalists, not specialists. Yet at the same time they were accountable for their work and politically vulnerable. Randall Dodgen has shown that efforts to expand the "irregular" bureaucracy in the Yellow River conservancy, necessitated by the heavy work load and need for expertise, led to the loss of control by the governor or governor-general over the whole process and the widening of opportunities for corruption.[265] In Zhili there was a similar tendency.

An imperial "campaign" was needed to shake the bureaucracy out of its routines. A major crisis would provide the reason to mobilize financial and bureaucratic resources. The emperor could use the campaign to clean up the bureaucracy, as in the Maoist-era campaigns, while at the same time addressing the very real need for flood control and famine relief.[266] The large campaign had its dangers, however. Huge infusions of funds provided greater opportunities for bureaucratic corruption and lower-level malfeasance, which in turn led to greater need to control the bureaucracy. The Daoguang era provided the perfect example of this process. In fact, managing the bureaucracy, not managing the rivers, became the principal focus and preoccupation.

When the bureaucrats tried to manage the rivers, the rivers themselves became bureaucratized. Xiong Xiling, who was in charge of reconstruction after the huge 1917 flood, said that this fragmentation of river authority at the end of the Qing was largely responsible for the abysmal condition of the river conservancy since it was the natural instinct of provincial officials to oppose the proposals of others. Xiong reportedly said that "engineers and surveyors reporting on the present situation are all unanimously of the opinion that the Chihli disaster is due to the malpractice of dividing the waterways into different sections and vesting the conservancy work in various hands."[267]

The eighteenth-century triumphs of hydraulic management—the stabilization of the Yongding River, the control of drainage around the Thousand-Li Dike, the diversion of silted waters to swamps, for example—only encouraged the intense use of the land on or near the swamps and dikes. Cultivators were willing to assume the risk of occasional floods because the silt-laden soil was very fertile. The state cushioned these risks by offering famine relief, which included generous tax remissions. As the population settlement became much denser, the human costs and risks became higher each time there was a natural disaster. To a great extent, then, the ecological crisis of the nineteenth century was a product of the very successes of imperial engineering of the eighteenth century, not of its failures. The changing riverbeds and topographical monstrosities described in the 1890s flood reports by Stanley were the legacy of centuries of channeling and diking. After any major rainfall, the terrain was "like a lake"—a description invoked constantly from the 1890s through the next half century at least. Even if it had been a different phase of the dynastic cycle, hydraulic cycle, or reign cycle, even a Kangxi or Yongzheng with ample financial resources could not have reversed the long-term environmental decline. Li Hongzhang's evaluation, given above, was painfully accurate. For all the millions of taels that had been spent, the tons of dirt, stone, and straw that had been moved, and the hours of backbreaking human labor that had been expended since the early Qing, the river situation had only deteriorated. The ambition of "eternal ease after one effort" was nothing but a hollow memory.

CHAPTER THREE

Population, Agriculture, and Food

FROM THE LATE SEVENTEENTH CENTURY to the end of the twentieth, Zhili's population expanded from about 10 million people to almost 90 million. Population pressure on land was severe. The early and mid-Qing successes in river conservancy and agricultural promotion had undoubtedly encouraged population growth, which, in turn, contributed to the decay of the river system. By the eighteenth century, a semipastoral economy had been transformed into a densely populated agricultural economy. In the nineteenth century, economy and society were increasingly vulnerable to human and natural crises. In the early twentieth century, North China experienced colossal famines, and hunger and poverty could be seen everywhere.

This history of North China seems to embody the specter envisioned by Malthus—that when population outstrips available land, famine would be "the last, the most dreadful resource of nature." Malthus believed "that the increase of population is necessarily limited by the means of subsistence," and "that population does invariably increase when the means of subsistence increase." He added that population growth could be contained only by "misery and vice." Short of mortality crises, only abject poverty, disease, infanticide, or "moral restraint" (late marriage), which he added later, could keep land and population in balance. Malthus frequently invoked China in his 1798 essay. "In some countries population appears to have been forced . . . to live upon the smallest possible quantity of food. . . . China seems to answer to this description. If accounts we have of it are to be trusted, the lower classes of people are in the habit of living almost upon the smallest possible quantity of food and are glad to get any putrid offals that European laborers would rather starve than eat."[1]

The world has evolved in ways not foreseen by Malthus, and most of his fundamental assumptions and predictions have proven to be incorrect. Technological improvements in agriculture have allowed higher yields from land. Industrialization and economic development bring greater security to many nations and people and have caused birth rates and overall population growth to decline. The poorest societies have the highest birth rates, while the richest societies have the lowest. Famines are not necessarily the logical outcome of scarcity; today they are more often the result of war or political misrule. Still, Malthusian ideas pervade contemporary discourse because the fundamental problem of population pressure on limited resources—not always agricultural—remains critical for many countries in the world.

In Chinese economic history, two classic studies address the issue of food and population. Starting from Malthusian assumptions, Ping-ti Ho's *Studies on the Population of China, 1368–1953* explains the population growth of China principally by its agricultural history. But unlike Malthus, Ho demonstrates that agriculture was not simply a function of land availability. In China, agricultural output grew not only through the settlement of new regions but also through the introduction of better seeds and new crops. The growth of the population in the mid-imperial period was dependent on the introduction of early ripening varieties of rice, which allowed for two crops a year, and the growth in the late imperial period depended on New World crops such as potatoes and corn. While admiring the resourcefulness of Chinese agriculture, Ho nevertheless accepts the Malthusian premise that food supply was an independent variable and population growth was the dependent variable.

Dwight Perkins's *Agricultural Development in China, 1368–1968* assumes a reverse causation, namely that population growth actually aided agricultural productivity. Like Ho, Perkins finds that China's traditional agricultural technology was extremely adaptable, but unlike both Ho and Malthus, Perkins does not view population growth as a negative force. Agricultural output expanded in the late imperial period and the twentieth century because additional labor inputs from the growing population produced higher yields. In this view population was the independent variable and agriculture the dependent. Perkins applies to China the insights of agricultural economist Ester Boserup, who showed that agricultural systems can adapt to population growth. The intensive use of labor in rice cultivation, for example, can raise yields.[2] Perkins concedes that the Boserup argument is stronger for South China, where rice yields are known to have improved over the centuries, than for North China, where wheat and millet yields probably remained unchanged.[3] Lacking historical data for agricultural output, Perkins uses accepted population figures for each period to estimate it, reasoning (somewhat circularly) that those who lived must have had enough to eat (or they would not be alive); thus, food supply must have expanded at least to the extent that population did.[4]

The history of the Hai River Basin conforms in some respects to each of these perspectives, but it also illustrates the limitations of their explanatory power when considered individually. Population pressure on limited resources, especially water and land, made the region increasingly vulnerable to famine, but Malthusian crisis was not inevitable, and the growth of population did not follow the simple geometric process posited by Malthus. Nor did food supply grow arithmetically, as Malthus predicted; instead, its expansion was the outcome of a number of factors, such as new crops and technology, that Malthus did not foresee. Ultimately crops such as sweet potatoes and corn did expand the food supply, as Ho points out. North China's agriculture did have a remarkable power to feed an ever-expanding population, but only at a subsistence level. A larger population did not result in greater land and labor productivity, contrary to the expectation of the Boserup-Perkins scenario. The dry-land crops of the north were not so responsive to increased labor inputs as rice was. And Perkins's reassuring logic that those who lived must have had, by definition, a sufficient diet, ignores the historical reality of those who did not survive famines, and the low standards of living that prevailed even when famines were averted.

Population and Land

How much did the population grow, and how much land was cultivated? Although the increasing pressure of population on the land was a trend observed by contemporaries as early as the eighteenth century, the exact quantification of population size and arable land before the early twentieth century relies on estimation rather than solid data. This section reviews the known sources, indicating areas of uncertainty and their significance.

POPULATION

The population of Zhili grew rapidly in the eighteenth century. Although there is a great deal of uncertainty about its exact size prior to midcentury, from 1751 until the end of the century it grew from at least 14 million to more than 24 million. Like the rest of the empire, Zhili's population may have doubled in the course of the eighteenth century. In Zhili this trend continued into the early nineteenth century, and the population may have reached 28 million by 1812. Following this, the population may have experienced a slight downturn in the middle of the century, not regaining its 1812 levels until the 1890s. This trend of no growth in the nineteenth century, and even a decline in midcentury, is also consistent with empirewide trends. The upward trend, regained perhaps by the 1870s, continued steadily through the 1930s, but it was interrupted by losses during the wartime period of the 1940s.[5] By 1953, the date of the first census taken under the People's Republic of China, the combined population of Hebei and the independent municipalities of Beijing and Tianjin had reached 43 million. After that a most dramatic expansion took place in the second half century of the twentieth century; by the end of the 1990s, the population had more than doubled to 89 million.

Table 3.1 presents some of the population figures upon which these generalizations are based. Although they document the trends described above, nearly every figure prior to the twentieth century raises some questions, and none should be taken at face value. Prior to 1953 there was no formal census, that is, an enumeration of the actual population. Numbers of households and population were routinely included in official reports of tax collection, the *baojia* mutual surveillance system, or grain storage, but such reports were not based on a systematic census.

TABLE 3.1

Zhili-Hebei Population, 1393–1999

(1,000s; brackets indicate figures of questionable utility)

Year	Population	Source
Ming		
1393	1,927	Liang Fangzhong, 203. Huang, *North China*, tab. B.1.
1491	[3,431]	Ibid.
1578	[4,265]	Ibid.
Late Ming	[12,759–16,088]	"guesstimates" by Heijdra, 440.
Qing		
1661	[2,858]	Liang, 258; Huang, tab. B.1.
1685	[3,197]	Ibid.
1724	[3,407]	Ibid.
1749	13,933	Ibid.
1751	14,021	QL 16/12/12, *GZDQLC* 2:190–91.[a]
1752	14,046	QL 17/12/14, *GZDQLC* 4:598–600.
1753	14,115	QL 18/12/12, *GZDQLC* 7:110–111.

TABLE 3.1 *(continued)*

Year	Population	Source

Qing *(continued)*

Year	Population	Source
1755	14,142	QL 19/12/21, *GZDQLC* 10:380–82.
1756	14,163	QL 20/12/22, *GZDQLC* 13:345–347.
1763	16,157	QL 28/12/11, *GZDQLC* 20:6–8.
1766	16,504	QL 31/12/8, ZPZZ, CZCS, 555-4-94, Box 505.
1767	16,541	QL 32/12/12, GZD 023616; also in *GZDQLC*, 29:1–2.
1768	16,581	QL 33/12/5, *GZDQLC*, 32:727–28.
1773	16,804	QL 38/12/3, GZD 027318.
1776	20,291	Huang, tab. B.2.
1777	20,523	QL 42/11/22, GZD 033371.
1779	20,708	QL 44/11/19, JJD 25413.
1781	21,756	QL 46/12/8, GZD 040257.
1782	21,977	QL 47/11/27, GZD 043360.
1784	22,302	Huang, tab. B.2.
1787	22,790	QL 52/11/27, GZD 052540.
1788	22,905	QL 53/11/24, GZD 055760.
1789	23,104	QL 54/11/21, GZD 058881.
1790	23,330	QL 55/12/3, JJD 46287.
1812	27,991	Liang Fangzhong, 400.
1820	22,622	Liang, 401 (total of yuan'e and cisheng; Ho, 56, gives the latter only).
1851	23,500	Perkins, 212.
1873	24,300	Ibid.
1893	27,200	Ibid.
1909–11	26,721	Liang, 268. Compiled in 1912.

Republic

Year	Population	Source
1913	29,600	Perkins, 212
1933	38,400	Huang, tab. B.1; adjusted from Perkins, 212.[b]
1948 [?]	38,400	*Quanguo hukou tongji*, national chart, and 24–27.[c]

People's Republic[d]

Year	Population	Source
1953	43,118	*Zhongguo renkou: Hebei fence*, 70; *Zhongguo renkou: Beijing fence*, 62; and *Zhongguo renkou: Tianjin fence*, 68.
1964	53,914	Ibid.
1982	70,490	Ibid.
1992	82,230	*Zhongguo renkou tongji nianjian 1992*, 4.
1999	88,600	*Zhongguo renkou tongji nianjian 1999*, 16.

[a] These *minshu gushu* figures do not include miscellaneous population categories sometimes reported separately. Each year the population of the saltworkers in the Changlu salt district was also given. Between 1766 and 1789, these figures grew from 145,000 persons (male, female, and children) to 167,000, always showing a small increment over the previous year. See further discussion in the text.

[b] Because Perkins's original source for 1933, Liu and Yeh, excluded Rehe, Beijing, and Tianjin from the Hebei total, Huang adjusted the figure by adding 1.6 million for Beijing, 1.2 million for Tianjin, and 5 million for Rehe.

[c] This source gives the totals 28.7 million for Hebei, 6.2 million for Rehe, 1.7 million for Beiping [Beijing], and 1.8 million for Tianjin. The total of 38.4 million is close to the 39,000 figure in Huang, tab. B.1, which is adapted from Guan Weilan. Guan, 68, gives 29,207,396 for Hebei, and Guan, 111, gives 6,196,974 for Rehe. Huang also adjusted the total for Tianjin and Beijing population to reach the total of 39 million.

[d] Under the People's Republic of China, Beijing and Tianjin are independent municipalities that report their populations separately. Fig. 12.2 in this book shows these separate figures; the totals are given here.

The first serious issue is that the figures for the late Ming and the early Qing are undoubtedly too low, as most historians acknowledge. If the figure of 2.8 million for 1661 is correct, then the growth in the first century of Qing rule would indeed have been phenomenal. After the 1393 census that shows Zhili population (then called Bei Zhili, North Zhili, to distinguish it from the southern capital area, Nan Zhili) to have been about 2 million; however, no reliable census was taken again in the Ming period. Martin Heijdra has shown that Ming population and land figures are consistently undercounted, and the early Qing officials relied on the erroneous Ming figures. Based on his understanding of the sources, he makes a series of population "guesstimates" for the late Ming period. For Zhili, his low estimate is 12,759,000 persons and his high estimate is 16,088,000. If even his low estimate is correct, this would imply that, contrary to general belief, the population hardly grew at all in the early Qing.[6] This seems difficult to reconcile with the qualitative evidence of settlement of the capital area after the Manchu takeover. Pastureland was gradually displaced by crops, and the ecological balance in the capital region shifted toward farming. It is possible that in the late Ming the population reached the levels estimated by Heijdra, and subsequently there was a considerable loss of life during the Manchu takeover, recovery from which was not reached until the early eighteenth century, but there is probably no way this will ever be known. The demographic history of Zhili in this period must remain largely conjectural, and the impression of a huge population explosion in the eighteenth century must be tempered by the uncertainty about the period before 1750.

Even after the first century of Qing dynastic rule, accurate censuses were not taken. Household registration was previously part of the tax collection record, but after 1711, when the Kangxi emperor declared that the *ding*, or head tax quota, should be frozen and merged with the land tax, there was no longer a need for an accurate household census since changes in household size or local population no longer affected the tax quota. In 1741 a proposal by the Board of Revenue to revive a house-to-house census was rejected by the high ministers. They declared that annual enumeration of the population was impossible to achieve. After 1741 "provincial officials need only to report annually in the eleventh month, the amounts of grain and the total numbers of households and mouths of their respective provinces, excluding the *liuyu* (that is, those who had taken up residence in localities which were not their officially registered ancestral counties) and aborigines. There is no need to make a door-to-door enumeration."[7] Thus Ping-ti Ho considers these household and population figures to be more "fiscal" than demographic, probably representing a considerable undercount of the population.[8]

There is some disagreement about whether the population figures for 1776–1850 became more reliable because the Board of Revenue wanted more accurate figures for the *baojia*, the mutual responsibility system.[9] G. William Skinner has shown how the official data for Sichuan Province for the nineteenth century was almost certainly fabricated by clerks and never questioned by officials. The data arouse suspicion because they show too regular a change from year to year, and the direction of the change is always the same.[10] The consistency with which this was done casts doubt on official data for other provinces as well, and Skinner suspects that the mid-nineteenth-century China totals usually given are almost certainly inflated.

Table 3.1 includes figures drawn from the population and grain (*minshu gushu*) reports found in the Qing imperial archives from the second half of the eighteenth century. Usually reported in the eleventh or twelfth month of each year, these figures are believed to be based on the *baojia* records. Each of these annual reports gives the number of households and "mouths" (*kou*, not *ding*) that includes subtotals for male adults, male children, female adults, and female children.

Additional figures are provided for the population in the Changlu salt district. One can observe how the numbers show a steady increment year after year, with a very low rate of growth, suggesting the possibility of a scribal addition to the figures rather than an actual count—very much in the same manner discerned by Skinner for Sichuan.

Of all the Qing data, Ho considered those published in 1820, based on a survey ordered by the Jiaqing emperor, to be the most reliable for the mid-Qing period.[11] But Cao Shuji and Jiang Shou have recently found that the *Jiaqing yitong zhi* contains many serious inaccuracies, including both over- and underestimates.[12] They maintain that the data from an empirewide survey in 1776 are more reliable. They also point to the previously dismissed "green registers" (*qingce*) of the Board of Revenue as a reliable source of population data.[13] Cao has reconstructed these provincial-level figures by disaggregating them, examining prefectural figures as well as county-level figures where available. Table 3.2 presents an expanded version of Cao's reconstructed population figures. The figures for 1776 and 1820 have been adjusted by Cao based on anomalies found in the prefectural figures. Still the figure for 1776 of 17.7 million is much lower than figures given in standard Qing compilations. The *Qing chao wenxian tongkao* gives a much higher figure of 20.6 million. And the Board of Revenue *qingce* for 1776 and the years after are in the range of 21.5 to 24.8 million. Cao's 1820 total of 23 million also poses difficulties. A figure for 1812 of 27.9 million, also from the Board of Revenue *qingce* and given in Table 3.1 here, is much larger than that for 1820 of 22,622,000. Although it is possible that this sudden decline could be attributed to the rebellion of 1813 in the southern part of the province, or to the various floods that occurred in the Jiaqing period, the gap still seems implausibly large.[14] Cao concludes his lengthy discussion of these anomalies with the sobering words: "Because of these careless editing mistakes and chaotic fabrication, all the documentary sources discussed above that have Zhili population figures are inaccurate."[15]

If the 1812 figure is inaccurate, or anachronistic, then it appears that the population size remained constant during the nineteenth century. If the 1812 figure is accurate, and Zhili population had reached 28 million, then we can say that the region suffered a population decline in the mid-nineteenth century, and recovery was not achieved until the end of the century or after the turn of the century.

In the Republican period, censuses began to be taken. The Nationalist government general accounting office undertook a survey of agricultural conditions.[16] Another survey, *Zhongguo nongye gaikuang tongji*, was sponsored by Zhang Xinyi (C. C. Chang). Both were used by the Tōa kenkyūjo in the 1940 Japanese publication, *Shina nōgyō kiso tōkei shiryō*, which is considered authoritative. Its data may be compared with those given in Table 3.3, and also form the basis for Table 3.6. Although *Shina* provides data on population and land for every county, it assumes an average household size that seems too large.[17] Less problematic household figures are found in *Hebei sheng gexian gaikuang yilan*, also used in Table 3.3.

Post-1911 population figures also raise the issue of changed boundaries for Hebei Province. In the Republican period, Hebei did not include Rehe Province, previously Chengde Prefecture. To the south, it yielded to neighboring Henan and Shandong certain counties formerly in Daming Prefecture. After 1949, the People's Republic of China also adjusted administrative boundaries. Most critically, it made Beijing and Tianjin independent municipalities having the same rank as provinces. Hence the figures for Hebei cannot be regarded as equivalent to those of the old Zhili Province; to them must be added the population figures for Beijing and Tianjin, as they are in Figure 12.1 in Chapter 12.

TABLE 3.2
Reported Population in Zhili Prefectures, 1776–1953
(1,000s)

Prefecture	1776	1820	1883	1953
Shuntian	1,987	3,860	4,250[a]	8,236
Xuanhua	746	839	851	2,119
Yongping	1,450	1,736	1,780	3,010
Baoding	1,932	2,304	2,199	3,918
Yizhou	346	412	244	656
Zunhua	540	702	816	2,309
Zhaozhou	658	767	632	1,153
Dingzhou	532	634	359	1,008
Shenzhou	447	533	695	848
Jizhou	632	750	1,236	1,268
Tianjin	1,343	1,601	1,976	4,745
Hejian	1,303	1,616	2,174	3,091
Zhengding	1,752	2,089	1,370	3,324
Shunde	835	952	1,053	1,290
Guangping	984	1,225	1,102	2,275
Daming	1,722	1,965	1,949	2,663
Subtotal	17,209	21,985	[22,686]	41,915
Koubei santing	9	117		253
Chengde	500	980	784[b]	597
Total	17,718	23,082	23,470[c]	42,765

SOURCES: For 1776, 1820, and 1953, Cao Shuji, *Zhongguo renkou shi*, juan 5: Qing shiqi, tab. 8.9, 349–50. See text for discussion of the origin and credibility of these figures. These totals vary from those in Table 3.1. Shuntian prefecture figures include Beijing; Tianjin prefecture includes Tianjin city. For 1883, *Jifu tongzhi* 1884, 96:24–61. Notes below indicate where and why adjustments have been made. Rozman, *Population and Marketing Settlements*, append. 4, and Huang, *North China*, 323, tab. B.2, are also based on this source Other sources that provide sub-regional or county-level population figures: for 1912, Liang Fangzhong, 268; for 1932, *Shina nōgyō kiso tōkei shiryō*, 15–16. 1953 figures can be compared with 1946 figures in Guan, 68–80.

[a] Adjusted to include Beijing population. The *Jifu tongzhi* figure for Shuntian prefecture of 3,474,000 does not include Beijing population, which in 1882 was 776,000 persons, counting only the Inner and Outer Cities. See Li and Dray-Novey, tab. 1.

[b] 1827 (DG 7) figure is provided in lieu of 1883. *Jifu tongzhi* 1884, 96:34a.

[c] Sum of above figures. *Jifu tongzhi* 1884, 96:25b reports 22,825,000 as the total for 1883. If the Beijing population of 776,000 is added to that figure, then the province total would be 23,601,000, a larger figure than what is calculated here. Some errors may be due to rounding, others to scribal errors.

PREFECTURAL TRENDS AND LOCAL RECORDS

Despite these many cautions, it is possible to have confidence in the basic trends from the mid-eighteenth through the twentieth century, and the general order of magnitude. Data from the prefectural and county levels allow one to confirm these trends. Table 3.2 reproduces the prefectural level figures for 1776, 1820, and 1953 from Cao's study, as well as the 1883 figures from the *Jifu tongzhi*, the provincial gazetteer. (The latter could represent data from an earlier date.) Despite the fact that the totals and subtotals may represent underestimates, Table 3.2 is useful in giving a sense of different rates of growth across the province.

Table 3.2 confirms the general stagnation of population during the middle part of the nineteenth century (here from 1820 to 1883). The prefectures of Tianjin and Hejian showed moderate growth. Zhengding showed a decline from 1820 to 1883. Other prefectures showed very little or no growth. The figures also show the rapid growth between 1883 and 1953, especially in the prefectures of Shuntian and Tianjin, where the cities of Beijing and Tianjin experienced development. Zhengding Prefecture to the west also had rapid growth, probably due to trade with Shanxi. The northern prefectures of Xuanhua and Zunhua also showed rapid growth, due to migration and industrialization.

Local gazetteers also provide occasional figures that help to confirm the provincial and prefectural demographic trends. Figures taken from various local gazetteers are presented in Table 3.3. Although most gazetteers do not provide statistics, a few provide a series of figures that seem to be at least internally consistent and reveal some trends. As with the prefectural figures, the most common pattern in the local examples was a rapid growth from the late nineteenth century into the 1930s. Three counties (Liangxiang, Shunyi, and Wei) show almost a doubling of the population in that period. Four others (Dingxing, Xinhe, Guangzong, and Guangping) show a more gradual, but still impressive, population increase. One can also see the slump of the nineteenth century. Two counties (Xinhe and Dingxing) show a distinct decline in population in the mid-nineteenth century, probably the result of rebellion, while a third (Guangzong) shows no net growth or decline in the entire nineteenth century. Yongqing County seems a distinct outlier in this sample of counties, suffering a drastic decline between the 1770s and 1870s, without full recovery even by 1930.

Conclusions about the eighteenth century are more difficult to draw—particularly since early Qing figures are considered unreliable. Xinhe may have had a threefold expansion during the eighteenth century if the early Qing figure can be believed. Guangzong's population may have grown two and a half times from 1670s until 1801 if the 1670s figure can be trusted. One county—Dingxing—gives enough information to show a more than 70 percent increase between 1778–1821, a period of slower growth for most other localities. Shulu's population grew sharply from the late eighteenth century through the first half of the nineteenth, but its figures seem to have jumped around inexplicably.

LAND

Historical information about cultivated acreage poses similar problems. The figures given in Table 3.4 are taken from tax records and thus should be interpreted as the amount of taxable land in Zhili since the Ming. As such they probably represent a serious undercounting of actually cultivated land especially in the Qing. In the first century of the Qing, the figures omitted banner land, which probably amounted to about 35 percent of the total cultivated land. Even when banner lands were eventually transformed and registered with civilian land, there was still considerable

TABLE 3.3
Local Populations, by County and Date

County (in Prefecture)	Date	Population	Shui Mu (tax mu)	Mu per person
Xinhe (Jizhou)[1]	Shunzhi	9,799		
	Kangxi	21,571		
	Early QL	23,115		
	QL 55 (1790)	69,234		
	JQ	69,293		
	XF	66,856		
	TZ	59,364		
	GX1 (1875)	61,496		
	GX2 [?] (1876)	82,852		
	Republic [?]	94,055		
	1928	87,120		
	1934	97,437[2]		
Liangxiang (Shuntian)[3]	Late Ming–KX55	2,670		
	GX 14 (1888)	40,179		
	1936	71,265		
	1934	75,986[2]		
Yongqing (Shuntian)	QL 42 (1777)	196,576[4]		
	GX 1 (1875)	77,298[5]		
	1934	149,940[2]		
Shunyi (Shuntian)[6]	Ming Wanli	12,960 (ding)		
	GX 9 (1883)	84,077		
	1931	165,521		
	1934	163,825[2]		
Dingxing (Baoding)[7]	QL 43 (1778)	95,924		
	DG 1(1821)	166,499		
	TZ 12 (1873)	122,756		
	1932	197,790[8]		
	1953	306,371[9]		
Wei (Guangping)[10]	Ming Jiajing (1522–56)	15,240	737,493	48.4
	Ming Wanli (1573–1619)	30,726	667,899	21.7
	Early Qing	38,777	667,950	17.2
	GX	76,199	821,505	10.8
	Republic	168,768	821,505	4.9
	1934	194,134[2]		
Guangzong (Shunde)[11]	Ming Wanli 21 (1593)	27,081		
	KX 15 (1676)	25,254 (ding)		
	JQ 6 (1801)	87,175		
	TZ 10 (1871)	89,188		
	GX mid	87,988		
	1931	101,968[12]		

TABLE 3.3 *(continued)*

County (in Prefecture)	Date	Population	Shui Mu (tax mu)	Mu per Person
Jiaohe (Hejian)[13]	GX period	235,640		
	1910	270,345		
	1915	255,569		
	1934	278,183[2]		
Guangping (Guangping)[14]	GX beg.	60,811		
	1934	82,155[2]		
	1937	85,679		
Shulu (Baoding)[15]	1762	177,614		
	1796	240,280		
	1850	332,840		
	1868	294,185		
	GX beg.	315,534		
	GX mid-late	260,000		
	1934	358,101[2]		
	1953	362,213		

SOURCES: Local gazetteers as indicated. Figures from around 1932 are provided by, or compared with, those from *Hebei sheng gexian gaikuang yilan* (1934). *Shina nōgyō kiso tōkei shiryō* (published 1940, but based on 1932 surveys) also gives figures for the period. See text for discussion of these sources.

[1] *Xinhe XZ* 1928, ce 2, 20a–21b.
[2] *Hebei sheng gexian gaikuang yilan.*
[3] *Liangxiang XZ* 1881/1889, 3:1–2, and *Liangxiang xian shiqing* (1939), 21.
[4] *Yongqing XZ* 1779/1813, 71a.
[5] *Yongqing XZ* 1875, huxubian 8:52ab.
[6] *Shunyi XZ* 1933, 6:2ab.
[7] *Dingxing XZ* 1890, 3:2ab.
[8] *Shina nōgyō kiso tōkei shiryō*, 15–16.
[9] See Cao Shuji, 343, for discussion of these figures.
[10] *Wei XZ* 1925, 4:7b; mu per person recalculated.
[11] *Guangzong XZ* 1933, 3:7ab.
[12] Almost identical to *Hebei sheng gexian gaikuang yilan.*
[13] *Jiaohe XZ* 1916, 2:1b.
[14] *Guangping XZ* 1939 7:10a.
[15] Various editions of local gazetteer, in Cao Shuji, 342-43; see text for discussion.

undercounting because of the custom of mu conversion, that is, combining portions of low-grade land into one taxable or cadasteral mu.[18] Yeh-chien Wang considers this practice "one of the major factors accounting for the downward bias of Ch'ing land statistics." For the government, the amount of taxable land was the principal concern, not accurate land registration.[19]

The land tax in Zhili was generally lighter than other provinces—although not uniformly across the province—because at least half of the land was alkaline or unproductive and also because labor services in the capital area were particularly onerous.[20] Knowledge of land ownership in Zhili was particularly confused because accurate land registration was lacking. The subbureaucrats were poorly informed about conditions in the countryside because they had no need for accurate information, and their superiors recognized and accepted this condition.[21]

TABLE 3.4

Cultivated Acreage in Zhili/Hebei, 1393–1957

(1,000s of mu)

Year	Mu[a]	Source
Ming		
1393	58,250	Liang Fangzhong, 346–47. Also Huang, *North China*, tab. C.1.
1502	26,971	Ibid.
1578	49,257	Ibid.
Qing		
1661	45,977	Liang, 380. Also Huang, tab. C.1.
1685	54,343	Ibid.
1724	70,171	Ibid.
1753	66,162	Ibid.
1812	74,143	Ibid.
1820	69,861	Liang, 401.
1840s	64,000	*Jifu shuili yi*, 8a.
1851	72,726	Liang, 380, and compare Brook, "Rice Cultivation," 679 n. 50.
1873	73,046	Liang, 380.
1887	86,652	Ibid.
Republic		
1914	95,400	Li Hongyi, 6309–12.
1932	103,432	*Shina nōgyō*, 16.
1933	118,000	Perkins, 236.
People's Republic		
1953	132,000[b]	Perkins, 236, listed under 1957. Also Huang, tab. C.1

NOTE: See discussion in text, as well as Huang, *North China*, append. C; and Perkins, append. B.

[a] In the Qing period, the mu was equal to 0.1518 acre, while in the Republican period and later it was equal to 0.1647 acre. See Perkins, 220. Thus the Qing acreage figures should be adjusted by about 8 percent to be commensurate with the Republican-period figures. See Li Hongyi, 6309–12, for other taxable land figures.

[b] The figure for 1953 may be overestimated. See discussion in Chapter 12 below.

The key issue is whether and when the cultivated acreage reached its limit in the Qing period. Several scholars have written that this happened in the eighteenth century. Dwight Perkins has assumed that for most parts of China a "saturation" point was probably reached by the mid-eighteenth century, and that the land figures for 1873 were probably no larger than those for 1766. For Zhili, Perkins calculates that the cultivated acreage in 1766 was closer to 120 million shi mu than the reported 68 million Qing mu.[22] For 1873, 1893, 1913, and 1933, he estimates the cultivated acreage at 120, 118, 120, and 118 million shi mu respectively. For 1957, he accepts the figure of 132 million.[23] In his book on North China, Philip Huang agrees with Perkins's estimate, arguing that if the reported Qing figures are increased by 29 percent for banner land and another 20 percent for undercounting, the eighteenth-century figures do become similar to those of the 1930s.[24] Wu Chengming, senior Chinese economic historian, estimates that Zhili's cultivated acreage was 111 million mu in 1873 and 109 million mu in 1933, and thus there was little change in that sixty-year period. For him, the "saturation point" was certainly reached by the late nineteenth century if not earlier.[25]

POPULATION DENSITY AND LAND OWNERSHIP

If cultivated land did not expand between the mid-eighteenth and the early twentieth centuries, population density must have increased no matter which population estimate is correct. If population increased by about 80 percent between 1766 and 1913—from 16.5 million to 29.6 million (see Table 3.1)—pressure on the land greatly increased. If a later date such as 1933 or 1953 is chosen, an even more serious picture emerges. If one adjusts the starting point to 1787, a slightly different rate emerges.[26] No matter which particular dates or estimates are chosen, the secular trend of increased population-to-land ratio is undeniable.

In the Ming period, large holdings of several hundred mu were not uncommon in North China. Usually only one crop per year was the common pattern, and much land was left fallow. The use of animals in farming was widespread.[27] After the Manchu conquest, Zhili was still an area of relatively low population density that supported herding and pastureland. During the next century, population increased steadily and more land was brought into cultivation. The Wei County gazetteer records a progressive increase in population density after the Ming period and implies that per capita landholdings declined thereafter (see Table 3.3). In the late Ming, there were 21.7 mu per person, in the early Qing 17.2 mu, and in the Guangxu period 10.8 mu. In the Republican period there were only 4.9 mu per person. (It is important to note, however, that the land figures given by this source are identified as "*shui mu*," or tax-mu, not as cultivated land.) Other estimates for North China have shown a more drastic decline: 9.56 mu per person in 1685; 4.35 in 1851; 4.89 in 1887; 4.04 in 1912; and 1.39 in 1920.[28]

Data from Huailu County shows that as early as 1725–50, landholdings were small. As seen in Table 3.5, 21,000 households owned 315,000 mu of land, which meant that each household owned on average 15 mu of land, hardly sufficient for subsistence. But if we count only the landowning households and exclude the 5,331 nonowners, taking them to be noncultivators (which was probably not the case), the farm population was 15,715, and each household held 20.6 mu, better but still inadequate. These figures imply much smaller landholdings than the Wei County data. They also show that land concentration was modest: 46.1 percent of households owned 15 mu or less of land; another 15.8 percent owned 16–30 mu. Fewer than 13 percent of households owned more than 30 mu of land. This pattern of small holdings is also found in Julu County in 1706–36; three surveys covering thousands of households showed the percentage of households holding more than 30 mu of land to be 10.2, 11.5, and 12.4 percent.[29]

The figures from 1820 provide confirmation that the pattern of small holdings seemed unchanged in the early nineteenth century. With a population of 22,622,000 persons and cultivated acreage of 69,861,000 mu, the average holding per person was only 3.08 mu.[30] But if we adjust by 50 percent the acreage figure to include the factors mentioned by Huang, total cultivated acreage would have been 105,000,000 mu, and the per person holding would increase to 4.64 mu. At five persons per household, the average per household holdings would have been in the range of 15–24 mu; at 5.71 persons per household, the number used in the 1930s *Shina* survey, the range would have been 17.5–26.5 mu.

Such figures from the eighteenth and nineteenth centuries differ little from the more reliable economic data collected in the 1930s, when the population was even larger. The survey taken by Zhang Xinyi for Hebei around 1932 shows that 103,432,000 mu of land were owned and cultivated by 4,223,704 farming households (they represented 85.5 percent of the total of 4,938,695 households), giving each farm household 24.4 mu on average.[31] Since the survey found that there were

TABLE 3.5

Land Distribution in Huailu County,
Early Eighteenth Century

(land in mu)

Land Owned	Number of Households	Percent of Households	Total Land Owned	Percent of Total Land Owned
0	5,331	25.3	0	0.0
<1	888	4.2	439	0.2
1–5	3,507	16.7	10,207	3.2
6–10	3,172	15.1	22,948	7.3
11–15	2,137	10.1	26,157	8.3
16–30	3,332	15.8	70,006	22.2
31–40	967	4.6	33,205	10.5
41–50	498	2.4	22,313	7.1
51–60	334	1.6	18,195	5.8
61–100	540	2.6	40,534	12.8
>100	340	1.6	71,225	22.6
Total	21,046	100.0	315,229	100.0
Average per household			15	

SOURCE: Huang, *North China*, 104. Originally found in Dai Yi, 1:346–47. Survey of households in 91 *jia* (mutual protection units). These figures are predominantly from the Yongzheng period, but some may date from the late Kangxi period or the early Qianlong period. The original source of these figures is not given. Comparable figures for 1706, 1736, and 1939 are found in Brandt and Sands, tab. 6.2, 183.

5.7 persons per household, this would mean that there were 4.3 mu per farming person, or 3.6 mu per person, if both farm and nonfarm households are included.

These findings are corroborated by local studies from the 1930s. Gamble's survey of Ding County from 1926–33 showed that with a population of more than 400,000 people, the average size family holding was 20.4 mu, and the average size family was 5.83 persons.[32] Thus there were 3.5 mu per person. But in a smaller sample of 400 families in the Ding County experimental village, he found that the average holding was 30.9 mu per household, with 6.3 persons per family. Thus there were 4.9 mu per person.[33] The Republican period data from Wei County in Table 3.3 also found on average there were 4.9 mu per person. In Sha-ching village in Shunyi County, a 1917 survey found that the average household owned only 14 mu.[34] In Ssu Pei Ch'ai village in Luan-cheng County in Zhengding Prefecture, cotton was a major crop by the 1930s, and there were some large-scale farms of several hundred mu each, but still two-thirds of farm households owned fewer than 50 mu.[35]

In the early eighteenth century, Sun Jiagan, the Zhili governor-general, estimated that it took about at least 30 to 50 mu for a family to have a comfortable living from the best land in the province.[36] It would appear from the examples cited above, however, that this standard was not generally achieved even in the eighteenth and nineteenth centuries, and certainly not in the twentieth century. In the 1930s, John Lossing Buck and other agricultural experts found that 25 mu of good land was needed to support a farm family of five, but these conditions were not always met, and many households had to seek additional forms of income.[37] Small holdings were not the only difficulty; the poor soil and difficult climate limited the productivity of the land, adding a greater degree of risk to subsistence farming and making large investment in land unattractive. Although much has been made of the phenomenon of managerial landlordism, in fact large-scale farms accounted for a small portion of the total.[38] Before collectivization in the 1950s, farming was overwhelmingly a small-scale family enterprise.

Land and Agriculture Under Manchu Rule

In imposing their rule over the capital area in the mid-seventeenth century, the Manchus caused tremendous destruction of property and lives, and they dramatically altered the geopolitical landscape of the Zhili region, at least for a while. They confiscated the extensive landholdings of the Ming court, princes, and nobles, converting them into estates for the Qing imperial court and the Eight Banners.[39] They also created banner lands (*qidi*) either by encirclement and appropriation, or through the voluntary surrender of lands by Han Chinese, and awarded them to bannermen for their livelihood.[40] Sometimes Chinese landowners commended their land to Manchus but continued to farm it, paying rents instead of taxes, which were becoming increasingly onerous.[41]

The bannermen became a kind of rentier class, living off the income from the land. Manchu princes and noblemen were forbidden to leave the Imperial City, so they could not have directly engaged in farming even if they had wanted to do so. In 1651, the year after the awarding of banner lands was supposed to have been completed, an edict was issued forbidding the bannermen to engage in farming themselves, thus requiring them either to seek estate managers or to rent out their fields to Han Chinese peasants to farm.[42] Apparently the latter course was the most common fate of banner lands.[43] In 1669 the Kangxi emperor declared a permanent end to the creation of banner lands.[44] Forbidden by law to farm the land and lacking technical expertise or experience, the bannermen were divorced from the land, and the structure of landholding eventually reverted to its preconquest pattern.[45] Even those relatively rare Manchu noblemen who were successful managers found that their holdings became more scattered, so that "eventually the banner estate system dissolved in a sea of private landlordism."[46] In 1737 half of the original land within 500 li of the capital was already in private hands, according to official estimates.[47]

According to the best estimates, in the early Qing period banner lands probably represented about 35 percent of the total cultivated land in Zhili, but by the end of the Qing only about 5 percent.[48] Most of the banner lands were concentrated in the capital area, principally in the prefectures of Shuntian, Hejian, and Baoding as well as in Zunhua, Yizhou, and Yongping.[49] Over time, the distinction between banner land and civilian land often became unclear. The 1884 gazetteer of Yutian County reported, "Here in Yutian, banner lands [*qidi*] and civilian lands [*mindi*] are often confused. Since old times the identity of *mindi* and *qidi* has been confused, and many false practices have arisen, such as the estate managers [*zhuangtou*] selling land. In this area there was originally more banner land than civilian land, but [now the situation is different]."[50]

Fairly early in their rule, the Qing emperors began to shift their focus in Zhili from banner land and the immediate interests of the bannermen, to the welfare of the Han population and to the "encouragement of agricultural production" (*quannong*). In putting a stop to the creation of banner lands, the Kangxi emperor expressed his regret for the hardship they had caused to the Han people.[51] In addition to river conservancy, Kangxi, Yongzheng, and Qianlong each paid attention to the issues of land tenure and agriculture. In the process, imperial policy facilitated, or at least did not resist, the transition from a lightly populated semipastoral economy, with sheep raising and horse riding, to a densely populated, sedentary agrarian economy.

Over time the Kangxi emperor seemed to appreciate the strengths of the north. He viewed the people of the south as weak, and their food and drink as less healthy than those of the north. He feared that northerners were beginning to imitate the dietary habits of the south, which would weaken them.

> Since the water and soil are good north of the great river, the people are also strong and robust. All of the food and drink is therefore always beneficial for the people. There is a definitive pattern regarding the water and soil in the celestial and terrestrial realm. Nowadays there are northerners whose opinion it is to follow the example of the south in food and drink, but this absolutely must be avoided.

Kangxi's injunction was based on the premise that it was not simply that the environments of north and south were different, but that the physiques of northerners and southerners were fundamentally different.[52]

The Yongzheng emperor, like his father, had an intense interest in agricultural prosperity and paid close attention to the reports on crops and weather that provincial officials were required to submit. Under him, Governor-general Li Weijun took an active role in promulgating policies to stimulate agricultural development. In 1724, he reported that Zhili's land was extensive, and there were definitely ways to expand cultivation, especially in the southern portions. In the north, where the banner lands were concentrated, there were lands in Bazhou (Shuntian-fu) and Xin'an that used to be horse pastures (*machang*) that could be cultivated, but people were afraid because it was government land. "This is really a pity," he commented. He suggested deputing representatives to talk to local officials about the problem.[53] A later survey of the land in thirteen counties in the capital area found there was a total of 20,744 qing of pastures, of which only 217 qing were already cultivated, and another 704 qing that could easily be cultivated, but there were 12,000 qing that were not suitable for cultivation, and the rest still needed to be investigated.[54]

The pastoral economy yielded slowly to encroachment by the agrarian economy. More than thirty years later, in 1756, Fang Guancheng also addressed the problem of reclamation of horse pastures, noting that settlers were afraid of being found guilty of privately opening up lands (*siken*). But, in fact, he pointed out, this process benefited everyone, and all such cases should be completely forgiven and more cultivation encouraged.[55] In 1764, Fang discussed the disruption caused by the grazing of sheep on wheat fields. This practice was particularly harmful because the hoofs of the sheep were sharp and damaged the wheat sprouts in the fall. The Muslim sheepherders from Shanxi and Shaanxi rode roughshod over the fields, striking villagers who tried to stop them. This practice was prevalent in areas south of Beijing where wheat was widely planted: Baoding, Hejian, Jizhou, and Shenzhou. In the future, he recommended, they should be redirected to Tianjin pastures.[56]

Most governors-general serving in Zhili in the Kangxi, Yongzheng, and early Qianlong reigns saw the need to encourage agricultural production in the capital area but also recognized the limitations of the natural environment. The weather was extremely variable, even from county to county, memorialized Liu Yuyi in 1732.[57] In discussing tax remission policy, Sun Jiagan, governor-general in 1739, argued that policies for Jiangnan were inappropriate for Zhili, where the best land in Shuntian, Baoding, Yongping, Tianjin, Xuanhua, Hejian, and other prefectures was given over as banner land, and the rest was dry or alkaline. In four other prefectures of Zhengding, Shunde,

Guangping, and Daming, there was no banner land, but the soil conditions varied. Zhengding and Shunde had stony soil as well as sandy soil. Guangping and Daming had good, but uneven, soil conditions. On the good land a family with 30 to 50 mu of land could do well. But on the sandy, alkaline, and poor soil, even 3 qing or 5 qing (300 to 500 mu) of land in a good year would provide only modest returns. In a year of drought or flood, those families with small holdings would inevitably become impoverished.[58]

Jifu's soil had been more fertile in ancient times, it was widely believed. One early Qianlong period official observed that in ancient times Zhili's land had been of average quality, but today the soil was unproductive (*jibo*). In the southeast, with 50 mu one could feed ten mouths, but here several qing of land would still not assure sufficiency.[59] Responding to the Qianlong emperor's edict ordering officials to consult a certain agricultural manual, *Caizheng nongshu*, another provincial official observed that in the south in the past, one could get 66 shi of unhusked grain from 1 mu. Today the yield was 20 shi, or at least 13 to 14 shi, provided there was irrigation and other investment. Even following the emperor's injunction, the result in the north could not match the 12 to 13 shi some were setting as a goal.[60] Fang Guancheng wrote in 1763 about the unfavorable growing conditions in the Tianjin area, where salinization and late rains limited crop choice and productivity. Only 60–70 percent of the land was cultivated. Each county had at least 1,000 or more qing of wasteland.[61]

Despite the recognition that growing conditions in the north were not so favorable, some officials could not resist trying to replicate the prosperity of the south. Xu Guangqi and other Ming agricultural experts were intensely interested in rice experimentation in the north.[62] In 1707, Governor Zhao Hongxie reported on an unsuccessful experiment to develop rice cultivation in the Tianjin area. Local people, he said, knew it would not work. "Besides, reports from each zhou and xian of Zhili's nine fu state that either the land is too alkaline, or it is too uneven, and the water won't drain off. Given these objections, we should probably do what is convenient for the people."[63] Another experiment brought low yields, of only 1 shi per mu at best, despite the high costs for capital and labor. "This is too big an investment for such a small result. It is all because the soil is alkaline and the climate unsuitable."[64] The Yongzheng emperor's irrigation project of 1727–30 involved thirty-nine counties and perhaps 6–7,000 qing of land.[65] "Jifu's soil is the most fertile in the empire," Prince Yi had said.[66] The bureaucratic fantasy of turning dry northern fields into beautiful paddyland kept recurring despite the harsh realities of northern China. Even in the nineteenth century, no less eminent a figure than Lin Zexu proclaimed the suitability of rice cultivation for North China, "The soil of Zhili is by nature suited for rice, and any place with water can be made into paddy fields."[67]

Emperors were the symbolic patrons of agriculture. The image of emperor as a leader in agriculture was just as ancient as the image of imperial river-tamer. The emperor made annual sacrifices at the Temple of Heaven. The Kangxi emperor wrote, "In bad droughts I have spent three days praying in a simple hut of mats, not even taking a bite of salted or picked vegetables, and then—after the fast—walked to the Temple of Heaven."[68] Emperors also sponsored publications promoting the latest agricultural techniques. Since Song times there had been various editions of *Gengzhitu* (Illustrations of farming and weaving). In the Kangxi reign, there was one edition (1696) containing forty-six illustrations by a court artist, Jiao Bingzhen. There were similar editions in the Yongzheng, Qianlong, and Guangxu periods.[69] In the Qianlong period a variation on the *Gengzhitu* was the *Mianhuatu* (Illustrations of cotton cultivation), accompanied by poems and imperial inscription, which was widely disseminated to promote cotton cultivation. The weaving sections of the previous *Gengzhitu* had all been focused on silk production. In 1765, Fang Guancheng presented an edition of the *Mianhuatu* to the Qianlong emperor on the occasion of the thirtieth year of his reign.[70] Such imperially sponsored publications may have had more symbolic than technological value. In the case of cotton, they demonstrated a bureaucratic as well as imperial interest in promoting this cash crop. In conjunction with seventeenth-century scholarly agricultural treatises such as Xu Guangqi's *Nongzheng quanshu*, or Song Yingxing's *Tiangong kaiwu*, such publications showed the great interest in agricultural improvement. One of the Xu's motives for undertaking his project, in fact, had been a concern about improving the agricultural productivity of the north so that the expense of grain transport from the south could be avoided, and he conducted some of his agricultural experiments in the Tianjin area.[71]

Agriculture: Grains and Other Crops

Agriculture in North China was based on multiple grain crops that were suited to its generally poor soil and the difficult climatic conditions. Throughout the Qing period the most important crops grown in North China were wheat, millet, and sorghum. A small amount of rice was grown, but it was not economically significant. Beans of many kinds provided food for people and feed grain for animals; they were also important in nitrogen fixation for the soil. Gradually, as population pressure mounted, corn and sweet potatoes played an increasingly large role in the ordinary diet. Vegetables supplemented the diet, and fruits and nuts became important cash crops in the late nineteenth and early twentieth centuries. Cotton was the major cash crop. Although growing conditions were not ideal, this diversity of crops helped to spread out risks and minimize damage from natural disasters. The dual cycle of summer and winter crops was critical in maintaining the food supply and contributed to the relative stability of grain prices in Zhili.

RICE

The visions of abundant rice fields held by successive high officials never really materialized in Zhili because the growing conditions were not favorable. At no point in time was the acreage or output very large. Lin Zexu estimated that in the 1840s, of the total cultivated area of 640,000 qing, 2 percent was planted in rice, or about 10,000 qing.[72] Local gazetteers record examples of rice cultivation. In Xiong County: "Rice is grown in all the villages bordering the lake [*dian*]."[73] In Xingtai County: "Some rice is grown in the southeast corner of this county, but the kernels are small and rough."[74] In Zunhua Prefecture: "Some rice is grown in villages near Shahe."[75]

The locally grown rice has always been considered fine and delicious. The emperor and the court actually ate rice that was produced locally—the excellent rice that was grown west of the capital, and not the stale rice that came from the grain tribute system.[76] Western travelers in the late nineteenth century observed rice growing near Beijing. "Rice is grown once in the year in the warm summer where rivers favor irrigation, and there is no better rice than that cultivated a few miles from Peking on the west where the Hwun Ho issues from the mountains, and has during myriads of years scooped out a valley of its own which now possesses a few alluvial tracts supplying excellent white rice for the wealthy families of Peking."[77] "Not a little rice is grown in this district," reported a Beijing gazetteer of the Republican period.[78]

Still, the idea that northerners did not like rice persisted throughout the Qing period: "Northerners don't like to eat rice and don't want to plant it."[79] Zhili's common people, it was said, were not used to eating rice, and Prince Yi's experiment had failed because northerners did not eat rice. At the time, officials suggested that the rice be purchased from the farmers with treasury funds and stored in the Tongzhou granaries. The farmers used the income to buy millet, which they preferred to eat.[80] In Beijing itself, grain tribute rice was traded in favor of fresh locally grown wheat or millet, but this was due to the issue of freshness as much as food preference.

In the early Republican period, the output of Zhili rice was estimated at about 1,350,000 shi, which might have been about 1 percent of total grain output.[81] Most rice grown in Zhili was of the dry variety, but according to a Japanese survey, near the shores of the Bai he (in the Tianjin vicinity) there was some wet rice cultivation. Only into the twentieth century, with new patterns of commerce and the influence of treaty ports, did rice become a significant part of the diet of the well-to-do, but that rice was imported from the south, and at Tianjin some rice was imported also from Korea.[82]

WHEAT

Wheat, or *mai*, was the important luxury grain in the north. It came in several varieties. *Xiaomai*, or winter wheat, was the most important, while *damai*, or barley, played a secondary role. *Qiaomai*, or buckwheat, was also planted in this region. Most gazetteers speak of wheat and barley. Although in many places both were winter crops, sown in the fall and harvested in the late spring, in Zhili barley seemed to be grown only as a spring-sown crop, and it was relatively unimportant.[83] A description frequently found in Zhili gazetteers is "The small [*xiao*] is planted in the fall and the large [*da*] is planted in the spring. . . . There is also spring wheat which has a short season."[84] Another description states:

> *Xiaomai* is planted in the fall and harvested in the spring. Its skin is thin and you can get a lot of *fen* [powder or flour] from it. *Damai* is planted in spring and ripens in the fall. So its skin is thick and its flour is sparse. It is not made into flour for eating. Sometimes it is made into wine. It is less than half the price of autumn wheat or *xiaomai*.[85]

Twentieth-century sources also refer to a type of summer wheat that was grown in the northern part of Zhili, Manchuria, and Inner Mongolia, while winter wheat came mainly from Shandong and southern Zhili. Winter wheat was of higher quality and more expensive. It was sown in September or October and harvested in May or June. Summer wheat was sown in March and April and harvested in autumn.[86]

Of *xiaomai*, there were red and white types (*hongmai* and *baimai*), of which white was the more important in the Zhili region. Fang Guancheng reported that *baimai* was high quality (*shangmai*), and *hongmai* was second in quality (*cimai*). The difference in price was usually more or less 1 qian.[87] Gazetteers do not list *hongmai* and *baimai*, but grain price reports before 1763 list *hongmai* and *baimai* prices separately. After 1764, only *mai* in general was reported, and probably this referred to *baimai*. In the twentieth century, red wheat was produced in northern Jiangsu and Anhui provinces, while white wheat was produced in Shandong. The latter was used in modern flour mills and brought a price higher by 10 to 20 cents a picul.[88]

In this study, the term wheat refers to *xiaomai*, or winter wheat, unless otherwise noted. Because wheat was planted in the fall and harvested the next spring or summer, it played an important role in the annual agricultural cycle, complementing the basic crops of millet in the north and rice in the south, both of which had a fall harvest. Wheat was harvested at the time when stocks of millet or rice were low, during the lean season that Chinese called *qinghuang bujie*, "when the green and yellow do not connect." This also permitted the land to be utilized more productively year round with crop rotations in North China usually allowing three crops in two years, a practice that originated as early as the Northern Wei period.[89] Because wheat matured during the winter, it was not affected by the summer floods and waterlogging that were characteristic of North China. Xu Guangqi wrote:

> In the north the worst category of land is the submerged. On it natives usually grow sorghum and can secure, on the average, only one crop in several years. For this reason they are poverty-stricken. I have taught them to grow wheat, which may not be affected by [annual floods]. For the flood usually comes in late summer or early fall and can do no harm to wheat. In the places where drainage is possible after the recession of the flood the land dries up in autumn and is therefore suitable for autumn wheat. In localities where drainage is not feasible, the land dries up in winter and is suited to spring wheat. . . . This method can practically assure nine crops in every ten years.[90]

In responding to an imperial edict inquiring about the shifting of the Hutuo River southward, where it now entered the Fuyang River at Ningjin in Jizhou (Shuntian Prefecture), Fang Guancheng personally went to inspect the situation. He observed, "All the fields here are of the *yishui yimai* type. Even if it were to flood, it would help the fall wheat. A popular saying says '*yimai di sanqiu*,' 'One wheat harvest can match three autumns [harvests],' and the people regard this as normal. Local officials since the Ming also know this tendency."[91] Fang Guancheng used the term *yishui yimai* numerous times.[92]

The expression *yishui yimai* occurs in other places as well and refers to the benefits of regular flooding. In Xiong County the local history recorded that "In times of flood there was the song of *yishui yimai*. After the wheat was harvested, no fall crops would be planted, and this is called 'land left for wheat, *liumaidi*.'" Land that was usually planted in the fall and harvested in the summer was left unplanted until the next spring, but spring wheat was not so fine as wheat planted in the fall.[93] J. L. Buck spoke of "lake land" that was "only free from water during the season that wheat can be grown."[94] An anecdote illustrating an unusually abundant wheat harvest after flooding is found in the Zhaozhou local history: in 1853 there was a huge rain in the seventh month; it rained day and night for seven days, and innumerable houses collapsed. On the new year's eve there was big snow. The next year in the summer the wheat crop was doubly abundant.[95]

The fact that wheat was so responsive to an abundance of water meant that it was vulnerable to dry conditions. Drought—which could mean the absence of enough snowfall during the winter growing months, as well as insufficient moisture retained in the soil from rainfall the previous summer—was not well tolerated by wheat. Until the twentieth century, the extent of irrigation in North China was quite limited compared with the south. Wheat was also a "comparatively low-yielding" crop requiring careful cultivation and rapid harvesting. In addition to adequate water, it required much fertilizer. It was also highly vulnerable to insects and disease and was therefore difficult to store for long periods.[96]

Although there is ample evidence of the importance of wheat in the North China agricultural economy, we cannot be absolutely certain how extensively it was cultivated in Zhili. Song Yingxing, the seventeenth-century author of the well-known agricultural manual, *Tiangong kaiwu*, thought that wheat constituted 50 percent of the northern Chinese diet, but this was an impressionistic judgment, not based on direct investigation.[97] According to Fang Guancheng, whose knowledge of Zhili was always based on direct personal observation and experience, in some other places in North China like Shaanxi ("*Qin Yong zhi di*"), 70 percent of land was planted with wheat, but this was not the case in Zhili. In Daming, Guangping, and nearby prefectures in the south, 50 percent of the land was planted in wheat; in Zhengding, Baoding, Hejian, Tianjin, and so forth in the central section, 30 percent was planted in wheat, and in Yongping, Xuanhua, Zunhua, and Jizhou, 10–20 percent was in wheat.[98] Fang added some details in 1764: "Wheat is grown in areas south and west of Beijing such as Baoding, Hejian, Shen, and Ji, but not in Tianjin area."[99] Fang also stated, "Not all of Zhili's soil is suited to wheat. The ordinary people do not eat it regularly. It cannot be compared to the two provinces of Henan and Shandong. Even there, out of every ten mu, only six or seven are planted with wheat. *In Zhili it is not even than half of that.*"[100] It then appears that Zhili was less productive in wheat than other parts of North China, and Song Yingxing's generalization overstated the role of wheat in Zhili's agriculture and diet.

The passage above suggests that wheat may have been cultivated more as a cash crop than for the farm family's own consumption.[101] In the 1920s and 1930s, wheat was considered the luxury grain— ground into flour and usually served as noodles or steamed bread. J. L. Buck wrote that peasants in North China in general sold half the wheat they grew and bought inferior grains for home consumption. In his estimate, one-quarter of the peasant family's food was purchased.[102] For the Qing period, references to food customs in Beijing support the idea that urban consumers created a huge market for wheat, which was an important part of the diet of the residents of Beijing's Outer City. "The people of Zhili most importantly value *gaoliang* and millet, and next spring wheat and buckwheat," observed officials. "Beijing has one million households, which eat a lot of wheat. . . . The more that is shipped the more that is sold, and [this] causes the market price to be level."[103]

Yet there are other references that point to the importance of wheat to the peasant diet. "The peasants most value wheat," for example.[104] There are frequent references to the widespread human suffering caused by poor wheat harvests. For example in 1778, when there was a poor wheat harvest in the southern part of the province, wheat was brought in for relief from Shaanxi, Henan and Fengtian, and Shengjing (Manchuria). If wheat had been only a cash crop, such steps need not have been taken.[105]

MILLET

Millets of various kinds had been the staple grain of North China since Neolithic times, and until the second half of the twentieth century, they were the principal source of subsistence for the peasants and urban poor of the north. There was an oft-quoted expression: "The people of the north use it daily and cannot be without it." There are green, red, yellow, or white types.[106] The expression, "northern people cannot be without it," is seen in many different gazetteers and is attributed to *Qun fangpu*, an early seventeenth-century compendium of botanical terms.[107] Colloquially called *xiaomi* (lit., "little rice"), today in North China, the unhusked grain is called *guzi*.[108] Generally speaking, in Qing sources, the term *sugu* refers to unhusked millet, while *sumi* refers to husked millet. One saying was, "In the field it is called *gu*, in the granary it is called *su*."[109] Another was, "*chu gu wei mi*" (Husked *gu* becomes *mi*).

The Latin name for this most common type of millet is *Setaria italica*, which is also known as foxtail millet. A second type is *Panicum miliaceum*, or broomtail millet, which in Chinese is called *ji* although the character *ji* was sometimes inaccurately used for *setaria* millet.[110] The glutinous form of *setaria* was called *shu*—a term later used for sorghum and maize; colloquially it was sometimes called *niangu*. The glutinous form of *panicum* millet was called *shu*, a different character of the same pronunciation.[111] A colloquial term for glutinous *panicum* was *mizi*. The confusion about the different terms for millet has rather ancient roots and has puzzled more recent scholars.[112] Further distinctions were made between sweet and nonsweet varieties of the different millets.[113]

The importance of millets is seen in the gazetteer of Xiong County, which also reveals the variations in local terminology:

> *Ji* [*panicum* millet]: the northern people call it *gu*; when it is husked they call it *xiaomi*. The people of the north use it daily and cannot be without it. In ancient times it was as important as *shu* [glutinous *panicum*]. . . . It is also called *su*. Its color can be red, white, yellow, or black. It is sown in the spring and harvested in the fall, but there is one type that is sown in the fifth or sixth month and ripens at various times in the fall; it is called colloquially "sixty days into the granary," and is planted during the dry years in great quantity.[114]

Other gazetteers also refer to the fast-growing type of millet. In Baoding Prefecture, it was said that traditionally millet was planted at *lixia* (May) and ripened at *bailu* (September), but these times were variable. In drought years one type was planted late and harvested early; it was called "sixty days into the granary."[115] Many other local gazetteers dwell on the different terms for millet.[116]

Millets were relatively hardy crops, considered to be heat tolerant and drought resistant. Yet they were vulnerable to pests and required good soil nutrients, sometimes derived from being rotated with legumes. Like wheat they needed to be harvested quickly before wind or rain disturbed the grains.[117] *Panicum miliaceum* was less important than *Setaria italica* in quantity, but historically it was probably important in opening up new lands in the early Qing period because it did not require much fertilizer.[118]

In general millets were a sturdy and reliable source of nutrition. According to Francesca Bray's authoritative study, "Millets are generally well balanced nutritionally, with relatively high protein content, and are often highly valued by rural populations as food for small children, nursing mothers and old people, even when their cultivation has largely been abandoned in favor of improved varieties of such large-grained cereals as wheat, maize or rice."[119] Western famine relief workers in the 1920s considered millet to be an excellent source of "a fine stable diet. While it has less protein than wheat, it has been found to have a considerable amount of vitamines and can advisedly be given in large quantities as procurable."[120]

SORGHUM

Sorghum was the other principal staple crop of North China. Its common Chinese name is *gaoliang*, but in older books it was often called *shushu* (lit., Sichuan millet), which suggests that it may have been introduced to China through Sichuan.[121] In the Qing period, it was grown extensively in North China. Bray suggests that it is "probable" that it was a relatively uncommon crop until the Yuan and Ming periods, and it may not have been extensively cultivated until the population boom of the eighteenth and nineteenth centuries.[122]

Sorghum can be grown on poor soil that is not suitable for wheat or millet. Because of its height, it is flood resistant and can be grown in low-lying areas where drainage may be poor. On the other hand, sorghum is not very drought resistant and has a relatively low yield.[123] Fang Guancheng encouraged the planting of sorghum in polder lands within dikes. In speaking of Jizhou, a district north of Baodi and west of Xuanhua in Shuntian Prefecture, Fang said that this was part of the *yishui yimai* land. "People plant fall crops and then ask for relief when the floods come. . . . Instead, they should be encouraged to plant *gaoliang*, not beans and other crops. We passed this word onto the local officials to tell the people."[124]

Sorghum's nutritional value is not high. In the twentieth century, medical personnel observed that in rural areas where *gaoliang* was a main part of the diet, cases of osteomalacia, bone softening due to Vitamin D or calcium deficiency, were frequent. *Gaoliang* also had low content of digestible protein.[125] In the 1920–21 famine relief effort, the nutritional guidelines recommended that, although it was plentiful, sorghum should not be given as the sole food for a long period of time because it was not as nutritious as millet.[126]

The portion of the Zhili land devoted to sorghum cultivation was extensive, and it may have been the leading grain crop in the early and mid-Qing. In a 1747 memorial discussing contributions to charity granaries, Nasutu mentioned that in Zhili the land was planted 20–30 percent in millet and 70–80 percent in *gaoliang* and beans.[127] In discussing the problem of restocking the granaries, Nayancheng memorialized in 1815 that "*Gaoliang* is the most planted grain in this area."[128] These two estimates seem high when compared with other references related to crop ratios, but they may well be accurate. In the northern prefectures, such as Xuanhua, *gaoliang* was the principal grain; very little millet was grown.[129] North of the Great Wall, in Mongolia and Fengtian, millet was grown, but *gaoliang* was the preferred grain.[130] In considering famine relief in 1812, officials suggested that *gaoliang* would be suitable since banner households, they said, were accustomed to eating it.[131] For Fengtian, *gaoliang* was always used as the standard for relief since that is what people ate. "Fengtian relief uses *gaoliang* as the standard."[132] In the twentieth century, *gaoliang* grown in Manchuria was considered superior to Zhili or Shandong *gaoliang* and sold at a higher price.[133]

Although Han Chinese did not rank sorghum as a preferred food grain, they greatly valued it when made into *gaoliang* liquor. (Mostly it was red sorghum that was used for this purpose.) The brewing of such liquor was extensive in the Qing period, but periodically officials tried to restrict this activity because they feared that it diverted food resources into a nonessential use. The appropriate policy to adopt toward *shaoguo*, or brewing, was a periodic subject of official discussion.[134] In the late Kangxi period, Zhao Hongxie, now the Zhili governor-general, argued that the prohibition on *shaoguo* should be enforced only when grain prices were high. He noted that when prices were low, it actually hurt the people not to be able to use grain to distill spirits for income. The practice of making wine from fruits, on the other hand, should never be prohibited.[135] In the following year he urged that the ban on making *gaoliang* wine be lifted until the spring, when prices would be high, arguing that this would benefit the people. The emperor's rescript said, "Let the local officials decide whether to lift the ban or impose it."[136]

In the Qianlong period, the subject of *shaoguo* was again raised. In 1737, Sun Jiagan, then president of the Board of Justice, argued that in North China suppressing *gaoliang* liquor manufacture would harm poor peasant households that depended on growing and selling sorghum for a significant portion of their income.[137] In 1751, Fang Guancheng expressed doubt about a suggestion that the breweries be licensed and then controlled. Closing the breweries only results in secret activities and having the functionaries extort money from them. Instead, in years of lean harvest, the amount of grain they could purchase should be limited. But two years later, he advocated that the practice of *shaoguo* be strictly banned. Thirty-eight districts had reported no evidence of hoarding grain or *shaoguo*. He hoped that officials would not be lax about enforcing regulations.[138] Like his fellow statesman Chen Hongmou, who supported prohibition only "in times of grain shortage," Fang was pragmatic.[139]

In the nineteenth century there were large distilleries in Manchuria, which soon became "the most important commercial enterprises in the frontier agricultural districts, doing a major share of the business in grain trade, milling, oil pressing, money lending, and the issuance of currency scrips. Some of the distilleries were built like fortresses to withstand the assaults of Manchurian bandits," according to a Western observer.[140] In the Republican period there were more than twenty *gaoliang* distilleries in Xuanhua alone. The business was quite profitable, especially after the construction of highways. In the ninth or tenth month, the Beijing merchants went to make their purchases, causing the price to rise immediately.[141]

BLACK BEANS

Beans of all kinds were extensively cultivated in Zhili, as well as in Manchuria, and were an important source of protein and other nutrients. Most gazetteers listed many different types of beans. *Huangdou*, "yellow bean," the soybean, was made into bean cakes, soymilk, soy sauce, and condiments.[142] The *qingdou*, "green bean," was used for similar purposes.[143] *Candou*, or broad beans (fava beans), were also important and frequently mentioned.

But of them only *heidou*, or black bean—not usually eaten by humans—was included in the grain price reports of Zhili officials. Important in the feeding of horses used in the military, black beans had strategic and economic significance. *Heidou* was a kind of *dadou* ("big bean"). It was the most drought resistant of all beans, and it could be grown under the worst conditions, even without irrigation. Like all beans, *heidou* was planted in the spring or summer and harvested in the fall.[144] It was used for feeding horses, but it could also be used as medicine or famine food, according to Qing-era sources.[145] Gazetteer sources often used these terms interchangeably. For example, "Black beans are also called *dadou*. They are actually shaped like a kidney and used for feeding horses. Also called *liaodou*."[146] Or in 1939, the black bean is "used for feeding horses, also for bean curd. It is the finest in texture of all the beans. Also called *ludou* or *liaodou*."[147] "Black beans are also called *liaodou*; they are mostly used for feeding cows and horses."[148]

According to a 1930 article on the bean trade in Manchuria:

> The black bean [*hei tou* and *wu tou*] has three varieties: when the epidermis is black and the inside green, it is called *Ta Wu Tou*. It yields oil or fat, and when boiled with millet or rice, it is used for food. When the epidermis is black and the inside is yellow and of much smaller size, it is known as *Hsiao Wu Tou*. It yields oil and is used for horse feed and the refuse for pig feed. When the epidermis is black and the inside yellow, the bean assuming a flattened and elliptical shape, it is called *Pien Wu Tou*, and is used for horse feed and when pickled for human food.[149]

According to present usage, the true *heidou* is round in shape and has a good taste. It can be used by humans as a food to survive the winter and is very nutritious. It is currently used for animal feed because it is less expensive than *huangdou*.[150]

Because black beans were necessary for feeding the horses used by the bannermen, an ample supply was considered strategically important. Officials also appreciated that in difficult times they could be used for human consumption. In 1737, the Zhili treasurer proposed to import beans to aid Xuanhua, "where the land is barren and the people are poor. Although black beans are used to feed horses, in times of distress they can be used as human food. . . . People in Xuanhua store beans and grain, and replace (or replenish) the supply every year. If there are no granaries, they use homes or temples. Black beans and the food supply of border people are mutually beneficial."[151] In 1751 Fang Guancheng suggested shipping black beans from Fengtian to Zhili.

> Black beans are needed for the feeding of horses. Yizhou in Fengtian has an excess supply of black beans of 13,000 shi each year. After distributing beans to estate managers [*zhuangtou*] for feeding their horses, etc., the remainder accumulates and mildews each year. I propose that we sell this surplus off at *pingtiao* [reduced] prices. The area east of the pass [Guandong] produces black beans, and the price is rarely high. It is an incomparable source of beans when the officials and soldiers at Beijing fall short. Each year 10–20,000 shi should be bought and stored for possible *pingtiao*, if the price is low, and 4–6,000 shi should be stored in each zhou or xian.[152]

Often in the eighteenth century, there were proposals to use granary surpluses—beans were mostly stored at Xuanhua—for human rations or famine relief. In 1728, it was proposed to substitute beans for grain when the latter was scarce, although the Board of Revenue had previously in 1726 rejected this idea.[153] In 1761 Fang proposed that beans be substituted for grain in military rations. "In Xuanhua's Wanquan xian there is not enough *bingmi* [military grain], but there is an excess of beans. In eight zhou and xian there is an excess of beans and a deficit of grain."[154] During the 1801 flood, however, the court turned down a proposal to use black beans in the banner and official stipends for the coming winter and spring, saying that people would not eat them even though the price of black beans was 0.50–0.20 taels lower than that of *mi* (millet). It would not benefit the people because the bannermen would simply turn around and sell their black beans and still would not have enough to feed themselves. Black beans, they argued, were needed in only a few places where horses were kept.[155]

Thus, despite their versatility, black beans were difficult to pass off as a food grain no matter how bad the situation was. Although soybeans and other beans did certainly play a supporting role in the diet—they did not rate a place in the grain price reports of Qing officials. From at least the mid-nineteenth century, however, beans of all kinds from Manchuria played a very large role in the export trade at Tianjin. They came from the Zhangjiakou area via railroad or ferries.[156] By 1928, bean exports of 2.4 million tons a year constituted 72.7 percent of China's agricultural exports, and they continued to be a major export commodity in the 1930s.[157] Beans were used principally for industrial purposes, not for food. Glycerine chemically extracted from bean oil was used in the manufacture of gunpowder, medicines, and toilet articles, and the fatty acid used in the manufacture of soap. It was also used as a petroleum substitute, in paints, and for numerous other purposes.[158]

CORN (MAIZE)

Corn was introduced to China in all likelihood in the sixteenth century, but its diffusion was gradual.[159] This important New World crop had the advantage of being suitable for poor and mountainous areas in the southwestern provinces like Sichuan, or the marginal lands of interior provinces like Shaanxi or Hubei. Its cultivation expanded in the Qianlong, Jiaqing, and Daoguang reigns. Because it allowed poor land even on hillsides to be used for cultivation, it expanded the food capacity of Chinese agriculture and supported the population growth of the eighteenth century.[160]

In the Zhili region, the earliest reference to corn is apparently in 1622.[161] Another reference appears in 1678 in a list of crops for Xianghe County.[162] It became commonplace in Zhili in the late Qianlong-Jiaqing period.[163] The earliest description of corn I have found is in a 1749 gazetteer of Dong'an County: "This is "jade millet [*yusu*]; among its green protective leaves are white hairs."[164] Other citations include Zunhua in 1793, Anxiu in 1808, and Nangong in 1827.[165] It was mentioned occasionally in nineteenth-century gazetteers of the region.[166] Maize was also called *yumi*, "jade rice," or *bangzi*, or *baomi*. As one gazetteer wrote, "*Yumi*. Its popular name is *bangzi*, or *baomi*. In the *Nongzheng quanshu* it is called *yushushu*. There are many types and colors. You can make cake out of it. The local folk all consider it *mi* [grain]."[167] The term *yushushu*, "jade sorghum," suggests the early association of corn with sorghum.

It was not until the twentieth century that corn was grown extensively in North China, probably at the expense of the other fall crops, sorghum and millet, with which it is classed.[168] In Shunyi County, corn became the most important food crop, although the traditional grains were

TABLE 3.6

Cropping Patterns in Hebei Province in the Republican Period

(percent of total output by volume, except as noted)

County (Prefecture)	Wheat	Millet	Sorghum	Corn	Cotton	Other
Region 2						
Zhuozhou (Shuntian)[1]	24.3	16.1	8.9	48.7	[?]	Peanuts
Ping'gu (Shuntian)[2]	18.8	33.8	9.8	26.3	—	Beans
Jinghai (Tianjin)*[3]	30	17	25	12	—	Legumes 14
Wangdu (Baoding)[4]	30	50	10	—	—	Beans, Barley
Wan (Baoding)*[5]	20	40	6	15	—	Rice, Beans, Barley
Region 3						
Gaoyi (Zhaozhou)[6]	30.5	36.5	19.3	.005	—	Beans
Guangping (Guangping)*[7]	12.5	50	0.1	12.5	2.5	
Cheng'an (Guangping)[8]	12.1	48.3	—	6.9	—	32.8
Qinghe (Guangping)[9]	18.3	24.8	40.2	0.9	—	15.8
Region 4						
Huailu (Zhengding)**[10]	26.9	55.7	4.2	3.6	7m jin	Beans
Gaocheng (Zhengding)*[11]	13	20	7	—	20	Beans 10
**[11]	10m	20m	5–6m	10m	10m jin	
Jingxing (Zhengding)[12]	39.7	33.3	4.0	7.8	—	15.0
Province Average	28*	22	20	14	7	Beans 9

* Percent of cultivated land.

** By weight (m jin), not volume.

NOTE: Regions refer to Map 7.1. Percentage figures are somewhat inflated because of undercounting of minor crops. They are calculated from gazetteer sections that are sometimes not precise about listing output of all crops.

SOURCES: Hebei figures calculated from *Shina nōgyō kiso tōkei shiryō*, 1:41–43. The figures in millions of mu are 31.3 million mu for wheat, 24.3 for millet, 21.7 for sorghum, 15.5 for corn, 9.8 for beans, and 8.1 million for cotton. See text for discussion of this source.

[1] *Zhuozhou zhi* 1936, 3:1a.

[2] *Ping'gu XZ* 1934, 3:27.

[3] *Jinghai XZ* 1934, 4:5ab.

[4] *Wangdu XZ* 1934, 1:35–40.

[5] *Wan XZ* 1934, 7:27–28.

[6] *Gaoyi XZ* 1933, 2:10–11.

[7] *Guangping XZ* 1939, 5:19ab.

[8] *Cheng'an XZ* 1931, 5:13.

[9] *Qinghe XZ* 1933, 2:68b 1934, 4:5ab

[10] *Huailu XZ* 1931, "Fangzhi wenchao," 58:151.

[11] *Gaocheng XZ* 1933, 1:4b–5a.

[12] *Jingxing XZ* 1934, 5:1–3. Percentages calculated from mu figures.

also important.[169] According to some estimates, by the 1930s, corn output in Hebei was almost equal to that of millet and greater than that of sorghum, but evidence in Table 3.6 suggests that estimate is too high even for the 1930s.[170] Corn was, however, consumed extensively in some places. In the 1870s, it was the cheapest grain product in Beijing.[171] In Ba County in the 1930s, 45 percent of total consumption was corn, 13 percent wheat, 10 percent millet, 13 percent various beans.[172] "In recent years new seeds and methods for cotton and corn only have flourished," recorded its gazetteer.[173] "People eat large quantities of it; therefore a great deal of it is planted," recorded another.[174]

Maize is highly nutritious in carbohydrates but less abundant in protein.[175] Nevertheless, it was, and still is, considered an inferior food by most Chinese. Corn bread, or *wotou*, unlike American-style corn bread, was very coarse, indigestible, often hard as a rock, and was eaten only as a necessity. Today in China, corn is used mostly as a feed grain. When it is eaten at home, it is considered more of a novelty food and treated more as a vegetable dish than as a grain product.

POTATOES, PEANUTS, AND FRUITS

The potato (*fanshu*), both white and sweet, was another New World crop that reached the southeastern coast of China in the initial twenty years of the Ming Wanli reign (1573–93). The first mention in any source of its being grown in Zhili is 1748.[176] Governor-general Fang Guancheng was a leader in this area as well, inviting twenty specialists from Ningbo and Taiwan to teach Zhili farmers how to grow sweet potatoes. In 1758, Fang ordered all the local officials to encourage peasants to plant potatoes.[177] In the Jiaqing and Daoguang reigns, sweet potatoes spread to the districts south of Beijing.[178] Like corn, the potato's water and soil requirements are not high. Because it could be grown on mountain slopes and in poor soil, it did not compete with grain crops for land.[179]

The peanut was another New World crop that became important as a cash crop in this area, gaining popularity probably in the late Qing period. In Guangping County, however, peanuts had been introduced at the beginning of the Kangxi period. All sizes and types were grown. By the 1930s, everyone in the county planted it.[180] Peanuts could grow on sandy soil, and because of their high nutritional content, they had a good market. They were used for cooking oil as well as food. In Tangshan County people started to plant peanuts on their sandy soil in the Xianfeng period. "In the last ten years or so [before 1881], both in the city and the countryside, all the sandy places are planted with peanuts. This is a superior strategy."[181]

In Shenzhou starting in the 1880s peanuts became the most important crop and brought a larger income than grains. They were transported to Fujian, Guangdong, or to foreign countries, where they were machine-pressed into oil and reshipped to China. (Later, peanut oil processing was taken up by Chinese producers.) In Shenzhou peanuts filled an important need since the rivers were heavily silted and the soil was loose, making agriculture difficult. Timber, fruits, and vegetables were the main sources of income. Some silk had been produced in the past, but very little by the late Qing. Cotton was not yet important in this district.[182]

In Sanhe County, it was said, "Commerce in this area has flourished. The biggest export from this locality is peanuts, followed by fruit products and cotton."[183] Another observed, "The number of people in the locality who are planting peanuts is gradually increasing. Recently a large-grain variety of peanut has been imported from the West."[184]

Fruits of various types also became important cash crops in the twentieth century. The gazetteer of Guangzong County wrote:

> The grains grown here are mainly millet, wheat, and *gaoliang*. Also some beans. Cotton is not grown here as much as in neighboring areas. This area is sandy and without water source. Sweet potatoes, peanuts, rape [*youcai*], etc. are grown here, and it is easy to grow fruit trees, like peaches, almonds, pears, dates, grapes. It takes 4–5 years to grow a tree. Tree planting started at end of Qing. More and more people are learning the technique.[185]

Other fruits included figs.[186]

COTTON

Cotton was the most important nonfood commercial crop in this area in the Republican period, but the extent of its cultivation before the twentieth century is a matter of some uncertainty. There is evidence from gazetteers that cotton cultivation had been introduced to many places as early as the Kangxi period.[187] In 1667 in Xinhe County, for example, the cotton was so abundant that it appeared as several inches of snow; this was recorded in the "unusual events" section of the gazetteer.[188] Cotton is recorded in the crops section of the 1679 edition of the Ningjin County history.[189] For other localities that record cotton cultivation, however, it was introduced in the eighteenth century or later.

In the mid-eighteenth century cotton was actively promoted by Fang Guancheng, who presented an edition of *Mianhutu*, sixteen illustrations of cotton, to the emperor. In the colophon he wrote, "In Jizhou, Zhaozhou, Shenzhou, and Dingzhou, eight or nine of ten peasants cultivate cotton [*yimianzhe*]. The output is greater than in the Lower Yangzi, and the quality of the weaving also matches that of Songjiang." In an often-cited passage, he stated that in the region south of Baoding, 20–30 percent of the land was planted in cotton. "When the new cotton comes to market, merchants from distant places gather, rubbing shoulders and tangling up each other's feet. The speculators line up at the market to accumulate it. The traders bring their carts for the market."[190] In 1808–9 the Jiaqing emperor spoke of the wide use and/or usefulness of cotton and expressed his interest in promoting it.[191]

Various gazetteers suggested the gradual process by which cotton production expanded. The 1749 edition of the Dong'an County gazetteer listed cotton as a local product, whereas the 1673 edition did not.[192] The 1868 edition of the Yanshan local history reports cotton production, whereas the 1671 gazetteer did not.[193] The 1757 edition of the Xinle County history lists cotton.[194] The 1766 Boxiang County gazetteer states that eight or nine households out of ten were involved in some form of cotton manufacture.[195] The 1830 edition of the Nangong gazetteer remarked on the expansion of cotton in the previous century and half.[196]

The 1779/1813 edition of the Yongqing County history reported that no one in the county grew cotton, but neighboring districts did grow some for a household's self-use. It was not marketed. Some cotton was imported from nearby Xincheng and Zhuozhou. Its price was 120 qian per jin.[197] The 1846 edition of the Luancheng (Zhengding) gazetteer, by contrast, stated that cotton was planted on about 40 percent of the district's fields and about 80 percent of it was marketed to merchants from Shanxi or Henan. After working hard all year, the farmers used the profits to buy grain.[198] The 1873 edition of Jinghai County history speaks of the benefits to this district of cotton planting, remarking that it was far more suitable than producing silk, which some officials had apparently advocated.[199]

These passages confirm the view that by the mid-eighteenth century, central and southern Zhili had become important cotton-cloth production centers, but closer examination suggests that while cotton production spread across a wider area, it did not account for a large proportion of Zhili's total agricultural production.[200] From Fang Guancheng's perspective, one of the great benefits of cotton was that the weaving could be a productive activity for women in the evenings and during the winter. The term "cultivate cotton" may also refer to the weaving or "manufacture" of cotton. (In other words, while 20–30 percent of the land in some areas was planted in cotton, 80–90 percent of the households engaged in the processing and weaving.) The scale of production in 1900, at the end of the Qing period, was rather small, perhaps 1–3 percent of total cultivated acreage, compared to 10 percent in the Republican period, according to two scholarly estimates.[201] In reviewing the scant information about Zhili's cotton production, another scholar has suggested the possibility that "North China grew considerably *more* cotton in 1750 than in 1870 or 1900" because population pressure and environmental decline forced peasants into grain production instead of cash crops.[202] Although it would be difficult to document, such a reverse trend would parallel the likely decline in wheat production in favor of coarse grains.

The situation by the 1930s was significantly different. Stimulated by the development of railways, in portions of the southern section of the province, cotton became more important than food grains by 1925. In Wei County cotton was the largest crop, followed by wheat. More than 3,000 qing were planted in cotton, producing 100,000 bales (*bao*) of cotton. As more people were planting cotton and fewer were planting grains, the price of grain naturally rose, causing hardship for the poor people—the landless or those having very little land—in the district.[203]

Cropping Patterns and Yields

Although wheat, millet, and sorghum were the most important crops before the nineteenth century, one cannot be certain about the quantities that were produced. The earliest and most reliable overall estimate of cropping patterns is found in the passages about wheat by Fang Guancheng. Fang's careful regionally differentiated estimate appears to be inconsistent with the observations of Nasutu and Nayancheng that sorghum constituted 70–80 percent of the crops planted in Zhili, or that it was the most widely planted grain crop. They can only be reconciled if we assume that Nasutu and Nayancheng were referring to the northern part of Zhili, as well as to Fengtian and Mongolia.

In the late 1920s and 1930s there were agricultural surveys that reported the following acreages for Hebei: wheat, 31.3 million mu (28 percent); millet, 24.3 million mu (22 percent); sorghum, 21.7 million mu (20 percent); and corn, 15.5 million mu (14 percent). Beans (*dadou*) were 9.8 million mu (9 percent); and cotton, 8.1 million mu (7 percent). (See Table 3.6.) These figures are roughly comparable to those from John Lossing Buck's well-known 1929–33 farm study for his winter wheat-*kaoliang* region, which included Hebei. The principal difference was that, as in the Qing, wheat played a proportionately smaller role in Hebei than in the rest of this region. In the Buck survey wheat accounted for 45.5 percent of crop area; millet, 23.1; sorghum, 18.5; corn, 16.3; soybeans, 13.4; and cotton, 8.6 percent.[204]

Table 3.6 shows the total provincial crop proportions, as well as cropping proportions of various counties in the Republican period. Although they are only estimates, these figures show a variation across the province. Wheat played a substantial role in all areas listed here, but compared with Fang's estimates for the eighteenth century, wheat did not amount to 50 percent of the crop in the southern prefectures, here designated as Region 3, but it did come close to the 30 percent for the central prefectures, here designated as Region 2. Millet had about the same relative importance in the twentieth century as two centuries earlier, but sorghum had a smaller role in the twentieth century; nowhere in the districts from which we have data did sorghum amount to anywhere close to 70–80 percent of the agricultural output. The most important change was the large role assumed by corn in most areas, amounting in some cases to more than 40 percent of total output. In addition, by the 1930s, cotton cultivation had become an important cash crop in the south and central regions of the province, displacing traditional grain crops. (This is not so apparent in Table 3.6, but will be discussed more fully in Chapter 11.)

Although North China's agriculture was never so abundant as that of the rice-growing south, the diversity of dry-land crops presented risk-minimizing advantages that could partly offset climatic risks. The flood-resistant quality of sorghum and to a lesser extent, wheat, and the drought-resistant qualities of millet afforded the possibility that bad weather in one season would not necessarily mean a poor harvest in the next. A summer or fall flood could harm the fall crops but contribute to an abundant wheat crop the next spring. A dry winter could negatively affect the winter wheat, but timely rains in the spring could still allow fall crops to be planted and mature. The seasonal diversity of the crops also ensured that there was a more constant food supply than in the south, where so much was dependent on the fall rice harvest, supplemented by the spring crop in the double-cropping areas. Biodiversity had its advantages in minimizing pests that favored one or another crop.

Rotation of crops contributed to soil replenishment in these densely populated agricultural economies, since the extensive fallowing of land that was practiced in Europe was not so feasible in China. Continuous cropping was a long-standing Chinese practice, and in both the north and south hundreds of different cropping patterns were practiced and identified in the twentieth century. Rotations usually included the basic grain crops, legumes, and oil crops, thus allowing for enrichment of the soil through nitrogen fixing. Interplanting of crops also allowed the land to be intensely cultivated.[205] Buck found the great diversity of crops in North China to be admirable, allowing not only for resource efficiency and less risk but also for soil maintenance and better seasonal distribution of labor. Rotations include a shallow-rooted crop, a deep-rooted crop, a cultivated crop, and a leguminous crop.[206] However, the early frosts in the northern part of Hebei limited the extent of double cropping. A 1930s survey revealed the index of double cropping as 122.6 for Hebei. A 1949 survey showed 116.3 for northeastern part of the province, 139.3 in central part, and 143.7 in the southern part.[207]

The many different patterns suggest adaptability. In Sanhe County, for example, three different cropping systems were used: (1) planting exclusively one grain crop; (2) planting two crops in one field, for example, black beans amidst corn or sorghum; (3) planting different grain crops in succession, for example, planting wheat after the fall harvest, and planting various types of beans amidst sorghum and corn after the spring harvest.[208]

In Zhili, Buck identified winter crops, planted in the fall; spring-planted crops that did not follow winter crops; and summer crops that followed winter crops. In Pingxiang xian, the winter crop was mostly wheat, with a small amount of barley. Together the two constituted 31.1 percent of the crop area. The spring-planted crops were *gaoliang* by itself, *gaoliang* with black beans, millet, vegetables, black beans alone, soybeans, and miscellaneous. They totaled 68.9 percent of the crop area. The summer crops were principally millet, with a small amount of hemp and indigo. This comprised 22.6 percent of the crop area. (These figures total more than 100 percent because of double cropping. The percentages of crop hectare area devoted to each season were 25.4, 56.2, and 18.4, respectively.) In Yanshan County, an important variation was that wheat represented a larger portion of the crop area, more than 50 percent. In addition, corn by itself, or in combination with soybeans, was evident, whereas none was grown in Pingxiang. The percentage crop area devoted to winter crops was 54.7 percent, spring-planted crops 45.3 percent, and summer crops following winter crops 52.7 percent. (The percentages of crop hectare area were 35.9, 29.7, and 34.4, respectively.)[209]

With poor soil and climatic uncertainty, the yields of major crops in North China in the mid-Qing were both low and widely variable. One can find some references to yields of 3 shi of unhusked grain per mu as an upward limit.[210] But more reliable sources suggest that 3 shi would have been highly unusual. Reporting an excellent fall harvest in 1754, Fang Guancheng wrote that for 1 mu the peasants got up to 2 shi, 4–5 dou, which, he said, was double the normal yield.[211] If this was a general rule, in the mid-eighteenth century, then the normal yield for millet must have been 1 shi and 2 or more dou per mu, that is, 12 or 12.5 dou. Other sources state that 5 to 6 dou per mu was the normal yield, and fatalism was the typical attitude. The Hejian County gazetteer observed that there were many poor people who were not able to make a good living. The land was seldom fertile, and by the end of the year of hard labor, their income was meager. If they got 5 to 6 or 6 to 7 dou for each mu, they considered it a successful year.[212]

In Yongping Prefecture, the peasants looked to fate for their harvest. "As far as drought or flood, they listen to heaven. If it rains in the third or fourth month, then the wheat will ripen. But if it rains excessively in the sixth or seventh month, and the ground becomes waterlogged, who knows what will happen to the agricultural work of the rest of the year?"[213] In Changli County, also in Yongping Prefecture, the agricultural conditions were unfavorable. "In this xian there are mountains to the northwest, and water to the east. There are almost no superior fields of fertile soil, but to the south the soil is *huangrang* (loess or yellow soil) and can be planted with grains and vegetables." In the face of this bleak situation, not surprisingly, the local peasants did not initiate changes. "The well-to-do farmers in particular do not work to irrigate the fields but rely on Heaven to determine their fate whether it be drought or flood," said the local history. "Each year each mu yields only 5–6 dou, . . . so at the end of the year they all have many debts and have stored little grain. In fortunate years, they like to go out and hire themselves out as a laborers."[214]

Yields of 12 to 13 dou per mu would suggest that there had not been much improvement since ancient times, but yields of only 5 or 6 dou would suggest a decline in productivity over time. Bray cites a passage from the Warring States period, which said that 1.5 shi (15 dou) per mu was the average yield for *setaria* millet. This would be the equivalent of 600 to 700 kg/ha in modern terms, not very high.[215] Wheat yields may actually have declined since ancient times. A study of agricultural data from the Kong (Confucius) family estate in Shandong seems to show a decline in wheat yields from the seventeenth century to the eighteenth and nineteenth.[216] This evidence is consistent with scattered impressions that wheat yields all over China declined in the late imperial period, and millet yields stagnated.[217]

In the twentieth century yields seemed to be about the same as those found in the mid-Qing. In the Republican period, especially in the 1930s, numerous excellent gazetteers included agricultural data. A survey of this evidence, as seen in Table 3.7, suggests that there had been little gain in millet yields since the mid-eighteenth-century norm of 12 to 13 dou. The millet yields for Wanping and Wangdu, near Baoding, are listed as 13 to 18 dou per mu—just a bit above what Fang said was the average for the area in the 1750s. In other parts of Hebei, millet yields in the 1930s were as low as 3–6 dou per mu. Wheat yields in Hebei were particularly poor. In 1930 Hebei yields were considerably lower than those in the south and even than those of Shandong.[218] The average yield of *gaoliang* grown in Hebei and Shandong in the Republican period was only 79 catties (*jin*) per mu, according to one source.[219]

In the 1930s, both Chinese and foreign observers commented on the seeming "conservatism" of farmers in their methods. In Shunyi County, even though farmers had adopted new crops and enjoyed a more prosperous lifestyle, the gazetteer still complained that peasants clung to their old ways, and they had not responded to new proposals to build dikes or dig wells to combat flood or drought. Ninety-five percent of the farmers still used old methods and animal labor.[220] Likewise

TABLE 3.7

Crop Yields in Hebei Province in the Republican Period

(dou per mu, or jin per mu)

County (Prefecture)	Wheat	Millet	Sorghum
Region 1			
Luan (Yongping)[1]	60–270 jin	70–180 jin	70–200 jin
Region 2			
Ba (Shuntian)[2]	—	5 dou, or 150 jin*	—
Wanping (Shuntian)[3]	3 dou	14 dou	—
Wangdu (Baoding)[4]	3–6 dou	13–18 dou	up to 10 dou
Wan (Baoding)[5]	5 dou	12 dou	8 dou
Region 3			
Gaoyi (Zhaozhou)[6]	110 jin	130 jin (4.3 dou)	90 jin
Handan (Guangping)[7]	—	100 jin (3.3 dou)	—
Guangping (Guangping)[8]	3 dou	4 dou unhusked (3 husked)	4 dou
Cheng'an (Guangping)[9]	3 dou	6 dou	—
Region 4			
Yuanshi (Zhengding)[10]	—	—	20 dou
Zaoqiang (Jizhou)[11]	3–5 dou (may refer to millet also)		—
Jingxing (Zhengding)[12]	60–70 jin	140–50 jin (4.7–5 dou)	145 jin
Hebei province and capital area[13]	4.6 dou	—	79 jin

NOTE: Dou was a measure of volume. 10 dou = 1 shi. Jin was a measure of weight. In Ba xian, 1 dou of millet = 30 jin. I have used this to estimate the equivalents of other millet figures quoted in jin. Regions refer to Map 7.1.

SOURCES:
[1] *Luan XZ* 1938, 15:1a–3b.
[2] *Ba xian xinzhi* 1934, 4:4.
[3] *Wanping xian shiqing diaocha* 1939, 46. Yields on best land.
[4] *Wangdu XZ* 1934, 1:35–40.
[5] *Wan XZ* 1934, 7:27b–28.
[6] *Gaoyi XZ* 1933, 2:10–11.
[7] *Handan XZ* 1932, in "Fangzhi wenchao," 64:227.
[8] *Guangping XZ* 1939, 5:19ab.
[9] *Cheng'an XZ* 1931, 5:13.
[10] *Yuanshi XZ* 1931, in "Fangzhi wenchao," 58:194.
[11] *Zaoqiang XZ liao* 1931, 2:16ab.
[12] *Jingxing XZ* 1934, 5:1–3.
[13] For wheat, Mai Shudu, 75, tab. 1. For sorghum, "Experiment with Drought-resisting Crops," 957–962.

in Ba County in the 1930s, agricultural techniques were also described as mostly old, although some new seeds had recently been introduced. "Only corn and cotton have prospered," the gazetteer recorded, while the yield of other grains had declined somewhat due to the lack of improvement in seeds.[221]

Wangdu County was mostly on a plain, and on the whole, the soil was barren and not fertile. Generally there was a great deal of alkaline land (*yanjian di*). In addition there was loam (or loess) soil (*rangtu*, also called *huangtu*), which was superior to black soil (*heitu*). On the loess soil one could plant the five grains as well as cotton, sesame, peppers, and sweet potatoes. The black soil was suitable for the five grains. The worst was alkaline soil, which liked dry conditions and hated wet. "In rainy years it produces not a hair," according to the gazetteer. But it produced a great deal of grapes and red dates. For these reasons, the local residents were receptive to agricultural innovation.[222] Yet, at the same time, Wangdu's local history recognized the benefits of flooding and expressed a fatalistic attitude toward it. "In the Tang River region around Gaoyang, where the Sha he flows into the Daqing he, the waters can be fierce in the summer and fall. The soil is white sand and the ground is barren, but after the rains, the rich mud and silt from the upper reaches creates fertile fields from barren ground."[223]

Diet and Standard of Living

In Zhili, and most of North China, during the Qing period peasants, small owner-cultivators or tenants, were engaged in farming primarily for their family's subsistence and not for the market. The typical rural diet was plain, and the standard of living was low by any comparison. Most households were not involved in commerce, although in some districts simple handicraft production provided supplemental income. These Qing-era conditions changed little until the early twentieth century, and with greater population pressure, the changes permitted only continuation of a low standard of living, not an improvement, for most people. Chinese local gazetteers prior to the Guangxu era usually listed local customs and local products, but they did not describe the standard of living. The few Qing-era gazetteers cited here are somewhat unusual in this regard. Two others, from Jingzhou and Nanpi, date from the 1930s and involve a comparison of contemporary conditions with those "in the past," probably meaning the late nineteenth century. They are intent on showing how much improved the conditions of the 1930s were in comparison with the recent past.

In Jingzhou (later Jing xian) in Hejian Prefecture the typical diet from the late Qing or early Republic was described in the 1932 edition of the local gazetteer: *in the past* in a year of good harvest the peasants all ate millet and corn. For breakfast and dinner they consumed them in the form of gruel (*xifan* or *zhou*); for lunch they ate corn bread (*wotou*) and pickled vegetables. Wheat was definitely something special. After the wheat harvest, or on special occasions, they would eat some noodles, but it was not something that families often had. In a year of poor harvest, they all ate corn noodles, or red or white *gaoliang* noodles, or even husks or chaff (*kang*). "You don't even need to mention meat." They drank cold water; only if they had guests did they drink tea or wine. Wealthy families ate noodles with one or two hot dishes, but still there were not many who ate meat regularly, or drank tea, and children were not supposed to spend money on food.[224]

The conditions in Nanpi in Tianjin Prefecture were quite similar. The local history described the county *in the past* as a place of simple living where the diet was coarse. When the day was long, the peasants ate three meals, but when the day was short, they ate only two meals. For breakfast, they made gruel (*zhou*) out of corn, millet, or *gaoliang*. Peasants usually relied on corn, *gaoliang*, millet, or beans as their main diet. Again, wheat was treated as a luxury. They ate wheat noodles for only a month or two after the wheat harvest. The thriftiest and hardest-working families gave the wheat to their workers, while they themselves still ate coarse grain. Otherwise, they stored the wheat and sold it in hard times, or if they had surplus, they exchanged it for coarse grain. Rarely did they actually enjoy wheat noodles themselves.[225] To accompany their main food, the people of Nanpi ate garden vegetables or wild vegetables with soy sauce, vinegar, or salt. They had sesame oil but rarely used it. Wine and meat were used only at weddings or funerals. Mustard plants and turnips were salted for pickled vegetables. In the winter, cabbage was consumed in great quantity. Melons and fruits in the summer and sweet potatoes (*hongshu*) in the winter were only supplementary foods (*fu shipin*).[226]

Luanzhou (later Luan xian) in Yongping Prefecture was a poor district that after the Xianfeng period benefited from commerce with the northeast. Still, the 1898 edition of its gazetteer said, "People here are plain and not ambitious."[227] The food and drink of the local people were frugal in the extreme. They economized by drinking only water, diluting their grains, and in the summer, only half-cooking their grain (in order to save fuel).

> In this xian the food and drink of the people were very frugal. In the winter and summer all drank water; only the elite and merchants [*shijia shanggu*] drank tea. People ate only *zhou*. Poor people ate millet just pounded into bits, not husked, and then boiled into *zhou*. This was called *pomi zhou*. Even the wealthy households [*xiaokang zhi jia*] and those thinking of economizing imitated this method. In the agricultural season they switched to *gaoliang*, which they boiled until half-cooked and then washed/rinsed in cold water; it's as hard as a rock and tough to swallow. This is called *huanfan*.

But when it came to preparing food and drink for special occasions, they would indulge in eating and drinking and were not stingy. Even in the poorest countryside people kept some wine to entertain their relatives and friends for special occasions.[228]

Some locations, such as Nangong in Jizhou, benefited from handicraft activities and commerce even in the early Qing.

> Nangong xian in Jizhou [Prefecture] is a flat plain without the benefits of being enriched by mountains and streams, but because it is at the important juncture between Jizhou and Zhaozhou, people are thrifty and know how to take advantage of opportunities. Men work in the fields or at manual labor, and women weave. Households that made a profit still save their money and work hard. That is why even though people are poor and weak, they do not freeze or starve.[229]

The 1673 edition of its gazetteer states that Nangong's soil was fertile—good for planting trees and growing grain, cotton, and fruits, some of which were taken by itinerant merchants to sell elsewhere. Their incomes were not bountiful, but one farmer working ten mu could support a family and be content.[230]

In late eighteenth and early nineteenth centuries, cotton growing and spinning became widespread in this district. "In the 156 years since the last edition of the gazetteer [1673?], things have naturally changed quite a bit," the 1830 local history observed. Women all worked at spinning. Men without work helped the women. Although the scale of production was not huge, still the sale of cloth and silk all permitted the district to become self-sufficient. This became the main occupation, and scholars, merchants, and artisans were next. The downside to this economic change was that rich households competed in an extravagant lifestyle and became lazy, in the opinion of the authors. There were also many legal disputes and false accusations, and ignorant people who sought redress through the yamen often were exploited by the crafty secretaries and clerks.[231]

By contrast, Yongqing County in the central swampy region of the province provides an example of a balanced but poor agricultural economy troubled by low yields and frequent waterlogging or flooding, and by possessing little of special value. "The soil of Yongqing is very thin and the people are poor. They do not make any unusual or valuable products to sell. In the distance of less than 2 *she* eastward to Tianjin, there are no peddlers that carry valuable or important goods. All the daily necessities are locally supplied."[232]

TABLE 3.8

Grain and Food Prices in Yongqing County
in the Mid-Qing Period

(prices are per shi unless otherwise indicated)

Commodity	Price
Grains and beans	
Rice	2 taels
Wheat	1.5 taels
Millet	7 qian
Panicum millet	7 qian
Sorghum and black beans	7 qian
Soybeans	7.5 qian
Green beans	8.5 qian
Other food commodities	
Meat	50 qian per 1 jin
Chicken	85–86 qian per 2 jin (for "a big one")
Bean sprouts	6–7 qian per 4–5 jin
Sesame oil	60 qian per 1 jin
Castor oil	33 qian per 1 jin
Lamb's fat candles	80 qian per 1 jin

SOURCE: *Yongqing XZ* 1779/1813, hushu 2:74b, 76a.

In the mid-Qing period Yongqing produced the full range of grains typical of the Zhili region including several types of millet; three types of sorghum; wheat, barley, and buckwheat; and corn. In addition several types of beans were represented, as well as melons, vegetables, and other fruits. No rice was grown in Yongqing, although apparently some was consumed. It was brought from paddies in nearby Wen'an, Bazhou, and Zhuozhou by itinerant merchants. Table 3.8, a list of food prices, shows the hierarchy of preferences and corresponds well with the prefectural and provincial grain market prices that will be discussed in Chapter 4.

Cotton was not planted by Yongqing people, except occasionally; the peasants used it mainly for making their family's clothes and marketed only any bit that might remain. On the whole women did not spin and weave; instead, they raised chickens. If they could not bear to kill the chickens, they exchanged them for cotton. The poor people of this locality did not boast of any special crafts or occupations. All the local products were about the same as the neighboring districts', without specialization. In the spring the poor looked for elmseeds or willow sprouts; in the summer they dug for *kucai* ("sow thistles"); in the fall and winter they looked for weeds and grasses for food. The struggle for survival was often desperate. "Among them are women of a bold nature who pick up chaff (bits from the ears of corn) or even steal crops. Even those who are employed expect calamity. The people's customs are plain and never extravagant or wasteful."

Despite this, Yongqing villagers did have two traditional crafts: willow baskets and reed mats. Basket weaving was a specialty in the eastern district (xiang), where the soil was so sandy and alkaline that in some villages people could not grow grain, but planted willow trees instead. They used the thick trunks for fuel and the thin branches for making willow implements. They made baskets for holding stones, for measuring grain, and for domestic uses. A family of eight, young and old, could rely on this craft for a living. So important was this skill that they did not teach it to girls because they feared that, if and when they married out to another village, they would divulge these techniques to their sisters-in-law and other women, and other villages would compete in this line of work.

In the southern district of the county—Xin'an zhen which abuts Wen'an and Bazhou, two other waterlogged places—villagers manufactured curtains and wove mats from reeds (*luwei*) harvested from the swampy marshes. A woman could make a mat of one zhang by four feet in two days and earn 160–170 qian. There was a good demand for this product, and the work produced critical income to pay off taxes and meet other needs. It could be done in the slack seasons and also in evenings. In the autumn and winter, when the days were short, the poor people either lit a fire or worked by moonlight. The neighbors could hear each other singing while working. By the time there was frost, the people would go out to market their goods.[233]

In the western district, some farmers raised pigs. Families would raise sixty or eighty, then sell forty or so and keep the rest for eating or for producing fertilizer, which the thin soil required. On the fertilized soil they grew linseed or sesame (*huma*) or melons. The really poor people in this section of the country also used grasses to make baskets or eating utensils, similar to the willow implements. In the northern district, along the Yongding River, the peasants were more passive. The Yongding River had no fish, shrimp, or crabs, but when there was a heavy storm and rough water, the people would rush out with nets to collect whatever came along. They could then market the fish; its flavor was very fresh and good. But, alas, according to the gazetteer, such opportunities were infrequent, so there was no specialization in this work.

The evidence from local histories presented here can leave little doubt that the standard of living of the Zhili peasant family was low—at the level of self-sufficiency or even worse in many cases. The opportunity to market agricultural commodities or handicrafts was generally very limited. Again and again the local gazetteers say that "people in this place are not accustomed to extravagant living," or "the people are accustomed to a plain way of life." To have grain that was fully cooked, and not diluted into a *zhou*, was considered a sign of well-being. To drink hot boiled water was also considered a source of satisfaction; some had to do with unboiled water. Tea was for the rich. Three meals a day were not taken for granted; often only two sufficed. Eating wheat was a sign of prosperity. Meat, rice, and wine were out of the question for most people, except on special occasions. Some, but not all, localities enjoyed fresh vegetables, mostly cabbage, and fruits. Cooking was plain; oil, vinegar, soy sauce, and spices were used sparingly.

Observations of conditions in Beijing and its environs were strikingly different. The capital had a population of a million, including the imperial court, the banner forces, officials, and other elites, who formed a large market for the countryside's meat, produce, and other goods. Westerners who traveled around Beijing and Tianjin in the late eighteenth and nineteenth centuries remarked on the agricultural abundance of the region. In fall 1793, as head of a British embassy, Lord Macartney observed the following crops near Tianjin: Indian corn, sorghum, millet, kidney beans, several varieties of rice, cucumbers, watermelons, apples, pears, plums, and peaches. Between Beijing and Rehe, he observed, "On each side every cultivable inch is cultivated." Sorghum, millet, beans, peas, and sesame were "all sown in drills between which another successive crop was often rising in the same ground."[234] Seventy years later, Robert Fortune, botanist and astute observer of the Chinese countryside, identified the following crops growing between Tianjin and Beijing: Indian corn, buckwheat, sweet potatoes, soybeans, eggplants, and "oily grain" five feet high and very productive.[235] Diplomat Freeman-Mitford noted about the same time rich crops of "millet and Indian corn, with undergrowths of beans or buckwheat, bordered with the castor-oil plant."[236]

Fortune also observed an abundance of meat: "Animal food appears to be consumed by these northern Chinese to a far greater extent than by their countrymen in the south. Butchers' shops are met with in all the towns, and both beef and mutton can be had anywhere."[237] Freeman-Mitford remarked, "The consumption of pork at Peking must be something fabulous. The streets swarm with pigs, and yet from every direction we saw large herds being driven into the town. The Chinese who can afford it eat pork at nearly every meal."[238] Other nongrain foods included meat, butter, and milk from Mongolia; pigs and poultry; vegetables from suburban and outer city gardens; fruit such as pears, apples, plums, cherries, and grapes from nearby sources; and fresh fish from Tianjin.[239]

As the imperial capital and a relatively cosmopolitan city, open to European Jesuits, Russian, Central Asian, and other traders and diplomats, as well as Chinese from all provinces, Beijing formed a market unique in North China in the Qing period. In the Zhili area, no other city came close to the capital in its political, cultural, and economic magnetism. Beijing depended on distant sources of grain supply, meats, and other food products, but it looked to its immediate region for vegetables, fruits, poultry, and fish, as well as a large share of its grain supply. The sharp contrast between the enthusiastic view of the Westerners and the sober perspective of the local gazetteers cannot be explained entirely by the difference between capital and countryside; the Western observations also reflect the generally favorable view of China by Westerners before the late nineteenth century; later Western observations of the countryside focused on its bleakness, not its abundance.

Not Quite a Malthusian Tale

The agricultural economy of the Zhili region experienced growth and change over the Qing period, but its fundamental limitations—varied and difficult growing conditions, low productivity, and low per capita output—only intensified. In the early Qing, there was rapid expansion of land under cultivation. In the mid-Qing, the population grew rapidly, and agricultural output must have increased, facilitated by water conservancy measures. With the relative efficiency of grain storage and relief measures achieved in the Qianlong period, the standard of living remained adequate. However, the role of wheat as a crop and a food probably declined, and there was a greater reliance on coarse grains, especially millet and sorghum. By the late eighteenth century, population pressure on the land, combined with environmental deterioration, probably created more hardship and uncertainty. Although yields of grain crops certainly did not improve, and may have declined, the greater use of "new" crops—corn and later sweet potatoes—expanded the caloric potential of the land and allowed a larger population to be sustained at minimal level at least.

By the turbulent mid-nineteenth century, the standard of living became more precarious in large part because of the political and military uncertainties. After the midcentury rebellions, the Guangxu era saw more natural disasters, which continued into the first half of the twentieth century. The diet of most rural areas continued to rely heavily on corn and sweet potatoes, as well as the coarse grains. By the aggregate measures of population-to-land ratios, it should also be clear that Zhili peasants in the nineteenth and early twentieth centuries could not have had, *on average*, a diet that was more than subsistence level. Although there were some improvements in the 1920s and 1930s, the generally low standards of living seem undeniable. By 1949, Hebei had the lowest per capita grain output of any province in China.[240]

The increasing population pressure on limited cultivable land need not have resulted in a lower standard of living if there had been improvements in agricultural technology, or if there had been major sources of nonagricultural income. Yet it is clear that Zhili's rural economy did not achieve any such break-through in productivity, and that the deterioration of water and soil conditions probably caused crop yields to decline somewhat. Unlike rice cultivation, which was amenable to greater inputs of human labor, fertilizer, and irrigation, the dry-land crops of the north did not respond to increased labor inputs, and irrigation was difficult in this water-poor environment. Philip Huang has described this process as "involutionary."[241] In a different context, Mark Elvin introduced the concept of the "high-level equilibrium trap," where increased labor inputs fail to increase productivity after reaching a certain level.[242] The situation in late Qing North China may more accurately be termed a "low-level equilibrium trap." The technological advances that would increase the productive capacity of the land were not achieved until after 1949. Prior to the twentieth century, moreover, the opportunities for cotton production on a substantial scale, or for other profitable handicrafts, were limited.

Although the story of Zhili agriculture from approximately 1700 to 1950 resembles a Malthusian tale, it also demonstrates that famine was not the only and inevitable outcome of population pressure, and that the ratio of population to land, while fundamentally important, was not the only variable. The multiple-crop system provided some protection against seasonal shortages, droughts, and floods. New World crops were introduced. The state intervened in key ways, and external supplies provided a lifeline. Although not inevitable, famine was, nevertheless, a frequent occurrence. Even without famine, agricultural work and rural life were nevertheless full of risks and uncertainties, and the margin between survival and failure was perilously thin.

CHAPTER FOUR

Food and Prices

GRAIN PRICES PROVIDE a unique lens through which to view and measure the economic and social impact of North China's agricultural system, its natural environment, and even state policies.
Since grain was the most important commodity in the economy, as well as the major part of the
human diet, its prices can reveal the secular trends in the economy, the cyclical or periodic trends,
and the effect of scarcities or surpluses. Prices *reflect* the economic interplay of supply and demand, but price historians want to explain what factors *cause* the movement of prices. Population
growth and monetary factors particularly engaged European historians, mostly of earlier generations, as factors explaining the long-term movement of prices, but in the short run, poor harvests
were the main cause of price spikes. These historians found prices and living standards to be so
closely linked that, in the absence of demographic data, they used prices to estimate possible
famine mortality. Here, we shall be particularly concerned with using grain prices to measure the
overall economic impact of natural crises and harvest failure in Zhili; their role in particular subsistence crises and famines will be studied in Chapters 8 and 9.

Based on earlier precedents, the Qing grain price reporting system began under Kangxi and
Yongzheng, but reached its fullest development in the early Qianlong period.[1] Every level of the
bureaucracy throughout the empire was involved. Every ten days, each county magistrate was
obliged to report to the prefectural government the prices of grains grown in his locality. The pre-
fect, in turn, summarized the various county reports and sent the results to the provincial government. Each month the provincial governor, or governor-general, summarized the information
from the prefectural reports and sent a summary grain price report to the central government.
The monthly lists provided the highest and lowest prices of each grain reported in each prefecture for the month. For example, the Zhili governor-general reported that in the previous month
in Tianjin Prefecture the price of wheat had ranged from a high of X to a low of Y, the price of
sorghum had ranged from X to Y, and so forth for each grain in each prefecture. For the seventeen prefectural-level units (fu and zhilizhou) in Zhili Province, five to seven grains were reported;
thus each price list had 170 or 238 separate data points. The recorded figures were accompanied
by a comment on whether they were higher, lower, or the same as those of the preceding month.
(See Appendix 2.)

Local officials were also required to submit twice-yearly harvest reports that ranked the harvest on a scale of 1 to 10, 10 being a bumper harvest, and 1 being a total harvest failure. Reports on rainfall and snow, the *yuxue fencun* and *qingyu lu*, were also required. These reports, supplemented by the records of granary stocks, gave officials a way to measure the extent of food supplies and to forecast impending scarcities. We have already seen how the Qing bureaucracy did little to collect systematic information on land under cultivation, or agricultural yields and output, and how, after the early eighteenth century, it ceased even to keep accurate household and population records—to a large extent because such records were no longer directly needed in the tax collection system. Thus it is all the more remarkable that the grain price, harvest, rainfall, and granary reports were kept so energetically at the same time that the other types of reporting were allowed to become moribund.

Grain price and weather reports were actively used by the central government and provincial officials in administering famine relief, recommending tax remissions, and managing the state granaries. A responsible bureaucrat such as Fang Guancheng constantly cited them in reporting to the throne on conditions in Zhili. This elaborate reporting system reflected the high priority placed by the state on maintaining an adequate level of food supplies. The Kangxi emperor was actively concerned about the threat to food supply posed by a growing population. The Qianlong emperor, in his early years at least, paid close attention to grain price reports—sometimes admonishing provincial officials for their ignorant or careless mistakes.[2] Like emperors of the past, he proclaimed his dedication to feeding the people, but unlike them, he actually seemed to do something about it. "Since the people treat food as if it were Heaven [*yishi weitian*], we in government must take agricultural production as our basic concern [*yinong weiben*]."[3]

It is reasonable to wonder whether these data were always faithfully collected and accurately recorded by local officials. Their accuracy varies according to time and region. At the end of the Qianlong period, officials themselves complained about the inaccuracy of the system, and they suspected that high prices were fabricated to justify postponing purchases for storage and to cover up corrupt granary practices.[4] Nevertheless, a number of scholars who have worked with the grain price reports have agreed on their essential accuracy at least for the eighteenth century.[5] Endymion Wilkinson, who analyzed district-level reports from Shaanxi Province, affirms the process at the district level: "While open to abuse and neglect at every level the entire system of price reporting was . . . subject to checking and scrutiny at every level."[6]

Zhili Province's grain price data may perhaps show the greatest degree of accuracy and completeness because it was the metropolitan province, politically central, and under the watchful eyes of the court, as well as of civil and banner officials. I have been fortunate to have obtained about 78 percent of the Zhili grain price reports, and I believe that they are highly accurate for the eighteenth century and largely accurate for most prefectures in the nineteenth century. A more detailed description of the Zhili grain price data, together with an analysis of their accuracy, can be found in Appendix 2. Because Xuanhua and Chengde were geographically peripheral, and the accuracy of their data appears to be more questionable, I have omitted their prices in the calculation of provincial averages for virtually all the statistical analysis done for this chapter.

No other civilization in world has left such a full record of grain prices systematically collected by a central government bureaucracy over such a long period of time. The well-known studies of European price history by the Annales school scholars and others drew their data from disparate, and often discontinuous, series from different localities of Western and Central Europe.[7] For Chinese history, the relatively recent opportunity to access the rich storehouse of grain price data in

Qing archives in Beijing and Taipei marks a new stage in the study of price history, which has previously been based on scattered local sources focused mainly on the Lower Yangzi area.[8]

Long-Term Price Trends

The Zhili grain price series offers a valuable insight into the overall economic trends in North China from the early eighteenth century until the end of the dynasty. Figures 4.1a–c show the movement of monthly wheat, millet, and sorghum prices from 1738–1911 in their original lunar-month form, while Figure 4.2 shows the grain prices converted to solar-month annual averages. As these figures show, the overall rise in grain prices during this whole period was not very great. When indexed against the base year of 1738 (= 100), prices by the end of the eighteenth century had risen to 151.4 for wheat, 128 for millet, and 123.9 for sorghum. By 1911 prices had risen to 313.5 for wheat, 253.6 for millet, and 244.5 for sorghum. If the last period of the dynasty—when inflation was very steep—is omitted, the overall trend is even less pronounced. Prices in 1894 were only 173, 162.9, and 153.8 for wheat, millet, and sorghum, respectively—not even doubling in two centuries.[9] By any of these measures the annual rate of increase was less than 1 percent: 0.35 percent for wheat prices for 1738–1894, 0.66 percent for 1738–1911, or 0.67 percent for 1738–1800.

The eighteenth century was characterized by great apparent stability and moderate inflation. This trend for North China was roughly comparable to what Wang Yeh-chien has found in his price studies of the Yangzi delta area in the Qing period. For the period 1700–1820, he calculates the annual growth rate in rice prices as 0.70 percent.[10] By comparison with contemporary trends in Western Europe, Chinese trends, both north and south, were moderate. Between the 1730s and 1810, prices in England rose 250 percent, in Germany 210 percent, in France 163 percent, and in the Netherlands 265 percent.[11]

After 1805, prices climbed steeply upward to 1814, when provincial average prices reached a high point for the entire period. This price spike was due largely to unusual political and economic conditions in the southern part of the province, as well as to drought. From 1815 to 1856, there was a steady secular decline in grain prices as measured in silver taels. This is evidence of the deflationary trend noticed by contemporaries and described by historians as the "Daoguang deflation," in which the monetary crisis of that period was likely the major factor. Following 1856, prices climbed to the late 1860s, fell briefly, and then spiked again during the great 1870s North China drought. After recovering from the drought crisis, prices fell and remained fairly stable from about 1880 through the early 1890s. Finally, prices began a steep inflationary rise from late 1893 to the end of the dynasty, which was due in large part to the decline in the value of silver internationally when most of the Western nations switched to the gold standard.

Although there were broadly similar price trends in North and South China, in the eighteenth century prices were not highly correlated, as Chapter 7 will show statistically. Although northern and southern prices became increasingly correlated in the nineteenth century, a large disjunction occurred during the midcentury Taiping Rebellion, which wreaked terrible devastation in the Lower Yangzi area, causing grain prices to skyrocket in the 1860s. This harvest effect was not felt in the Beijing-Zhili area—which, however, did experience a monetary crisis in midcentury. (See Figure 7.4 and Table 7.6 in Chapter 7.)

As early as 1683, however, the rising prices of grain caused official concern. Statesmen like Li Guangdi felt certain that population growth was causing the inflation, and this was increasingly assumed to be true in the early and mid-eighteenth century. Even the Kangxi emperor worried

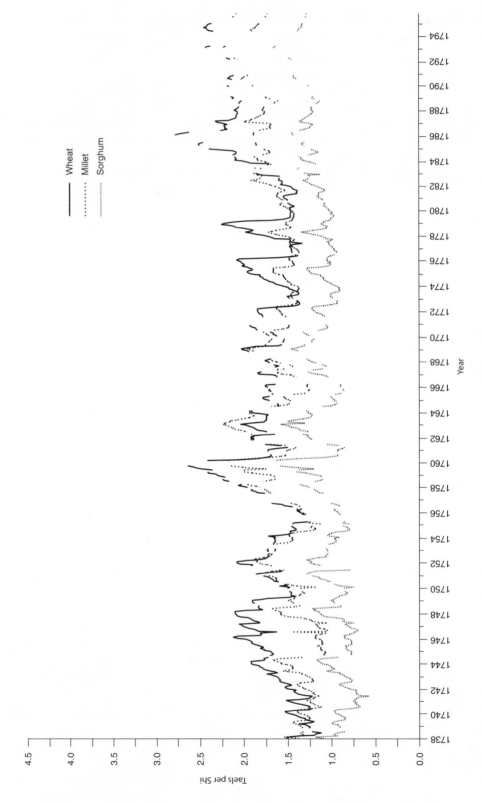

FIGURE 4.1A. Zhili grain prices, 1738–1795 (lunar monthly prices, excluding Xuanhua and Chengde)

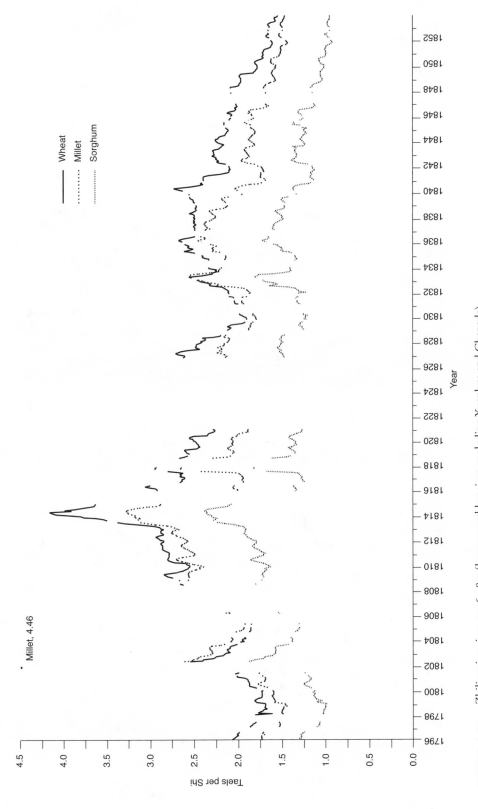

FIGURE 4.1B. Zhili grain prices, 1796–1853 (lunar monthly prices, excluding Xuanhua and Chengde)

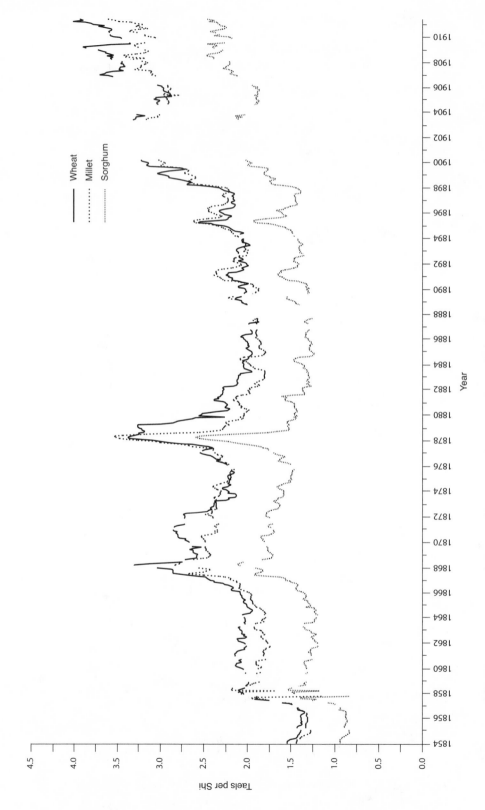

FIGURE 4.1C. Zhili Grain Prices, 1854–1911 (lunar monthly prices, excluding Xuanhua and Chengde)

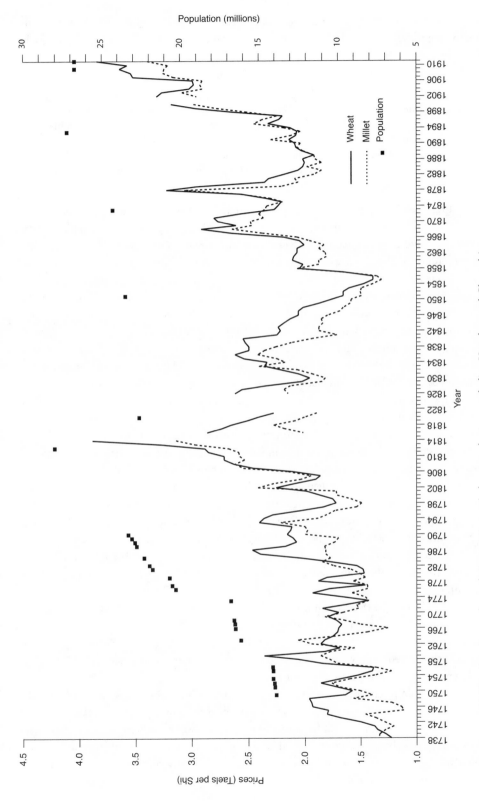

FIGURE 4.2. Zhili grain prices and population, 1738–1911 (solar annual prices, excluding Xuanhua and Chengde)

that population was raising prices.[12] By the 1740s, there was an active policy debate at the court and among high-level provincial officials about the possible causes of the perceived steady rise in prices. Many thought it was due to population growth, but the Qianlong emperor himself questioned this view.

> If it is pointed out that population is multiplying, We reply that the recovery and growth since Kangxi times should have been accompanied by a gradual increase in prices. Why is it that only at the present time there should have been this sudden increase? If one invokes regional calamities, such as floods and droughts, these too have always been with us. Why is it that prices such as those found now have not been heard of previously? Besides, it is to be expected that places which suffer poor harvests have high prices, while places with good harvests enjoy low ones. Why is it that irrespective of the state of the harvest, the predicament is everywhere the same?[13]

Citing an example directly from Zhili, the edict noted, "Or again, take Zhili, which has always been dependent on the grain of Bagou [north of the Great Wall, east of Chengde]. This year the Metropolitan Province [Zhili] has in fact had a harvest, yet Bagou also is experiencing high prices because too much has been transported from it."[14] In response to the emperor's call for a discussion of this phenomenon, the high officials of the time offered various other explanations for the perceived inflationary trend. A leading concern was that government grain storage had perhaps become excessive, and restocking helped to drive up prices.[15] This policy debate had little defined outcome since granary restocking continued apace, as did population growth.

With the benefit of historical perspective, the concern over price inflation seems unjustified or unnecessary. From either a historical or comparative perspective, eighteenth-century inflation was relatively mild. With relatively unreliable population figures, it is difficult to test whether population was the driving factor in price rises. In Figure 4.2, population figures from Figure 3.1 are plotted along with annual prices. Some correspondence can be seen, but there is so much missing population data for the nineteenth century and so many questions about the eighteenth century that one should be cautious about drawing any conclusions. A rough comparison of population and price trends from 1749 (when the population figures become reliable) to 1893 (before extreme price inflation set in) reveals that while wheat prices rose 15.8 percent, and millet prices 25.8 percent, population increased 46.6 percent. (This is a blunt instrument of measure since it is sensitive to which endpoints are chosen. Price trends were by no means linear.) By these measures, grain prices did not rise as steeply as population. Robert Marks reaches a similar conclusion in his study of eighteenth-century Guangdong: "When the trend of rice prices is seen in the light of population growth, . . . the annual rate of increase of rice prices through the Qianlong period was .55 percent, or *less* than the .68 percent rate of population increase. The problem that needs to be explained, then is not why rice prices increased, but why *rice prices increased so little relative to population growth*."[16]

Yet for us the real interest of the debate about price inflation is the deeply held assumption that grain prices should remain low and stable, and price rises were inherently harmful. Although it was acknowledged that low prices were not necessarily beneficial, it became a "cardinal assumption" that high grain prices were even more detrimental.[17] Keeping prices low and stable was the major objective of grain storage and other grain policies. According to tradition, the normative price was 1 tael per shi of grain, and the normal exchange rate was 1,000 wen copper coin to 1 tael (or ounce, liang) of silver. Deviations from this were a matter of concern. In their restocking operations granaries were expected to follow the *lijia*, "prices set by precedent," even when they would be inadequate given much higher market prices.[18]

The underlying assumption that low grain prices benefited the people and that high prices were harmful follows the dominant perspective of the Qing state. However, while low prices may have contributed economic and political stability in China, they might also suggest stagnant or no growth in the economy. In the 1660s–80s, especially in the southeastern provinces, the low prices of grains had led to serious economic problems, causing an economic slump, now termed the Kangxi depression, that affected wages and land values. Low agricultural prices caused a slump in demand for other commodities, and general commercial stagnation resulted. There were even cases where many people died of starvation despite low grain prices. This was described as a *shuhuang*, a crisis of abundance. Kishimoto-Nakayama Mio has attributed this principally to the decline in silver supply.[19] By contrast, when there was mild inflation, the economy was prosperous. Wang Huizu, author of a well-known administrative handbook, wrote at the end of the Qianlong period, "Rice is always expensive now, but people enjoy life. For in the past the high cost was confined to rice, but now fish, prawns, vegetables, and fruit are all expensive, and the small traders and farmers can all make a living."[20] As early as the Han period there was already an expression, "Expensive grain hurts the people, cheap grain hurts the farmers."[21] But in the late Ming and early Qing, according to Kishimoto-Nakayama, the emphasis shifted to "expensive grain hurts the people," and the issue of "cheap grain hurts the farmers" was generally not considered important.[22]

In European history the long-term secular movement of grain prices is seen to represent historical trends in the economy. The "late medieval agrarian depression" following the Black Death of the fourteenth century, the "price revolution" of the sixteenth century, the "crisis" of the seventeenth century, and so forth—are now regarded as basic chapters in the economic history of Europe, but the timing and causes of these trends, as well as their human impact, remain controversial.[23] The liveliest debate among European economic historians focuses on the causes of price revolutions, especially that of the sixteenth century, with monetarists on one side, and nonmonetarists, who argue for population and velocity as key factors, on the other.[24] Some, like Wilhelm Abel, see population growth as the leading factor, an independent variable, that causes agricultural price inflation.[25] Malthusians, on the contrary, see that population growth depends on agriculture.[26]

In European history good harvests have been associated with upswings in the economy, and poor harvests with recessions. However, C. E. Labrousse also thought that scarcities led to high prices, which in turn led to depressions. Abel, on the other hand, thought price revolutions were periods of prosperity and price equilibria were periods of depression.[27] Slicher Van Bath provided a more widely acceptable description of the social effects of agricultural booms and slumps in European economic history. "An agricultural depression means a shift in income in favour of townspeople and wage-earners." By contrast, "When high cereal prices are combined with low real wages, as the result of a rise in population and the consequent labour surplus, the farmer gets a double benefit: from the cereal prices, with their tendency to soar to the highest point, and from the wages he pays his unskilled labourers."[28]

The social and economic conditions assumed by Slicher Van Bath's generalization—a certain degree of commercialized agriculture and larger landholdings—were similar to those embodied in the idea that "expensive grain hurts the people, cheap grain hurts the farmers." A clear distinction between agricultural and urban interests may have existed in early modern Europe and in South China, but they did not prevail in North China during the Qing. The vast majority of cultivators in North China were small-scale owners or tenants working for subsistence; managerial farming and large-scale landlordism were rather limited. There was no real distinction between the "people" and the "farmers." The Chinese state's economic policy and famine-prevention methods took as their goal the maintenance of subsistence, or perhaps moderate prosperity, for the small-scale peasant cultivator, not for the commercialized, entrepreneurial farmers.

Any monocausal explanation of trends in price history, or history in general, is likely to lead to disappointment. Similarly the cyclical behavior of prices that has been observed in European history has also eluded satisfactory explanation.[29] In Zhili eighteenth-century prices were characterized by medium-term cycles of about five years each. (These can be seen in Figure 4.1a and even more clearly in the eighteenth-century solar price data.) These medium-term cycles have the appearance of modern business cycles, but more likely they represented the impact of weather on an agrarian economy. Without detailed weather data, however, the cause of these cycles can only be a matter for speculation. What is more important and productive than a one-size-fits-all explanation for price behavior is to examine how various factors impacted price behavior in different periods of history, and how price behavior can help inform the understanding of economic processes and historical change.

Multicropping and Seasonality

MULTICROPPING

The planting of multiple grain crops was one of the basic features of the agricultural system in the north. The winter wheat crop and the summer-fall crops of millet, sorghum, and later corn, not only took advantage of varied soil conditions but also provided diversification of risks and protection against climatic variability. As Figure 4.1 reveals, wheat was the most expensive grain in almost all periods, millet the next most expensive, and sorghum the least expensive of the grains. Millet and sorghum prices were almost perfectly correlated, and their prices always remained separated, with millet the more expensive. Although wheat was usually more expensive than millet, there were periods when the prices of the two grains were very close. This seems especially so in the second half of the nineteenth century. There were a few exceptional periods during which the price of millet actually exceeded that of wheat—in the early 1760s, in the early 1780s, in the early 1800s, and the early 1890s—all of which were crisis periods.

These relationships may be seen in a more formal way by comparing the correlations of the monthly prices of the three grains for each decade. The correlation between millet and sorghum was constant, more than 0.90 for every decade. The correlations between wheat and millet, and wheat and sorghum, however, were more changeable. One way of describing the correlations is to say that they tended to be fairly high—in the range of 0.70–0.85, with the exception of the 1738–49 initial period, and the decades of the 1770s, 1840s, 1870s, and 1880s. In short, there was no trend toward increasing correlations of price *movements* of grains, but this does not override the observation that wheat and millet price *levels* were often quite close, especially in the late nineteenth century.

Figure 4.3 illustrates another aspect of the relationship among the prices of the different grains. Here, millet, sorghum, and black bean prices (five-year averages) are graphed as a percentage of the wheat price in the concurrent period. Millet and sorghum are shown to have maintained their separation from each other and to have displayed a fluctuating relationship to wheat. They were especially expensive relative to wheat about 1770, 1780, 1805, 1830, 1850, 1875, and 1890. Most striking here is the advancing relative cost of black beans. Although they were initially close in

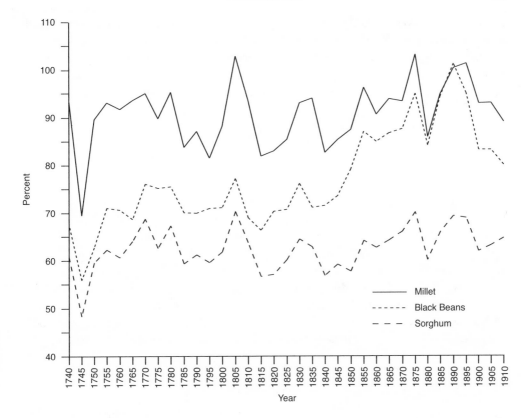

FIGURE 4.3. Relative grain prices, 1738–1910 (five-year averages) (percent of price of wheat in same period)

price level to sorghum, by the end of the period black beans were almost as expensive as millet. This trend probably reflected the increasing domestic and foreign demand for Chinese beans as an industrial product.

Although millet sometimes reached or exceeded the price of wheat, in general the price separation of the grains shows that the diversity of crops provided a buffer against the extreme effects of harvest failures and subsistence crises. In his work on early modern England and France, Andrew B. Appleby suggested that one reason England overcame subsistence crises earlier than France is that its mixed farming system, with animal husbandry and multiple grains, worked to minimize the effects of harvest failures because people could choose to eat inferior grains, like oats and barley, usually reserved for livestock, instead of wheat and rye, the preferred grains—eating down the food chain, so to speak. To a greater extent than in France, English farmers increasingly planted more spring grains providing a better balance of risks between spring-sown and winter crops. When the price of various grains followed the same trend, Appleby argues, there was a greater likelihood of famine, but by the late seventeenth century, he finds that various grain prices in England followed different trends—so that in case of a high price in one, people could purchase another. "In short, the evidence suggests that a symmetrical price structure and subsistence crises went hand in hand. When all grains were costly at the same time, food shortage had an impact on both mortality and fertility."[30]

For China, especially North China, the agricultural system did not include extensive animal husbandry, as in Western Europe. Presumably people could eat down the food chain—which would explain why millet prices sometimes rose to the level of wheat prices—but the elasticity of demand for different grains was probably less than in the European system, in which meat was important in the diet. The prices of grains were fairly well correlated—so higher prices in wheat almost always meant higher prices in millet, resembling the English situation before the late seventeenth century, but unlike England this pattern did not fundamentally change. Multicropping in the north, with different seasonalities, presumably allowed for a more stable system, with lesser risks, than monocropping would have, but it certainly did not eliminate famines.

REGRESSION ANALYSIS

In order to measure the effects of various factors on price movements, the technique of multiple linear regression analysis was employed. Appendix 3 provides a more detailed explanation of the technique and the variables used in each regression, as well as explanation of the measures of statistical significance. In Tables 4.1a–b, the results of a regression of several variables on the wheat and millet price in a given year are presented: the solar months of the year, a flood crisis (CriFld) if there was one for that year, a drought crisis (CriDrt) if there was one that year, and size or rating of the harvest in Baoding Prefecture (BDHarvest) for that year. Prices used in the regression analysis have been converted to solar-year prices to better reflect seasonality. They have also been detrended, that is, the effect of inflationary or deflationary subperiods had been removed in order to measure the effect of other variables more accurately.

SEASONALITY

The results of this regression enable one to see the seasonal effects of solar months on price. The monthly coefficients are graphed in Figure 4.4 to give a visual impression of the annual agricultural cycles.

Grain prices had a marked seasonal cycle, as expected. In Zhili wheat was usually planted in the fall, in September and October.[31] It was harvested in the early summer, in May or June.[32] The wheat price in Zhili reached its annual peak in April or May (the *qinghuang bujie* lean season), before the harvest, after which it fell to its low point in August and September, when it came to market.[33] It then began to rise in the autumn, flattening out in December and dropping in January, before rising again in the winter months of February and March.

Millet and sorghum were planted in the spring (in April) and harvested in the fall (around September). The millet price reached its annual peak in June and July before starting to fall, reaching its low point in January. Like the wheat price, the millet price had a brief November–January minicycle, before starting to climb in the early winter months. In May the price dipped slightly before climbing again to its June–July top price. Sorghum followed the same cycle as millet.

Wheat prices started to fall at the time of the harvest and afterward, taking about three to five months to reach the bottom of the cycle, but fall crop prices started to fall in June or July *before* the harvest and reached their low point at the time of the harvest. This seems to show that the price of millet and sorghum during the summer months was affected by the spring wheat harvest, and that there was an interaction between their seasonal price cycles.

The brief November–December–January blip for both summer and fall crops (which shows up consistently in repeated versions of the regression equation) is most likely an exchange-rate reaction, resulting from the demand for copper coin at the end of the year, when people in North

TABLE 4.1A
Regression of Wheat Prices on Seasonal and Climatic Variables, 1738–1911

Variable	Zhili Province*	Yongping Prefecture	Tianjin Prefecture	Daming Prefecture
Constant	-3.054	1.3892	8.3261	8.5334
	(t = -12.97)	(t = 3.65)	(t = 35.34)	(t = 22.03)
Year	0.003	0.0002	-0.0039	-0.0041
	(t = 22.22)	(t = 1.01)	(t = -31.12)	(t = -20.18)
February	0.017	0.0309	0.0093	0.0153
	(t = 0.59)	(t = 0.64)	(t = 0.31)	(t = 0.31)
March	0.032	0.0387	0.0222	0.0325
	(t = 1.07)	(t = 0.80)	(t = 0.75)	(t = 0.67)
April	0.059	0.0650	0.0334	0.0490
	(t = 2.05)	(t = 1.38)	(t = 1.15)	(t = 1.03)
May	0.062	0.0826	0.0248	0.0316
	(t = 2.13)	(t = 1.75)	(t = 0.85)	(t = 0.66)
June	0.030	0.0804	0.0137	0.0055
	(t = 1.03)	(t = 1.71)	(t = 0.47)	(t = 0.12)
July	-0.020	0.0346	-0.0313	-0.0526
	(t = -0.66)	(t = 0.72	(t = -1.05)	(t = -1.08)
August	-0.027	-0.0031	-0.0426	-0.0716
	(t = -0.88)	(t = -0.06)	(t = -1.41)	(t = -1.44)
September	-0.029	-0.0062	-0.0529	-0.0546
	(t = -0.96)	(t = -0.13)	(t = -1.78)	(t = -1.11)
October	-0.019	0.0134	-0.0322	-0.0455
	(t = -0.64)	(t = 0.28)	(t = -1.09)	(t = -0.93)
November	0.008	0.0384	-0.0183	-0.0795
	(t = 0.26)	(t = 0.80)	(t = -0.62)	(t = -0.61)
December	0.007	0.0522	-0.0064	-0.0340
	(t = 0.23)	(t = 1.07)	(t = -0.21)	(t = -0.69)
CriFld	-0.015	-0.0870	0.0192	0.0214
	(t = -1.01)	(t = -3.52)	(t = 1.26)	(t = 0.85)
CriDrt	0.196	-0.0031	0.1187	0.1953
	(t = 10.16)	(t = -0.10)	(t = 6.15)	(t = 6.16)
BDHarvest	-0.033	-0.0350	-0.0122	-0.0067
	(t = -8.58)	(t = -5.50)	(t = -3.12)	(t = -1.04)
R^2	0.375	0.040	0.414	0.245

* Excludes Xuanhua and Chengde prefectures.

TABLE 4.1B
Regression of Millet Prices on Seasonal and Climatic Variables, 1738–1911

Variable	Zhili Province*	Yongping Prefecture	Tianjin Prefecture	Daming Prefecture
Constant	4.182 (t = 23.05)	-8.5077 (t = -24.34)	5.9145 (t = 26.91)	9.2226 (t = 30.23)
Year	-0.002 (t = -17.31)	0.0055 (t = 31.00)	-0.0026 (t = -23.44)	-0.0045 (t = -29.14)
February	0.013 (t = 0.63)	0.0336 (t = 0.81)	0.0095 (t = 0.36)	0.0097 (t = 0.27)
March	0.021 (t = 0.97)	0.0209 (t = 0.50)	0.0104 (t = 0.40)	0.0229 (t = 0.63)
April	0.044 (t = 2.12)	0.0566 (t = 1.39)	0.0221 (t = 0.87)	0.0510 (t = 1.45)
May	0.042 (t = 1.99)	0.0724 (t = 1.77)	0.0195 (t = 0.76)	0.0422 (t = 1.19)
June	0.063 (t = 3.04)	0.0657 (t = 1.62)	0.0426 (t = 1.68)	0.0650 (t = 1.84)
July	0.061 (t = 2.90)	0.0975 (t = 2.35)	0.0461 (t = 1.78)	0.0448 (t = 1.25)
August	0.057 (t = 2.61)	0.0784 (t = 1.85)	0.0388 (t = 1.47)	0.0158 (t = 0.43)
September	0.034 (t = 1.61)	0.0526 (t = 1.26)	0.0173 (t = 0.66)	0.0094 (t = 0.26)
October	0.007 (t = 0.32)	0.0465 (t = 1.12)	0.0033 (t = 0.13)	-0.0117 (t = -0.32)
November	0.004 (t = 0.17)	0.0476 (t = 1.14)	0.0060 (t = 0.23)	-0.0209 (t = -0.58)
December	0.008 (t = 0.35)	0.0421 (t = 1.00)	0.0103 (t = 0.39)	-0.0235 (t = -0.64)
CriFld	0.018 (t = 1.59)	-0.0041 (t = -0.19)	0.0394 (t = 2.92)	0.0443 (t = 2.37)
CriDrt	0.118 (t = 8.71)	0.0419 (t = 1.60)	0.1372 (t = 8.36)	0.1408 (t = 6.16)
BDHarvest	-0.008 (t = -2.11)	-0.0134 (t = -1.92)	0.0010 (t = 0.22)	-0.0108 (t = -1.77)
R^2	0.221	0.434	0.323	0.400

* Excludes Xuanhua and Chengde prefectures.

China paid their debts. The May dip in the price of millet (which shows up in all versions of this regression analysis) may represent the annual spring sell-off of old grain stocks from the ever-normal granaries (*changpingcang*), and/or the Beijing and Tongzhou tribute granaries, prescribed by the regulations to take place by the third and fourth lunar months of each year, that is, April or May, or possibly the effect of seasonal fluctuations in the exchange rate due to the arrival of grain tribute boats from the south.[34] Additional grain on the market at the time of *qinghuang bujie* dampened the steeply rising millet prices just before the wheat harvest came in to alleviate the seasonal shortage. Even when the data were split into two time periods, pre- and post-1821, the seasonal pattern for the later period still shows the April–May dip in millet price, perhaps implying that granary stocks continued to play a role in the grain market after 1821. (An alternative explanation is that this price dip anticipated the forthcoming wheat harvest.)

As shown in the figure (and also Tables 4.1a–b), the seasonal coefficients are in a small range: for wheat, the difference between the high price in April–May and the low price in August–September being only about 0.09 taels on the average. For millet, the span was even smaller, about 0.06 taels. In other words, while the seasonal price cycle was important in the short run, it had little impact on the overall determination of price levels and trends.[35]

Figures 4.5a–b graph the seasonal coefficients of wheat and millet for selected prefectures representing different regions of the province: Yongping, Tianjin, and Daming. Their seasonal patterns each had a distinctive pattern, but the magnitude of the differences was not great. From

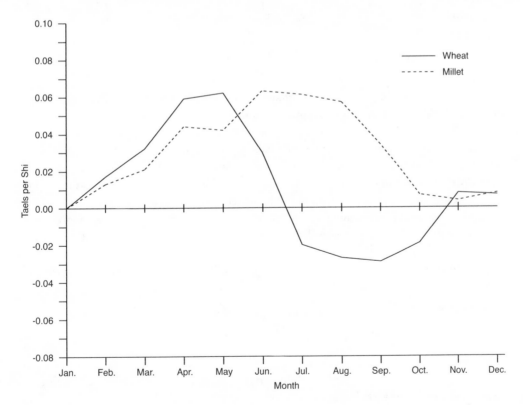

FIGURE 4.4.   Seasonal variation of grain prices in Zhili, price relative to January price (provincial average, excluding Chengde and Xuanhua)

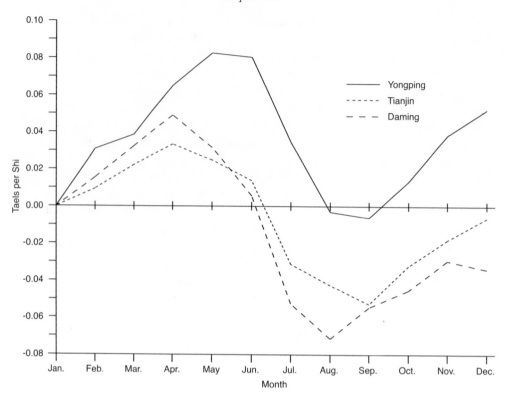

FIGURE 4.5A. Seasonal variation of wheat prices by prefectures, price relative to January price

north to south, the timing of the harvest could vary by a month, affecting the price cycle. For example, the high price of wheat in Yongping was a month later than elsewhere, reflecting a later harvest, or possibly imports of wheat into the prefecture. The low price of wheat in Daming, in the wheat-growing southern part of the province, was in August, a month earlier than that in other regions. Millet seasonal patterns showed even greater variation from the provincial average, especially in the first half of the year. Some regional variations can also be observed at the end of the year; Tianjin wheat prices, for example, did not seem to have a year-end minicycle.

Seasonal patterns did not seem to change very much during the period from 1738 to 1911. As detailed in the Appendix 3, the data were divided into two time periods—1738–1820 and 1821–1911—in order to perform a statistical test on the monthly coefficients. This test revealed that in no case were the coefficients in the two different time periods significantly different from each other.

Natural Crises and Harvests

HARVEST-PRICE RELATIONSHIP

The harvest ratings submitted twice yearly, in spring and fall, allow one to see the extent to which grain prices were determined by the size of the harvest. The ratings of 1 to 10 were made before the harvest and after it; one was a forecast and the other a report. Most likely a rating of 8 meant a harvest of 80 percent.[36] Officials, at least in the eighteenth century, took the ratings seriously and used them together with prices to form a judgment about agricultural conditions and to prepare for the

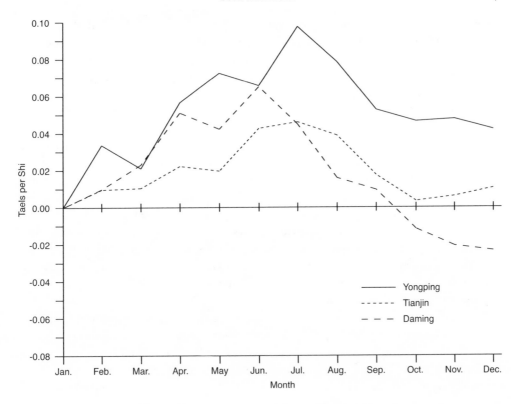

FIGURE 4.5B. Seasonal variation of millet prices by prefectures, price relative to January price

season ahead. Fang Guancheng, the model governor-general, regularly did so. In the ninth month of 1754, for example, he reported with satisfaction that the fall harvest was very good, and there was local prosperity:

> For one mu of dry field, the peasants got up to 2 shi, 4–5 dou, more than double the normal yield. Only in Daxing or Wanping had there been any concern because of heavy rain. The former had a 7-point [*fen*] harvest in the seventh month, the latter got 7.5-point harvest. [But] in the 8th month they both got 8-point ratings. Everywhere the price of grain was low and stable. In Baoding city, the millet price was 1.05, the best in over ten years.[37]

In the regression analysis shown in Tables 4.1a–b, the harvest ratings for Baoding, the provincial capital and prefecture, were regressed on the prices of wheat and millet for the entire province (except Xuanhua and Chengde). Baoding's harvest rating had a strong statistical relationship with prices all over the province (which is indicated by the *t*-values).[38] The regression coefficients for "BDHarvest" show that high harvest ratings in Baoding were associated with significant decreases in wheat and millet prices *for the province as a whole*. For each one-point increase in their respective harvest ratings, the price of wheat fell by 0.033 tael and the price of millet by 0.008 tael. For example, the difference between a bumper harvest of 9 and a poor harvest of 4 would account for 0.165 tael increase in the wheat price, and 0.040 tael increase in the millet price. When regressed onto the prices for three individual prefectures—Yongping in the north, Tianjin in the central section, and Daming in the south—Baoding's wheat harvest had a strong statistical relationship with Yongping and Tianjin, but a weak relationship with Daming. Baoding's millet harvest had a statistically weaker relationship with all three prefectures (*t*-values under 2) than with the prices of the province taken as a whole. Although prices were affected by the size of the harvest in Baoding, the sizes of the coefficients were also low. These results confirm that harvests and prices were inversely correlated, but the harvest and price ratings, which are based on particular prefectures, are only rough measures of change.

When the Baoding harvest ratings are graphed together with the wheat prices from Baoding, a strong visual impression of the inverse nature of the relationship is gained. Figure 4.6 shows the fall harvest ratings for wheat at Baoding prefectural city, which was the provincial capital where data collection presumably was undertaken faithfully. One can easily see that years of poor harvests corresponded with years of high prices, and that years of especially good harvests sometimes corresponded with relatively low prices. (There is missing price data for 1806, 1821–25, and 1900–1901.) For example, major price spikes occurred during the following years when harvests were rated only 4 or lower (that is, 40 percent or less than a full harvest): 1759, 1814–16, 1867, 1870–71, and 1877–78. These were years of well-documented droughts, and sharp price rises are what one would expect. Comparing these results with Figure 1.1 (Rainfall at Beijing, shown in Chapter 1), one can see that these years of extremely poor harvests in Baoding correspond well with the years of extremely deficient rainfall in Beijing.

By contrast, there were quite a few years of poor harvests (3 or 4) that were not accompanied by particularly high prices: 1737, 1744–45, 1752, 1762, 1778, 1789, 1794, 1843, and 1847. The absence of a discernible price spike for 1744–45 is of particular interest since the drought of 1743–44 was extremely severe, but it was also the time of a major famine relief campaign under the leadership of Fang Guancheng. When examining this period more closely with monthly rather than annual data in Chapter 8, one can see that there were price surges in these years, but viewed in a larger perspective here, they do not seem very dramatic. The year 1762 was a very wet year, at least at Beijing (see Figure 1.1), and the Baoding harvest was only a 4, and yet there was no price spike. This may have been because the previous year 1761 had seen a bumper harvest rated 10. Examining the other poor harvests in detailed context may reveal reasons why the price reactions were sometimes muted.

Looking at years of excellent harvests (9 and 10), one can see that price dips were definitely associated with most: 1754–55, 1769, 1772–73, 1776, 1781, 1797–99, 1804–5, 1837, and 1863. There were also two years with ratings of 8 that were associated with price dips: 1831 and 1863. Yet there were other years of allegedly bumper harvests that did not see discernible price drops: 1761, 1786, 1793, 1795, and 1801–2. Of these the last is the least expected since this was a period of the Jiaqing flood—showing the second-highest amount of rainfall in this period (see Figure 1.1)—and should not have had a high harvest rating. Official ratings of famine severity, with 10 as the most severe, show that eight counties in Baoding Prefecture were severely affected by famine (with ratings of 10 or 9), and seven others were somewhat affected by famine (with ratings of 8, 7, or 6). In this case at least, the accuracy of the harvest ratings are extremely suspect, and the famine ratings more plausible because they are supported by other evidence.

A few other anomalies require discussion. It is striking that in the nineteenth century there were no harvests rated 10 and few rated 9. This coincides with the decreasing amounts of rainfall reported in the second half of the nineteenth century. The investigators at the Institute of Geography who developed this data are also puzzled by this nineteenth-century trend and are not certain whether it represents a climatic shift, or a change in the methods of recordkeeping.[39] In the nineteenth century we have already observed that the data on prices, as well as harvests and rain-

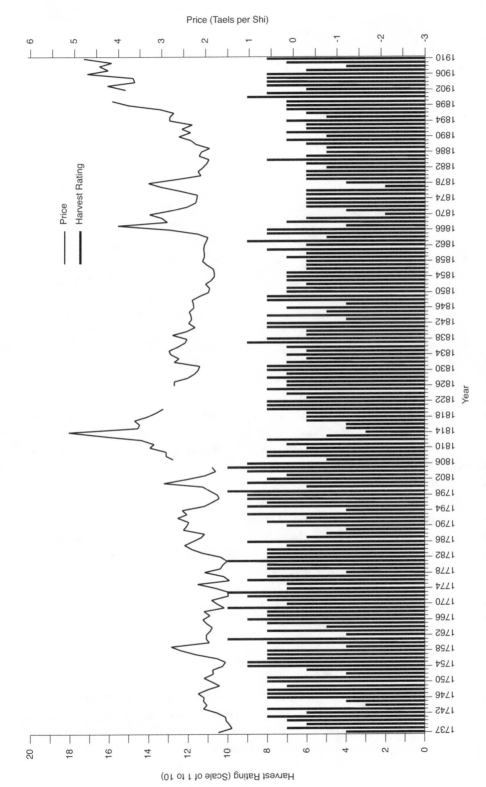

FIGURE 4.6. Harvest rating and wheat prices in Baoding (annual average of solar prices)

fall, were not so accurately recorded as in the eighteenth century. (See Appendix 2.) Possibly for these reasons and others, in Figure 4.6 the negative relationship between harvest size and grain price is more clearly seen in the eighteenth century than in the nineteenth. This is particularly the case in the middle decades of the nineteenth century (1840s–70s) when a monetary crisis caused prices measured in silver to be artificially depressed.

Another possible explanation is not that the reporting system declined, or that monetary issues distorted actual price changes, but that grain prices came to be determined not by harvest size alone but also by other economic factors, that is, that there had been a fundamental shift in the economic system. An English economist, Gregory King (1650–1710), believed that there was a fixed relationship between harvest size and price. For example, a 10 percent harvest shortfall would result in 30 percent rise in grain prices, a 20 percent shortfall would result in a 80 percent price rise.[40] These fixed relationships assumed no external trade effects; the harvest entirely determined the food supply. King's Law reflects a well-understood economic principle that the demand for food, especially grain, is usually quite inelastic: people need to purchase food regardless of its price because it is a necessity. Because of this, small changes in the supply (due to harvest variability) re-sult in large changes in the price. (This principle is illustrated in Figure 7.2, Model of Supply and Price Elasticity Behavior, in Chapter 7.) This is particularly true in preindustrial economies when the local harvest was the only source of food. In modern times Engel's Law—that as its income rises, a family will spend a smaller share of it on food—illustrates the reverse implication of the fixed demand and need for food.

Not surprisingly historians have shown that in Europe after a certain point, grain prices were increasingly determined by market factors and less influenced by the harvest.[41] King's Law no longer applied. In South China, Robert Marks has found that the relationship between harvests and prices weakened over the course of the eighteenth century, and that the sensitivity of Guang-dong rice prices to harvest yields was weaker than in England, and less than what King's law would have predicted.[42] Guangdong was, and still is, endowed with highly favorable climatic and soil conditions, and its harvests were never less than 6 in ratings.[43]

Figure 4.6 and the regression analysis show that there was a definite relationship between har-vest size and grain prices in Zhili, but it was not so fixed as King's model would suggest, perhaps because of the influence of external sources of grain and also market mechanisms. In Chapter 7, however, a more formal test of whether the relationship between harvest size and price changed between 1737 and 1895 shows that the relationship did not decline as expected, with the exception of wheat prices in Tianjin, which was more exposed to interregional and foreign trade after the 1870s. (See Table 7.4 in Chapter 7.) South China's increasing commercialization is well known, but markets in North China were for the most part poorly developed outside the major cities. Whereas the price volatility of grain declined in South China by the second half of the eighteenth century, in North China volatility and instability only increased.

RAINFALL AND NATURAL CRISES

The vulnerability of the natural environment of the Hai He Basin to floods and droughts suggests that rainfall should have been the most important variable in the variation of grain prices, and that either floods or droughts would cause prices to rise sharply. However, various tests of rainfall and grain prices reveal that the relationship was far more complicated than might be expected.

In the regression analysis presented here in Tables 4.1a–b, dummy variables were created for floods and droughts (CriFld and CriDrt) based on rainfall data and documentary reports of crises. (See Appendix 3.) Drought crises always show the expected positive effect on price, that is, droughts caused prices to rise. In the regression on the provincial average price, droughts, on average, were associated with a 0.20 tael per shi rise in the price of wheat. When this regression was performed separately for selected prefectures, drought had a negligible impact in Yongping, possibly because little wheat was grown there, about a 0.12 tael impact in Tianjin, which grew relatively little wheat, and a 0.20 tael impact in Daming, where a great deal of wheat was grown. For millet, droughts had a 0.12 tael impact on the price for the province as a whole, 0.04 for Yongping, 0.14 for Tianjin, and 0.14 for Daming.

Floods, by contrast, did not always have the anticipated effect on prices. For the province as a whole, floods had a negligible effect on both wheat and millet prices (the coefficients -0.015 and +0.018 are both insignificant, with t's well under 2). For individual prefectures, the results are mixed; sometimes the coefficient has the expected sign (positive), and sometimes it is statistically significant (t over 2), but only in two cases, millet in Tianjin and Daming, is there a significant result in the expected direction: floods were associated with a 0.04 tael increase in the price.

A separate procedure provides another perspective on the relationship between rainfall and price that confirms this point. Rainfall of more than 900 mm (which should roughly constitute excessive rainfall) does not seem to have an impact on the price. On the other hand, rainfall under 900 mm does seem to have an incremental impact on price. A variable termed "Dry" was created and defined as (900 mm − actual rainfall)/100, thus measuring how far short the actual rainfall was of 900 mm. For example, if 600 mm of rain had fallen, the variable would be (900−600)/100 = 3. Thus the number is higher as the actual rainfall goes down. In a regression of detrended prices with year, a constant, and months as dummy variables, and Dry as the single other variable, the coefficient for Dry was 0.032 (t = 8.43) for wheat and 0.011 (t = 4.13) for millet, showing that decreasing amounts of rainfall had the effect of steadily increasing the price. (See Appendix 3.)

In Figure 4.7, the price effect of dryness in a given year and each of the successive four years is shown. This was based on a regression in which the amount of "dryness" in the year the crop was harvested and sold, the year the crop was growing, and each of the three years before that were successively measured. The results show that a given amount of dryness in a year increased the price to some extent in the year before the harvest, and had the greatest impact in the year of the harvest. In the year after the harvest, it was associated with a decrease in price, and by two and three years after the harvest, there was little or no effect in either direction, as prices regained their normal levels. While the main significance of this analysis is to show that rainfall, or its lack, had an effect beyond the current year, the further implication is that in any given year, the price was affected by the *cumulative* effect of rain or dryness of the last few years. These trends were true of both wheat and millet.[44] (See Appendix 3.)

These results underscore the fact that droughts and floods operated in different ways. The old expression that flood disasters were like a thread, while drought disasters were like a sheet, has some bearing on the way floods and droughts impacted the environment. "Drought," a deficiency of rainfall, tended to affect larger areas and could be anticipated because it was the end result of cumulative and observable lack of rain. Deficient rainfall had a greater negative impact because this was already a semiarid region with low average annual precipitation. It had a greater price impact on wheat than on millet. This finding is consistent with the known facts about wheat cultivation. Wheat had more demanding water requirements than millet. (By contrast, above-average rainfall tended to have a greater price impact on millet than on wheat.)

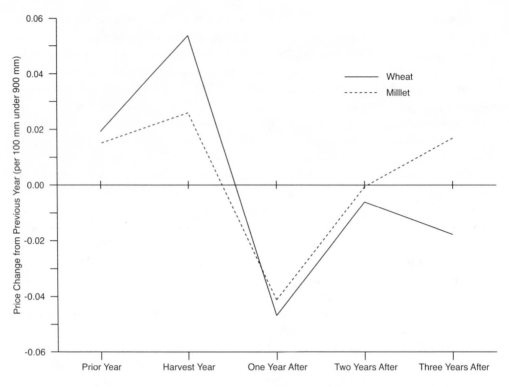

FIGURE 4.7.   Effect of dryness on Baoding grain prices in subsequent years

"Flood," an excess of rain, on the other hand, was a far more differentiated experience. Excess rain in Beijing (the principal source of our rain data) did not necessarily mean excess rain elsewhere.[45] Even in the directly affected region, above-average rainfall would affect different localities quite differently; localities on high ground would continue to have excellent harvests, while those in low-lying areas could be waterlogged or inundated. Impact would vary with the timing and intensity of the rainfall. Above-average rain at a certain point in the growing season might ruin a crop, whereas at another time it might only diminish the yield. If the rain fell suddenly and in a concentrated period, the impact would be more severe than if it fell gradually over a longer period of time. A "flood" was not always caused by local rainfall; some disasters arose from runoff from upstream.

Despite the frequent reports of floods in the Hai River region, *on the whole* rainfall was good for crops in this semiarid region of China. Even though natural disasters were disruptive and perhaps tended to lower overall productivity in this region, more rain was generally better than less rain, and above-average, excess rain might not really have been excessive in the sense of having a negative impact. Excess rain in a given year would create the expectation of higher yields the following year because of the renewal of the soil, and thus keep prices from rising too high. We have already seen that people were unwilling to move from flood areas because flooded lands were fertile. In Xincheng in Baoding Prefecture the people were not worried when the Daqing River overflowed; their attitude was that when the water receded, the soil would be fertile, and the next spring the wheat harvest would be bountiful. The local saying, "*yiman yimai*"—each overflow means another crop of wheat—was a variation on the phrase "*yishui yimai*."[46]

SUBSISTENCE CRISES

These statistical measures should not obscure the fact that there were frequent natural crises in North China that resulted in subsistence crises that should be called "famines." Those crises (see especially Table 1.2 in Chapter 1) reflect the historical reality more meaningfully than statistical indicators alone. The largest of these historical crises are well associated with the reports of harvests, rainfall, and prices, as the present study shows.

The most serious of the North China crises did result in sharp price spikes. In 1759 the average monthly wheat price reached 2.36 taels; in 1814 the highest price was 4.14 taels; and in 1878 the price reached 3.25 taels. When measured against the trend for their respective subperiods, 1759–60 prices reached about 170 percent of normal, 1814 prices reached about 240 percent of normal, and 1878 prices were 165 percent of normal. (See Figures 8.3a, 8.4a, 9.1a, 9.2a, 9.3a, and 9.4a in Chapters 8 and 9. Provincial averages include Chengde and Xuanhua prefectures.)

Although grain price rises of such magnitude are unquestionably indications of social and human hardship, such famine prices are not so extreme as those recorded for other famines in world history. In the "great famine" of 1315 to 1322 that spread widely through Europe, prices in some places rose to 800 percent of normal.[47] The French subsistence crises of the seventeenth century, well studied by the Annalistes, saw grain prices three to four times or more than their normal levels.[48] In 1816–17, the "last subsistence crisis" to strike all of Europe, prices rose 200 percent on average, and as high as 300 percent in some places.[49] According to historian John Post, a subsistence crisis should be defined as a doubling or tripling of grain prices.[50] In the tragic Bengal famine of 1943, when 3 million perished despite good harvests, grain prices rose to 300–500 percent of normal.[51] In Bangladesh in 1974, prices rose as high as 200 percent.[52]

Chinese defined a "famine" as a harvest failure, not by price levels. By the price standards just cited, there were relatively few Chinese subsistence crises that could qualify as major famines. The fact that the price effects did not usually double or triple suggests that factors other than the climate and harvests entered into the determination of prices. Grain storage, external supplies, market forces, and various forms of state intervention tended to cushion the price impact of natural disasters. Others such as monetary factors and political events, however, tended to increase price volatility and instability.

The Copper Coin–Silver Exchange Rate

Although grain prices were reported in silver ounces or taels, for most daily transactions the copper "cash" or "coin" price was much more relevant. China employed a bimetallic or duometallic monetary system consisting of silver and copper.[53] Silver—in the form of ingots or sycee—formed the basis for official transactions, especially tax collection, and wholesale transactions, while copper cash or coin, qian, was used for retail transactions. In fact, Qing coins were made of an alloy of copper and lead or zinc, but for convenience the term "copper" is used here.[54] The older practice was to refer to qian as "cash," but "coin" is more accurate and has been used by recent English-language authors. The theoretical relationship between the two was 1,000:1, that is, 1,000 copper coins were the equivalent of 1 ounce (liang or tael) of silver. In reality, however, the exchange rate fluctuated according to the market and varied from locality to locality and region to region.

The term *qianjia*, or price of coin, was used to refer to the exchange rate between silver and copper coin. So if the coin-silver exchange rate was 800:1, this would be called expensive coin or cash. If the rate was 1,200:1, that would be called cheap coin. As Helen Dunstan has pointed out,

"In contexts where it would come naturally to us to speak of 'exchange rates,' Qing officials consistently spoke of the 'price of coin.' People went to coin shops to buy coins. And officials thought of coin as if it were a commodity, just as they thought of grain as a commodity."[55]

It was commonly observed by officials that the price of copper coin and the price of grain moved in the same direction. Whenever there was a poor harvest, and the price of grain rose, the price of coin also rose (that is, the copper-silver exchange rate was low, for example, 800:1). This was because coin was used in the agricultural sector for the purchase of grain. So when more coin was needed for grain purchases, the price of coin would go up, that is, the price of silver would fall. In other words, the coin-silver exchange rate had an inverse relationship to the price of grain.[56]

Seasonal fluctuations of the exchange rate reflected the agricultural cycle and other annual events. Fang Guancheng said that the price of coin went up every spring when the tribute boats arrived at Tongzhou, reflecting the need for coin at that time. Reports of conditions in nineteenth-century Beijing showed an annual cycle: "rates" were higher in March and October, lower in January and February, just before Chinese New Year, according to the observation of W. F. Mayers and N. B. Dennys, British consular officers.[57] High "rates," meaning high exchange rates, or cheap coin, in March and October may have reflected the lowered price of grains around the time of the spring and autumn harvests, respectively, or, more likely, low prices at the time of the government's below-market sales (*pingtiao*) of old grain in the government granaries, which, according to regulation, took place in the tenth lunar month in nearby Tongzhou, and the third or fourth lunar months in Beijing. The low "rate" before the New Year, or expensive cash or coin, reflected the peasants' need for money to settle debts and pay taxes. There was also a monthly cycle, with low rates, or expensive coin, between the fourth and tenth day of each lunar month, reflecting the payment of silver stipends to bannermen on the fourth, fifth, or sixth; the influx of silver, they said, caused the value of coin to rise.[58] Presumably this was because the bannermen all sought to exchange their silver for coin.

At least part of this pattern persisted into the twentieth century. Sidney Gamble shows the exchange rate in Ding xian dropped dramatically at the time of lunar new year, in the eleventh, twelfth, and first months—23 percent from the first day of the eleventh month to the end of the twelfth month for 1930–31, for example—because of the demand for money at the New Year. Even in 1930 city markets and exchange shops still used the lunar calendar.[59]

THE EXCHANGE RATE AND GRAIN PRICES: QUANTITATIVE ANALYSIS

Quantitative analysis clearly confirms the testimony of contemporary observers. Figure 4.8 shows the coin-silver exchange rate for the Beijing area from 1738–1911, plotted against the Zhili provincial wheat price in silver. For the eighteenth century there are not any annual data for exchange rates, but the figure shows the stable but slowly rising exchange rate. The data for the nineteenth century show the dramatic rise in the exchange rate at the start of the century, peaking in the 1850s at a level of over 2,200 wen per tael.[60] Although there was some volatility in the 1860s and 1870s, the overall trend in the last decades of the dynasty was a steady decline in the exchange rate.

The inverse relationship between the exchange rate and grain price is clearly seen for the nineteenth century. When the exchange rate was high (that is, coin was cheap), the grain price in silver was low, and when the exchange rate was low (that is, coin was expensive), the grain price was high. For the eighteenth century, the relationship does not show clearly on these figures because of the absence of annual exchange rate data.

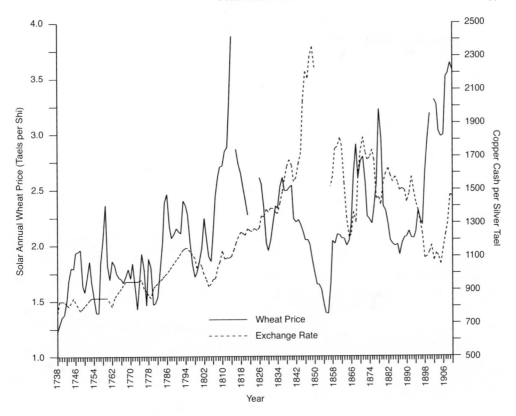

FIGURE 4.8. Wheat price (in silver taels) and exchange rate, 1738–1910

When this relationship is tested in a regression analysis, the results are unambiguous. The result of regression analysis, as seen in Tables 4.2a–b shows the strong relationship between the exchange rate and the silver price of wheat and millet in the nineteenth century. For the entire period 1799–1895, omitting the highly abnormal years at the end of the dynasty, the coefficient for the exchange rate regressed onto wheat prices was -0.3748 (t = -7.67), and -0.5494 (t = -13.32) for millet prices. This means that for each 1 tael increase in the annual wheat or millet price, -0.38 or -0.55 tael, respectively, was contributed by the exchange rate. The results of the same regression run on three subperiods show similarly valid and strong results in the anticipated direction, but in the middle period 1841–70, the coefficient is smaller than for the other two periods. (This may reflect missing exchange rate data for the 1850s.)

In short, quantitative analysis confirms the strong negative or inverse relationship between exchange rates and grain prices. Moreover, in comparison with the regressions with weather and harvest variables in Tables 4.1a–b, the coefficients for the exchange rate are larger than those for flood, drought, or harvest, and the t-values are as strong as those for droughts, and much stronger than those for floods.

When wheat prices in silver are converted to copper coin prices (and indexed), as seen in Figure 4.9a, one can see that up to about 1837, the two followed the same trends. After 1837, however, grain prices in silver and coin diverged dramatically, and they did not regain a harmony until the drought crises of 1878. Thus the mid-nineteenth century, 1838–78, can be seen as a period of in-

TABLE 4.2A

Regression of Zhili Wheat Prices on Cash-Silver Exchange Rate, 1799–1895

(monthly wheat prices, annual exchange rate)

Variable	1799–1895	1799–1840	1841–1870	1871–1895
Constant	5.1163	-42.5906	-12.2843	96.4551
	($t = 5.49$)	($t = -3.77$)	($t = -3.21$)	($t = 18.79$)
Year	-0.0012	0.02584	0.0080	-0.0480
	($t = -2.32$)	($t = 3.99$)	($t = 3.94$)	($t = -18.26$)
Exchange Rate	-0.3748	-1.5618	-0.2355	-2.4295
	($t = -7.67$)	($t = -3.89$)	($t = -3.99$)	($t = -14.17$)
R^2	0.112	0.049	0.223	0.562

stability during which the grain prices in silver and in coin followed two different trends. From 1878 until the end of the dynasty, the two once again followed the same trends.

The divergence in price behavior can be seen even more clearly in Figure 4.9b, which compares the silver and copper coin prices of millet from 1799 to 1911. Here prices in coin show clearly the volatile effect of midcentury political crises in 1839, 1848, and 1861, and the natural crisis in 1871, whereas the prices in silver show no impact, or far less impact, during these particular years. To be specific, in millet, crises in 1848, 1861, and 1871 seen in coin prices are barely visible in silver prices. In wheat, one can see smaller peaks in silver for 1839, 1861, and 1871, but 1848 crisis in coin seems to have no counterpart in silver.[61] By the great drought of 1877–79, however, exchange rates had begun to fall, narrowing the difference between coin and silver prices.

CAUSES OF SECULAR TRENDS IN EXCHANGE RATE

The causes of the basic monetary trends in China from the sixteenth to the nineteenth century were poorly understood at the time and are a subject of ongoing scholarly debate as well. The early Qing period, until about 1715, was a period of stable exchange rates, based on an ample supply of copper, supplemented by imports from Japan from 1685–1715. The eighteenth century, however, was a period of copper scarcity (*tonghuang*), and the coin-silver exchange rates were low (or put another way, the price of coin was expensive). Most explanations have focused on the scarcity of copper supply as the fundamental cause. After 1715, the Japanese severely restricted copper exports. The Yunnan mines started production in the 1730s, but their output did not effect a shift in the situation until the 1780s, when the parity of 1000:1 was reached.[62] Recent scholarship, however, rejects the supply-side explanation for monetary imbalances and instead attributes the rising value of coin in the eighteenth century to the expansion of commercialization into rural areas that increased the demand for coin.[63]

In the early nineteenth century (from the Jiaqing period onward), the balance shifted so that coin became cheap while silver became expensive. Statesmen of the era thought, and most historians since then have assumed, that this was due principally to the outflow of silver caused by the opium trade. During this period, much alarm was expressed by officials, who saw that the social and economic impact of the silver drainage was very damaging as peasants made their daily transactions in copper coin but were required to pay land taxes in silver that was now far more expen-

TABLE 4.2B
Regression of Zhili Millet Prices on Cash-Silver Exchange Rate, 1799–1895
(monthly millet prices, annual exchange rate)

Variable	1799–1895	1799–1840	1841–1870	1871–1895
Constant	-0.4138	-51.2658	-25.2768	62.4378
	($t = -0.53$)	($t = -5.92$)	($t = -8.27$)	($t = 10.41$)
Year	0.0018	0.0309	0.01487	-0.0307
	($t = 4.13$)	($t = 6.22$)	($t = 9.16$)	($t = -9.99$)
Exchange Rate	-0.5494	-2.1302	-0.2267	-1.6333
	($t = -13.32$)	($t = -6.92$)	($t = -4.82$)	($t = -8.15$)
R^2	0.183	0.137	0.478	0.280

sive. Most scholarly opinion has followed this view of events.[64] An American scholar, however, has emphasized that the shift in exchange rates began at the start of the nineteenth century, and its timing did not correspond with that of the opium trade. In his view, it was the shortage of copper supply that caused the debasement of copper coins, which in turn caused the rise in the copper-silver exchange rates.[65] Recent scholarship casts doubt on both the opium trade and debasement as causes of the monetary crisis, providing a more complex explanation that places weight on the decrease in copper and copper coin supply.[66]

In the late nineteenth century, after the crisis years of Xianfeng and Tongzhi, a new chapter in monetary history was marked by Europe's adoption of the gold standard. For China this step caused even greater monetary complexity. As the world demand for silver declined and production increased, the price of silver in China also declined while the price of coin went up. With the gold standard, commodity prices in silver gradually rose. If China had been on the gold standard, there would have been no inflation.[67] When Zhili grain prices for 1862–1911 are converted in gold standard (pounds), as seen in Figure 4.10, the truth of this assertion is clearly confirmed. By the international gold standard, there was no inflation of Zhili grain prices in this period, but the depreciating silver tael caused the domestic prices in silver to rise sharply. The value of copper coin, in turn, became dearer with respect to silver, and the coin-silver exchange rate plummeted in the 1890s before rising again in the last years of the dynasty.

POLICY CONCERNS

The Chinese bureaucracy considered the maintenance of cheap coin a fundamental part of economic policy. In North China, copper coin was much more widely used than in the south, and the maintenance of a stable exchange rate in Beijing and Zhili was especially important to metropolitan and provincial officials.[68] The problem of expensive coin was a major topic in the policy debates of 1744–45 where the relative merits of interventionist measures as opposed to market-driven laissez-faire measures were argued.[69] The problem centered at Beijing, where most transactions were made in coin, and where the government was particularly concerned to maintain cheap coin. Officials were convinced that the high cost of coin at Beijing was due to drainage from the capital and hoarding by households in rural Zhili.[70]

Some examples from Fang Guancheng's tenure as governor-general illustrate the extent to

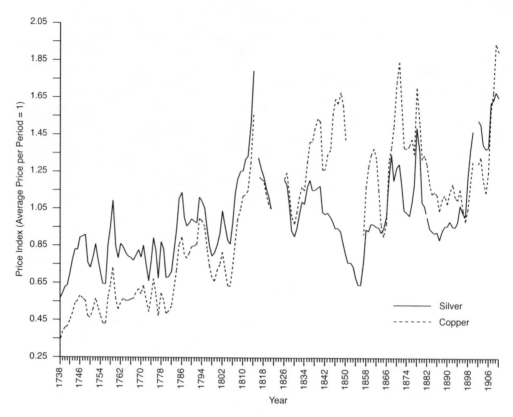

FIGURE 4.9A. Indices of Zhili Province wheat prices in copper and silver, 1738–1910

which coin was used in economic transactions and the close relationship that officials saw between the exchange rate and economic well-being. During the 1750s, the scarcity of coin in Zhili continued to be a grave concern. In 1752, as Zhili governor-general, Fang Guancheng waged a campaign to stop the hoarding of coin by rich households, which he believed was a prevalent practice in North China and caused the price of coin to rise and hurt the ordinary people. "The rich like to use coin because it is convenient, and because it is heavy, it is less tempting to robbers than silver, which is much lighter. *So for all transactions, including the sale of land and houses and the purchase of grain, everyone uses coin, up to several hundreds of taels.* They bury the coin in a hole in the ground, or they hide it among the grain."[71] By offering awards, he encouraged households in Shuntian and other places to turn in their coin for silver. Local reports said that the price of coin had "fallen" to 800 wen per tael.[72] The next month Fang reported that more people were complying by turning in their coin. The price of coin was 830–870 wen per tael, and he was hopeful that the custom of hoarding would disappear. However, within 100 li of the capital *the rents were collected in coin*, so people were not willing to change to silver. Moreover, during the winter, when the price of grain would rise, he was not confident that the price of coin would not rise again.[73]

However, the following spring, because of excellent growing conditions over the winter, Fang was pleased to report that the price of both coin and grain had continued to fall. Coin was "down to 830–870 wen per tael of silver" because of the policy of forcing people to stop hoarding, he said.

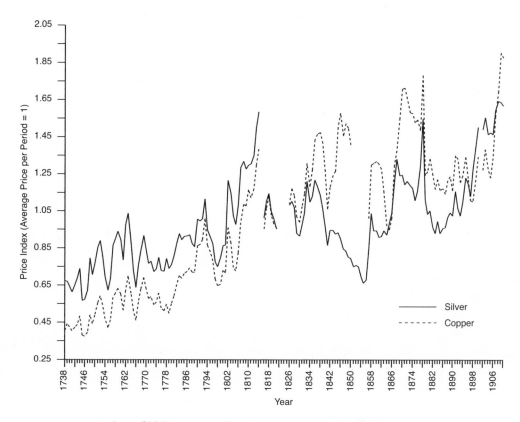

FIGURE 4.9B. Indices of Zhili Province millet prices in copper and silver, 1738–1910

> *Usually the price of coin goes up every spring when the boats arrive at Tongzhou.* Usually the price of grain goes up every spring, but this year, because of abundant snow, the wheat harvest is plentiful. Fields have been planted early, and plenty of grain is being marketed by the people. The price of millet and *gaoliang* near Baoding is especially low. According to local reports, the need for *pingtiao* is slight this year. The price of hay [grass] and beans is normal. Near Baoding it is lower than in the winter. The feeding of horses by the military and banners will be easy.[74]

This memorial reveals the interdependence of the different types of grain prices with the exchange rate and also the close relationship of horse feeding and human feeding.

In the next winter, the price of coin remained low and stable. Fang reported that in the winter season, "ordinary households and banner estates will all need silver to pay their taxes," implying that coin prices would stay low.

> Recently people have stopped hoarding coin, and the price has gone down and stabilized. As we enter the winter season, the ordinary households and the banner estates [*zhuang*] *all need silver* to pay their taxes. In most places like Tianjin, Baoding, Hejian, Shunde, Guangping, etc., and also beyond Great Wall, the price of coin is 880–890–900 wen per liang. In other places it is 850–860. 1.4 liang is the price of millet [*sumi*] near Baoding in recent days.[75]

This example from 1752–53 points to the importance of coin in the North China rural economy, and the extent of bureaucratic concern with its stability and supply. Fang's memorials show clearly that important payments such as rents and the sale of land and houses, as well as daily

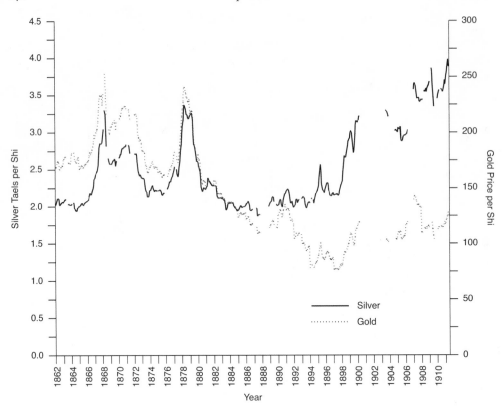

FIGURE 4.10.   Zhili wheat price in gold and silver, 1862–1911

transactions, were paid in coin. According to Fang, only taxes were paid in silver, but after the mid-eighteenth century, it appears that in the north, at least, even taxes were commonly paid in coin.[76]

Because of the importance of coin in the north, in the early nineteenth century the impact of the "Daoguang deflation," whether due to silver outflow or to the debasement of coins, may have been felt less severely in the north than in the south, where silver was more often used in transactions.[77] But this situation changed during the Xianfeng-era monetary crisis in the Beijing. In 1854 (XF 4/3), the circulation of *daqian* ("big cash"), which were debased coins, created bottlenecks: the prices of ordinary goods in Beijing were so high that shops had to stop business.[78] The use of big cash was only one conspicuous example, however, of the overall problem of debasement in this period.[79] During the Taiping Rebellion, Beijing's supply of copper from Yunnan was cut off, and Beijing itself was occupied by foreign troops in September 1860. Both events contributed to a serious monetary crisis at the capital.[80] A foreign observer wrote on June 13, 1861, that "Peking currency is becoming a growing evil, thanks to the depreciation of the copper coinage. . . . Government steps nine years ago have compelled people to use big cash, which is presently worth only three ordinary tchen [qian](although nominally worth ten)."[81] Not only did the people's purchasing power decline, but grain shortages caused the price of ordinary grain to double, forcing the poor to eat spoiled rice. When the court fled to Rehe, grain merchants found they could get a higher price there, even including the cost of transportation.[82]

THE SOCIOECONOMIC IMPACT OF EXCHANGE-RATE FLUCTUATIONS

If exchange rates had remained relatively stable, it would probably have mattered little in the long run whether prices were figured in silver or in copper coin because economic activity can adjust to long-term trends. But exchange rates were prone to volatility. Short-term or seasonal variations could cause temporary hardship and inconvenience, and a secular crisis, such as that of the mid-nineteenth century, was deeply disruptive.[83] Although some economists, such as Milton Friedman, have argued that bimetallic monetary systems may be stabilizing in their effect, Chen Chau-nan (Chen Zhaonan) has given several reasons why the Chinese system was inherently volatile and unstable.[84] Because "silver taels and copper coin were by no means perfect substitutes for each other," there was a dual price system. Some commodities were priced mainly in terms of coin and others in silver. "Because of this particular structure, whenever the demand-supply conditions of one of the chief commodities in the economy changed, the exchange rate fluctuated in response."[85] Chen regards the Chinese system as duometallic rather than bimetallic because "a fixed exchange parity between the two kinds of currency is necessary if the bimetallic system is to have a single monetary unit and single price system." In the Chinese system there was not a fixed parity, but "a double monetary standard accompanied by a double price system."[86]

However, Chen agrees with Wang Yeh-chien that for the eighteenth century at least, North China's exchange rates were more stable than those of other regions because of the government's large role in the metropolitan region.[87] Wang argues that "the purchasing power of coin remained more or less stable" through the early nineteenth century.[88] Lin Man-houng uses price data from a store in Ningjin, Zhili, 1800–50, to show that commodity prices were more stable in coin than in silver even though exchange rates were unstable in this period.[89] The mid-nineteenth-century monetary crisis centering on Beijing, however, greatly disturbed this balance.

The lack of monthly exchange-rate data makes difficult a reliable statistical test of grain price variation measured in coin prices. However, it seems that from year to year, copper prices of grain were more volatile than silver prices. As seen in Table 4.3, if the coefficient of variation of annual prices is used as a measure, during the entire period 1737–1910, copper prices showed 57 percent more variation from year to year than silver prices. When the coefficients of variation are calculated for different subperiods, the results show that prices in coin showed greater annual variation than silver prices in each subperiod.

For the grain market, it was probably the case that wholesale transactions at Tianjin were made in silver, but everyday transactions in rural areas involving small amounts of grain were all in coin.[90] Consequently, it might appear that the impact of the monetary crisis in the rural areas may not have been so severe because farmers/peasants were both selling and buying grain in copper coin, and virtually all their usual business was done in coin. Those who could pay taxes in coin, as well as tenants who could pay their rents in coin, may not have been so gravely affected by fluctuating exchange rates. However, the widely held view has been that most peasants suffered because they received any income from sales of grain or produce in cash, and they had to pay their taxes in silver, at least until the nineteenth century, but the evidence for this varies. Tax collectors might have passed on the exchange costs onto the coin-paying farmers. Chen Chau-nan terms the coin sector the "poor people's money" for which the demand was inelastic just as the demand for grain was inelastic.[91] In a bad harvest, grain prices would rise, thus creating a greater demand for coin and raising its value—creating a double hardship for the small buyer. Thus, on the whole it would appear that the operation of a duometallic system worked to create a harsher and more volatile

TABLE 4.3

Variation of Annual Wheat Prices in Cash and Silver, 1737–1910

(coefficients of variation, expressed as percentages,
provincial* average over time)

Period	*(a) Copper Cash*	*(b) Silver Taels*	*Ratio (a)/(b)*
1737–1795	25.44	17.01	150
1796–1840	24.68	19.35	128
1841–1895	16.18	13.85	117
1896–1910	22.63	15.44	147
Entire period	38.35	24.36	157

* Average of seventeen prefectures in Zhili.

economic situation for most North China peasants, the overwhelming majority of whom were small-scale cultivators, as well as for urban workers.

Normally, fluctuations in exchange rates might also affect those whose incomes were fixed in the one currency that was losing value. In Beijing, for example, official and banner stipends were paid in silver. So theoretically, stipend holders should have been in an advantageous position during the mid-nineteenth century, when silver was expensive compared to coin. In reality, however, stipends were not fully paid from the mid-nineteenth century, so the grave economic situation of most of the bannermen was not relieved by the exchange rates that should have been favorable to them.[92] In the late nineteenth century, however, with the declining value of silver on the world market (with respect to gold) and domestically (with respect to copper coin), the livelihood of workers whose incomes were fixed in silver—including government functionaries as well as laborers—was severely affected.[93]

Conclusion

Grains were the major agricultural crops in North China and virtually the entire focus of agricultural activity. Grains were also the major component of the human diet, except perhaps for elite families. Grains were thus the key part of the economic system. The uncertainties of the climate combined with the deterioration of other environmental conditions meant that the annual harvest was never a matter of certainty. A variable supply combined with an inelastic demand meant that prices were subject to volatility, and both rural and urban families were vulnerable to hardships.

In North China there could never be any doubt that good harvests and low-stable prices were beneficial to the farmers as well as to the "people." Good harvests meant not only sufficiency for the farm family but also the possibility of a surplus to be sold. A very small cultivator might be able to consume some wheat, for example, as well as selling some for extra income, or to trade for coarse grains. Poor harvests, or dearth, meant less to eat and less to sell. Prices did matter. Even the very poor farmers were rarely completely divorced from market transactions.[94] Volatility in the exchange rate increased the vulnerability of the farmers to poor harvests and high prices because high prices also meant more expensive cash.

The long-term trends in prices also provide another kind of insight into the historical decline from the eighteenth century to the nineteenth century. The greater capacity of the state to control the environment, to relieve subsistence crises, to support substantial grain reserves in the eighteenth century—all provided some price stability within the context of agricultural uncertainty. Population growth, environmental deterioration, and declining state involvement—all worked to make prices less stable and subsistence more of a challenge in the nineteenth century. In addition, the political shocks of the mid- and late nineteenth century, when combined with the monetary crisis, added to the uncertainties of subsistence.

Yet the analysis of grain prices shows that there were some factors that moderated the price effects of too much or too little rainfall, very bad harvests, and even extreme dearth and famine. For excess rainfall in particular, negative effects resulted only in extreme cases of widespread and multiyear conditions. Years of known floods and droughts do show price spikes, but they were not so extreme as the documentary record might lead us to think, and not so extreme as subsistence crises in other historical situations. The multicrop system reduced the impact of a single season of bad weather. State intervention also must be credited with doing some good, at least in the eighteenth century if not later. Finally, Zhili was not completely dependent on its own harvest. Throughout the Qing period, it received substantial grain supplies from external sources, particularly from the Lower Yangzi region and Fengtian Province. The location of the imperial capital right in the center of this region played a major role in attracting these grain imports—both through government channels and from trade.

CHAPTER FIVE

Provisioning Beijing

BEIJING, THE QING CAPITAL, was situated at the center of the Zhili Province and was certainly its political core, if not also its economic and social magnet.[1] The entire capital region, Jifu, was the dominant portion of Zhili, the metropolitan province. By the eighteenth century Beijing's population had probably reached a million, including the court, the banner population, and high officialdom as well as a large number of ordinary Han Chinese, many of whom served the capital's elites. The grain tribute system, brought to Beijing millions of shi of grain each year, mostly from central and southern China for the purpose of provisioning the court, the banner population, and other stipendiaries. The food security of the capital was of paramount importance, and imperial and local authorities monitored the supply, storage, and circulation of grain with vigilance. Tribute grain also entered the regional market where it supplemented local resources; this reserve grain supply was one reason why the region was not entirely at the mercy of the weather and the local harvest. Beijing residents, for their part, relied on regional and local sources of grain and foods for their diet, not just tribute grain, and were by no means segregated from the regional economy. The relationship between the capital city and the region was thus unusual and complex. The capital did not drain resources away from the countryside; rather, it served as a stabilizing force for the entire region.

Beijing and Grain Tribute

Since the tenth century Beijing had been the site of dynastic capitals of the Khitan Liao, the Jin, and the Mongols. When the Ming dynasty decided to move its capital to the north from Nanjing, it chose the site of the Mongol capital and constructed the city that the Manchus took over in 1644. The grand physical plan of the city, based on nested walled areas, is what remains the historic center of Beijing today. (See Map 5.1.) The innermost core was the Forbidden City, which housed the emperor and his court. Surrounding that was the Imperial City, which contained the palaces of the imperial clan, government offices, and residences of high officials. Outside the Imperial City was the extensive remainder of the Inner City, where the banner forces, the main military support of the Qing dynasty, and their families lived. Although the Inner City residents were

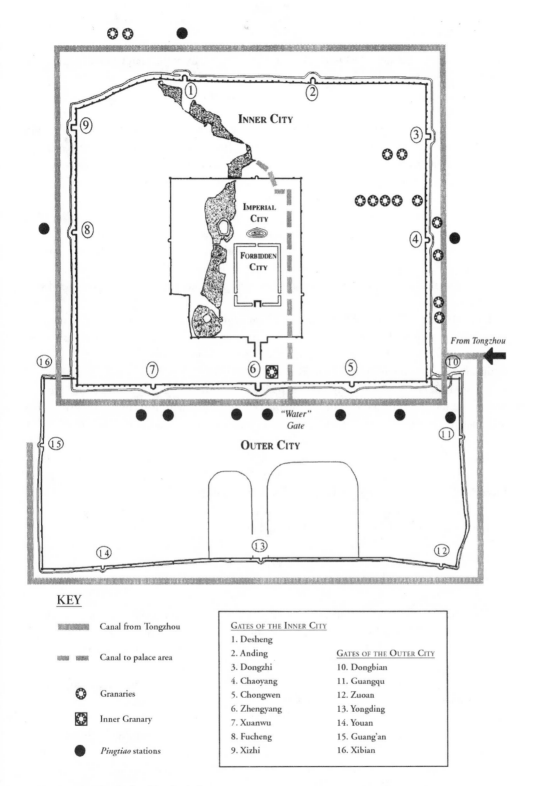

INNER CITY

IMPERIAL CITY

FORBIDDEN CITY

From Tongzhou

"Water" Gate

OUTER CITY

KEY

▧▧▧ Canal from Tongzhou

▨ ▨ Canal to palace area

⊛ Granaries

◈ Inner Granary

● *Pingtiao* stations

GATES OF THE INNER CITY
1. Desheng
2. Anding
3. Dongzhi
4. Chaoyang
5. Chongwen
6. Zhengyang
7. Xuanwu
8. Fucheng
9. Xizhi

GATES OF THE OUTER CITY
10. Dongbian
11. Guangqu
12. Zuoan
13. Yongding
14. Youan
15. Guang'an
16. Xibian

MAP 5.1. Beijing in the Qing Period

SOURCE: Li and Dray-Novey, "Guarding Beijing's Food Security," Figure 1,998. See its notes for sources and also *Shuntian fuzhi 1885, juan 10.*

predominantly bannermen, the Outer City was largely the locale of the Han Chinese population, which had been forcibly displaced from the Inner City at the time of conquest.

Qing-era Beijing in its time was one of the world's most populous cities, matched in size and prosperity only by Edo, the shogunal capital of Tokugawa Japan. The population grew from about 660,000 at the beginning of the Qing dynasty to well over a million at its end. In the eighteenth century, about two-thirds of the population lived in the Inner City, but by the late nineteenth century, the Outer City and the suburbs had gained substantially. In the early twentieth century, the Inner City population had declined even further, but the metropolitan total continued to increase (469,000 in the Inner City; 316,000 in the Outer City; 343,000 in the immediate extramural suburbs; total close to 1,129,000).[2] For almost all of the Qing period, the banner (Manchu, Mongol, and Chinese or Hanjun) population, including families, constituted more than 60 percent of the people of Beijing, defined as the two walled cities and their immediate suburbs, but a much smaller percentage if the larger metropolitan region is considered. Although concentrated in the Inner City and found in small numbers in the Outer City, bannermen also increasingly resided in the nearby suburbs.[3]

Located in the agriculturally unfavorable environment of North China, Beijing could not have been fed by the regional economy. Following the practices and precedents of earlier dynasties, the Qing emperors looked to the economically abundant provinces of the empire to provision the capital and its large population. The importance of the grain tribute system in Chinese imperial history and the immense quantity of its supplies during the Ming and Qing periods are well known. Yet the variety of grains available and the range of instruments by which the court and bureaucracy manipulated them to maintain the food security and stability of Beijing and the entire metropolitan region have not received the attention they deserve.

The grain tribute system originated in the sixth and seventh centuries when the Sui dynasty built the first Grand Canal linking the Lower Yangzi valley to its capital at Loyang near the Yellow River. In the thirteenth century, when the Mongols placed their capital at Beijing, the canal was rebuilt and redirected to reach near the city. In the Ming and Qing periods, the grain tribute achieved a scale much larger than that of the Sui and Tang. Grain tribute was a form of tax required of the Lower Yangzi and southeastern provinces of Jiangsu, Anhui, Zhejiang, and Jiangxi; the central Yangzi provinces of Hunan and Hubei; and the northern provinces of Henan and Shandong, adjacent to Zhili.[4] Of these, the Lower Yangzi and southeastern provinces contributed the largest share.

The broad base from which tribute grain was drawn ensured a constant supply; a poor harvest in one region could be offset by agricultural bounty from another. It also ensured a diversity of grain types. Although tribute grain consisted fundamentally of various grades of rice from the south, Henan and Shandong also had a small quota for beans and millet, and, in the late eighteenth century, wheat. The principal categories of rice were *baimi*, *gengmi*, *xianmi*, and *suomi*. *Baimi*, sometimes also called *bailiang* or *bailiangmi*, was superior white rice. It was intended for the court's consumption and also was given as stipends to imperial princes.[5] *Gengmi* was ordinary, nonglutinous rice, and it constituted the bulk of the rice from Jiangsu and Zhejiang. Apparently, glutinous rice, or *nuomi*, sometimes was included with it. At times *xianmi* was allowed to be substituted for *gengmi* or mixed with it, but *xianmi* was considered inferior.[6] *Suomi*, never well defined in any source, clearly was considered inferior to *baimi*, *gengmi*, and *xianmi*. In fact, it is implied in some references that *suomi* was not even considered a type of paddy rice (*daomi*).[7] Millet, or *sumi*, always was considered inferior to any grade of rice, but definitely was included in the tribute system. Wheat, or *mai*, was not formally listed as part of the grain tribute. From the late eighteenth century, however, wheat that had previously been shipped from the provincial granaries for relief sales but had remained unused was allowed to be substituted for millet or inferior rice (*sumi* or *suomi*) in stipend grain. Beans, mainly black beans, were allotted for horses. In theory, 1 shi of black beans was allotted monthly per horse.

Not only were there diverse types and sources of grain tribute, but each year the timing of their arrival at the capital area was deliberately staggered. Tribute boats arrived from various embarkation points at specified times of the year. At the outset of Qing rule, boats from the south would cross the Huai River annually during the winter in the twelfth, first, or second lunar months. They would arrive at Tongzhou—the terminus of the Grand Canal—between the third and sixth lunar months. For example, from the Jiangnan region, the boats would cross the Huai in the first month and arrive in Tongzhou in the fifth lunar month.[8] In 1753, the regulations were altered to say that henceforth tribute grain might arrive between the fourth and eighth months.[9] Wheat from Henan and Shandong, nearer to the capital, arrived in the third month.[10]

The tribute grain arrived at Tongzhou, about 12 miles from the capital, where it was either unloaded and transferred to boats bound by canal for the Beijing metropolitan granaries or retained for the Tongzhou granaries. In Qing-period Beijing there were, at various times, ten to fifteen granaries with a total of 956 buildings (*ao*). Tongzhou with only two granaries containing 222 buildings had less than one-quarter the storage capacity of the capital. With an average capacity of 10,000 shi per building, the combined capacity of Beijing and Tongzhou granaries was 11,780,000 shi in 1,178 buildings.[11] In addition the Northern Granary (Bei cang) at Tianjin stored tribute grain in transit to or intended for the Zhili provincial granaries. It had been established in 1724 and had 48 buildings at its height.[12]

The difference in functions between the Beijing and Tongzhou granaries is nowhere, to our knowledge, explicitly stated, and the balance between them seems to have changed frequently during the Qing period. The Inner Granary (Nei cang) in Beijing, under the overall supervision of the Board of Revenue, had the special function of provisioning the Imperial Household Department and certain related agencies within the Imperial City.[13] The other Beijing granaries also functioned under the Board of Revenue, but their activities were supervised directly by the Army of the Eight Banners, which controlled the distribution of banner stipends; these granaries were guarded by the joint banner/Chinese gendarmerie. (Map 5.1 indicates the approximate locations of granaries in the eighteenth century.) The Board of Revenue, however, managed the stocks at Tongzhou that were given out as salary stipends to both civilian and military officials, and possibly also to imperial princes. The Board of Revenue also played a role in diverting relief grain to the state civilian granary system within Zhili Province. The governor-general of Zhili, however, controlled the stocks of the Northern Granary at Tianjin, which he could divert for relief within the province.[14] Although regulations for grain tribute specified the types and amounts of grain to be stored in each of the metropolitan granaries, actual practice allowed for considerable flexibility among the granaries in the allocation and distribution of types of grain.[15]

The amount of the grain tribute that was delivered each year was immense. In the Ming period, the target amount was 4 million shi per year, but in the later fifteenth century, it may have reached 5.2 million shi.[16] Under the Qing, the annual quota for the grain tribute was 4,372,614 shi.[17] This total probably applies to the early Qing, at least through the first part of the Qianlong reign (1730s–50s). In 1753, 2,750,000 shi of grain were received for the capital granaries and 500,000 for the Tongzhou granaries, making a total of 3.25 million shi.[18] Again, in the early nineteenth century, the total amount of grain tribute levied was 5.5 million shi, but the amount expected to reach the metropolitan granaries was only 3.5 million shi per year.[19]

The quantity stored at Beijing and Tongzhou from the early Qing through the eighteenth century was staggering. In 1721, at the end of the Kangxi reign, all granaries together held 5.8 million shi in reserve. There was so much grain at the Tongzhou granaries around this time that shipments were diverted or temporarily suspended.[20] In the Yongzheng period, 13–15 million shi were in storage. Through most of the long Qianlong reign, even until the end of the eighteenth century, 6–10 million shi were stored. Even in the early nineteenth century, during the Jiaqing reign, reserves of 3–6 million shi still were maintained. Only in the Daoguang reign did inventories begin to fall to 3 million and under. Following many mid-nineteenth-century disruptions—the gradual disuse of the Grand Canal due to silting, the use of sea transport, the Taiping Rebellion, poor harvests in the Lower Yangzi region and tax resistance—grain tribute storage in the capital area fell precipitously to amounts under a million shi in the Xianfeng and Tongzhi periods. Some of the metropolitan granaries were reported to be in terrible disrepair in the early nineteenth century.[21] In the late nineteenth century, commercial purchases boosted grain stocks once again to over a million, but for all practical purposes, grain tribute was a shadow of its former self after midcentury.[22]

Had the Beijing food supply system been a simple and closed one, there is no question that grain tribute received would have been more than sufficient to feed the million or more people in Beijing and its environs during most of the Qing period. Even in the first half of the nineteenth century, a supply of 3.5 million shi a year would have been sufficient to feed the capital population.[23] No other grain supply would have been needed if direct consumption had been the only function of grain tribute. Yet it is clear that much of the tribute grain circulated either commercially or through official channels to the nonstipendiary population in Beijing and in the entire region. On the other hand, stipend recipients did not restrict their diet to tribute grain, preferring to purchase regionally grown grain for their own use while selling their stipendiary grain. In this manner, the tribute grain became part of the circulation of grain for the entire region.

According to one estimate, in the early Qing, only about 60 percent of the grain tribute was used in the payment of stipends for princes, officials, and bannermen (*fengmi* and *jiami*). Another 10 percent was needed for wages of government workers and artisans (*jiangmi*), and 1 percent for the imperial family (*enmi*).[24] This would have left 29 percent (more than 1 million shi) for discretionary use. A more conservative estimate concludes that about half a million shi remained each year after the stipend grain had been distributed.[25] Yet another source states that 2.4 million shi were distributed as stipends to the banners and 350–360,000 shi to officials, a total of about 2.75 million shi per year.[26] In fact, these totals show such a surfeit of grain in the Beijing and Tongzhou granaries that it is likely that the state had an amount far greater than half a million shi at its disposal.

Most of the reserves formed an important source of relief grain in times of crisis, supplementing the stores held in the ever-normal granary system in the province of Zhili. Grain tribute also was diverted to other regions of China, or retained in the province of origin, to meet critical shortages.[27] In 1744, the Qianlong emperor explicitly cautioned against overuse of the practice of diverting grain tribute to other regions: "In fact, although the Metropolitan Granaries' stocks are said to be enough for five years if not ten, and to be required, in principle, only for official salaries and military rations, if one reckons with the capital's whole population, it is to be feared that they will not suffice for so much as a year or two."[28]

When grain reserves were used within Beijing, they were released principally through the mechanism of *pingtiao*, or reduced-price sales, which provided a useful mechanism for maintaining the stability of grain prices within the city and in the region. Grain that was used in government-operated soup kitchens every winter and for emergency relief also came from the tribute granaries. In addition to these uses of reserves, much of the stipend grain not consumed by its recipients was sold on the local market. One estimate states that in 1750, 30–40 percent of the stipend grain was consumed by officials and bannermen themselves, 20–30 percent was bought by government bureaus, and the rest was circulated outside officialdom; in other words, up to 60–70 percent of banner stipend grain, perhaps 1.2 million shi, reached the market.[29] Through these routes—use of reserves for reduced-price sales or soup kitchens, and sale of stipends—a substantial amount of the total grain tribute, perhaps 2 million shi, circulated on the grain market of Beijing and its environs. This market was not entirely "free," because the chief source of the grain, the timing and manner of its entry, and its price were closely monitored and regulated by the authorities. Nonetheless, tribute grain helped greatly to supplement the food supply and support the stability of the entire region, not just the capital.

Recipients had several reasons for selling their stipend grain. Whether or not they had a surplus, they often preferred fresh, locally grown grain to granary grain that was often stale. Although one cannot construct an exact flow chart of grain movements, one can surmise that Beijing residents consumed a substantial amount of regional, nontribute grain, including millet, sorghum, wheat, and later corn grown in Zhili Province. Agriculture surrounding the capital seemed abundant to foreign observers; additional supplies were provided by adjacent provinces. Henan and Shandong provinces in particular sent wheat and millet commercially as well as through the grain tribute system. Fengtian, in Manchuria, also became a major source of millet for the capital region. In the early eighteenth century, the dependence of Beijing on Fengtian grain already was clear to the Kangxi emperor.[30]

The recent work of Chinese scholars such as Wu Jianyong and Han Guanghui supports the view that regional supplies were important in supplementing grain tribute and contributing to price stabilization.[31] Just as food prices within Beijing were sensitive to the distribution and sale of stipend grain, they were vulnerable as well to fluctuations in local and regional harvests, which in turn depended on highly variable weather conditions. In one example, in 1751 a Shuntian Prefecture official reported that the price of grains in the seventh month had risen quite high. The grain brokers (*mihang*) in the city told him that because of recent rains, the various local grains could not reach the market, and the inventory of the shops was low. Later questioned about why prices had fallen after the sixteenth of the month, they said that the shops had heard that the granaries would be opened on the twentieth.[32] This example demonstrates the sensitivity of the market to both tribute supplies and local agricultural conditions. Despite the formidable gates and walls of the city and the efforts of the gendarmerie, Beijing's economy was not hermetically sealed off from its hinterland. Although there is no grain price data for the city that can be analyzed at this time, it seems almost certain that Beijing's prices were well integrated with those of the surrounding region.[33] Economic logic suggests that even a small amount of grain moving in and out of the city gates would have created some price integration.

Table 5.1 reproduces a grain price report from 1778 and shows the clear hierarchy of preferences in the capital grain market. Two grains of local and regional origin—high-grade white wheat and capital rice—fetched the highest price. Millet and *laomi* were close in price. *Suomi* and *cangmi* were only a little more expensive than the regionally grown *gaoliang*.

During years of normal harvest the movement of small quantities of grain was, in all likelihood, relatively unrestricted as the sale of stipend grain was counterbalanced by the marketing of

TABLE 5.1

Beijing Grain Prices, 1778 (QL 43/7/11)

(price in silver taels per shi)

Jingmi (capital rice)	1.90
laomi (old tribute rice)	1.50
suomi (low-grade tribute rice)	1.20
cangmi (granary grain [?])	1.00
xiaomi (millet)	1.42
shang baimai (high-grade white wheat)	1.98
gaoliang (sorghum)	0.90
heidou (black beans)	1.07
ganmian (dry noodles)	21 wen cash per jin
qiemian (fresh noodles)	20 wen cash per jin

Exchange rates: yuanbao silver, one tael = 925 wen zhiqian (cash)
fenglu silver (stipend silver), one tael = 917 wen

SOURCE: Price list for Beijing found as enclosure near memorial of Zhili Governor-general Zhou Yuanli, dated QL 43/7/11, JJD 20508, Taipei, National Palace Museum.

regional grains, both within the Outer City and just outside the thirteen external gates of the Inner and Outer Cities. During years of poor local harvest, however, when outside prices would rise, the authorities probably became more vigilant in guarding the gates to see that no stipend grain was taken out for sale beyond the city—which would cause Beijing prices to rise even higher. Gendarmerie documents show that gate restrictions were especially emphasized in hardship years.[34] Under such circumstances, officials also would become alarmed about sales of stipends at Tongzhou, preferring that grain be brought into the Inner and Outer Cities to help lower prices within the gates. In addition, Beijing grain shops would be subject to more inspections to guard against "hoarding" (*tunji*).[35]

Grain Stipends: Distribution, Timing, and Sales

The original purpose of the grain tribute was to provide stipends to the imperial family, court nobles and functionaries, high officials, and bannermen living in the walled capital and its suburbs. Stipends for princes and officials were called *fengmi*; those for bannermen were called *jiami* or *bingmi*. Levels for both were fixed by rank. From the beginning of the dynasty the stipends had consisted of two parts: silver and grain. The highest-ranking Manchu princes received annually 10,000 taels of silver and 5,000 shi of grain.[36] By contrast, banner stipends were more modest although in the early postconquest period, they were "more than ample to meet the needs of the time." Bannermen were given a monthly stipend in silver and an annual grain allowance distributed twice a year. In addition, beans were allotted for the bannermen's horses, allowing three to six horses per man. Grain stipends ranged from twenty shi per month for a general-in-chief to one shi for an infantry private. The assumption was that the private would support a family of four while a general-in-chief would have a large household of eighty or more staff and servants.[37] After 1686 the amounts of stipends and allowances were standardized. For example, for corporals in certain banner divisions, the silver allowance was 4 taels per month and the grain allowance was 46 hu (or

23 shi) per year; for cavalry privates, 3 taels and 46 hu; for infantry corporals 2 taels and 22 hu, and for ordinary privates, 1.5 taels and 22 hu.[38]

Rank also determined the kinds of grain received. Originally, grain stipends for princes and officials consisted of various proportions of *baimi*, *gengmi*, and *suomi* (different kinds of rice) and *sumi* (millet); stipends for bannermen did not include the superior *baimi*.[39] According to a precedent of 1737, the banner stipends consisted of 50 percent *gengmi*, 35 percent *suomi*, and 15 percent millet.[40] In reality, however, minor short-term substitutions and adjustments often were made. If there was an excess of one kind of grain, it could be substituted for another kind. For example, in 1744 too much *gengmi* was stored and not enough *suomi*; therefore, for a limited number of months, only *gengmi* was to be distributed.[41] In 1782, officials reported that there was too much *baimi* in one granary but too little *suomi* and millet. Citing precedents from 1742 and 1763, they suggested that in issuing stipends to Manchu and Chinese officials, old *baimi* be substituted for *suomi* and millet.[42] In these substitutions, one motive of the authorities was to use up grain that had been stored too long. In 1768 officials wrote, "If grains are mixed up and cannot be separated into three categories (*gengmi*, *suomi*, and millet), distribute it all until you reach the bottom, using the old grain first."[43]

Great attention was paid to the timing of grain stipend distributions because they had a strong impact on market prices. Officials feared that if the stipends were not distributed evenly throughout the year, or if they were so distributed but not promptly collected, hoarding would lead to price manipulation. The original schedule called for distributing both official and military stipends twice a year, in the second and eighth lunar months (spring and autumn). Each distribution was to be completed in three months. In 1704, the autumn military stipend was moved to the tenth month, and both spring and autumn distribution periods were limited to two months. Officials were severely punished for any delays. In 1709 the Zhili governor-general urged that the emperor authorize the early release of second-month *guanmi*, as well as commercial grain from Shandong, so that "millions" of people in the capital could get through a difficult winter season.[44] In 1723 the official grain was given out in the second and eighth months as before, but the military distribution was divided into three payments in the third, seventh, and eleventh months. Duration of both official and military distributions again was limited to two months.[45] Thus there were distributions in the second, third, seventh, eighth, and eleventh months each year.

In 1752 the payment schedule for the different banners was staggered: the yellow and bordered-yellow banners received their allowances in the first, fourth, seventh, and tenth months; the white, red, and bordered-white banners received theirs in the second, fifth, eighth, and eleventh months; and the bordered red, blue, and bordered-blue received theirs in the third, sixth, ninth, and twelfth months.[46] The purpose of balancing out the stipend payments throughout the year was to reduce opportunities for hoarding and manipulation. As the 1752 edict stated, "In the past the banner stipends were given out four times a year, and it was the practice of the merchants to take advantage and hoard the grain." Failure to collect stipends promptly often posed a problem, and the importance of prompt collection of stipend grain was emphasized periodically.[47]

When market prices already were high because of a poor harvest, an early distribution of stipends could be authorized to allow prices to level off. An edict of 1758 reported, "Recently the price of rice in the capital has gone up and is quite expensive compared to last year. Usually the stipend grain of the capital officials is given out in the eighth month, but this year let us do it a month earlier. Let us open the granary in the seventh month to allow grain to be abundant and prices both inside and outside the capital to level off and then decrease."[48] The year 1824, which followed an extensive Zhili flood disaster, had an intercalary seventh month, usually an occasion for an extra month's banner stipend. An early distribution of that bonus was authorized in the third month as a sign of imperial blessing to provide famine relief. The edict remarked, "If we wait until the intercalary month, people will have a difficult time."[49]

Stipendiaries of all ranks sold at least part of their stipends for different reasons. At the high-status end, princes, nobles, and high-ranking officials received as stipends far more grain than they and their households could possibly consume. If they sold it, they received additional income, and if they sold at Tongzhou, they avoided the cost of transporting the grain into the capital.[50] At the other end, bannermen of inferior rank sometimes were forced by financial hardship to sell their stipends for cash, even when the grain was barely sufficient for their needs. With the cash they could purchase coarser, less expensive grains, and/or make other urgent expenditures.

The Yongzheng emperor believed that many Manchus did not know how to manage their household incomes and had become too extravagant:

> They want to eat meat every day, drink wine, and wear beautiful clothes. . . . The price of meat is 100 *wen* per jin. . . . If a large number of people would buy less, the price would go down. . . . The Han people know how to be thrifty. Even among the rich households, very few eat meat every day. The poor people pursue their daily livelihood and have just enough to eat. If the Manchus et al. could be thrifty, stay in their respective positions, reduce their meat consumption and eat only veg-etables with each meal, they could save some of their monthly cash stipend, have a small surplus, and make a budget; then they would naturally prosper and become self-sufficient.[51]

A far more fundamental factor, however, was the distinct preference of bannermen, and other northerners, for the coarse grains of millet and sorghum, and later for wheat—the staple crops of the north—over rice. "The people of Zhili most importantly value sorghum and millet, and after that spring wheat and buckwheat," observed the officials. "Beijing has 1 million households, which eat a lot of wheat. . . . The more that is shipped the more that is sold, and [this] causes the mar-ket price to be level."[52] In 1812, proposing that sorghum be used instead of millet for relief at Chengde, Manchuria, one official justified the change by saying, "We know that banner house-holds are accustomed to eating *gaoliang*."[53] In the nineteenth century, Western observers, too, re-ported that Beijing residents preferred wheat and coarse grains to rice.[54] It was not just a question of taste preference; much of the stipendiary rice was stale by the time it had been stored for two or three years and distributed. In fact, the local term *laomi* ("old rice") described precisely this kind of rice. Although a common part of the Beijing diet, it understandably was not the preferred grain.[55] If bannermen sold their rice stipends rather than eating them, they could use the cash ob-tained to purchase fresh local wheat or millet for their own consumption. And, as shown in Table 5.1, millet was about the same price as *laomi*, and sorghum was less expensive.

For all of the above reasons, the sale of stipendiary grain was practiced almost from the begin-ning of the dynasty, periodically causing policy debates among Qing officials. During the Kangxi period, bannermen would sell their stipends immediately upon receipt to merchants, who might hoard the grain. The same bannermen later would be forced to the market to buy grain, which they now absolutely needed, at higher prices than they had received for their stipendiary grain. To address this problem, in 1728 twenty-four Eight Banner grain bureaus (Baqi miju) were set up in Beijing and two additional ones at Tongzhou. With annual funding of 8,000 taels, each bu-reau was to buy grain from the bannermen at current prices and sell it back to them when they needed it at a *pingjia*, or stable price. By purchasing, storing, and reselling grain, these bureaus in principle formed a closed circuit and were intended to serve the interests of the banners exclusively. But in reality it was not a closed system. Some bannermen must have continued to sell grain directly to merchants, and the buyers of the *pingjia*, or stable-price, grain were not necessarily bannermen. One source suggests that the old banner grain was bought also by outsiders, including "bannermen and people from near and far," as well as "people in search of food, itinerant laborers, government functionaries and various types from other areas."[56] These bureaus operated for more than twenty years before they were disbanded in 1752. They had not actually kept prices stable, in officials' view, and moreover the danger of forced purchases (possibly from bannermen by corrupt officials) was too great.[57] When the bureaus were initiated, grain supply was plentiful and prices low, but when prices were higher in the 1740s and 1750s, there seemed no benefit for any party in trying to restrict stipend sales to government-run bureaus. In fact, there is some suggestion that the fine grains stored by the bureaus were not much in demand and sometimes rotted.[58]

In 1787 a proposal to revive the grain bureaus was defeated. Three reasons for this decision were given in the imperial rescript: (1) with population growth and pressure, it was not possible to stop inflation; (2) if the circulation of grain were to be impeded, the benefit would fall to the merchants, not the people; and (3) the bureaus lent themselves to official corruption. In the opinion of Wu Jianyong, this decision marked a shift in state policy that reflected the greater respect for merchants and trade in the Qianlong reign, quite different from that of the immediately preceding Yongzheng period. By the 1780s, the banner bureaus were seen as too repressive of trade. Moreover, it was true that they had afforded plenty of opportunity to profiteering officials.[59] Helen Dunstan argued that the disbanding of the bureaus marked a shift from the Yongzheng-early Qianlong "supply protectionism" that was "intensely interventionist" to a belief in the free circulation of grain that has the appearance of a kind of economic liberalism.[60]

When one considers, however, the intense suspicion with which grain merchants continued to be viewed by officials, and the extreme measures that the latter sometimes used to restrict the activities of the former, one should be cautious about attaching great significance to the abolition of the Eight Banner grain bureaus and viewing the decision as a vote for economic liberalism. The bureaus did not accomplish the goals for which they were established, and they may have interfered with the circulation of grain and hence with price stability. The authorities recognized implicitly that it was impossible to cordon off the economy of the bannermen from that of the city and the metropolitan region, and they also saw the interest of the state in providing food security for the population at large, not just for the banners and the court.

The official position from the mid-eighteenth century on was that the sale of stipend grain was desirable because it allowed for circulation. Somehow, after 1752, stipendiaries low and high sold their grain without the formal institution of banner bureaus. But the mechanisms by which this was done are not clearly documented. The official statutes of the Board of Revenue expressly forbade the operation of private *miju*. "Mean merchants and hoarders at Tongzhou or near Beijing who privately set up *miju* to purchase *fengmi* are to be strictly apprehended and punished by the managing officials, but clerks and runners are forbidden to interfere with those private stores that sell grain in the markets."[61]

Despite the general endorsement of stipend sales, officials continued to urge vigilance against hoarding by merchants. The sale of grain to brewers was a particular problem. In 1752, Fang Guancheng, governor-general of Zhili, memorialized:

> In addition to this year's second month salary, the fall salary and next year's second month official stipends all are being given in advance. It is hoped that the Manchu and Han officials will not sell

[the stipendiary grain] to the merchants, who will hoard it, or to the brewers. The situation should be watched. Every month cases of hoarding and/or brewing should be reported by local officials. In the third month, 38 zhou and xian [districts or counties] have reported no hoarding.[62]

Stipend sales at Tongzhou were usually encouraged. An example is found in an edict of 1775, which was usually issued each year: "Hitherto it has been permitted that bannermen's extra grain be sold in Tongzhou to give them extra income. . . . If in addition to what bannermen are given as regular pay there is extra grain, those who want to sell it are permitted to do so in Tongzhou. Thus the bannerman should be happy, the amount of local grain will increase, and the market price of grain will benefit."[63]

At other times, however, authorities regarded Tongzhou sales with suspicion. Requiring princes and high officials to collect their stipendiary grain at Tongzhou was thought to contribute to problems springing from grain sales because the Tongzhou disbursement was less supervised than that of Beijing. For example, the following document is from 1809:

If all the princes et al. were to sell their surplus grain inside the city [Beijing], the price could level off, and the people would benefit. Transport costs also would be saved. But if grain is sold in Tongzhou, the grain does not flow into the city [Beijing], and city prices rise. The mean merchants take advantage "to hoard grain and raid the granaries" [*tunji huicao*]. As a result, if the granaries are lacking grain, it is because of this.[64]

As a result of a corruption scandal at Tongzhou, it was decreed:

All grain must be shipped into the city and not sold outside the city. If anyone violates this [rule], his stipend will be cut off permanently. As for the others—high civil and military officials—who go to Tongzhou to get their stipendiary grain, as well as those officials and soldiers who get their grain at capital granaries outside the walls, we should devise inspection methods so as to be certain that they transport their grain into the city and do not sell it at Tongzhou.[65]

All the *miju* were given three months to move into the city. Evidence in the case further revealed that there had been many private *miju* located near the granaries outside the Chaoyang gate and other locations in the Inner City.[66]

Sales by officials and bannermen made the Tongzhou granaries, in effect, wholesale depots for commercial grain. Officials often were admonished to guard against cheating at both the Tongzhou and Beijing granaries.[67] Sometimes merchants tried to bribe granary attendants to falsify measures used to weigh grain.[68] Merchants were so bold as to place orders even in advance of distribution of stipends.[69] Banner officials sometimes sold their stipend tickets (*mipiao*) to the merchants instead of claiming the grain in person.[70] In another case in 1794 merchants in collusion with clerks in charge of grain distribution forged names of soldiers and tried to take government rice directly in payment of loans. When the authorities uncovered the case, the soldiers concerned were flogged, and officials ruled that the borrowed sums need not be repaid.[71] Although shop owners were supposed to stay away from the granaries, their porters and carts often entered there despite the rule.[72] At granaries in both locales, loan-shark Shandong merchants waited where soldiers were paid and demanded that payment on previous loans be made in grain. Interest rates were high and soldiers could never finish paying on their loans, so most of their grain went to the merchants.[73] In the view of the authorities, brazen merchants forever sought new stratagems in their constant efforts to hoard grain and raise prices.

Collusion between merchants and granary attendants or watchmen (*huahu*) was endemic in the Jiaqing and Daoguang periods. The following passage from 1802 describes the situation:

It has not been forbidden for officials and military to sell the extra portion of stipendiary grain that they do not need to consume themselves. But when the price of grain is high, the shop owners [*puhu*] wish to benefit, and the granary watchmen [*huahu*] take advantage and extort a high price, causing the market price to increase. When this happens the granary officials [*cangchang shilang*] and the censors inspecting the granaries need strictly to forbid this practice, etc., and those watchmen who collude with the shop owners should be strictly apprehended and investigated.[74]

This document was issued during the 1801–2 flood, when grain prices skyrocketed, and it illustrates why violations of the norm were most likely during periods of inflationary crisis, when the temptation to cheat was greatest. It was at such times that the authorities invoked prohibitions against sales at Tongzhou and required stipend grain to be transported into Beijing before being sold, as seen in the 1809 example above. That particular case involved substantial shortages that were discovered in each of the granary buildings at Tongzhou. After investigation it was found that princes and noblemen were in the habit of selling their grain or their tickets at either Tongzhou or Beijing. The *miju* who bought the tickets then resold them to two or three head watchmen (*huatou*), who then could use them to get more than the allotted share. This is probably the meaning of the form of malfeasance known as "hoarding grain and raiding the granaries," mentioned above.[75]

Pingtiao *and the Beijing Market*

Pingtiao, sale at reduced prices, was another way that tribute grain entered the market. Although it was an administrative tool applied throughout the empire, in Qing-period Beijing *pingtiao* was practiced with resources and regularity unmatched anywhere else. When there was a shortage of grain and prices were high, either because of regular seasonal variation or poor harvest conditions, grain from the tribute granaries was sold at grain stations (*michang*) in Beijing. In official documents these were referred to as "*Wucheng shichang*," or the ten stations of the Five Districts, but over time their numbers increased and some of their locations shifted.[76] In 1738, seven of these were in the Outer City and three were just outside the west, north, and east Inner City walls. (See Map 5.1, page 145.) In the next year, however, so many famine refugees were flocking to the city that the Outer City stations were moved outside the gates.[77] In 1744, a year of serious drought, four more stations were added in the nearby suburbs: Lugou Bridge, Tongzhou, Shahe, and Huangcun.[78] Again in 1748, the emperor authorized *pingtiao* stations in the suburbs, citing a precedent of 1737.[79] In the early nineteenth century, *michang* were established on occasion at seven locations in Daxing and Wanping counties.[80]

The consistent pattern of few if any stations in the Inner City, several in the Outer City, and several more in the suburbs reveals the basic purpose of *pingtiao*: to support the food security of the entire metropolitan population, not just that of the bannermen and other stipendiaries. During their period of operation up to 1752, the Eight Banner grain bureaus also participated in this expanded *pingtiao*, but they were run by the banner authorities and by the Imperial Household Department. The Five Districts grain stations, however, were operated by the Board of Revenue, under the supervision of the censors of the Five Districts, the gendarmerie, Shuntian Prefectural officials, and banner authorities.[81] The *pingtiao* stations outside the city walls were supervised also by the local district authorities.[82]

In the practice of *pingtiao*, prices always were set a certain amount below the current market price.[83] In 1759, a year of crisis, for example, "The price of grain in Beijing is very high. Thus 50,000 shi are being distributed from the capital granaries and stations are being set up for *ping-*

tiao. At present the market price of one shi of *laomi* is 1,550 cash; *suomi* 1,340 *wen*; and millet 1,170 *wen.* Each price should be reduced by 100 *wen.*"[84] In general, the Board of Revenue's rules for reduced-price sales provided that

> the Board of Revenue should determine, according to the market price, how much the price should be reduced. Representatives of each of the ten stations in the Five Districts should go to the granaries to get the grain. (They should assume the costs of transport.) In selling the grain, each person should get 2 dou per day. It is not permitted to go above that limit.[85]

In addition to providing relief, these sales helped to rid the granaries of surplus stocks that were stale. There was an established schedule for semiannual *pingtiao* sale of old grain once after the tenth month and again between the third and fourth months.[86] According to the Board of Revenue's regulations, the adulterated grain (*chengse mi*) that was left from the metropolitan granaries' summer and fall distributions, and from the Tongzhou granaries' spring distributions, was to be sold off after the tenth month. The adulterated grain left over from the metropolitan granaries' winter and spring distributions and the Tongzhou granaries' fall distributions should all be sold off by the third or fourth month.[87]

Because the most important function of *pingtiao* was to keep grain prices stable, Beijing officials also paid close attention to the price of cash (*qianjia*), and reported on it too when they reported grain prices, as Table 5.1 shows. Since cash was the currency for small retail purchases, a shortage of cash (that is, when 1 tael of silver would buy less than the nominal 1,000 cash) was as damaging to overall price stability as was a shortage of grain. The cash from *pingtiao* sales was supposed to be closely guarded and returned to the Board of Revenue.[88] Alternatively, on some occasions, merchants were invited to buy up the cash, and the silver that they paid was sent to the board.[89] On occasion, local officials would in effect make up the deficit caused by an unfavorable exchange rate. In 1762, when grain and cash prices were both high, the gendarmerie was ordered to see that river workers who were to be paid 1,000 cash were given 1 tael and 2 qian of silver (nominally equal to 1,200 cash).[90]

Pingtiao sales were intended for individuals. The authorities were always anxious that grain shops might make illegal purchases and then hoard the grain, impeding circulation. Yet, under some conditions, they allowed limited sales to peddlers or merchants in order to promote circulation. One 1737 report pointed out the need to allow small retailers to purchase *pingtiao* grain because some old and weak people, or women, could not travel a long distance to take advantage of reduced-price grain sales. Thus officials recognized the need for small-scale retailers who would sell grain by carrying it around on their shoulders. But these merchants would be limited to storing no more than 50 shi of rice. Officials suspected merchants of deliberately hoarding rice in multiple places at once and with families bearing different surnames; thus, they kept a close watch on operations of extremely limited size even while recognizing their usefulness to the people.[91]

Relief sales apparently included not only tribute grain but also wheat that may or may not have been part of the tribute system. In 1759—a crisis year—not only granary stocks but also wheat shipped from Henan and Shandong to Beijing were ordered to be distributed to the ten grain stations of the city for reduced-price sales. Representatives of flour shops went to the stations to receive tickets to buy wheat and grind it into flour for sale to the people. A standard amount of purchase was 5 shi. The market price of wheat at the time was 2,124 wen per shi; when reduced by 325 wen, it equaled 1,800 wen for reduced-price sales. The time limit for these sales was from the twenty-sixth day of the third month to the fifteenth day of the intercalary sixth month.[92]

When they were allowed to participate in *pingtiao* sales, merchants found their role strictly controlled by the authorities. Merchants from families regarded as upright and financially well established were chosen. Announcements would be posted informing everyone that hoarding and raising the price of grain were prohibited, and violators would be punished seriously. When the merchants went to the government grain stores to get the grain, officials would be present to observe them. If the merchant did not have enough room to store all the grain that he wished, he could obtain certain limited amounts from the government at a time. For example, in 1813, another year of crisis, he could take 2,500 shi once in five days, selling 500 shi each day; the quotas varied with circumstances. Transport fees were paid by the government from money paid for the grain. The rest of the funds went to the Board of Revenue for military expenses.[93]

Retailers got little profit from *pingtiao* business. The money that they collected had to be handed over to the government immediately. If they were found to sell the grain at a higher price than that set by the government in order to get more profit for themselves, all the grain that they owned, including nongovernmental grain, would be confiscated and sold on a *pingtiao* basis. In addition, the merchants would be punished as criminals. Profits to the merchants appear to have been mainly leftover rice. Having sold 80 percent of the grain or polished white rice (*ximi*), for example, they could keep 20 percent, mostly *suimi* (odds and ends, broken fragments, chaff). This would be their fee for handling *pingtiao*.[94]

In some instances, the court explicitly ordered that private shops rather than the official stations be used for reduced-price sales. In an edict of 1787, the emperor, or those who wrote in his name, directed that an additional 50,000 shi of grain be released for reduced-price sales to meet the relatively high prices that prevailed. According to custom, this grain should be given to the Five Districts to set up stations. But the expenses would be bothersome (*jingfei zhi fan*), and it would also be difficult to prevent officials, clerks, runners and their hangers-on from colluding in fraud (*chuantong zibi*). Reduced-price sales then would be in name only, but without substance:

> In my [Imperial] opinion it would be better to have each of the Five Districts depute a high official jointly to select both inside and outside the city wealthy large grain shops to sell the official grain at reduced prices at each place. . . . If the shops do not respect the government-set price and still conduct private sales to make extra profit, not only will the government grain be given to another selected shop to *pingtiao*, but the shop's own inventory will be confiscated at the same time and sold at reduced price, and the merchant will be punished.[95]

In 1806, during a period of excessive rains, the reduced-price sales were once again conducted by the government-operated stations. An edict had ordered that 40,000 shi each of rice and wheat be released for reduced-price sales in the Five Districts to help the poor during a period of rain and relatively high prices. The Board of Revenue complied, stating:

> The present market price of *gengmi* is 1,850 wen [per shi]. It has been decided to reduce it by 250 and sell it at the reduced price of 1,600. As for the wheat, wheat is hard to store. Previously it had been requested and granted to take 60,000 shi in granaries to be used for banner stipends. Now it can all to be sold at reduced-price sales. The present price of wheat is 2,800 wen, so reduce it by 300 wen and it will be 2,500 wen. As for the rice sold at reduced price, each person each day may buy from 1 or 2 sheng up to 1 dou. As for the wheat sold, each person is allowed to buy from 1 or 2 sheng up to 2 dou. They are not allowed to exceed that amount.[96]

In 1810 wheat was sold directly to shops to be ground into flour:

> Because wheat does not store long, it should be given over to the Board of Revenue for sale in the city to help the people [in the amount of] 74,000 shi. For tribute wheat [*caomai*], the market price is 2,850 wen per shi, and should be reduced by 600 wen to 2,250 wen. For white wheat [*baimai*]

the market price of 2,950 wen per shi should be reduced by 700 wen to 2,250 wen. . . . Because the ordinary people do not have any grinding instruments, . . . [it has been proposed to] reduce each shi of both kinds of wheat to 1,600 wen and sell it to the shops and allow them to resell it at 1,750 wen, 500 wen less than the original price. Afterward the shops can grind it and retail the flour at 20 wen per jin. In the Five Districts, publicize the price so people will know it. If the people purchase according to the [set] price, their subsistence will benefit and the shops will also taste a bit more profit.[97]

Social Unrest, Pingtiao, *and Soup Kitchens*

Soup kitchens (*zhouchang* or sometimes *fanchang*) normally operated in Beijing every winter, and in the nineteenth century, soup kitchens also were increasingly used for emergency relief.[98] (*Zhou* was a gruel made of rice or other grain.) The regulations of the Board of Revenue stated that in Beijing's Five Districts every winter—from the beginning of the tenth month to the twentieth day of the third month—soup kitchens were to be set up for relief. For each district each day, 2 shi of *mi* plus 1 tael for fuel were to be provided. Other provincial capitals and localities were directed to follow this example.[99] These official soup kitchens, initially ten, were located at strategic points in the Five Districts and just outside the gates, mostly on the grounds of temples.[100] Gendarmerie records show seven locations in the Outer City and three in the Inner City.[101]

In times of harvest crisis in the region, additional use of soup kitchens was employed as the principal form of relief within the city and the adjacent suburbs. Although this provided food security for impoverished local residents, soup kitchens and other resources also attracted famine refugees to Beijing, creating great fear of disorder for the local authorities. Refugee problems were not entirely new. In the well-documented drought crisis of 1743–44, so many crowded into the city that extraordinary measures were taken. But during the crises of the nineteenth century, even larger numbers flocked to the capital seeking relief. During the huge flood of 1801, officials tried to stem the tide of refugees by trying to let them know that relief was available in the local areas.[102] The next spring, when the soup kitchens were extended for another month to 4/20 from their usual 3/20 closing, an imperial edict decreed that the soup kitchens of the Five Districts all move their operations outside the city, noting that it would be inconvenient for peasants to come to the city as the agricultural season was getting busy, and that the roads would be crowded.[103] Reduced-price sales often were used alongside the soup kitchens in times of crisis. In 1811, reduced-price sale grain stations were set up outside the city gates to give relief to the poor. Once again the decree said that "if poor people come into the city to get *pingtiao* grain, it is a hardship [for them] because they need to travel far and sometimes when they arrive, it is too late." Left unsaid was the obvious advantage to the rulers of keeping impoverished grain recipients outside the city wall.[104]

In the 1813 drought crisis, the same year as the assault on Beijing by White Lotus rebels, grain prices reached an all-time high, and *pingtiao* was offered in desperation:

> Around the capital area it has been very dry since spring. Prices are very high and people are suffering. The Board of Revenue has permitted 40,000 shi of wheat newly arrived at the granary this year to be sold at reduced prices at the ten stations in the Five Districts. Each shi will be reduced by 600 wen to a price of 2,100. Each person may buy from 1 or 2 sheng to 1 dou daily.[105]

There also seems to have been a decision in 1813 to give grain directly to shops for reduced-price sales, citing the precedent of 1810, when wheat had been given to shops to retail. "Find rich shops to do this," said the instructions.[106]

In 1819, during a flood crisis, soup kitchens were recommended for the counties around Beijing. In 1823–24, at the beginning of the Daoguang reign, when Beijing and the entire region were confronted with tremendous floods, preceded by a serious cholera epidemic, significant quantities of grain were released for reduced-price sales at Beijing: 50,000 shi in each year.[107] This grain also was given to selected merchants to sell. In addition, the authorities set up soup kitchens where gruel was served to the poor. To save famine victims the hardship of daily trips to the soup kitchens, they were allowed to collect five days' rations at once. Normally each adult got three he of grain and each child half that amount per day.[108] In this crisis, each adult could collect one sheng, five he of grain and each child, one-half. The magistrates of Wanping and Daxing were ordered to purchase grain from Henan.[109] Soup kitchens in effect became food-ration (*kouliang*) distribution centers. Additional soup kitchens were set up in some of the usual locations in the suburbs: Lugou Bridge, Huangcun, Dongba, and Qinghe. Shelters for the refugees were erected.[110] Despite these measures, however, many famine refugees still crowded into the capital, and there were even incidents of violence, of grabbing food by force, which alarmed the emperor and officials.[111]

Problems of vagrancy and beggary seemed to abound in the capital; gendarmerie documents of this era, especially for 1830–50, show many problems related to control of "people of unknown background," or "floating population."[112] A persistent concern of local authorities was to stem the tide of poor people coming to the capital in search of relief. Demand for this relief was so great that sometimes people were crushed to death while waiting at soup kitchens, and the police were punished for failing to prevent it.[113]

The grave social and political problems that started in the Daoguang period and lasted through the 1860s appear to have changed the emphasis in food security measures from *pingtiao* (eighteenth century) and gate restrictions (early nineteenth), which emphasized price stabilization, to soup kitchens, which emphasized direct relief. Soup kitchens became far more frequently the major means of famine relief and crowd control in the nineteenth century.[114] At the same time, *pingtiao* was less frequently employed because of the diminished capacity of the government to hold large reserves of grain. Also, there was an increasing tendency to locate soup kitchens outside the city walls. More soup kitchens were opened at even more temples.[115] By the Guangxu period, many soup kitchens were privately operated, as part of a general trend toward private charitable organizations filling any vacuum left by the government.[116] The shift toward private charity reached such an extent that a few decades later, Sidney Gamble, a close observer of Beijing, mistakenly believed that under "the Empire, the poor relief [in Beijing] was carried on almost entirely by individuals or private associations."[117] He interpreted the assumption of responsibility for these activities by the government and the modernized city police as a new departure rather than (as it was) a return to the Qing-era pattern.

How effective were these regular and emergency uses of *pingtiao* and soup kitchens, and how many people were directly affected? Without detailed price data, one cannot quantify the extent to which prices were stabilized by the reduced-price sales of grain. It is highly unlikely, however, that these considerable measures would have been continued throughout two centuries if they had not achieved noticeable economic and social benefits. The amounts for *pingtiao*—ranging from 40,000 to 74,000 shi each time—were substantial. If we use the adult famine ration standard of 0.005 shi of husked grain per person per day, such an amount would have produced 10 million adult rations. In the course of a month, this would be enough to sustain—at bare subsistence level —330,000 adults. Looking at soup kitchens, we know the regulations called for ten stations, two in each district, and each district was provided 2 shi of grain daily. Using the same minimum stan-

PHOTOGRAPH 5.1.   Boys at soup kitchen in Beijing, c. 1920s. Courtesy of Sidney D. Gamble Foundation for China Studies.

dard of 0.005 shi per day, these 10 shi would have provided 2,000 meals per day, or 60,000 meals a month (soup kitchens served one meal a day). Of course, in the nineteenth century there were many more than ten official stations routinely in operation, as well as numerous privately run soup kitchens; furthermore, the thin gruel that they served may have used even smaller amounts of grain. So, in fact, far more meals must have been dispensed.

We can compare our calculations to the figures cited by Gamble for the early Republican period. Adding the figures reported to him by various local police authorities responsible for relief, we can see that 550,000–640,000 meals a month were dispensed at twelve soup kitchens. In the month of January 1918, more than 700,000 meals were served.[118] Six hundred thousand meals a month would have meant about 20,000 meals a day on average—a figure ten times the normative Qing standard of 60,000 meals a month, or 2,000 meals a day. During winter 1925 another source said that soup kitchens served 30,000 people a day.[119] (See Photograph 5.1.) The greater need for soup kitchens in the Republican period reflected not only the more chaotic political conditions—with warlord rivalries, greater foreign presence, and more displaced persons seeking food and shelter—but also the breakdown of other aspects of the food security system that the Qing state had provided for Beijing.

Markets, Merchants, and Gendarmerie

To a greater extent than anywhere else in the empire, in Beijing the Qing state maintained a tight control over the supply and marketing of grain. The state, however, did not try to substitute itself for the market so much as to control and limit it as effectively as possible and with minimal expense to the government. Prices in the *pingtiao* stations were set by officials, but in accordance with the prevailing market price. Government documents conventionally deprecated merchants as *jianshang*—"evil merchants"—but their necessary role was always acknowledged. An ambivalent tone about merchants was characteristic; for example, in a revealing reflection, one memorialist commented that, after all, merchants too were one of the four social classes (scholar, farmer, artisan, and merchant) and deserved Heaven's goodness. But in the next sentence he castigated merchants for their continual hoarding, which showed them to be "really hateful."[120]

In several ways officials tried to limit or control the activities of grain merchants: by regulating their purchases at Tongzhou and the other granaries, by limiting their profits in *pingtiao* transactions, and by limiting the amount of grain that could be taken out the city gates. Because of their great fear of hoarding by merchants—especially hoarding grain that could be held over for more than one season—local officials also limited the size, location, and inventories of grain shops. In 1737, even amounts of 40–50 shi supposedly held by "crafty" people for brewing (*shaoguo*) were forbidden because of the concern that grain supplies would be affected and prices would rise. The regulations stated, however, that "those who just carry a few shi away on their backs should not be investigated." The fear was that "the small, ignorant people do not know anything about storage and just take the first price for wheat [instead of storing it until the price goes up]. Thus the merchants monopolize or corner the market and do not concern themselves about the food supply of the little people." This practice was considered to be especially severe in Linqing in Shandong and Zhenjiang in Jiangnan, so it reflected an empirewide concern.[121]

In theory, there were limits placed on the inventories of grain shops, and violations were punished. But exact limits showed some flexibility. Regulation of stocks always was aimed at the prevention of hoarding, but the amounts varied in each instance. For example, an 1813 document states that if the grain accumulation was *not* judged to be for hoarding, the merchant could store even more than 160 shi, but if hoarding and profit were the goals, he could be prosecuted even if he had *less* than 160 shi.[122] In the 1801 flood, the authorities already had acknowledged that some leniency toward merchants was necessary:

> According to regulations, the grain shops in Beijing's Five Districts are not supposed to have more than 80 shi of each type of grain. If they exceed this amount, they are considered to be hoarding and should be punished. But in this crisis, it is important to keep grain circulating. *According to secret investigation*, grain shops in and outside the capital hold from several hundred to several thousand shi. Now we are raising the limit to 160 shi. The rest we will permit to be sold at a stable price [*pingjia*] and [we] will not permit any hoarding. Do not let the functionaries make the slightest excuses.[123]

Secret inspections of shops were carried out by the gendarmerie, particularly in connection with commerce in grain in shops located near the city gates. Special attention was given to gates located near granaries.[124] In 1810 a censor's memorial led to a secret police investigation of grain shops near the Xizhi gate in the western wall of the Inner City. The censor had feared that merchants were taking grain outside the city wall to hoard and sell later at a higher price. Police officials reported that thirty-two shops did business inside the gate and twenty outside; those inside had much larger reserves of grain, bought at city markets. But gendarmerie headquarters reported that all this commerce was legitimate. Grain stayed in the capital area. It went through the gates by permit to the Western Hills on the backs of donkeys, as rations to the summer palace at Yuanmingyuan, to storage at two granaries near the Xizhi and Desheng gates at the northwestern corner of the Inner City, and on the backs of peasants from nearby areas in small amounts for their own use. Moreover, the captain-general of gendarmerie reported that Wuying (nonbanner Chinese) police regularly monitored all grain shops in the gate area.[125] But all grain shops, not just those near gates, were closely watched. For example, in 1856 when prices had risen high in Beijing, shops were told to sell off all their grain within ten days and not to hoard any.[126]

Because of the bulkiness of grain, it was relatively easy for the authorities to be aware of shipments as they occurred and to stop those that were unauthorized. Shifts of gendarmerie continuously guarding the city gates could, if so ordered, permit only small amounts of grain bought by peasants to pass through.[127] Elaborate planning and precautions were devoted to official grain shipments, such as transports of grain through a gate to one of the government granaries.[128] Grain leaving the city gates as official rations for soldiers outside the city had to be accompanied by a pass from the captain-general of gendarmerie. Gate officers kept one part of the pass, and the other part needed to be returned for cancellation after the rice was consumed.[129] A good example comes from the confession of Cao Fuchang, a Chinese bannerman whose father was the 1813 White Lotus rebel leader Lin Qing's sworn brother. Lin Qing and Cao's father often ate together at the Chongxiang restaurant on the south side of the Chashi alley outside the Xuanwu gate. During the winter of 1808, one could not leave the city carrying grain. Because Lin Qing lived outside the city, Cao's father gave him an authorized paper falsely saying that the grain was for soldiers' rations, and so they let him go through. In the summer and winter of the following year he did this twice more.[130]

Pingtiao grain was not supposed to be moved outside the city wall; if it was carried through a gate, it needed to have a license and official stamp.[131] Gate officers were warned not to extort, hoard, or smuggle grain and not to create counterfeit passes. When grain was confiscated at the gates, it was either used as a reward to the confiscators or as food for prisoners at the gendarmerie yamen.[132] Authorities also were concerned about grain leaving the capital *region*; the banner component of the gendarmerie was responsible for keeping track of grain in transport inside the gates, and the Green Standard component outside them.[133] As with other regulations regarding grain, these were enforced most strictly during times of poor harvests and high prices, when the fear was that grain merchants would be tempted to seek higher prices outside the city, thus causing city prices also to rise. During normal years the enforcement of this prohibition was probably relaxed. Beijing's gendarmerie played a major role in enforcing all these regulations. Knowledge of merchants, prices, and market conditions obtained by open and secret surveillance enabled the authorities to respond in a flexible, timely manner.

Another means of maintaining indirect control of the grain market was to keep the scale of marketing relatively small.[134] There were over a thousand small shops run by Shandong merchants called *duifang* that polished rice (often stipend grain that reached the market through *pingtiao*) and then peddled it in the neighborhoods of the city.[135] Qing-era Western visitors consistently noted that all kinds of grain and other foods were sold in small-scale shops and by peddlers up and down the streets of both Inner and Outer Cities.[136] A well-regarded late Qing Japanese gazetteer noted that Beijing merchants were mostly small-scale; large merchants were very rare. Grain shops were located, among other places, inside the Qian (Zhengyang) gate, Qiaozi hutong, inside the Xizhi gate, and also inside the Qihua (Chaoyang) gate.[137]

Elsewhere in the capital region the same small-scale grain commerce prevailed, even at the wholesale level. At Tongzhou, where officials were vigilant against manipulation of the market, merchants were constantly under surveillance, and every attempt was made to limit their scale of business. According to Governor-general Zhou Yuanli in 1778, there were 220 "guest" merchants at Tongzhou, and each had a stock of about 100 to 1,000 shi of wheat. There was a total stock of 200,000 shi. Although he considered this a desirable situation, he thought that newly arrived merchants should not be compelled to limit their inventories lest they be discouraged from doing business there.[138] Nevertheless, there was an investigation of the warehouses that normally stored the large shipments of wheat from Henan, Shandong, and Jiangsu and sold the stock gradually to retailers in Beijing and Tongzhou. Such a large inventory remained in 1778, however, that officials were suspicious that merchants were withholding stocks in anticipation of a poor harvest. After a thorough investigation, the authorities concluded that the eighty or more merchants suspected were not guilty of actual hoarding and therefore should not be punished. Under pressure, however, the merchants volunteered to sell the whole of the remaining stock within two months at a price of 0.2 taels per shi below the current price. The emperor then reduced this self-penalty to 0.1 taels.[139]

Like many means, direct and indirect, employed by the Qing state to control and limit commerce in grain, the atomization of the trade was not limited to the capital and its region. In the metropolitan region, however, the state's capacity to enforce it was greater. At Tianjin, the major seaport, and Baoding, the provincial capital, the grain trade also was small in scale, at least until the nineteenth century. Differing from trade in salt, silk, or other important commodities, the grain trade of the Chinese empire never had large-scale merchants who achieved economic influence and personal stature. An examination of more than 100 local gazetteers from Zhili Province does not reveal even one grain merchant mentioned by name. Other sources refer to a few large dealers in Tianjin in the early nineteenth century.[140] There were no Chinese counterparts of the Cargills or Thellussons of the West. Unlike authorities in eighteenth-century France, Chinese officials had no need to negotiate with large grain magnates.

Some historians both inside and outside China have seen a trend toward liberalization of trade in the mid- to late Qing period, spurred by an ideological transformation, a recognition of the importance of free markets and respect for merchants.[141] The decline in government intervention can certainly be seen in the grain trade, even in the capital area, where the state's role was greater than elsewhere, but it was prompted more by circumstance than by ideology. The decline of the grain tribute system and the other aspects of Qing fiscal weakness meant that the state simply could not command the resources that it had marshaled in the eighteenth century, and it could no longer successfully enforce a free circulation of grain by restricting inventories and controlling hoarding. When the state turned to merchants to perform functions previously undertaken by the state, it was not because of a more positive view of merchants, but because its fear of bureaucratic corruption became more immediate than its fear of merchant connivance. In effect, corruption was part of the cost to the state of its intervention in the grain market. When this cost rose too high under either governmental or private auspices, the government switched to alternative channels to reduce it. In the flood crisis of 1823–24, the emperor ordered officials to purchase grain from as far away as Taiwan and Fujian, but he ordered the purchases to be delivered not to local functionaries, but rather to merchants recruited for the occasion to ship the grain to Tianjin and Beijing.[142]

Conclusion

Through single-minded determination and clever statecraft, the Qing rulers achieved an impressive degree of food security for Beijing. Even after the prosperity of the late seventeenth and eighteenth centuries had passed, overall price stability and food security were maintained even during most of the nineteenth-century difficulties of the Qing dynasty that included frequent local harvest crises and some major disasters.[143] Only in the period of monetary instability, rebellion, and foreign invasion in the 1850s and early 1860s was this stability seriously threatened. Despite this crisis, and despite the periodic danger posed by famine refugees crowding toward the city, food never became a cause of popular uprising. Food security was achieved not simply by the adequate provisioning of the city, but by maintaining a public confidence that the authorities would provide food.

The Beijing populace never seized upon food scarcity or high food prices as causes of dissatisfaction with the Manchu rulers. There was an annual and highly visible inflow of tribute grain, even though much of this was not consumed by those for whom it was intended. This situation can be contrasted with the experience of London in the early eighteenth century, when urban residents could see vast quantities of grain being exported by grain dealers to foreign destinations, thus causing local scarcities.[144] With the approval of the crown, Britain remained a major grain exporter until it faced the necessity of feeding concentrated urban factory populations in the mid-nineteenth century.[145] In Beijing, however, massive granaries along the eastern and northern walls of the city and at nearby Tongzhou, as well as the constant busy traffic of grain junks on the canal, were ever-present visual reminders of the capital's food supply and the unshakeable political will to maintain it. Even after the grain tribute was increasingly transported by sea, the late Qing government tried to avoid social disturbance due to food scarcity. Although there are some instances of food-related protests in other parts of China—for example in Hunan in the eighteenth century—the urban food riot was not part of the political life of Beijing.[146]

Protecting the food security of Beijing, however, was not entirely the same as maintaining the economic security of the bannermen and their families or preventing poverty among urban dwellers. The Qing state did not meet these latter challenges so successfully as it did the first. The inadequacy of banner stipends was felt as early as the late seventeenth and early eighteenth centuries.[147] The impoverishment of the bannermen over the course of the dynasty has often been described. Prevented for long periods from working at nonmilitary occupations, bannermen were heavily dependent on stipend rates set in the seventeenth century and cut in the nineteenth century.[148] They were frequently the victims of sharp Chinese merchants; the Shandong rice-polishing shop owners often tried to shortchange the bannermen who relied on them to polish their rice.[149] Han Guanghui shows a gradual increase in banner numbers and growing banner poverty as some did not receive stipends and some Chinese bannermen or Hanjun even returned to the life of commoners.[150]

The irony of banner decline in the much-protected Beijing dynastic stronghold underscores once more the primacy accorded the goal of food security for the capital as a whole, not just its ruling elite; the emperors cannot be said to have accorded the bannermen any economic advantages. This larger view of food security may be contrasted to the policies of the Tokugawa authorities in Edo in the same period. As James McClain and Ugawa Kaoru observe, the "Tokugawa regime . . .

went to considerable lengths to create mechanisms to supply water, food, and other essentials to all of Edo's residents, but within that framework it paid particular attention to the needs of the samurai estate."[151] Because the incomes of the Tokugawa retainers were dependent on the value of their grain stipends when sold on the market, the authorities pursued a policy of keeping grain prices high, even in years of natural crisis such as 1733. Only when faced with evidence of widespread starvation did they lift the ban on imports of grain from neighboring regions.[152] The Edo commoners expected the state to protect them; on each of the three occasions in the Tokugawa period (1600–1868) when they rioted against grain merchants, they assumed that the state stood behind the merchants.[153] Qing food policy differed fundamentally from that of the Tokugawa shogunate in that the interests of the ruling class were not put first. Unlike the Tokugawa shoguns or feudal lords, the Qing rulers wanted low, not high, grain prices. What the two had in common, however, was a highly political view of food security, one that emphasized control of distribution more than development of agricultural production.

The Qing dynasty achievement in maintaining Beijing's food security, particularly in the eighteenth century, stands in sharp contrast to the fate of revolutionary-era Paris, where bread prices became the most visible focus of political contention. Parisians habitually convinced themselves that every food crisis was the result of a government plot. Although they were not necessarily less well fed than Beijing residents, the Paris population, by contrast, saw food as a source of grievance against the authorities. There were, to be sure, striking similarities in the food security of the two cities. In Paris as in Beijing, policing of grain merchants and bakers was central to the control of the grain trade, even after the short-lived "liberalization" of 1763–64. French authorities regarded bread as the most vital link in the security of Paris, just as Beijing authorities placed great importance on guarding grain supplies.[154] Both French and Chinese rulers recognized that wholly taking over the grain trade by means of a "leviathan machine" or "master-plan" was both undesirable and beyond governmental capacities.[155] But after the building of Versailles in the late seventeenth century, Paris was no longer the seat of government. It had only about 3,000 police compared to Beijing's 33,000. Paris had no city wall after the seventeenth century to control grain movements. Paris authorities did not store grain in large quantities, subsidize grain supply, or run soup kitchens (a task they left to the church). Because of a history of "extensive commercialization before state power became concentrated and centralized," the French bourgeoisie had "some independent bases of power and some forms of alliance with landlords."[156] In Beijing, by contrast, the grain trade was kept to a small scale; grain merchants did not have a sense of class identity and did not oppose the state or police in a collective way. And in Beijing, unlike Paris, the local population did not seize upon hunger or high grain prices as a source of political grievance. They did not think they were the victims of a terrible conspiracy. Most of all, their rulers did not dismiss their need for cheap grain proclaiming, "Let them eat cake."

CHAPTER SIX

Storing Grain: Granaries as
Solution and Problem

THE ENTIRE CAPITAL REGION, indeed Zhili Province as a whole, received substantial benefit from of the provisioning of Beijing. Tribute grain reached the Zhili market indirectly through the private sales of stipends, the government-sponsored reduced-price sales, and famine relief. In addition, tribute grain was frequently diverted to the Zhili state granaries to address scarcities resulting from poor harvests. The state granary system itself was the second means by which the state augmented Zhili's grain supply.[1] The ever-normal granaries (*changpingcang*), supplemented by community granaries (*shecang*) and charity granaries (*yicang*), were part of an empirewide system that required the storage of grain in each county of each province for the purpose of price stabilization and famine relief. Zhili's ever-normal granaries were among the best stocked and received the direct attention from the nearby court and high bureaucracy.

The very substantial amounts of grain storage represented by both systems—grain tribute and state granaries—meant that Zhili was not entirely dependent on its own uncertain harvests for its subsistence. In the eighteenth century, there were 3–5 million shi of *unhusked* grain (*gu*) reserves in the state granary system, in addition to the estimated 6–10 million shi of *husked* grain (*mi*) stored in the metropolitan granaries of the grain tribute system (about 3.5 million received each year).[2] These large reserves shielded the local people from what surely would have been highly volatile price fluctuations resulting from poor harvests, and they undoubtedly account for the relative price stability shown in Chapter 4. The price analyses presented in Chapter 7 will provide an indirect but unambiguous demonstration of the favorable effect of government intervention in the high Qing. Chapters 8 and 9 will show the impact of famine relief during crises of the eighteenth and nineteenth centuries. In sum, Zhili was a poor region that benefited from large, state-subsidized transfer of resources that was part of an empirewide redistribution of income.[3]

Despite these positive outcomes, both the theory and practice of state-sponsored grain storage were controversial. In the mid-eighteenth century, at the height of the system, the Qianlong emperor and some high officials began to question whether storage on such a large scale was responsible for the price inflation they detected, and whether market forces alone might not be more effective in maintaining low and stable grain prices. There was, moreover, the inevitable question of whether the benefits of storage were reaching the targeted population, the urban and rural poor, or whether reduced-price sales merely benefited the larger households, merchants, or corrupt functionaries. Indeed some sharp critics observed that restocking the granaries created so many abuses that granaries ended up harming the very people they were intended to benefit. By the end of the eighteenth century it was difficult to see how the state could sustain the enormous financial costs of this institution, as well as the political costs of bureaucratic corruption. Periodically, high officials sought to shift the burden of grain storage and famine relief from the state to local elites, which would at the same time deny local functionaries the opportunities for graft. Yet the efforts to pump up local activism and moral economy only revealed the weaknesses of local society and economy in North China.

Granaries in Chinese History

The concept of the ruler's obligation to encourage grain storage, like the concepts of river control, had ancient origins in China. The classics such as the *Book of Rites*, or the book of *Mencius*, all spoke of the importance of storing grain against the inevitability of famines. The ever-normal granary, named *changpingcang* in the Han dynasty, bought grain after the harvest, when it was cheap, and sold it at below-market prices during the lean season (*qinghuangbujie*) in the late winter or spring.[4] Wang Anshi, the controversial reformer-statesman of the Northern Song, promoted the practice of "green sprout loans," which would extend credit to peasants during the difficult late winter and spring period, to be repaid after the fall harvest.[5] Distrusting state activism, the philosopher Zhu Xi favored entrusting local elites with the responsibility for community granaries.[6] Although there was no clear resolution of this Song policy debate, grain storage continued to be a theoretical responsibility of the state, but the actual responsibility of local elites if they could manage it. The first Ming emperor decreed that four "preparedness" granaries (*yubeicang*) should be set up in each county, but few could be found after the mid-Ming.[7] Charity and community granaries were evident in some localities, and ever-normal granaries were revived to some extent in the sixteenth century.[8] In the Qing period, state-managed granaries reached their most developed form in Chinese history. In constructing the massive grain reserves of the eighteenth century, the Qing rulers and bureaucracy rested on more than two millennia of theoretical principles and institutional precedents, but they implemented this system with a consistency, intensity, and degree of centralization unknown in previous eras.

The ever-normal granary was by far the most important of the three prototypes. Its principal function was price stabilization through *pingtiao*—the seasonal purchase, storage, and sale of grain at reduced prices. Its second function was to provide emergency relief during times of food scarcity. It also made seasonal loans. Established in each county or district (xian or zhou), the ever-normal granaries were theoretically self-funded, but were in fact heavily subsidized by the state, via the Board of Revenue and the provincial governments, and they were managed by the local government staff.[9] Because these granaries were located in the county seats, presumably they targeted the urban population of workers, artisans, and shopkeepers, but the line between urban and rural recipients was difficult to maintain.[10]

The community granary, inspired by Zhu Xi, emphasized the local, nonofficial, community management of granaries established in rural areas and funded by private contributions.[11] The *shecang* was engaged in making seasonal loans to peasants, rather than the sale of grain. Despite strong central government encouragement of such granaries, few were established before the Yongzheng period, with the exception of Zhili, where some were in operation in the late Kangxi period.[12] In the Qianlong period, state sponsorship of such granaries in many provinces gave them life, while eroding the principle of nonofficial management. Officials tried to increase the reserves of the community granaries "as the first line of defense against food supply instabilities," either complementing or substituting for the ever-normal granaries.[13]

The charity granary in the Qing period was "an urban repository financed by private contributions and offering reduced-price sales and loans." During the eighteenth century, salt merchants in Jiangnan and elsewhere were active sponsors of *yicang*. In the mid-eighteenth century in Zhili, Nasutu, the governor-general, and Fang Guancheng, then provincial treasurer and later governor-general, promoted the establishment of charity granaries in the countryside to supplement the ever-normal granaries, which were located in the xian cities. Thus, they were somewhat like community granaries, but they were engaged in famine relief as well as loans.[14]

Kangxi-Yongzheng Origins

The Kangxi emperor did not begin to promote grain storage until around 1680. In these early years "contributions" toward purchased degrees were very important in stocking the granaries, but by the 1720s, provincial funding played a larger role, and grain tribute diversions were another important source. Sometimes silver was stored rather than grain itself.[15] In 1691 the quotas established for the ever-normal granaries were 5,000 shi for large counties; 4,000 shi for medium-size counties; and 3,000 shi for small counties. In 1704 quotas were raised to 10,000, 8,000, and 6,000 shi respectively.[16] Unlike the grain tribute system that transported and stored husked grain (*mi*), principally rice, the state granaries stored unhusked grain (*gu*). Generally the ratio of unhusked to husked grain was 2:1.[17] The procedures for the operation of the granaries were not firmly established until later and were always adapted to meet circumstances. For example in 1719, when Zhili Governor-general Zhao Hongxie suggested that granaries be restocked through treasury funds, rather than contributions, while prices were low, the emperor ordered him to wait until the seventh or eighth month, when the prospects for the fall harvest would be clear.[18]

Part of the Kangxi plan was to supplement the ever-normal granaries with community granaries.[19] Although in Zhili there were community granaries by 1702, earlier than elsewhere, and they had relatively more success than in other provinces, the *shecang* experiment did not flourish.[20] Experiments were conducted in the capital area and then extended elsewhere. In 1708 Governor Zhao Hongxie, reporting on the contributions to community granaries since 1702, requested that the emperor consider ending the call for contributions because local officials placed an undue pressure on people to contribute even in prosperous years.[21] Three years later, in 1711, Zhao again reported that the results of the *shecang* experiment had been poor, with very small contributions. "In inquiring, I find that there are few people who are willing to contribute, and there are few local officials who are good at complying with the orders. The village elders are not virtuous, and the fraudulent practices multiply."[22]

In 1714, Zhao again reported poor results. "The *shecang* was originally a good idea, but its execution was not skillful and the result was that it burdened the people," he memorialized. "So the emperor had entrusted the matter to officials, but then the opportunities for cheating became numerous. But if you entrust the matter to the people's contributions, then the rich will scheme . . . and not be willing to help others, and then the poor will not have enough for daily use." Zhao then proposed that the rich households be given exemption from corvée labor services, while the gentry be given rewards if they contributed grain. Those who showed willingness but lacked sufficient means to contribute would have their names recorded, and they would be eligible for any future tax remissions granted the locality. Those who were unwilling to contribute would be ineligible for any tax remission. "As for grain already donated to the granaries, we should take last year's stock, and sell it at *pingtiao* [reduced] prices at the middle of the year, and change it for new grain at the end of the year and distribute it as relief, and thus the functionaries will have nothing with which to cheat and steal."[23]

Such carrot-and-stick incentives revealed the difficulties of raising donations. Zhao's successors in the next decade seemed to have no more success with community granaries than he had. Governor-general Li Fu memorialized in 1726 that although his successor Li Weijun had reported that 100,000 shi of grain had been collected for *shecang*; in fact, it was not so. He elaborated on the difficulty of organizing labor for construction, rowdyism among workers and soliders.[24] In short, it seems that there was little enthusiasm for contributing grain, and that such granaries were difficult to control. Although the annual population and granary reports showed a steady volume of reserves in the *shecang*, there is hardly any reference either in memorials or local gazetteers to their actual physical existence or operation. Most likely, these holdings were managed by officials together with the ever-normal granary reserves in the county seats and nominally called community granary holdings. Will and Wong observe that "government intervention in the administration of community granaries generally increased during the eighteenth century, ultimately rendering them just another sort of 'public' reserve from which officials could draw at will."[25]

Although the hopes for local contributions were not realized, granary reserves as a whole had been steadily accumulating. In Zhili, there were 1.6 million shi total reserves stored by 1721.[26] The creation of enormous reserves empirewide was the "the principal achievement" of this formative period of Qing granaries, not price stabilization or famine relief.[27] In the Yongzheng period, more granaries were built to accommodate the larger stocks of grain.[28] Granaries were well stocked; people were reported to be content.[29] In fact, granaries were sometimes overstocked, and spoilage was a concern. In 1726, Li Fu reported that local granaries held over 2 million shi of grain, not counting sorghum and beans. He requested that no more restocking be done, particularly since there had been a poor harvest due to flood in the previous year, and since restocking would allow the price to rise higher and cause hardship.[30] By 1729, storage facilities were insufficient. "At present, in sixty or more counties, granaries have various amounts of grain," wrote an investigating official. In many places grain was inadequately stored and rotting. In Guangping Prefecture's Qinghe County, there were only eleven rooms in the granary, some big and some small, that stored only 12,000 shi out of more than 60,000 shi held in the county. The rest was stored in forty-six mud huts, twelve family homes, and two temples, unprotected and rotting. The official recommended that several new granaries be built.[31]

Ever-Normal Granaries in the Qianlong Period

At the very outset of the Qianlong reign, the emperor and his advisors made an unequivocal commitment to maintaining large-scale storage in all of the provinces. Zhili's reserves were among the highest in the empire, about 7 percent of the total; Henan's reserves were much higher, while Fujian, Sichuan, and possibly Guangdong's were slightly higher.[32] During the second half of the eighteenth century, reserves of all the civilian granaries in Zhili totaled 2.9 to 5.4 million shi of grain (generally unhusked), of which the ever-normal granaries represented the largest share. Although the charity granaries played a supporting role, in Zhili it was the ever-normal granary system that

TABLE 6.1
Storage Balance and Rates of Distribution from All Granaries in Zhili Province, 1749–1792

Year	Ever-Normal Granaries			Community Granaries			Charity Granaries			Total Reserves
	opening balance	disbursals	rate	opening balance	disbursals	rate	opening balance	disbursals	rate	
1746[1]	3,090,362	1,276,145	41	271,524	158,387	58	—	—	—	—
1748[2]	3,665,300	1,669,736	46	277,463	167,496	60	181,818	1,116	1	4,124,581
1749	3,322,044	1,118,988	34	294,744	120,105	41	206,688	27,375	13	3,823,476
1751	3,194,282	1,548,743	48	301,113	168,944	56	236,604	93,054	39	3,331,999
1752	2,716,779	923,208	34	310,719	137,989	44	306,278	35,802	12	3,333,776
1753	2,744,990	817,228	30	328,411	112,065	34	333,363	36,505	11	3,406,764
1754	2,794,377	620,573	22	333,187	102,687	31	381,328	44,987	12	3,508,892
1755	2,729,650	477,593	18	342,659	76,844	22	376,759	89,443	24	3,449,068
1756	2,633,701	493,718	19	346,102	102,844	30	405,550	106,261	26	3,385,353
1763	4,515,140	3,147,117	70	375,499	176,354	47	501,792	260,529	52	5,392,431
1764	2,981,353	1,307,734	44	399,756	134,222	34	461,437	157,190	34	3,842,546
1765	3,120,374	905,404	29	415,626	95,152	23	498,597	109,023	22	4,034,597
1767	3,202,272	652,706	20	426,747	88,196	21	558,223	130,915	23	4,187,242
1768	3,171,376	894,962	28	433,223	103,414	24	594,328	200,040	34	4,198,927
1773	2,572,163	839,821	33	441,642	95,967	22	664,402	161,988	24	3,678,207
1777	2,648,821	756,790	29	458,201	98,937	22	599,653	190,749	32	3,706,675
1778	—	—	—	—	—	—	625,165	234,013	37	—
1779	2,839,768	1,010,635	36	465,707	178,533	38	595,677	279,617	47	3,901,152
1780[3]	2,719,925	966,556	36	470,879	270,879	58	605,163	194,327	32	3,795,967
1781	3,784,762	966,457	26	411,695	108,529	26	541,889	212,032	39	4,738,346

TABLE 6.1 (continued)

Year	Ever-Normal Granaries			Community Granaries			Charity Granaries			Total Reserves
	opening balance	disbursals	rate	opening balance	disbursals	rate	opening balance	disbursals	rate	
1782	2,348,941	1,021,749	44	415,690	124,052	30	551,297	209,839	38	3,315,928
1783	2,461,776	1,047,886	43	418,910	120,983	29	555,779	217,276	39	3,436,465
1784	2,328,501	454,291	20	422,870	72,742	17	563,188	157,267	28	3,314,559
1785	2,266,621	657,741	29	422,757	97,639	23	564,921	168,921	30	3,254,299
1786	2,728,045	919,161	34	418,916	129,653	31	564,969	237,709	42	3,711,930
1787	2,530,369	737,062	29	396,190	92,247	23	523,238	157,953	30	3,449,797
1788	2,510,558	561,092	22	398,091	79,520	20	529,121	142,455	27	3,437,770
1789[4]	2,484,254	567,405	23	398,561	87,717	22	531,419	142,372	27	3,414,234
1790[5]	3,504,749	2,017,130	58	392,570	127,800	33	530,088	226,832	43	4,427,407
1792	2,096,070	919,926	44	363,885	106,011	29	458,577	179,596	39	2,918,532

NOTE: Disbursals as a percentage of opening balance. Disbursals include both amount distributed and amounts owed. See notes to Will and Wong, tab. 9.8. All other figures in shi.

SOURCES: Based on Will and Wong, *Nourishing*, tab. 9.14, with exception of 1746, 1748, 1780, 1789, and 1790, as listed below. Data from 1789 corrects errors in Will and Wong, tab. 9.14. The original source for all data is *Minshu gushu* memorials (on population and grain storage). See Will and Wong, append. and notes to tab. A.1 for details.

[1] QL 11/11/30, ZPZZ CZCC, §6:10–12.
[2] QL 13/10/29, ZPZZ CZCC, §6:1588–91.
[3] QL 45/12/3, JJD 29002.
[4] QL 54/11/21, GZD 05888I.
[5] QL 55/12/3, JJD 46287.

held the largest amounts of grain and played the dominant role in food security during the eighteenth century. Reserves of community granaries ranged from a low of 271,000 shi in 1746 to a high of 471,000 shi in 1780. Reserves of the charity granaries ranged from a low of 182,000 shi in 1748 to a high of 664,000 shi in 1773. In terms of annual disbursals (which included the outstanding loans owed to the granaries), ever-normal granaries represented at least two-thirds, and generally between 70–88 percent of the total. Yet, if the records are assumed to be correct, there was a slight trend toward an increasing share being held by the other two types of granaries.[33] (See Table 6.1.)

In 1738, when he was governor-general of Liangjiang, Nasutu, who was a close advisor to the emperor, surveyed the ever-normal granary system throughout the empire and identified the three principal functions he thought they ought to serve: to provide relief during poor harvests by reduced-price sales, to adjust seasonal fluctuations in price also by *pingtiao*, and to sell off stale grain to assure a constant turnover.[34] The basic guidelines for the *pingtiao* operations of the ever-normal granary stipulated that 30 percent of its stock should be sold off each year, but this norm could be adjusted according to conditions in different provinces. In case of disaster, the 30 percent quota could be exceeded. In case of stable prices, less could be sold; in Zhili 10 or 20 percent would be all right. In normal times, the market price should be reduced by 5 fen per shi, but in lean times 1 qian per shi was permitted. And in a serious crisis, larger reductions were permitted. Reductions of 5 fen or less were at the governor's discretion, but anything over 5 fen had to be reported.[35] Regulations stated that the type of grain to be stored depended on the agricultural conditions of each province. Rice, wheat, beans, millet, or sorghum could all be stored, but in the accounting they should be converted into *gu* (unhusked millet) equivalents.[36] Quotas were established for each county of each province.[37]

Seasonal loans of grain were also a practice of the ever-normal granaries, although theoretically this function was assigned to the community and charity granaries. There is little documentation of the process by which loans were made, but it is clear they played a large, perhaps even dominant role, in the process of turning over stocks and the seasonal adjustment of prices. The role of loans seems to loom larger than that of sales, at least for the late eighteenth century.[38] Generally, ever-normal granaries in Shandong, Zhili, and other northern provinces, lent more grain than they sold.[39] In Shandong, loans were made only to landowners, not tenants (the latter estimated to be 10–30 percent of the rural population). By contrast, reduced-price sales were available to all.[40]

In 1746, Zhili Governor-general Nasutu reported that during the lean season the price of wheat was soaring. He advocated either selling grain at reduced prices or extending loans to be returned after the harvest. He said that the people were willing to borrow grain and return it later using the formula of one part husked grain to two parts unhusked grain. He said that it would benefit the people the most if they borrowed *mi* now and returned *gu* later. Evidently, Zhili had received some 300,000 shi diverted from tribute grain (*mi*) and 50,000 shi from Tongzhou, as well as 200,000 shi of wheat from Shandong and Henan in the previous year for drought relief, and apparently some *mi* was still in the granaries. He reported a total of 2,240,000 shi of *gu*, or its equivalent, in storage in Zhili's ever-normal granaries.[41]

Zhili's ever-normal granary reserves in the second half of the eighteenth century, until 1792, ranged from over 2 million to 4.5 million shi of theoretical reserves. (See Table 6.1.) The annual disbursal rate ranged from a low of 18 percent to a high of 70 percent in 1763. In general, it seems that the 30 percent sell-off rule was maintained except in years of hardship such as 1763. Every year, there were loans in arrears, so the actual reserves were about one-third or less than the theoretical reserves.[42]

These large reserves were maintained despite considerable doubts raised by midcentury about the wisdom of storage on such a large scale, including the problems of restocking. In the early eighteenth century, when supplies were generally abundant, the stocking problems were minor. In 1735, for example, the governor-general, Li Wei, urged a quick purchase of wheat from the bountiful harvest that was anticipated. (Thirty-seven counties in Xuanhua, Baoding, Guangping, Zhengding, and so forth already had harvest ratings of 8.) Not only would the price be low, but he feared that if the officials did not buy up the grain, greedy merchants would hoard it. He observed:

> *The peasants do not have the habit of storing grain.* They just sell it off right away no matter what the price is. We repeatedly persuade them to save and economize. . . . The price of *mi* is normally between 1.30–1.40 and 2.00 liang [taels]. This year the price is especially low. So when the wheat is harvested, the price will be even lower. Unless we take preventive measures, the hoarders will take advantage of the low price and wait half a year, and then sell very high. The people will suffer. When wheat seeds mature, they can be stored one or two years without harm. We request that several tens of thousands of taels be issued from the treasury to buy wheat from willing families and store it in the locality. If the fall harvest is good, wait until next spring to sell it off. If this is done every year, it will be very effective.[43]

Although initially it was not difficult to find adequate supplies to purchase locally or from other provinces, restocking—large-scale government purchases—had an impact on the local market.[44] Thus, ironically, the very institution that was intended to keep prices low and stable was seen as responsible for causing them to rise. In 1748 the emperor and high officials became concerned about the apparent inflation in grain prices all over the empire. Although some suspected population growth was the culprit, others, including the Qianlong emperor, suspected that the government had stored too much grain, leaving not enough for the people's needs.[45] He noted that in recent years the price had been rising steadily and had not fallen despite prosperous harvests. He ordered each governor-general to investigate and present a report. The grand secretary Zhang Tingyu and others advanced the idea that near a provincial capital or along waterways less grain needed to be stored because merchants had easy access. Fertile areas also needed to store less grain. But localities that were remote, or subject to waterlogging or dry conditions, needed to store more grain. In remote areas, it would be difficult and costly to transport grain in an emergency. In addition, the grand secretary pointed out that areas that were at the crossroads of adjacent regions should store more grain so that mutual assistance could be rendered. For example, if Linqing and Dezhou stocked more grain, they could assist the three adjacent provinces of Shandong, Henan, or Zhili.[46]

In response to the court's invitation, Nasutu, recently the Zhili governor-general, presented a detailed report on the metropolitan province's situation. Although Zhili's Zhengding, Shunde, Guangping, and Daming prefectures, and the independent zhou of Ji, Zhao, Shen, Ding, and so on were all near Henan's borders, there were not any good roads (implying there would be no reason to store extra grain in these locations since there was no easy way to export this grain to Henan). There were, however, localities—such as Huailu and Jingxing counties (both in Zhengding Prefecture) and Wan and Tang counties (both in Baoding Prefecture)—that were fertile areas near the mountains but well positioned on major thoroughfares, and therefore easily accessible (and thus needed no extra reserves). The other (central) prefectures of Shuntian, Baoding, Hejian, Tianjin, and so forth were near water; thus, transport was not difficult. Moreover, the areas of Yongping and Zunhua could be assisted easily by the (tribute) granaries at Tongzhou and Tianjin and were also in communication with the grain-producing regions at Guandong (Liaodong) and

Rehe and therefore did not need to increase their grain storage either. Only Xuanhua Prefecture had need for additional grain storage since transportation was not easy. In sum, Nasutu mounted an effective argument against increasing the quotas for Zhili's granaries.[47]

In the previous year, Nasutu had already argued against a proposal to increase Zhili's grain stocks. He reported that the holdings of the Zhili ever-normal granaries were 3,306,046 million shi (of *gu*), which included 1,928,607 shi in actual storage, plus 1,377,439 shi that had been lent out and should be returned. Nasutu pointed out that this exceeded the target quotas originally set in 1732 of 1,996,216 shi by 1,151,156, and it reflected the new granaries that had been built since that time.[48] He noted that the Yongzheng guidelines had excluded substantial sections of Zhili—the metropolitan granaries; Guangchang xian, which was then attached to Shanxi Province; the granaries of Baoding, Zhengding, and Daming prefectures, which were grouped under the military commander of Tianjin; Cangzhou, which was under the maritime customs jurisdiction; Shanhaiguan jurisdiction; and Rehe Bagou, which was under the Fourth Banner jurisdiction. It should also be noted that the districts of Daxing and Wanping in Shuntian Prefecture did not have ever-normal granaries until 1760 or later.[49]

In the short run the proposal for Zhili to purchase more grain was overruled, at least theoretically. "In recent years the price of grains has been rising in all the provinces. No one knows why. But it is a worry for stocking the granaries. The general opinion is that there has been too much *caimai* (official purchase), and this has caused grain prices to rise. So we should cut back to the quotas of the Kangxi and Yongzheng period. Zhili should adhere to the Yongzheng period quota of 2,154,524 shi of *gu*."[50] Although the 1748 guidelines and targets remained the standard for the rest of the dynastic period, the actual reserves in many provinces, as well as Zhili, were much higher.[51] In 1752 the emperor once again asked provincial governors to respond to a proposal to reduce the level of granary restocking, but some governors resisted giving their direct agreement, arguing for the specific needs of their regions.[52]

In Zhili, Nasutu's resistance to higher levels of restocking was supported by Fang Guancheng, newly appointed as governor-general, who argued that Zhili was somewhat different from other provinces because the strong winds and dry soil allowed unhusked grain to be stored for a long time without spoiling. Therefore Zhili's granaries need not adhere strictly to the guidelines; they did not necessarily need to sell off 30 percent each year, nor did they need to store 70 percent. The selling of grain at reduced prices needed to take place only when the market price was high.[53] In deliberations among the governors-general about *pingtiao* guidelines, he repeatedly emphasized the principle that reduced-price sales should never result in a net loss for the granary system, that is, sales should not take place until the market price was so high that the reduced price would not be lower than the price at which the grain was originally purchased. In Zhili, he wrote, the price of grain within the province varied a great deal, and the original buying price also varied. So it was important to follow the market price (*shijia*) and not just the (government-set) seasonal price (*shijia*).[54] Fang also emphasized the need to adapt the general granary guidelines to the agricultural patterns of Zhili. He stressed flexibility or fungibility in the types of grain to be bought, lent, or sold and returned to the granary. In 1762, for example, he recommended that borrowers of unhusked millet be allowed to repay their loans with wheat at the rate of 6 dou of wheat for one shi of unhusked millet. In the fall, the peasants could return unhusked millet and borrow wheat. This particularly made sense because at that time, the fifth month, there was a bumper harvest of wheat, but the previous autumn there had been a poor harvest of other grains.[55]

Nasutu and Fang Guancheng's strong views on local restocking seemed to derive from a genuine concern with the negative local effects of the restocking process and may also have reflected a protectionist posture, defending Zhili's interests against those of other provinces. Another persistent concern was that the annual restocking process would be conducted in a coercive manner, with functionaries forcing a low price on the peasants. Yinjishan, Liangjiang governor-general, memorialized in 1764 against the evil of short prices (*duanjia*):

> Ever-normal granaries in all provinces are supposed to sell [*pingtiao*] in the spring and restock in the fall (30 percent) to avoid rotting. In each xian and zhou when the fall purchase is made, it is supposed to be at the government-set seasonal price. *But sometimes the functionaries force a short price onto the peasants and cause them to suffer.* When I was governor of Jiangnan and Jiangxi this often happened, and so we ordered the price to be publicized widely so the functionaries could not cheat.[56]

He also proposed flexibility in other procedures. The 70/30 rule should be relaxed; in some lean years, it might not be necessary to purchase as much as 30 percent. If the set price of 1.20 taels was too low, the local officials should apply for additional funds from the provincial treasury. "If each province has 1.5–1.6 million shi in storage, it will need to buy 400–500,000 shi (which will definitely affect the price), so the rules should be flexible."[57]

In Zhili, restocking was always done through market purchases (*caimai*) and not through "allotted purchase" (*paimai*), as was the practice in some other provinces, which often forced below-market prices on local farmers.[58] Still there were instances of coercive practice. In 1773 Governor-general Zhou Yuanli reported a case of suicide that resulted from such coercion. In Laishui County the magistrate needed 1,000 shi of *gu* to replenish his granary stocks and deputed two granary functionaries, Wu and Wang, to go to the periodic market to purchase that amount. There they happened upon a Yang Shichen, who was selling grain. (He is described as nominally or falsely calling himself an attendant on the district inspector of schools, *guaming mendou.*) Wu and Wang asked him whether he had any grain stored at home. He replied that they still had 20–30 shi that they were willing to sell. Wu and Wang reported this to the county yamen and ordered Yang to take his grain there. Wu then paid him 0.70 taels per shi for 20 shi, for a total of 14 taels. When Yang returned home to tell his father what had happened, his father, who was ill at the time, got angry and said that he had not intended to sell all the grain at once and demanded that his son return to the yamen to get it back. Yang went back to town but was not able to get his grain back; in desperation he took some poison and died. Subsequently, the magistrate and other local officials were dismissed, and an investigation of granary accounts was ordered. In commenting on this case, the governor-general stated that the precedents for granary stocking forbade allotted purchases, and that the magistrate should not have allowed this to happen; when the functionaries went to the market, they should have offered the market price.[59]

In 1779, Zhou Yuanli reported a case of local resistance against the forced purchase of grain. In Jingxing xian, the local magistrate had authorized the restocking of granaries through market purchase of 3,000 shi of *gu* at the price of 9 qian and 3 fen (0.93 taels). Since payment was to be made in cash, the magistrate converted silver into cash, but only at the rate of 600 cash (6 qian) per tael. If the common people did not question it, the functionaries did not give them the additional 3 qian and 3 fen due to them. Later when a case was brought to the magistrate, he ordered the functionaries to compensate twenty-eight hamlets (*zhuang*) with the additional cash owed. But leaders of four other hamlets declined to go to the yamen to get their money, and instead sent representatives to the prefectural city to make a charge against the magistrate. The magistrate was unable to refute the charges against him.[60]

As early as 1738, the Qianlong emperor had authorized the purchase of grains from other provinces as an alternative to local restocking.[61] Thereafter special purchases were made by the government from southern and western provinces, particularly for relief in Beijing and Zhili.[62] In fact, as already seen, grain shipments from Shandong and Henan also played a role in relieving price rises in Beijing. In 1742 the emperor reaffirmed the right of buyers' access to markets in other regions, ruling against provincial protectionism.[63] For Zhili this encouraged the increasing dependency on Shandong, Henan, and especially Fengtian for special purchases. It had become the practice to purchase 100,000 shi per year from Fengtian—50,000 for *pingtiao* in Beijing and 50,000 to be stored in counties along the rivers. The retention or diversion of grain tribute for use in Zhili, as well as the increasing practice of deploying grain from Fengtian for relief in Beijing and Zhili, was questioned by some grain tribute officials.

In 1775, however, responding to an edict ordering discussion, Zhou Yuanli favored the continuation of local purchases. He stated flatly that in years of high grain prices, such as 1743–44, 1751, and 1762, deputies had been sent to Fengtian to purchase grain, which was shipped by sea to Tianjin and used in *pingtiao* and loans. But usually, it was still easy to make purchases within the province. Grain shipped by sea was already salty and damp when it arrived and thus did not store well. The Board of Revenue's rate for *caimai* was 7 qian (per shi), but in recent years Fengtian's grain prices had risen, and the cost of transport had to be considered as well. He recommended that the counties that needed grain after the fall harvest should try to restock at the board's rate and look to Fengtian only if necessary; they should not exceed price limits of the board.[64] In a separate memorial later that year, however, Zhou Yuanli acknowledged the need to consider shipments from Henan in particularly bad years.[65]

Despite the theoretical commitment to local purchases, the relatively easy availability of Fengtian grain proved an irresistible temptation. In 1780, Governor-general Yuan Shoutong stated plainly, "In Zhili, after the fall harvest, sometimes the price is too high, and it is not convenient to restock." The alternatives of purchasing from other provinces, especially Fengtian, or diverting grain tribute could be employed.[66] The total amounts transported from Fengtian in the late Qianlong and Jiaqing periods reached substantial proportions and proved invaluable to maintaining all the functions of the granary system in Zhili.

Ever-Normal Granaries in Jiaqing and Daoguang Periods

At the outset of his reign, the Jiaqing emperor was aware of the abuses of restocking or government purchase by functionaries. He knew that government purchases caused the price to rise and hurt the "little people," and he ordered the governors to make sure that the local officials did not take advantage of the people under their jurisdiction.[67] On the death of his father in 1799, the emperor reaffirmed the importance of maintaining the state granary system. He said that many provinces had not even restocked 20–30 percent of their quotas when it came to the fall harvest; either the local officials were afraid to harm the people with their purchases, or else their funds were insufficient for the purchases. But the emperor said that the point of granaries was to help the people. If money were stocked instead of grain, as some advocated, it would only cause the price to rise higher.[68] He ordered governors to go to neighboring localities that had good harvests to purchase grain for restocking at the government-set price. They were not allowed to *paimai* in their own localities.[69]

But for Zhili, the general directive to make purchases in neighboring regions still met objections. In 1800, Governor-general Hu Jitang memorialized, "In Zhili, most of the zhou and xian are not on water routes. The cost of transporting the grain 10–100 li sometimes exceeds the purchase price of the grain. . . . Furthermore, Chengde and Xuanhua are beyond the Great Wall [*kou*] and have no neighboring localities. And the transport from there is especially difficult. Therefore I request that in the future we purchase grain locally."[70] The emperor approved this exception: "What Hu Jitang says is correct. If such transport abuses arise, the policy designed to keep the people will end up burdening them still more. From now on, the provinces not on water routes will be exempt from the policy of purchasing from neighboring districts and will be allowed to purchase grain locally."[71] Comparing the arguments in this discussion with those raised by Nasutu and Fang Guancheng half a century earlier, one can see how the context had changed. In 1749–50, they had argued that no increase in reserves was needed in almost all of Zhili's districts because of the *ease* of water transport; in 1800, Hu Jitang argued that it would be costly to import grain because of the *difficulty* of water transport. What had changed was the deterioration of the water routes in Zhili, as well as the contraction of the state's fiscal means.[72]

During the Jiaqing and Daoguang periods, the ever-normal granaries became increasingly difficult to replenish by any means, and their stocks dwindled dramatically. Any attempt to restock caused market prices to rise—thereby creating a problem rather than solving it. In the aftermath of the great flood of 1801, the granaries had become depleted. Of the quota of about 2.2 million shi, there was a shortfall of about 900,000 shi reported. Although the next year's harvest was bountiful and prices fell, the provincial officials were afraid to restock too quickly since some areas had not completely recovered, and they were afraid to cause difficulty by trying to restock. The target was set at 300,000 shi.[73] In 1806, there was a proposal for a temporary slowdown of *caimai* all over the empire; some urged that the practice should be halted so that the functionaries would be denied the opportunity to extort money from the people. *Caimai* should definitely not be practiced in the several provinces where had been a series of lean years. According to an edict, however, in Zhili there had been good harvests since the 1801 flood, so *caimai* would be a good idea.[74] But the next year, 1807, Wen Chenghui, acting governor-general, nevertheless requested another temporary slowdown of purchases: "My predecessor Yanjian memorialized in Jiaqing 7 [1802] that he was ordering *caimai* of 300,000 shi to fill up the deficiencies in Zhili's *changpingcang*. . . . I tried to follow this, but this year there was a poor wheat harvest, so official purchases would only hurt the people's livelihood. In any case, outside merchants are not coming here and prices are high. So we ask a slowdown of purchases. 150,000 shi have already been purchased, the remaining 140,000 can wait."[75]

In 1815, however, Nayancheng, the next governor-general, proposed a renewed effort to restock the ever-normal granaries after an excellent harvest.

> The *changpingcang* in Zhili are supposed to stock a quota of 2,218,300 shi. Because of repeated droughts and floods, the emperor has repeatedly forgiven the debts owed to granaries. In Jiaqing 7, Yanjian proposed replenishing the granaries by a purchase of 300,000 shi, and deputed personnel to purchase 15,000 [150,000?], but Wen Chenghui requested postponement of the other 14,000 [140,000] because of bad harvests. This year, however, except for a few swamps [*wa*] that have not yet dried out, Zhili has had the best harvest in more than ten years. . . . We propose purchases. If some places have more sorghum, buy sorghum, millet, and all grains together and find the right conversion rate.[76]

False reporting and various other types of abuses had been a well-known and seemingly unavoidable aspect of the state granary system from the early part of the dynasty. At the beginning of the Yongzheng reign, there had been a great shakedown of the Zhili granaries. It came to light that in forty-two of Zhili's counties, the granaries had deficits (*kuikong*). The emperor not only ordered a thorough investigation but also was brutally frank about the ultimate causes of the widespread corruption, sparing few his wrath and scorn. In scathing edicts, the emperor had said that Zhili's granaries had been empty and in disrepair for a long time, and that officials had covered up numerous malfeasances and had misappropriated grain for their own profit. The former governor-general, Li Weijun, had been inattentive to this problem, and the new governor-general, Li Fu, was authorized to investigate the entire matter. But Zhili was a complicated place; the edict described a volatile social situation. There were bannermen and families all over, cunning clerks tampered with documents (*huali wuwen*), eunuchs and their families and hangers-on abounded; amidst all were the imperial estates and the estates of various princes and nobles—all of whom could run circles around the somewhat hapless local officials. When a new local magistrate arrived on the job, the secretaries and clerks concealed all the records from him. Since the interests of the various princely estates extended into the Imperial Household Department, his authority was necessarily limited.[77]

In general, the regulations and precedents of the Board of Revenue concerning granaries openly acknowledged that there were three persistent granary abuses: first, "crafty merchants" hoarded grain for themselves; second, people were coerced into selling grain at low prices; and third, rich families took advantage of the cheap grain.[78] The first was a grave concern for the metropolitan granaries, and the second issue was a continual concern in Zhili in the eighteenth century. Yet, for the most part, corruption had been kept in check through the vigilance of the emperor and his top officials. From the late eighteenth century, however, corruption became far more pervasive and difficult to control. Lack of stocks and corruption were mutually reinforcing. Sometimes deficiency in stocks could be linked to mismanagement, but as grain scarcity became more of a general problem in the nineteenth century, it made cheating even more tempting. Coercive practices continued to be a problem. Adulteration of grain supplies was another persistent problem. Often the Beijing grain supply was adulterated. It was reported that "people pick over the grain, a practice that should be forbidden."[79]

False reporting was the most troublesome issue for the court. There are numerous suggestions in the records, such as the 1815 case described above, that granary reports and accounts for the nineteenth century were not necessarily to be trusted. In another case, in 1792, when the Zhili governor-general reported that granaries in Zhili's southern part, which had a meager harvest, were in fact virtually empty, the Qianlong emperor responded that this showed that the (previously) reported amounts were only a fiction. This was due to the malpractice of local functionaries, who extorted grain from the people and sold it, he said.[80] The emperor used this case as an opportunity to berate the governors and governors-general all over the empire for their failure to investigate abuses and prevent false reports.[81] Although reports from Zhili were presumably subject to more bureaucratic scrutiny and thus more accurate, this did not appear to be the case in the late Qianlong and Jiaqing periods. Xiong Mei, a key figure in the 1801–2 flood relief campaign, found extreme laxness in the Zhili financial reporting. He reported that "the magistrates in Zhili are among the most remiss in the empire," and that this situation had been the case "for several decades."[82]

During the Daoguang period, falsification may have been the rule rather than the exception. In many provinces restocking simply was not done. "Sometimes the officials falsely report that granaries are full when they are not. Sometimes they take funds but do not purchase the grain. When it comes to a flood, the unworthy officials falsely report certain districts are flooded. So in the case of partial disaster [*pianzai*], the officials use their treasury silver, convert it to cash, and give it out as relief."[83] Two years later, in 1833, Zhili reported a total actual inventory of 616,037 shi, including 275,719 shi in the ever-normal granaries, 13,874 shi in the community granaries, and 326,383 shi in the charity granaries.[84] However, Qishan, who served as Zhili governor-general from 1831 to 1840, just before his involvement in Anglo-Chinese negotiations during the Opium War, commented that in the previous year, an investigation had been conducted because Zhili's granaries were supposedly depleted. The current report, he said, might not be accurate either, and further investigations would be made. Zhili, he said, had meager harvests for years, and the price had never really fallen.[85]

Later the same year Qishan and others responded to the investigatory report that recommended postponing the restocking of Shuntian prefecture granaries even though they had been found to be almost empty. This interesting and complex memorial revealed the dilemmas facing the granaries. First was the hardship imposed on peasants.

> The fall harvest was plentiful, and we ought to be able to stock the granaries, but in fact *caimai* hurts the peasants. At the government-set price [*shijia*], the large counties would be able to purchase 6,000 shi, the medium-sized counties 5,000 shi, and the small counties 4,000 shi. With 24 counties in Shuntian, more than 100,000 shi would need to be purchased. The price of millet in Shuntian prefecture in the tenth month ranges from 1.60 to 2.83 taels per shi. With the ratio of *yimi ergu*—one unit of *mi* equals two units of *gu*—each shi of *gu* would cost 0.80 taels, but the *lijia* or regulation price is only 0.70. Besides this grain is damp and will not store well. To obtain dry *gu*, you would need no less than 1.30–1.40 per shi.

Second, there was the problem of abusive practices.

> There is also the problem of the innumerable cases of abuses by functionaries in burdening communities [by coercing purchases]. Furthermore, Shuntian Prefecture does not produce a lot of grain, and the people are not likely to have a surplus to sell. If you order all the district magistrates to purchase grain at the same time, the merchants will take advantage, and the prices will rise. The benefits will accrue to the wealthy, and the people's food will become more expensive than if no restocking had been done.

Then there was the problem of transport costs.

> If you order purchases to be made in other parts of the province where the price is stable, there is the problem of transport since right now the rivers are frozen up and the cost of land transport is high. We have repeatedly discussed this matter with merchants, but at the moment purchases will be difficult.

He concluded, "Let's wait until after next year's summer and fall harvests, when hopefully the quantity on the market will be sufficient for the regulation price, and *the people's food supply* [*min-shi*] *and grain storage* [*cangchu*] *will both benefit.*" In effect he stated what had been obvious for over a century, that grain storage was often in conflict with the interests of the peasants.[86]

Despite the overwhelming evidence that the ever-normal granary system no longer functioned at the same level as before, the official policy throughout the Daoguang and Tongzhi reigns was to maintain the granaries and to continue restocking. In 1864, the Tongzhi emperor issued an edict reaffirming the commitment to grain storage. "Of all the essential functions of government, the first is sufficiency of food," he declared. Because of the recent military disturbances [the Taiping and other rebellions], bandits abounded, and the granaries had been pillaged and were all destroyed. He enjoined the governors and governors-general to take seriously the rebuilding and restocking of the granaries.[87]

In reflecting on the history of granaries in Daming Prefecture, its local history noted that the ancient principle of price stabilization was wise. "When the price of grain is low you can buy it an elevated price to help the farmer [*linong*]. When the grain is expensive, you can lower the price and sell it to benefit the people [*limin*]." Yet, the authors saw that granaries had engendered abuses that outweighed their benefits.

> Our dynasty inherited these methods, and for over two hundred years [the people] have received the imperial largesse, and have not needed to worry about natural disasters turning into famine and destruction. The dynasty has generously provided funds to relieve famines, support the people's livelihood, store grain, and so forth. However, what is worrisome is that those who have authority are not virtuous—whether it be misappropriating funds for military use, lining the pockets of officials and functionaries, . . . or other evil practices. . . . This is turning what were originally good policies into tyrannical government.[88]

Community and Charity Granaries

Community and charity granaries seemed so attractive to Qing officials for the same reasons they had appealed to Song statesmen. In principle, not only would they relieve the state of the fiscal and bureaucratic burden of maintaining reserves and restocking, but they might also avoid the seemingly inevitable problems of corruption and mismanagement whenever large amounts of public funds were involved. The leadership of a moral, energetic, and, most of all, generous local elite was essential to the ideal social order. Such a "moral economy" would also benefit and embrace the common people. Among the important eighteenth-century statesmen-thinkers, Chen Hongmou was a particularly strong proponent of community granaries. In Zhili Province, Fang Guancheng was a great promoter of the charity granary, but his charity granaries functioned much like community granaries, being located in the countryside rather than in the county cities.[89]

FANG GUANCHENG'S CHARITY GRANARIES IN THE QIANLONG PERIOD

The big push for charity granaries occurred in the mid-eighteenth century, when the ever-normal granaries were at their height. The *yicang* were seen not as a substitute for the *changpingcang*, but as an important complement to the state granary system. In response to the imperial edict of 1746 ordering that charity granaries be established, Fang Guancheng, then governor-general, presented in 1753 a comprehensive plan, together with maps, for establishing a network of charity granaries in Zhili. His purpose was to extend the granary system to rural areas away from the xian cities so that people would have easy access to grain. As Nasutu had said, 70 to 80 percent of the community granaries in Zhili were located near the ever-normal granaries in the cities instead of the countryside where they were supposed to be.[90] The charity granaries would be managed by local leaders, free of interference from government clerks. This would most benefit the people. This was a concept having ancient roots. As Fang pointed out, this particular concept of *yicang* was the same as Zhu Xi's notion of *shecang*. "Zhu Xi advocated it. He called it *shecang*, but actually it is similar to *yicang*." Contributions of more than 285,300 shi of *gu* had already been made.[91]

According to this plan, which was based on guidelines worked out by Nasutu, the former Zhili governor-general, in 1747, charity granaries were to be set up in market towns (*jizhen*) and large villages (*cun*). Awards of various titles or ranks should be made to contributors, the local gentry, depending on the size of their contribution. If they gave 10 shi or more, they would receive an award (*huahong*); more than 30 shi, an inscribed plaque (*bian'e*); more than 50 shi, an additional reward mentioned in the official report, and so forth. Their names would be recorded in a book. If the harvest was below a 6 rating, no contribution would be expected. Nasutu had emphasized that local elites should be given other incentives as well. The previous year had seen a bumper crop; in such times, he said, the bannermen and people would gladly contribute charity grain. And the emperor had completely forgiven the regular tax. He suggested that in every year after a bountiful harvest, officials step up their efforts to solicit contributions.[92]

"An upright local person" should be chosen as manager for each granary having at least 500 shi of *gu*. If there were more than 1,000 shi, then a second manager should be appointed. They should be excused from corvée, and so forth.[93] They were not to be degree-holders, and they were to report directly to the local magistrate, bypassing the functionaries, who were not permitted to go to the granaries, according to some local regulations. In the first month of each year they would be invited to the yamen to be rewarded with wine and food. If they served faithfully and honestly for a three-year rotation, they would be given awards by the local magistrate; after six years an award would be given by the prefectural treasurer.[94]

Loans were to be made on a seasonal basis. Every year at the last third of the third month, at the *qinghuang bujie* lean season, half the holdings were to be distributed. Each household could borrow up to 2 shi of unhusked millet or mixed grains. Those who had already borrowed from other granaries were not allowed to borrow. Those who were unemployed were not allowed to borrow. Also those villages without contributing households were not allowed to borrow. The grain was to be returned after the tenth-month harvest. If the harvest was above 8, the interest rate was 10 percent. If the harvest was 6 or 7, no interest was charged except a surcharge of 3 he of wastage grain (*haogu*) per dou. If the harvest was 5 or below, repayment of the loan could be postponed until the next year.[95]

According to Nasutu's plan, Zhili's 144 counties, containing 39,687 villages, were to have 1,005 granaries. Each granary would service an area from 15 li to 40 li distant, the latter being quite exceptional, so that it would be accessible to people. Most counties had granaries within 20 li of each village.[96] In Tianjin County, for example, there were 299 villages, with one granary every 20 li. Ten were listed in the 1898 edition of the prefectural gazetteer.[97] *Jifu tongzhi*, the provincial gazetteer, presents a comprehensive list of granaries by county, undoubtedly compiled from local gazetteers, but their dates of operation, amounts stored, and other details are rarely given.[98] Local gazetteers that include a section on granaries tend to follow a certain format. There is frequent reference to the preparedness granaries of the Ming. This may or may not be followed by some mention of an ever-normal granary, sometimes indicating the year of construction, and the official who was in charge. Pingxiang County left the following record: "*Changpingcang*: the quota is 14,000 shi. The old granary was outside the Yimen Gate of the xian yamen and has long been defunct. In Kangxi 45 the magistrate Liang Shijin constructed another one inside the Small Eastern Gate, with twenty buildings [*ao*]. In Yongzheng 12 the magistrate Li Shixian added seven buildings on the north. In Qianlong 4, twelve more buildings were added on the south. In Daoguang 30 the magistrate Kong Qinggui again repaired it."[99] Entries concerning ever-normal granaries often end with the phrase *yifei* or *jiufei* ("already defunct" or "long defunct").

Community granaries are seldom mentioned, which contributes to the suspicion that community granaries were not actually a separate system, but rather were treated as part of the ever-normal granary system. Charity granaries received the most attention in gazetteers, which almost always mentioned the initiative of Governor-general Fang Guancheng—often quoting at length the regulations from his *Jifu yicang tu*, or even reprinting its text.[100] *Yicang* were also the embodiment of a sense of community or local pride, highlighting local initiatives.[101] Quite often that section would also close with the note that these granaries had long ceased to operate. Frequently the phrase "*youming wushi*" ("in name, but not in reality") appears after a list.

It is difficult to evaluate the accuracy of the reports of total charity granary holdings even for the second half of the eighteenth century, when the record is purportedly complete, and when reserves were the highest. As seen in Table 6.1, the total reported reserves for charity granaries rose from about 200,000 shi in 1749 to between 500–600,000 shi between 1765 and 1790. In this same period, disbursals from charity granaries represented about 15–20 percent of the annual totals disbursed from all granaries in Zhili.[102] Although *yicang* activity is regularly mentioned in the records of famine relief during the Qianlong period and even later, the total volume of reserves cannot be verified. Almost certainly, if the charity granaries did hold reserves to the extent reported, they were probably subsidized by the state, and private contributions were unlikely to have been their sole origin. Scattered records show that new contributions each year were not large; at about 46,000 shi at the beginning of Fang's campaign, they dwindled over the next few decades down to about 2,000 shi a year, which certainly suggests that charity granaries could not have depended solely on charitable contributions.[103]

REVIVAL IN THE JIAQING AND DAOGUANG PERIODS

The charity granary became the focus of granary reforms in Zhili on a few occasions in the nineteenth century. As the ever-normal granaries could no longer be well supported by the central government, provincial governors-general looked again to local resources not as a supplement, but as an alternative. Two attempts to revive the charity granaries were made by Governor-general Nayancheng. In 1815, he memorialized the throne for permission to revive the charity granary system (in addition to advocating restocking the ever-normal granaries).[104] "Zhili originally had a *yicang* system, but in recent years *yicang* have not stored much grain, and I hear they are really defunct. At Shahe County, they have been rebuilt. There are also other places, but I observe that, although the *yicang* was basically a good idea, its implementation resulted in graft, and the like, or else no one would contribute. Now we are trying to revive it again." To address the needs of the drought in Daming Prefecture, he proposed repairing the old granaries and setting a target of 207,000 shi. Later he claimed 210,000 shi had been accumulated within a year. Nayancheng said that a considerable amount of the grain stocks was used to open soup kitchens for the famine refugees, and the result had been very good.[105]

In 1826, he again sought to revive the charity granaries, based on the Fang Guancheng model and the 1815 experience. The ever-normal granaries in Zhili's 147 zhou and xian, he wrote, had depleted their reserves because of a succession of disasters in the region, and replenishments could not be purchased in time to address emergencies. The community granaries, based on people's contributions and for their direct use, were few in number and not well stocked. Instead provincial officials were forced to ask for grain tribute diversions or shipments of millet from Fengtian, but this was a drain on the imperial treasury and too slow for emergency use. Thus, he concluded the ideal solution would be to solicit grain from within the province in bumper harvest years and to locate the granaries in the rural areas for the convenience of the people. The 1753 model of Fang Guancheng's charity granary—1,005 granaries storing 285,000 shi—should be revived. Only 164,000 shi remained in the granaries the previous year, and the buildings were all leaky and decayed after several rainy years. He said that there had been an excellent fall harvest the current year, and gentry, merchants, and ordinary people had contributed generously, from 300 up to 800 shi each. Although the totals were not yet in, he estimated that 200,000 shi had been collected, enough to address a flood or drought crisis. It had taken Fang Guancheng, he said, eight years to reach his target of 285,000 shi, but in 1815, 210,000 shi had been stocked within a year, and now he hoped another 200,000 shi could be accumulated by the end of the year for a total of 400,000 shi.[106]

The following year Nayancheng reported in detail about the results: 29,720 shi of unhusked millet had been contributed by officials; 218,100 shi had been contributed by gentry, merchants, and other people. In addition several thousands of taels had been contributed to fix up the granaries. Together with the inventories carried over from the previous years, amounting to 247,824 shi, there was a grand total of 418,910 shi stored in the charity granaries. Again he boasted that it had taken eight years for Fang Guancheng to meet his target, but in 1815, and now twelve years later, 1827, it had taken less than a year to meet the same target. The purpose of his memorial was to request rewards and ranks for those individuals in all the counties for their contributions. In making such awards, he felt sure that even more contributors would be encouraged to come forth. The emperor granted all the requests.[107]

The veracity of statistics reported in this period cannot be assumed. In 1833, Qishan had questioned the reports that had been submitted.[108] The figures given here by Nayancheng showing over 400,000 shi theoretically stored in *yicang* are in line with the full granary account of 1833, cited earlier, which said that there were over 300,000 shi in the *yicang*, more than the total figure for the *changpingcang*.[109] In any case, the charity granaries represented the only hope for the granary system in the Daoguang period, and official efforts were centered on trying to sustain them.

Although these fulsome official reports may not have been accurate, local gazetteers do provide evidence that at least some localities did respond to this call for voluntary efforts, "persuaded" by local officials. In Rongcheng County, for example, a charity granary was established in 1815, which operated for ten years or more with local contributions amounting to 100,000 shi; the names of contributors were posted on a plaque outside the granary. The granary was run by local gentry (*shenshi*), not by functionaries (*xuli*). "Although the district is small, everyone is virtuous."[110] At Xingtai County in the Jiaqing period, a granary of four buildings and eight chambers was set up within the city's temple. In 1825, the officials, gentry, and people were again ordered to make contributions. More buildings and rooms were added. Sixty-four hundred shi of unhusked millet was stored, with additional amounts in various villages. Money was given to merchants to earn interest.[111] Huailu County also experienced a revival of charity granaries in the Daoguang and Tongzhi periods. Sometimes money was entrusted to merchants, and the interest from the loan was used for the granary.[112] At Gu'an County in 1825 a local degree-holder persuaded the upright gentry and people to contribute unhusked millet to the charity granary, following the suggestion of the governor-general, Nayancheng. In 1853, the magistrate followed this example.[113]

Other gazetteer records show continued efforts by private individuals to raise funds or grain, but the scale tended to be modest.[114] Still, as late as 1834, a request by the Board of Revenue to use charity grain in the Zhili drought was granted, suggesting that there were still sufficient reserves to be useful. To counteract the possible, or likely, chicanery of functionaries, it was suggested that "those places using charity grain should have it posted in yellow so everyone will know and the functionaries will not cheat."[115]

GUANGXU-ERA REVIVAL

During the Guangxu period, there was another significant revival of interest in charitable granaries, particularly after the great 1870s drought famine. Around 1879 Li Hongzhang ordered local officials to enlist the help of local gentry and merchants in a revival of *yicang*. Gentry leaders were urged to contribute grain and also to be managers of the granaries (*shendong*), and merchants were sometimes entrusted with funds to invest, with interest to accrue to granary operations. Local officials did respond to this order, and gazetteers provide ample evidence of this effort to promote local activism.[116] In Ding xian, previously Dingzhou, the quota of 10,000 shi was met by contributions from the gentry and people. North and south granaries were set up within the county city. The 6,000 shi contributed from the rural districts were stored there.[117] Some counties responded with an unusual degree of activism in reviving charity granaries in the countryside, especially with interest from funds given to merchants for investment.[118] In Tongzhou in 1879 the magistrate donated funds of 6,000 taels, from which 5,400 taels were distributed to merchants and 600 taels to salt merchants, minus fee, and he also contributed 3,800 shi of gu to distribute among various temples and homes in the district. In 1883 another magistrate built a new granary at the site of the old *changpingcang*.[119]

Noteworthy is the fact that in many localities there were no facilities for storing the grain that had been contributed. So the grain was stored in various places, or turned over to gentry leaders to store.[120] At Dong'an, in 1881 the magistrate solicited contributions totaling 2,000 shi of unhusked millet and distributed it for storage in thirteen places; three were charity granaries and the other ten were in homes, shops, or temples. The charity granary storage was managed by the granary manager and assistant, but the other ten places were all managed by gentry managers.[121] In most counties, however, the Guangxu effort had no lasting effect. In Yuanshi County, all granaries of any type were defunct by the Guangxu period. The few remaining buildings were relegated to the county government.[122] In Xinhe County, there had previously been six charity granaries outside the city, but all had been long defunct by the Daoguang period, except one that was repaired in the early Guangxu period.[123]

The following succinct history of granaries in Xiong County epitomizes the experience of the entire province:

> The *yubeicang* and old *changpingcang* in this county from the early Ming and early Qing are already defunct. Otherwise there are *shecang* and *yicang*. *Shecang* were started in YZ 12 [1734]. The principle was to persuade people to contribute grain. A *shezhang* [granary head] and assistants were publicly selected, but supervised by officials. *Yicang* were more or less the same as *shecang* but based on voluntary contributions of gentry and people, with an elected granary manager and assistant, who were occasionally investigated by the local official. The accounts of the *changpingcang* and *shecang* both had to be reported to the throne [*zouxiao*], but the *yicang* could avoid this. The *changping* and *shecang* were mostly in the xian city. *Yicang* were scattered around the rural districts. In Xiong, after the official granaries declined, granary grain was divided and stored at the Wenchang pavilion and Jiexiao temple. *Yicang* were reestablished in QL 38 [1773] after Zhili governor-general Fang Guancheng's memorial, with four districts, each having one granary. . . . In DG 10 [1831], the magistrate Peng made a record on the plaque on each cang. . . . The four districts gathered 1,660 shi. After Tongzhi period, there was no longer any grain stored. In GX18 [1892], the magistrate Wang established a *yicang* at the county seat, but it did not succeed in gathering any grain and was disbanded. In GX 24 [1898], the magistrate Hu again urged the contribution of *gu* in the four districts, each of about a thousand shi. After the year of the Boxer disturbance [1900], this grain was quickly used up, and the granaries fell into disuse. Only the granary within the xian city still had grain in storage.[124]

Although it was not true that granaries were all defunct in nineteenth century, it was certainly the case that few survived. The Shuntian prefectural gazetteer of 1885 said that of the granaries established in the previous hundred years, only two or three out of ten *yicang* remained. *Changpingcang* and other granaries had fallen into decay. Conceding the limitations of local resources and initiatives, the essay conceded that the revival of granaries should be the responsibility of virtuous officials.[125]

A greater degree of local activism was seen in the Guangxu period than in previous decades and possibly a greater involvement of merchants as well as traditional local elites. However, in every case it was the local magistrate who took the initiative, based on directives from the province or the central government, to solicit contributions of grain. The objectives for encouraging charity granaries were not realized either in terms of significantly expanding grain reserves, or in terms of shifting the burden to local society. The semiprivate granaries flourished best when the ever-normal granaries also flourished, in the late eighteenth century, rather than after the latter's demise. And even though they gave "lip service to the ideal of decentralization and community (as opposed to bureaucratic) control, a fair degree of official supervision was felt to be indispensable to prevent abuses from mushrooming."[126] In Zhili, the weakness of semiprivate granaries had less to do with poor local management than the scarcity of well-endowed local elites. As in the case of river management, the state was by necessity in a stronger position than local society.

External Grain Supplies

Zhili's limited agricultural resources could largely account for its disappointing experience with local granaries, but fortunately in the eighteenth century, and in part of the nineteenth, the metropolitan province could also draw upon the abundant external resources of the grain tribute system, as well as official and commercial purchases of grain from the nearby provinces of Shandong, Hebei, and Fengtian.

TRANSFERS FROM GRAIN TRIBUTE

The reserves of the metropolitan granaries were tremendously advantageous for stocking the ever-normal granaries in Zhili during periods of local dearth. Substantial transfers were easily and frequently made from the grain tribute system to the Zhili granary system, either from reserves already in the Tongzhou granaries, or by "diversions" (*jieliu*) from grain in transit from the south. During crisis years, the court drew freely upon tribute reserves. For example, in 1717, the Kangxi emperor allowed a transfer of 200,000 shi of grain from Tongzhou to Zhili's local granaries—prefectural, county, and district—because of bad harvests due to floods of the previous fall, citing the target that "ideally every fu should have 10,000 shi, and every zhou and xian several thousands."[127] In the 1743–44 famine relief, 1.4 million shi were commandeered from various sources for ten grain distributions within Zhili. About 53 percent of this came from regular tribute grain from the south, 21 percent from Henan and Shandong, and 12 percent from Fengtian.[128] In 1745, 300,000 shi were diverted from grain tribute, 50,000 shi from Tongzhou, and 200,000 shipped from Shandong and Henan.[129] In other crises, grain tribute was diverted or retained for use in Zhili, sometimes in very substantial quantities and sometimes in moderate quantities. One source stated that between 1753 and 1762 more than 5.4 million shi of tribute grain had been "retained" for aiding the people (all over the empire), and in Beijing alone, 460,000 shi had been used for *pingtiao*.[130] Another source recorded that for Zhili alone 150,000 shi had been diverted in 1763, 200,000 in 1764, 600,000 in 1765, and 1.3 million in 1766.[131]

However, during his tenure as governor-general, Fang Guancheng sometimes met resistance to transfers from the metropolitan granaries, controlled by the Board of Revenue, to the Bei cang, Northern Granary, in Tianjin, which was under the province's control. Alternatively, he had to argue for allowing tribute grain stored at the Bei cang to be used elsewhere in Zhili. In 1756, he acknowledged, "Tribute grain is not like *changping* or *shecang* grain that can be taken out and used at any time." He argued, however, that the unused portion of 200,000 shi of southern tribute grain that had been diverted and stored at the Bei cang in 1753 be deployed to Yizhou and other areas for immediate use before it spoiled.[132] A few years later, in 1759, Fang proposed retaining 400,000 shi at Tianjin rather than shipping it on to Tongzhou because the water in the Bei River was low and transport would be difficult. The court granted permission, but required Fang and the grain tribute commissioner to report in detail about the security measures for the transfer of the grain supply from grain tribute vessels to the Northern Granary. This seemed to betray its sensitivity about relinquishing control over such a large supply of grain.[133]

In the nineteenth century, grain tribute was frequently used for relief in the major crises of the Jiaqing and Daoguang periods, especially in 1801 and 1823. Grain tribute was still being used in 1867 and later, even though resources were much more limited. Even in the Guangxu period, modest amounts of tribute grain were authorized on several occasions.[134] These substantial diversions from grain tribute were the most conspicuous and tangible way by which the resources intended to support Beijing were important to the entire metropolitan region.

HENAN AND SHANDONG

Diversions of grain tribute often came from Henan and Shandong, but these two provinces frequently served as a direct source of grain for Zhili's ever-normal granaries as well. Although as northern provinces, they suffered some of the same climatic risks in their agriculture as did Zhili, their good and bad years were not necessarily the same as Zhili's, except in the case of a major drought that affected the entire north, such as what occurred in the 1870s. Geographically, they were very much linked with the southern prefectures of Zhili—Daming, Guangping, and Shunde.[135] Grain was transported through internal waterways, such as the Wei River, which were linked to the Grand Canal. During the Qing period Shandong exported 1 to 2 million shi of grain a year to Zhili and Henan, while receiving grain from Jiangnan and regions to the south.[136] In times of dearth, Shandong in turn received assistance from Zhili and Fengtian.

The close links between conditions in Henan and Shandong and food prices in Zhili were well known. In 1709 Governor Zhao Hongxie memorialized that the high prices in Beijing could be attributed to conditions in Henan and Shandong.

> I observe that Zhili's food supply has always been sold by the itinerant merchants from Shandong and Henan. This year Henan's summer was wet and the autumn harvest was slightly reduced. The supply of food was small. Also, after winter set in, there was a lot of rain and the roads were covered with mud, and that made it difficult to get through. Since the ground has now frozen, traffic will be unimpeded. I have heard that whenever official rice [*guanmi*] is distributed, the price of grain drops. I request that your majesty take the rice scheduled for the second month and distribute it now in the twelfth month. Between the guest-rice [*kemi*, that is, commercial rice from external sources] and the official rice, the price should stabilize and lower itself. The millions of people of the capital would receive the imperial benefit.[137]

In 1716, Zhao Hongxie responded to another imperial inquiry.

Your Majesty was concerned about the high price of grain in the Jifu region because of the hoarding by wealthy merchants. So following the precedent of Jiangnan's purchases from Huguang [Hunan and Hubei provinces in central China], I was ordered to report the amounts of grain arriving in Zhili from Henan and Shandong by [internal] water routes each month. Accordingly I have made it known that an imperial edict forbids rich merchants from buying excessive amounts of grain and storing it. I have also noticed that along the way local officials are not allowed to use their names [positions] to intimidate the merchants. According to the circuit intendant Li Weijun, the amount from the two provinces in the sixth month was 110,760 (41,972 from Henan and 68,430 from Shandong). Based on my experience as Tianjin circuit intendant, there was also grain shipped by sea. I am awaiting a report on that.[138]

The emperor continued to question the figures reported by Zhao and to express concern with hoarding by merchants along the way. The next year Zhao tried to clear up the matter.

Your majesty was suspicious that the reason that grain [*mi*] prices are not very stable or low even though last year more than 2 million shi of grain was supposedly shipped by water route from Henan and Shandong was that there were dealers along the way who were hoarding the grain. According to the reports I personally received, last year there were 597,355 shi shipped (332,091 from Shandong by sea, and 264,964 from Henan). But according to the two governors, from the sixth through the twelfth months, 232,739 should have arrived from Henan, and 437,097 from Shandong, for a total of 666,836. The difference of 69,481 is because merchants must have sold some grain en route.[139]

The emperor was not satisfied. "But in reality I have not received any report of 2 million or more shi. Zhili is a populous place, and grain from outside should be easily consumed although every spring the grain price must necessarily rise. I am afraid there are hoarders. I am ordering an investigation so that the rich households can root out this evil."[140]

In the Qianlong period, Henan and Shandong, together with Fengtian became the major source for restocking Zhili's granaries. The figures for 1743–44 have been cited above. In 1759, to take another example, because prices were rather high in the capital area, the emperor ordered the governor of Henan to purchase wheat in regions that had an abundant harvest and ship it to Beijing for *pingtiao*. He asked him to consult with Fang Guancheng about the method of transportation. This shipment of 100,000 shi was in addition to the regular grain tribute which was arriving from the south at about the same time.[141] In 1763, considerable stocks had to be purchased to replenish the granaries depleted because of emergency *pingtiao* in the crisis of the previous year. An edict ordered the purchase of 400,000 shi of *mi* from Fengtian and 200,000 shi each from Henan and Shandong before Zhili's own wheat crop was to be harvested.[142]

BEYOND THE GREAT WALL: FENGTIAN AND MONGOLIA

During the Qing period, Fengtian (Manchuria) rapidly became an agricultural bonanza for the Qing court. In the early Qing, the settlers found the soil so rich that they could grow bumper crops without the application of fertilizer. "Throughout the Ch'ing period the Manchurian frontier was a land of opportunities for those willing to brave the hardships of a pioneer life."[143] By the eighteenth century Fengtian was supplying Zhili at least a million shi of grain a year through official channels. Unlike the grain from Henan and Shandong, Fengtian grain was used mainly to stock the ever-normal granaries, not the metropolitan granaries, and as such it became the mainstay of famine relief grain dispensed in Zhili.

In the Kangxi period, the dependence of Beijing on Fengtian grain was already clear. In 1709, an edict to the grand secretaries noted that the price of grain in the capital was very high: 1 shi of millet cost 1.2 taels, and 1 shi of wheat 1.8 taels. Although Li Guangdi, previously Zhili governor and now a grand secretary, had speculated that the price rise was due to population growth, the emperor noted that many Henan, Shandong, and Zhili peasants had gone to open up new land in the border areas, and the grain supply of the capital was often dependent on cheap and plentiful supplies from beyond the Great Wall, *kouwai*, where sorghum was only 2 qian and millet only 3 qian.[144] In 1725 during a flood period in Zhili, and at other times in the Yongzheng–early Qianlong period, grain shipments from Fengtian were permitted.[145] Sea transport was banned, but the prohibition was suspended on many occasions: once in 1737, and again in 1749 with the limitation of 200 shi per large ship and 100 shi per small boat. By 1762 it seems to have become a regular practice although one document gives the date as 1773.[146] A sum of 1.3 million shi was reported to customs shortly after that data, but the actual total per year was probably higher.[147]

The cost of grain in Fengtian (Manchuria), and at other locations north beyond the Great Wall (present-day Inner Mongolia), was considerably less than in Zhili. The region in Chengde or Rehe, administered partly by the Zhili governor-general after 1778, was an agriculturally productive area and also a collection point for grain from Fengtian. In 1751, Governor-general Fang Guancheng reported to the throne that although the cost of millet at the Siqi Santing District in Bagou at Rehe was slightly higher than in previous years, the market price was still under 8 qian per shi, and even with transport costs, it would be relatively cheap to purchase for *pingtiao* in Zhili. He had received authorization for 80,000 taels to buy grain at Rehe, but because commerce there had been brisk, by the time he received authorization the price had risen as high as 9 qian. Although official purchases of several thousands of shi had already been made, he was concerned that the officials would not be able to purchase the targeted amount. He suggested that half of the 60,000 shi of grain in storage at Bagou's Siqi Santing be delivered to Tongzhou, in addition to the amounts already purchased, for distribution. This would be helpful to the hungry people, he argued, and would be returned in the fall after the harvest. In justifying this demand on the Rehe grain stocks, he pointed out that after every fall harvest beyond Gubei (a pass in the Great Wall in Shuntian Prefecture in Miyun County, northeast of Beijing), the price was only 6 or 7 qian, implying that the Rehe granaries could easily restock next fall.[148]

The Qianlong emperor, like his grandfather, was constantly worried about price manipulations by merchants of such large quantities of grain. In 1752, he asked for reports from the various governors about restocking the granaries. In the previous year considerable treasury funds had been expended on restocking the granaries all over the empire, and as a result, the prices had risen and the people were harmed. The court feared that when the brokers knew there was going to be government purchase, they would raise the price. The imperial edict recommended that if granaries had 30–40 percent in actual holdings, they did not need to purchase more grain that year. There were ample reserves in all the provinces. If the need arose, stocks could be transferred from elsewhere.

In response, Fang Guancheng made a case for the uniquely favorable circumstances for large purchases in Fengtian and Mongolia even though there was no urgent need in the present year.

> I wish to observe that the conditions of other provinces are different. Jiangnan is linked by water to Hankou and Xiangtan. When the merchants get word of this, they raise prices, with bad consequences for the people. But the situation here in the north is different. We buy grain at Bagou from Fengtian and beyond, where the price is between 0.70–0.80 up to 1 tael. *At Bagou they grow mostly millet. In Mongolia and Fengtian, most residents eat gaoliang more than millet.* So even though there is official purchase, the prices won't go up and the people won't suffer. This year there will be

an abundant harvest in most parts of Zhili, probably an 8 or 9 [harvest rating]. So after the fall harvest it should be possible to purchase grain at local markets to restock the granaries while the price is low. *This is completely different from using treasury funds and buying grain from other places, and will not harm the people.* However, in the Bagou region every year after the eleventh month the Mongolian grain price is low. So the Bagou granaries ought to make an estimate and purchase grain to store for the needs of *kounei* [area within the Great Wall].[149]

Later that year, Fang continued to defend the practice of government purchases north of the Great Wall. He wrote:

I have previously memorialized about how Zhili differs from the south and how grain can easily be bought from Fengtian or Bagou. I believe that the practice of *caimai* should not be stopped, because it helps people, but its method should be altered. The governor of the buying province should secretly communicate with the governor of the province supplying grain. The latter in turn should use provincial funds to allow local officials to buy up the grain while the price is still low. When the price rises, they should go to the next place to buy grain. The other province can pay later or report to the Throne. In the past, the rules have been too restrictive. The buying officials have not had the latitude to go where the prices are lowest. *In this way, official purchase can continue without disrupting market forces.*[150]

Despite Fang's enthusiasm for Fengtian purchases, one should remember the reservations expressed in 1775 by Zhou Yuanli of the excessive cost and trouble of shipments from Fengtian by sea. Although transport costs remained an issue, actually Fengtian millet prices remained considerably lower than Zhili millet prices until about 1805, although there was a price spike in about 1784 and another around 1789, which sent Fengtian prices up to the level of Zhili's. (See Figure 7.5 in Chapter 7.) Still, in crises, Fengtian was the place of first resort. In 1801, when Zhili had its megaflood and 106 out of 122 xian needed relief (only those in the north did not), 150,000 shi were ordered from Fengtian, in addition to 150,000 shi already purchased from Shandong in preparation for next spring's relief (*qinghuang bujie*). Fengtian was reported to have had an excellent harvest.[151]

In the Jiaqing and Daoguang periods, large shipments continued to be made, but with more difficulty to the Fengtian population. Fengtian itself was sometimes needy. In 1807 Fengtian itself needed to sponsor *pingtiao*, and bannermen were reported to be experiencing difficulty buying food. In this memorial officials observed that Fengtian's principal crops were millet and sorghum.[152] In 1812 Fengtian experienced hardship, and famine victims fled to Zhili, which offered some relief.[153] In the same year, officials recommended using sorghum, not millet, for relief of the banner population, saying that banner households were accustomed to eating sorghum.[154] In 1822 sorghum and millet shipments from Fengtian were temporarily halted because the prices in Fengtian had been high. "Conditions in Fengtian were not bad last year, but crafty merchants hoarded grain in preparation for sea transport to other provinces, with the result that this spring the price went up. Shipments from Fengtian are made by sea, but when local conditions are poor, the people there will suffer if shipments are made."[155]

Yet even when Fengtian banner populations were experiencing shortages, Zhili continued to receive emergency transfers of grain. For example, in 1810, 157,000 shi was received for relief in nineteen waterlogged districts in central Zhili.[156] And in 1825, a period of great crisis, 200,000 shi of millet was authorized to be purchased from Fengtian province; at the price of 2 taels per shi, this was estimated to cost 400,000 taels.[157] Even in the Tongzhi period, *caimai* was ordered for the relief of drought in Zhili. Officials in Fengtian and Shengjing were ordered to see if millet could be purchased there.[158] In all, the total amounts of grain shipped to Zhili from Fengtian in the late eighteenth and early nineteenth centuries sometimes exceeded 1 million shi a year. A memorial from the Zhili governor-general Wen Chenghui in 1810 stated plainly, "At Tianjin, ships come from Fengtian carrying from *700–800,000 shi up to 1.3–1.4 million of mixed grains* [zaliang] *per year.*"[159]

Conclusion

Until the publication of Pierre-Etienne Will's *Bureaucracy and Famine* and of Will and R. Bin Wong's *Nourish the People*, both Chinese and Western scholars had tended to dismiss or underestimate the Qing state granary system's historical importance. Influenced by the ample evidence of the nonfunctionality of the system in the nineteenth century, scholars like Hsiao Kung-chuan did not see how well the system had functioned during the earlier period, and how extensive the state's claim on grain resources had been.[160] The state granaries did not always meet the intended objectives, and the operation of this massive system created as many dilemmas for policy makers as it solved. Yet, as one of the most ambitious and sustained attempts at state economic intervention in world history prior to the modern era, the Qing granaries deserve far more appreciation, not only of their successes and failures, but also of their more subtle and indirect historical significance.

Above all is the fact that puts everything in perspective: the sheer quantity of grain controlled by the state was immense. In Zhili and Beijing, at their height around 1749–92, the ever-normal granaries themselves held at least theoretical reserves ranging from 2 to 4.5 million shi of unhusked grain, and the total reserves including the community and charity granaries ranged from 3 to 5.4 million. (See Table 6.1.) In most years total recorded reserves were between 3 and 4 million shi. If we add to this figure, the 6–10 million shi of husked grain stored at the tribute granaries at Beijing and Tongzhou in this era, counting the ratio of unhusked to husked grain as 2:1, we can see that the total amount stored in the Zhili region under the state's control *could* have reached the equivalent of 24 million shi of unhusked grain. Even if we count only the amount of grain tribute reaching Beijing annually, about 3.5 million shi of husked grain—instead of the accumulated reserves—the total, conservatively estimated, was still in excess of the equivalent of 10 million shi of unhusked grain.

In addition to these amounts in storage, there were frequent calls for additional purchases of grain from Henan, Shandong, and Fengtian, for emergency use in the capital itself or in the surrounding prefectures. Although these purchases are not recorded in a systematic way, and there is necessarily some overlap with the figures for granary reserves cited above, they should also be included in the consideration of how much grain was under the state's control. The total amounts traded from Henan and Shandong were extensive. For example, as cited above, 600,000 shi a year were traded around 1717. Throughout the eighteenth century, it was not unusual for the court to call for 100,000 or 200,000 shi from Henan and Shandong whenever the need arose. Fengtian trade was in the range of 700,000–1,400,000 shi a year in the early eighteenth century. In addition there were amounts of grain traded from Mongolia at the major passes—Zhangjiakou in the northwest and Gubeikou north of Beijing—as well as Bagou in Rehe. (See Map 7.2 in Chapter 7.) These amounts are more difficult to estimate, and technically Rehe or Chengde was part of Zhili after 1778. Earlier these quantities may have been substantial, but since overland transportation was difficult and expensive, they seem to have declined once Fengtian sea transport became more feasible in the second half of the eighteenth century. If we estimate conservatively that these amounts from outside the grain tribute system totaled at least 2 million shi per year, then the grand total of grain directly under the government's control was in the range of 12 to 26 million shi (unhusked grain or equivalent), probably closer to the lower figure. (Because the latter figure assumes that there were 10 million shi of grain tribute stored in the metropolitan granaries, which was probably an inflated figure; the first figure assumes only 3.5 million shi of husked grain was actively in storage.)

This large quantity of grain was at the state's disposal for use in Beijing or Zhili, available almost at any time, and meant that Zhili, no less than Beijing, was not entirely dependent on the local harvest with its great variability and vulnerability. Indeed, Zhili benefited immensely from Beijing's huge stock. Zhili's total agricultural production in the eighteenth century was probably considerably less than its 1930s output of 100 million shi.[161] But if it had been 100 million, then 12 million shi of reserves would have represented about 10 percent of the total available supply of food within the region. If the reserves were larger, and local output smaller, then the importance of reserves would have been proportionately greater. Even at 10 percent, the economic impact had to be considerable, regardless of the manner by which that supply reached consumers (as stipends, resale of stipends, famine relief, reduced-price sales, and so on). Since the demand for grain was so inelastic, even a small change in supply (whether from harvest or imports) could have a significant impact in lowering the price. Indeed, even if the grain remained in storage without being touched, its presence was a buffer, real and psychological, against panic and price shocks.

This proportion of external grain supply would have had an economic impact no matter what, but the direct control of the state over these supplies meant that it had considerable flexibility to implement a number of key policy objectives. First, the court had the capacity to direct resources to relatively needy regions of the empire from relatively well-endowed regions. In an era of limited means of transportation, the state's subsidizing of regional needs enabled it to use nonmilitary means to unify and strengthen the empire. This was true from province to province, as well as within a given province, especially within the metropolitan province where a politically strategic population presented special challenges.

The large reserves also permitted the state to pursue more concrete objectives that provided economic security and political stability through social welfare. Specifically this included famine relief, overall price stabilization, and reduction of seasonal fluctuations. Again and again grain reserves were used effectively in the crises of the eighteenth and early nineteenth centuries. Overall price stability cannot be so easily proven, but the results shown in this study suggest strongly that granary reserves, and outside grain supply in general, did seem to diminish the overall impact of natural disasters. Whether grain storage helped to ease seasonal fluctuations of price, however, is doubtful because roughly the same seasonal price movements occurred in the nineteenth century, when granary stocks were low, as in the eighteenth century, when storage was high.[162]

Despite these positive effects of storage, the granary system was subject to considerable criticism, or at least skepticism, even at its height. The Qianlong emperor himself began in the 1740s to question the wisdom of so much state storage, and the governors-general responded thoughtfully to his call for discussion. Although the immediate concern was that overstocking had contributed to price inflation, the more general concern was whether grain storage impeded commercial activity and the free circulation of grain—which was known as *liutong*. Some argued that by being so active in grain transport and storage, and almost regulating prices and limiting merchant inventories, the government was discouraging merchants from participating in the grain trade. If merchants were not so restrained, they and the "market," in today's terms, might have attained the same outcome, low and stable prices, at a lesser "transaction cost" than the government. Much of this "subsistence policy debate" of 1742–53 focused once again on the role of "evil" merchants whose ambition was to "hoard." Chen Dashou, as governor of Jiangsu, memorialized in opposition to the Board of Revenue's banning of grain hoarding. He argued that merchants performed a service; their storage of grain had a function similar to the state's. When prices were high, they released the grain, helping to alleviate the shortage and the local area: "Once the price is high, the rice is sold, and thus remains available for consumption in the local area. The market does not run short of rice; the market price is kept from rising even higher." The only thing to "detest" is "continued refusals to sell even after the market price has risen."[163]

In the early nineteenth century, Yang Jingren also argued for the importance of commercial exchange. His essay on "*tong shang*" (freedom of commerce) is based on imperial documents concerning grain shipments to Zhili from distant places.[164] Another author, Hui Shiqi, also argued for the importance of encouraging merchants. If prices were kept artificially low, it would only keep them away and end up harming the people. It would also encourage private hoarding. Grain should circulate in the world the way blood circulates in the body, he said. "To stop the flow of grain is like stopping the ocean," he wrote, mixing his metaphors.[165] One astute critic, Yang Xifu, when he was governor of Hunan in 1748, observed that despite the prosperity of his era, people had become more impoverished. This he attributed to population growth, extravagant customs, large landholdings by the rich, and large-scale grain storage, which, he asserted, had contributed to an inflationary price rise. The only justification for storage, he argued, was for famine relief. Excessively large storage under any conditions only contributed to shortages and high prices.[166] Another critic in this early Qianlong era debate was Yang Eryou, censor, who memorialized in 1742 about the high prices caused by such purchases. First, he said, "when the official buying starts, . . . the price of grain immediately rises." Secondly, "because there is grain being made available through the stabilizing sales, the merchants bind their feet and fail to come forward, with the result that grain is even dearer, the folk plagued even more."[167]

Chen Hongmou, previously intendant in Zhili, and in 1748 Shaanxi governor, expressed a contrary opinion. Although he has been regarded as an economic "liberal," Chen Hongmou was apparently alone in asserting the importance of maintaining granary reserves, and he recognized the necessity of prohibiting grain exports from a province that was experiencing a famine.[168] Despite the doubts expressed by others about grain storage, Chen kept building stocks in Shaanxi Province. Although he respected market mechanisms, Chen also had "a highly activist willingness to use the resources of the state to participate in that market to achieve desired social ends," according to William Rowe.[169] Chen and others tried "to influence the market through market means themselves."[170]

Historian Wu Jianyong has argued that these debates signified a widespread official recognition of the importance of the circulation of grain, *liutong*, in order to stabilize prices across the empire, to adjust the supply and demand for grain, and to prevent both real famines (caused by shortages) and "glut famines" (*shuhuang*)—crises due to low prices and lack of markets. He estimates that the commercial circulation of grain outstripped government control of the market by 4:1.[171] But one should be careful not to equate the concept of *liutong* with the modern concept of markets. Although the debates of 1748 and later marked a kind of intellectual juncture in the theory of state grain storage—an end to the unquestioned support for state storage—they did not mark a turning point in its practice. Although reserves were not supposed to exceed the level of 1748, in fact until the end of the eighteenth century grain reserves in all but the more commercialized provinces far exceeded the 1748 levels.[172] The empirewide total reported reserves for state civilian granaries in the 1790s was 40 million *shi*.[173] However, as Will and colleagues have pointed out, the spatial distribution of grain storage was not uniform. The provinces having the largest reserves—Zhili, Henan, Fujian, Sichuan, and perhaps Guangdong—represented those regions where, for different reasons, the state was heavily committed to intervention. On a per capita basis, however, frontier provinces such as Gansu, Guizhou, and Yunnan had higher reserves than Zhili and Henan and were about the same as Sichuan, Guangdong, and Fujian. "This pattern suggests that Qing leaders made clear commitments to inhabitants of less accessible areas to develop the governmental means of influencing food supply conditions."[174] By this reasoning, the northern provinces of Henan and Zhili received less attention than these border provinces, but if grain tribute supplies are taken into account, the direct commitment to the capital region was clearly paramount.

For the capital region, the commitment to government storage was unquestioned because of its strategic importance, and the rest of Zhili was usually considered exceptional as well. It was sometimes exempted from the general criticisms of storage. The disruptive aspects of local restocking were offset by the increasing dependence on external sources of grain. The investments made by the state in river conservancy and in the granary system created a situation that had the same effect as market integration, as Chapter 7 shows. Circulation of grain was facilitated, not impeded, through these state-subsidized networks. Officials intervened to balance the needs of one region against another. In 1766, for example, authorities were puzzled about high grain prices in the counties of Daxing and Wanping in which Beijing was situated. Since there had been several years of bumper harvests in the capital region and there was an 8–9 harvest rating at the present time, the emperor wondered whether the high prices might be caused by Shandong merchants making large purchases for shipment to Shandong where harvests had been poor. Yet officials were uncertain whether direct intervention to restrict merchants and bring prices down might have the unintended effect of giving functionaries an opportunity to interfere and make private gains. After investigation, the provincial governors including Fang Guancheng reported that indeed Hejian and Tianjin merchants, hearing of the situation in Shandong, had made large sales to merchants from Dezhou and Linqing, along the water routes to Shandong. He recommended that they be stopped.[175] In this case, the authorities gave the food security of Beijing and its environs a higher priority than the interests of Shandong and overcame the theoretical concern for maintaining *liutong*.

In the absence of the state's intervention, would market networks have done the same job? Did the state's activity keep merchants from flourishing and thus inhibit commercial development? In fact, without state grain reserves, would individual peasant households have been motivated to store grain privately? Even more intriguing, in the absence of state reserves, would higher grain prices have provided an incentive to Zhili's better-off peasants toward agricultural innovation rather than continuing their fairly simple crops and technologies? Although counterfactuals can never be proven, it seems unlikely, knowing the difficult terrain and growing conditions in Zhili, that commercialized farming or agricultural commerce would have developed in any case. The potential for commerce seen by the mid-eighteenth-century political economists did not seem to describe North China very well.[176] Small-scale subsistence farming prevailed into the twentieth century, except for fruit and cotton growers in the late nineteenth and early twentieth centuries.

Grain storage has been a topic of considerable theoretical interest to economic historians of medieval and early modern Europe. In a controversial article, McCloskey and Nash theorized that in medieval England grain storage and interest rates were implicitly related. Since they reasoned that no one would store grain if they could sell it and get a higher rate of interest elsewhere, the opportunity cost of grain storage was the rate of interest. Since this cost was high, stores of grain must have been low.[177] Komlos and Landes in a sharply worded critique said that McCloskey and Nash's "picture of the medieval world is essentially ahistorical" because it assumed that "well-functioning money and product markets were characteristic of the medieval economy."[178] Echoing earlier debates centering on the views of Chayanov's peasant economy, they sided with the view that the peasant family was more likely to be risk-averse than rational market-calculators. "As a group, rural commoners were the last to move toward the open calculation, monetary decision making, and speculative risk taking characteristic of 'modern' man."[179] This issue is also represented in the debate between James C. Scott, who posited a "moral economy" among Southeast Asian peasants, and Samuel Popkin, who argued that peasants were just as "rational" in their economic choices as anyone else.[180]

For North China we know that private storage, if it existed, had to be a risk-minimizing move, and not a profit-motivated calculation. Of all the pronouncements against hoarding, for example, none is directed toward storage by individual peasant households, even large ones; all are directed against merchants. Li Wei's observation in 1735—"the peasants do not have the habit of storing grain. They just sell it off right away no matter what the price is"—could apply as well to peasants in 1835 or 1935. While a family in comfortable circumstances might store enough grain for their own consumption to get them to the next harvest, most families were forced to sell some of what they harvested to meet present expenses, or to sell small quantities of fine grain such as wheat to exchange for coarse grains for their own consumption. Amounts that were sold at the periodic markets were very small indeed. In the 1773 example of forced sales cited above, the hapless victim's family had reserves of 20–30 shi, which was an unusually large amount. Two shi was the maximum amount that a household could borrow from a community granary.[181]

In South China the situation was, of course, entirely different. In Guangdong Province, Robert Marks argues that despite the reported figures, the state granaries stored little or no grain after the 1760s and instead held an equivalent in silver. Private storage and commerce were increasingly important.[182] In neighboring Guangxi Province, which had a grain surplus, peasants in the eighteenth century seemed to have stored "substantial" quantities of grain and sold off their unused stocks after the next harvest. Landlords and lineages, as well as individual households, also stored grain. Merchants from neighboring Guangdong came in numbers to purchase grain.[183] In South China, government intervention declined as markets became more important, but in North China markets were dependent on state intervention; when the state retreated, some markets also declined.

If private storage on a significant scale had been possible, it is extremely unlikely that the Qing state would have lavished so much money on an extensive state granary system. Similarly, as Will and Wong have argued, if they had been profitable and self-supporting, state granaries could be seen to have displaced commercial activity. When the state retreated from grain storage in the nineteenth century, merchants would have stepped in to take advantage of the new opportunity. But they did not. The fact is that "the state subsidized granary storage through its continuous allocation of funds. This created a redistribution of income because the people funding the granaries—tax-payers, especially the wealthy ones—overlapped only partly with those people receiving benefits from the system."[184] Nowhere in the empire was this more true than in the Zhili region, which was the chief beneficiary of the interregional reallocation of resources, as well as the partial redistribution of wealth to the poor.

The state civilian granary system was unquestionably important to the economy and to the political system in the eighteenth century. Although seriously dysfunctional in some highly visible ways, grain storage played a definite, and sometimes measurable, role in several key functions—

price stabilization, famine relief, interregional transport networks—that otherwise would not have been met.[185] Yet, the nineteenth-century aftermath of the high Qing state activism requires one to consider whether in the longer historical perspective such state activism did not also leave a negative legacy by creating larger problems and unrealistic expectations. Grain storage brings into historical focus the strengths and the weaknesses of the Qing bureaucratic management of the agricultural economy, just as river management highlighted the strengths and weaknesses of the Qing management of the environment.

CHAPTER SEVEN

Markets and Prices

QING EMPERORS AND STATESMEN understood and respected market forces, but they did not regard the "market" as an end in itself.[1] They wished to use market forces to promote the circulation of goods, but when market forces were blocked, they generally did not hesitate to intervene, particularly in the grain market, which was so vital to the state's interests. State granaries were seen as a means of correcting the negative effects of price fluctuations, but stocking the granaries was controversial because it often seemed to create abuses as great as those it was intended to correct. Merchants were regarded ambivalently. Although Fang Guancheng counted on them to facilitate trade, he often acted against "evil merchants" or "evil brokers," making a clear distinction between reasonable profits and illicit profits.[2] The ideal was to encourage the participation of many small-scale merchants in the grain trade, but to restrict large traders who could monopolize or "hoard" supply and raise the market price. Unlike the salt merchants or the Canton merchants—who often became fabulously wealthy and influential—grain merchants were rarely well known and influential, at least in the north.[3] Because of the restrictions placed on the grain trade, it was unlikely to have been so lucrative.[4]

Market development and economic growth were important aspects of the "high Qing" era of the eighteenth century, and of the late imperial period in general. Chinese historians have increasingly, since the 1980s, focused on the positive aspects of economic change, whereas the earlier generation of Marxist historians had emphasized the suppression of "sprouts of capitalism" by "feudal" classes and imperialist oppressors.[5] Western scholars have drawn attention to agricultural and commercial developments of the high Qing and to the general prosperity that resulted. Studies of merchants and commerce, in particular, have worked against the older, essentialist view that traditional Chinese culture was hostile to science and capitalism.[6]

An important measure of economic development is the extent to which markets are integrated. Classical economics places great importance on the free flow of goods between markets. The economist expects that the development and integration of markets advanced by improved transportation and the reduction of transaction costs of all sorts will allow comparative advantage to work and the "Law of One Price" to prevail. Likewise in the spatially uniform world of central place theory, modernization can be achieved only through modern transportation, which obviates the need for closely spaced standard markets and allows consumers to purchase goods from more distant, higher-level markets.[7]

In Europe from the seventeenth to the nineteenth century, grain prices of different regions became increasingly integrated and prices more stable. The regulation of markets declined, and so did food riots.[8] In China important scholarship has demonstrated that different regions were becoming increasingly integrated through trade. Wu Chengming's book on marketing has been particularly influential.[9] William Rowe's work on Hankow shows the broad economic reach of this central entrepôt. Using quantitative analysis of grain prices, Yeh-chien Wang has convincingly shown a correlation of prices between key regions of China during the eighteenth century, and Loren Brandt has done the same with data from the late nineteenth and early twentieth centuries.[10]

The historical evidence for an empirewide market challenges some of the implications of G. William Skinner's macroregional approach. Skinner's application of central place theory to Chinese realities models a nested hierarchy of markets (standard, intermediate, and central) and urban places that form a discrete system within each of eight macroregions of China that he defined by physiographic criteria. He asserts that the macroregions, rather than administrative units such as provinces, are the "proper units for analyzing urbanization."[11] Although the dynastic cycle had some impact, he suggested that "the developmental cycles of the various regions had their own distinctive rhythms" and had "relative autonomy."[12] In North China, Skinner has noted, subregions have changed over history (one might add that this was because the river systems were unstable), and "the superior potential for production and exchange enjoyed by particular subregional systems has depended as much on imperial favor as on physiographic endowment."[13] North China was among the least urbanized of the macroregions of China, and it had "remarkably low levels of rural commercialization."[14]

Although the work of Wang and others on long-distance marketing seems to contradict the notion of relatively autonomous macroregions, their results may have been over-interpreted. Interregional trade suggests a prosperous and integrated national market and implies concurrent market development within each region as well. Skinner's model also suggests an integrated hierarchy of markets should be the norm. But there are many empirical lacunae to be filled, and *interregional* market connections have been easier to document than *intraregional* networks. Few studies of interregional trade deal with internal trade networks below the regional centers.[15]

An alternative hypothesis is that interregional trade networks may form without necessarily resting on well-developed internal trade networks—they may form a two-tiered trading system rather than an integrated one. Wu Chengming showed effectively that there were important networks of long-distance trade—mostly in grain rather than handicraft or industrial products—before the nineteenth century, but he also emphasized that villages in most regions were still "natural economies" that had not yet developed into "market economies."[16] Rowe has shown that in the nineteenth century, the city of Hankow, the key market in central China, conducted flourishing trade with other macroregions but at the same time exhibited "an unusually low degree of embeddedness" in its immediate hinterland.[17] Similarly, Rhoads Murphey argued that there was a gap between treaty ports and interior China in the nineteenth century. The rise of foreign trade at the treaty ports, and of substantial trade among them, did not necessarily affect the internal Chinese marketing networks.[18]

Zhili Province grain price data provide an excellent opportunity to measure quantitatively the extent of market development and integration. Results of the analyses suggest that market integration within Zhili declined from the eighteenth century to the nineteenth, but that the province's

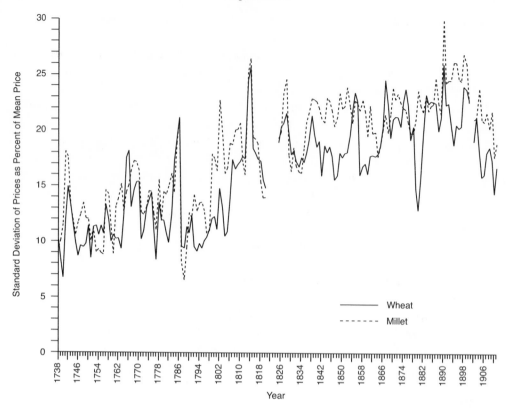

FIGURE 7.1A.   Coefficients of price variation, all prefectures, 1738–1911

markets simultaneously grew more closely integrated with external markets—first that of Feng-tian, and later that of the Lower Yangzi region. These results support the alternative scenario of market development just described. They cannot be predicted by economic theories or models, but they can be understood in the historical context of state policies, dynastic decline, and environmental degradation.

Although the prefectural-level grain price data can provide insight into the interrelationship of grain markets among prefectures within the province, and between the province and other provinces, we lack the constituent county-level price reports. Even if local prices were available, they still would not tell us about the operation of the thousands of periodic markets below the county level. Consequently grain prices alone cannot give us a detailed picture of rural marketing. Evidence from local gazetteers and official documents suggests a relatively low degree of commercialization in most localities, with only very small-scale marketing of grains in periodic markets, and little large-scale or wholesale handling of grain. The integration of these local markets, as well as their scale, appears to have been slight.[19]

Market Integration Within Zhili

This chapter uses two common statistics to measure the development of market integration within Zhili over this period: correlation coefficients and coefficients of variation. If transportation and

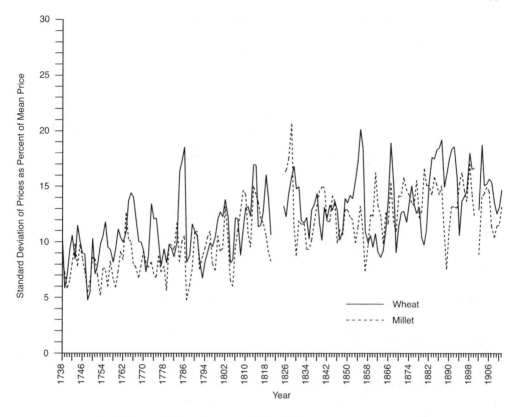

FIGURE 7.1B.   Coefficients of price variation, excluding Region 1, 1738–1911

markets in Zhili were efficient, then prices should have been well correlated across prefectures. Of course, correlation might also have resulted from similar weather conditions in areas not actually connected by transport and markets, or from common inflationary or deflationary trends, but high correlations are at least a necessary, if not a sufficient, indicator of market integration. A second way to study price variation over time is to use the coefficient of variation (the standard deviation expressed as a percent of the mean), which measures the dispersion of data at one point in time. If there is wide dispersion, the coefficient of variation is high; if observations are clustered around the mean, the coefficient is low. If it decreases over time, then that is a strong sign that market integration has occurred.

Formal testing of prefectural prices in Zhili using the coefficient of variation, however, does not provide evidence of growing integration. We computed the coefficient of variation for each year from the annual prices (that is, the mean of the monthly price observations) of Zhili's seventeen prefectures. Figure 7.1a, which tracks the coefficients of variation for wheat and millet, shows that they almost doubled between the eighteenth and nineteenth centuries—very much contrary to what one would expect with market integration. To measure more formally this trend, we regressed the coefficients of variation on the variable for year (or time). The resulting regression coefficients were all positive and significant: 0.068 (t = 14.77) for wheat; 0.077 for millet (t = 17.53); and 0.052 (t = 9.94) for sorghum. These values are the amount by which the coefficients of variation increased, on average, year by year. However, the process was not continuous: a sharp increase in the coefficients in the period 1800–20 stands out, probably reflecting the serious flooding in the Jiaqing period as well as banditry around 1813.

It appears that some of the rise in the coefficients can be attributed to the weakening ties between Zhili proper and its northernmost prefectures: Yongping, Xuanhua, Chengde, Zunhua, and Yizhou. Exclusion of these five prefectures reduces the coefficient of variation for the later years (see Figure 7.1b) such that the overall regression coefficient for the year on the annual coefficients of variations falls to 0.037 ($t = 9.50$) for wheat, 0.042 ($t = 12.26$) for millet, and 0.023 ($t = 4.80$) for sorghum. A comparison of these two figures shows the greater magnitude of the coefficients of variation when the northern prefectures are included and also the steeper rate of increase. But, even excluding the northern prefectures, the fact remains that prices in Zhili experienced a clear and significant increase in variation from 1738 to 1911.

To examine further the relationship among the regions of Zhili, we may divide the prefectures into four groups, taking into rough account differences in soil, topography, and climate. This grouping can only approximate these differences. Variations in topography and climate range across prefectural boundaries, even across county boundaries. Unfortunately, the data are aggregated by prefectures. (See Map 7.1.)

Region 1 consists of the five northern prefectures already named, which share a topography of mountains and high plateau areas. Xuanhua and Chengde, north of the Great Wall, were markedly different from the rest of the province; in addition, the data for Chengde are particularly sparse and poor in quality.[20] This region includes the agricultural zones I, II, III, IV, V, and VIII. (See Map 1.3 in Chapter 1.)

Region 2 consists of the politically and commercially central prefectures of Shuntian, Baoding, Hejian, and Tianjin. These prefectures straddle the piedmont and the low-lying, easily waterlogged districts of Zhili. Because these prefectures constitute the drainage area of the Hai River Basin, and they include the key urban centers of Beijing, Tianjin, and Baoding, Region 2 may be considered the "core" of the Hai River Basin subregion of Skinner's North China macroregion. However Region 2 includes agricultural zones V, VI, VII, and VIII (see Map 1.3 in Chapter 1).

Region 3 consists of the four prefectures of Shunde, Guangping, Daming, and Zhaozhou, which formed the quite distinct southern leg of the province, nicely gerrymandered between Henan and Shandong. This region had a different climate and was more suitable for the growing of wheat than other parts of Zhili. It straddles agricultural zones IV, VI, and VII.

The remaining four prefectures—Zhengding, Jizhou, Shenzhou, and Dingzhou—are more difficult to classify. Although they also straddled agricultural zones IV, VI, and VII and included some fertile land in the piedmont, parts of these prefectures were often waterlogged and impassable terrain. They were central in location but economically peripheral. This is Region 4. In most cases, prices in this region behaved similarly to those in Region 2, but sometimes they were more like Region 3. The region also includes three different agricultural zones.

Correlations of the first differences of annual prices of these four regions are displayed in Table 7.1. The "first difference" is the difference between the price in two successive years. Correlation of first differences, instead of the price levels themselves, strips away the covariance that results from a shared time trend. As anticipated, Region 1 in the north was moderately correlated with the adjacent Region 2, at a level of about 0.7, but generally less correlated with Region 4 in the center, and poorly correlated with Region 3 in the south. This was the case with all three grains. Overall, the strongest correlations were between prices in Regions 2 and 4—measuring over 0.8 in all three grains, and between Regions 3 and 4. On the whole, correlations of wheat and millet

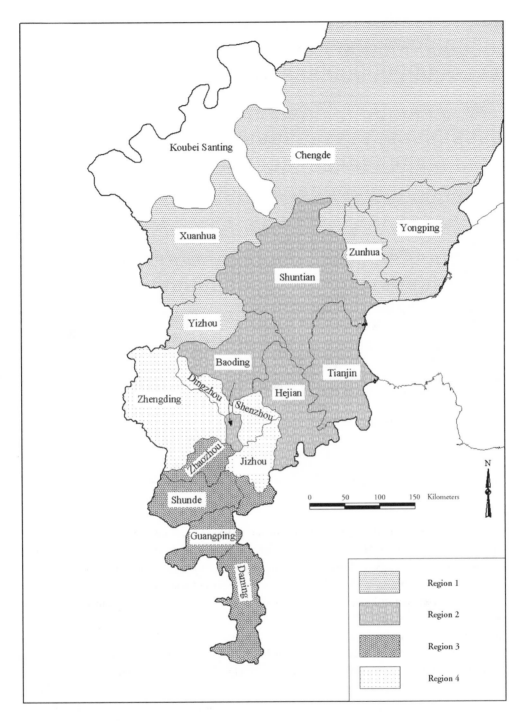

MAP 7.1. Prefectures and regions in Zhili Province

TABLE 7.1

Correlation of Grain Prices Within Zhili, 1738–1911

(first difference of annual average solar prices)

(coefficients over 0.700 indicated in bold type)

Wheat

	Region 1	Region 2	Region 3	Region 4
Region 1	1.000			
Region 2	**0.734**	1.000		
Region 3	0.524	**0.776**	1.000	
Region 4	0.634	**0.836**	**0.822**	1.000

Millet

	Region 1	Region 2	Region 3	Region 4
Region 1	1.000			
Region 2	0.693	1.000		
Region 3	0.409	**0.722**	1.000	
Region 4	0.584	**0.862**	**0.779**	1.000

Sorghum

	Region 1	Region 2	Region 3	Region 4
Region 1	1.000			
Region 2	**0.727**	1.000		
Region 3	0.377	0.696	1.000	
Region 4	0.559	**0.851**	**0.736**	1.000

NOTE: All correlations have a significance of 0.01. See text and Map 7.1 for definition of regions.

prices were stronger than those of sorghum, which is to be expected given that sorghum was a subsistence crop while wheat and millet were partially commercialized. This summary view of correlations among the regions confirms the separateness of the northern prefectures, and the importance of geographical proximity in determining the strength of relationships overall.

To see if these relationships changed over time, correlations were taken on the first difference of prices divided into twenty-year periods, as seen in Table 7.2. Wheat-price correlations among the four regions experienced no strong secular trends, with the exception of marked deterioration in all relationships in the final decade of the dynasty. Region 2 in particular evinced a steady and strong correlation of wheat prices with all other regions, including Region 1. Regions 2, 3, and 4 had a strong relationship with each other, but there was some deterioration in the period 1801 to 1820. Millet price correlations were less stable on the whole than wheat prices, but they too followed no overall trend, only a dip between 1780 and 1820, but there were still strong ties between Region 4 and Regions 1 and 2. Sorghum price correlations were similar to those of millet, with the exception of the correlations between Regions 2 and 4, which increased slightly in the last decade, rather than decline. Sorghum price correlations were slightly less constant over time than millet correlations.

Interregional correlations give a perhaps misleading impression of stability because the data are

TABLE 7.2
Correlations of Grain Prices Within Zhili, 1738–1911, by Subperiod
(first difference of average annual solar prices)
(coefficients over 0.800 indicated in bold)

	Regions	Wheat			Millet			Sorghum		
		1	2	3	1	2	3	1	2	3
1737–60	2	.650			.690			.741		
	3	.543	**.870**		.513	.773		.513	.798	
	4	.661	**.901**	**.908**	.720	**.936**	**.840**	.649	**.914**	**.809**
1761–80	2	.675			**.885**			**.883**		
	3	.604	**.907**		.699	**.812**		.571	.754	
	4	.531	**.941**	**.926**	**.857**	**.934**	**.873**	**.804**	**.934**	**.853**
1781–1800	2	**.892**			.597			.738		
	3	.661	.783		.037	.537		.117	.541	
	4	**.836**	**.919**	.736	.501	**.844**	.682	.572	**.877**	.527
1801–20	2	.786			.686			.697		
	3	.377	.768		-.034	.549		.107	.594	
	4	.677	.771	.675	**.851**	**.918**	.647	.662	**.811**	.693
1821–40	2	**.822**			**.933**			**.908**		
	3	.554	**.807**		**.845**	**.926**		**.832**	**.938**	
	4	.619	**.838**	.742	.534	.718	.749	.539	.780	.734
1841–60	2	**.804**			.622			.716		
	3	**.807**	.789		.759	**.833**		.671	.715	
	4	.796	.795	.778	.731	**.945**	**.867**	**.845**	**.867**	**.800**
1861–80	2	**.853**			**.924**			**.861**		
	3	.589	.740		.729	**.855**		.549	.763	
	4	.756	**.863**	**.927**	**.835**	**.913**	**.876**	.707	**.913**	**.831**
1881–1900	2	**.838**			.795			**.836**		
	3	.793	**.886**		.502	.745		.400	.636	
	4	**.871**	**.894**	**.831**	.485	.759	**.889**	.562	.779	**.846**
1901–11	2	.780			.282			.287		
	3	.415	.554		.240	.263		.014	.566	
	4	.657	.597	.790	-.036	.499	.238	.069	**.875**	.391

NOTE: See text and Map 7.1 for definition of regions.

so highly aggregated. Looking more closely at correlations among specific pairs of prefectures we see greater variability over time. For this we have singled out four key prefectures: Shuntian (politically central); Baoding (the seat of the provincial government); Tianjin (commercially important); and Daming (productive, but, unlike the others, geographically peripheral). Table 7.3 shows changes in these correlations by twenty-year intervals.

Taken as a whole, these results do not show any clear trend toward price integration, but interesting patterns emerge when the pairs are looked at separately. Most prominent is that the grain prices of Baoding and Tianjin were highly correlated throughout the eighteenth century, with cor-

TABLE 7.3

Correlation of Grain Prices Among Selected Zhili Prefectures, 1738–1911

(first difference of annual solar prices)

(coefficients above 0.800 indicated in bold type)

	1738–1911	1738–1760	1761–1780	1781–1800	1801–1820	1821–1840	1841–1860	1861–1880	1881–1900	1901–1911
Wheat										
Shuntian-Baoding	.734*	—	—	.489	.727	.738	.784	**.871**	**.880**	.652
Shuntian-Tianjin	.702*	—	—	**.803**	**.871**	**.849**	**.843**	.744	.683	.366
Shuntian-Daming	.562*	—	—	.530	.597	.578	.652	.492	.750	.573
Baoding-Tianjin	.653	**.870**	**.889**	.740	.701	.773	.668	.784	.669	.109
Baoding-Daming	.563	**.801**	.716	.524	.477	.466	.456	.581	.701	.552
Tianjin-Daming	.638	.704	**.870**	.768	.386	.636	.478	.590	**.844**	.587
Millet										
Shuntian-Baoding	.616*	—	—	.406	.702	**.871**	.664	.606	.660	.221
Shuntian-Tianjin	.556*	—	—	.437	.579	.690	.399	**.821**	.705	.302
Shuntian-Daming	.292*	—	—	-.254	-.068	.682	.429	.642	.541	.473
Baoding-Tianjin	.709	**.914**	**.815**	**.906**	**.866**	.653	.619	.661	.773	.115
Baoding-Daming	.425	.653	.603	.477	.111	.645	.666	.678	.740	-.346
Tianjin-Daming	.479	.650	.689	.483	.229	.669	.474	.702	.662	.127
Sorghum										
Shuntian-Baoding	.655*	—	—	.786	.622	.715	**.850**	.619	.701	.532
Shuntian-Tianjin	.601*	—	—	.568	.648	.738	.441	.539	.745	**.819**
Shuntian-Daming	.204*	—	—	.073	-.028	.405	.527	.315	.182	.578
Baoding-Tianjin	.589	**.865**	**.806**	**.844**	.698	.658	.585	.639	.587	.375
Baoding-Daming	.299	.548	.578	.330	.088	.658	.578	.436	.370	-.041
Tianjin-Daming	.405	.545	.628	.481	.124	.408	.315	.417	.496	.542

* 1781–1911.

NOTE: All correlations are significant at the 1 percent level. Shuntian data missing 1738–80.

relation coefficients on the first difference of prices in all three grains of over 0.8. Also striking is the decline in these coefficients in the nineteenth century. The strong link between these markets was undoubtedly due to the investments in water control and transport that were made during the Qianlong period; when these waterways deteriorated in the Jiaqing and Daoguang periods, so did the connection between these markets. This occurred as the state was also reducing its stake in grain storage. (Because there are no Shuntian price data before 1771, we cannot see a similar trend for Shuntian-Baoding and Shuntian-Tianjin coefficients.)

Noteworthy also is the extended period of high correlations of wheat prices in Shuntian and Tianjin, from the 1780s through the 1860s. These high correlations may reflect Beijing's steady demand for wheat, which may have been transshipped through Tianjin from Henan, Shandong, and the Lower Yangzi area. After the occupation of Beijing by foreign troops in 1860, roads in this area deteriorated—as did the correlations. On the other hand, wheat-price correlations between Shuntian and Baoding show steady improvement until 1901.

Lastly, these results confirm that Daming Prefecture was not very tied into the markets of the core and was indeed the result of what Skinner has called "high-level gerrymandering" that severed its natural ties with the trade of Henan and Shandong.[21] With the exception of a couple of periods, correlations were not high and showed no particular trend. None of this indicates a trend toward increasing market integration. In such a case one would expect prices at Tianjin, at the very least, to be more closely correlated with those in the other key prefectures. This clearly was not the case, and in fact evidence for its declining integration with Shuntian and Baoding for wheat and with Baoding for the other two grains is quite clear. The opposite seems closer to the truth, especially for the late nineteenth century.

We can further confirm this result by analyzing harvest size. Regression analysis and other tests in Chapter 4 showed that harvests in Baoding did have the expected relationship to grain prices all over the province: better harvests were associated with a decrease in grain prices. In the ideal economic world, however, as markets expand and a region becomes less dependent on its own produce, the quantity-price relationship should weaken.

In order to test the hypothesis that the price effect of harvests would decline over time due to increasing market integration, we constructed a model of price determination.[22] Our model of the supply and demand for grain (Figures 7.2a–b) shows the effect of harvest fluctuations on price, *ceteris paribus*. Figure 7.2a illustrates a theoretical situation in which the grain supply is completely inelastic because the region is isolated and imports (and storage) are impossible. Demand is fairly inelastic because grain is a necessity, and it is assumed that it does not shift significantly for the time period under consideration. Thus small shifts in supply result in large changes in price (and decrease in quantity consumed). A shortfall in the harvest from Q_0 to Q_1, for example, results in a significant price rise from P_0 to P_1. Figure 7.2b illustrates a situation in which supply is relatively elastic due to external trade. Elasticity means that a shift in supply of similar magnitude (from SS_0 to SS_1) arising from a poor harvest results in a smaller change in the price (P_2 rather than P_1) and a lesser decline in quantity consumed (Q_2 rather than Q_1) than in the top figure.

In order to test whether such a shift occurred in the harvest-price relationship in Zhili Province, the relationship of prices and harvests may be estimated on the basis of the following model:

$$P_c = e^{\beta(H\mu - Hc)}$$

where P_c is the current price, e is the base for the natural logarithm, H_μ is the mean harvest rating for the time period in question, and H_c is the current harvest. P_c is indexed so that it will equal one

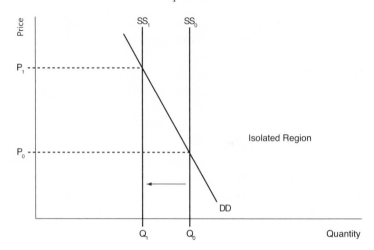

FIGURE 7.2A.　Model of supply elasticity and price behavior, isolated region

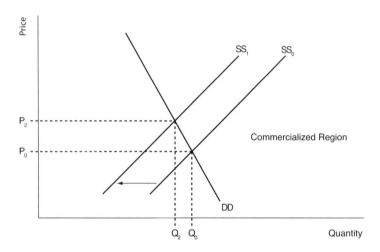

FIGURE 7.2B.　Model of supply elasticity and price behavior, commercialized region

for an average harvest. (So, for example, if the average price for the period 1736–95 was $2 and the actual price for 1750 was $3, the data point for 1750 will be $3/$2 = 1.5.) The key to the model is β, which captures the sensitivity of price to shifts in the supply curve. This model allows for a nonlinear relationship where extremely poor harvests have a magnified effect on prices (such that the price change in going from a harvest of 6 to 1 of 5 is much less than that in going from 3 to 2). However, for the values of β well below unity (such as those reported in Table 7.4), the relationship described by the equation is approximately linear. Taking the natural log of both sides yields the equation

$$\ln P_c = \beta(H\mu\text{-}Hc)$$

The coefficient β can then be estimated by ordinary least squares (OLS) regression analysis.

This model may be applied to the data from Tianjin and Baoding. The harvest ratings are matched with the detrended price data from the year preceding the harvest (assumed to be June

TABLE 7.4

Harvest-Price Relationship (β) in
Tianjin and Baoding, 1737–1895

Period	Tianjin Wheat	Tianjin Millet	Baoding Wheat	Baoding Millet
1737–1795	0.040	0.067	0.036	0.042
1796–1840	0.078	0.036	0.046	0.053
1841–1895	0.005	0.011	0.033	0.051
F-statistic for significance of differences				
1737–1795 vs. 1796–1840				
	1.623	0.927	0.198	0.093
1796–1840 vs. 1841–1895				
	4.853	0.714	0.360	0.044

NOTE: A Chow test on the stability of coefficients from one period to the next shows that only the coefficients for Tianjin wheat were significantly different between time periods. The *F*-statistic that resulted was signficant for Tianjin wheat at the 1 percent confidence level. For the other three grains presented—Tianjin millet, Baoding wheat, and Baoding millet—there is not a statistically significant difference in the coefficients at the 10 percent confidence level.

for wheat and September for millet).[23] The data for our final analysis are split into three subperiods, 1737–95, 1796–1840, and 1841–95, taking into account relevant historical periodization as well as the desirability of dividing the data into samples of roughly equivalent size.[24]

Estimates for β for these subperiods are given in Table 7.4. The most striking results are those for Tianjin wheat: in the eighteenth century, when the state was heavily involved in grain transport and storage, the sensitivity of Tianjin wheat prices to local harvest conditions was fairly low; in the 1796–1840 period, when there was a decline in state involvement, wheat prices were substantially more sensitive; and in the 1841–95 period, when Tianjin became important as a treaty port, they were the least sensitive of all. For Tianjin millet, a more expected pattern of continuous decline in sensitivity is found. For Baoding wheat and millet, however, only small changes in the harvest-price relationship are seen from one period to the next. Grain prices continued throughout to depend on local harvests to roughly the same extent and did not show evidence of increased external market influences. Thus, only Tianjin Prefecture conforms to the expectation of decreasing harvest-price sensitivity over the mid- to late Qing period. And only in the case of Tianjin wheat are the changes from one period to the next statistically significant.

GRAIN MARKETS IN ZHILI

With the exception of Tianjin's apparently decreasing price responsiveness to local harvests, all the results presented thus far reveal a trend of declining market integration, or at least the absence of increasing market integration. The trend toward higher coefficients of variation overall, and the weaker correlations between particular locations, corresponds with the history of both the grain tribute and the state-sponsored granaries, and the internal waterborne transport system. Fang Guancheng had observed that "in Zhili the prices of grain within the province varies a great deal, and the original buying price also varies. So it is important to follow the market price (*shijia*) and not just the government-set seasonal price (*shijia*)."[25] The state's policies in the eighteenth century helped to overcome these natural variations in price and undoubtedly explain the strong price correlations. Subsequent dynastic decline changed all this: as the level of storage and the maintenance of internal waterways declined in the early nineteenth century, so did the strong price integration of key centers such as Baoding, Tianjin, and Shuntian. The decline of state intervention also led to the deterioration of internal water transport routes, which were important for cheap intra-provincial transport. Without a strong state presence, local markets revealed themselves as rather underdeveloped and unintegrated.

State policy in the eighteenth century encouraged the circulation of grain by allowing interregional trade and discouraging centralization of markets, even to the point of atomization. Officials tried to ensure the adequate stocking of the granaries by imports from other provinces (Shandong, Henan, and Fengtian, and more traditionally from central and Lower Yangzi regions via the grain tribute system). At Beijing and to a lesser extent at Tianjin, officials placed limits on grain merchant inventories so that no one merchant would be able to affect prices by "hoarding," which officials regarded as a threat to food security. "In Tianjin, the grain shops do not store more than 60 or 70 shi at the most, or 30 to 40 at least. Because the nearby [grain tribute] warehouses are easy to get to, there is no need to hoard," reported Liu E, Zhili governor-general in 1787.[26]

At Tianjin and also Tongzhou there were brokers, merchants who were designated by local authorities to facilitate trade and to collect taxes if needed. They were a type of *yahang* or *jingji*—general terms for brokers in any commodity; grain brokers were sometimes called *douhang*, and later *doudian* (a "*dou*" being an instrument to measure grain).[27] At Tianjin *doudian*, grain brokerages on a larger scale seem to have originated in the first half of the nineteenth century. There were between 800 and 1,000 grain shops in Tianjin, and the *doudian* served to coordinate or monitor their activities. The east, north, and south warehouses at Tianjin each had four *doudian*. The east and north collected grain from the Ziya, Daqing, and Yongding River regions, while the south received grain from the Grand Canal. After the Boxer Uprising, these businesses suffered a decline.[28]

Elsewhere in the province, the scale of grain marketing was even smaller, mostly transacted in periodic markets selling locally grown grain. Even in Baoding, the provincial capital, there were many small shops with modest inventories or none at all. "All around Baoding's four gates, there are grain markets [*miliang jishi*]. Every morning farmers bring grain to the markets on donkeys and carts. The shops simply buy and sell as things go along; there are none who hoard grain."[29] Near Tianjin, grain was regarded as a good line of business, but the merchants held a small inventory, enough to sell in the local area. If they relied on the outside ("guest") merchants for buying and selling, they might find that in times of warfare, the grain merchants would not come, or the rivers would be dried up so that boats could not navigate, and profits would be reduced.[30]

Outside of the major cities, the grain trade was highly decentralized. Few prefectural or county cities on major trade routes had identifiable grain brokers or retail grain shops. Local gazetteers often identified salt merchants and pawnbrokers, but rarely grain merchants.[31] Indeed, the great majority of Zhili's counties appear not to have had any resident grain traders, and to the extent that they had any external trade, they relied on outside merchants, both larger-scale dealers and small-time local itinerants who visited the periodic markets. The gazetteer of Yongqing County enumerated the numbers and types of *yahang* in the various periodic markets in the county. Altogether

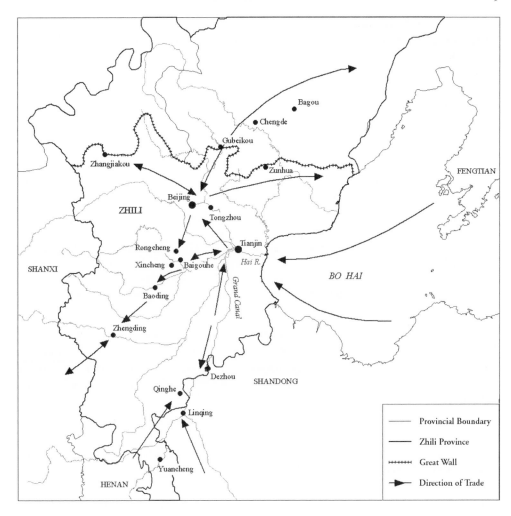

MAP 7.2.   Trade routes in Zhili

there were 67 *yahang*, who collected taxes amounting to 85 taels; of these 25 were *douhang*, or grain brokers, usually one or two at each market.[32]

There were 2,000 merchants of various types in the "region" (probably meaning Jifu or the capital region), but Beijing and Tianjin cities had the greatest number; few resided in other cities and market towns, according to the Xiong County history.[33] At the juncture of Baoding, Shuntian, and Tianjin Prefectures and on the main north-south road, Xiong County's commerce in the late Qing was active. Grains were locally consumed or sold to neighboring districts experiencing drought or floods. Sorghum that was not consumed by the peasants themselves was shipped to Baigou, Rongcheng, and other places for distilling. Wheat flour was carried by human-drawn carts or by camels to be sold in Beijing, or by large carts to Baigou he to be transferred to boats, or by boat to Tianjin, or by cart to Baoding.[34] From Tianjin many routes emanated north to Fengtian and south toward Shandong. (See Map 7.2.)

In addition, some localities in Zhengding Prefecture where cotton was grown depended on outside merchants from Shanxi and Henan to provide grain.[35] Many local sources attest to the importance of Shanxi merchants and Shanxi trade to the local economy from at least the mid-Qing period. The big merchants were all from Shanxi and dealt mostly in grain, salt, and pawnshops.[36] Other gazetteers from Zhengding stated that the salt and pawnshop merchants were from elsewhere, mostly neighboring Shanxi, while the grain brokers (*douhang yahu*) were local folk.[37] But in a later edition of the same county's gazetteer: "None of the merchants here are local people. The locals sell fruits and vegetables as needed. This is a very poor area."[38] In another county in Zhengding, the land was barren and the people poor; trade in grain or cloth was conducted at the periodic market every five days; there were no big merchants.[39]

By contrast, Zunhua, which was well positioned on trade routes by land to Chengde and by sea to Tianjin and even Taiwan, seemed exceptionally responsive to the market as well as local harvests.

> There are many grain shops [*liangdian*]. In this rural district people buy grain in the fall and sell it in the spring in order to gain a profit. By selling grain in the market they are able to know its supply, its quality, and to know how finely to have it milled. . . . But the price of grain is still determined by the Chengde region. Depending on whether the harvest is abundant or lean, they know which district has insufficiency and can be supplied by another. But there are those wholesalers who are speculators and commit crimes; it is important to constantly be on guard, and prevent them [from doing harm].[40]

It seems that peasants rarely stored grain themselves. After the harvest, outside merchants purchased grain and transported it, by water where possible, to Tianjin, or elsewhere. Or local folks took it away on a small scale, but this could hardly be considered "commerce," in the view of one Chinese historian.[41] Most areas apart from the major trade routes describe their isolation from trade. According to the gazetteer of Gaoyi County (Zhaozhou Prefecture), "People here are isolated and enjoy plain things. Consequently the merchants do not come here very often. Periodic markets are held. All the big merchants come from outside. Clothing merchants are all Shanxi people."[42] Changli County (Yongping Prefecture) was not on the main trade routes and had no large merchants. At the periodic markets, no precious commodities were traded, just cotton cloth, fish, and salt. "People just try to get by," said the local gazetteer.[43] Numerous other local gazetteers of the Qing period, and even some dating from the Republican period, stated that the local grain trade was left to small-scale merchants (peddlers), while the larger merchants were mostly in the salt trade or pawnshops.[44] Often grain is not mentioned in the list of commodities traded.

PERIODIC MARKETS

In most places, except Beijing, Tianjin, and some other centers, grain "shops" were in fact itinerant merchants who carried their small inventories among designated market places. Being itinerant meant that their inventories were small.[45] There is a lack of information about exactly how transactions were carried out in rural areas, and how the itinerant merchants replenished their stocks, but we do know that grain was the most important commodity in the periodic markets.[46] Temple fairs were also important in some localities.

The operation of periodic markets has been well described in the academic literature.[47] In North China, periodic markets met every five days.[48] In some localities they may have met more frequently. In Nanpi County, the periodic markets met traditionally on the fourth and ninth days of a ten-day cycle, but in the late nineteenth century, they began to meet on the third, sixth, and ninth days. In only one or two locations were there retail shops that were fixed.[49] In one locality at Shunyi County, a big market (*gan daji*) met every sixteen days, and a small market (*gan xiaoji*) every three days.[50] The market was not only a place where necessities could be purchased but was also a gathering place for folks both good and bad. As one gazetteer put it, "People gather to eat and drink, and to gamble for the fun of it. The unemployed, the bandits, and other bad types all gather."[51] Another old saying was that periodic markets were good because they were convenient, but they were bad because they caused endless disputes.[52]

North China periodic markets concentrated on the basic necessities such as grain, livestock, fruits and vegetables, and cloth and other household necessities. There were few commercial crops to sell and few luxuries to buy. There were more periodic markets in North China than in the south because there were fewer market towns.[53] Population growth created a need for more periodic markets. In 1814, a censor was granted imperial permission to look into increasing the number of periodic markets in Shuntian Prefecture. He argued that in the previous hundred years or more the population had increased vastly; in addition, the collapsed southern dike of the Yongding River had not been repaired, and the local people had to walk even greater distances to reach markets. He estimated that there were more than 100 villages or hamlets from which the round trip to the nearest market could be as great as 40–50 li, or even 60–70 li. The time and energy spent in carrying goods on their backs greatly interfered with the peasants' agricultural activities, he argued. Moreover, he had heard that in Wuqing County additional periodic markets had been established at the site of coal stations and had greatly benefited the local people, so he asked that the same be done in other places.[54]

The number of periodic markets in the Zhili area did increase greatly during the Qing period. On the basis of local gazetteers, Ishihara Jun has shown that the density of the periodic markets increased from 0.95 markets per square kilometer in the Ming, to 1.44 in the early Qing, 1.71 in the later Qing, and 2.50 in the Republican period. Although his survey does not include all editions of gazetteers, Ishihara's work shows a clear spatial differentiation. The less commercialized northeastern section of the province had a lower density of periodic markets, while the more commercialized southeast had a higher density.[55]

Whether such market *intensification* signifies greater market *integration* is a difficult question, but an important one. Market integration should be seen as one aspect of economic modernization whereby larger and larger trading networks become integrated with each other, thereby reducing costs to the consumer. The key to this change is modern transportation. In his articles on marketing and social structure in rural China, Skinner characterized modernization in a general way that seems appropriate to the situation in Zhili.

> True modernization occurs only when a modern transport network is developed *within* an already commercialized central marketing system to the point where the standard markets of the system are obviated and die. By contrast commercialization without intrasystemic transport improvement amounts to a kind of false modernization. It means an increase in the total volume of trade at each market, with results in no way different from those predicted by the theory of traditional change already presented: existing markets increase their frequency and new markets are formed. And the *traditional* periodic marketing system flourishes as never before.[56]

TRANSPORT ROUTES AND COSTS

Unlike southern China, the north was not blessed by a dense water transportation network, and land routes were mostly rudimentary. Yet during the high Qing, the state's maintenance of the Grand Canal and other waterways allowed for cheap water transport. In Zhili, the key water transport routes were the Grand Canal and the major rivers and canals.[57] The Grand Canal served not only as the major transport route between north and south but also as the major artery of internal commerce, linking Tianjin, Tongzhou, and other localities within Zhili to key urban centers in Shandong, such as Dezhou, and beyond. Wheat shipped from Henan and Shandong to Beijing for reduced-price sales sometimes came by internal water routes. In 1762, boats transporting wheat from Henan entered Zhili by Yuancheng in Daming Prefecture, and from Shandong by Qinghe in Guangping Prefecture.[58] Even after the Grand Canal was eclipsed by the sea route for interregional trade, locally it still served to distribute grain and other commodities from Tianjin to other localities along the Wei River.

During the mid-eighteenth century the intensive water conservancy projects still allowed swamps and basins in the central part of the province to provide adequate drainage for this waterlogged area; at the same time, dredging and dike construction facilitated water transportation from Tianjin to Baoding. Surely this water transport network accounts for the high price correlations of this period. By the Daoguang period, however, many canals and dikes had fallen into disrepair, and the passage from Tianjin to Baoding was so heavily silted that boats often ran aground.[59] The breakdown of the internal network formed an obstacle to trade that accounts for the decline in the Baoding-Tianjin price correlations found in Table 7.3 and may account for the higher level of the coefficients of variation found after 1820 in Figures 7.1a and b.

Government postal routes, the main land routes in the region, radiated out from Beijing. To the north, they linked the capital to Yongping and beyond the pass to Manchuria, to the immediate northeast with Chengde, and to the northwest with Xuanhua and Zhangjiakou (Kalgan) and beyond the Great Wall to Mongolia. To the south, one road traversed Baoding and Zhengding, where it intersected an east-west road leading to Shanxi Province. Another trunk line to the south linked Tianjin with Dezhou and other centers in Shandong and beyond.[60] (See Map 7.2.)

Most of the region's other land routes were fairly primitive. In the 1860s British diplomats W. F. Mayers and N. B. Dennys described the sorry state of transportation even on the well-traveled route from Tianjin to Beijing via Tongzhou. The distance from Tianjin to Beijing was about 80 miles (or 240 li). The "preferred way of travelling" was by boat to Tongzhou, and then by cart or horseback the last 13 miles to the capital.[61] Usually the trip took four days to Tongzhou and could be pleasant, they said. If coolies were kept tracking all night, it could be done in three days. But since the river was not navigable from early December until end of March, one had to proceed either by horse or by cart. Carts were hard to come by because they were in demand by the government for troops. The trip to Beijing took thirty-six hours if you were lucky, but after heavy rain, it might take up to three days.

> To call the wretched tracks, which in many places form the only available highway of communication, *roads*, is certainly to make use of a misnomer. The beauties of these delightful "roads" are however only to be seen to advantage during the wet weather. The ruts being occasionally two feet deep, and the whole of the surface being covered with mud and water in a uniform level. . . . It will hardly be believed that in some parts of the high-road between the capital and its nearest seaport there is only room for one cart to pass at a time.[62]

The American missionary Arthur Smith—a sharp observer of rural life—decried the decay of the roads and canals in Zhili, which were impassable several months of the year, and the lack of public spirit to build them. "Intercourse between contiguous villages lying along a common 'highway' is often for weeks entirely interrupted." He told the story of an elderly woman in the central part of the province whose land was flooded annually. "The evil was so serious that it was frequently impossible to haul the crops home on carts, but they had either to be brought on the backs of men wading." She paid for a raised road to be built. Although it benefited the entire locality, the next winter, when there was an influenza epidemic, the villagers blamed the highway for it.[63]

Of course, poor roads and unsettled conditions in the mid- to late nineteenth century may have been caused in part by the various internal disturbances and foreign military occupations of Beijing. In later decades, of all the lines of commerce, including salt, wood, cloth, and so on, the grain trade was considered the most stable, but those who marketed grain locally did not earn much profit. If they depended on guest merchants to supply them, they experienced great difficulty whenever warfare broke out, or when the rivers became unnavigable.[64] Despite the contempt shown by the foreign observers, they were no doubt accurately describing the challenges of both land and water transport in the interior of North China.

Generally speaking, water transport was always much cheaper than land transport. In the early Qianlong period (and perhaps later), the standard rate for internal water transport was set at 1.5 fen per shi (1 fen = 0.01 tael) for every 100 li (1 li = approx. 0.3 miles).[65] When new canals and basins were constructed in the mid-eighteenth century, Fang Guancheng pointed out that the cost of transport from Tianjin to Baoding had become quite cheap.[66] Since the distance was about 415 li, the total transport cost would have been only about 6 fen per shi. Land transport costs varied. According to one statement, whenever a county received relief grain in the early nineteenth century, transportation cost 1 qian (10 fen) per shi for each 100 li. So the same 415 li trip from Baoding to Tianjin would have cost 40 fen per shi rather than 6 fen. In a drought year, when the rivers were impassable, as in 1817, the cost of transport greatly increased.[67]

The cost of land transport from beyond the Great Wall was even higher. In 1754, in discussing how to get military grain from beyond the Great Wall, Fang Guancheng found that for ox-drawn carts, 3 taels were needed for each shi of grain, for a grand total of 60,000 taels, a considerable sum of money.[68] We can compare this with an earlier memorial by Fang in which he said that he had personally gone to the "koubei" area, beyond the Great Wall, to check on the supply of camels and the costs of transporting grain. He found that for every shi of grain, he would need to budget 10 taels for a haul of 800 li (equivalent to 1.25 taels per shi per 100 li). He suggested that it would be cheaper to give each soldier a stipend to allow him to purchase his own grain on the market, thus saving the government the high transport costs.[69] It was for the same reasons that in 1800 Governor-general Hu Jitang sought and received permission not to restock granaries from neighboring areas, pointing out that "in Zhili, most of the zhou and xian are not on water routes. The cost of transporting the grain 10–100 li sometimes exceeds the purchase price of the grain."[70]

These sources and others provide evidence that land transport in Zhili was rather underdeveloped in the Qing period, and both land and water routes deteriorated in the late Qing and early Republican periods. Modern transportation did not play a role until the introduction of the railroad in the early twentieth century.[71] The increase in periodic markets during the Qing period may appropriately be seen as an example of the "false modernization" described by Skinner because it was not accompanied by improvement in transportation. Evidence from grain price analysis also supports the notion that in the Qing period there was no continual improvement in internal market integration in Zhili. In this sense the price convergence of the eighteenth century might be called a "false market integration" in the sense that the state played a role in adjusting supply and demand. The Law of One Price was enforced not by improved transport or technology, but by direct bureaucratic intervention.

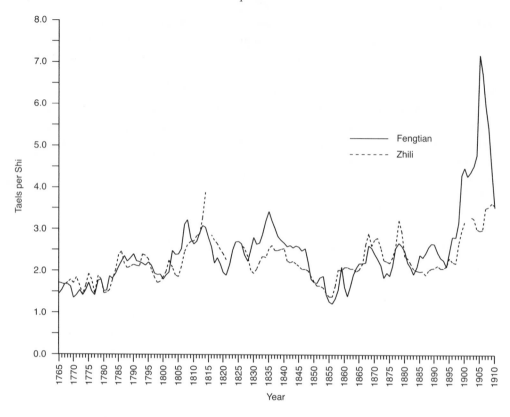

FIGURE 7.3A.   Wheat prices in Zhili and Fengtian, 1765–1911

Price Integration with Other Regions

Although there was no trend toward greater integration of prices among markets within Zhili, the province as a whole was definitely tied to external markets from which it received grain supplies. Zhili grain prices exhibited a strong relationship with Fengtian and an increasingly strong relationship with Lower Yangzi rice prices after the opening of Tianjin as a treaty port in 1860, which expanded direct coastal trade to Shanghai and other treaty ports.

In the Qing period, Zhili became very dependent on Fengtian's increasingly abundant agricultural production to support its growing population. By the late eighteenth century, Fengtian was supplying Zhili at least a million shi of grain a year through official channels, used mainly to stock the ever-normal granaries, the mainstay of famine relief grain dispensed in Zhili. The cost of grain in Fengtian was considerably less than in Zhili, and the expansion of sea transport greatly reduced the total cost. Although the Qing court initially forbade sea transport from Fengtian, in the Yong-zheng and early Qianlong periods the ban was frequently lifted to relieve harvest shortfalls in Zhili. Although these suspensions were considered provisional, sea transport became the regular practice, and after 1773 the ban on sea transport lifted.[72] The Tianjin-Liaodong maritime trade expanded from ten ships in Kangxi period to hundreds in Jiaqing period, allowing Fengtian grain to become increasingly important for Zhili.[73]

Responding to an imperial inquiry in 1785 about the practice of official purchases for relief, the

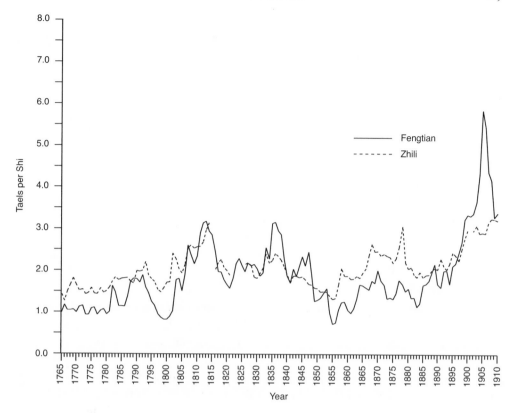

FIGURE 7.3B. Millet prices in Zhili and Fengtian, 1765–1911

provincial official Liang Kentang said that in fact there was no need to depute officials to Fengtian. Each year at Tianjin and Ninghe districts, there were more than 1,000 merchants who applied for licenses to transport grain from Fengtian. The government, he argued, need only purchase grain from these private traders and thereby save the cost of sea transport. On arrival, the grain was usually transferred to outside merchants, who rented small boats to transport it via the Grand Canal to Shandong, or further via the Wei River to Daming in Zhili and Linzhang in Henan. It was not Zhili alone that benefited from Fengtian's grain supply, but also all the districts in Shandong and Henan along the river routes. In the current year, the Tianjin intendant had reported that 800 boats had gone to Tianjin, and together they would transport a total of hundreds of thousands of shi of grain.[74]

In 1810, in response to the Jiaqing emperor's inquiry about rumors of large congregations of merchants at Baigou he and Tianjin, Governor-general Wen Chenghui replied:

> Xincheng and Rongcheng Counties [in Baoding Prefecture north of Gaoyang] have joint jurisdiction over Baigou he, which . . . commands the [internal] routes to the *dian* (swamps) and also to Tianjin on the south, . . . but no big merchants congregate there; there are only five grain shops with a total inventory of 31,000 shi wheat and 800 shi of beans. There is no rice and no *zaliang* [mixed grains]. But at Tianjin, ships come from Fengtian to Tianjin carrying *zaliang*, 700,000–800,000 shi a year, up to 1.3–1.4 million. Only a small amount is rice. . . . There is only one grain market at Tianjin outside the East Gate. Nearby at Yangliuqing there is one relatively large market town, and its small shops do not sell much rice either.[75]

TABLE 7.5A
Regression of Zhili Wheat Prices on Fengtian and Lower Yangzi Grain Prices, 1765–1895
(solar monthly data for Zhili and Fengtian, solar annual average for Lower Yangzi)

Variable	1765–1895	1765–1798	1799–1869	1870–1895
Constant	-0.4963	4.1641	7.2441	64.5611
	(t = -1.14)	(t = 1.09)	(t = 5.29)	(t = 18.73)
Year	0.0006	-0.0022	-0.0036	-0.0341
	(t = 2.5)	(t = -1.02)	(t = -4.85)	(t = -18.36)
Fengtian Wheat	0.6048	0.7659	0.5171	0.4925
	(t = 30.11)	(t = 13.41)	(t = 17.99)	(t = 9.33)
Lower Yangzi Rice	0.0983	0.1230	0.1519	0.4825
	(t = 5.75)	(t = 3.08)	(t = 6.52)	(t = 7.55)
R^2	0.521	0.592	0.511	0.606

Although this memorial was intended as an argument against conducting official granary purchases at Tianjin, it also reveals how important sea transport had become, far overshadowing internal land or water transport of grain from beyond the Great Wall. This continued into the twentieth century. "Honan and southern Chihli used to be the granary of north China," reported the *Chinese Economic Journal*. "In former times the bulk of the cereals marketed at Tientsin was imported by junk from the interior of Chihli and Honan. In recent years owing to famine and unsettled conditions, the supply from this source has been decreasing, while imports from Manchuria and the Mongolian border have been on the increase."[76]

The integration of Fengtian and Zhili, particularly through sea transport, is well reflected in grain price behavior. As seen in Figures 7.3a–b, Fengtian prices exhibited the same broad secular trends as Zhili's, although they were by no means highly correlated in every period. In the 1895–1911 period, prices of both provinces rose steeply, but Fengtian's price spike far exceeded Zhili's. The Zhili price series may be better understood by regressing it on grain prices in Fengtian and the Lower Yangzi for the period from 1765 (when the Fengtian data begin) to 1895 (after which point severe inflation would greatly distort the results). The coefficients reported in Tables 7.5a–b reveal that Fengtian wheat prices had a stronger influence than did Fengtian millet prices, and that both were more influential than Lower Yangzi rice prices. Regression coefficients were 0.605 for Fengtian wheat and 0.098 for Lower Yangzi rice, and 0.408 for Fengtian millet and 0.035 for Lower Yangzi rice. (See Appendix 3.)

When divided into subperiods, Fengtian prices remain important, but the estimated coefficients decrease over time. For wheat it declines from 0.766 in 1765–98 period to 0.517 in 1799–1869, to 0.492 in the 1870–95 period; for millet it rises slightly from 0.325 for the first period, 0.364 for the 1799–1869 period, and then declines to 0.149 for the final period.

Lower Yangzi rice prices were less strongly related to Zhili's overall, but the connection increased over time. In the regression of Zhili wheat prices, the coefficients on Lower Yangzi rice increase from 0.0123 in the 1765–98 period to 0.482 in the 1870–95 period. The Lower Yangzi rice coefficients in the regression on Zhili millet prices rise from 0.083 in the 1765–98 period, to 0.650 in the 1870–95 period. All these results are statistically significant at the 2 percent level, at least, and the overall validity of the regressions is represented by high R^2s.

TABLE 7.5B
Regression of Zhili Millet Prices on Fengtian and Lower Yangzi Grain Prices, 1765–1895
(solar monthly data for Zhili and Fengtian, solar annual average for Lower Yangzi)

Variable	1765–1895	1765–1798	1799–1869	1870–1895
Constant	-3.1067 (t = -8.00)	-11.0454 (t = -5.92)	8.2069 (t = 7.70)	45.4765 (t = 12.09)
Year	0.0024 (t = 11.24)	0.0068 (t = 6.52)	-0.0039 (t = -6.79)	-0.0238 (t = -11.76)
Fengtian Millet	0.4076 (t = 27.07)	0.3251 (t = 9.96)	0.3642 (t = 20.10)	0.1493 (t = 2.56)
Lower Yangzi Rice	0.0354 (t = 2.25)	0.0834 (t = 3.17)	0.1396 (t =7.51)	0.6496 (t = 8.73)
R^2	0.505	0.453	0.571	0.427

Figure 7.4 graphically displays the changing relationship between grain prices in the Lower Yangzi and in Zhili. In the eighteenth century, a close correspondence of medium-term cycles and peaks is evident, but in the nineteenth century these relationships break down. Most striking is the huge rice price shock in the 1860s, caused no doubt by the Taiping Rebellion's devastation of the Lower Yangzi area. Equally striking is the lack of impact this had on Zhili grain prices.[77] This may reflect either a breakdown in transport in the post-Taiping recovery, or inaccuracies in Zhili's data collection during this decade. After 1870, however, restoration of peace, the rise of Tianjin as a treaty port, the growth of coastal steam transport—all combined to bring North China and Lower Yangzi prices more in line with each other than ever before.

These trends in the relationship between Zhili and Lower Yangzi prices are echoed in the correlations of prices (price levels, first differences of annual prices, and percentage change from previous year) for three periods: 1738–98, 1799–1869, 1870–1911. There was substantial, secular convergence of price levels, whereas price differences were more weakly correlated in the second period than in the first, but a good deal more closely correlated in the third period than ever before, as seen in Table 7.6. Not surprisingly, wheat shows the strongest correlation, millet next, and sorghum the least.

Conclusion

The strong integration of Zhili grain prices with those of both Fengtian and the Lower Yangzi confirms the view that has long been advanced by Yeh-chien Wang. Beginning with his article "The Secular Trend of Prices during the Ch'ing Period (1644–1911)," published in 1972, and through many subsequent studies, Wang has convincingly demonstrated that during the Qing period prices in key regions of China followed broadly similar long-term trends. In other words, there was a nationwide market for grain. Thus the Zhili-Fengtian and Zhili–Lower Yangzi price integration found here may be seen as part of a national network linking major centers.

This price study employs data from only Zhili, Fengtian, and the Lower Yangzi region. If Henan and Shandong price data were included, there is every reason to believe that the grain prices from those two provinces would be even more closely correlated with Zhili prices, particularly those from

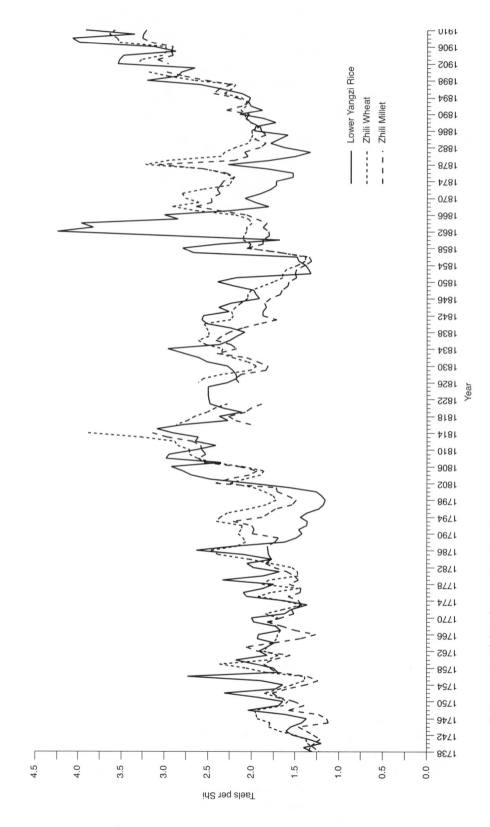

FIGURE 7.4.　Grain prices in Zhili and Lower Yangzi, 1738–1911

TABLE 7.6

Correlation of Zhili Grain Prices with
Lower Yangzi Rice Prices

*(solar annual prices; Zhili provincial average
excluding Xuanhua and Chengde)*

Period	Wheat	Millet	Sorghum
	Price Level		
1738–1798	.094	.142	.134
1799–1869	.287*	.318**	.295*
1870–1911	.819**	.834**	.795**
	First Difference of Prices		
1738–1798	.150	.118	.178
1799–1869	-.052	-.052	-.065
1870–1911	.407**	.308*	.244
	Percentage Change from Previous Year		
1738–1798	.157	.176	.219
1799–1869	.060	.094	.090
1870–1911	.441**	.318*	.258

* Significance LE .05
** Significance LE .01

Zhili's southern sector. Shandong prices were in turn closely linked to Jiangsu's. Such strong integration was apparent as early as 1805, when officials commented on the integration of Shandong prices with Jiangsu prices and deputed officials to go to Jiangsu and buy grain for relief.[78] We have already documented other instances when Shandong grain was deployed to Zhili, either through official or commercial channels. A recent study of Shandong in the Ming and Qing further confirms the fact that Zhili, Hebei, and Shandong formed a close trading network centering on Linqing, on the Grand Canal. In years when there were high prices in one area, suggesting a poor harvest, the amount of grain circulated might have reached 5 or 6 million shi, or even 10 million shi. Even in years of stable prices and lower demand, the volume traded was 1 or 2 million.[79]

Unfortunately, the price data used in this study halt at 1911. But if they continued into the 1930s, they would no doubt reveal continued, and possibly increased, integration with grain prices from south and central China. Grain prices from south and central China from 1870–1937 have already been shown by Loren Brandt to have been closely linked to prices in the major Southeast Asian markets, with which there was major coastal trade from the late nineteenth century.[80] Even beyond that, recent studies have revealed the strong connection between rice and wheat prices in Asian and world markets in the late nineteenth and early twentieth centuries.[81]

But despite some empirewide integration in grain prices, evidence from Zhili shows that intraprovincial market integration did not follow the same trend. To a great extent this conclusion resembles the argument advanced by Rhoads Murphey about the essential gap between treaty ports and interior China in the nineteenth century. Murphey cites the example of trade at the port of Tianjin, emphasizing that even in particular years in the late nineteenth and early twentieth centuries when serious floods and droughts devastated Zhili-Hebei, trade at Tianjin continued to flourish, unaffected by events in the interior.[82] The results in this chapter demonstrate the relationship among major coastal ports was quite strong even prior to the nineteenth-century treaties, while the integration of markets within the Zhili region first improved and then deteriorated. Yet, they also show that Fengtian and Lower Yangzi prices had a strong effect on prices in the whole province, not just at Tianjin. The disintegration of internal markets did not mean that they were unaffected by external markets.

Markets in North China experienced a highly uneven development, with many facilitating factors as well as many obstacles. While transportation through the central part of Zhili was increasingly difficult, the trade of this province with areas beyond the Great Wall was flourishing. Only the political disruptions involving Russia and Japan at the turn of the twentieth century disrupted trade with the Manchurian region. Man Bun Kwan has richly documented this trade and described such trade routes as "dendritic" rather than spatially uniform as central place theory predicts. Focusing principally on the early twentieth century, he concludes "Tianjin's commercial hinterland extended asymmetrically in long paths over provincial boundaries, mountains, and steppes, connecting peasants, nomads, foreign and Chinese traders into a functional region within the world economy."[83]

Quantitative analysis confirms the strong role that the state played in promoting economic stability during the high Qing. It did so by supplying large amounts of grain to Beijing and Zhili, maintaining price stability through measures such as price equalization, grain storage, and famine relief. Yet it is clear that none of these steps led directly to the development of the internal market system—nor, hence, to long-term economic change—in the rural interior of Zhili Province. For this to happen, considerable investments in infrastructure—principally the introduction of rail transport (begun in 1905) and the intensification of irrigation and water conservancy (especially since 1949)—were needed.

CHAPTER EIGHT

Famine Relief:
The High Qing Model

LARGE GRAIN RESERVES played a role in preventing harvest failures from turning into major subsistence crises, but their most direct and important function was in famine relief and reconstruction rather than prevention. During the "high Qing period" the state mounted large-scale relief campaigns to meet crises in various parts of the empire, utilizing the large stocks of grain and well-developed techniques of famine management, and motivated by the commitment of emperors and bureaucrats to maintain economic and social order. Zhili Province was one of the major recipients of famine relief. The successful relief of the drought of 1743–44 was documented by Fang Guancheng in his *Zhenji*. Based in part on earlier precedents, this experience provided guidelines that supplemented the regulations of the Board of Revenue. In 1751, the emperor enjoined all provinces to use Fang Guancheng's fourteen rules of famine relief as a model.[1] Fang was the provincial financial commissioner during the 1743–44 crisis; the record was published in 1754 when he was governor-general. So remarkable were these famine relief campaigns that the eighteenth century has been described as "the golden age of late imperial famine administration."[2]

The *Zhenji* was only one of a substantial corpus of bureaucratic writing about famine relief during the Qing period, but it was exceptional because of the imperial favor that was shown it. Writers in the mid-Qing period included the Manchu statesman Oertai (1680–1745), who published essays on famine relief, *Kangjilu*, in 1739. Chen Hongmou (1696–1771) included famine relief and river control as key topics in his collected essays, *Peiyuan tang oucun gao*. The Manchu official Nayancheng (1764–1833) recorded his experience with famine relief in Gansu Province in 1810 in a work also entitled *Zhenji* (1813). (Nayancheng was governor-general of Zhili in 1813–16 and 1829.) Yang Jingren (1762–1828) wrote *Chouji bian* (On planning relief) in 1823 based on his own experiences in Jiangsu Province. This work was used successfully in 1831 to provide relief in Hubei Province, and in 1877, it was reprinted and used in the Shanxi-Henan drought relief. Essays by these and other authors were included in well-known collections. In his widely consulted work on local administration, *Muling shu* (1848), Xu Dong devoted three *juan* to famine relief, including essays by Chen Hongmou. In the important compendium of statecraft, *Huangchao jingshi wenbian*, edited by He Changling (1785–1848), substantial space is devoted to essays on famine relief, including those by Chen Hongmou, Fang Guancheng, and Yang Jingren.[3]

These essays and records were full of practical advice about how officials should administer famine relief. In almost every case, the author or compiler had substantial experience with famine relief as a local or provincial official and was able to combine "erudition with experience."[4] As governors-general, Fang Guancheng, Nayancheng, and Chen Hongmou were among the highest-ranking statesmen whose advice was solicited by the emperor himself. Although the methods of famine relief they discussed, such as soup kitchens or *pingtiao*, had been part of a familiar repertoire of antifamine techniques, what was new in the high Qing was the assumption of direct central government responsibility over matters that in the past had been considered local responsibilities. Whereas the rhetoric of imperial benevolence toward the people had ancient roots, the reality of state-funded and state-managed famine relief campaigns meant that it was the high-ranking bureaucrat, not the local official or gentry leader, who was in charge. The extent to which the state supported an empirewide granary system and effected huge interregional transfers of grain was unprecedented in Chinese history. The amounts expended on famine relief and tax remissions in the eighteenth century were also unprecedented.

In other ways, the Qing rules on famine relief were not so different from those of earlier eras. Especially since the Song dynasty, famine relief was a subject of great importance to bureaucrats and scholar-gentry. In official dynastic compilations, sections on grain storage and famine administration, *huangzheng*, were customary, and in the writings of statesmen-scholars from Zhu Xi onward, the theory and methods of famine relief were given serious examination. Many of the Ming-Qing works drew on the Song-dynasty work *Jiuhuang huomin shu* by Dong Wei.[5] Some raised theoretical issues, discussing the philosophy or assumptions behind certain practices, but for the most part these famine relief treatises describe commonly encountered dilemmas and suggest practical techniques for resolving them. Certain issues were frequently discussed: (1) the leadership that should be exercised by officials and gentry, and with respect to the latter, how to encourage donations by the rich families; (2) the relative importance of cash versus grain in giving relief; (3) how to prevent cheating; (4) how to keep people from fleeing their homes, and (5) how to use price stabilization methods without discouraging farming and commerce, and so forth.

Most of the works from the late sixteenth and seventeenth centuries, the late Ming period, were authored by scholar-gentry figures from the Jiangnan, Lower Yangzi, region. Although some wrote in their capacity as local magistrates, even more were members of the local elite. Famine relief was but one aspect of their dedication to charitable work in general, a development characteristic of the late Ming period. Previously local officials bore the responsibility for famine relief activities, but from the late Ming, several new types of charitable institutions and practices developed. "Unlike Buddhist monasteries and lineages, they were wholly dedicated to philanthropy. Unlike state-sponsored institutions, they were set up and managed by members of the local elite (. . . retired officials, scholars, and wealthy residents)" whose main motive for doing good works was to show their generosity and virtue, according to Joanna Handlin Smith.[6] In the 1640s, when Qi Biaojia and his fellow gentry members in Shanyin County, Jiangsu Province, mounted a famine relief operation, they assumed a leadership role independent of the local magistrate. Yet at the same time they sought his support for their plans.[7]

The distinction between local gentry-led famine relief initiatives and large-scale state-financed famine relief campaigns was certainly not absolute. Even the statecraft essayists of the Qing, which included those with abundant bureaucratic experience, dwelt constantly on the need for elite involvement. As a practical matter, contributions from well-to-do local residents, whether landlord or merchant, were always sought; grain, clothing, and money were all needed. Elite assistance in maintaining soup kitchens was necessary because subofficial personnel were insufficient or unreliable.[8] In fact, Yang Jingren wrote about the importance of flattering the rich. The rich households should be cultivated even in normal times so that in hard times they would be easily persuaded to contribute grain.[9] Lu Shiji, another statecraft essayist, wrote that in famine prevention pacifying the rich (*anfu*) was second in importance only to promoting agriculture.[10]

Still the state-organized campaigns of the high Qing, as well as the scholar bureaucrats who engaged in discourse about famine relief techniques, adopted a far broader perspective than that of the local elites. They were far more concerned with the interests of the state and the balance of resources spread all over the empire. For them the goal of famine relief was to restore agricultural production and to avert or relieve social disorder—not to earn individual merit and local prestige. Rather than focusing on individual acts of charity, they took a rather hardheaded, practical approach to this important aspect of administration and governance. It was truly a matter of famine administration—*huangzheng*—and not of charity.[11]

To accomplish these goals, Qing officials had a number of key tools at their disposal that they could apply according to the circumstances and to the extent authorized by the court. Some, such as soup kitchens or reduced-price sales, were familiar local practices, but systematic investigation of famine conditions and the distribution of "general relief" were more ambitious endeavors that only the central government could authorize and undertake. Fang Guancheng's fourteen rules for famine relief provided the general guidelines, but there was a great deal of flexibility in the application of all the techniques.

Famine Investigation

The investigation and classification of districts and households was one of the most important aspects of the 1743–44 effort and the subsequent campaigns.[12] The regulations of the Board of Revenue stated that when a harvest crisis occurred, the governor should report it. A summer disaster had to be reported by the last ten days of the sixth lunar month, while an autumn disaster had to be reported by the end of the ninth lunar month (except in Gansu Province, where the dates were later). The governor or his deputies should personally go to inspect the disaster areas; in an especially severe disaster, the governor should go in person. The local officials should prepare a register of fields and households and their degree of disaster. In the fall months, whether or not the flood or drought turned into a disaster, the governor should report the conditions, and at the same time open up the granaries to feed the people. No matter what the degree of severity, he should give one month's relief. Within forty-five days, further relief should then be given according to the degree of disaster. There were deadlines for each phase of reporting.[13]

The most important step after reporting famine was a survey of conditions in the localities. The survey and classification of regions was similar to the routine semiannual harvest reports. In rating degrees of crisis or *zai*, a 10 meant the most severe disaster, and a 5 meant a 50 percent disaster, below which no relief was deemed necessary. This process was known as *kanzai* or "investigating crisis." A locality with a rating above 5 was deemed *chengzai*, or "developed into a crisis," others were *kan bu chengzai*, "investigated, but not developed into a crisis." (In theory, the investigation of crisis should have taken place after the harvest failure, but one suspects that the same investigation that produced the harvest rating also produced the crisis rating.) Those localities that had mixed conditions were described as "partial disaster," or *pianzai*.[14]

The second aspect of famine investigation was the survey and classification of households by degree of need, called *chazhen*, or "survey of relief needs." Although examples of elaborate classification systems are cited in the earlier famine relief literature, in Zhili only two classifications were assigned: "very poor" (*jipin*) and "less poor" (*cipin*). The distinction between the two groups was based on an assessment of the extent of crop loss in the field as well as damage or loss of tools and farm animals.[15] Records of famine relief in other parts of China suggest that the amount of property owned by the family and the size of a family were key considerations.[16] The amount of relief to which a household was entitled to receive was based on a combination of the locality's crisis rating and its household classification.[17]

Famine investigation was crucial because it determined who was fairly entitled to what amount of relief, but its second function was to avoid misappropriation of funds by officials or functionaries. "The total lack of confidence in the personnel that were supposed to serve as the connecting link between government and the people explains why, in eighteenth-century practice, it was considered necessary to provide special supervision in times of famine and to supplement the local administration with regular officials especially commissioned for the purpose." Indeed, the *Zhenji* shows that an impressive number of officials were assigned to supervise the 1743–44 famine investigation: in addition to the magistrates of the 16 severely affected counties were 16 other officials, their 69 assistants, and 85 assistant officials brought in from other counties.[18] In the final analysis, the total number of personnel employed in the effort was 245.[19]

The problem of honesty was recognized in the previous decades. In 1715, Governor-general Zhao Hongxie stressed the need for secret memorials when requesting famine relief; if the communication was routine, the danger was that word would get out and functionaries would take advantage of the advance knowledge.[20] A few months later he requested more personnel to inspect the distribution of relief. "Only if the officials are capable will the people benefit from relief."[21] During the flood of 1725, another governor-general, Li Weijun, planned a household investigation in villages in the most heavily affected counties in order to distribute famine relief of 3 he of grain (*mi*) per adult and 2 he per child. This was an early step in building the high Qing model.[22] In 1732 another governor-general, Liu Yuyi, commented that the distribution of relief was not difficult, but the household inspection was. Local officials should make sure that the names of the poor were put in a separate record, not the usual *baojia* records. Through personal experience he had discovered that local officials sometimes concealed the fact that there were hungry people. Liu's team of twelve personally went to each locality to investigate the poor people, under the pretext of reduced-price sales, but they felt they had not learned the truth.[23]

Although there was a chronic and justifiable fear of malfeasance on the part of the functionaries, famine investigation may have been done with greater rigor than the collection of population and land data and received more official scrutiny.[24] The crucial principle was that famine investigation be kept separate from the distribution of relief.[25] Severe sanctions were applied against those found cheating. Publicity was a technique frequently used in famine relief: public announcements concerning the dates and terms of relief distribution, posting of a household's rating on its door, so it could be matched with the records, and so forth.[26] Posting of notices was to minimize subbureaucratic misuse of relief supplies and funds, and was recommended in other measures such as silver/cash exchange rates or tax remissions.

General Relief

After investigation of the districts and classification of households, famine relief could be distributed according to the prescribed regulations. The purpose of *dazhen*, or general relief, was that households should be sustained throughout the winter. However, in severe crises such as the 1743 drought, *jizhen*, or emergency relief, (also called *puzhen*) was given in the eighth month in order to provide immediate assistance before famine investigation and regular relief could begin. In the case of the old, ill, or abandoned, *puzhen* continued for two additional months. Usually general relief would commence in the eleventh lunar month and continue until the second or third lunar month of the next year, with the possibility of extension.[27] In 1743 *dazhen* began in the eleventh lunar month but continued until the fifth lunar month of the next year, for a total of seven months of relief. This was particularly generous, and eventually overlooked the distinction between "very poor" and "less poor" households and the statutory limit of four months' relief for the partially ruined counties.[28] In the *Hubu zeli* (Regulations and precedents of the Board of Revenue), the term *dazhen* was not used, at least not in the nineteenth-century editions; instead the term *zhengzhen*, "principal relief," was used for the first month's relief; and the later months of relief were *jiazhen*, "additional relief."[29] This and evidence in the case studies below suggest that general relief was not the normal expectation after the late eighteenth century.

According to the statutes, the rate of relief was 5 he of *mi* per day for each adult and half that amount for a child (those under twelve *sui* were considered children). The amount should be doubled for *gu*, or unhusked grain.[30] If a household had too many mouths, then the amounts might be commuted into silver.[31] Thus the monthly grain ration for adults was 7 sheng, 7 he, and the monthly amount for children was 3 sheng, 7 he, 5 tiao, if the rate was half grain and half money.[32] This standard of rations was frequently not met in relief efforts later on. On the other hand, privately published famine relief manuals recommend even more generous rations.[33]

The number of monthly rations was proportionate to the degree of disaster severity and the household's level of poverty. In the most severely affected localities that had experienced 100 percent harvest loss, or a rating of 10, the very poor households would receive four months of relief, and the less poor would receive three months of relief. In the localities that lost 90 percent of the harvest, or a rating of 9, very poor households received three months of relief, and the less poor two months. In localities rated 8 or 7, the very poor households received two months and the less poor one month. In localities rated 6, the very poor households received one month of rations, and the less poor received none. In localities rated 5, households were permitted to borrow rations to be repaid in the spring.[34]

The purpose of general relief was not social welfare, but agricultural assistance. *Zai*, or disaster, meant a harvest failure, nothing more and nothing less. The purpose of relief, as Will first pointed out, was to compensate for agricultural loss and to aid the restoration of agricultural production. The *Zhenji* was explicit on this point, giving a well-reasoned explanation.

> When the crops in the fields encounter disaster, then dispensation of merciful relief [*zhenxu*] is put into effect. Because of the relief, agriculture can be saved. Farmers [*nongmin*] toil all year long and the taxes they pay benefit the public [*gong*]. The accumulated contents of the treasuries and storehouses of the empire are the result of the farmers' labor. That which is used for relief in disasters is only that which was contributed by them in abundant years.[35]

Here is the same idealistic but practical logic that Fang used in his arguments about labor relief, or grain storage; these state-sponsored programs were essentially self-funding, not gifts by the state to the people. It is in these ideas that the term *huangzheng* reaches its fullest expression. Sometimes translated as "famine relief," but by Will as "famine administration," it implies that a harvest failure, *zaihuang*, could and should be regulated or managed (*zheng*) by the rulers.

Famine relief, according to this logic, was only for producing farmers, and not general charity for others who might also be poor. The *Zhenji* was explicit, even harsh, on this point.

> Those who are poor [*pin*] but not on account of disaster [*zai*] should not count as farmers [*nong*]. . . . To provide relief also to those who are impoverished, but not because of disaster, is to confuse relief with broad general acts. It is not necessary to give relief to the infirm and elderly who are poor. This mistakenly regards relief as a method of supporting the elderly. If beggars get to eat their fill during poor years, will this not give them the attitude of rejoicing in disaster? If workers get to eat by simply sitting comfortably [and doing no work], will this not slacken their body's industriousness? If the farmer is starving, then everyone will starve. If grain is expensive, then all other goods will also be expensive. This is why simply spreading imperial benevolence widely is not the basic meaning of administering relief.[36]

To promote the quickest restoration of production, relief measures emphasized the loans of seeds, in this case wheat seeds, to aid in planting. Considerable importance was also attached to measures to prevent the sale of oxen by peasant households.[37]

Other special social groups were also excluded from general famine relief. Estate managers and workers (*zhuangtou, zhuangding*) and their servants on the banner estates were not eligible. Nor were bannermen in general. Exceptions could be made for those bannermen who actually engaged in farming as an occupation and had no sons who were officials. Other exceptions were often made. For example, in 1809, special relief was requested for bannermen in Beijing because they were especially poor.[38] *Zaohu*, or brewers, were registered as merchants and therefore ineligible.[39] Poor "students," *shengyuan* degree-holders studying for higher degrees, were also an exception; a limit of one-third of them could be given relief, with the assumption that there were only three adults in the household.[40]

Grain Versus Cash / Millet Versus Sorghum

The high Qing model of famine relief emphasized state distributions of grain, with silver as a supplemental portion. Under certain circumstances, the grain portion of the ration could be commuted to monetary distributions. There is evidence from ancient times of the use of cash, justified in terms of the convenience of the people.[41] However, most previous arguments about using cash or silver instead of grain were likely based on the experience in the Lower Yangzi provinces, which were relatively commercialized. The use of abundant grain surpluses in the eighteenth century allowed grain to be the normal and preferred form of relief. By the turn of the nineteenth century, however, the use of cash in famine relief was increasingly practiced. Although giving money was usually justified in terms of convenience to the people, it also served the interests of the government since the cost of grain storage and distribution could be avoided.

In 1743–44, grain played the major role, but even then 1 million taels of silver were used as relief. In 1757, when Fang Guancheng jointly investigated a waterlogging disaster in four counties in Henan, he and Tuerbina jointly recommended that relief be given in cash at the rate of silver 0.60 taels per shi of *gu*. The usual ratio they said was 70 percent *mi* and 30 percent silver. Expanding the silver portion, they argued, would benefit the people.[42] In 1799, Governor-general Hu Jitang requested that relief be completely given in cash, as a convenience to the people. Of thirty-seven counties inspected because of flooding, *dazhen* was requested for twelve. The remaining granary stocks should be saved for *pingtiao* in the spring, he argued.[43]

During the 1801 crisis, a considerable amount of grain was used for relief, but cash was used to a much greater extent than previously. "In dispensing famine relief, using silver is not as good as using grain, using grain is not as good as using cash," they argued. Silver had the problem of fineness and weight, while grain had the problem of cheating on measures, but in using cash, the authorities could decide on the amount and make a public announcement so everyone would know, and "the officials and functionaries won't have an opportunity to cheat."[44] The acting governor-general, Chen Dawen, requested giving cash relief instead of purchasing grain from Shandong and Henan. Although an imperial edict had stated that in principle the giving of grain was better than giving cash, he argued that transport costs would be too high. If 100,000 taels of the 1.5 million the emperor had allocated for relief were used for grain purchases, the costs would double those of giving cash. (The price of Shandong and Henan grain at the time was 1.20 taels.) There was, moreover, enough reserve grain both in grain tribute and regular state granaries that could be released for famine relief, without employing government purchases.[45] In later years, cash was increasingly substituted for grain in relief operations. For example, in 1819, cash was substituted in a Beijing relief operation.[46] In 1820, cash was permitted to be given during a relief operation in Fengtian principally because grain stocks had been depleted in the previous year's relief. The conversion rate suggested was the average of the last nine months' sorghum prices.[47] In 1857, after multiple disasters, the distribution of cash, after some grain, was promoted.[48]

A related tendency was to use sorghum as the basis for conversion to silver. For example, in 1812, it was proposed that sorghum be used instead of millet for relief at Chengde. In this case, as in many others, the justification for this change was, "We know that banner households are accustomed to eating *gaoliang.*" Additionally, since sorghum was less expensive than millet, it would stretch the budget further. If given as relief, however, the price would rise. Thus, the argument concluded that cash, at the rate of current sorghum prices, would be the most efficient.

> The granaries' stock has not been replenished, so we need grain from elsewhere. We know that banner households are accustomed to eating *gaoliang.* We observe that the monthly report from each *cheng* [county capital] shows each *cangshi* [granary shi] of millet is worth 4.18 to 2.20, and *gaoliang* 2.28 to 1.13. So each 8 dou of millet is worth one shi of *gaoliang.* So the price would be worth 2.85 to 1.41. Compared with millet you can save 1.33 to 0.79 per shi using sorghum. If we give out millet, we don't have enough. If we buy sorghum, the crafty merchants will raise the price. *So the best thing is to give out money calculated according to the market price of sorghum.*[49]

The same procedures were used in Fengtian relief in 1818 and 1819.

> We ought to give relief in kind, but the granaries in Fengtian are empty. So let's give cash. In the ninth month millet [*sumi*] was 2.24–1.27, and *gaoliang* was 1.36–0.52. If one shi of *gaoliang* is worth 8 dou [of millet], and one shi *mi* costs 1.70–0.65, so you could save 0.62–0.54 over millet. We have discussed this and agree that since Fengtian's banner population are accustomed to eat *gaoliang* . . . , if we convert at the *gaoliang* price, we can allow the households to receive Imperial grace. We request conversion rates [*zhese*] half according to old *sumi* precedents and half according to the current price of *gaoliang* so that people can purchase various grains.[50]

Although justified on the basis of efficiency and convenience, it is clear that such measures only reduced the actual value of the relief that famine victims received.

Soup Kitchens

Soup kitchens, or *zhouchang*, were centers that distributed rice or other gruel to famine victims and had a long tradition in China. Operating such centers was a function of the local elite in the south, and much of the traditional famine relief literature centers on their appropriate method of operation. Not only did they relieve local hunger, but also soup kitchens were considered to be the finest act of either Buddhist-inspired charity or Confucian-inspired community philanthropy.[51] In Beijing soup kitchens were operated every winter and were used increasingly as a famine relief measure. Provincial capitals and other localities were encouraged to follow Beijing's example.[52] Normally soup kitchens were used in urban centers rather than the countryside. In the famine relief regulations, which focused on the countryside, soup kitchens were accorded a lesser role than grain and cash distributions. In the Fang model, soup kitchens were expected to play an auxiliary role only, being used as a bridge before the commencement of general relief and after it ended. In practice, however, even in the eighteenth century local officials found soup kitchens easier to manage than direct distributions, and in the state famine relief operations of the nineteenth century, soup kitchens played an even larger role.[53]

In the late Kangxi period the virtues of soup kitchens were advocated by Governor Zhao Hongxie. Although the fall harvest was reported to be excellent, he requested setting up soup kitchens in nine places where the water from previous flooding had not drained off. He said that soup kitchens were better than giving grain to people at home because it would be possible to prevent bandits from causing trouble by falsifying identities. If you get the grain and cook it and serve it, you will get the most effective result, he argued. Those willing to show up in person would be truly poor. If the supervisory personnel were upright, the poor will really be benefited by this method. He proposed using grain from granaries to set up soup kitchens from 11/15 to 3/1 of the next year. "After the fall harvest next year, I and other local officials will donate our salaries to return those items borrowed from the granaries. That way the granaries will not be deficient and the poor will be able to benefit," he memorialized.[54]

Half a century later, Fang Guancheng advocated soup kitchens in the context of charitable granaries, which were located in the countryside. His regulations for *yicang* state that soup kitchens should be set up when people are starving. There should be one feeding per day, and women should be served before men. The ration of *mi* should be 5 he for adults and 2.5 for children. Thus 1 shi of *mi* could feed 200 or more people. Five shi a day could feed 1,000 adults and children. It should be given to nearby people only.[55] In 1819, when Governor-general Fang Shouchou advocated soup kitchens for counties around Beijing in order to stop refugees from flocking to the city, he considered that 3 he of *mi*, not the previously recommended 5 he, was sufficient to address one day's hunger.[56]

Although they provided the most direct form of famine relief, there were those who argued that soup kitchens did less good than they should have. In the essays on famine relief in *Huangchao jingshi wenbian*, much doubt is cast on the value of soup kitchens. Wei Xi wrote that soup kitchens were necessary only when conditions were too critical to give out only grain.[57] Zhang Boxing wrote that in his experience operating a soup kitchen was dangerous because of the mobs that pressed in. It was the officials who usually gave out gruel, not the gentry, who would like to do it but did not dare.[58] Hui Shiqi wrote that to pass out gruel was one of the four evil practices of famine relief. "It is supposed to save people, but it really kills them," he said. "Petty functionaries take it up. The strong get the rice, and the old and weak do not. . . . Only two or three out of ten will survive, and the others will die. Besides when several thousands crowd into the city, and steam rises, disease is bound to spread. And many thieves will emerge."[59] Huang Mao wrote that giving grain rations was better than giving out gruel. It saved the cost of transportation. It prevented people from having to go back and forth every day. Men could go collect the rice every five days; women did not have to leave their homes and enter the public places. Rich households would be more willing to contribute grain.[60] Most of these passages seem to represent situations in the south, where the expectation of local elite leadership still prevailed.

Pingtiao

Pingtiao, or reduced-price sales, functioned both as famine prevention and famine relief. In principle, the ever-normal granaries, annually sold off 30 percent of their stocks at the time of *qinghuang bujie*, or the lean season just before the summer harvest. They restocked after the fall harvest, when prices were the lowest. During times of crisis, however, reduced-price sales served as another way to lower prices. *Pingtiao* was supposed to be undertaken in every province, but rarely did it match the regularity and frequency of its use in Beijing.

Pingtiao rates and regulations were set by the Board of Revenue, with some allowance for regional differences, and adjusted only rarely. In crises the governor or governor-general was allowed a certain amount of discretion. The regulations for *pingtiao* as found in *Hubu zeli* stated:

> The general rule is to keep 70 percent and sell off 30 percent, but the conditions in each province differ and so should the ratios. In Jiangsu, for example, the rate is 3 and 7. Fengtian, Guizhou, and Jiangxi have no limits on the amounts they can sell at any one time. In case of disaster you can exceed the quota. In case of stable prices, you need not necessarily sell 30 percent; you could sell 10–20 percent. Within 5 fen the governor can set the price or the level himself. Above 5 fen he needs to report. But he cannot just empty out the granaries. In normal times, the price should be reduced by 5 fen per shi, but in lean times, by 1 qian per shi. In a big crisis, reduction should be greater. For those rural districts [*xiang*] and villages [*cun*] too distant to go to the city's markets to buy grain, two officials should be deputed to set up stations on the roads to distribute the shipped *pingtiao* grain.[61]

During the eighteenth century, the regulations about *pingtiao* during famine relief were: if the market price was 1.50–1.80 taels, it should be reduced by 0.10; if it was 1.80–2.00 taels, the price should be reduced by 0.20; if it was over 2.10 taels, the price should be reduced by 0.30. Prices under 1.50 taels did not require relief. At the Northern Granary in Tianjin the rate was 5 fen (0.05 tael) per shi, but in lean years, it was 1 qian (0.10 tael).[62]

In the early nineteenth century, *pingtiao* continued to be used during harvest crises, but since prices were significantly higher, new rates were established. In 1811, the *pingtiao* practices in Zhili were reported by Wen Chenghui.

> The price of grain in Bazhou and other districts is daily increasing. Lesser-grade millet [*cisumi*] has gone up to more than 3 taels per shi. We request that the stipend grain [*fengmi*] left over from last year—28,000 shi—be used for *pingtiao* sales. According to JQ 14 [1809] precedent, if the price is between 1.80–2.00 taels, reduce it by 0.20; if it is 2.00 to 2.50, reduce it by 0.30; and if it is 2.60 to 3.00, reduce it by 0.40. If over 3.00, then every shi should be sold at the set price of 2.50. If the price is less than 1.80, then follow the old rules. Ask officials to watch out for hoarding by merchants and mischief by functionaries. If there is not enough grain, then use cash conversion rate of 1.40 per shi. After the fall harvest, the grain should be returned but no interest should be charged.[63]

In 1814 a memorial from Zhili governor-general Nayancheng confirmed new guidelines for *pingtiao*, identical to the 1811 guidelines, except that even under 1.80, the price should be reduced by 0.10 taels.

> I observe that in Xingtai and other counties last fall the harvest was meager, and there is little grain, and the prices are high. Only if we conduct reduced-price sales will the people be able to eat. I request 22,000 shi or more of stipend grain [*fengmi*] stored in excess at the Northern Granary be left in Zhili for use in *pingtiao*. At Xingtai and other markets *the price of millet is over 5 taels.* . . . If this is done, the price must go down gradually. If neighboring districts can help out, the province will pay transport. I will order each district to *prevent merchants from hoarding grain and yamen underlings from practicing corruption.*[64]

These memorials around the time of the 1813 crisis, when grain prices reached unprecedented heights, reveal the ongoing practice of, and faith in, the efficacy of *pingtiao*.

Throughout the Qing, however, arguments against *pingtiao* were raised. Most were focused on the problems of restocking and on the hardships that might create either locally or in the areas of purchase. In the mid-eighteenth century the censor Xu Yisheng memorialized at length on the wastefulness and corruption in the practice of *pingtiao*, which raised prices rather than lowering them. He felt that the granaries should be maintained only for famine relief.[65] Others said that reduced-price sales did not benefit poor people directly, since they might not have enough cash with which to purchase any grain. The real beneficiaries, critics said, were unscrupulous dealers or hoarders, who could come in and buy up the grain for future sales.[66] Because of this concern the statutes said, "When the time comes for the *pingtiao* sales, the governor must tell the local officials to strictly forbid the practice of hoarding. If they do not, they will be prosecuted."[67] Almost every directive about *pingtiao* admonished local officials to be vigilant against unscrupulous merchants.[68]

The efficacy of seasonal *pingtiao* in maintaining stable prices in normal times has been questioned. In Beijing, reduced-price sales were important both for seasonal and emergency use, but elsewhere the 30 percent target was not often met, and the amounts of reduction were not great. Still, Zhili's ever-normal granaries were probably more functional than those in other provinces.[69] *Pingtiao* was more effective in crisis management. After the Daoguang period, however, *pingtiao* was rarely used for emergency relief, even at Beijing, and given the much diminished granary stocks of the period, seasonal *pingtiao* also ceased to be practiced. At exceptionally critical times, however, reduced-price sales, together with soup kitchens, were the remaining tools available to the authorities. During the crises of the 1870s, Li Hongzhang ordered *pingtiao* in Beijing. During the flood of 1917, *pingtiao* was ordered by the flood relief committee.

Tax Remissions

Tax remissions or reductions were a major tool in the state's arsenal against famines and hardship in general. The regulations of the Board of Revenue describe several types of tax forgiveness.[70] First there was general cancellation of taxes for the empire for the entire year, *pujuan*. In 1710 the emperor declared a general cancellation to be effective in the next year and extending over the next three years, including all unpaid back taxes. The total amount forgiven was 38 million taels. During the Qianlong period, general forgiveness was declared on four occasions for land taxes (*difu*)—in 1745, 1770, 1777, and 1790—each for the following year or years—and three times for the forgiveness of grain tribute (*caofu*). On the latter occasion, the imperial edict urged the local officials to persuade the rich landlords to pass on the benefit to their tenants.[71] In the last year of the Qianlong emperor's reign, he declared general forgiveness of all land taxes, which was spread out over the first three years of the Jiaqing period, and totaled about 28 million taels. This was the last time the dynasty declared general forgiveness.[72]

Second, there was the permanent cancellation or reduction of taxes for particular areas because they were places of chronic hardship, or *yongjuan*. Most of the cases cited in regulations of the Board of Revenue refer to Jiangnan area, but in 1746 Zhili's Qingyun County received a 30 percent reduction of its annual land tax quota because of its poor land, and its inability to recover from repeated disasters.[73] Based on this precedent, in 1802, Wen'an County received a 30 percent permanent reduction after the big flood of the previous year.[74] Wen'an was surrounded by a dike and was frequently inundated. Fifty-one of its 360 villages were within its *dawa* (big depression); the villages were to receive annual inspection to see if their rates needed further adjustment.[75]

Third, there was the cancellation of accumulated back taxes. This was called *pumian jiqian*, or *enmian jiqian* (imperial forgiveness of accumulated back taxes). In 1735, all land taxes owed from before 1734 were forgiven, although some argued that this would help landlords more than the unemployed poor people.[76] In 1794 as part of a general forgiveness of accumulated taxes, Zhili's back taxes were forgiven. Its accumulated unpaid debts totaled 2.9 million taels, plus 1.2 million shi of *cangliang* (granary grain), and 42.5 thousand bundles of straw (*su*), and 796.4 thousand wen of *zhiqian* (copper cash). The total for all provinces amounted to 17 million taels and 3.75 million shi of grain. The six provinces that had no back taxes to forgive were to get 20 percent reduction of their taxes for the next year.[77]

Under subsequent reigns, there were other instances of tax forgiveness. In the Jiaqing period, there was forgiveness of back taxes in 1799 amounting to 83,380 taels, and 29,000 plus shi of grain. In 1809, all seed and feed lent out was forgiven, amounting to 17,354 taels, and 5,351 shi of grain. In 1818, there was forgiveness of back taxes and taxes delayed because of disaster, totaling 1.029 million taels.[78] In 1835, the fifteenth year of Daoguang, a general forgiveness of back taxes up to 1830 was declared. This amounted to 472,628 taels and miscellaneous grain for Zhili.[79] This was repeated in 1845 for all land taxes, surcharges, delayed taxes, and lent-out seed and feed for debts up to 1840. For Zhili this amounted to 94,312 taels and miscellaneous grain and other items.[80] In the Xianfeng period, there was a similar complete forgiveness of back taxes up to 1850. The amount for Zhili was 1.3 million taels and miscellaneous grain and straw.[81] In 1862, the first year of Tongzhi, there was a forgiveness for Zhili and Henan provinces of taxes accumulated up to 1859, for grain tribute and lent-out seed.[82]

Lastly, there was the specific reduction or postponement of tax obligations of particular counties because of disasters in the current year. In the records, these steps are called variously *juanmian*, *huomian*, *huandai*, or *juanhuan*. This type of tax remission was the most directly related to famine relief. The amount of tax reduction was based on the assessment of the extent of damage suffered by each county. Households in the most severely affected counties, those rated 10, were to have their taxes reduced by 70 percent; 9th degree districts by 60 percent; 8th degree by 40 percent, 7th degree by 20 percent; and 6th and 5th degree by 10 percent. The districts rated 8–10 could postpone their payments over three years, the 5–7th degree areas over two years, and districts below 5th degree were allowed to postpone paying until after the wheat harvest of the following year, or a similarly appropriate harvest or event. The collection of "meltage fee" surcharges (*haoxian*) could be postponed at the same rates. In Zhili the "rents" from banner lands were also reduced or postponed according to disaster ratings.[83]

In the Jiaqing period, there were frequent tax postponements or remissions for Zhili. In

1807–10 there were various postponements of taxes. In 1811 in addition to the one-third of the land tax for that year that was forgiven, all those accumulated postponed taxes for twenty-two counties, plus unpaid banner rents, for 1805–10 for eight districts, and all silver lent out in lieu of grain, and so forth were forgiven.[84] In 1819, taxes were completely forgiven for Gu'an and Yongqing counties because of flooding that submerged most fields. A yellow plaque was posted so people would know this.[85] Yongqing County, one of the chronically flooded counties on the Yongding River, benefited frequently from tax remissions. In the Qianlong period, according to the local history, remissions were granted only about three times, all at the end, but in the Jiaqing period remissions were constantly granted, reflecting the decline in the river system. Tax forgiveness was granted numerous times in the Daoguang, Xianfeng, and Tongzhi periods, when the record halts.[86]

As with *pingtiao*, such declared remissions provided opportunities for local functionaries and officials to profit illicitly. In 1811 a censor proposed that remissions be stopped because of these malpractices. He said that although tax remissions were supposed to commence on the day of the imperial order, in fact officials could take advantage of the period between the issuing of the re-script and the receipt of the information locally to collect taxes and pocket the amount themselves. The Board of Revenue therefore recommended that each governor should publicize the date of the rescript and make sure that the people knew about it.[87] Three years later the board ordered provincial treasurers to conduct secret investigations to see if the procedures for tax remission were actually being carried out.[88]

The amounts involved in such special remissions, together with the general forgiveness of taxes, were quite substantial, but another criticism was that they benefited primarily the rich landowners and not the poor independent or tenant farmers. In the early Qianlong period, two governors, Sun Jiagan and Nasutu, successively questioned the usefulness of tax remissions in Zhili. In 1739, after receiving imperial permission for remissions for Zhili in the amount of 900,000 taels, Sun argued that the practice of granting remissions according to the amount of land under cultivation was unfair because it benefited the rich households, who did not necessarily pass the benefits onto their tenants. "The present method does not distinguish between rich and poor households." Further, he argued that the policy for Jiangnan was inappropriate for Zhili, where the best land in Shuntian, Baoding, Yongping, Tianjin, Xuanhua, and Hejian prefectures was banner land, and the other land was dry or alkaline. Sun suggested that a rent-reduction policy be promulgated. This would benefit the poor households.[89]

While he had been governor-general of Liang Jiang, Nasutu also criticized the tax-remission policies. Nine hundred thousand taels tax relief had been granted to Zhili, 1 million for Suzhou (Jiangsu), and 600,000 for Anhui, but such tax remissions, he argued, mainly benefited the large landlords, especially in the Jiangnan area. The small owner gained only a small benefit. He suggested a kind of progressive scale for remissions.[90] Although there is evidence that the Qianlong emperor sympathized with this view, it does not appear to have been applied more than once or twice, if at all.[91] In 1748, when he served as governor-general of Zhili, Nasutu argued for the forgiveness of the loans of the landless poor for 1744.

> At that time Hejian and Tianjin had meager harvests, but by last year the harvest was normal and most villages were in good condition. But Qingyun, Yanshan, and other places still had partial disaster [*pianzai*] and needed tax relief and other relief. The governor-general Liu Yuyi went according to precedent and lent grain and seed, but only to peasants with land so that they could return it after the fall harvest. The poor without land were not aided. But the emperor permitted loans to be made to those poor who really had no employment and were experiencing daily hardship. In

QL 9 a total of 9,287 shi of *gaoliang* was lent to the landless poor of these two counties. These people really do not have regular employment, and some have moved away and are hard to pursue. So we request forgiveness.[92]

This makes it clear that Qing officials and emperors recognized the limited social reach of famine relief and tax remissions, and in this last example at least, a small step was taken to correct a problem. During the Kangxi and Yongzheng periods, Jing Junjian has found a few examples of remissions whose benefits were meant to be shared by landlords with their tenants, in the form of rent reduction. The formula of 70/30 was a standard invoked, that is, 30 percent of the benefit was to be passed on to the tenant. In the Qianlong period, great emphasis was given to tax remissions, but landlords were not bound by any formulas; they were merely encouraged to give rent reductions. At the beginning of the dynasty, tax remissions formed part of the policy of *quannong*, encouragement of agriculture, but by the Qianlong period, maintaining the support of the landowners, particularly those of South China, was more important to the dynasty, in his view.[93] For Zhili, and North China in general, with lower levels of tenancy and smaller private holdings, the direct benefits of tax remissions may have extended to more farm households. Whether such benefits in turn reached agricultural laborers and other landless people is another issue.

Shelters and Famine Refugees

The aspect of a subsistence crisis most dreaded by officials was vagrancy, which in turn could develop into social and political unrest. "People's readiness to take to the roads whenever they faced starvation, or simply the fear of starvation, may well have been the most specifically Chinese aspect of a crisis situation."[94] From the Zhili area, migration north of the Great Wall, either to Fengtian or to areas in present-day Inner Mongolia, was common. Together with Shandong refugees, Zhili famine victims also went to Fengtian by sea. In the Kangxi and Yongzheng periods, the policy had been to try to send famine refugees back to their homes. One basic principle of crisis management was to try to keep people in their homes and to avoid the specter of famine refugees on the roads or crowding into urban centers, where they would create trouble or spread disease. *Zisong*, or sending refugees home with a cash travel allowance, was a practice used by beleaguered local authorities. In 1704, when many refugees from Shandong Province sought relief in Beijing, the Kangxi emperor ordered the Zhili governor to send home as many as possible. The Yongzheng emperor issued similar orders in 1723 and 1726, but he began to realize that migration from food-deficit areas to other areas was impossible to stop. The Qianlong emperor also saw that it was cruel to stop people from going outside the Great Wall. Yet in the 1743–44 crisis the emperor's orders to provincial officials to allow people to migrate beyond the Great Wall were supposed to be kept secret so that it would not start a stampede of refugees to the north.[95]

The flow of refugees to Beijing was viewed with greater alarm. In every crisis in this region, poor people flocked to the capital to seek food, and the *zisong* allowance was another incentive. Sometimes, including in 1743, the cash allowance was considered by officials as too generous and misused by its recipients, who regarded it as a dole.[96] In 1754–55, Fang Guancheng memorialized the throne, requesting a return to the lower rates of 1740. He said that in the 1743 drought in Henan and Shandong, many poor people fled to Beijing. According to the 1736 precedent, each person received 6 fen silver per 100 li of distance from home. The old and infirm that could not walk would get 3 fen more. Since such allowances amounted to double that given for relief, it often attracted famine refugees to the capital, even those from neighboring provinces. The lower rates of 1740 were 20 wen cash for each adult and half of that for each child.[97]

Imperial policy seemed to shift from *zisong* to *liuyang* in the 1740s as the emperor ordered provincial officials to try to provide for refugees rather than sending them home. Related to this was the promotion of shelters that would operate on a regular basis, not just in response to particular crises. Starting in 1748, Fang Guancheng promoted the establishment of shelters throughout Zhili Province. These *liuyangju* (also called *liuyangyuan* or *liuyangtang*) were intended principally to provide shelter during the winter months. In 1759 he reported that 561 shelters had been set up since 1748. They all operated during the winter months. When the ice melted, the poor people were sent away, except for those with serious illness or crippling disease, who were sheltered continuously. In 1759 these numbered only seventy people. All the fuel, food, clothing, medicine, and so forth was contributed by the local officials. "Because the managers give the money to merchants to earn interest, the gentry, merchants, and people all compete to contribute. And salt merchants and pawn-shop owners are happy to manage the shelters," he said. One hundred forty districts in Zhili contributed 45,500 taels to invest, and 143 qing and 9 mu of rental land to generate income.

> Up to now, the amount that officials and people contribute has increased yearly, and there are still more shelters being set up. Each shelter is managed by the elders. It does not go through the hands of functionaries. I observe that in the past, during the four [winter] months from tenth to the first month, there used to be 1,100–2,000 dead bodies reported, but in recent years, there has only been about a hundred or so. Like the relief homes, these places used to be managed by local officials, but now [1759] they are becoming gradually a joint [public] effort of the literati and the people [*shimin gongzhong zhi ju*].[98]

From gazetteer evidence, it appears that *liuyangju* were indeed established throughout the province in the Qianlong period.[99] The shelter gradually changed from being an officially sponsored institution to a local gentry and people-led institution. The Zhengding prefectural gazetteer gave some basic rules for *liuyangju*: in every city, market town, or crossroad, wherever there was a shelter, there should be a large sign where the three characters "liuyangju" were to be clearly written so that everyone, even those coming from outside the district, could read it. It appears that shelters were scattered around the countryside. At the Zhengding County seat, for example, there was one shelter with eight rooms. Ten li to the south there was another shelter with six rooms, and a third with six rooms. All were located at temples. Warm padded clothing and quilts were to be distributed. The basic rations were 8 he of *mi* per adult, and 4 he for children, considered to be under 10 sui, which was more generous than the standard rations for famine relief. Adult rations were to be distributed daily, together with fuel, vegetables, and even 4 wen cash, but the numbers in the shelter were large, then gruel, *zhou*, should be cooked twice a day.[100]

Shelters were financed with the interest from funds or property donated by local gentry or merchants, often salt merchants. Examples for Zhengding Prefecture's counties show that the local magistrate set an example, and then local gentry and merchants contributed land or money, the interest from which was used for the shelters. The Wangdu County gazetteer reports that the local magistrate Yang Fengtai initially donated in 1748 the sum of 50 taels. Given to merchants to invest, at the rate of 3 percent per month interest, it yielded 18 taels a year, and by 1755, it had accumulated 140 taels. Another magistrate contributed the amount of 150 taels, which invested at 2 percent per month interest, accumulated to 258 taels, and so forth. The shelter was renovated in the Guangxu period.[101]

Other types of shelters also developed extensively in the eighteenth century, particularly after the Yongzheng emperor decreed in 1724 that localities should establish *pujitang* and *yuyingtang*.[102] *Pujitang* were shelters in larger urban centers for the elderly and the sick. The Board of Revenue directed that officials were to be responsible for managing them, and the funds should come from both public sources and private donations, especially from merchants. Rations and allowances varied by province.[103] In addition there were the *yuyingtang*, which were shelters for abandoned babies that were to be set up in all large cities. They were supposed to be financed by the local gentry.[104] Of the close to 1,000 *yuyingtang* listed in Qing gazetteers, only 9 were in Zhili, 5 of which were in Tianjin.[105]

In Beijing, reports of mismanagement of the *pujitang* surfaced in the early Jiaqing period.[106]

> Pujitang are supposed to be have funds every year at the beginning of winter, and they are supposed to be granted grain and cook gruel from it. . . . But we hear that some of the responsible people are not virtuous and take coarse grain and substitute it for government grain [*guanmi*] so that the gruel is inedible, and the homeless and poor cannot benefit. Thus it is broad assistance [*puji*] in name, but not in substance. From now on, the *pujitang* should follow the example of the soup kitchens [*fanchang*] of the Five Districts [Wu Cheng]. Manchu and Han censors, two people, should be appointed to oversee the work.

In Beijing at least, the *pujitang* continued in the Daoguang and Xianfeng reigns to be very important. The number of poor people supported by the *pujitang* in the Xianfeng period was especially great.[107]

Yangjiyuan, frequently mentioned in gazetteers, also housed the orphaned, widowed, and crippled, in each district. As ordered by the board, local officials were responsible for having such shelters to house the widowed, orphaned, childless, crippled, and ill persons. In disaster years, more funds could be requested.[108] Such institutions had existed in the Ming dynasty; every county was ordered to shelter such people. In the Hongwu reign (1368–98), Xinhe County, for example, had fifteen *yangjiyuan*. They were repaired in 1593 and 1678. In 1823, after the big flood, the buildings collapsed. Later it became a Buddhist institution.[109] According to the statutes, orphans and poor were to be investigated and given a tag to wear on their waists. Steps were taken to make sure that people were not falsifying their names to get the rations. In Beijing's Five Districts and Daxing and Wanping counties, 906 were registered. In Zhili, 7,362 were supported by the state in these homes. Each person received 3 taels, 6 qian annually; the total reported expenditure was 25,099 taels, which was supposed to be deducted from the land tax.[110]

In Beijing in each of the Five Districts there were also shelters for vagrants, *xiliutang*. "All those who come from outside the city and have no clothes or shelter should be registered and sheltered." They were to be given one sheng of *mi*, as well as oil, coal, vegetables, and so forth, worth 15 wen cash. In the winter those who lacked a cotton-padded jacket should be given one. An allowance of 5 qian silver should be paid to a responsible person in each district to look after the shelter. If the vagrant died of illness or expired along the road, the official should provide 8 qian for a wood coffin and burial.[111]

All of these public shelters had roots in earlier periods, and they had proliferated in the late Ming period, especially in the Jiangnan region. In the Qing period, and particularly in the eighteenth century, the state played a large role in promoting their spread. In Beijing, the authorities directly funded the shelters, but elsewhere the state authorized local officials to find local elites to contribute funds and management. Liang Qizi has described this as the "bureaucratization" of charitable organizations in the eighteenth century.[112] Fang Guancheng's sponsorship of *liuyangju* in Zhili in the 1740s and 1750s followed this example. The initiative was a bureaucratic one, and it appears that the funds were advanced as part of the broader famine relief effort under his stewardship. It seems clear, however, that additional funds were advanced and invested primarily by salt merchants, and that some shelters were managed by them as well. This arrangement could be described as official supervision and merchant management of a charitable organization, *guandu shangban*, similar to what Liang describes as official supervision and popular management, *guandu minban*, of other types of charities in the eighteenth century.[113]

1743–1744: Famine Relief Model

The 1743–44 crisis was the textbook case for famine relief procedures. The relief campaign was occasioned by a drought that affected twenty-seven counties, sixteen of them very gravely, concentrated primarily in the prefectures of Tianjin and Hejian in the eastern-central part of the province. In the spring of 1743, spring rains never materialized, causing the failure of the wheat crop. At the same time, drought parched the soil and prevented the sowing of the autumn crops. By the fall of 1743, a crisis (*chengzai*) was officially declared. After an entire winter's general relief, *dazhen*, the next spring there was still no rain, and another spring crop failed. There was no harvest until autumn 1744, and it was quite meager.[114] Although it was not geographically extensive, the 1743–44 drought was intense and lengthy, spanning two years.

Relief was distributed to the sixteen "completely ruined" and eleven "partially ruined" counties over the winter and spring of 1743–44.[115] (On Map 8.1 they are labeled "most severe" and "less severe.") The relief campaign was a model effort in several respects. First, it involved a complete investigation and classification of the famine districts and the famine victims. Each district was evaluated on a scale of 1 to 10, with 10 representing the most severe catastrophe, or *zai*. Households were classified as extremely poor (*jipin*) or less poor (*cipin*).[116] The information about the rating, the numbers in the household, the village, and county were all recorded on a tally, or *piao*, which could be presented at the grain distribution center at the appointed time.[117]

Second, it involved the distribution of monthly rations, primarily in the form of grain, over the winter months. The number of months for relief was determined both by the classification of the district and the rating of the household.[118] In 1743–44, a preliminary round of relief, *puzhen*, was distributed to some districts in the eighth lunar month, and the very elderly and the sick received additional relief, *zhezhen*, in the ninth and tenth months, to tide them over until the general relief, *dazhen*, commenced in the eleventh lunar month.[119] This was followed by distributions in the first, fourth, and fifth lunar months. The actual distribution was done in ten installments that extended over an entire calendar year from August 1743 through July 1744.[120] Since the sixteen severely affected counties were concentrated in Hejian and Tianjian prefectures along the Grand Canal, the distribution of this grain was considerably easier than if more distant counties had been affected. The grain was mostly wheat or millet, with a few exceptions.[121] The guidelines indicated that when grain was insufficient, silver should be substituted.[122] During the *puzhen* phase, in the eighth month, half was given in grain and half in silver.[123] During the general relief both grain and silver were distributed in each of the affected counties.[124]

The grain-distribution stations, *zhenchang*, were located in each county seat, and in villages within 20 to 30 li to each side, or along key roads where the population was most concentrated. The goal was to allow people to get back and forth easily in a single day. If there were locations beyond 30 li, additional stations should be established. The guidelines recommended how the stations should be supervised, how wide the door should be, and how the crowds should be man-

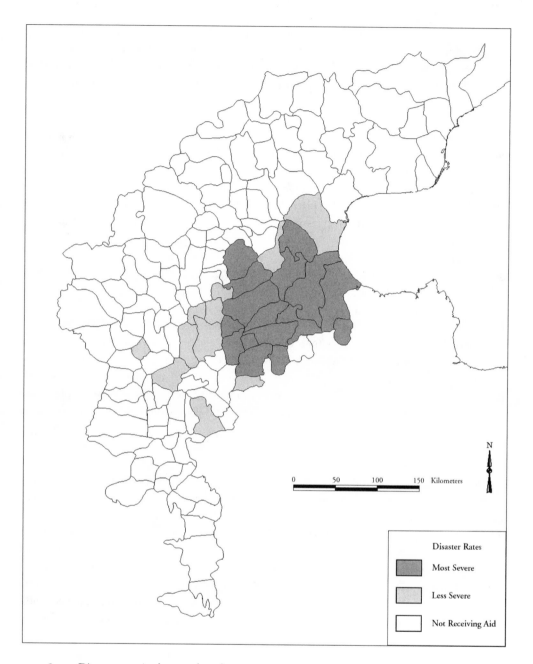

MAP 8.1. Disaster areas in the 1743 drought

SOURCE: Fang Guancheng, *Zhenji*, juan 8. Used also by Will, *Bureaucracy*, 31.

NOTE: "Most severe" counties (sixteen total) had disaster ratings of 6, 7, 8, 9, and 10. "Less severe" counties (eleven total) had disasters ratings of 5, 6, 7, 8, and occasionally 9 or 10. For identification of counties, please refer to Appendix 1 and Map A.1 (Prefectures and counties in Zhili Province).

aged. A few days before each village's turn for monthly distribution, notices should be posted. People should line up in an orderly manner, with women before men, and old and weak before the young men. However, relatives of the old and infirm with no young man at home were allowed to collect their share for them. Each recipient should bring the family's tally and the transaction should be recorded. Exchange shops should be located nearby so that the poor could exchange their silver allowances for cash.[125]

The grain distributions were intended not simply to feed the rural population but also to encourage peasants to remain at home, or to return home if they had already fled in search of food elsewhere. "In 1743, for instance, people 'left in droves' . . . as early as the sixth month, at the height of the agricultural year."[126] Many fled to locations in Shuntian Prefecture; others went to Yongping Prefecture, or to Rehe and other places beyond the Great Wall. Many people were crowding the roads. The officials feared this type of disorder more than anything else, and they sought to publicize the availability of relief in their home districts.[127] Migration to Beijing was rapid and intense. Panic was what the authorities feared most and first, but disease was a distinct possibility during the winter. Although thousands were sheltered in the fall, between the eighth and the eleventh month, 1,600 had been sent home. Still more people arrived. The censors of the Five Districts requested increased grain supplies for the ten stations and tried to discourage others from entering the city. They reported that the lines at the soup kitchens were orderly.[128] There were probably about 4,000 or 5,000 famine refugees fed by them over the winter, and perhaps as many as 10,000.[129] In order to prevent crowding and disease in Beijing, two additional soup kitchens on the outskirts were set up, one at Tongzhou to the east and the other at Liangxiang to the west. After winter, vagrants were to be given allowances to return home, *zisong*, in time for the spring planting. Outside of Beijing and its environs, soup kitchens played a relatively minor role. In the period before the commencement of general relief, local gentry outside the city were encouraged to take the responsibility. At Wuyi County, for example, five soup kitchens helped feed more than a thousand men and women.[130]

To restore agricultural production after both the spring and fall harvests had failed, the authorities concentrated on returning people to their homes and lending them wheat seeds to plant in the fall for next spring's harvest. In fact they encouraged planting double the usual amount of wheat to make up for the grain deficits.[131] But the determination of each farm household's needs required great caution and ingenuity, particularly because farmers frequently claimed more than they actually required, hoping to sell seed rather than plant it. Since only about 30 percent of the land in Zhili was planted in wheat, the directives stressed that a farm of 100 mu should be lent no more than seed for 30 mu, at the rate of 5 sheng per mu. But the actual situation varied, and officials needed to go in person to villages to make sure that the functionaries had not been falsifying the records and colluding with the locals.[132]

The ambition of the grand model of famine relief extended the reach of the state to the household level, but the extent to which the functionaries could actually conduct investigations so completely over such a large population is highly doubtful.[133] Yet the goal of supporting the rural population at the village level must have been met to a certain extent. By the end of the relief campaign, the population that had received relief totaled 664,890 households, amounting to more than 2 million individuals. Those who had been fed by soup kitchens amounted to 944,000 people. In total 1,100,720 shi of grain (both *mi* and *gu*) had been used, as well as 1,105,670 taels of silver.[134] Grain shipments totaled 1,387,951 shi. The largest share, 53.3 percent, was diverted from the grain tribute coming from the south. Another substantial portion, an estimated 21 percent, was ordered from the neighboring provinces of Henan and Shandong. Another large share, perhaps 12 percent, came from Fengtian. Only 4.6 percent of the relief supplies originated from Zhili itself.[135] The restrictions on sea trade were suspended to allow grain to enter the province from Fengtian, while other supplies originated from Gubeikou, Bagou, Rehe, and Siqi santing.[136]

According to contemporary and later judgment, the results of this campaign were highly successful. It was said that no one lost their homes, or that there were no homeless during this crisis.[137] This suggests that famine mortality may have been limited, but this is difficult to prove. The records do not usually mention mortality, although Fang Guancheng asserted that because of timely preliminary relief in the eighth month, and follow-up relief in the ninth and tenth months, many of the orphans, widows, elderly, and sick had survived.[138] The drought and heat conditions were very severe. There are an unusually large number of references from local gazetteers to deaths due to sunstroke. Many gazetteers report the unusually hot conditions in the fifth and sixth lunar months of 1743, and how large numbers of people and animals died of sunstroke, *hesi*.[139] However, for the following year, when drought conditions persisted, there is relatively little mention of mortality in the gazetteers. In the Gaoyi and Guangzong gazetteers alone, there is mention of deaths resulting from "big hunger" (*daji*). In the next year, 1745, there was continued drought (*han*) and crisis (*zai*) in many places, but only a handful of mentions of hunger (*ji*).[140] From this evidence, it would appear that mortality due to heat was quite severe in 1743, but that there were few deaths resulting directly from hunger or starvation.

Grain prices provide another way to assess the effectiveness of famine relief campaigns. Figures 8.1a–b show the monthly price of wheat and millet in this period compared with the "predicted" price, which represents what the price of grain would have been in the absence of a harvest crisis. The graph of the predicted price takes into account the secular price trend for the period and the seasonal fluctuations of price. (See Appendix 3.) The effect of this drought is clearly seen. The price of wheat, which had been advancing steadily since 1741, rose to over 1.90 taels in 1744, and then dropped back to 1.68 in 1745. The price of millet, which had not experienced the same rising trend, rose from a low of 1.20 taels in 1742 to a high of about 1.60 in 1744, and then fell precipitously to 1.07 in 1745. Also visible is the effect of another drought in 1745–46, which affected wheat prices greatly, but seemed to have almost no effect on the price of millet, perhaps because of the timing of renewed rainfall.

The next pair of figures, 8.2a–b, shows the price of wheat and millet, indexed to a base year, compared with the percentage of normal rainfall for the period. This provides another way of assessing the magnitude of the price effect of the drought. Here one can see that rainfall was only about 40 percent of normal in the 1743–44 drought, while the wheat price was less than 40 percent over the base-year price, and the millet price less than 20 percent of the base-year price. In the 1745–46 drought, rainfall was deficient to about the same extent. Wheat prices rose to about 50 percent above normal, but millet prices stayed at normal, showing little impact from the drought. Although there is no reason to expect that price rises in harvest crises should be directly proportionate to the shortfall or excess in rainfall, this case study shows that the price impact of this drought was measurable, but relatively limited, and it appears that the 1 million shi of relief grain may have accounted for the moderated impact in millet prices especially.

Although the crisis was concentrated in twenty-seven counties in Hejian and Tianjin prefectures, grain prices of the seventeen prefectures of the province did not experience greater than normal variation. Region 1 to the north (see Map 7.1 in Chapter 7) usually had distinctly lower prices and continued to do so in this crisis. Wheat prices were highest in Region 4, which included

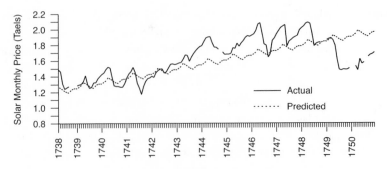

FIGURE 8.1A. Actual and predicted wheat prices, 1738–1750

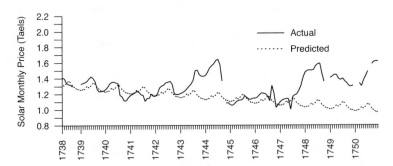

FIGURE 8.1B. Actual and predicted millet prices, 1738–1750

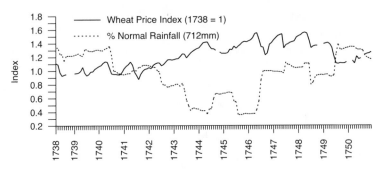

FIGURE 8.2A. Wheat price and rainfall, 1738–1750

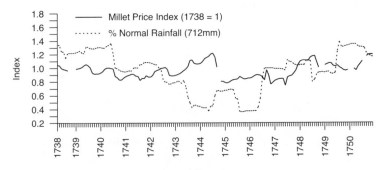

FIGURE 8.2B. Millet price and rainfall, 1738–1750

Zhengding Prefecture. Millet prices in Region 2, which included Hejian and Tianjin, were higher than normal, as expected.[141] Yet prices in all regions followed the same trends. The coefficients of price variation, graphed in Figures 7.1a–b (in Chapter 7), show the greater variation before the crisis, in 1741 and 1742, when all the prefectures are taken into account. Without the northern prefectures, there was not a pronounced increase in variation during the crisis years. Although a low or stable coefficient of variation might indicate that the impact of a crisis was uniformly felt, in this case it appears to show that grain distributions helped to moderate price volatility and, thus, interregional variation.

Not all price spikes were weather related. The price rises of 1747–48 in both wheat and millet occurred when rainfall was apparently at normal levels. Gazetteers do not record any unusual disasters for those years.[142] In 1746, forty-six counties had been investigated for flood damage, of which thirty-two were declared partial disaster districts, but this was not really a crisis.[143] Perhaps the price spike was caused by a rise in rice prices in the Lower Yangzi area—seen clearly in Figure 7.4 (in Chapter 7). Although Zhili prices were less strongly correlated with Lower Yangzi prices in the eighteenth century than they would be in the nineteenth (see Tables 7.5a–b and Table 7.6 in Chapter 7), the correspondence in 1748 (and also in 1752) is striking. Regions 3 and 4 in Zhili were most affected, suggesting some problem with grain tribute shipments that year.

1759: Disaster Without Relief

The 1743–44 campaign had been declared a model and was frequently invoked in the eighteenth century. Yet the harsh experience of Zhili in 1759 reveals that there were instances even in the high Qing when the model was not followed. As Figures 8.4a–b show, in 1759 there was a severe drought in Zhili, as severe as that of 1743, with about a 60 percent shortfall in rain. Prices reached much higher levels than in either 1743–44 or in 1761–62—about 50–70 percent over normal. The effect was more serious for wheat prices than for millet. Figures 8.3a–b show that wheat prices rose to about 2.60 taels per shi on average, while millet prices rose to about 2.05 taels. The highest reported prefectural wheat price was 2.93 in December 1759. (There are five months of missing data for January to May 1760.) The extent of actual crisis is also revealed in Figure 8.3a, which shows a massive single wheat price spike starting about 1757 and rising to a peak in 1759–60; prices then dropped suddenly, returning to normal levels until 1761. For millet, in Figure 8.3b, there was a drop in prices in 1759, followed by another surge in 1760–61. This crisis seems to have been uniformly experienced all over the province; unlike 1743–44, price levels were about the same in all the prefectures. The coefficients of variation in Figure 7.1b (in Chapter 7) were at a low point for 1758–59 for both wheat and millet, confirming that this was not a crisis limited to one part of the province. Rainfall at Beijing was only 312 mm in 1758, but increased to 550 mm in 1759, and 631 mm for 1760. (See Figure 1.1 in Chapter 1.) Harvests in 1759 were in the range of 40–60 percent for the summer wheat and 50–80 percent for fall crops.[144]

The social conditions of these years leave little doubt that this was a genuine human tragedy. Gazetteers have frequent references to high prices and to hunger. Many people left the area to look for food. Conditions in 1760 became more severe. Reports of severe hunger (*daji*) were accompanied by reports of death from pestilence from all over the province. Xingtai and other counties reported deaths in large numbers, very unusual in such accounts.[145] Despite these conditions, there is no record of a large-scale relief campaign to meet this crisis. The Fang Guancheng model so well applied just before and just after these years does not seem to have been fully activated to meet this

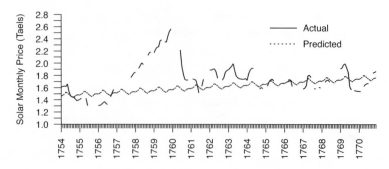

FIGURE 8.3A. Actual and predicted wheat prices, 1754–1770

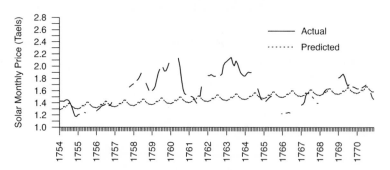

FIGURE 8.3B. Actual and predicted millet prices, 1754–1770

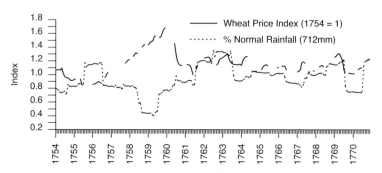

FIGURE 8.4A. Wheat price and rainfall, 1754–1770

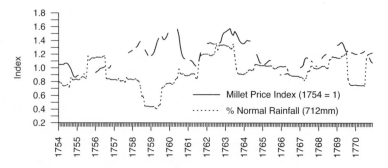

FIGURE 8.4B. Millet price and rainfall, 1754–1770

crisis. In the sixth month, the emperor had expressed concern for a prolonged drought of recent months. He expressed special concern for the unemployed who were leaving their families in search of relief or work. The state granaries might not be able to provide the level of relief needed. The experience with *zisong* and *liuyang* policies recently had met with problems of abuse. Fang memorialized in response saying that people should not be forbidden to find work outside and especially to seek labor on public works. He also said that people should be encouraged to fish in the rivers and lakes and also to borrow grain through *pingtiao*.[146]

The overflowing of multiple rivers in the second half of the year turned this into a classic spring drought–summer flood situation. "In the twenty-fourth year [of Qianlong], there was a big drought in the spring and summer, with no wheat harvest. Only in the intercalary sixth month, on the twenty-fourth day, did it finally rain."[147] For the rest of the year, floods in all parts of the region are what attracted official attention. In the next month Fang complied with an imperial order to investigate flood conditions in the lower reaches of the Yongding River. He personally went to inspect an area that had turned into a lake, extending 17 li from a breach in the river banks to Tianjin, including seventy-three villages in Gu'an County, sixty-two villages in Yongqing County, and six villages in Bazhou—about 30 percent of them were surrounded by water on three or four sides. Some *gaoliang* stood on the high ground, and he predicted that replanting would not be difficult. For the seriously affected larger households, 4 dou of husked grain was allotted for relief; for the smaller households, 3 dou. There is reference to further disaster investigation and rating in the fall.[148]

In the ninth month the provincial treasurer Sanbao reported partial disaster conditions in the southern part of the province due to a rise in Zhang, Wei, and other rivers. There were twenty-five counties in Daming, Shunde, Guangping, and so on that were relatively heavily affected. He requested permission to give relief according to the precedent established earlier for the flooded counties in the Yongding River flood: 4 dou of grain for households of more than five persons; 3 dou for those of four persons or fewer. Repairs of houses and boats should also be subsidized. For the seventeen lightly affected counties, like Julu, no emergency relief should be given, but they should be put in the general relief category, and *pingtiao* loans could be given according to precedent. There were twenty-six counties, such as Tangshan, which were inspected but found to be without disaster conditions. He requested no relief but some tax remissions for them. Altogether he requested 300,000 shi of grain be deployed from the Northern Granary in Tianjin.[149] There is no reference to the drought that had preceded the flood.[150]

Given the ample documentation of other relief efforts during Fang Guancheng's tenure as governor-general, the lack of further documentation for 1759–60 seems significant. Compared with the elaborate steps taken in other crises of this period, there seems to have been relatively little acknowledgment or action in this crisis. Despite the intention expressed, it does not seem that any *dazhen* was provided in the winter months. The most likely explanation is that grain and other resources were diverted to the northwest, and Zhili was bypassed in terms of grain and other supplies. In 1758–61, there were huge military campaigns against the Eleuth Mongols and a large deployment of troops and supplies to the northwest. In Gansu Province, the military situation combined with drought to cause a spectacular food crisis.[151] In 1759 Zhili was on the periphery of a major drought that centered in Shaanxi, Gansu, and other parts of the northwest.[152] The Qing state placed high priority on provisioning the northwest, which was critical for defense against the Mongols. Zhili and other northern and western provinces regularly supplied large quantities of grain and other material to the northwest, so much so that Peter Perdue has argued that Gansu's markets became well integrated with those of North China.[153]

The diversion of resources to the northwest is the most likely explanation for the paucity of famine relief within Zhili during 1759–60, and the failure of relief in turn contributed to severity of the crisis in Zhili.[154] Multiyear droughts tended to be the most serious of the natural crises. The drought conditions in Zhili itself were not of such duration, but this turned out to be a multiyear crisis because it was greatly exacerbated by the drought in the northwest, the effect of which spread to neighboring provinces. The greater impact on wheat harvests and prices is not surprising since wheat was more dependent on rainfall than millet or sorghum, and there was no wheat harvest that year.

1761–1763 and Later: Relief with and Without Disaster

By contrast, during the period of severe flooding in 1761–63, the grand model was put into action, again under Fang Guancheng's direction. The first round of heavy rains came in 1761. In the following year, the rains came particularly early, overflowing the dikes of the Yongding River; the flooding was even more serious than in the previous year, with fifty-three counties affected. The flood was classified as a serious one, *zhongzai*, and not just a partial flood, *pianzai*.[155] The affected area included the low-lying areas centering on the prefectures of Shuntian and Baoding. Forty-five counties were recorded as having *jimin*, people who were starving.[156] Rainfall at Beijing was over 950 mm in 1762, not a record, but certainly much higher than normal. (See Figure 1.1 in Chapter 1.) In local gazetteers, extreme hunger and starvation are noted. "In the autumn of the twenty-seventh year [of Qianlong] there was a large flood that started on the high ground and then waterlogged the lower ground; many people died of starvation [*jisi*]."[157] High prices are sometimes mentioned. In 1761 in Hengshui County, the price of one dou of *mi* was 700 wen. In 1763 in Jizhou District the price of 1 dou reached 2,400 wen. More frequently there are references to *minji*, starving people, even to people eating grass. However, the picture was mixed. In 1762 and 1763, many counties had good harvests, even as others suffered.[158]

As in the 1743–44 crisis, classification of districts was undertaken. Twenty-three districts received emergency or preliminary relief, *jizhen*, in the eighth lunar month of 1762. General relief for all affected counties began in the eleventh month, as required, but the extent to which direct household investigation was undertaken is not clear. In a report in the twelfth month, Fang stated that in the seventeen heavily affected counties, the very poorest, *jipin*, households in localities with disaster ratings of 10 received general relief up to the second month of the next year; the less affected and the *jipin* and *cipin* of the 9-rated villages received relief up to the end of the first month. Thirty-six additional counties experienced partial disaster and did not need further relief, although some were still experiencing difficulty during the winter.[159] The wording of the official report implies that there was some way to distinguish poor from very poor households.

Soup kitchens were operated until the third lunar month, but were extended by imperial order for another month. They were set up in districts that were adjacent to those in which relief was being given, as well as the districts designated for general relief. Women and children especially went to them. They seemed to play a larger role in this crisis than in previous years. Fang argued that soup kitchen relief (*zhuzhen*) and general relief (*dazhen*) were mutually supportive.[160] In the winter of 1761, seventy-three locations provided *zhou*, thus reaching some famine victims who were not given grain distributions. Fang pointed out that such districts were often adjacent to each other. He was pleased that the soup kitchens were located at the charity granaries, and not more than 15–20 li from each other.[161] However the proximity of soup kitchens to nondisaster areas also invited trouble. Later that year there was a case of three cousins from an area not receiving relief who went to a soup kitchen in the next county and extorted grain. They were caught and punished.[162] *Pingtiao* sales also played a larger role in this relief effort than in the 1743–44 campaign. The scale of price reduction was that cited above.[163] Labor relief also seemed to play a larger role in this campaign than in others. It was at this time that Fang Guancheng was heavily engaged in overseeing river construction, including the Thousand-Li Dike.[164]

Because of recent demands on the granaries, silver may have played a larger role in the earlier part of the relief campaign. According to Fang's report, 1.6 million taels of silver had been appropriated for relief.[165] Fang ordered that both grain and silver be distributed so that people would have enough to eat but prices would stay low, but this also reflected the diminished grain supplies on hand.[166] As in 1743–44, the relief grain came principally from the diversion of grain tribute, some 700,000 shi by the fourth month of 1763. In addition, as in previous years, substantial purchases were made from Fengtian, Shandong, and Henan. In the fourth lunar month of 1763, Fang reported that because the *pingtiao* sales and loans from the ever-normal granaries had been so extensive, much grain had to be purchased to restock the granaries, especially before the wheat crop came on the market. Harvests in these neighboring provinces had been plentiful, and so 400,000 shi of *mi* (husked grain) was ordered from Fengtian, and 200,000 shi each from Shandong and Henan.[167] Together with the grain tribute of 700,000 shi, this amounted to a total of 1.5 million shi of husked grain used altogether—approximately the same as the 1.4 million shi used in 1743–44.

The heavy use of granaries in 1763 is seen in the very high rate of disbursals, 70 percent, from Zhili's ever-normal granaries. (See Table 6.1 in Chapter 6.) The report of holdings at the end of the year showed that the total actual holdings of the three types of granaries together had been reduced to 1.8 million shi of *gu*, of which 1.4 million was held in the ever-normal granaries—which was unusually low for this period.[168] By 1767, however, the actual holdings were raised to 3.5 million shi of grain, of which 2.6 million were held in the ever-normal granaries.[169]

By the winter and spring of 1763, Fang was rather sanguine about conditions and the prospect of an excellent wheat harvest. Right after the lunar new year, he reported on his direct observations from touring the flood districts. Since the new year, he said, grain prices in all places had remained stable. Near Tianjin the price of white flour was 17–18 wen cash per jin, not very high. Every market still had both wheat and millet. People were relying less on grain to fill their stomachs and were turning toward the streams and rivers to find food. Labor relief was also available. So all those poor people who cannot farm, he said, have some means of surviving. He also observed refugees from Zhili and Shandong migrating, even though relief measures were available, saying they wanted to go beyond the Great Wall (Gubeikouwai) to find their relatives. Their clothes and shoes seemed to be warm and thick, he reported.[170] He found that in the prefectures of Daming and Guangping, in the south of the province, the areas that had been flooded were about to have double their usual wheat harvest, having borrowed seed from neighboring areas.[171] In short, he concluded that the disaster victims had not lost their homes and livelihood.[172] In the fifth month, he reported that there had been good rains during the month, that wheat was sprouting, and wheat prices had fallen greatly. In Baoding capital city, in the third month, a jin of wheat flour cost 24 wen; now it cost only 14 wen. For both breakfast and dinner people were substituting wheat flour for millet; therefore, the price of millet had not yet risen.[173] People were peaceful and seemed to be without need.[174]

The grain price data corroborate most of what Fang reported. Figures 8.3a–b show the distinct effect of the flooding on both wheat and millet prices. In the case of wheat, however, the effect was more moderate, and the seasonal effect of the wheat harvest of 1762 is still apparent. In the case of millet, however, prices remained high throughout the crisis—because there was a meager harvest in autumn 1762. (The harvest size for Tianjin was 50 percent, according to harvest reports.) Its price kept climbing until winter 1762–63, when it was almost 60 percent above normal, as seen in Figure 8.4b; rainfall was about 40 percent above normal. Millet prices continued to remain high during the year. These prices do not show the trend that Fang identified in Baoding, when he said that wheat was so cheap that millet prices could also stay low. Possibly this phenomenon was particular to the provincial capital. (Sorghum prices as usual followed the same seasonal trend as millet, but they were still considerably lower than those for wheat.) These figures do suggest, however, that after the good wheat harvest came in June, the prices of coarse grains also started to come down, although they were still significantly higher than their normal levels. As Figure 4.1a (in Chapter 4) shows, this was one of the few periods when the price of millet actually exceeded that of wheat.

After Fang's death, in 1768, his successors continued to invoke the grand model of famine relief even when there was not a serious crisis. In 1774 there was a meager wheat harvest due to drought in sixteen counties in Tianjin, Hejian, and Shuntian prefectures. In the seventh month Zhou Yuanli, the new governor-general, requisitioned 120,000 shi of grain from Henan to be used for *pingtiao* sales, even though the price of wheat, ranging from 1.6 to 2 taels, was not much higher than Henan's average price of 1.4 taels, and transport costs were 0.2 taels per shi.[175] In the ninth month Zhou reported that the drought was only a partial disaster, with only 10 percent of the province affected, but he requested one or two months of relief in the form of 100,000 shi to be diverted from Tongzhou. In the following month he raised the disaster ratings of some districts and asked for "additional relief" (*jiazhen*) to start in the first month of the new year.[176] In the following year, 1775, the Yongding River overflowed both banks, and by the fall fifty-eight counties or districts were in need of relief.[177] In 1776, thirteen counties were granted relief in both silver and grain, fifteen counties were relieved through loans, and all were permitted to postpone their tax payments.[178]

The 1775–76 fall harvest ratings for five locations in Zhili ranged from 8–10 for millet, and 6–10 for wheat and spring crops, suggesting that floods did not diminish the harvests in any significant way, if at all. When the average wheat price reached 2.08 taels in 3/1776, it was not very much over normal levels for that period. Millet prices were normal or below average.[179] Figure 4.1a (in Chapter 4) shows a cyclical inflation in wheat prices from 1.39 taels per shi in 7/1773 to 1.39 taels in 7/1776. In short, the events of 1774–76 did not constitute a crisis if measured by size of harvest, grain prices, or recorded social consequences, but the governor-general took advantage of the available resources and famine relief opportunities to deliver more resources to the province and in so doing may have prevented a further price rise.

Overall Evaluation

As these cases illustrate, price behavior during crises depended not only on the local weather and harvest conditions but also on the geographic extent, severity, and timing of the disaster. The application of the various means of famine relief, particularly general relief, seems to have limited the extent of price impact as well as the social and human consequences of harvest shortfalls. The cases of the 1743–44 drought and the 1761–63 flood show that a massive infusion of grain relief contained the effect of the crisis, and normal conditions were soon regained. The case of the 1759 drought, by contrast, shows that the absence of famine relief caused, or at least contributed to, a more acute and prolonged inflation of wheat prices. It is impossible to measure quantitatively the precise outcomes of particular policies and measures, but the overall conclusion that famine relief—with its related institutions and practices—was fairly effective seems undeniable.

Crop failures, or harvest shortfalls of 40–60 percent, were certainly serious, and price rises of 20 to 70 percent over normal could have grave social consequences. Yet by comparison with the worst European famines where prices doubled, tripled, or quadrupled, they were moderate. By European or other standards employing price measurements, these subsistence crises should perhaps not be called famines. By the criterion of elevated mortality, it is also questionable that these were "true famines." Demographic information is not available, but anecdotal reports of deaths from starvation are practically nil; even the mentions of severe hunger, *daji*, are relatively few. Of course the absence of anecdotal evidence does not necessarily prove that mortality was not elevated, but the lack of graphic descriptions of hunger, deaths, cannibalism, and sales of children forms a striking contrast to descriptions of late Ming famines as well as those of the late nineteenth and twentieth centuries. And virtually absent from the descriptions of the crises of the eighteenth century are references to victims resorting to extreme measures to feed themselves with roots, bark, or other famine "foods" that were well described for the late Ming period and often mentioned in the great famine of 1876–79, or the Great Leap Famine of 1959–61.

Other factors may have helped limit the damage from these crises. The multicrop system, with a mixture of spring and fall crops, made it possible for a harvest shortfall in one season to be followed by a good harvest in the next. Although all grain prices rose during these crises, they did not all rise to the same extent. This did not quite conform to Appleby's idea that "a symmetrical price structure and subsistence crises went hand in hand"—because the prices of various grains generally followed the same trend, but with the brief exception of the 1760s, when they did converge and millet became more expensive for a while; the fact that prices maintained their separation meant there was still some element of choice left in the grain market. In a real "crisis" people become unable, or unwilling, to pay for the exorbitant price of an expensive grain; therefore, they substitute it with an inferior grain, which in turn drives up the price of the second grain.[180]

The moderate impact of harvest crises shows the effectiveness of the famine relief techniques and the flexibility with which they were applied. Although there were guidelines, the kinds of relief given in each crisis depended on the available resources and the particular circumstances. Although regions or counties were differently affected by harvest crises, famine relief helped to redistribute resources and target them to the needy areas. Some counties got more in relief than they normally owed in taxes, three to ten times as much, and "a drastic redistribution of public revenue within a much larger area" may have resulted.[181] However, it is doubtful that the ambition of proportionate and fair distribution down to the household level was actually achieved, even when it was attempted in 1743–44. Such a degree of social engineering would have required a highly efficient subbureaucratic local organization that simply did not exist. Although it was the intention of Fang Guanchang's famine relief program, as well as his charitable granary project, to extend state relief into rural villages, there were still enormous advantages to those who could walk to county capitals to take advantage of grain sales or soup kitchens.

The grand model of relief was possible because of the vast resources of the Qing state in the eighteenth century. Above all it was the massive diversion of grain supplies from the grain tribute and from Fengtian and other external sources that was critical in the relief efforts. The location of the capital at the center meant that there was another source of grain available as a reserve. Grain in the form of distributions or sales was a direct antidote to the problem of hunger, and it kept prices from skyrocketing and staying high for a long period. It was both an economic lever and a psychological tool. The very fact of ample supplies alone might have accounted for any favorable price effects—regardless of how the grain reached the famine victims, whether by direct household distribution, *pingtiao*, or soup kitchens.

The quantities of money spent by the state, as well as monies not collected by the state, were enormous. The totals recorded for Zhili in the entire Qing period were at least 11 million taels of tax remissions plus 14.5 million taels and 7.5 million shi of grain.[182] Zhili was exceptionally well treated, but it was not unique in the quantities of relief it received. Other provinces, such as Jiangsu, Anhui, Hunan, Hubei, Shandong, and Gansu, also received a million or more taels in relief on occasions in the eighteenth century.[183] In one year alone, 1766, the state spent 34.5 million taels on relief in various parts of the empire, or approximately 12 percent of its total expenditures for the year.[184] The amounts of tax remissions granted were even greater than those for famine relief. Relief tended to be given in larger amounts for relatively serious disasters, but tax remissions were frequently granted for more isolated situations affecting a particular county or two. There were at least twenty times in the early to mid-Qing period (through the Daoguang period) when tax remissions larger than 1 million taels were granted, totaling 46 million taels. According to one generous estimate, the total amount of tax remissions granted in this period, including both large and small cases, may have amounted to 150 to 200 million taels, while the total amount of famine relief may have amounted to 446 million taels.[185]

The grand model of relief depended also on imperial and bureaucratic leadership to initiate it and bureaucratic efficiency to sustain it. Fang Guancheng or Chen Hongmou, with the emperor's support, had the ambition to master these crises and the resolve to oversee the lower bureaucracy and subbureaucracy to carry out the tasks. Yet even Fang was not above criticism. In 1763 when he was criticized by censors for not being timely in investigating the recent floods, the emperor commented sympathetically that famine relief administration was such a demanding task that it was no wonder Fang could not attend to both at the same time. Several lesser officials, however, were dismissed for neglecting the river work. The emperor expressed discouragement: if such trouble could develop in the capital area, where circuit intendants and prefects followed the lead of the governor-general and were continually fearful, then imagine what happened in other provinces.[186] The great ambition and elaborate detail of the grand famine relief model thus set an extraordinarily high standard of performance for a thinly staffed bureaucracy, one that was difficult to meet even under the best circumstances and with the best people.

Their guidelines were written with constant attention to the problems of getting accurate information and preventing collusion and cheating. Yet the infusion of such large amounts of grain or money inevitably provided opportunities for both petty theft and major corruption. This was a frequent problem in the major river conservancy projects. Starting in the 1780s, the extent of bureaucratic corruption expanded—a well-known phenomenon of the late Qianlong reign. In famine relief, the largest scandal was revealed in 1781 in Gansu Province—a case that involved the systematic and large-scale embezzlement of both famine relief "contributions" and state-issued funds. In this shocking case, Gansu officials solicited "degree-donation grain," commuted to silver, from would-be degree candidates for use in famine relief, but instead they pocketed the funds. They also received state famine relief based on reports of fabricated droughts. Fifty-six officials, including the governor-general, were executed, and dozens of others were given lesser punishments.[187]

In Zhili, cases of bureaucratic mismanagement of river funds in the 1780s and 1790s were later revealed during the reign of the next emperor Jiaqing. At the same time, not coincidentally, major floods occurred in 1780, 1789, 1790, and 1794 (as well as drought in 1792). Rainfall was greater than usual, and the geographic scope of damage wide. During those years, the governor-general reported the extent of damage, but only very limited relief was provided.[188] By the end of the Qianlong reign, the golden age of famine administration seemed to be over. Not only had there been a failure of imperial will and a breakdown of bureaucratic conduct, but demographic pressure, environmental decline, and the fiscal weakness of the state had raised the stakes in famine relief. The next emperor determined, however, to revive the practice of the grand famine relief model. Relying on his own leadership, rather than that of leading officials, the Jiaqing emperor intervened in 1801 to underwrite one of the most ambitious famine relief campaigns on record. The structure of high Qing model was maintained even in the Daoguang period, as seen during a crisis in 1822. At the end of the nineteenth century, it was revived with new energy and new inputs by the last important governor-general, Li Hongzhang.

CHAPTER NINE

Famine Relief:
Nineteenth-Century Devolution

THE NINETEENTH CENTURY in Chinese history has been regarded as the century of dynastic decline, the period of the unequal treaties with the West, the period of "opening" to the world, or perhaps the beginning of "modern" China. The demands of Western nations in the Opium War and the unequal treaty system were unprecedented in Chinese history, but in other ways, the nineteenth century, with its rebellions, natural disasters, and subsistence crises, conforms well to the classic picture of the end of a dynasty. The decline of imperial talent and authority from the Jiaqing emperor to the last, child-emperor Xuantong (Puyi), could not have formed a more striking contrast with the vigorous and powerful rulership of Kangxi, Yongzheng, and Qianlong in the eighteenth century. Closer examination of the facts, however, complicates the simple picture of straightforward decline. Although struggling against diminished resources and bureaucratic inertia, the Jiaqing and Daoguang emperors nevertheless maintained much of the form, if not the content, of famine administration. In midcentury human suffering and economic dislocation were caused more by political and military crises, both foreign and internal, than by natural disaster. For the rest of the century, a faltering court and bureaucracy had few traditional resources with which to face the natural disasters that followed in rapid succession. Although some of the traditional tools against famine unexpectedly survived, by the turn of the century, they seemed not only insufficient but actually outdated, as famines assumed even graver proportions and significance.

The 1801 Flood

In 1801 the Hai River Basin experienced one of its greatest floods of all time. It was unprecedented in its geographic extent and amount of rainfall. (See Figure 1.1 in Chapter 1.) Unlike the floods of 1761 or other years, it affected virtually every county in Zhili Province. The conditions were so unusual that the rising waters were described as a strange occurrence. Fields everywhere were flooded. In the flat areas, there were fish and shrimps in the water.[1] The sheer force of the floodwaters swept away thousands of homes and even some people. In a village-by-village survey of three counties at the outset of the crisis, the totals for Wanping County were 8,700 adults and children "affected by disaster." More than 2,300 houses were swept away, including 35 persons. In Liangxiang County, there were 9,800 disaster victims, and more than 2,800 houses collapsed. In Zhuozhou there were more than 9,050 disaster victims, and 3,200 houses destroyed.[2] The crisis presented a new challenge for the Jiaqing emperor, who was eager to prove his merit. He used the occasion to launch a full-scale campaign for river conservancy and famine relief that had as its real objective the reassertion of imperial control over a bureaucracy that had proven itself so dissolute and negligent that some local officials had not even reported the crisis conditions when they first occurred in the sixth month. Publication of *Xinyou gongzhen jishi* (The record of riverwork and famine relief in 1801) was a tribute to this effort. The emperor's personal dedication to the management of the crisis and the disciplining of the bureaucrats and functionaries was extraordinary.[3]

The grain commandeered by the imperial government formed the central focus of its general relief program, which lasted from the tenth month of 1801 through the first month of the next year and was then extended to the fourth month.[4] General relief included the distribution of money as well as grain, but reduced-price sales and soup kitchens were more important than direct household distribution. Neither was done on a wide scale until the first month of the lunar new year, but the total material resources concentrated on the famine relief effort were extraordinary in magnitude, equaling, or possibly exceeding, the amounts employed in 1743–44. By the second month of 1802, the governor-general, Chen Dawen, reported that more than 2 million taels had already been spent on relief in addition to the million taels spent on river conservancy.[5] The amounts in 1743–44 had been 1.1 million taels and 1.1 million shi of grain.[6]

At the outset of the flooding, in the sixth month of 1801, Chen Dawen reported that of the 122 counties affected by the flood, 106 needed relief. Only the sixteen counties of Xuanhua, Yongping, Chengde, and Yizhou were not needy. It was necessary to purchase grain for the next spring's relief (*qinghuang bujie*). Each county, he estimated, would need 2,000–4,000 shi for a total of 300,000 shi. Aside from 150,000 that had already been purchased from Shandong and Henan, he proposed buying another 150,000 from Fengtian, which was reported to have had an excellent harvest. At that time, he anticipated this amount would be sufficient for spring *pingtiao*.[7] Tongxing, the Zhili treasurer, reported that although there had been a good wheat harvest, the floods destroyed the stocks. There was little grain in storage and little in the way of cash for upcoming needs.[8]

Within days of deputing officials to all localities to investigate the flood, in the sixth month, the Jiaqing emperor ordered 600,000 shi of tribute grain to be set aside for relief, as well as 100,000 taels of silver for immediate distribution.[9] Later, in the eighth month, Chen Dawen reported to the emperor that the ninety-nine counties deemed in need of relief had a population of 10 million people, and they would require 1.8 million shi of *mi* to get through the winter. Beyond the 600,000 shi already allocated from tribute grain, he would need 1.4 million taels to purchase the additional 1.2 million shi of grain. In addition he requested another 100,000 taels for the repair of houses, bringing his total request up to 1.5 million taels. The emperor permitted 1 million taels from a fund contributed by Liang-Huai salt merchants to be used for this purpose.[10]

Later that month, Chen Dawen estimated that 300,000 shi more would be required to satisfy the next year's needs. Half of this amount had already been ordered from Henan and Shandong, while the other half was to be ordered from Fengtian. Of this amount, 40–50,000 shi would be *gaoliang* and the rest millet.[11] In the next month a survey of the fall harvest in all counties revealed that more than 50 percent of land had no harvest at all. Of the remaining 40 percent or more counties that had fall harvests, the average rating was 5, 50 percent, and many had ratings of 3, even 2.[12] In the eleventh month Chen Dawen reported that in the general relief for eighty-eight counties, 800,000 shi of grain had been used so far, coming from state granaries as well as from tribute grain. He estimated that the costs of general relief to date had been 1.5 million taels.[13] In the twelfth month Chen Dawen gave a summary report of conditions.[14]

> There are 128 zhou and xian in Zhili, of which 90 had disaster ratings of 6 to 10 and need relief (38 others have disaster ratings of 3, 4, or 5, and have already received tax postponements and loans and need no further discussion). For the 90, I have been discussing general relief [*dazhen*] with the provincial treasurer. 1.5 million taels have been allocated for relief, together with 600,000 shi in retained grain tribute.

Still he was concerned that one or two months' relief would be insufficient, and merchants and others should be urged to make contributions or to sell grain at reduced prices. In addition, in the eleventh month shelters were set up, and soup kitchens began operations. He felt that soup kitchens would be more efficient and get around the problem of distributing grain to those who were not truly needy. "The emperor has already shown great favor this fall by widely extending soup-relief as a form of comfort [*zhuzhen yidai fuxu*]."

> I propose taking the sixty counties with ratings of 9 and 10 [in Shuntian fu, Baoding, Hejian, Tianjin, Zhengding, Yizhou, Zhaozhou, Shenzhou, Dingzhou, and so on] and starting with the first month next year, to continue or set up soup kitchens until the fourth month wheat harvest. As for the other thirty districts that have ratings of 6, 7, and 8, their situation is slightly different from that of the sixty counties. They have already received relief, and if upon further investigation they need more soup relief, the details can be reported.

Thus it appears that the 1801–2 relief effort tended to substitute soup kitchens for repeated distributions of grain prescribed in the *dazhen* model. This shift seemed to reflect several new realities. There may have been doubt about the ability of the sub-bureaucracy to manage the household distributions, as well as doubts about their integrity in effecting such a wide-scale distribution. In addition, the passage reveals fear of wasting grain on households that might hoard or otherwise misuse it. Finally, it may have reflected a concern with social unrest and vandalism, particularly in Beijing. Although some considered giving cooked food less effective than giving grain, it was more direct and reliable since it kept people near their home localities and prevented any misuse or hoarding of grain.

In this memorial Chen Dawen referred to a grain shop theft in Xincheng:

> A native of Gu'an and two others took guns and tried to plunder a grain shop in Xincheng xian, but they were killed by store workers. There were more than 1,000 ruffians trying to plunder the store. 11/7 happened to be a market day in the town. These folks were on their way to look for work, but because of the hardships this year, there was no work to be found. They tried to beg for food, but the grain shop was not willing to lower its price. Some people seized wheat, sorghum, and black beans.[15]

Of even greater concern than local violence was the fear of disorder in Beijing, which was attracting refugees in large numbers. The officials were ordered to try to get out the word that relief was available in local areas.[16] In the seventh month, tens of thousands of refugees were reported in Beijing, and despite efforts to keep them away, they were reported to be increasing at a rate of 8,000 or 9,000 a day, largely women and children, hovering by the city gates.[17] Reduced-price sales were begun in the middle of the second month of 1802, with ten stations within Beijing, where each person was allowed to purchase up to 2 sheng of rice each day at reduced prices. Twenty-six thousand shi of different types of grain were made available.[18] On the twenty-seventh, the grain sales were to be extended to seventy-seven counties that had insufficient supplies of grain. The

300,000 shi authorized from Fengtian, Shandong, and Henan were to be used primarily for this purpose.[19] The scale of prices was revised on the seventeenth day of the fourth month. Beijing and Zhili grain prices were still high, but prices at Fengtian, Henan, and Shandong were not.[20]

Tianjin also attracted a large number of refugees during the summer, and by the winter months, it was estimated that there were 208,600 people in distress in that city, and that 23,400 shi of grain had already been distributed, as well as 35,000 taels.[21] There was also significant migration to Manchuria, which persisted in a small and steady stream, largely unhampered despite the attempts of some officials to curb it. By the third month, it was reported that 15,500 had migrated.[22] For these reasons, more soup kitchens in local areas were set up. On 2/15, Chen Dawen reported that 265 *zhouchang* would be opened in sixty-seven counties in the outlying areas, and on 2/19, four more counties were added to the list. Each kitchen served 2,000 to 7,000 persons a day, while the ten in Beijing attracted 25,000 a day.[23] Chen Dawen documented the need for more soup kitchens.

> I observe that last year there were 265 soup kitchens set up in sixty-seven counties, 2 to 15 per county. Each served 2–7,000 people daily. 33,000 shi of *cangmi* were used. 216,700 taels of banner rent were used to finance this. Altogether the relief effort cost more than 2 million taels. Now we propose to set up another 100 soup kitchens for another 100,000 taels. But we must carefully monitor them to see that there is no cheating by officials.[24]

On this memorial the emperor wrote, "Yes!" He further commented, "Of the 26,000 people now in the area, most are from nearby areas, but half are from outside. We cannot but add soup kitchens at the crossroads. Giving out food is not the most enlightened policy, but it is necessary for emergency relief."

Although they were scheduled to close on 3/20, the emperor granted an extension of their operations until 4/20.[25] In the fourth month, the soup kitchens still operating in Beijing were reported to be functioning in an orderly manner. As many as 80–90 percent of the people were women and children; the other 10–20 percent were the elderly men or young boys.[26] In the fifth month there were seven soup kitchens still in operation in the Beijing area, including the Five Districts, Daxing, and Wanping, serving more than 18,000 people a month.[27] In addition to the provision of money or grain, officials collected a total of 85,000 padded cotton garments to be distributed for use in the winter. Some 62,000 of these came from 300 pawnshops; about 3,000 were donated by officials; and another 20,000 were from a single rich merchant.[28] It appears that Beijing was the center for both the collection and the distribution of these garments.

Tax remissions, either complete or partial, were granted for eighty-one counties in the sixth and seventh months of 1801, as well as postponements of tax collections for forty-three counties in 1802.[29] In approving the request for the tax remissions, the emperor asked that the announcement be postponed until after the eighth month in order to minimize the opportunity for cheating by the functionaries.[30] In the record of tax remissions for Zhili Province, those of 1801–2 were the most extensive and generous, with the exception of remissions to seventy-one counties in the 1725 flood, and general remission given in 1877–79 because of drought.[31]

In 1803 the new governor-general, Yanjian, frankly acknowledged the eclectic nature of the relief campaign, which had been conducted with a great deal of local variation.

> *The practices of the 1801 relief effort did not entirely conform to precedents.* As far as giving relief [*fuxu*], there were several methods: each household got several sheng to several dou of husked grain [*mi*]. In some places they prepared noodles [*mian*] and distributed it. Some places gave cash and instructed people to buy food. There were other places where there was not enough in the granaries, but grain was purchased locally and distributed. Even more places bought grain and

cooked it. In the eighth and ninth months, some places gave out only grain, while others gave both grain and cash. *Some gave according to the registered household population,* [hukou], *while others gave only to the widowed, orphaned, and so on.* There were different methods, grain and cash. *But the amounts as reported are different from the precedents.* The price set by the Board [of Revenue] was 1.40 [taels] per shi, but the famine relief precedent was 1.20. Each zhou and xian requested permission to report according to the market price of that year, which did not correspond to the precedents. I ordered strict reporting, but according to the provincial treasurer, this flood was one that had not been seen in decades, and the situation differed in each locality. From JQ 6/6 to JQ 7/4, the price of millet [*sumi*] all over the province ranged from 1.50 to 4.46 per shi. Last year's rain was unusual, and the relief effort could not be compared to normal relief operations, and the costs cannot correspond to precedent.[32]

This report describes the relief campaign as *fuxu*, "giving comfort," rather than *dazhen*, "general relief," the official standard. It confirms that household investigation was not attempted; if there was household distribution of grain or money, it was done on the basis of the household registration records—which accounted for the number of adults and children in the household but were not necessarily up to date—rather than a new investigation. These eclectic practices reflected the impossibility of matching the standards for comprehensive micromanagement prescribed by the *Zhenji.* Yet the emperor did impose high standards for accurate information gathering and reporting by local magistrates. For example, in the eleventh month, he refused the request of some counties for relief, saying their conditions were quite good and warranted only tax remission.[33] Complaints that relief was not being properly administered in some counties were investigated and found to be invalid.[34] Complaints against the magistrate of Wen'an, one of the hardest hit districts, were also investigated. Governor-general Chen Dawen recommended rewards and punishments for several magistrates based on their performance of famine relief duties.[35]

The emperor took a keen personal interest in every aspect of the relief effort and seemed to have an extraordinary grasp of detail, as exhibited in his command of river conservancy. His interlinear comments on memorials were chatty and encouraging. With regard to price gouging by grain shops, he wrote knowingly, "Instances of shops holding back goods to raise the price are commonplace." Sometimes he wrote, "Yes, indeed!" or "Very good!"[36] He exhorted, "Everything that is undertaken should be part of a complete plan [*tongpan chouhua*], not just done from one perspective."[37] In particular, he seemed to be very familiar with the personnel involved in the relief effort, having knowledge of even the lower-ranking officials. He often chastised officials in colorful language. Commenting on a memorial by the Zhili provincial treasurer Tongxing, he wrote in vermilion rescript, "Don't bother with this empty language; just let me see the results."[38] On another memorial he wrote, "Don't have a tiger's head and a snake's tail [*hutou shewei*]," in other words, "don't talk big and do little." He admonished, "It is also important to take care of these matters secretly."[39] In a comment on a Grand Council letter to Chen Dawen, he wrote, "This is not a trivial matter. You cannot do this, and then do that, without regard to the basic matter."[40]

Throughout the crisis, or campaign, the emperor constantly expressed the need for surveillance of local functionaries and officials, but he was also quick to reward meritorious service.[41] In Wen'an, one of the most seriously damaged districts, a local monk reported that low-ranking officials had extorted money from residents while registering households for general relief.[42] Two or three local officials at Rongcheng and Dacheng were impeached for allowing false reports about needy households.[43] At Tongzhou, one of the grain brokers was found to have cheated on measurements and to have forced lower-than-regulation prices on sellers, pocketing the difference.[44] In another case in the summer of 1801, two wall posters had been posted in Tianjin, one complain-

ing of corruption by the magistrate of Wen'an County, the other complaining that rewards promised for donations made in 1793 had never been paid. After investigation, it was found that there
was no basis for these complaints. The author of the posters, a disappointed scholar, was sentenced
to death by hanging, and his accomplice was given eighty lashes.[45]

The emperor must have been extremely pleased with the campaign results. A bumper harvest
followed in the next year, and "people are overjoyed."[46] In addition to authorizing publication of
the relief record, he ordered Shandong provincial officials to follow the model of the Zhili campaign.[47] He continued to follow both agricultural and river conditions closely, chastising officials
for false or inaccurate reporting.[48] In 1805 he praised a relief effort in Shandong that had followed
the Zhili model, but he continued to crack down on false reporting.[49]

The extent of destruction of crops and property during this flood was reflected in the prices of
grain. Grain price reports for the key months of the crisis (JQ 6/6 through 7/3) are missing, but
Yanjian's report stated clearly, "From JQ 6/6 to JQ 7/4, the price of millet [*sumi*] all over the
province ranged from 1.50 to 4.46 per shi." He did not mention wheat, consistent with the timing of the flood, which affected the fall crops principally. Wheat stocks had either been damaged,
or they were exhausted. Figures 9.1a–b reflect the known data, but if the highest reported millet
price of 4.46 is taken into account, it is readily apparent how serious the crisis was. A millet price
of 4.46 was about three times the norm for the period.

As Map 9.1 shows, this flood was very extensive, including most of the counties in Region 2,
about half in Region 4, and three in Region 3. The major river systems of the Bei, Yongding,
Daqing, and Ziya rivers were all affected. The price impact was widespread, and the prices of all
four regions were closely integrated. Looking back to the coefficients of variation displayed in Figures 7.1a–b (in Chapter 7), one can see a sharp peak for both wheat and millet in 1802. Yet the actual coefficients were not very elevated compared with the previous year, except in the case of millet when Region 1 was included, which confirms the separateness of the northern prefectures. In
the following year, 1803, all coefficients of variation fell to pre-crisis levels. Although there is missing data for several months, it appears that the crisis did not cause greater than usual price variation except in 1802. This suggests that the impact of both the crisis and the relief effort were experienced uniformly.

No matter how well a crop developed in 1803, the recovery from such an extensive flood could
not have been quick. Flooded fields, loss of livestock, damaged houses, and other physical destruction compounded the social dislocation. As a consequence of the flood, some households sold off
their land at low prices. Value of land may have fallen as few new landowners wanted to assume
the tax burdens of the previous owners.[50] On the other hand, the mortality toll may have been
limited by the relief measures and by better harvests in the next year. For 1801–3, there are very few
references to starvation, *ji*. In 1802 there are references to pestilence, *yi*, and the following year,
there was some outbreak of locusts, *huang*.[51] Although it is difficult to draw a firm conclusion on
the basis of negative evidence, there is little reason to believe that the 1801–2 flood resulted in elevated levels of mortality.

The 1813–1814 Crisis

In 1813–14 Zhili suffered what was undoubtedly the most severe drought crisis during this period.
Rainfall was about 55 percent less than normal, and both wheat and millet prices were more than
double their normal levels. (See Figures 9.2a–b.) Average provincial wheat price peaked at 4.14

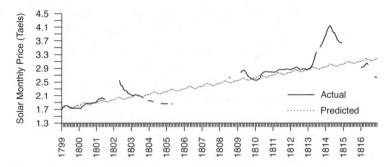

FIGURE 9.1A. Actual and predicted wheat prices, 1799–1816

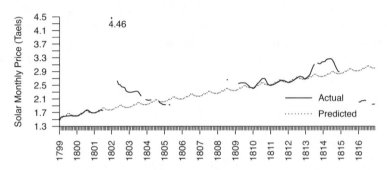

FIGURE 9.1B. Actual and predicted millet prices, 1799–1816

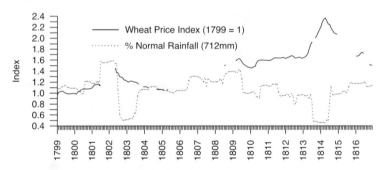

FIGURE 9.2A. Wheat price and rainfall, 1799–1816

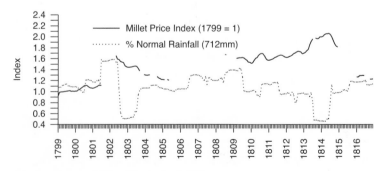

FIGURE 9.2B. Millet price and rainfall, 1799–1816

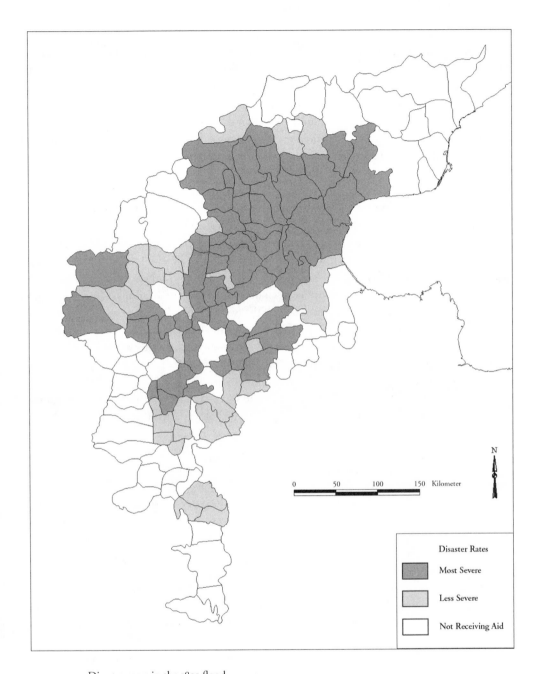

MAP 9.1. Disaster areas in the 1801 flood

SOURCE: Data from JQ 6/12/2, GZD 006858.

NOTE: For identification of counties, please refer to Appendix 1 and Map A.1
(Prefectures and counties in Zhili Province).

taels in April 1814, while millet reached 3.28 taels in June 1814. (See Figures 9.1a–b.) During spring and summer 1813 there was little rain in the south of the province—in Shunde, Guangping, Daming, and Zhaozhou—and almost no wheat was harvested in the summer. Because the fall crops could not be planted in a timely fashion, there was no harvest in the autumn either.[52] The governor-general, Wen Chenghui, recommended relief using 40 percent grain and 60 percent cash distribution and requested for some counties one month's emergency relief (*jizhen*) in the ninth month before general relief was to begin in the eleventh month.[53] For other counties he requested that general relief begin one month earlier, in the tenth month. Although he said he was deputing staff to investigate households, there is no evidence that a household survey was undertaken in this crisis.[54] Rather, it appears that there was limited distribution of silver rations in the heavily stricken areas, as well as reliance on soup kitchens. Since the drought extended to Henan and Shandong, these neighboring provinces were unable to provide relief grain.[55]

Acting Governor Zhang Xu reported at year's end that fifty-six counties had had experienced drought. Of them twenty-one eventually received some rain and had no difficulty with the fall harvest. The other thirty-five counties had meager harvests, and four others had hail. In addition, nine counties in Baoding Prefecture had crop failures in the fall from multiple causes, making a total of forty-eight districts that required relief. Of the twenty-one lightly affected counties, mostly in the central part of the province, tax postponements had already been given, and spring seeds could be lent. No further assistance was planned. The twenty-seven other counties had disaster ratings of 5 to 9 and had already been given relief. These included Pingxiang, Nanhe, Guangzong, Quzhou, Guangping, Jize, Wei xian, and so on—all in the southern part of the province.[56] Fifteen additional counties had 3–4 degree harvests and had crisis ratings of about 5. According to the statutes, they were not entitled to relief, but Zhang Xu had ordered that these districts, also in the southern sector, should be allotted some surplus stipend rice for use in soup kitchens.[57] In Changhuan, which was troubled by bandits, he ordered a soup kitchen to be set up. In each zhou or xian in Shunde Prefecture, Guangping Prefecture, and Zhaozhou, plus Dongming, Kaizhou, and Changyuan, three counties at the southern tip of Daming Prefecture, two months' rations should be given in silver (at the conversion rate of 1.40) to the jobless poor, widows, and so forth.[58] In order to finance the two months' rations, 290,000 taels were allocated from the treasury since grain from the granaries was already depleted. In addition grain tribute of 40,000 shi had been distributed to the poor.[59]

In the following year, the new governor-general Nayancheng requested tax remission and other relief because in 1813, in forty-five counties the fall harvest had been affected by drought, flood, and hail. Three counties—Kaizhou, Dongming, and Changhuan—had been overrun by bandits. In 1814, forty-two counties were affected by drought during the wheat harvest. So he had requested postponement of tax and other payments (rents, amounts owed to granaries, and so on) until after the fall harvest. Since it turned out that the fall harvest all through the province averaged only about 70 percent, people did not have enough to pay their debts. Thus he requested further tax postponements for next two to three years.[60] (See Map 9.2.)

Although the drought conditions in 1813 were extremely serious, this crisis was made far more critical by rebellion in Henan, Shandong, and the adjacent southern leg of Zhili. One group of the rebels was from southern Zhili-Henan and did not make it to Beijing with the main group that reached the city walls that year. The three districts of Zhili that were affected were precisely Kaizhou, Dongming, and Changyuan—on the boundary of Henan, the main focus of the rebellion, and also of Shandong. Wen Chenghui, the Zhili governor-general, was appointed special

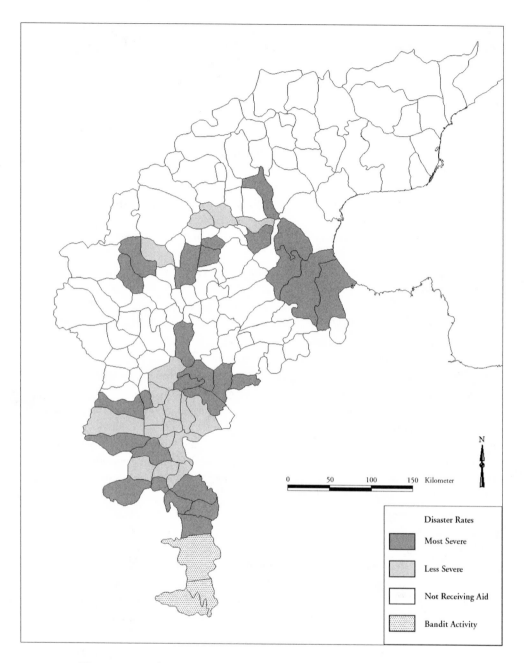

MAP 9.2. Disaster areas in the 1813–1814 drought

SOURCE: Data from JQ 19/11/23, GZD 016996.

NOTE: For identification of counties, please refer to Appendix 1 and Map A.1
(Prefectures and counties in Zhili Province).

commissioner to put down the rebellion, only to be replaced by Nayancheng. In the tenth month Green Standard soldiers entered the xian city of Kai.[61] The Eight Trigrams rebels had seized ample food supplies, and "their occupied cities and villages became storehouses for grain and provisions." Famine victims often joined the movement, but Susan Naquin feels that "famine alone was not a sufficient condition for successful recruitment."[62]

This situation helps to explain not only the unusually high price spike in this crisis but also the large regional differences. Although wheat prices were elevated throughout Zhili Province, and millet prices were high everywhere except Region 1 in the north, the most elevated prices were found in Region 3 in the south. The price of millet surpassed 5 taels in Xingtai and other places.[63] Yet the province as a whole (and the adjacent areas of Shandong and Henan) suffered negative consequences from the drought and rebellion in the south. Figure 1.1 (in Chapter 1) reveals 1813 to have been a year of extraordinary drought in the Beijing region, and Figures 4.1b and 4.6 (in Chapter 4) show the extreme character of the price inflation for the entire province between 1813 and 1815.

With prices so inflated and granary stocks depleted, it is not surprising that there were grain dealers and shops that engaged in smuggling from the grain tribute granaries. A scandal involving the private sales of grain from the Beijing granaries came to the attention of the authorities. Quantities of tribute grain had leaked out of Beijing and had been directed toward shops in Tianjin. Upon investigation, the authorities found that altogether at least 14,600 shi of *suomi* had reached the Tianjin shops, eighty-nine of which were found to have purchased less than 100 shi each, while thirty-six had purchased quantities ranging from 100 to 600 shi each. This crime of "raiding the granaries," *huicao*, was one that had become familiar.[64] In this case, however, the special needs of the city dwellers of Tianjin played a role. Nayancheng noted that Tianjin was at the crossroads of routes from north and south, and that there were many merchants and residents from the south residing there. With grain prices so high north and south of the capital, as well as in Tianjin itself, there was a steady traffic of boatmen and small merchants, in collusion with banner soldiers, plying the waterways from Beijing to Tianjin. The major culprits were apprehended and punished accordingly.[65]

Political unrest combined with drought to create extreme social consequences. Banditry, migration, homelessness, and alienation of land were more evident in this crisis than in others. Relief given for the three districts of Kaizhou, Dongming, and Changhuan were for people whose houses had been destroyed by bandits, rather than for famine as such. Refugees were given money to get home.[66] In the wake of the drought and military disaster, houses, equipment, and stored grain had all been plundered. Zhang Xu feared that merchants would be discouraged from entering the area because of bandits and vagrants, and especially because "Zhili doesn't have a lot of water routes." He discussed with Nayancheng the proposal to send soldiers to patrol.[67]

Population movement, migration due to civil and economic disturbances, was rampant throughout this period, and difficult for officials to contain. Yongping Prefecture had experienced a lean harvest in the fall of 1811 and a heavy snow in the winter of 1812. Relief was difficult, and the wheat crop in this area was late. In the past people could go north through Shanhaiguan to seek a living, but now the pass was closed. Two months' rations and other relief were to be given to the needy in the stricken counties.[68] In Shandong Province, famine victims were reported to be fleeing in great numbers by boat to Fengtian in order to find a living. Officials at each Shandong port were ordered to try to stop this migration by setting up soup kitchens. But they knew the movement was hard to contain because Fengtian had experienced a particularly good harvest the previous year.[69]

Loss of homes and property was widespread.[70] During the crisis, many peasants sold their land at low prices. They had not been able to get a very high price for their land; good land sold for 1,000 to as few as 100 wen (cash) per mu, and poor land was worth 300–400 wen per mu. In prosperous years their value would have been ten times as much. Land values in good years and bad in this area could vary by a factor of ten.[71] Nayancheng proposed a plan to help peasants to buy back their land while the conditions for planting were good. He proposed that the redemptions be made "between the last wheat harvest and the next one so that the peasants can get back their land, but the people who bought the land can also make some profit." The profiteers were identified as outside merchants and rich households who had purchased the cheap land.[72]

This crisis, and the years immediately following, resulted in severe human suffering and high mortality. Not only do gazetteers refer to 1813 as a *zai*, crisis, but there are many references to *ji*, or starvation. Some gazetteers record that people ate bark. Another speaks of the selling of children. And there is at least one reference—from Daming County, the geographic center of the crisis—to cannibalism.[73] Another speaks of people starving to death in huge numbers, a highly unusual statement for the record of famines in the Qing.[74] In 1814, there was reference to pestilence as well. People were so weak they could not farm.[75] Just a few years later, in 1817, references to starvation or *ji* were numerous.[76] That year 105 counties were affected by drought, hail or frost, of which 53 were deemed *chengzai*, and 29 of them were relatively heavily affected.[77]

It is evident that the resources available to address this disaster were extremely limited, particularly in comparison with the relief effort of 1801. Although there were references to general relief, *dazhen*, its actual application seems to have been limited to two months' rations in the three most critically affected districts. In this crisis, and most others in the mid-nineteenth century, granary stocks were depleted, and the state's ability to command supplies from the grain tribute or other provinces was diminished. Crises in other provinces around 1814 competed for scarce state resources. Fengtian, Hubei, Anhui, Jiangxi, Zhejiang, and Gansu all had multiple disasters including floods, drought, hail, locusts—some occurring simultaneously within one province.[78] For the remaining years of the Jiaqing reign, famine relief was quite circumscribed. Although general relief is mentioned in the surviving documents, there is no evidence that it was enacted. *Pingtiao* was sometimes employed, but at higher rates. Instead, there was greater reliance on tax remissions, soup kitchens, and trying to shelter and then send refugees home. When *pingtiao* was mandated, the amounts were trivial compared to the hundreds of thousands of shi deployed in previous crises. Even though millet prices reached more than 5 taels in Xingtai and elsewhere in 1814, Governor-general Nayancheng was able to call up only 22,000 shi of stipend grain stored at the Northern Granary in Tianjin to be used for *pingtiao*.[79] He also requested postponement of taxes, rents, and other debts until the fall harvest in some areas, and longer in others.[80] He reported that soup kitchens had been supplied with contributions from local gentry and people, and he recommended awards for thirty-one of them; in addition officials in Daming Prefecture had made contributions from their *yanglian*, or "nourishing-honesty" income.[81]

The silting of waterways in Zhili compounded the difficulty of transporting relief grain and in turn the supplying of soup kitchens. Although in 1817 an imperial edict had ordered the setting up of soup kitchens and shelters (*liuyangju*) in addition to tax postponements, Fang Shouchou memorialized that there was inadequate funding for these efforts. Because of drought, the water routes had to be changed to land routes, greatly increasing the costs. On top of this burden, localities all over the province were now being asked to set up shelters. There had been money contributed by officials and given to merchants to earn interest, but the interest was not sufficient to meet the costs. Nor was there enough money to buy cotton clothes. There were also insufficient funds to send refugees home.[82]

Soup kitchens became the only significant means of providing relief. In 1819 during flooding of the Yongding and other rivers, which affected ten prefectures, including at least fifty counties, Fang Shouchou once again expressed his preference for using them.

> In my opinion, the best method is to give cooked food. Three he of *mi* is enough for one day's hunger. I have given orders to the affected counties . . . to set up soup kitchens. If they have granaries, they should take granary grain and mill it. If they do not, they should buy grain and cloth. They should do this until the commencement of *dazhen* in the 10th month. For those places where the roads are blocked, famine victims should be given steamed bread or cash: small boats should be used to transport functionaries to give these out.[83]

General relief, or *dazhen*, was mandated, but again the resources were limited. Fang estimated that he would need 200,000 taels to carry out general relief, which he could get from the treasury. As far as grain, aside from the supply from Tongzhou next spring, there was also grain at Tianjin's Northern Granary left over from the 1817 relief campaign, plus 66,000 shi of millet from Henan and Shandong, amounting to a total of 81,000 shi in storage.[84] The stipulated ration was: each household with five mouths or more was to receive 4 dou of *mi*. Households with four mouths or fewer were to receive 3 dou.[85] Although he referred to these as Qianlong precedents, in fact they were differently stated than those prescribed in the *Zhenji* and other regulations. In any case, it is unlikely that any form of general relief was actually carried out.

Daoguang Crises and Corruption

Like the three previous reigns, the Daoguang reign commenced with a huge natural disaster—a flood affecting 104 districts, 92 of which needed relief. The impact of the flood was widespread. The three most severely affected districts were Gu'an, Yongqing, and Dong'an—in Shuntian Prefecture, just south of Beijing, in the swampy center of the province. Twenty-three counties were heavily hit and were granted one month's ration in the ninth month before the commencement of general relief. Households in localities with a disaster rating of 7 or higher could get allowances to fix their houses; for example, for brick homes, 1 tael each; mud and straw houses, .5 tael each. Since there was not much grain stored in local granaries, the governor-general suggested that grain from the Northern Granary or from neighboring localities should be used.[86] Tax remissions, or complete forgiveness, were extended in 1822 to forty-three counties having disaster ratings of 5 to 10. Fifteen counties were given some remission, and thirty-three counties were given none.[87]

In the next year, the wheat harvest failed for lack of rain, and in the beginning of the sixth lunar month, torrential rain fell in sheets, causing conditions that were worse than those of the previous year. All rivers were affected, including the Grand Canal. In eighty-one counties there were reports of fields being submerged in water; people's houses, city walls, and yamen buildings all collapsed under the force of the water. Of these fifty to sixty were deemed to be deserving of relief. The situation was very much like that of 1801, it was said, but then ninety counties received relief.[88] Because the flooding was particularly heavy, the emperor authorized the commencement of *dazhen* a month earlier than usual, in the tenth month. Since the 400,000 shi of tribute grain ordered to be diverted for famine relief had not arrived, he authorized the use of silver payments instead, at the rate of 1.40 taels per shi. The twenty-one most severely affected counties were centered in the Beijing-Tianjin corridor and the swampy heartland of the province.[89] Earlier in the year the insufficiency of tribute grain at the Northern Granary had already caused the emperor to order the use of wheat and silver instead.[90] In subsequent years, the court again ordered the substitution of silver for grain, or their concurrent use, due to insufficient grain supplies. In one case, Nayancheng argued that giving out this converted ration, *zhese kouliang*, was not so good for those who were unemployed and hungry as setting up soup kitchens, but the weather was so hot that they were afraid the food would spoil.[91]

As before Fengtian was an important source of additional grain. But at the start of 1822, grain shipments from Fengtian were stopped because of shortages and high prices there. Officials believed this was because "crafty merchants have started to hoard millet, causing the price to go up."[92] Nevertheless, Fengtian served as a reserve of critical importance. In 1823, the Grand Council authorized additional purchases of 350,000 shi of grain from Fengtian—partly from military reserves—citing precedents of 1813 and saying there was still much stored at Shengjing. Some 400,000 shi of tribute grain diverted earlier in the year was insufficient.[93]

Despite these diminished resources, the records seem to show very large expenditures in this crisis. In total, it appears that the government spent at least 1.8 million taels for general relief and river work, and perhaps another 780,000 shi of grain was commandeered for relief. The plan was to draw on many extraregional sources for financial support of up to 1 million taels. This included 490,000 taels from the Canton Customs (Yue haiguan), 150,000 from Jiujiang Customs, and smaller sums representing customs or land tax revenues from Tianjin, Shandong, Henan, and so forth. The remaining 800,000 taels would come from the Board of Revenue. In addition, there were the Fengtian millet "contributions" because 400,000 shi of grain diverted from grain tribute was insufficient.[94] Later in the crisis, the emperor approved a suggestion to acquire and ship cheap grain from Taiwan and Fujian.[95]

On paper at least, the final amounts used in 1822–23 were as large as those in 1801. The Daoguang emperor invoked the standard of generosity set by his father in 1801 and other relief efforts, and he claimed he would spare no effort in extending relief, often using paternalistic language, such as "I feel your pain."[96] In 1824, he concluded that over several consecutive years of disaster in Zhili, he had spent more than 1 million taels and diverted hundreds of thousands of shi of tribute millet. In addition he had kept open soup kitchens in Shuntian and deployed *pingtiao* on two occasions.[97] New sources of funding had been employed. Bannerland rents were used until grain tribute arrived from the south.[98] Customs revenues totaling 1 million taels from eight ports, including Canton and Jiujiang, had been diverted for relief in Zhili. In addition, 800,000 taels had been allocated by the Board of Revenue. These funds were for general relief in the winter and also for river construction.[99] For relief, 180,000 shi of Henan and Shandong grain tribute had been retained, with wheat and silver substituted for some of the millet.[100] Two hundred thousand shi of millet had been used from Fengtian, and 400,000 shi of grain tribute from Jiangxi had been retained at Tianjin.[101]

Despite all these expenditures, however, the emperor observed that there were still many famine refugees crowding into Beijing, and there were even incidents of violence, grabbing food by force. There were countless others who were fleeing beyond the Great Wall. To him, this was a sign that the local officials had not done their work of distributing famine relief in the countryside; if they had, then people would have no need to leave their homes. If more bandits and *liumin* appear, then it would be a sign that the local officials were being contemptuous of the suffering of the masses, and they should be punished.[102] The previous fall, he ordered that the exodus of refugees beyond the Great Wall should not be blocked. In the Qianlong and Jiaqing periods, the ban was lifted only as a temporary measure. Famine refugees needed to have a pass (*piao*), and many questions were asked. He ordered that people be allowed to leave more freely; after all, they would want to return home next spring to tend to their fields.[103]

It is difficult to get a clear picture of the other social consequences of this beginning-of-era flood, partly because documents from the Daoguang period are conspicuously missing from the archives. The effects of the flood were intertwined with a devastating cholera epidemic that had swept through the Zhili area in 1821, the first year of the reign. Mortality during this period must have been extremely high, due more to the epidemic than to the floods. Records from all districts indicate the horrible extent of death. A common description was terse but unmistakable: "Epidemic swept through during the summer; most people died"; "the number of dead was incalculable"; "the number of dead was huge"; "those who were exposed to the epidemic all died." The epidemic reached Beijing in the seventh lunar month. The death rate was more than 1,000 per day.[104]

During 1822–23, mortality continued to be recorded, but the numbers seemed to decline. In some cases, mortality was attributed to recurrent episodes of disease. In Wangdu County, for example, "In the summer and fall [1822] there was a big epidemic; people died in masses." In other cases, famine was the clear cause. For example in Luan County, "In the spring there was a big hunger [*daji*]; the number of dead was very numerous." But in other cases, flood and epidemic were indistinguishable as causes. In Yongping Prefecture, for example, "There was a big famine and epidemic [*dajiyi*]. People died in great numbers." In 1823, epidemic seemed to have revived in quite a few places. In Wen'an County, "There was a big flood, a dou of grain was a thousand cash, and in the fourth month, epidemic/plague was rampant. People died in rapid succession; there was no time for mourning."[105]

Despite trying to emulate the model of his father, the new emperor could hardly have regarded the Zhili floods and epidemic as an auspicious start to his reign. In fact the entire Daoguang reign was characterized by floods and droughts in several different regions of the empire in every year. Together with the better-known challenges of the Opium War—accompanied by social unrest, bureaucratic factionalism, and corruption—famines and natural disasters have contributed to the historical judgment that the Daoguang period marked something of a turning point in the fate of the Qing rulers.[106] The record of the 1822–23 flood reveals that despite all the funds that had allegedly been expended on relief, the management of the crisis had not been good.[107] Relief and investigation took place in the multiple crises of 1832–34 period as well, with the emperor continually concerned with the widespread corruption that impeded any relief effort.[108]

Misuse of public funds in connection with river projects, granaries, and famine relief in general was nothing new, but cases from the late Qianlong and early Jiaqing periods reveal the widespread misappropriation of funds for famine relief. In the Jiaqing period, the emperor himself exercised personal vigilance against malfeasance by officials administering relief or managing river work. Throughout his reign, he continued to pay attention to the problem of corruption, but it nevertheless became an increasingly pervasive phenomenon all over the empire. In Shanyang, Jiangsu Province, in 1808–9, the embezzlement of famine relief funds was commonplace.[109] In Zhili also in 1809 the emperor demoted the governor-general Wen Chenghui and the provincial treasurer Fang Shouchou for failing to investigate cases of fraud in use of famine relief funds. In one instance, 20,000 taels out of 40,000 taels that had been allocated for famine relief in Baodi County during the floods of the previous year, 1808, had been embezzled by the local magistrate. The emperor despaired, saying, "If one county is like this, then how can we trust the others?" Beyond this, it was clear that even honest higher officials sent to investigate localities were paid off.

"They did nothing but mutually divide the fat," and they became entangled in the network of corruption.[110] Later Wen Chenghui, who had been retained in office, reported that corruption had not spread further beyond Baodi. "I appointed officials who had not been involved in the relief operation and were known to be upright. They actually went into the xian and to households in poor villages to see if relief had actually been administered," he claimed.[111]

In 1814, a discussion of famine relief frauds in all provinces took place:

> The management of famine relief in many provinces has not been ideal. In investigating disaster, officials use pretexts or extortion. The treasurer issues money but withholds a portion. In making up the relief registers, the functionaries do not report a household's being empty, so they can profit. In setting up soup kitchens, they don't take distances into account, so people are exhausted before they get there, or else they find it preferable to become *liumin*.[112]

Other malpractices included distributing relief at the wrong times, mixing sand and dust with the rice gruel, and shortchanging people on the exchange rates. In a general review of famine relief practices in 1826, some common forms of cheating in famine relief included functionaries' taking advantage of missing households and pocketing their share of relief; officials' not announcing tax remissions to the relevant districts; officials' reporting districts with good harvests as disaster districts in order to collect taxes but not remit them to the central government. The edict enjoined provincial governors to publicize famine relief decrees and to order local officials to keep accurate household registers so that famine relief could be fairly distributed. The amount of relief to which each household was entitled should be posted on their doors, indicating whether the household was "very poor" (*jipin*) or "less poor" (*cipin*).[113]

In Zhili, local magistrates sometimes cheated on granary transactions—making false reports, exchanging bad grain for good, selling to merchants, and so forth.[114] Every spring there were malpractices at the district and county level when it came to the lending of seeds. When the loans were due in the fall, the local functionaries would make them pay double. Or else, in dispensing rations, they would make up names and take the grain themselves. "The governors should look into this and not indulge the functionaries," an edict stated.[115]

Tax remissions provided another fertile area for corruption. In 1818, for example, there was cheating on the forgiveness of back taxes that had been granted. A local official overreported the amount still owed and pocketed the difference.[116] In 1821, the first year of Daoguang, an imperial edict cautioned, "In the cancellation of taxes because of flooding, the officials should strictly look out for cases of intimidation of the small people and other offenses."[117] There was also evidence of cheating by functionaries, who were continuing to collect taxes when they had been declared cancelled or postponed by the court. Local officials were ordered to publicize the tax remissions so that the poor people would not allow themselves to be cheated in this way.[118]

The necessity to convert silver prices into copper cash rates, and also the commutation of grain payments into cash payments, provided additional opportunities for malfeasance. This may have become more important because more relief rations were converted to monetary payments. In 1822, the proportions were 50/50, 40 percent grain/60 percent silver, or 30/70, depending on local conditions.[119] In 1810, for example, Wen Chenghui was determined to prevent the corrupt handling of relief for nineteen districts. In nineteen districts that needed relief, 157,150 shi of *mi* had arrived. He consulted with each district about whether to give grain and money together, or only money. He deputed the big officials (*daotai* and prefects) to take their chops and set up stations to give out relief at once, whether the district was scheduled for one to three months. Also to prevent local officials from profiteering off the silver/cash exchange, they took the original silver and cut it up, and marked it with each household's name. He estimated that for *dazhen* they needed 18,000 shi of grain and 204,000+ taels of silver, as commuted from grain.[120]

To avoid malpractices in the silver/copper conversion in famine relief in 1822, a Grand Secretariat censor proposed using copper cash in famine relief. In Anhui, he pointed out, it had long been the practice to use cash because it was easier for the uneducated women and children in the countryside. For disaster-struck households eager to buy food, silver was inconvenient because it had to be converted to copper cash. To exchange the money, the poor people had to go into the city, where the prices were higher than in the countryside. "But let's prohibit the money changers from making a profit from this, and the functionaries from taking a cut. The exchange rate should be posted on the streets and thoroughfares so that the country people can be informed."[121] In Zhili there was always talk of the importance of deputing high officials to make sure there was no cheating in such transactions. "The commutation rate (of grain to money) should be made to cash, not silver, and posted so all will know."[122]

Midcentury Political Crisis

In the Daoguang reign attention was increasingly focused on famine refugees surging to Beijing, raising fears of crowding and unrest in the capital itself. Successive political disturbances in the capital area in the nineteenth century threatened the actual security of Beijing and the entire region as well as its food security. With declining grain reserves and the greater pressure of refugees near the capital, both provincial and Beijing authorities resorted to a greater dependence on soup kitchens than ever before. This was simply relief, not part of an ambitious plan to restore agricultural production. Although the major floods and droughts of the Daoguang reign were accompanied by an increasingly empty ritual of famine relief procedures, the few resources left to the state were focused on the critical area of the capital itself. From 1853 until 1858, locusts spread all over the province, but the crisis went unreported and neglected.[123]

Although agricultural and natural vulnerabilities were the underlying cause of Zhili's seemingly perpetual state of crisis, political disturbances caused the greatest human and social hardships. In 1813, the Eight Trigrams uprising and attack on Beijing itself was an event that had enormous economic repercussions all over the region, as well as being a highly daring assault on the dynasty itself. In 1853, after establishing their kingdom at Nanjing, the Taiping rebel forces entered Zhili, reached Tianjin, and threatened the capital. Occurring at the same time that the Yellow River was shifting its course northward and completely halting the already diminished Grand Canal tribute traffic, this constituted a grave disruption to the food security of the capital region. In 1860 British and French forces fought their way from Dagu (Tianjin) to the capital, destroying and looting the imperial palaces at Yuanmingyuan and terrorizing the city for a short period. The emperor Xianfeng fled the capital for the summer palace at Rehe (Chengde), causing grave apprehension about his own fate and that of the dynasty. He never did return to the capital and died in Rehe the following year.[124]

The very presence of either rebels or foreign troops in the region was enough to cause the price of food to rise. But compounding the disruption in grain supplies was the monetary crisis of this era. Shortage of copper supply from Yunnan due to these political events caused the government to gradually debase the standard coins in circulation and then issue the infamous "big cash"—a practice that started in Fujian and other provinces and spread to Beijing in 1853. At the same time the government began to issue paper money, both for cash and for silver. Its circulation was largely confined to Beijing despite attempts to extend its use to the provinces.[125] In order to meet the many expenses in putting down the rebellion, as well as its routine expenses, the government was in effect printing money that had not much backing. It also started to issue iron coins, which were even less popular than paper money.[126]

In Beijing this monetary system wreaked havoc with all types of transactions. The pricing system was chaotic. Shopkeepers had no way to make change with money or bills of large denominations. The saying was that if one had "big cash," one could not buy grain. Grain merchants would not come into the city, and grain shops closed down. Shopkeepers were afraid to accept paper money and hoarded their stocks. Even pawnshops shut down. Farmers in the region were afraid to bring their produce to the capital. People holding only big cash could only cry; the poor became beggars, and the beggars became corpses in the streets—according to the local lore.[127] In the region generally, the combined effect of political disorder and monetary instability caused an economic slump that required decades of recovery.[128]

Prices of grain rose precipitously even with good harvests. In 1854, despite a good harvest in the capital region and low prices, there was a food shortage inside the city. A catty of wheat was 16 to 17 standard cash outside the city, but 37 or 38 within.[129] The price of rice in Beijing in 1848 had been 2.1 taels per picul; by 1851 it was about 5 taels; in 1857 it was almost 10 taels, and there was crop failure in the surrounding region. Commercial rice imported to Tianjin increased eightfold from 1856–57. By 1860, rice prices fell back to 1 tael per picul.[130] However, prices rose again in 1861. David Rennie, staff surgeon to the first British embassy, reported that since the court had fled to Rehe, the price of rice was so high—double its normal price of 1 tael—that ordinary people could purchase only inferior or spoiled varieties. War had raised the cost of daily necessities, but, in addition, grain merchants had directed their supplies to Rehe, where the court had fled, leaving Beijing undersupplied. "This grain question is agitating the public mind a good deal at the present time, as they say they have troubles enough without it."[131] Paper money inspired no confidence; laborers would not accept it as payment of wages. The daily fluctuations in its value caused much uncertainty. "Every morning the exchange shops are besieged by crowds endeavouring to convert paper money into cash." Rennie observed that even the wealthy were in a state of economic distress, a fact that he observed as various antiques were brought into the embassy for sale. "Provisions are said to be rapidly approaching famine prices, and indications of distress continue amongst the higher classes, judging from the character of the property which continues to be offered for sale at the Legation."[132]

The Beijing monetary crisis had a wide impact on the entire region despite the reports of higher prices in the city. Gamble was surprised to see little evidence of the Beijing exchange rate trend in the Ding County records, but Figure 4.8 (in Chapter 4), which employs the exchange rate series from Ding County, shows clearly the profound effect of exchange rates on grain prices in the period from the 1830s until the 1860s.[133] Although grain prices reported in silver taels took a steep dive from the 1840s until the 1860s, it is actually the cash prices that reflected supply and demand in this period. Peaks in grain prices as measured in cash seen in 1839, 1848, 1861, and 1871 reflected either harvest shortfalls or political unrest.[134] (See Figures 4.9a–b in Chapter 4.) In 1839 there were drought conditions in some parts of the province with reports of deaths; the previous years were also difficult for many areas, but the harvest ratings in Baoding were not particularly bad.[135] In 1871, high prices reflected floods. In 1861, however, the price spike for both wheat and millet prices are seen more clearly in cash prices than silver prices, and the spikes clearly reflect the political crisis in Beijing and at the court. The interpretation of the price spike in 1848 is more ambiguous. It was not a year of particular crisis in North China; although there were floods in the Yangzi valley that year, the rice prices in our series do not reflect any particular disturbance.[136]

Although the depreciation of cash was an empirewide phenomenon, the Xianfeng crisis centered on Beijing and North China generally. Some denominations of cash coins were minted only in the north. Large coins did not circulate much in the provinces. Iron coins were restricted to Beijing. Paper money, however, did circulate for a long time in Zhili and continued to be used in tax payments together with silver. Although urban residents were seriously affected, peasants were generally more vulnerable because their income from grain sales was received in copper cash, but their tax payments were in silver; so the result was an increase in their actual tax burden.[137] The duometallic monetary system tended to increase the vulnerability of North China peasants. The tremendous discrepancy between grain prices in cash and prices in silver from the 1840s until the late 1870s, as seen in Figures 4.9a–b, is in itself evidence of the economic dislocation of this period.

The 1871–1872 Floods and the Li Hongzhang Era

In the last third of the nineteenth century, Zhili and much of North China suffered what seemed to be a perpetual crisis. Floods and droughts succeeded each other in rapid succession, blending seamlessly into what seemed like an endless catastrophe. The early 1870s witnessed massive flooding, which was followed by the great North China famine of 1876–79. In the 1890s, Zhili's rivers, now almost out of control due to silting and decay of the dike system, constantly inundated the central plain of the province. Finally, prolonged drought in 1899–1900 weakened an already fragile social and economic infrastructure, leading to one political crisis at the turn of the century, the Boxer Uprising, and then another in 1911, when the dynasty fell.

The increasingly scarce resources of the central government were again unable to cope with the mounting crises, but to a surprising extent the Qing famine relief administrative procedures were revived and employed throughout this period, even to the very last year of the dynasty. (It is possible that the reporting of crises continued on a regular basis in the Xianfeng and early Tongzhi periods, but few records remain.) In large measure this was due to the leadership of Li Hongzhang, who served as Zhili governor-general from 1870 to 1895 and who was the single most important statesman and diplomat in this era. Having secured his reputation in the suppression of the Taiping rebels in the Lower Yangzi region, Li became the key figure in China's negotiations with foreign powers in this period and was also known for his support of Westernization projects such as the first cotton mill, telegraph company, and steamship company. His post in Zhili gave him easy access to the court and contact with Western powers at Beijing and Tianjin, where he served also as Superintendant of Trade for the Northern Ports. In fact, he spent more time in Tianjin than the provincial capital at Baoding. At a time when there was no adult emperor exercising power, and the court was mired in various intrigues, the authority and influence of Li Hongzhang was far greater than that of previous governors-general.

The new governor-general seemed to be very aware of the continual state of crisis in Zhili and of the pervasive social unrest that had developed.

> Ever since the harvest-disaster of Tongzhi 6[1867], people have been roaming around homeless. Households rarely store grain, and there have been several years in a row of disaster. Every winter since the general relief of TZ 6, the setting up of shelters has been ordered. This fall, although the harvest is called average [*zhong*], in fact there are a lot of poor people, so I request changing the soup kitchens [*zhouchang*] into grain stations [*michang*] because there is *gengmi* left in storage from TZ 6.[138]

In 1871 torrential rains reached over 1,000 mm in the Beijing area, almost the level of the 1801 floods, and about 80 percent above the average rainfall for this period. (See Figure 1.1 in Chapter 1, and Figures 9.4a–b, below.) Grain prices soared to unprecedented levels; in fact the cash price of wheat was higher in 1871 than it would be in the crisis of 1878. (See Figures 4.9a–b in Chapter 4.) The index of wheat prices, measured in copper cash, rose to 1.85 in 1871, and 1.71 in 1878. The index of millet prices was 1.71 in 1871, and 1.78 in 1878. Grain prices measured in silver showed no such spike for 1871, as seen in Figures 9.3a–b and also in Figure 4.1c (in Chapter 4). This is a clear proof that in this period of time, cash was a more relevant measure of value than silver.

Li Hongzhang was relentless in memorializing the throne for relief, even though the initial damage was relatively light. There was more rain in the seventh and eighth months. Six counties were heavily hit (Tianjin, Cangzhou, Wen'an, Baoding, and so on), seventeen were less heavily hit, and sixty-five were relatively lightly affected. For the six worst districts, he recommended that relief should be given in the ratio of 70 percent grain and 30 percent silver. For one month this would require 140,000 shi of grain and 80,000 taels of silver. In requesting relief, Li was skillful at citing precedents and figures from past crises in order to support his request for relief.

> I observe that this is like two or three months' relief of the past. In Daoguang 3 [1823], when the wheat harvest was hit by hail and drought, and the fall harvest was flooded, Jiangsu and Guangdong tribute grain supplied 550,000 shi and the Fengtian granaries supplied 150,000 shi. Also customs revenues from various ports, and contributions of 1 million taels silver were collected from other provinces, and 800,000 taels from Hu Bu. In TZ 6 [1867], when the fall harvest was affected by drought, Fengtian and Shandong supplied 200,000 shi millet by sea tribute, and the Board of Revenue gave 200,000 taels for relief. This year's flood is the biggest since JQ 6 [1801], and the crisis more serious than those of DG 3 and TZ 6. The local gentry and rich have contributed generously, but only half the amount of 1867. I observe that Zhili's treasury has never been large, and help from the south is necessary.[139]

Not only was Li Hongzhang aware of the levels of past relief, but he also understood the classical model of famine relief. For the first time since 1801, the practice of famine investigation was renewed (but probably not at the household level). In the tenth month, he requested relief for thirty-three counties that had by then experienced heavy damage and tax remissions for ninety-five counties that had been affected. He then enclosed in his memorial a list showing the detailed results of the famine investigation: including the number of villages affected and their disaster ratings from 3 to 9. Villages with ratings of 5 to 9 were considered in the disaster category (*chengzai*), while ratings of 3–4 were counted as "lean harvest" (*qianshou*). He then cited previous regulations for granting relief: one month's ration should be given to the desperately poor (*jipin*) of 6-degree disaster areas and the moderately poor (*cipin*) of the areas of 7–8-degree disaster areas. Two months' ration should be given to the *jipin* of the 7–8-degree villages and the *cipin* of the 9-degree villages. Three months' ration should be given to the *jipin* of the 9-degree villages.

> This year the flood disaster situation is especially severe. Fields and crops have been submerged. Dwellings and boats are all washed away. The small people are leaving their homes. It is in reality the worst situation in several decades. Because winter is approaching, we humbly begged for (and received) imperial permission to divert 80,000 shi of tribute grain and 20,000 shi of millet from Fengtian. In addition 20,000 taels were diverted from the treasuries of military bureaus in the cities, the Changlu salt treasury, and the Tianjin customs. In addition I have repeatedly asked for permission to order 40,000 shi of grain from provinces of Jiangsu and Zhejiang, as well as 50,000 taels more from the treasury of Changlu Salt Bureau, and 200,000 taels from military rations.

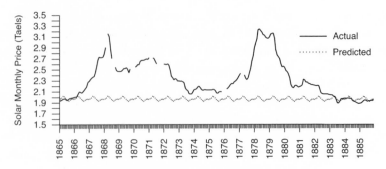

FIGURE 9.3A. Actual and predicted wheat prices, 1865–1885

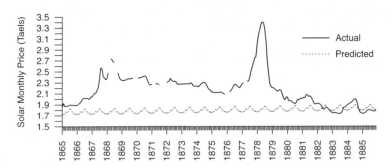

FIGURE 9.3B. Actual and predicted millet prices, 1865–1885

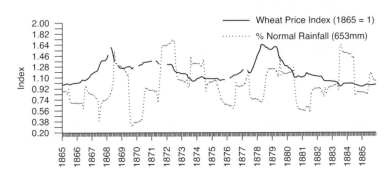

FIGURE 9.4A. Wheat price and rainfall, 1865–1885

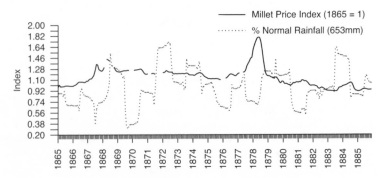

FIGURE 9.4B. Millet price and rainfall, 1865–1885

He also asked permission to persuade local officials and gentry as well as Jiang-Zhe gentry and merchants to contribute grain, cotton clothes, and other goods. The area affected was quite broad and the expenses would be great, he argued. He had also received imperial permission to increase the amount of relief from grain tribute by 30,000 shi and relief payments by 40,000 taels. But this was still not enough to conduct *dazhen* in the nineteen counties. So he requested more funds from the Board of Revenue. In addition to these funds, Li requested tax remissions so people could re-build their houses and boats: 10 percent for villages of 5–6-degree disaster, 20 percent for 7-degree, 40 percent for 8-degree, and 60 percent for 9-degree disaster areas. Again he cited the precedent of DG 3 (1823).[140]

The year 1872 brought continued heavy rains; at first, it seemed that they would do limited damage to crops. In the ninth month, however, Li Hongzhang reported that seventeen low-lying counties at the center of the province had several inches of water on the ground and were going to lose their fall crops. In the twelfth month, he reported that thirty-eight counties had villages with disaster ratings of 5–9 as well as villages of "lean harvests" with ratings of 3–4. Another thirty-five counties had (only) villages with "lean harvest" ratings.[141] In the spring of the following year, 1873, there was an early thaw, and some rivers started to rise. In the sixth month, there had been heavy and unceasing rains, and the downpour from the mountains was great. The Yongding, Daqing, Zhulong, Zhang-Wei, and other rivers were all rising. The four prefectures of Shuntian, Baoding, Hejian, and Tianjin experienced catastrophe; other areas were partly affected. Altogether there were seventy-one counties affected: thirty-three were lightly affected; twenty-nine not only lost their fall crop but also would have no wheat crop the next year. Li then presented a detailed report of the classification and rating of villages within the twenty-nine stricken counties. He noted that the districts that had been hit by disaster this year had repeatedly in recent years been storage-deficit areas, and the common people rarely stored grain themselves. They must be given relief, he stated. He further memorialized about the relief that the thirty-three lightly affected counties were to receive, appending a list of how many 3- and 4-degree villages were in each county.[142]

This documentary record reveals that Li Hongzhang was able to exercise his tremendous in-fluence—both with the court and with the provincial-level bureaucracy in the south—to com-mand resources for famine relief and river conservancy in Zhili. Although the quantities of assis-tance deployed were not so large as those of the 1743–44 or 1801, they were not trivial. Li could, more easily than others, request the diversion of resources from other regions to Zhili. The devel-opment of steamship transport for the grain tribute shipments in the 1870s was a boon in this re-gard. Several times over these years, Li boldly demanded that tens of thousands of shi be diverted to Zhili for famine relief. He also asked repeatedly for the governors of southern provinces—es-pecially Zhejiang and Jiangsu but also Fujian—to help him make large purchases of grain. The relatively easy access to grain from Fengtian continued to be a great boon to Zhili. The extent to which Li could act on his own authority was impressive. He was authorized to decide how much money should be contributed from each province for repairs on the southern bank of the Yong-ding River, which had overflowed in the seventh month of 1873, totaling 400,000 taels (Jiangsu, Hubei, Zhejiang, Fujian, Guangdong, and Anhui). Again, he ordered officials to go to Niuzhuang (Newchwang) in Fengtian and Daokou in Henan to purchase *zaliang* (mixed coarse grains) for the winter's relief.[143]

In dealing with famine relief, Li Hongzhang employed a combination of traditional and new techniques. In reviving the practice of village investigation and famine ratings, he implicitly drew on the assumptions of the past about famine relief: that it should be bureaucratically managed, and that it should be directed to the household level if possible. In using the concept of *dazhen*, he invoked a grand vision of bureaucratic effectiveness, while at the same time recognizing that lower goals might have to be set. In asking for tax remissions, he employed a common technique of the past intended to reduce the economic burden of stricken households and districts. Yet he acknowledged that the full-dress famine relief campaign of the past was hardly feasible. According to him, in XF 11 (1861) the concept of *zhen* (relief) had been changed to *fu* (comfort). Although he argued for a return to the level of relief implied by *zhen*, Li seemed to be acknowledging that something more modest would have to suffice. He cited the phrase, *gaizhen weifu* ("changing relief into comfort"), which he said was first used in 1861, when relief had been delayed. In 1871 he said that in fact *fu* had been used as *zhen: yifu weizhen*.[144]

A relatively new dimension of this, however, was the preference that Li often expressed for the use of cash instead of actual grain transfers. An edict in the seventh month of 1871 had ordered Liang Jiang Governor-general Zeng Guofan and Jiangsu Governor Zhang Zhiwan to send 20,000 shi of rice, but Li Hongzhang then said he preferred cash because northerners like to eat coarse grains. Send cash to Tianjin, he said, and we can go to Fengtian to buy grain. Zeng and Zhang calculated that the cost of Shanghai's rice plus transport costs would be 2.50 taels per shi, so they would send 50,000 taels to Zhili.[145] Other relatively minor innovations were made. In 1870, instead of traditional soup kitchens, Li Hongzhang reported the establishment of two factories to make *mo* (steamed bread), one ounce each one, one per person (adult or child) per day.[146] Soup kitchens at the six gates of Beijing were still set up.[147]

Recognizing that state resources were limited, Li Hongzhang also put pressure on officials to make donations as individuals and on gentry and merchants to show their merit. He repeatedly requested rewards for gentry and merchant contributors, including Hu Guangyong, a prominent merchant-philanthropist from the Lower Yangzi region.[148] The government practiced *zhaoshang*, calling upon merchants to ship grain. The gentry and the rich were asked to contribute money, set up shelters, and collect cotton clothing.[149] In 1873, for example, Li Hongzhang reported that from the seventh month of 1872 to fifth month of 1873, grain, cotton clothes, and silver, totaling 130,278 taels in value had been received, and suitable rewards should be given to the official and gentry contributors, such as the Soochow Imperial Textile Commissioner. The conversion rates used to get cash-equivalent contributions were 2.50 per shi of rice and 1.80 per shi of millet.[150]

The 1876–1879 North China Famine

Of the many catastrophes in the history of North China none can match the great drought famine of 1876–79. It was unquestionably the most severe and geographically extensive natural crisis of the entire Qing period, and perhaps ever in Chinese history.[151] Starting first in Shandong and Zhili, and then spreading to Shanxi, Henan, and Shaanxi provinces, the crisis left an estimated 9.5 million to perhaps 13 million or more dead and imposed great hardship on the survivors. For Zhili alone, the estimated toll was 2.5 million deaths, in Henan 1 million, and in Shandong .5 million. Shanxi and Shaanxi experienced the greatest suffering.[152]

The famine was extraordinary also because of its duration of three or four years. Following several years of flood conditions, the great drought struck a rural society in Zhili already bereft of any reserves or resources. Foreign missionaries and diplomats familiar with the North China plain had seen the region transformed from what they regarded as relatively prosperous agricultural environment to one unable to yield any crops at all.

This enormous plain was once famous for its fertility, but since the floods of 1871–75, when it was nearly covered with water, owing to the bursting of the [Grand] Canal and Peiho [Bei River], its character has been changed. The floods destroyed nearly all trees which had been left standing, the usual ditches for irrigation were obliterated, the river courses altered, and when the foundation was succeeded by the rainless yeas of 1876–77, the plain became parched up and incapable of bearing even a moderate crop. Dr. Frazer, a gentleman of many years' experience at Tientsin, asserts that the appearance and character of the country, as far as his observations extended, has undergone a complete transformation since the floods. The herbage and crops are now poor and coarse, and the farms very much less productive. The inhabitants, once well to do and contented, are poverty stricken and improvident.[153]

The author, R. J. Forrest, British consul at Tianjin, also noted the extent of salinization on the plain.

The winter wind covers the ground with dust . . . and the ground becomes covered with a white saline exudation fatal to all fertility. At Chu-lu hsien is a considerable tract of land so thoroughly impregnated with salt, that if the soil is mixed with water and left to dry in the sun, a considerable crust of salt results. . . . It is simply monstrous that a large and generally fertile plain should be allowed to dry up into a saline desert, when the accidental bursting of the banks of one of the rivers traversing it can flood it in a week with fresh water.[154]

The social consequences of the drought were appalling and included all the stages of human catastrophe. First households sold their clothes and other property. Next they gave up their homes and their land. Men went off elsewhere to seek work, leaving their wives and children behind. Or whole families were forced to roam around in search of food. Children were frequently sold, girls bringing higher prices than boys, and younger women higher prices than older. Prices ranged from 9,000 wen cash for an eighteen-year-old woman to 6,000 wen for a twenty-eight year old.[155] Such responses within families to famine scarcity severely tested the normal Confucian social bonds.[156]

Illness often accompanied starvation. During this period, typhus was a frequent visitor to poor families. Typhus broke out in the winter of 1877 and killed "thousands and thousands" that the famine had spared. Several famine relief workers died this way. Such conditions also led to suicide, which became very common. According to reports, as many as half of the villagers in some places had died. In Shanxi, Timothy Richard, a missionary, observed a 30 percent mortality in his village; someone else observed that three-quarters of the villagers had died. In some severely stricken areas, it was said that 60–90 percent of the population died. In Zhili, some reported that one-fifth had died; others one-third.[157] In northern Shanxi, people said that 50 percent of the people died, 20 percent were sold or fled, leaving only 30 percent at home.[158] Local gazetteers contain reports of high mortality, especially in 1877 and 1878 in Zhili. All over the province grain prices soared, reaching 2,000 wen per dou. People were eating grass and bark, and they were dying "in large numbers" of starvation. The stock phrase about "bodies filling the roads" occurs several times. In some places more than half the people died. In addition there are references to contagious diseases and reports of cannibalism (*ren xiangshi*).[159]

Famine victims resorted to famine "foods" that had no nutritional value but provided a sense of fullness.[160] People were seen eating clay or a soft stone that they pounded to pieces, mixed with millet husks, and then baked. Trees were stripped bare and the bark sold for 5 to 7 cash per catty. Ingesting such foods caused people to die of constipation. Grain was three to four times the usual price.[161]

When there was no grain and no more bark, cannibalism was the last resort. It was widely observed by missionaries in Shanxi, but less so in Zhili.[162] They reported that in some places the eating of human flesh was a regular occurrence, and one only hoped that the victim was dead before being eaten.[163] In some places human flesh had become commoditized. "They sell human flesh almost publicly, not only in buns, fritters, but also without being mixed with herbs or anything." Traffickers could be prosecuted, but the practice was too widespread to contain. Some villagers rationalized that it was better to consume human flesh than to leave the corpses to the wolves.[164] To prevent their loved ones from being eaten, families rushed to bury their dead before animals or people seized the body, but there were even reports that family members sometimes consumed each other, contrary to the Confucian notion of "exchanging your children and eating them [*yizi er shi*]." Such stories suggest the disintegration of the social order during this crisis.

These extreme and horrible conditions were found mostly in Shanxi, but there is no doubt that parts of Zhili also experienced extensive social degradation. The gazetteer of Tangshan County (Shunde Prefecture) describes religious and antiforeign disturbances in 1877, accompanied by *daji*, great hunger. In that year, there had been an unusual crisis, and many people starved to death.[165] In 1878 there was drought from spring to summer. In addition to withered crops, people suffered from epidemic disease. The price of *mi* was up to "1,000 qian per dou."[166] The Daming *daotai* gave 2,000 taels to the county to set up a *pingtiao* bureau and deputed "upright gentry" to Shandong to buy grain to distribute for relief. In the third month he requested opening up the several "preparedness granaries," *yubeicang*, and distributing grain to villages. There was an unusual example of a locality where there were some reserves and local leaders took initiatives; a number of local gentry helped directly with the relief effort and distributed grain from the granaries.[167]

Migration and vagrancy were widespread. Many from Shandong fled to Manchuria. Shanxi refugees also fled north beyond the Great Wall. Zhili and Henan vagrants fled also to Jiangsu, Anhui, and Shandong. Altogether one observer said there were hundreds of thousands on the road.[168] Suicides and deaths were frequent. The situation was precisely what traditional famine relief measures had sought to prevent. Not only were there famine refugees, but government measures to bring grain to Shanxi and other inland areas produced a heavy traffic in carts and animals as well as humans. The road from Tianjin via Huailu County through the Guguan Pass into Shanxi was a nightmare to travel. Full of ruts, it was difficult for the myriad carts and pack animals carrying commercial or relief grain to make much progress.

> During the winter and spring of 1877–78, the most frightful disorder reigned supreme along this route. . . . Fugitives, beggars, and thieves, absolutely swarmed. . . . Camels, oxen, mules, and donkeys were hurried along in the wildest confusion, and so many perished or were killed by the desperate people in the hills for the sake of their flesh, that the transit could only be carried on by the banded vigilance of the interested owners of grain.

Murder was common, and it was dangerous to travel at night. Corpses were strewn along the way.[169]

Although the situation was overwhelming, official famine administration was brought into play. Both Li Hongzhang in Zhili and Governor Zeng Guoquan in Shanxi were fully engaged in trying to deal with the crisis. Compared with the major relief campaigns of the past, the level of state funding in this crisis was small, but not insignificant. In 1876, the court authorized 100,000 taels for the purchase of grain from Fengtian for relief in Zhili. Li Hongzhang came up with another 100,000 taels to encourage the purchase of grain from Fengtian, Jiangsu, Hu-Guang, and so on. An additional 100,000 was found from the provincial treasurer, and 120,000 taels were found from other sources. This total of about 400,000 taels was used mostly for work relief (312,000 taels in 1876), as well as for soup kitchens and *pingtiao*. The work relief was targeted at Hejian Prefecture, which suffered the most damage during this crisis. In addition, about 140,000 shi of tribute grain was used for relief.[170] In Shanxi, Zeng Guoquan managed a surprisingly energetic state relief operation and reportedly raised through official and voluntary sources as much as 10 million taels and 1 million shi of grain. As many as 4 million people may have received some amount of state relief.[171]

In all five provinces, some effort to set up soup kitchens was made, and there was also some effort to contain the flow of refugees. In Henan and Shanxi, there was a famine classification of some sort, perhaps not based on actual investigation, with the distribution of *kouliang* (rations) according to the ratings of *jipin* and *cipin*.[172] In Zhili, however, there is no record of household investigation. At Beijing *pingtiao* was conducted with grain shipped from Fengtian. After arrival at Beijing, the grain was distributed through the Zhaoshangju (Bureau for Soliciting Merchant Contributions), which in turn sold the grain to small shops in Beijing, reducing the price by 1–2 qian per shi. Beijing continued to receive the most attention, with many famine refugees converging. It was estimated that 30–40 percent of the recipients of famine relief were outsiders, while 60–70 percent were local residents. Because of the desperate conditions in the countryside, Li Hongzhang gave strict orders forbidding other districts from coming to Beijing to purchase grain.[173]

Having become the major treaty port of North China, with extensive trade and a large foreign community, Tianjin assumed importance in this crisis as a haven for famine victims in search of relief and shelter. In the fall of 1877, at the outset of the crisis, 100,000 refugees poured into the city.[174] Soup kitchens that also served as shelters were set up. Of a total of fourteen soup kitchens, two were exclusively for men and nine for women. The total numbers sheltered were 43,900 adults and 7,400 children, for a total of 51,300 people. In 1878, the court allocated 20,000 taels for the purpose of sending home refugees who had fled to these cities and other centers. Refugees from Zhili and Shandong were allotted 1 tael each to get home. Those from Henan, Shanxi, and Shaanxi were allotted 4 taels. In the Tianjin/Hejian area adults got 2 dou of grain, children 1 dou, plus 1,000 Tianjin cash for transportation.[175]

Despite these various efforts, some concluded that most of the relief never reached its intended recipients. This was particularly true in the inland provinces of Shanxi and Henan. These two provinces had traditionally relied on central China for their grain supply, but found these routes cut off. Transport over inland dirt roads in Shanxi became virtually impossible.[176] Corruption was also pervasive. He Hanwei finds that the relief effort was impressive, but the results poor.[177] Zhili's situation was a bit more favorable because of the relative accessibility of shipments from Fengtian, which, once again, played a key role in relief supplies. In 1874 the ban on exporting grain from Fengtian was lifted in order to give relief to starving people within the Great Wall in Zhili. The price of millet (*mi*) had reportedly gone up to 7,000+ cash per dou! Li Hongzhang had petitioned about the traditional and critical role of the Fengtian grain trade in the survival of Zhili residents.[178]

Officially reported grain prices did not reach the levels of these anecdotal reports of local prices, but Figures 9.3a–b leave no doubt that prices were extraordinarily high. The highest provincial average grain prices were reached in May 1878 at 3.25 taels for wheat and 3.40 taels for millet. This was about 60 percent above normal levels for wheat, and 80 percent above normal for millet, as Figures 9.4a–b show. Prefectural price data confirm that the drought was most pronounced in the southern part of the province.

Despite the hardships and tragedies of this famine period, substantial quantities of grain reached Tianjin. According to the foreign observers, when the 1877 autumn harvest failed in Shanxi and in much of Zhili, Henan, and Shaanxi, there were plentiful supplies of grain at Tianjin from "every available port." "The Bund was piled mountain high with grain, the government storehouses were full, all the boats were impressed for the conveyance of supplies toward Shanxi and the Ho-chien districts of Chihli, carts and wagons were all taken up, and the cumbersome machinery of the Chinese government was strained to the utmost to meet the enormous peril which stared it in the face." One hundred thousand refugees poured into Tientsin.[179]

Even as conditions worsened, markets usually worked, according to the foreign relief workers. "As long as there was money to buy grain, the supply was always equal to the demand, and indeed, at no time during the whole history of the famine was there a failure of supplies for those who had the means to purchase them." This is why relief was generally given in money, not grain. "When money began to fail and general starvation commenced, the Government stepped in and began to import as fast as it could, impressing into the service all the carts and animals that could be secured." The government at first did not offer enough for transport, and few came forward to transport the grain. When they raised the rates to market levels, there was a positive response although it was sometimes too late.[180]

Even in inaccessible Shanxi Province, Timothy Richard, the renowned famine relief leader, felt that cash relief was preferable to direct distribution of food. Roads were difficult to traverse, but not blocked. "Give sufficient money and time, and the merchants *all the world* will vie with each other for the market." When cartage rates were raised, everyone wanted to participate. "We never found an actual want of grain in any of the *hiens* [xians] we distributed in, though we visited *marketplaces* in them where grain could not be bought." When markets were empty it was because merchants did not want to have grain stolen in mountain villages and also because no one had any money to spend. Once villagers had cash to spend on food, the merchants responded accordingly, explained Richard.[181]

Since official sources of funds were so limited, Li Hongzhang and Zeng Guoquan, and other provincial officials, made extraordinary efforts to raise funds through irregular, but still official, means. Contribution bureaus were set up in all the southern and central provinces to raise funds for famine relief. The major sources of funds were surtaxes on *lijin* (internal customs) revenues, contributions from officials and functionaries, sale of titles, and voluntary contributions.[182] In this way, considerable funds were raised for Shanxi and Henan, in particular. Although Zhili was badly hit by the disaster, its situation was relatively favorable compared to these others, and in fact Zhili itself contributed funds for Shanxi relief.[183] Grain supplies for Shanxi were channeled through bureaus established in Zhejiang, Jiangsu, and Fengtian, under the direction of Li Hongzhang, who established at Tianjin the Chouzhenju (Bureau for Raising Famine Relief Contributions).[184]

Foreign relief workers played a significant role in famine relief during this crisis, and their firsthand observations and accounts form an important historical record. They were active not just in the distribution of relief but also in raising contributions from the foreign community and overseas. In March 1877 the Shantung Famine Relief Committee was established in Shanghai in order to solicit contributions from both Chinese and foreigners, but particularly the latter. By the end of the year the committee had collected 30,000 taels for use in famine relief. The following year, the committee reconstituted itself as the Committee of the China Famine Relief Fund in order to expand its scope of action and its fund-raising. Appeals were made to England and the United States, and contributions came from many churches. In all, the committee collected more than 125,000 taels.[185]

Foreign relief workers used effectively the power of the press to appeal for contributions from overseas. The China Famine Relief Fund was established in England and vowed to send remittances by telegraph, a new form of communication, to China on a weekly basis. The fund had published a set of twelve Chinese woodblock prints "Pictures Illustrating the Terrible Famine in Honan that Might Draw Tears From Iron." James Legge, renowned Sinologist then teaching at Oxford, translated the accompanying text.

The pictures and accompanying explanations which are given in the following pages, are of purely native origin. The little Chinese book from which they were taken, was composed solely for the purpose of appealing to the compassion of benevolent persons amongst the Chinese for help. It has been thought, however, that the re-publication of the book in England . . . might help carry home to English hearts a sense of the dire distress from which these unhappy people are now suffering.[186]

The distribution of these foreign relief funds was assigned to thirty or more people, following the leadership of Timothy Richard, who later played an important role in encouraging reformers in China through the translation and publication of important English-language works. In Shanxi in 1878, Timothy Richard and his colleagues organized the distribution of cash to needy famine victims. At first they gave cash on a house-to-house basis, which they called the "retail" method, but later, to save time, they issued the cash "wholesale," that is, to a representative of each family who would come to a central distribution point. The amount of relief was usually 500 cash, sometimes as much as 800 cash, per person. Zeng Guoquan had given them permission to distribute funds in the company of government functionaries. Of the 200,000 taels raised through Shanghai, 120,000 taels were used in Shanxi, and the other 80,000 were used in Shandong and Zhili.[187]

Although the foreign relief workers were sometimes contemptuous of the Chinese relief work and of the inability of the Chinese authorities to cope with the famine, Richard himself realized that "great as the efforts of foreigners were, they were a mere drop in the bucket compared with what the Chinese Government itself did."[188] However, the focused and well-publicized foreign philanthropic effort of this crisis led the way to still greater foreign involvement in famine relief that continued until the 1930s. For the Chinese victims and government, this represented some direct and immediate benefit, although later there would be serious debates in the Western community about the long-term consequences of famine relief. For the Western missionaries, famine relief presented them with "unprecedented opportunities for the reaching of the Gospel," in the words of Timothy Richard.[189]

The 1890–1895 Floods

During the period from 1890–95, there was excessive rain in almost every year. According to meteorological records, in 1890, 1,043 mm of rain fell in the Beijing area, and in 1891, 1,401 mm—exceeding even the record of 1801, when 1,112 mm of rain fell. Following an average rainfall in 1892, the next two years, 1893 and 1894, also saw rain in excess of 1,000 mm in each year. (Figure 1.1 reminds us that this was an unusually wet decade.) The sense of perpetual crisis was unavoidable. Missionaries provided vivid descriptions of the flooded terrain in central Zhili and around Tianjin. Although this was a period of considerable unrest in North China, and state resources were even more limited than before, the rituals of investigation (however nominal), reporting, and appeals for relief funds continued even amidst the dynasty's last throes. Each year, Li Hongzhang, still governor-general, was relentless in describing the desperate circumstances within Zhili Province, and he pleaded for some dispensation.

In 1890, all the rivers were overflowing their banks. Li Hongzhang, described an area of several hundred li as a lake, about 2 zhang deep. Many people and animals drowned.[190] People were fleeing to Tianjin by the tens of thousands. Low-lying areas were all affected, and there was little hope for a fall harvest. He predicted that prices would soar.[191] In the summer he reported that 60,000 taels had been disbursed from the Board of Revenue, and that some tribute grain and some millet from Fengtian were coming in. But all the rivers were rising, and the situation was serious. He estimated that the cost of construction and relief the following spring would be 2 million jin [?]. He memorialized:

> Zhili is a deficient area. All the treasuries are very empty. Also this place, unlike the southeast, has few rich people from whom to solicit donations. In recent years people have been asked to give again and again, and their resources are exhausted. Even if they contribute the amount will be limited. We don't dare to go to the Board of Revenue again, but ask Imperial favor to give out more awards to those who contributed more than 1,000 pieces of cotton clothing.[192]

At end of year, Li Hongzhang reported that since the amounts collected so far were insufficient, and there was only 100,000 (taels[?]) left to repair the Yongding River, he had telegraphed all the governors to tell them about the situation; they responded by donating a total of 592,480 taels.[193] During a two-year period a total of only 289,000+ taels, modest amounts of grain, and some clothing had been contributed privately.[194] The following spring Li reported that some areas had dried out, but low areas were still waterlogged, and he requested more assistance from grain tribute, citing precedents of GX 10, 13, and 14, when, because of flood, 100,000 shi from Jiang-Zhe spring grain tribute were diverted for relief.[195]

In 1892, he memorialized that the situation was very similar to that of 1890 and requested the same measures, including contributions from southern provinces.[196] He noted that since the Qianlong period, the rivers had become more silted. Also, the population had increased. People and water were competing for land, and the situation was getting desperate. He again asked 100,000 shi from Jiangsu and Jiangbei. Li's credibility was called into question, and in response, he provided a detailed report of famine ratings in each village and of the numbers needing relief.[197] The terms *dazhen, jizhen,* or *puzhen* were not used in this period, and new terms *zhenfu* (relief and comfort) or *chunfu* (spring comfort) were employed, perhaps tacitly acknowledging the fundamental inability of the government to provide genuine relief on a household basis.

In 1893, the situation was probably worse. "Since spring there has been continuous rain and the rivers are all overflowing," memorialized the governor-general in the sixth month. "It is like a vast lake for several hundreds of li, and the force of the water is so powerful, something not seen for over ten years."[198] He described, "This is the worst situation in recent years." Several millions need relief. Officials have been delegated to every xian to verify the numbers of people and households (*hukou*) in preparation for the winter relief. Again, citing precedents, he asked for more relief.[199] It is unlikely that the famine investigation ever took place. In 1894, the situation was described as similar to that of the previous two years. Water was several feet to one zhang deep. Houses and fields were submerged.[200] At least 1 million people need to be relieved, he estimated, again ordering an investigation of households, and he requested that 120,000 shi be diverted from Jiangsu sea grain tribute. But this time, he recommended that the allocation be converted to 60 percent cash and 30–40 percent grain. Because northerners preferred *zaliang,* cash would be convenient. Forty percent should be allocated to Shuntian Prefecture, and 60 percent to Zhili.[201]

In 1895, the new acting governor-general, Wang Wenshao, reported that Zhili had not yet recovered from the big crisis of 1890, nor the additional crises of 1892 and 1893 that were even wider in scope. More than sixty districts required relief. He commented on a new element in famine relief: the participation of voluntary agencies from the south, including some foreign relief workers. According to Wang, the southern relief societies started to work in Zhili in 1892. Officials and gentry went there to manage *yizhen* (charitable relief). Eating relief food had become habitual. These officials were vigilant about possible fraud. Tens of thousands of people were helped. The victims all survived, countless of them. Zhili received this relief more than twenty times.[202]

As Zhili became more regularly dependent on outside relief agencies, it had also set up a provincial contribution bureau, Chouzhenju. The totals received for GX 18/6–19/5 (1892–93) were 2,514,816 taels, 619,043 strings Tianjin cash, plus some grain and cotton clothing. These had aided several millions of famine victims in 1892.[203] However, as in 1876–79, these "contributions" were really exactions from irregular, but still official, sources—for example, from the provincial treasury, from various bureaus, or from salt merchants. From 1892 until the end of the dynasty, "contributions" thus became incorporated into the official structure of famine relief and were included in the governor-general's reports. They took the form of cash, grain, or cotton clothing. In 1897, for example, the report of contributions from GX 20/6 (1894) to GX 21/#5 (1895) showed a net total of 2,557,877 taels as well as 473,885 Tianjin cash (juan) for relief and river repairs. Of these totals raised from various sources, the largest share—1,872,311 taels—was from the general category of "officials, gentry, merchants, and wealthy people" from Zhili and other provinces. The report listed how many households were relieved in each county and what repairs were supposedly made on river works.[204]

In the post-1900 period, contributions from the southern and central provinces, as well as from overseas Chinese sources, were used in the reconstruction effort.[205] Such "irregular" contributions from the central and southern provinces continued the historic practice of transferring resources from the south to assist the north. While the formal extractive powers of the central government, in the form of the grain tribute, had waned, the informal forces of empire still compelled a significant transfer of resources from south to north.

The raising of relief funds in the south was undertaken by gentry leaders and formed an important focus in the late 1870s and 1880s of what Mary Rankin has termed "elite activism." The Shanghai newspaper *Shenbao* provided an important medium for raising public consciousness about the famine and regularly published accounts of the famine, accompanied by editorials, as well as lists of donors. As such, the famine in the north was seen not as a regional problem, but as a national one. "A sociomoral commitment to philanthropy led to the idea of people from all regions working together to preserve the social stability of the country."[206] Some southerners traveled to the north to participate directly in dispensing famine relief. In 1877 and 1878 several groups went to Henan to give out relief; they became "professionalized" in their techniques and wrote about their experiences.[207]

The charitable institution of the Guangrentang (Hall for Spreading Benevolence) was revived at Tianjin by Li Hongzhang in 1878 to shelter women and orphans rendered homeless by the crisis. Originating probably in the mid-Qing period, the Guangrentang had been a shelter for orphaned and homeless children, but it had been allowed to lapse.[208] Although official sources credit Li Hongzhang with the Guangrentang's revival, this was just another of several ways in which the energies of southerners were channeled into benevolent work in the north. In fact the Guangrentang was modeled on the benevolent societies (*shantang*) of the Lower Yangzi region.[209] Motivated in part by a charitable spirit toward famine refugees, the southern merchant and gentry leaders in Tianjin also advocated social reform and education. With a strong sense of regional pride, they had "both pity and contempt for what they saw as the crude, impoverished North and the chaotic city of Tianjin."[210]

In Beijing, there was a similar burst of private charitable initiatives, supported in part by local officials. Funds donated to officials were turned over to the new gentry-led institutions to administer. In 1880 a Guangrentang was established in Beijing under such circumstances. Four Jiangsu sojourners constructed a hall similar to Tianjin's and then sought and received operating funds

PHOTOGRAPH 9.1.   Flood refugees in Beijing, 1890. Courtesy of Forbidden City Press, Palace Museum, Beijing.

from the local authorities.[211] Other civic activities abounded. During the 1890 flood, which affected the immediate suburbs to the southwest of the walled city, a coordinated public and private effort was made to deal with the many famine refugees that sought refuge inside the gates. A new relief bureau (Zhenfuju) was established to give out soup relief. Six gentry-led benevolence halls were created to transport grain outside of the city and to bring relief to victims. Sometimes the local leaders performed useful services in the outlying flood zones. This type of activity stands in contrast to the traditional model in which refugees came toward Beijing to seek relief; here relief was taken from Beijing to neighboring flood regions.

Such efforts were considered meritorious; in 1892, the *Jifu zhenni quan tu* (Fully illustrated account of the flood relief in the capital region), with a set of woodblock prints, was issued to commemorate the relief effort. The publication was sponsored by sojourners from the south.[212] Photographs also recorded the famine relief and shelter given to refugees from the countryside. Photograph 9.1 shows a group of mostly women and children waiting outside a clinic set up at a temple.

In other localities in Zhili, various shelters, such as *liuyangju*, seemed to have been reactivated or rebuilt in the late nineteenth century. In 1872, the local magistrate of Yongnian County had the local *yangjiyuan* repaired and the local *liuyangju* revived.[213] In Yongqing County the local magistrate "persuaded" the local gentry and rich to contribute funds for a *yangjiyuan* to shelter the widowed, orphaned, and so on. It was to be managed by gentry-managers chosen from among the upright local citizens.[214] At Luanzhou, it had been the custom to use interest from a fund to shelter the needy, but only in 1879, through the initiative of a former magistrate named Guo Ren was a new shelter, or *liuyangju*, built. It contained ten rooms and was to house the needy from the eleventh through the first lunar month each year. Funds were contributed by the shop owners and merchants of the city, and the disbursal of funds was to be controlled by the gentry-managers of the local academy.[215] In Tianjin in 1880, a Relief Preparation Society (Beijishe) was set up, with income from contributions from the rich. In addition, a certain tax was charged onto boats arriving at Tianjin.[216]

Although these charitable institutions were privately funded, they were mostly initiated and sponsored by local magistrates. Strictly speaking, it would be incorrect to call them private charities. However, there were some exceptions. An example of an entirely private initiative was the building of an infirmary (*yangbingtang*) in Dong'guang County on the initiative of one individual, Ma Dezan, who, in turn, got people in nearby villages to contribute.[217] For Wen'an County, which was particularly troubled by waterlogging, there were some interesting cases of aid being brought by individuals from Tianjin or other provinces for local relief, but in the Republican period, this custom would become more pronounced.[218]

Conclusion

Such famine relief activities in North China and elsewhere seem to be signs of the new elite activism, or perhaps even the emergence of a type of civil society. Yet since almost all the voluntary activities that originated in the north were sponsored by officials, or coordinated with officials, very much like the well-known "government-sponsored, merchant-managed" (*guandu shangban*) business enterprises of the earlier decades, they could be regarded as "government-sponsored, gentry-managed" civic activities. They appear to be part of a "Guangxu Restoration," similar to the "Tongzhi Restoration" that is an accepted historical era. Starting at the end of the Tongzhi period, the leadership of Li Hongzhang at Tianjin reinvigorated the traditional imperial and bureaucratic forms of famine relief, including the revival of charitable granaries. The warm response of the merchants and gentry in the region, as well as those from the south, was a sign of a heightened national awareness of the seriousness of the crises and the government's declining capabilities.

Whether funded officially or privately, famine relief at the end of the nineteenth century was, even at best, merely *relief*, that is, the provision of food or money, and sometimes shelter and clothing, to the needy. No longer was the intention so grand as the restoration of agricultural production, or the "once-and-for-all" reconstruction of the river systems. No longer was Beijing the stable and secure center of the region's grain supply system; the food security of the capital itself, always the highest priority, was threatened in every major natural and political crisis since 1813 although only in the 1850s and 1860s was there a fundamental food crisis. The somewhat surprising survival of Qing famine administrative procedures, as well the new signs of nongovernmental initiatives and social conscience, complicate the conventional understanding of an unremitting political decline at the end of the dynasty. The historical periodization of the nineteenth century, as emphasized initially, was not straightforward. Yet amidst these twists and turns, the decay of the natural environment and the mounting social disorder were quite inexorable.

Environmental degradation and social turmoil went far beyond the traditional signs of dynastic decline and would require more than a restoration or even new dynasty to overcome them. Near Tianjin in 1890 foreign missionaries observed the seemingly perpetual state of flood and famine. The destitute relied on stalks, roots, and grass. "The examination of these villages revealed a condition of poverty that beggars description. I know of no standard by which to compare it that would be intelligible to foreigners. The food we found them eating consisted mainly of the poorest quality of the lowest grade of large millet, ground up 'husk and all,' with which was mixed such weed and reed seed as can be gathered from the marshes or scraped together in any other way."[219] Three years later, another missionary described the countryside south of Tianjin with villages surrounded by water as far as the eye could see.

> Fortunately, relief has been extensively given from native sources, and actual starvation to the point of dying for want of food, has no doubt been largely prevented. Native benevolent societies, partly official and partly private, have distributed money and food. The government has done the same on a considerable scale, besides distributing some supplies of warm, substantial clothing, and the immense sum of 200,000 dollars is reported to have been sent north by an official in the south to be used in giving aid.[220]

Although famine occurred in other parts of China, the north was by far the most affected, and Zhili Province experienced China's highest rate of natural disasters in the nineteenth century.[221] Famine not only led to destruction of agricultural production and productivity by also to enormous social and psychological disruption. Chi Zihua has argued persuasively that famines helped to spread superstition, rumor, and overwhelming sense of insecurity and indebtedness.[222] Repeated harvest failures and crises led to just the kind of social unrest, even chaos, that the Chinese rulers feared the most. The Boxer Uprising of 1899–1900 had multiple causes, but drought was one important factor that foreign observers cited. "The Boxer movement might never have amounted to much, except for the long continued drouth [sic], extending over the whole of North China. This left farmers and others with little to occupy their time. And this drouth, which was recognized as an unmitigated evil, was easily laid to the charge of the foreigners and their employees, the native Christians."[223] Paul Cohen describes the phenomenon of "hunger anxiety" that made people more willing to risk their lives and "more susceptible to religious constructions of reality." Zhili was ripe for antiforeign activity because of the large presence of foreign missionaries and other foreigners and because of its economic distress. In fact, Boxer activity converged on what he calls the Tianjin–Beijing–Baoding triangle, which was the main flood region.[224] The drought of 1900 was similar to that of 1876. The writer-missionary Arthur Smith observed, "The drought was great and practically universal. For the first time since the great famine in 1878 no winter wheat to speak of had been planted in any part of northern China. . . . The ground was baked so hard that no crops could be put in, and at such times the idle and restless population are ready for any mischief."[225]

The links connecting hunger, social disorder, and political dissent were by no means simple or direct. The Boxers and other rural poor were not consciously invoking food entitlement as a source of their grievance; these were not food riots by any means. Nor were the Boxers demanding the fall of the dynasty; indeed, in the end, the court supported them. It is often said that hunger more often causes political apathy rather than political action, or that "hungry men don't rebel," yet by the turn of the century, a traditional and familiar cause of dynastic decline—repeated natural and subsistence crises—had become intertwined with a new kind of political unrest in the form of antiforeignism and nationalism.

CHAPTER TEN

The "Land of Famine,"

1900–1949

FOR NORTH CHINA, particularly Beijing and Zhili, the Boxer Uprising of 1900, followed by the Allied occupation of the capital in 1901, and the flight of the court to Xian for two years, were cataclysmic. For the empire as a whole, these events signified a fundamental shift into political crisis and final dynastic decline.[1] The revolution of 1911 toppled the Qing dynasty and with it the entire imperial system of government that had prevailed for two millennia. Destroying the old system was, however, easier than establishing a new one. The new Republican government faltered in the face of weak leadership, contending military factions, and pervasive threat of further foreign domination of the government and the economy. Although the Nationalist Party, the Guomindang under Chiang Kai-shek, brought a superficial end to the warlord struggles and established a new capital at Nanjing in 1928, its control over the nation was challenged and ultimately destroyed, not only by the surviving warlords but more seriously by Japanese military and economic penetration and, at the same time, by Communist insurgency. After eight years of war with Japan, from 1937–45, and four more years of civil war with the Communists, the Nationalists retreated to the island of Taiwan in 1949.

This half century was also marked by a succession of natural and man-made disasters resulting in famines. (See Table 10.1.) So frequent and geographically extensive were these crises that the view that China was the "Land of Famine," a term coined by Western relief workers, was shared by Chinese people as well.[2] Throughout the 1910s, 1920s, 1930s, and 1940s, every region of China experienced large-scale "famines"—crises of subsistence and security caused by both natural and political factors. In 1915 flooding in the Pearl River Basin in South China, submerged more than 10 million mu of fields, creating 6.5 million flood victims. In 1920 the great North China drought severely affected the entire north, causing high mortality. From 1928–30 an even more severe drought affected the northwest as well as the north, causing enormous suffering. In 1931, the great Yangzi River flood included the Huai River Basin as well and affected eight provinces of central and eastern China. The Yellow River, known as "China's Sorrow," flooded in 1925, 1933, and again in 1935, but the greatest damage was done in 1938 when the Nationalist forces bombed the dikes at Huayuankou in order to block the advance of the Japanese army. The resulting shift of the riverbed of the Yellow River from north back to south caused great human dislocation and suffer-

TABLE 10.1

Major Disasters and Famines: China and Zhili-Hebei, 1850–1950

(Zhili-Hebei in bold)

Year	Location	Type	Provinces	Disaster Victims	Mortality (est.)
1855	Yellow River	Flood, shift course	1	7 million[a]	—
1876–79	**North China**	**Drought**	**5**	**—**	**9–13 million[b]**
1912	**Hai River Basin**	**Flood**	**1**	**1.4 million**	n.e.
1915	Pearl River (Guangdong)	Flood	1–2	6 million	60,000
1917	**Hai River Basin**	**Flood**	**1**	**5.6–5.8 million**	n.e.
1920	**North China**	**Drought**	**5**	**30.3 million**	500,000
1924	**Hai River Basin**	**Flood**	**1**	**1.5 million**	n.e.
1928–30	**North and Northwest**	**Drought**	**8–9 (299 counties)**	**57.3 million[c]**	10 million
1931	Yangzi River, and others	Flood	8–15	61 million[d]	422,499
1933	Yellow River	Flood	6+	8.2 million	18,293
1935	Yangzi (mid)	Flood	2	12.7 million	142,000
1938–47	Yellow River	Flood, shift course	3	6.2 million	893,303
1939	**Hai River Basin, etc.**	**Flood**	**4**	**4.5 million**	**13,320**
1942–43	Henan	Drought, war	1	11–16 million	2–3 million[e]

SOURCE: With the exceptions noted below, these figures are found in Xia Mingfang, *Minguo shiqi ziran zaihai*, append. tabs. II, III.1, and III.2, 384–403.

[a] The Yellow River began to suffer breaks in its dikes starting in 1851 and changed its course in 1855 from south of the Shandong peninsula to the north. Shandong was principally affected, but parts of Henan and Anhui were also affected. This estimate of flood victims was made in *Zhongguo jindai shi da zaihuang*, 43–44, based on the Shandong governor's report of disaster damage in Shandong villages. A total of 7,161 villages were rated as having damage of 6–10 degrees (to being the worst). Assuming that each village had two hundred households of five persons each, the authors calculate that seven million people were direct victims of the flood.

[b] This is the range of estimates by Western relief organizations for 299 counties. See *Zhongguo jindai shi da zaihuang*, 98. See also Chapter 9 of this book.

[c] This was the estimate of the China International Famine Relief Commission. See text of this chapter.

[d] This figure includes victims of all disasters in China in 1931, most of which were directly or indirectly related to the Yangzi flood. Xia Mingfang, *Minguo shiqi ziran zaihai*, 389.

[e] *Zhongguo jindai shi da zaihuang*, 272–78. White and Jacoby, 166–78. The total population of Henan was 30 million; 11–16 million were destitute.

ing, as well as loss of farmland and crops. This was the ultimate example of the combining of human calamity and natural disaster, or in the Chinese phrase, *tianzai renhuo.*[3] In 1942–43 an extensive drought famine in central China was made more horrible by the conditions of warfare. In their classic of wartime reporting, *Thunder Out of China,* Theodore White and Annalee Jacoby described graphically how millions starved in Henan Province in 1943 while tons of grain in neighboring provinces were blocked by opposing military factions, and meanwhile the Guomindang ignored the tragedy.

Although all regions were affected by such disasters, it was North China that was the most constantly affected.[4] In the Hai River Basin, the flood of 1912 was particularly threatening to Tianjin itself, while the great flood of 1917 affected 105 counties and attracted much attention. Shortly after this, all of North China, including Zhili, experienced a drought in 1920–21 of the same proportions and intensity as the 1876–79 drought. In 1924, another large flood struck the same area, affecting at least sixty counties and leaving more than 1 million people destitute.[5] Following this, the 1928–30 drought, often referred to as the Northwest Drought, affected the southern portion of Zhili very harshly. In 1939 another great flood affected 116 counties in the Hai River Basin, and wreaked havoc in Tianjin.

Although the central government had few means to combat these disasters, there still was organized response—in varying degrees—to these human tragedies. After 1900, both the foreign involvement and the Chinese voluntary efforts expanded while the formal government role decreased even more. The foreign role was legitimized in the China International Famine Relief Commission (CIFRC), which played an increasingly larger role in the 1920s. During the 1927–37 decade, however, the Nanjing government began to curtail the relative independence of the CIFRC and insisted on asserting greater Chinese authority.

These organized responses, however, could neither cure nor mask the fundamental deterioration in the order of "Heaven, Earth, and Man." Viewed from a traditional Chinese perspective, the continuation of natural and human disasters could be seen as a sign of the failure of a new dynasty to secure the Mandate of Heaven. Yet viewed from the present, one can see with greater clarity that these events of the first half of the twentieth century—or indeed the entire century from 1850–1950—were not merely part of a dynastic transition, but rather that they were evidence of a fundamental historical shift—the outlines of which were just being recognized. The scale and frequency of famines were greater, but more importantly, their political significance had been magnified through the lens of the newly emergent Chinese nationalism. "Natural" crises were increasingly seen as having direct political causes, as well as revealing deeper economic and social origins.

1917 and Later Floods

The 1917 floods were regarded as the worst in at least thirty years, and the devastation in and around Tianjin was particularly serious. Rains in July caused the Yongding River to silt up heavily, which in turn caused the Hai River to shoal up so that the water barely flowed. Finally the dikes of the Yongding River broke and the surrounding countryside was submerged. In August a second set of downpours resulted in the flooding of southern rivers, including the breaching of the Nan Yunhe, which resulted in the flooding of the plain to the south and west of Tianjin.[6] By September, the city of Tianjin itself was flooded, with seven inches of water along the west bank of the Hai River. Later the water rose to as much as 1.8 meters in some sections.[7] Panic set in. "Junks of quite big size are now sailing on the main roads in the Japanese Settlement," reported the

Peking Daily News.[8] "The country between the Grand Canal and Paotingfu [Baoding fu] is virtu-ally a lake," reported the *North China Daily News*.[9] For a while it was thought that the flooding was caused by breaks in the Yellow River dikes at Kaifeng, and there was a widespread fear that the Yellow River might be shifting its course northward and threaten the city of Tianjin itself.[10]

At its maximum extent, the flood affected 105 counties, including at least 40 that were severely affected. As many as 5.8 million people were estimated to be destitute, with 46 million mu (12,000 sq. miles) of crops damaged. Torrential rain destroyed numerous houses, and thousands of refugees crowded into Tianjin. The city itself was estimated to have 400,000 people in need of as-sistance.[11] In late October, the American Red Cross reported that there were 55,000 homeless in the city, and 1 million altogether in the region.[12] During the winter the homeless in Tianjin reached 100,000.[13] An estimated 40–50,000 were unemployed.[14] The Peking-Hankow railway suf-fered washouts in 600 places on the northern half of the line. Because of the vast plain between the railway and Tianjin, water remained on the ground, flowing very slowly if at all, and as the cold weather set in, whole villages including their houses were frozen under a sheet of ice. As the spring thaw approached, areas once again were soaked, and more houses collapsed.[15]

Flooding was not simply the result of excess rainfall, but rather the vulnerability of the rivers to overflows because of the narrowing of the channels and the accumulation of silt. An earlier flood, in 1912, was at the time considered the most serious in many years, flooding the regions to the west and north of Tianjin. In late August, with 24 counties or districts reporting, 300,000 peo-ple were estimated to have suffered the destruction of their crops.[16] The recorded annual precipi-tation at Tianjin was 796 mm. But in 1917, the total rainfall was only 415 mm, far less than in 1912, and below the average annual rainfall of 499 mm for the period 1894–1922.[17] The rainfall at Bei-jing was also less than in other historic floods. In 1801, the estimated precipitation was 1,112 mm, but in 1912 only 732 mm fell, and in 1917, 782 mm. (See Figure 1.1 in Chapter 1.) Of 140 counties in the 1917 flood region, 41 were rated as heavily damaged, 63 as lightly damaged, 23 had no dam-age, and 11 did not report. In 1801 10 million people were in need of relief; in 1917, 5.8 million.[18] In the 1939 flood, considered the worst in a hundred years, only 681 mm was recorded at Beijing, but nearby areas recorded 1,137 mm.[19]

LEADERSHIP AND ORGANIZATION

To an unprecedented degree, the leadership of famine relief in 1917 was shared and its funding eclectic. In 1917, there was no emperor or traditional bureaucracy and even fewer official sources of funds than before. The natural crisis coincided with a turbulent series of political events at Bei-jing. The warlord government was challenged by an attempt at monarchical restoration. The war-lords Feng Yuxiang and Duan Qirui thwarted the attempt, but other warlords forced their resig-nation. Coup followed coup. By October 1918, the new administration of President Xu Shichang had replaced all the earlier contenders.[20] Under these circumstances it was no wonder that the at-tention of the Beijing government was not fully focused on flood relief. Its choice of Xiong Xiling in late September 1917 to be director-general of flood relief and river conservancy was nevertheless wise; despite his checkered political career and his brief and unhappy tenure as premier in 1913–14, he was admirably suited for this new role in philanthropy and social work.[21]

By the time of Xiong's appointment, the devastation from the flood was already acute. The Ministry of Finance had already appropriated 300,000 yuan (Chinese dollars), but the govern-ment could provide no more. Xiong's main responsibility was to raise funds and to coordinate the work of existing private charitable groups. His directorate was also to supervise the flood conservancy and reconstruction. It had offices both at Beijing and Tianjin, but only a small staff. Instead he would rely on Chinese officials and gentry as well as foreign officials to advise him on policy, and on foreign and Chinese engineers to advise him on technical matters.[22] Xiong also had the responsibility for collecting information on local conditions.[23] At the conclusion of the campaign, in a manner reminiscent of the imperial compilations of the past, he ordered the publication of the record of reconstruction, *Jingji shuizai shanhou jishi*.

There was an explosion of activity that could be seen as an example of "civil society." Several associations of regional leaders assumed the responsibilities for providing relief. The main coordinating group was the Shuntian-Zhili Relief Bureau (Shun Zhi zhuzhen ju). At Tianjin there was the Tianjin Shuntian-Zhili Charitable Relief Society (Tianjin Shun Zhi yizhen hui).[24] The former had already raised 1.2 million yuan by October and was active in the distribution of food, working closely with the Tianjin group.[25] Other Chinese groups included the Chinese Red Cross Society, the Shanghai Chinese Red Cross Society, Chinese Life-saving Society, and Tientsin (Tianjin) Army Medical School.[26] The Tianjin Chamber of Commerce played a large role in famine relief, particularly in organizing the purchases of grain from other provinces.[27]

The Metropolitan Union Flood Relief Committee coordinated the relief work of the many Sino-foreign charitable organizations that were already active. Xiong chaired the committee, while Roger S. Greene, resident director of the Rockefeller Foundation in China, and Liu Jo-sen, former governor-general of Zhili, were vice chairmen.[28] Various Chinese and foreign civic leaders served on the council.[29] The American Red Cross Relief Committee was probably the most active on the foreign side and helped to coordinate other local groups.[30] The North China Christian Flood Relief Committee was the umbrella group coordinating the work of various Christian agencies. Among them, the Tientsin Christian Union Flood Relief Committee set up a refugee camp in Tianjin, while other groups worked in Wen'an.[31]

Money, not grain, was the single most critical need in the relief effort. In October it was estimated that 5 million yuan would be needed for relief, but only 2 million was available.[32] In addition to the 1.2 million raised by the Chinese organizations, and the 300,000 from the Ministry of Finance, the American Red Cross donated 50,000 U.S. dollars, with a promise of a total of 200,000.[33] Ambassador Reinsch failed to secure further U.S. assistance because of the war in Europe.[34] Appeals to provincial governments also failed. It was clear that the relief effort would depend principally on private Chinese funds.[35] Chambers of commerce in all provinces, banks, overseas Chinese associations, Shanghai industrial leaders, and Japanese groups responded to fundraising appeals.[36]

FAMINE RELIEF

The famine relief campaign employed some traditional methods as well as new approaches. The sale of grain at below-market prices and the operation of soup kitchens were familiar methods, while new methods emphasized the economic rehabilitation of families and communities. Compared with the Qing bureaucracy at its height, however, the 1917 authorities had neither the direct command of the grain market nor the control over local officials needed to enforce effectively the new relief measures.

In the fall the major effort was the purchase and shipment of grain from Fengtian and Jilin, where, as in the past, there were ample grain supplies. Now they were shipped by rail, with half the transport costs subsidized by the Ministry of Transportation.[37] Initially the directorate put down 440,000 yuan for the purchase of grain from Fengtian and Jilin in Manchuria for *pingtiao*, and that sum was supplemented by 40,481 yuan from the Ministry of Finance. A report dated about January 16, 1918, shows that a total of 209,925 shi of grain (121,766 of red sorghum and 88,159 shi of corn) had been sold through the *pingtiao* method at seventy-two places, yielding total income of 588,892 yuan.[38] Regulations stated that only two types of grain—sorghum and corn—were to be distributed.[39] Red sorghum, usually for making *gaoliang* liquor, was used, but it was less nutritious than white sorghum. Previously sorghum for Tianjin came from Shandong or south Zhili, but in the 1920s Manchuria became a more important source.[40] On June 26, 1919, in its final report, the directorate stated that a total of 858,635 yuan had been spent on grain purchases, plus transportation costs of 41,645 yuan, for 84,236 shi of grain.[41] In addition, Tianjin grain merchants had arranged for the purchases of 804,000 yuan worth of grain from Anhui, and 250,000 shi of grain from Jilin. In 1917 alone, Tianjin grain merchants were responsible for purchasing from other provinces a total of 1.7 million yuan worth of food products, mostly grain.[42]

The cost of grain was supposed to be passed on to the county governments, each of which was to assess its need and depute officials to Tianjin or Baoding, where the government had collected most of the grain. While each county was to determine the fair selling price according to its local conditions, the price was not to be set so low as to discourage merchants. Rich households should be persuaded to sell their grain at the same price.[43]

In addition to *pingtiao*, about 600 soup kitchens in 56 or more counties were set up at a total cost of 189,902 yuan.[44] Direct charity also included the distribution of clothing and fuel and the establishment of shelters.[45] The remission of taxes in 1917 to 110 counties, covering a total of 25,482,265 mu, was another measure that the authorities could easily extend, although it could not bring direct relief.[46]

During the winter and spring, the directorate's focus shifted to the distribution of cash relief rather than grain. Through various other agencies, the directorate provided a total of 1,160,000 yuan for winter relief, while the Tianjin and Beijing branches of the Shuntian-Zhili Relief Bureau raised 370,023 yuan, for a total of 1,660,000 yuan.[47] The bureau administered the distribution of relief by dividing the flood area into fourteen relief districts and rating each village according to the seriousness of its devastation. In principle, all households were also rated as in desperate need, or simply in need; the former would get 2 yuan per adult and 1 yuan per child, while the latter would get 1 yuan per adult and .5 yuan per child.[48] This winter relief program, however, encountered many problems. The Zhili Relief Bureau apparently misrated many villages, permitting relief to be given to those who did not need it and denying relief to others desperately in need.[49] As a result, the directorate raised 140,100 yuan more to be given to 4th and 5th degree villages, which were in fact as much in need as those of the 6th and 7th degree. The responsibility for administering the spring relief was transferred to the second organization, the Tianjin Shuntian-Zhili Charitable Relief Society, which raised about 200,000 yuan to supplement the 500,000 raised by the directorate.[50]

The records of the spring relief distribution show how difficult it was to avoid malfeasance and corruption. Relief workers were cautioned against taking the word of local leaders regarding local conditions without conducting a separate investigation. The county magistrate was supposed to supervise the distribution of relief funds in conjunction with local organizations and leaders. It was forbidden to let village authorities make these decisions unilaterally.[51] The rules for *pingtiao* also stipulated that grain should be sold directly to individual households, and not wholesale to village elders to resell.[52] Yet at the same time local magistrates were not to be entirely trusted either; the authorities knew of their corruptibility, noting that not all magistrates regarded the welfare of the people as their first priority.[53]

Despite the use of grain and cash distributions, there was the conviction that direct charity had limited usefulness, and that efforts should be directed toward increasing the purchasing power of the flood victims. Magistrates were urged to set up loan societies both in the county capitals and the countryside. They were to solicit funds from banks as well as local leaders and merchants in order to extend low-interest loans to help flood victims get back on their feet.[54] At the end there were 309 such societies that had aided 44,000 flood victims with total capital of 316,213 yuan.[55] Magistrates were also to set up charitable pawnshops. They were to raise the capital from local public and private sources in order to buy land from the flood victims, although it does not appear that this institution was widespread.[56] If local funds were insufficient, the authorities could apply to the directorate for funds. On 12/14 the directorate issued a notice to all counties to follow the example of Baodi, where, after several meetings had failed to raise any funds, the magistrate set an example by donating 1,000 yuan, after which others followed with 20,000 yuan in contributions.[57]

Work relief was seen as a way of providing income for the destitute and getting cheap labor for the flood reconstruction. It appears that several counties, such as Baodi, Ba, and Xianghe, were designated as work relief sites. The regulations prescribed the method for conducting investigations of flood victims and issuing coupons to the able-bodied that would enable them to find work; women, the elderly, and the disabled were to receive other types of relief. It is not clear how well these plans were carried out, or how extensively work relief was tried elsewhere. Cases of abuse of laborers by county officials were reported.[58]

The most imaginative relief measures were directed toward reviving the cotton-weaving industry since the flood districts included the cotton-weaving centers of Raoyang, Gaoyang, Xian, and Suning. The directorate estimated that there were 100,000 idle looms in the region that could support 800,000 people, assuming eight to a household.[59] The directorate proposed the guarantee of loans to cotton merchants to revive the market, the distribution of cotton yarn to cotton-weaving counties, and the signing of contracts with Mitsui Trading Company for the guaranteed purchase of cotton yarn for distribution to weaving households. The chamber of commerce was exhorted to persuade the cloth merchants to buy as much cloth from the weavers as they normally would; the merchants would be advanced loans on easy terms.[60] The emphasis on economic recovery of household industry forms a striking contrast to the Qing emphasis on restoring agricultural production and reflects the commercialization of some local economies in this region.

CHINESE AND FOREIGN ACTIVISM IN THE RURAL AREAS

In 1917, private initiatives flourished, and numerous Chinese as well as foreign groups, even individuals, raised money and rushed to the Zhili region to dispense relief. Many were based in Shanghai, including the Shanghai branch of the Shuntian-Zhili Flood Charitable Relief Society, the Shanghai Red Cross, and the Shanghai Guangrentang (Hall for Spreading Benevolence). Others originated in Hong Kong and Japan.[61] Social activists from the Shanghai area played a particularly large role, as they had in the 1876–79 North China drought.

Tang Zongyu and Tang Zongguo, two brothers from Wuxi, raised funds and distributed relief in Zhili, inspired by the example of their late father, Tang Tongqing, a Zen Buddhist believer, who had traveled to several provinces in his lifetime to dispense famine relief and had written some rules for famine relief. The sons also lived frugally and practiced charity. In Zhili they were drawn to the four of the most severely distressed counties: Baodi, Ba, Wen'an, and Gu'an. Since a Shanghai silk merchant had already contributed a considerable sum to Baodi, the Tang brothers decided to concentrate on Ba and Wen'an counties; they heard that many at Ba County had died. They gave out both money and garments, but soon they discovered that the destitute actually preferred grain. Ultimately they were able to purchase 9,000 shi of grain and also to distribute 29,400 yuan. Their account reveals the eclectic nature of the relief effort and the apparently easy networking among different charitable organizations and agencies. The Tang brothers were in direct communication with the Shuntian-Zhili Relief Bureau and the Beijing-Zhili-Fengtian Charitable Society, but knowing that the relief effort's success would depend on private initiatives, they raised money among those whom they personally knew and also cooperated with Buddhist and Christian organizations, as well as the Guangrentang.[62]

The impact of these various initiatives is difficult to measure. Wen'an was one of the worst regions. The entire county lay in a geographical depression, or *wa*. After the 1912 flood, it took three years for the water to drain off. In the 1917 flood, many families had fled, and homes and crops were destroyed. Christian missionaries estimated that in the summer of 1918 about 30 percent of the population had fled, and about 100,000 of the remaining population, mostly women and children, were in desperate need.[63] The positive effect of Chinese and foreign relief efforts is recorded in the Wen'an local history, which names five organizations as particularly important in 1917: (1) the Shanghai Guangrentang contributed a great deal of money, and distributed tickets to the very poor to allow them to get some cash, clothes, cottons, and medicine. It also gave out flour and set up soup kitchens. (2) The North China Christian Flood Relief Committee donated a large amount of money; the American clergyman Lei-si-de (John Leighton Stuart[?]) came to supervise the distribution. Foreigners and Chinese cooperated to run soup kitchens at thirteen locations, to repair the Thousand-Li Dike, and to fix the road to Beijing. They used labor relief and saved the lives of countless poor people. They set up hospitals and gave out seed. They donated a total of 36,000 foreign dollars and 80,000 shi of grain. This scale of money was rarely seen before. (3) The Shanghai Red Cross sent a deputy. (4) The Tianjin branch of the Shuntian-Zhili Relief Bureau also distributed a total of 37,000 yuan at Wen'an: 1 yuan for adults, and 50 cents for children, and double the amount for the very poor. (5) Shuntian-Zhili Charitable Relief Society donated 30,000 yuan for Wen'an in 1918.[64]

Xinhe County in Jizhou also suffered badly from the flood. Rains started 6/5, and the entire county was affected. Thirty-five thousand houses collapsed, and more than twenty people drowned. Emergency relief was distributed in cash from local charity granary funds. In the spring, the provincial government donated funds for labor relief. In addition villages were granted tax remissions, depending on the severity of their disaster.[65] Because of the extensive relief, this crisis was considered to have been less devastating in its effect than the 1920 drought, when many died from epidemic disease as well as hunger. In 1917 there was still relative prosperity. People still had reserves and were willing to help each other, according to the local history.[66]

In Ding County, the facts recorded by the American social scientist Sidney Gamble seem to indicate that the directives of the directorate were carried out faithfully. Crops were damaged in 335 out of 453 villages, of which 197 had no crops or less than 10 percent of the normal output. About 40 percent of the land suffered damage, with about 25 percent of the population reporting serious or very serious damage. Tax remissions were granted on a sliding scale. A few soup kitchens were set up, and *pingtiao* was practiced in a few districts. Cash distributions seemed to play a larger role. The local authorities sold off the grain reserves from local granaries and used the 3,727 yuan in proceeds, plus an additional 1,954 yuan in donations, to distribute cash to the poor.[67] The emphasis on cash grants, rather than grain distribution, seems to suggest that the grain market was fully functional during the crisis.

Although not so severe in human and social devastation as the 1876–79 drought or the one that was to follow in 1920, the 1917 flood was nevertheless extremely damaging. The low-lying districts in the Yongding River region, between Beijing and Tianjin, were practically in a chronic state of crisis. In Gu'an County, for example, the Yongding River had broken out of its dikes regularly since 1904. By 1912 the district was like a swamp, *zeguo*, and people had nothing to eat. Because of the repeated flooding, the silt had accumulated to a height of five to six feet so that the district that used to be moderately fertile was now barren. In fact the level of the land within the xian city was lower than the surrounding countryside by five to six feet and was shaped like a cauldron or kettle, *fudi*, from which there was no way for the water to flow out. The yamen and other buildings within were all toppled.[68] Mortality estimates or figures were rarely cited. People did not die from drowning, but from the accumulated effects of hunger, disease, cold, migration, and so forth. Scattered local records for 1918 speak of *daji*, or starvation—or alternately, people eating tree bark. The price of grain reached 4 yuan per shi in some places. More significantly, in the fall of 1918, epidemic disease in some places claimed many lives. In Wen'an, in the ninth month, "innumerable" people died.[69]

The homeless were of greatest concern. Shelters were set up by local authorities and also by gentry, merchants, or church groups. The record shows there were altogether 170 shelters in 62 counties. About 40,000 people were housed, at a total cost of 225,000 yuan.[70] As in Qing times, a paramount concern of authorities was to try to keep people in their home localities and prevent them from roaming around. Many refugees fled to Tianjin by land or water from distances up to 200–300 li. The authorities feared that if they stayed on, they would become vagrants. The directorate advised that they be given free transport and stipends and sent home. But since some returned for another dole, the police were advised to take and issue picture identification to refugees and to keep a photographic record of them.[71]

In this crisis, as in 1876–79 and other well-documented early twentieth-century disasters, a common act of desperation was the sale of young children or women. In 1876–79, Western observers reported the large-scale sales of northern Chinese women, even transporting them to the south. Most of the thousands of refugees that fled to Tianjin in that crisis were probably women and children. The Guangrentang sheltered them from not only hunger and disease but also from the danger of being kidnapped or sold.[72] In 1917 there was only indirect evidence of the sale of women or children. On 1917/10/11 the directorate cabled all county magistrates to forbid the sales of young children. Many such cases have been reported, said the cable. Two other notices followed in November advising magistrates to set up orphanages for the care of children, and the military to guard them.[73] There is no reference to infanticide, but evidence from other disasters suggest that this was a frequent but never acknowledged social practice.[74]

CHINESE AND FOREIGN ACTIVISM IN TIANJIN

Far more than in previous crises, the 1917 flood was Tianjin-centered. Not only was it the geographic center of the flooding itself—the point at which the five key rivers converged—but also it was the center of the Chinese and foreign relief efforts. Despite the aid available in some rural areas, Tianjin offered tremendous advantages to those Zhili flood victims who could find refuge there. As it had developed as an industrial center, many migrants from the hinterland sought economic opportunity as factory workers and service laborers. Ninety-seven percent of the workers in the Santiaoshi industrial district were from Hebei, mostly from Hejian Prefecture (especially Wuqiao, Jiaohe, and Ningjin).[75] In times of crisis, refugees swelled the population of the city. In the winter of 1877–78, 100,000 people had been sheltered and fed in Tianjin.[76] In 1917–18, the numbers may have been smaller, but they were still significant. Tianjin police estimated in September 1918 that 284,349 people had been destitute in Tianjin city, with another 66,679 in outlying districts.[77]

Although missionaries were active in the countryside, foreign relief efforts were more concentrated at Tianjin. The foreign residents had charitable impulses, but, with the presence of so many refugees, they were also motivated by fear for their own personal safety and health. In addition, the flood threatened their businesses and shipping. Foreign relief efforts included a few showcase examples, such as the American Red Cross Flood Relief Camp, which was open from November 13, 1917, to March 31, 1918. The camp, built in the German Concession, contained about a thousand huts designed by "Mr. Harry Hussey—of the well known architectural firm of Shattuck and Hussey of Chicago."[78] It was run along the lines of a military camp, with inmates issued identification tags and ration cards and forced to submit to morning inspections, baths, and schools. Each person was medically examined upon entrance, his or her clothes sterilized and hair shaved or washed with kerosene oil. In all, the operators were proud that they had taken care of "4,800 homeless, destitute Chinese of the lowest and poorest order, already weakened by long exposure to flood and cold, and only *one* case of an infectious disease ever appeared in the camp."[79] The Tientsin Christian Union operated another refugee camp consisting of 2,000 huts housing 7,000 refugees. Xiong's directorate financed the construction, but the Christian group assumed the responsibility for running the camp, where they maintained a high sanitary and medical standard. "Vaccination against smallpox and regular bathing are provided for and encouraged while the latrines are cleaned daily. The proportion of sickness is extremely low." Women were kept busy making clothing and bedding and reed mats. Classes were established for adults as well as children.[80]

Other cities held fund-raising events. In Beijing the Chinese power-elite of warlords and others did its part by sponsoring fairs and raffles.[81] In Shanghai the Sino-foreign community sponsored a five-day "charity fete" in Mr. S. A. Hardoon's garden, which included a balloon ascension, a lantern parade, Chinese dramatics, acrobatics, bazaar entertainments, cinema shows, and pyrotechnic displays. However, "most of the evening was given over to feasting while watching the shows in the theatres." Not only the foreign community, but "Chinese from the tall northerner to the thin, short Cantonese, poor and rich, all were there contributing their share to help their needy brothers."[82]

At Tianjin, civil society and social activism were evident in each subsequent crisis. In 1939, when there was a massive flood accompanied by fierce winds that devastated Tianjin and surrounding localities in Hebei, its effects were felt even in Shandong, Henan, and Shanxi. Within the city, the water reached some rooftops, and more than 100,000 people had to evacuate their houses. Sampans ferried passengers along the streets that had become waterways. Municipal authorities and civic organizations banded together to organize a large relief effort. Some grain inventories were available within the city, but as in the past, shipments of grain, especially corn, from Manchuria proved critical. Including thirty-nine cities, districts, and townships outside Tianjin, a total of 406,500 households, or 1,688,800 persons, received relief in this crisis.[83]

The foreign concessions were directly affected and mounted their own relief efforts. In the Italian Concession, 3,000 refugees were sheltered in tents set up in the park, but there were an estimated 1,000–2,000 others who could not be accommodated and eked out a living in back alleys or on the streets. By late October, all the refugees were given allowances and sent away, presumably because there was no way to shelter so many people over the winter. Funds were raised from local residents, both Chinese and foreign. And as in almost all these relief campaigns, careful accounts were maintained, and many photographs were taken of the refugees and the staff that looked after them, such as the sanitation brigade, the soup kitchen staff, and the barber.[84] The final report proudly enumerated the accomplishments of the relief effort, down to the last steamed bun and each serving of gruel dispensed. Special attention was paid to sanitation and the prevention of infectious disease. Donations from civic groups, including the Japanese, amounted to more than 1 million dollars, not including donations in kind. Ultimately only 889,000 yuan were spent, leaving a surplus of about 300,000 yuan—another source of pride.[85]

RIVER CONSERVANCY: THE FOREIGN ROLE

It was in the area of river conservancy that foreign advisors made the most distinctive contribution, motivated by the protection of their own economic interests. The 1917 flood prompted the most sustained foreign involvement to date in river conservancy. Although the Chinese authorities had already spent 560,000 yuan on dike repairs by October 19, 1917, they knew that foreign assistance would be needed.[86] At Tianjin foreigners had been active in conservancy problems since the turn of the century. In 1901 the Hai Ho (He) Conservancy Commission, a Sino-foreign advisory body under the Chinese government, had been formed, composed largely of foreign engineers and financed with customs and river revenue and a tonnage tax on all vessels using the harbor.[87] It had made an excellent start in surveying the flood areas, although its jurisdiction did not extend beyond the Hai River. In 1912, after terrible floods, the commission made recommendations for relieving the pressure on the Hai River and its tributaries. Its focus was not just the immediate Tianjin area but the entire basin, and recommendations included cutting other outlets to the ocean, the creation of canals that would facilitate drainage, reforestation, and construction of reservoirs upriver.[88]

The 1917 flood, however, seemed to be a real wake-up call for the foreign diplomats and businessmen in Tianjin. They recognized that continual silting and flooding of the waterways around the port threatened their commercial interests, and thus they needed to take a wider view beyond the treaty port itself in order to keep the port navigable. Further, they recognized that international cooperation was essential. "Tientsin has taken a very limited view of its responsibilities, and indeed of its own danger. . . . There is only one solution of the flood problem, and that solution is full co-operation."[89] Another editorial noted that the advent of railways had made the foreign community more aware of the suffering in the interior because localities were easier to get to. "So the Chihli floods have come again. But this time with a difference. Where they have merely affected the native before, they have this time very boldly and badly hit the foreigner." Because of this, the Chinese population would benefit from steps the foreigners would take to guard the rivers.[90] The fear that the city would be entirely flooded was the most compelling reason for action. One foreigner referred to "the coming end of Tientsin." There was also concern about disruption of the Peking-Hankow rail line. The French consultant engineer, G. Bouillard, conducted a survey and concluded that the only way to avoid future damage to the railroad was to adopt fundamental measures such as "reafforestation" and the building of storage basins.[91]

H. Vanderveen, the consulting engineer for the National Conservancy Board and author of many reports on the Zhili River problem, saw the Zhili River crisis as a political and historical issue, not an engineering one. "Human interference, the direct cause of the present conditions" was the subtitle of an essay written in 1917. He argued that the two main problems—the "silt evil" and the inadequacy of outlets—both had their historic origins in the diversion of tributaries into the main rivers to protect the Grand Canal. For example, the diversion of Chao River into the Bei River in earlier centuries placed too much pressure on the latter, which in turn affected the Hai River. The Yongding River was the major problem. In order to prevent the river from bringing to the Grand Canal a huge quantity of silt, it had been diverted to the then-existing swamps, which acted as storage basins until, in the course of centuries, they had filled up. At the same time, the riverbeds also become elevated because of the restricted outflow of water. "The result is that the Hun Ho [another name for the Yongding River] is now a menace to the entire country and in destruction is only surpassed by the Yellow River."[92]

On October 12, 1917, a new Commission for the Improvement of the River System of Chihli (Zhili) was created by the Chinese government and the diplomatic body. Xiong Xiling was appointed president and its members consisted of foreigners and Chinese, with a generous representation of engineers. Its main functions were providing technical advice on river improvements and controlling expenditures of funds supplied by diplomatic agreement. River conservancy posed a type of challenge that appealed to the Western, particularly American, reformers. Engineers such as O. J. Todd traversed the countryside, surveying, measuring, and supervising work when possible. From 1917 until 1927, the commission conducted extensive surveys of the river system and undertook certain projects, including the "Cathedral Cutting," north of Tianjin, which straightened out one bend of the Bei River, removing a danger to one section of the city.[93] Together with the China International Famine Relief Commission (CIFRC), established in 1921 to coordinate foreign relief efforts, it helped to build dikes along the Daqing and Ziya rivers and to sponsor local self-help projects, as well as the Shilu irrigation scheme, which was largely completed in 1927 and which helped to irrigate 70,000 mu along the Yongding River, west of Beijing.[94] Another successful project was at "West Lake" (Xi dian), about 30 miles east of Baoding fu, where extensive diking was undertaken at the cost of 300,000 yuan. In 1927 a successful harvest was achieved there, whereas in 1924 and 1925 the entire district had been covered with floodwater. A third success was the repair of a major break along the Thousand-Li Dike, which made farming possible within the Wen'an wa.[95]

Dated September 2, 1922, Photograph 10.1 shows work on the diversion of the Bei River under the supervision of the Chihli River Commission. Notable is the combination of modern engineering technology with old-fashioned human labor.

More ambitious engineering projects were beyond the commission's means. One major construction project recommended but never carried out by the CIFRC was the digging of a channel from the Grand Canal near Duliu to the sea, which would provide a second outlet for the southern river systems. This project would have cost 6 million yuan and required 100–200,000 laborers.[96] Map 10.1 reproduces a CIFRC survey map, dated January 1926 and signed by O. J. Todd, showing a proposed flood channel at Duliu (Tuliu). In its final report, the commission recommended not only a southern outlet for the Yongding River but also major improvements in northern and southern rivers, at a total estimated cost of 100 million yuan. As the commission disbanded, it acknowledged that not much net gain had been made, and in its current state the Yongding River would repeat the disaster of 1917.[97] The Hai River Commission reached the same conclusion, namely that unless the Yongding River were put under central government control, "provincialism" would offset any river conservancy attempts.[98] Despite its limitations, the Chihli River Commission had a good record. O. J. Todd commended its survey work and smaller projects, but larger projects had to be postponed for the future, "when China has a government," he

PHOTOGRAPH 10.1.   Laborers at river site, 1922

SOURCE: Chihli River Commission, *Reports*.

wrote. "The problems of this one Commission alone would keep an able staff of foreign engineers busy for twenty years with a reasonable annual appropriation at hand to carry out the work of construction and necessary maintenance."[99] Most of the large projects suggested by the commission were eventually undertaken after 1949. Today's Duliu jianhe, for example, is exactly what was suggested in the 1920s. Yet, the commission itself had not been able to effect fundamental change. Just a few years later, in 1924, another large flood struck the same area, affecting at least sixty counties and leaving more than 1 million people destitute.[100] In 1939 it flooded even more seriously.

The 1920–1921 Drought and International Aid

Barely recovered from the flood, Zhili in 1920–21 bore the brunt of the great drought that extended all over North China. The conditions were similar to those in 1876, and the same five provinces of Shaanxi, Shanxi, Shandong, Henan, and Zhihli were principally affected. The sections of Shantung and Honan and Chihli, north of the Yellow River and south of the line drawn between Peking and Tientsin were the worst. The total number of destitute was estimated to be 20 million; 8.8 million of them were in Zhili, the largest number of all provinces. The Zhili destitute were found in ninety-seven counties, whose combined population was 18.8. million.[101] In the autumn of 1920, thirteen counties had 90–100 percent of their population in distress, thirty-

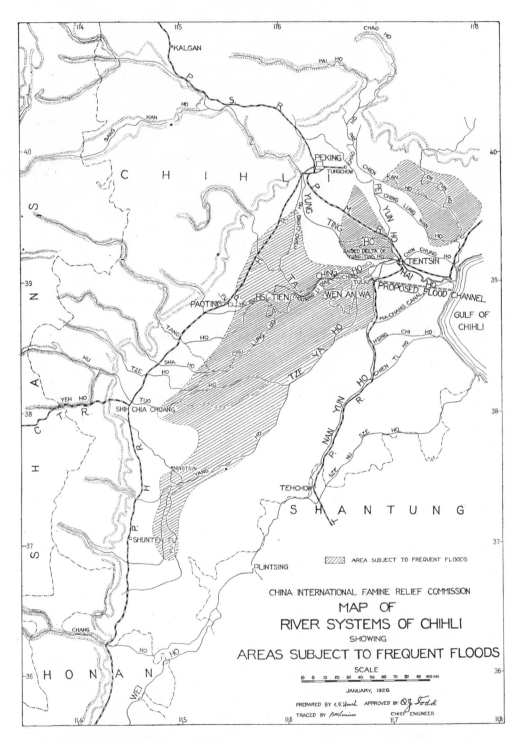

MAP 10.1.   Areas subject to frequent floods, 1920s

SOURCE: China International Famine Relief Commission, reproduced from Mallory, 159.

two had 70–89 percent, eighteen had 40–69 percent, while nine had 20–39 percent in distress; the remaining 25 counties had under 20 percent, or the percentage was unclear.[102] (See Map 10.2.)

SINO-FOREIGN FAMINE RELIEF

The famine relief effort inspired both Chinese and international assistance of unprecedented proportions. Several foreign relief organizations formed an executive committee, supported by the diplomatic community, while several Chinese voluntary and semiofficial organizations combined to form the North China Famine Relief Society. The Chinese and foreign groups together formed the Peking United International Famine Relief Committee. Together with the North China International Famine Relief Committee of Tientsin, these groups coordinated activities in Zhili. The first had responsibility for western Zhili, and the Tientsin group for the eastern part of the province. Similar groups were established at Shanghai, Jinan, Kaifeng, and other cities. Each had its independent jurisdiction, but the overall coordination was given to the Peking group, which had a semiofficial status.[103]

Fund-raising in the United States, Hong Kong, Canada, Britain, and other countries was enthusiastic, and donations for relief were substantial. In total 17.4 million Mex. dollars were raised by international committees. American donations of 6.5 million dollars provided the largest share. Another 4 million was raised through a loan based on a surtax on the Chinese Maritime Customs.[104] There was a tremendous outpouring of generosity in the United States. Led by banker Thomas W. Lamont, appointed by President Woodrow Wilson, the China Famine Relief Fund mounted a vigorous nationwide fund-raising campaign, collecting more than 4 million dollars, which were transferred to the Peking United International Famine Relief Committee.[105] Fund-raisers used slogan after slogan to nag the American conscience. "Famine relief is a sermon without words," their posters said. "Pick a Pal in China." "Give China a chance to live!" "15 Million starving—Every minute counts."[106] In both the Chinese and Western communities in Beijing and Tianjin, there was also a "contagion of philanthropy." According to John Earl Baker, an American missionary, "it became the socially correct thing to donate bridge winnings to some relief fund, and one became sure of a moment in the spotlight by letting it be known that shortly one was 'going down to the famine area.'"[107]

The 17.4 million raised through the international committees represented only one part of the total of 37.1 million dollars spent on relief. Another 2 million was raised by various missionary bodies—the American Presbyterian Church, Catholic Missions, and so on—and administered separately.[108] Another 2.4 million was raised through the American Red Cross. The remainder came from Chinese Government Relief Bureau, the Ministry of Communications, and various Chinese voluntary groups, which donated 8 million. Since 44 percent of the international committees' funds actually came from Chinese donations, the final report estimated that 60 percent of the total of 37 million in relief came from Chinese public and private sources. In addition, the government provided free transportation for relief and relief workers valued at an estimated 9 million dollars.

METHODS OF FAMINE RELIEF

Unlike 1917, when the emphasis was on economic recovery of households, in 1920–21, relief focused overwhelmingly on the distribution of grain, not money. Although grain distribution posed a more complicated challenge, the committee hoped that large quantities of imported grain would discourage profiteers and keep prices down.[109] There were ample supplies available from Manchuria that

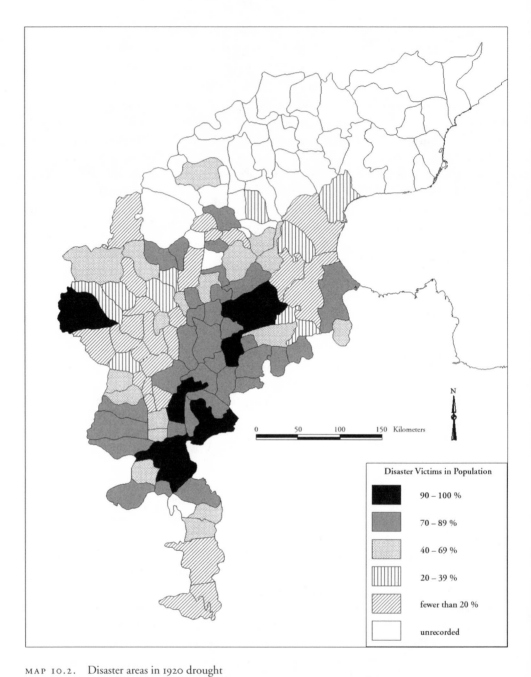

Disaster Victims in Population

■ 90 – 100 %

▨ 70 – 89 %

▧ 40 – 69 %

▥ 20 – 39 %

▧ fewer than 20 %

□ unrecorded

0   50   100   150 Kilometers

MAP 10.2.   Disaster areas in 1920 drought

SOURCE: Adapted from Bergère, 1367–72, based on *Report on Famine Conditions, November 15, 1920* (North China International Society for Famine Relief, Tientsin).

could be transported by rail: the Peking-Kalgan, Peking-Mukden, Peking-Hankow, and Tientsin-Pukow lines. The government paid the cost of freight. When the line to Manchuria became too congested, the Peking committee turned to the grain markets along the Peking-Kalgan line. Some supplies also came from northern Jiangsu and Anhui. The Peking Committee purchased altogether 53,152 tons of grain—mostly *gaoliang*, but also some millet, corn, and beans—which were distributed to Baoding, Shunde, Daming, Zhengding, Dingzhou, and elsewhere.[110] As in the past, the easy availability of large grain supplies in Manchuria, and now Mongolia, was a precious resource, indeed a life-line, for Zhili.

The railways were seen as the main factor in limiting the loss of life. For North China as a whole, the estimated mortality was half a million victims, a terrible human toll, but far less than the estimated 9–13 million victims of the 1876–79 famine. A mild winter and effective relief measures also helped.[111] Even so, some famine areas received nothing. "Yet the communications are not sufficient. How hard it is for some to understand how there should have been famine in China when the stations in Manchuria and other districts were filled with grain awaiting shipment. There was an abundance of food supplies to meet all the needs had the conditions been favourable for transmission to the affected districts and had there been money to make purchase."[112]

Relief was administered through subcommittees of foreign and Chinese members, and channeled through local Chinese groups, either local leaders or Christian church members. International committees aimed at guarding against malfeasance supervised all stages. Under the Peking Committee, there were subcommittees for Baoding, Dingzhou, Zhengding, Shundefu, Daming, and Beijing.[113] Altogether there were 537 foreign famine workers and 5,761 Chinese workers covering the five provinces.[114]

The first step in administering relief was the direct investigation of households and their classification into the destitute and near destitute. Because so many households had split up or been abandoned, this was a difficult task. Lists already prepared by the magistrate were sometimes used after spot-checking them. Although investigation resembled the methods of the Qing famine relief model, the guidelines for relief distribution placed greater emphasis on saving lives rather than restoring agricultural production. The guiding principle was that

> relief should be given in sufficient amount to sustain life until harvest time, when the people would be able to get along on their own resources. This policy was necessary owing to the prevalent practice of distributing the relief available to all the sufferers, no matter how little each one got, thus not benefitting [*sic*] any individual sufficiently to sustain life till the resources of the next harvest were available. The International Committees felt it was better to choose a few however, and help them effectually than to give any such small quantities as to be of no effectual help.[115]

This reflected a rather harsh but practical triage mentality: there was no point in giving relief in such small quantities that the recipients would still die.[116] In other words, relief should be given only to the "truly destitute," who often happened to be women and children. The "near destitute" by definition had just enough to pull through. "This group comprised the backbone of the country life and were the ones who, if helped, would be of the greatest good in the country. Humanitarian grounds however compelled the passing by of this group and the giving of relief to those completely destitute even though they might be of less value to the community."[117] In Daming Prefecture, the tickets were given to those families chosen by lot from among the list of the very poor provided by the magistrate. "The pressure of the Chinese to distribute the relief very thin so that all might have a part was very great, but we adhered to the principle that relief should be sufficient to maintain life until the harvest." In one town the beleaguered relief worker resorted to benevolent deception by making a small speech before departing, "saying that the official had in-cluded all the poor, that as all could not be helped there were not tickets enough those who were lucky were chosen by chance (the idea of luck makes a great hit)." A list of all those chosen for re-lief was posted in a public place—"this prevents the headman from doing something different, and also absolves him from the responsibility of choosing households."[118]

Although in Baoding and Zhengding local organizations were used as grain distribution centers, in the other areas, grain was distributed only at the prefectural city. On distribution dates, thou-sands of people filled the roads, traveling three or four days to get their grain. Despite the crowds, these mass distributions were managed efficiently, according to the report. As a matter of policy, soup kitchens were discouraged.[119] Money was distributed only to nursing and expectant mothers, in emergencies, and in mountainous areas. Only half a million dollars was spent in cash relief.

The ration for grain relief was 20 catties of grain, usually *gaoliang*, sometimes millet and corn, for each person each month. This was a fairly generous allowance since the medical experts said that 8 ounces of millet (about half a catty) or of *gaoliang* was sufficient as a daily ration. It is dif-ficult to compare this standard with the Qing famine of 5 he of *mi* per day per adult, later reduced to 3 he. Technically the he or ke was a measure of volume, while the catty or jin was a measure of weight. The standard of 8 ounces per day may have been comparable to the Qing ration of 3 he per day if there were about 180 lbs of *mi* per shi. It was consistent with the principle that the truly destitute be aided "until they were able to procure a good harvest off their lands."[120] Distributions were made from February until May 1921. Altogether 2 million or more people were aided in the western Zhili region with 7.4 million monthly rations, averaging three to four months of relief for each person.[121]

In the end, the international relief committees had a positive assessment of the work they had done. They estimated that their efforts, along with those of the Red Cross, had relieved a total of 7.7 million people. Of these, 2.7 million were from Zhili Province.[122] The Peking Committee praised the Chinese side of the relief effort. "It is probable that there has never been in the past such a large interest and support in relief work by the Chinese for their own people." It also com-mended the spirit of cooperation between Chinese and international groups, and the willingness of the Chinese authorities to entrust their funds to international administration.[123]

NEGATIVE SOCIAL CONSEQUENCES

However successful the relief campaign was deemed by the foreign relief workers, it could only ad-dress one part of the suffering of the population. If, by its own calculation, 2.7 million were served by the relief organization, then there were another 6 million who did not receive this type of re-lief. By Peking Committee's own account, as well as the independent observations, this crisis was severe and long lasting. Local conditions varied widely, even in the heavily affected areas. One lo-cality might survive because of good water supply, while a neighboring district might be "barren and destitute." But rural investigation showed that grave hardship was experienced widely. Around Shunde, one-third of the population of about 1 million were "in direst need and there were 31,286 deaths from hunger and cold." In Ding County during a three-week period in the winter, there were an average of 110 deaths a week in a district of half a million people. In Handan, 5 to 80 per-cent of residents were "destitute."[124] Local histories identify the crisis as a crop failure resulting in severe hunger, *daji*; only occasionally do they mention death from hunger (which does not mean it did not occur), and there are no references to cannibalism, as there had been in 1876–79.[125]

Famine foods included *kang* (chaff) mixed with wheat blades, flour made of ground leaves, fuller's earth, flower seeds, corn cobs, roots, sweet potato vines, elm bark, and so forth. "Some of this food was so unpalatable that children starved, refusing to eat it. Yet so common was dependence on this food that in many districts relief workers investigating thousands of homes, very rarely found any store of grain commonly used in food. It is very true that many millions of people were able to eke out their existence by the reliance on food such as the above."[126]

Another measure of famine distress was large-scale migration. The Peking Committee's report estimated that at least a million people had left their villages, sometimes using the railroads to migrate to Mongolia, Manchuria, Shanxi, or Shaanxi.[127] The absence of men in villages was common and especially noticeable in areas of Hebei and Shandong from which migration to Manchuria was possible. This was part of a trend that had begun in the 1890s. Each year hundreds of thousands migrated from Shandong and Hebei in search of employment in Manchuria, thus providing an important escape for poor peasant families. Fleeing a specific disaster was one reason for migrating, but not so important as general economic hardship.[128] In 1876, 900,000 migrants fled to Manchuria, escaping the great drought, but the statistics for 1920 and 1921 do not show a great increase during the years immediately before and after; in each of these years about half a million migrated to Manchuria.[129] In 1927–29, when drought again struck North China, and 1939–42, when the Japanese war broke out, there were exceptionally large numbers.[130]

The sale of women and children was "surprisingly extensive."[131] One relief worker said in twenty years in Henan he had never seen so many children sold. In Shunde fu, 25,000 children were sold.[132] Numbers of children sold equaled the number that had died. Some children were taken to big cities in other provinces, but Shijiazhuang in Zhili was one of the big centers. Girls and women were sold, even up to the age of forty, as wives, concubines, servants, or prostitutes. Boys were sold as adopted sons. Prices were 3 to 80 yuan, and in one case, 150 yuan.[133] The Peking Committee took a special interest in this issue, sending investigators to the countryside. Some attempts at relief or prevention were made, including paying students in a school 1 or 2 yuan monthly to make them economically valuable to their families.[134]

Xinhe County was one of the thirteen counties reported as having 100 percent of its population destitute.[135] Its experience is exceptionally well described in its gazetteer. The year 1920 was simultaneously a natural and a human disaster. Many people died in an epidemic that broke out in the seventh month. Grain prices rose sharply: millet was 8,200 wen per dou; *gaoliang* was 4,100 wen; and cotton 680 wen per jin. Everyone panicked. In the ninth month, the local leaders established a relief-grain bureau. The province contributed a total of 26,414 yuan. A total of 12,000 yuan was borrowed to use for *pingtiao* sales twice. Beijing relief bureaus donated 500 yuan of cotton garments, and so forth. Grain was distributed three times, with rations of 4 sheng for adults and 2 sheng for children.[136] Unlike the 1917 flood when people still had reserves and were willing to help each other, in 1920 by contrast, people were not able to help each other. Banditry was widespread, and officials and police could not keep order. Families fled, some taking refuge in other places or seeking shelter in the county seat. The harvests of 1922 and 1923 were good, but it was hard to hire agricultural workers because so many had gone to the cities. In 1924 there was another flood, but it was not as serious and or as damaging as the crises of 1917 and 1920. In the following year, 1925, the wheat harvest was great.[137]

Ding County, one of the less severely affected counties, had only 20 percent of its farmland affected by the drought (in 36 percent of its villages), but it also experienced crop loss from locusts that year. Twenty-five percent of the families were classified as very poor or poor. Aid came from various sources: the provincial government, local relief associations, the CIFRC, the American Board Mission, and the American Red Cross. In 1921 and 1922, these organizations helped to support the digging of about 460 wells in Ding County and 3,100 more in neighboring counties.[138] The gazetteer of Wan County also recorded famine relief received from various sources, but did not comment on its efficaciousness. Relief was received in 1920 from the local government, from a temple, from the Shuntian-Zhili disaster relief committee, from the Zhili Charitable Society, and from a Confucian charity. In 1929–30, 3,000 yuan was received each year from the Hebei Civilian Affairs Bureau.[139]

CHINA INTERNATIONAL FAMINE RELIEF COMMISSION

An outcome of the generally successful international cooperation in famine relief was the formation of the China International Famine Relief Commission in September 1921.[140] The commission became a permanent relief organization composed of the existing famine relief groups.[141] Funded partly by an embarrassing surplus of 2 million dollars of unexpended funds, the CIFRC functioned for almost two decades as the key private voluntary organization for relief operations. Its directors and constituents were both Chinese and foreigners, and it had branches and projects in most of the provinces. The CIFRC saw itself not as an emergency relief group but as an organization dedicated to seeking a "permanent improvement" of conditions in China. It sought to define famine broadly, as a condition "where drought or flood has reduced any considerable portion of the respectable countryside to a diet of unwholesome substitutes." Relief should be given in such conditions, even if there was no increase in the death rate. In addition, the CIFRC stressed that the principle of labor relief, rather than free relief, should be applied whenever possible. Beyond emergency relief, the prevention of famines, particularly through river control projects, was emphasized.[142]

The CIFRC devoted its greatest efforts to public works projects, particularly the building of roads, bridges, and dikes. John Baker had set a high standard of productivity in 1921, when he supervised the construction of 128 kilometers of mountain road in Shanxi Province in 164 days by 20,000 laborers. This two-lane paved road crossed five mountain ranges, ranging between 750 and 1,500 meters in height, and crossed twelve rivers.[143] By 1936 the CIFRC had built a total of 3,200 kilometers of new roads in fourteen provinces, repaired 2,000 kilometers of old road, sunk 5,000 tube wells, dug three large irrigation canals, and built 1,600 kilometers of river embankment. The CIFRC also promoted social reform. The establishment of rural cooperatives of various types— primarily credit cooperatives—became a major thrust of its activities in the 1930s, and by 1936, some 20,000 cooperatives had been sponsored. Between 1922 and 1936, the CIFRC disbursed a total of about 50 million Chinese dollars, of which more than half went to such rural reconstruction projects, and about 22 million was spent on direct relief. More than half of the CIFRC funds came from the Chinese government or individual Chinese donors.[144]

Although famine relief work had become fully secularized, the overwhelming majority of Americans involved in it were missionaries, and there were close ties between church groups and famine relief organizations. Ninety-five out of 125 foreigners on CIFRC committees were missionaries.[145] There were still some hard-core evangelical types who criticized missionary participation in famine relief work on the grounds that it drew attention away from spreading the Gospel, but most missionaries saw relief as charitable work, a "ministry of loving deeds," that must be performed, even if no evangelical gains resulted.[146] More critically, missionaries saw that fundamental structural reform of the Chinese economy and society would facilitate the long-term prospects for Christianity in China. To this end, they engaged in a wide range of secular activities in addition to famine relief, such as the building of hospitals, schools, and universities. Most missionaries also understood that famine relief campaigns were extremely useful in attracting the American public's support for church work in China.[147] Their critics, in turn, accused them of creating "missionary famines" simply to raise more funds for missionary work.[148]

Whether their motives were religious or secular, Americans approached famine relief and reconstruction with characteristic energy and enthusiasm. Despite the grim conditions in China, Americans were invariably full of optimism. O. J. Todd, the chief engineer for the CIFRC from 1923 to 1935, perhaps best exemplified this "can-do" attitude. Known as the "River Tamer," he supervised numerous flood control and road-building projects. He regarded the Chinese as hardworking and easy to teach; traditional Chinese methods, he felt, needed only the extra benefit that could be provided by Western technology and good leadership. So spectacular were his accomplishments, and so large his ego, that in the foreign community he was known as "Todd Al'mighty."[149]

The 1928–1930 North China Drought and National Crisis

In 1928–30 another devastating drought struck across northern and northwestern China, including Gansu, Shaanxi, Shanxi, Henan, and Shandong. During the late 1920s dry conditions prevailed over North China, particularly in southern Zhili and western Shandong.[150] In December 1927, a million-dollar campaign was authorized by CIFRC. About seventy counties with 4 million people were affected, it was estimated. Conditions described as "worst in years," or "worst in 25 years." Gentry and elders appealed to CIFRC for help. "The long line of pedestrians moving day after day from this to other sections speak louder than words of the impossibility of trying to pass through the winter in this section of Shantung and Chihli. Many thousands are now using cottonseed, while others are forced to use chaff, leaves, and weeds, mixed with a little grain, for food. . . . Even the middle class [that is, landowners] have been forced to go out to beg."[151]

Grain prices were said to be higher and conditions worse than in 1920–21. "Land is sold at a cheapest price, and in many cases a buyer cannot be found. Houses are being torn down in order to sell wood and buy grain. Girls are being sold for a few dollars, charitable institutions are filled to capacity, and can do no more. Roots of trees, wheat-sprouts, and chaff are the daily food of hundreds of thousands."[152] The following year the drought continued with scorching temperatures, and the disaster reached its height, with 117 out of 129 counties and an estimated 6 million people in Zhili affected.[153] Grain prices in the spring in the Shandong-Zhili border area had risen two to four times the previous year. For example, *gaoliang*, which had been 2 yuan per 100 catties, had risen to 8 yuan, millet, from 3 to 10 yuan, and wheat from 3 to 7 yuan. Relief workers reported that in villages in this area, most existed on cotton seed and chaff. People were unable to sell land at any price. Many had gone out begging or left for Shanxi or Manchuria. In one relatively large village of 500 families, at least 200 people had left. Children and even wives had been sold off to pay for traveling expenses. Or, in other cases, women, children, and elderly had been abandoned to fend for themselves; the able-bodied men had left. In yet other cases, entire families had left together.[154]

As before, the specter of children and women being sold attracted Western concern. "The only thing they are able to sell is women and children." Boys cost 10 yuan, girls 10–30 yuan, while young women brought in as much as 100 yuan or more. "Men from Shansi are living in each inn in the village buying them up." In another market town, boys were sold for 4–10 yuan, girls and young women for 10–100 yuan. In another village children were being sold "constantly." Some had died. In another village, seven girls from ages six to eight had been sold in two days for 12–15 yuan each. In that village, "deaths by starvation" were common. A poignant tale was reported by a relief worker who gave bread to a dying man, who instead "tottered off to give it to his old mother."[155]

Although famine in Hebei was confined mainly to the southern portion, overall the 1928–30 North China drought was more geographically extensive than that of 1920–21. A total of 299 counties, with population of 57,350,000, were affected. "Severest" conditions (where there was "already high death rate") prevailed in 129 counties with a population of 21,015,000. This included Gansu, most of Shaanxi, and part of Henan. "Severe" conditions ("all except indigent can survive") were found in 84 counties, with population of 17,197,000, scattered in Shanxi, Shandong, and Hebei. "Less severe" ("death rate will be high before harvest") existed in 86 counties having a population of 19,137,000, in parts of Shaanxi, Shanxi, Hebei, Shandong.[156] The government classified famines into five grades, A to E. To be graded A, all six conditions—drought, flood, insects, hailstorm, military, banditry—had to be experienced by two-thirds of the counties for successive years. Hebei was classified into group C: at least one-third of the counties had experienced three conditions. Thus, Hebei was not as bad off as Shandong, Henan, and Chahar in Group B, or Shaanxi, Gansu, Shanxi, and Suiyuan in Group A.[157] By spring 1929, however, the Beijing-Tianjin area had experienced a good spring wheat crop. By fall, Hebei as a whole was off the famine list, although the Daming area still slightly affected.[158]

Although Hebei was relatively well off, the toll in Gansu, Shaanxi, and Henan was very severe. In Gansu the estimated mortality was 2.5 to 3 million in an already sparsely populated province of only 6 million people.[159] In Shaanxi, out of a population of 13 million, an estimated 3 million died of hunger or disease during this three-year period; another 6 million fled the province.[160] For the entire affected area, one estimate places the total mortality as high as 10 million. Although there is no hard data on the actual mortality, there is little doubt that the 1928–30 disaster was, on the whole, more severe than that of 1920–21. Conditions in the northwest have been described as "a living hell." Already pitifully poor peasants found grain prices to have risen five times their normal levels, and they resorted to the famine foods of desperation: tree leaves and bark, grasses and weed, and cottonseed. Those who had not fled sold their children if they could. As the very last resort, cannibalism was practiced.[161] Vagrancy and banditry were widespread.[162]

These nightmarish conditions were directly related to the battles between Chiang Kai-shek and the warlords Feng Yuxiang, Yan Xishan, and others, which prevented relief from reaching the most needy areas in Shaanxi and Henan.[163] Not only were militarists preoccupied with their military campaigns, but scarce grain supplies were used to feed soldiers first. Extensive opium cultivation, especially in Shaanxi, Gansu, Rehe, and Suiyuan, took valuable land away from foodgrains.[164] Of ninety-two counties in Hebei affected by famine in 1928, eighty experienced military activity at the same time.[165] These and other political issues greatly interfered with Chinese and international efforts to mount a major famine relief campaign. Relief efforts, both Chinese and foreign, were more modest than before, and warfare and civil unrest made the delivery of relief, particularly inland, virtually impossible. Rail traffic from Manchuria in particular was seriously disrupted by warlord rivalries. Some warlords intervened on behalf of the grain shipments, but most did not.[166] In the summer and winter of 1928, General Chu Chin-lan arranged military escort for grain to be transported to Hebei to assist in relief of landlocked counties stricken by various forms of disaster, following the evacuation of Shandong-Zhili armies. Large quantities of grain were also sent to Shandong.[167]

Compared with 1920–21, the absolute level of resources available—both Chinese and foreign, public and private—was much lower. Between the summer of 1928 and spring of 1929, the Chinese government distributed 4.5 million yuan. Ultimately the Chinese government raised a total of 11 million yuan. Most distributions were made to other northern and Manchurian provinces. Hebei got a relatively small amount. Two-thirds was derived from relief bond issues. Other sources of funding included overseas Chinese; a customs surcharge of 2.5 percent; and contributions made by government officials according to a sliding scale, for example, officials salaried at 400 yuan or more "contributed" one month's pay. The Ministries of Railways and Finance provided free transport for grain and materials.[168] Although some of the formalities of traditional famine relief were still observed, such as county-by-county surveys, it is unlikely that much relief actually reached the needy.[169] Private contributions were substantial, and many Chinese charitable groups aided the relief effort where possible.[170] As in previous disasters, groups in Shanghai, as well as the Shanghai press, mobilized to raise famine relief funds, some using techniques of photojournalism and pamphleteering.[171] Some Shanghai papers, however, held back because they felt that any contributions for famine relief to the northwest would only be used to support Feng Yuxiang's soldiers.[172]

Negative publicity about military and political interference posed a problem for both Chinese and international fund-raising after 1920–21. The Western-language newspapers in China covered the continuing tragedies with bold headlines. "Flood Waters Creeping Over Shantung, 80 Square Miles, One Foot Deep Every Twenty-Four Hours; Losses Enormous," screamed one headline in 1925.[173] On the same date, however, another newspaper wrote an editorial, "China's Sorrow and China's Shame," that asserted, "Not all of these calamities are beyond human control." There were "a few noble-minded Chinese," but "the main burden of organization and disbursement of relief has had to be shouldered by foreigners, for so indecently corrupt are most of China's politicians and officials that few of them can be trusted with funds for the succour of the striken."[174] The same editorial accused the Zhili provincial governor of trying to sabotage the work of the river commission. The *New York Times* reporter Hallett Abend faulted the Nanjing government for failing to act in any effective way even though the famine had been predicted for months. The CIFRC was reaching only 175,000 out of an estimated 20 million needy. In the face of grim reports from Gansu and Shaanxi, "Nanking is not only inactive but is logrolling and playing politics."[175] Fundraising posters and articles were still bold—"Famine: 10,000,000 Face Starvation in China. China's Plight, America's Opportunity"—but they were less successful than in previous campaigns.[176]

Famine and famine relief became increasingly politicized after the establishment of the Nanjing government in 1928. On the one hand, the government tried to impose its authority over foreign participation in famine relief. The CIFRC and other Sino-foreign organizations continued to function, but with the clear understanding that foreigners participated under Chinese supervision. On the other hand, some Americans were uneasy about the close association between their charitable efforts and the new government. In 1929 the American Red Cross attacked the CIFRC for transcending its original objectives and becoming a permanent, all-purpose philanthropic organization. In its report, the Red Cross asserted that famine relief should be given only in disasters where the cause was unmistakably "natural," that is, a flood or drought, and not in cases where the cause was demonstrably "political." If China could count on foreign assistance under any circumstances, then a dangerous situation of dependency would develop. The Chinese government should assume full responsibility for the type of public works sponsored by the CIFRC, and it should not rely on foreign assistance.[177]

The CIFRC's official response was that it was a Sino-foreign organization representing Chinese interests as well as foreign. Moreover, the criterion for the giving of relief should always be need, and not politics. The basic causes of recent disasters were fundamentally "natural"; politics had merely exacerbated the situation. Privately, however, the CIFRC staff regarded the Red Cross report as an attack on the Nationalist government.[178] William Johnson, an American missionary active with the CIFRC, drafted a sharp rebuttal entitled "Politics and the Red Cross," in which he denounced the report as politically motivated. "The American Red Cross has lost its soul," he wrote.[179] More moderate members of the relief community suppressed the publication of Johnson's article fearing that negative publicity would interfere with fund-raising.[180] Indeed, there had already been considerable reluctance to launch a major fund-raising campaign for famine in northwestern China because the American public's interest was at a low ebb. The foreign relief organizations all recognized, however, that the American public would more readily contribute to disaster relief than to long-term development projects.

The great 1931 flood of the Yangzi River provided the Nationalist government with an opportunity to assert its control over disaster relief. Considered a hundred-year event, it was probably one of the most extensive floods in world history. The Yangzi disaster affected all of central China and parts of the north and east, covering a territory of 87,000 sq. kilometers and resulting in damage of billions of dollars of property. At the same time other rivers, particularly the Huai River Basin, were also affected. Eight provinces were seriously impacted and others partially so. In the eight provinces of Anhui, Hubei, Hunan, Jiangsu, Zhejiang, Jiangxi, Henan, and Shandong, an estimated 60 percent of the 642 counties, about 30 percent of the fields, and 25 percent of the population of 214 million people were affected. Some 422,500 people died by drowning. The economic loss was valued at 2.3 billion yuan, about five times the size of the national government budget.[181]

The National Flood Relief Commission asserted the government's sovereign authority, but it also employed many foreigners. Its director-general was Sir John Hope Simpson, who had long experience with relief administration in India and Greece. John Earl Baker, Dwight W. Edwards, and several other Americans active in the CIFRC were also appointed to the commission as advisors to the Chinese government, and the chairman of the commission was T. V. Soong, minister of finance and brother-in-law of Chiang Kai-shek. The relief effort was greatly aided by the purchase of 450,000 tons of wheat and flour from the United States. Although the costs of shipment and other relief work were substantial, the commission received only about 1.25 million dollars from foreign donations and raised the rest—a sum of 20 million dollars—through private Chinese contributions and a 10 percent customs surcharge.[182] This relief effort was remarkably successful on the whole, at least according to the authorities. No serious food shortage resulted, and the price of grain was kept low. Repairs to 7,000 kilometers of dikes were completed by June 30, 1932. The Nationalist government and its foreign supporters regarded these accomplishments as another sign of its political legitimacy.[183] Like the emperors of the past, the Nationalists celebrated their success in river control through the publication of a commemorative volume.[184]

Nationalism played a role in famine relief elsewhere. One striking example was a massive relief effort in Shandong Province after the 1935 Yellow River flood. Under the unlikely leadership of the warlord governor Han Fuju, about 400,000 flood victims were sent out from the flood district in the western part of the province to counties in the east where they were provided with food and shelter over the winter. The entire operation was conducted according to the Spartan values espoused by the New Life Movement of the Nationalist government. Refugees were to obey orders, follow discipline, rise early, and be diligent. Not content with these general guidelines, Han Fuju ordered male refugees to cut off their queues (if they still had them) and women to unbind their bound feet (if they had them). Cleanliness and sanitation were stressed. Idleness was forbidden;

all able-bodied refugees were expected to work. All were to receive education. Refugees were also to get plenty of exercise and recreation, including singing. Vital records were maintained of all the deaths and births in each shelter in each province every day.[185]

From the late 1920s through the 1930s, the numerous natural disasters were unavoidably connected with political and economic crises; the world depression, warlordism, and Japanese invasion followed in succession. Although warlords and Guomindang were held responsible for obstructing aid, or ignoring relief, they were not seen as the only cause of the disasters. The famine in Henan Province during the anti-Japanese war, however, was unambiguously caused by human factors. Although there had been poor harvests and drought in 1942, the government had continued to tax the farmers, leaving them with no reserves. There were ample grain supplies in neighboring Shaanxi Province, but the government took no steps to deploy the grain. Theodore White and other foreign correspondents described the most abject famine conditions, with people eating bark and husks, begging and dying on the roads. They estimated that "of 30,000,000 people of Honan [Henan], probably 2 to 3 million had fled the province, and another 2 or 3 million had died of hunger and disease. It was the greatest disaster of the war in China, one of the greatest famines in the world."[186] Historians deem the mortality rate of this crisis to have exceeded that of the Guangxu famine in Henan sixty years earlier. At least 2 million died out of 11–16 million people who were destitute.[187] They point to the government's certain complicity in this tragedy by citing evidence that it suppressed and denied the reports of famine published in the respected newspaper *Da Gong Bao*.[188]

Conclusion

The Guomindang government did not base its legitimacy on river control, famine prevention, or agricultural prosperity, but even so, it was held responsible for failures in these traditional dynastic functions. The 1931 Yangzi flood relief campaign could not compare with the river-taming efforts of Kangxi or Qianlong, but even they could not have restored the status quo ante. The problems of natural and human catastrophe that the Nationalists encountered were historically unprecedented and cannot be understood simply as the nadir of a cyclical process. The frequency and the scale of the disasters of the Republican period far exceeded anything that had occurred previously. The late Ming period and other periods of dynastic decline had also experienced a succession of disasters, but level of devastation and the human toll simply could not have been so great, and eventually the status quo ante was restored. In the Republican period, events took place so frequently and violently that even under better political circumstances there could not have been restoration of the environmental conditions of the past.

Environmental decline, especially the siltation of the major rivers, was also historically unprecedented, not simply the result of the ruler's shortcomings. The cumulative effect of centuries of deforestation, intensive land use, and excessive control of the rivers posed a problem of greater magnitude than had ever been experienced. The increasingly frequent floods of the Hai River Basin were a small and intense version of the problems in the larger Yangzi and Yellow River systems. The silting of the Yellow River and its instability were legendary. The shift of the riverbed in 1852 to the north of the Shandong peninsula from its ancient southern course to the south was the most dramatic manifestation of the fundamental dilemma of a riverbed precariously higher than the surrounding countryside; frequent smaller breaks of dikes caused hardship for peasants in this critical region. The Yangzi River, by contrast, deeper and more stable, had experienced only two major floods in the period 1583–1840, that is, from the late Ming to the late Qing. But in the century from 1841 to 1949, it experienced nine major floods including the megaflood of 1931.[189]

The human toll from large-scale natural disasters in the first half of the twentieth century certainly exceeded that from any other period in the last few centuries. If the century 1850–1950 is taken as a whole, the case is overwhelming. In his recent study, Xia Mingfang attempts to quantify this trend. Famine mortality in the second half of the Qing period he estimates at about 17 million, and in the Republican period, 21 million. His estimate for the entire Ming period is 3 million, and for the first half of the Qing period, 1.2 million.[190] For the Republican period, the mortality from natural disasters was far in excess of mortality from internal warfare—including all the warlord battles and the 1946–50 civil war between the Nationalists and the Communists—which he estimates at 6 million. The mortality from the war against Japan was 35 million, which did certainly exceed the mortality from famine.[191]

In the past, floods and droughts, even major ones, were regional in scope, even though they may have had dynastic significance. In the 1920s and beyond, the catastrophes were larger in scale and national in significance. The droughts of 1920–21 and 1928–30 were geographically extensive, affecting several provinces at once. The 1931 Yangzi and Huai flood was a hundred-year flood that affected eight provinces at the geographic center of the country and had a truly national character.[192] The shifting of Yellow River in 1938–47 affected 62 million people in three provinces. (See Table 10.1.) No region was spared major catastrophe in these decades. Because of newspapers and radio, knowledge of these events was widespread, at least in the cities. The examples of civic and nationalistic response show clearly that the public considered a crisis in any region to have national significance. And with increasing levels of international participation in famine relief, and famine relief campaigns overseas, such crises, wherever they occurred, assumed even more of a national identity. Both assigning blame and providing relief became political.

Insofar as there was a growing Chinese public attention to famines, one can see that there were hints of new ideas about them, at least on the part of the urban educated elite. The very attention to the quantification of famine mortality and other social indicators marked a change from the past. The need for applying "scientific" methods to famine relief, under the influence of Western famine relief workers, manifested itself not only in documentation and quantification, but in attention to nutritional requirements, public health, and mass education, at least in fortunate areas such as the treaty ports or territories under the control of unusual warlords like Han Fuju. Thus, in addition to the easy and obvious blame attached to the political authorities, one can perceive a change in the way in which famines were viewed. Rather than accepting them as an inevitable part of the natural and political order, modern opinion saw famines as the outcome of deeper economic and social forces. Thus the outlines of a paradigm shift could be discerned in two ways: in the phenomenon of disasters themselves (their frequency, extent, and consequences), but also in the understanding of their causes. The conditions were worse, and new approaches and solutions seemed to be required.

This new view of famines was barely emerging in the 1930s. In his path-breaking book *China: Land of Famine*, published in 1926, Walter H. Mallory, the secretary of the China International Famine Relief Commission, analyzed the various causes of famine. Mallory understood that in earlier periods of history the Chinese state had effectively used preventive measures such as public granaries and relief measures such as tax remissions, but the new Republican government he found to be so weak that it had neglected key functions such as river control. Instead, banditry, militarism, excessive taxation, and opium traffic flourished in the absence of strong central authority. But Mallory did not think that political causes were solely responsible for the repeated famines. He identified economic, natural, and social causes as well, devoting separate chapters to each. Among economic factors he named rural poverty and indebtedness, population density, and poor transportation. Among the natural factors, he pointed to deforestation, the pattern of rainfall, and the instability of the rivers, paying special attention to the Zhili rivers. Among social issues, he identified reasons for the population problem, which he blamed on social customs, such as ancestor worship, the preference for sons, and the practice of early marriage. Moving into the more subjective areas of Chinese "conservatism" and "waste" (including waste due to ceremonies and feasts, waste due to overeating, waste of time), he began to sound more like the earlier generation of missionaries such as the acerbic and straight-talking Arthur Smith, author of books such as *Chinese Characteristics*.

Just as Smith's negative characterizations of Chinese social attitudes were taken to heart by the writer and social critic Lu Xun, so too Walter Mallory's epithet "Land of Famine" sent shock waves among Chinese intellectuals and social scientists, who recognized its appropriateness and yet, at the same time, were ashamed by it.[193] When the young Deng Tuo (Deng Yunte) hastily wrote *Zhongguo jiuhuang shi* (The history of famine relief in China), which was published in 1937, he invoked Mallory and other Western writers, as well as scores of traditional Chinese sources. Deng's book was the first modern Chinese work on the problem of famines.[194] Although he was already a Marxist at the time, his approach to famine was rather eclectic, and he seemed to be searching for solutions whether they were in modern Western books or in ancient Chinese essays.[195] He urged the application of "scientific" methods to the problem of famine, rather than accepting the fatalistic attitude of the common people.[196] Deng's history of famine relief was republished many times, most recently in 1998, and drew attention to the problem of famine. He did not deny the characterization of China as the "land of famine" [*jihuang de Zhongguo*].

CHAPTER ELEVEN

Rural Crisis and Economic Change, 1900–1949

FOR THOSE WHO SAW CHINA as the "Land of Famine," the evidence of underlying rural poverty, low agricultural productivity, and social degradation was everywhere and made all the more striking in contrast to the modernity found in cities such as Shanghai and Tianjin. In the Qing, the management of famine (*huangzheng*) had as its principal goal the restoration of agricultural production after a crop failure; the assumption was that the restoration of social order would naturally follow. By the 1920s and 1930s, however, many recognized that there were fundamental social and economic problems that made peasants chronically vulnerable to floods and droughts. Reformers, both Chinese and foreigners, addressed the causes of rural poverty and low agricultural productivity rather than focusing only on famine relief and restoration of the status quo ante.[1] The British socialist, R. H. Tawney, wrote incisively in his classic *Land and Labor in China* (1932):

> Famine is a matter of degree. . . . If the meaning of the word is a shortage of food on a scale sufficient to cause widespread starvation, then there are parts of the country from which famine is rarely absent. . . . There are districts in which the position of the rural population is that of a man standing permanently up to the neck in water, so that even a ripple is sufficient to drown him. The loss of life caused by the major disasters is less significant than the light which they throw on the conditions prevailing even in normal times over considerable regions.[2]

The image of "the man standing permanently up to the neck in water" so perfectly captured the dilemma of rural poverty that it has invariably been quoted in descriptions of this era. The 1920–21 Famine Relief Committee spoke more bluntly: "In the Western world, famine means something unusual—a most rare calamity. In semiarid North China, it is a state more or less chronic. Thus in certain districts, like those about Tingchow or Shuntefu in Chihli, famine is almost a permanent condition and times of the most intense suffering are different from normal only in degree."[3]

Chinese and Western reformers proposed a range of possible solutions or approaches to what most regarded as a rural crisis. Most respected among the Western reformers was John Lossing Buck, Professor of Agricultural Economics at the University of Nanking, and later dean of the agricultural school. His monumental, three-volume work, *Land Utilization in China*, was drawn from a survey of thousands of farms and farm families in twenty-two provinces conducted between 1929 and 1933.[4] Although his study amply documented the low yields, small farm holdings, and other aspects of rural poverty, Buck's attitude was positive. He admired the "efficiency" of resource use in the Chinese farming system. "It has been stated that the peoples who produce most efficiently will inherit the earth. China's rural economy is one of efficient use of the land in that the large consumption of vegetable products requires less land to support a given population." He believed in the value of family farming, and resisted ideas of collective or other large-scale agricultural organization. Instead, Buck advocated river conservancy, land reclamation, and forestry. He proposed technical improvements in agriculture, such as plant and animal breeding, crop improvement, and so forth. In particular, he suggested the creation of institutions such as agricultural schools, experimental stations, and rural banks.[5]

Under the influence of Western social science, Chinese reformers focused on the social and economic aspects of rural reform. Ding County in Hebei was the center of Y. C. James Yen's Chinese Mass Education Movement, and there Li Jinghan (Franklin C. H. Lee) conducted a survey of all aspects of village and farm life.[6] By the 1930s the Ding xian project included agricultural experimental stations, public health campaigns, and even the production of local plays to raise the cultural standard of the villages.[7] Another important rural reconstruction project was Liang Shuming's Zouping (Tsou-ping) project, which placed students in counties in southern Shandong Province.[8] Although Liang's approach was more traditional or "nativist" than James Yen's, he shared the assumption of the liberals that rural reconstruction had to go beyond the technological aspects of agriculture to address education and rural organization.[9]

These reformers did not regard the land tenure system and landlordism as the chief causes of peasant impoverishment or "immiseration." Speaking of China as a whole, Tawney wrote, "The question of land tenure is less important in China than that of credit. . . . Landlord and tenant are parties to a business contract, not members of a distant class based on privilege and subordination." This he found to be in great contrast to the conflicts that "kept European villages simmering for over a thousand years."[10] Likewise, "in Buck's opinion, the popularly perceived problem of farm tenancy was exaggerated." Although some practices of landlords were abusive, especially sharecropping, Buck felt that tenancy was far less of a problem than the lack of rural credit.[11] Consequently reformers emphasized the importance of establishing credit institutions and even cooperatives to reduce the burden of debt and the influence of traditional institutions such as pawnshops.

In contrast, a few social scientists, such as Chen Hansheng, saw the unequal distribution of wealth as the leading cause of rural poverty.[12] More importantly, the Communist movement stressed class relations as the fundamental cause of rural poverty and oppression. Although the Communist Party often moderated its line for tactical purposes, its worldview called for radical and ultimately revolutionary change. Mao Zedong and Liang Shuming met during the war and appeared to share a view of rural life that stressed the potential for change and growth from within, rejecting Western models.[13] But the fundamental, irreconcilable, difference between all the reformers and Mao was that the Communists could not accept the possibility of gradual change through rural cooperatives and the emphasis on village unity and cohesion. Instead, the realization of class conflicts was a precondition for any meaningful change.[14]

Mao Zedong first wrote about the importance of the peasantry in the revolutionary process from his home province in Hunan, central China. His "Report on and Investigation of the Peasant Movement in Hunan," written in March 1927, is recognized as the earliest expression of Mao's vision. In it, he defended the revolutionary potential of the peasantry. "The main targets of attack by the peasants are the local tyrants, the evil gentry and lawless landlords, but in passing they also hit out against patriarchal ideas and institutions, against the corrupt officials in the cities and against bad practices and customs in the rural areas. In force and momentum the attack is tempestuous; those who bow before it survive, and those who resist perish." He famously predicted, "In a very short time, in China's central, southern, and northern provinces, several hundred million peasants will rise like a mighty storm, like a hurricane, a force so swift and violent that no power, however, great will be able to hold it back."[15]

It took more than two decades for Mao's prescient words to achieve reality. In history and historiography the actual cause of Communist success will always be a matter for debate and conjecture. Whether it was the Japanese invasion and occupation of northern and eastern China that mobilized the peasantry to rise up against landlords and other authorities, or whether it was the failure of the Guomindang to address adequately the poverty of the countryside will always remain a central issue of twentieth-century history. The Chinese Communist Party's own view is that it succeeded because it understood that suffering of the rural masses was caused by the unfair structure of landlordism coupled with foreign imperialism. But by the 1930s and 1940s, no matter where one stood on the political spectrum, there was hardly anyone—Chinese or foreigner, liberal or Marxist, Nationalist or Communist, northerner or southerner—who did not think that China was in an agricultural crisis, and that resolving it was not an urgent necessity.[16]

In Western scholarship in the late twentieth century, the radical "distributionist" approach found much support. Philip Huang's *The Peasant Economy and Social Change in North China* adopted an analytical framework that emphasized class differentiation through a process of "involution" and "semi-proletarianization," caused by declining returns to farm labor and the consequent necessity to engage in handicrafts and wage labor, which he termed "dual crutches." Recognizing that landlordism was not so important in North China, he cast the peasant as an oppressed wage-earner rather than a victimized tenant.[17] By contrast, Ramon Myers in *The Chinese Peasant Economy: Agricultural Development in Hopei and Shantung, 1890–1937,* found that "the fundamental problems of agriculture had nothing to do with rural socioeconomic relations," and that Chinese agriculture was fundamentally sound and only in need of technological improvements. "North China's food supply problem was never critical," except in war and natural disasters, which were setbacks from which the economy quickly recovered.[18]

In recent decades, others have gone even further to question whether there was an agricultural crisis at all. They hold a strikingly positive view of the economy of the Republican period, noting the considerable advances in transportation, industry, banking, and even agriculture.[19] China, far from being a "land of famine," was a nation where commercialized agriculture and rural industry produced significant gains in per capita income.[20] Since the economic reforms of the 1980s, some Chinese scholars too have reassessed the 1930s. In North China, they see increasing prosperity experienced by those localities that turned to cotton and other commercial opportunities, as well as the dynamism of treaty ports like Tianjin.[21] In the revisionist interpretations, the world depression in the 1930s set back these promising new trends, and the Japanese invasion of North China after 1937 completely reversed them. Economic growth was overwhelmed by the combined forces of warfare and revolutionary conflict.

The first half of the twentieth century remains the most difficult challenge for historians, with both facts and interpretation in contention. It was no more a time of coherent or unilinear development economically than it was politically. *If* warlordism, Japanese invasion, and civil war had not occurred, it is possible that significant economic changes *may* have overcome the seemingly chronic condition of famines. Instead, by 1949 the issues of hunger and rural poverty had acquired even greater urgency and political meaning than they ever had before.

Famine and Poverty

LAND AND AGRICULTURE

By the 1930s relatively accurate data confirm the picture of poverty, if not "most intense suffering" in Hebei, and in North China generally. Tables 3.6 and 3.7 and the discussion in Chapter 3 summarize available data about population, landholdings, cropping patterns, and crop yields. Population density had increased since the early eighteenth century, and average family landholdings, always low, were barely at levels needed to provide self-sufficiency—considered by Buck to be 25 mu per household. By the 1930s the average land per household ranged from about 20–25 mu, or possibly a bit more. If each household had an average of five to six persons, the average per capita holding was about 4 mu.[22] In Wei County it was under 5 mu.[23] In Ba County in Shuntian Prefecture, 6 mu per person was the norm, better than average, but this was still regarded as insufficient.[24]

The productivity of the land in Zhili as measured by yields of grain does not seem to have been any better in the 1930s than it had been in the early Qing and may have deteriorated. Less amenable than rice to increasing labor inputs, the dry-land grains of the north grown on poor soil did not yield more than the levels of earlier centuries.[25] Irrigation in the form of wells or canals would have increased yields substantially, but they were not widely used. In the 1930s, only 7 percent of land, mostly in the central and southern, or piedmont area, was irrigated.[26] Deterioration of the river system further inhibited productivity. The periodic overflows of the rivers did not enrich the soil and lead to abundant harvests the next year, as they had in the past. In some areas flooding only produced sand that covered the fertile loam so that the land was no longer suitable for grain crops. In one village in Wanping County, near the Yongding River and about 25 miles from Beijing, the flood of 1892 had left a layer of white sand over the loam. Afterward, the farmers planted peanuts and trees instead of grain crops. According to sociologist Sidney Gamble, "While one would ordinarily see an almost endless sea of grain when approaching other North China villages, the area around [this village] showed nothing but trees. . . . Peanuts, which do well in sandy soil, were one of the main annual crops." Of 12,700 mu of land in this village, 7,700 mu was considered to be poor grade, while only 2,000 mu were good and 3,000 were rated average.[27]

The increased planting of corn and sweet potatoes, both New World crops, greatly helped to counteract these negative trends and to sustain a larger population on poor soil. In the 1930s the percentage of land in Hebei devoted to corn was 14 percent, ranging from 3 percent in the southern section to as much as 49 percent in parts of Shuntian. (See Table 3.6 in Chapter 3.) Corn and sweet potatoes were usually grown for self-consumption and not for the market. At Ding xian, for example, families consumed 430–465 catties of sweet potatoes per person, even more than millet, the most important grain. Gamble found that the amounts of millet, sweet potatoes, other grains, and vegetables did not vary much by the income of the household.[28] At Ba xian, the crops and diet were more varied than Ding xian's. Still, corn constituted about 45 percent of the agricultural output and family diet; wheat was 13 percent, and millet 10 percent.[29] In this county, the yields of grains had declined due to lack of seed improvement; only corn and cotton seemed to be gaining.[30] The planting of commercial crops—particularly cotton, but also fruits and peanuts—increased the income of farming households but also decreased the acreage that could be devoted to grain crops.

FAMILY INCOME AND NUTRITIONAL STANDARDS

Surveys of the 1920s and 1930s measured the standard of living for farm families by estimating family income, rather than landholdings. Attempts at quantification varied, but all supported the widely held impression of the marginal standard of living of most rural households. Surveys by J. B. Tayler of Yenching University, followed by those of the CIFRC, showed that more than four-fifths of families in North China villages they studied (in Zhili and Shandong) had annual incomes below the poverty line, which they set generously at 150 yuan. A total of 62.2 percent of the families had incomes of less than 50 yuan (representing value of crops raised as well as cash income from village industry).[31] A national government survey of 1935 found that rural families in Hebei earned 124 yuan a year on average.[32] At Ding County, of the 400 families in an experimental district, average total family income was 347.30 yuan a year, high by provincial standards, but the value of their own labor was included in the calculation.[33] Owner families had the larger incomes, part owners a lesser amount, and tenant families the least. Of thirty-four families *not* in the experimental district, the average annual family income from all sources was 226–460 yuan, about 20 percent of which came from profit from home industries such as weaving or food preparation. The proportion of income spent on food decreased as the income increased, from 65.5 percent to 54 percent.[34] On the whole, Ding xian families were better off than other rural families and Beijing families.

Beijing in the Republican period had a large population of poor people; about 12 percent of Beijing's population—or 97,000 people—were classified as "poor" or "very poor." Gamble and John Burgess found that among those classified as poor, 93 yuan a year was needed for a family of four. Of a small sample of poor Chinese and Manchu families, the median income ranged from 90 to 109 yuan a year; most of the Chinese families falling as low as 50–70 yuan a year could survive; for Manchus 90 yuan seemed to be the minimum required. These poor families spent as much as 90 percent of their income on food, which generally consisted of two meals a day of cornbread and turnips.[35] In a 1926 survey of 283 Chinese families in Beijing, families spent from 65 to 20 percent of their monthly income on food, with the poorest spending the greater proportion on food, as expected.[36] In other studies of Beijing and Shanghai families, the range was 87 to 42 percent of the family budget. In a study of Beijing by L. K. Tao, the proportion spent on food was found to be 71.2 percent.[37]

The amount of grain consumed by Beijing families also varied according to their incomes, but only up to a certain point, after which a greater portion of their food budgets would be spent on vegetables, meats, and condiments. On average working-class families consumed 1.2 catties (1.6 lbs) of grain per person per day, although they aimed at 1.5 catties a day. Although needs varied according to occupation, gender, and age, such a diet was just about at the subsistence level. Field workers in the CIFRC estimated that laborers required 1.5–2 catties of grain per day. Buck estimated that in the rural population of Zhili, there was only 1 catty of grain per adult male equivalent, or 1.1 catties per person, and this is consistent with what was said about Ba County.[38]

When household income was insufficient or barely sufficient, indebtedness was commonplace and greatly increased the family's vulnerability. For Gamble, Buck, and Tawney alike, the single greatest economic problem for peasants was the crushing weight of debt they assumed. In Ding County between 1929 and 1933, the number of farm households that took out loans in each year doubled to 58 percent. The interest rate varied considerably by location, but in Hebei in general the annual rate of interest was 29 percent. In other parts of North China it was much higher: 46

percent in Shanxi, and 51 percent in Shaanxi.[39] In Hebei in 1933, 51 percent of households had cash debts and 33 percent owed grain.[40] Indebtedness was caused in great measure by the increasing number and levels of taxes imposed by the provincial government eager for new revenue.[41]

DEMOGRAPHIC CRISIS?

Life expectancy and infant and childhood mortality are also critical measures of the standard of living. In the first half of the twentieth century life expectancy was very low, and infant and childhood mortality very high. In his investigation of farm families, Buck and his associates found that life expectancy for males and females at the time of birth was only about 35 years.[42] Although it was the most comprehensive and scholarly survey of rural conditions ever attempted in China, the Buck study has been criticized for an unrepresentative sampling technique that may have been biased toward politically stable and wealthier localities. Taking these factors into account, demographers Barclay and Coale have reconstructed the data and concluded that life expectancy was even lower than what Buck had estimated: overall life expectancies were lower than 25 years for both sexes in all of China. North China life expectancy was higher than that for South China: 29.4 years for males in North China and 26.5 for females.[43] In a recent study of population in Liaoning Province in the Qing period, life expectancy at birth was judged to be in the high 20s for women and in the low 30s for men, higher than the Barclay and Coale reconstruction, but not as high as the Buck study's estimate.[44]

High childhood and infant mortality rates were the major contributors to the low life expectancies. Less than 60 percent of those who were born alive survived to age 10. Infant mortality, estimated by Buck at 155 per thousand for North China (152 for males and 159 for females), and 156 for all China, was the largest factor.[45] Other studies "support the internal evidence that the rate of 156 was too low." Barclay and Coale's reconstruction concludes that there was "a very high level of infant mortality, in the general range of 300 deaths per thousand births."[46] In Ding xian, the infant mortality rate varied from 185 to 199.[47] The infant mortality rate is considered by demographers to be the most sensitive indicator of economic development.[48] Infectious disease, compounded by poor nutrition and sanitation, is the general cause of high infant and childhood mortality. The leading fatal diseases in China were smallpox, typhoid, dysentery, tuberculosis, and cholera.[49]

The practice of infanticide was also a major factor in the infant mortality rate. There is uncertainty about the extent of the practice, as well as its cause and significance. In a study based on data collected at famine refugee camps in Shandong in 1935, I concluded that the infant mortality rate among those born during a four-month period was at least as high as 265 per thousand, and perhaps as high as 410. The record of births at the camps showed 1,935 boy babies and 1,303 girl babies, producing an unnaturally high sex ratio of 151. Because these records were kept on a daily basis, and because there was a bonus food allowance for newborns, it is unlikely that the missing girls were due to underreporting, and far more likely that at least part of the missing had been the victims of female infanticide.[50] In other words, as many as one-third of all the girl babies may have been killed. Because these Shandong data were collected during a crisis, I assumed that both the high rate of infant mortality and the probable rate of female infanticide were outcomes of famine, but these rates, may have reflected a normal situation among Shandong's rural poor in the 1930s. After all, no registration was maintained in normal times, and the famine refugees were receiving far better treatment than those who remained at home. Of an estimated 2.3 million in need, only about 300,000 were sheltered by the government, leaving close to 2 million without official protection.[51] If there had been a registration of births and deaths among this unsheltered population, it might reveal even higher rates of infant and childhood mortality. But in either case, infanticide was motivated by desperate circumstances, as well as a decided preference for boys.

James Lee, Cameron Campbell, and Wang Feng argue that infanticide was not an act of desperation, but a method of fertility control. They have estimated that between one-fifth and one-quarter of all females in a village in Liaoning in the late Qing died from infanticide, and one-tenth of all female babies in the Qing imperial lineage may have been killed at birth.[52] In their view, the peasants acted not out of economic need, but from a desire to control the size and desired gender mix of their families. "Peasants used female infanticide to respond to short-term changes in economic conditions," they maintain. Infanticide was not a Malthusian "positive" check, but rather was used as a "preventative check" to control fertility after birth as "a form of post-natal abortion."[53] It "was a product of rational decision making embedded in a peculiar cultural attitude toward life."[54] "In consequence, the Chinese demographic behavior during the late imperial period exhibits a form of rationality that was in many ways proto modern."[55]

Infanticide may have been "rational" and voluntary, but it was practiced in situations of dearth and desperation more frequently than in situations of prosperity. Both contemporary observation and subsequent discussion have all concurred. In Hebei and Shandong, anecdotal as well as statistical evidence points to infanticide as both a "normal" practice and a response to famine or other crises. Likewise, "overpopulation," which Lee and colleagues regard as a "myth," was hardly an abstract concept, but a simple reality understood by the very poor: one more mouth to feed when there was not enough food to begin with left only bad choices. In his critique of the Lee's "revisionist" thesis, Arthur Wolf argues that the relatively low fertility of Chinese couples was not due to deliberate limitation but to a combination of "poor health, inadequate nutrition, heavy labor, and poverty-induced spousal separation."[56] There can be no greater indicators of poverty, disease, and hunger than high infant and childhood mortality, which prevailed in rural China until the late twentieth century.

Changes in the Economy

In the face of undeniable evidence of rural poverty, there were nevertheless signs of economic change. Developments—such as railroads, the expansion of cotton industry, the rise of Tianjin as the dominant regional center—altered the methods of production, trade, and consumption for North China. While many localities remained isolated and unaffected by these changes, others experienced greater opportunities to escape the cycle of poverty.

RAILROADS

Railroads were the single most important change to the economy of North China. They were more concentrated in the north than in any other region of China and made the biggest impact there. Through the new rail lines, Beijing and Tianjin and their hinterlands were connected to the northeast, the northwest, central China, and Shanghai. The first to be constructed was the Peking-Hankow (Beijing-Hankou) Railway, completed in 1906. Running along the north-south spine of Zhili Province, it connected Beijing with Shijiazhuang, Henan cities, and then down south to the Hankou, the major port on the central Yangzi River. (See Map 10.1 in Chapter 10.) For the Zhili-Hebei region in the twentieth century, the railroad was as important in linking north and south as the Grand Canal had been during the Ming and Qing. It had an even greater impact on the interior of the province than sea transport at Tianjin. In the Qing, the key land transport routes in North China had been government roads that centered on Beijing, and the key water route, the Grand Canal, also had Beijing as its eventual destination. When the rivers running from west to east were dredged and navigable, Baoding was linked to Tianjin, which in turn was linked to Beijing. In the twentieth century, however, the railway made Baoding less important as a trade center while elevating Shijiazhuang and Handan as key trade centers. Grains, especially wheat, sorghum, and millet, from the southern Zhili prefectures could be exported southward. Cotton growing and cotton handicrafts became much more widespread in the twentieth century because of the easy access to rail transport. Other agricultural products such as tobacco, peanuts, sesame, and fruits of many varieties—pears, apples, figs—now had a viable market both outside the region and within it.[57]

To the northeast the key route was the Peking-Mukden (Beijing-Shenyang) Railway. Originating in 1881 as the first actual rail line in North China, a six-mile route from the Kaiping mines at Tangshan to the Beitang River, this line was extended in 1889 south to Tianjin, and later north to Shanhaiguan and Liaoning, and still later as far as Vladivostock.[58] Completed by 1907, it was one of the important rail lines that supported the industrial development of Manchuria. The Tianjin-Shanhaiguan segment, as well as the other three lines in this region, was operated by the Chinese government—in contrast to the heavily foreign-invested lines in Manchuria and elsewhere in China. This connection rendered Tianjin an even more important treaty port, greatly strengthening the commercial links that previously depended on sea transport.

The Tientsin-Pukow (Tianjin-Pukou) Railway, completed in 1912, also enhanced Tianjin's economic importance, playing a major role in transport to the south by providing a reliable alternative both to the Grand Canal and to sea transport. It linked Tianjin to Shanghai via Pukou just to the west of Shanghai, where goods could be transshipped on the Shanghai-Nanjing rail line. Shanghai could now be reached in two days instead of twenty-five on the Grand Canal route.[59]

To the northwest, the Peking-Kalgan (Beijing-Zhangjiakou) line was constructed by 1909, linking Beijing by rail to the important trade centers beyond the Great Wall in northern Shanxi and present-day Inner Mongolia. Later the line was extended to Suiyuan and was known as the Peking-Suiyuan line. By 1923, the line was extended further to Baotou. The first and most important link to Kalgan at the Great Wall, the principal gate to trade with Central Asia, the railway greatly facilitated commerce. Previously, the trip from Beijing to Zhangjiakou by mules or camels took one to two months; now, it took eight to nine hours.[60] In general railroads greatly reduced transport costs and made the greatest difference in the north and northwest where water transport was scarce. The cost per ton/mile was 0.56 yuan by donkey, for example, or 0.48 yuan by mule, as compared with 0.09 by rail or 0.08 by steamboat.[61]

COTTON

The expansion of cotton cultivation southward along the Peking-Hankow railway from Baoding affected principally the prefectures of Guangping, Shunde, Zhaozhou, Zhengding, and Baoding that were on the plains and in the piedmont area. Cotton cultivation was stimulated by the introduction of cotton-spinning factories that required greater supplies of cotton. According to the best estimates, cotton output between 1900 and 1936 expanded three to five times. Its portion of the total cultivated acreage in Hebei may have risen from about 2–3 percent to as much as 10 percent in this period (and 6 percent in Shandong). In certain counties the figure was as high as 30 percent.[62] The sandy soil of many localities in Hebei was well suited for cotton, although irrigation was a major asset in raising yields.[63] In all, in 1934 Hebei cotton acreage represented about 17 percent of the total acreage in China and about 25 percent of the output.[64] Although it provided a good income for Hebei farmers, its development was uneven, and cotton yields were hindered by man-made and natural disasters in the 1930s.[65]

Cotton cultivation was most concentrated in the Lower Yangzi region, especially in Jiangsu Province. The first Chinese modern cotton mills were established in Shanghai in the 1890s after years of bureaucratic difficulty and delay. Machine spinning required longer fibers and greater tensile strength than Chinese cotton could provide; so in fact about one-third of the factory demand for raw cotton was fulfilled by imports from the United States and India.[66] Some counties in Hebei, particularly in the southern part, began to plant Western grades of cotton with success.[67] The shorter-staple "native" cotton was used for spinning coarser cottons, usually in handicraft or domestic production.[68] Most of the cotton grown in Hebei Province was either retained for domestic spinning, or was exported through Tianjin. These coarser Chinese cottons were used overseas for padding, pharmaceutical cotton, gunpowder, and mixing with other fibers.[69]

The introduction of handloom weaving at Gaoyang around 1906 represented an import-substitution initiative by the Zhili provincial government and local chambers of commerce. Importing iron looms and machine-spun yarn, local entrepreneurs devised a putting-out system that was remarkably successful. The Gaoyang cotton cloth was collected, dyed, and processed by factories and then marketed within Hebei and also localities toward the northwest and northeast, such as Zhangjiakou and Harbin.[70] This enterprise built on the tradition of domestic weaving, but it developed its designs for the modern marketplace and vastly expanded the scale of output. Neighboring localities like Baoding and Renqiu also participated, but Gaoyang was the distribution center for the region; there were 157 cloth dealers based there. Although most of the farmers worked within the putting-out framework, some had sufficient capital to weave cloth "on their own account."[71] The types of cloth woven at Gaoyang included varieties of drills, calicoes, pongees, muslins, poplins, and so forth. They reached markets in more than twenty provinces, plus Outer Mongolia and even Southeast Asia.[72] Production reached its height between 1917 and 1919, declining after 1920 due to civil warfare.[73] After a "temporary retrenchment" that lasted until 1925, there was a second boom, lasting until 1929. In the early 1930s there was a decline due partly to internal warfare but also to the world depression.[74]

Gaoyang was the showcase example. It benefited from proximity to the Peking-Hankow railway, as well as from its official designation as a hand-weaving district. A similar experiment at Baodi, located north of Tianjin, in 1934 had four cotton mills, ten representatives of cotton textile firms, and numerous other cotton merchants in residence who marketed its cloth to Zhangjiakou, Suiyuan, Shaanxi, Ningxia, Gansu, and other locations in the northwest, but its production and quality had declined since 1923.[75]

TIANJIN

The transformation of Tianjin into a major commercial and industrial center for all of North China was another key development. In the early and mid-Qing periods, Tianjin served as the first destination and key transfer point of the Grand Canal as well as a sea port receiving and sending goods to Liaodong and to Shanghai and beyond. As the major treaty port and key entrepôt in North China, Tianjin's foreign trade developed rapidly, especially between 1903 and 1923, when the total volume of imports and exports grew from 1.5 million U.S. dollars to 12.5 million.[76] After 1905, Tianjin also became a manufacturing center, with both Chinese and foreign-owned companies. Cotton-spinning mills, flour mills, carpets, and matches were particularly important businesses. Although the capitalization and management of these new industries suffered from inexperience and unfavorable political conditions, Tianjin outstripped all other North China cities, including Beijing, in economic importance.[77]

The railroads, more than anything else, accounted for Tianjin's dominant position in the region. As the rivers had ceased effectively to connect Tianjin to its Zhili-Hebei hinterland, the various rail lines after 1905 drew Tianjin closer to the interior. In 1912, 53 percent of the value of goods between Tianjin and the hinterland was carried by rail and 44 percent by rivers; by 1921, more than 70 percent was carried by rail.[78] The hinterland included not just the adjacent regions of Zhili, but beyond Zhili to Shanxi and the northwest, to Mukden and the northeast, and south to Shanghai and Hankow. As Linda Grove has pointed out, the trading networks reached the frontier areas before they included the immediate hinterland. In the early treaty port days, Tianjin served as a transshipment point for goods from outside the region, and only later did it serve as the market for goods produced within North China itself.[79] Liu Haiyan has argued that railroads not only benefited the hinterland but also brought the countryside closer to the cities, especially Tianjin.[80]

As the population of Tianjin grew, it became a major market for the agricultural and handicraft products of the interior, as well as a labor market for both men and women from the countryside. Now the fruits, nuts, and vegetables from the interior could be conveniently and cheaply shipped to Tianjin, not waiting for roads to dry up or rivers to become passable. In the 1860s the English botanist Robert Fortune observed, "Pears are perhaps the most abundant amongst all the autumnal fruits in Peking. They are exposed for sale in every direction, in shops, in stalls, on the pavement, as well as in the basket of the hawker. . . . Curiously enough, this fruit, excellent though it is, is as yet unknown at Tientsin, a place only about 70 miles distant."[81] In the 1920s and 1930s it was unimaginable that one could buy something in Beijing that could not also be purchased in Tianjin. Similarly one can recall the description of Yongqing County in the mid-Qing: although less than 60 miles from Tianjin, there had been virtually no commerce between the two, and all necessities had been locally supplied. In the twentieth century, however, even the poor districts near Beijing or Tianjin benefited from trade.

WHEAT FLOUR

Tianjin became the starting point for an important change in the North China eating habits: the use of factory-milled flour for the noodles, steamed breads, dumplings, and other favorite foods of northerners. Flour mills were the second most important modern factories in China, after cotton mills. Introduced by the Japanese in 1896, they spread rapidly in Shanghai, Hankou, Tianjin, Wuxi, and Jinan, and most particularly in Manchuria, where so much grain was produced.[82] At Tianjin there were four main factories, one jointly owned with a Japanese company, one Western, and two Chinese-owned, and these were later joined by three others by 1930.[83] The wheat for the mills came in part from the United States and elsewhere, as it was often cheaper to import the wheat than to obtain it from distant places within China. Indeed, the demand for flour could not be met by China's flour mills, and wheat imports included processed flour as well as the raw grain. Although the amounts fluctuated a great deal, depending on domestic and foreign conditions, by the 1920s, the totals were substantial. For the year 1928 at Tianjin, a total of 21.7 million bales of wheat were "consumed": 32.9 percent was Western flour; 46.7 percent was Shanghai flour; 4.1 percent from other locations, and only 16.2 percent was locally milled.[84] Wheat flour also became more important to Beijing's working families. According to one study, for all but the poorest and the richest, wheat was the major food grain. The poor still depended on millet grain, or millet or corn flour. For the well-to-do families that earned 200 yuan a month, rice became a more important staple.[85]

The taste for wheat flour spread rapidly to the interior. In Wei County in Guangping Prefecture, the local history noted, "In the old days people ate millet and beans, and only the upper or middle class people ate wheat; since the Republican period, there have been shifts in clothes styles and diet, and those who eat wheat have gradually increased."[86] In Qinghe County, also in Guangping, wheat was eaten only by the rich or by merchants. Its principal form was *mantou* or *baozi*, but it was also made into noodles.[87] Manufacturing *mantou*, known colloquially as *momo*, became a local specialty.

> For several hundred li in every direction, there are Qinghe people producing *mantou*. The local people are particularly fond of boiled dumplings, and eat them on New Years or on other holidays. At the periodic markets to the southwest, those who like boiled dumplings and fried *baozi* are numerous. Along the Grand Canal, spiral biscuits, *xuanbing*, are very popular, and in the winter people give them as gifts to relatives and friends. . . . In the spring people in Han family village make toy people, swallows, or tigers out of flour and sell them at the temple fairs for folks to give to children. Some people use flour to make gifts; a hundred jin makes quite a nice gift.[88]

GRAIN IMPORTS

The growing preference for wheat flour, particularly in the cities, was blamed by some for the increase in grain imports into China in the 1930s.[89] By the mid-1930s, rice imports amounted to 2.6 percent of Chinese rice output, and wheat imports about 5.5 percent of Chinese output. The average annual wheat imports in 1929–33 was double the average for the previous five-year period. Wheat imports were only 2,000 piculs in 1913; they were 17.7 million piculs in 1933.[90] Although these proportions may not seem large now, they appeared alarming at the time. Leading economists like C. C. Chang discussed "China's Food Supply Problem," while government officials like Chen Kung-po, then minister of industry, wrote about "Self-Sufficiency in Food Supply."[91] They feared that grain imports were the start of a trend that could only worsen.[92] For them China's increasing dependence on grain imports was prima facie evidence of the failure of Chinese agriculture, and a manifestation of the rural crisis. The four northern provinces of Shanxi, Hebei, Shandong, and Henan, for example, were about 20 percent deficient in grain, and this was reflected in the imports of grain at Tianjin.[93]

Some foreign analysts, however, questioned whether the increase in imports reflected a fundamental inadequacy of the Chinese agricultural system. One argued for the comparative advantage of trade, saying, "The fundamental and inclusive reason for China's imports of food stuffs is that it is more profitable to produce other commodities and buy the imports." Ironically, he concluded, "China is too poor a country to attempt a policy of self-sufficiency."[94] Another foreign observer rebutted this view, citing short-term and temporary reasons for the recent rise in imports: the world surplus of grain caused grain prices to fall, and some "dumping" onto the Chinese market had occurred. In addition, the Yangzi flood created a demand for relief supplies. Furthermore, the world depression of the 1930s had ruined the market for some Chinese agricultural products such as raw silk.[95] Another agreed that the immediate world market conditions were principally responsible for the grain imports, but he saw the new urban demand as a second reason. Harvest failures within China, such as the famine in the northwest, by contrast, were less of a factor in the level of grain imports than some had thought.[96]

Grain imports in the 1920s and 1930s did not constitute a fundamental change in the economic system, but the debate about them shifted the thinking about food supply problem, just slightly, beyond the realm of agriculture itself. The dominant Chinese view, however, remained that food and grain deficits were a domestic agricultural problem, and grain self-sufficiency was the first sign of a strong economy.

MIGRATION

Another fundamental change in economic life, perhaps not quite structural, was the growth in migration to Manchuria, starting with the North China famine of 1870s and steadily increasing through the Republican period. The introduction of rail travel in North China greatly facilitated the migration of workers from the western part of Shandong and the adjacent parts of Hebei. Although sea transport was still used by most Shandong migrants, some used rail travel to get to a port such as Jinan or Qingdao, from which they could transfer to a boat. Others took trains directly to Manchuria from Jinan, Tianjin, and onward to Liaoning. Between the 1890s and 1920s, the migrants from Shandong peninsula and those from Hebei and western Shandong were about the same each year, but the numbers from the latter area were more variable and began to increase steadily and sharply peaked between 1927–31.[97] The totals reached 0.5–1 million men a year. This meant that after 1927 as many as four to nineteen out of each thousand in the population left for Manchuria each year.[98]

Each time there was a major disaster, large numbers of people, especially men, fled their homes. In a 1930s survey of migrants from Shandong, 27.3 percent of the respondents named disasters—including banditry and warfare as well as natural disasters—as their reason for migration, while 69 percent gave economic reasons, including too little land, debts, homelessness, and so forth. Thus, large-scale disasters alone cannot account for the scale of migration throughout this period.[99] Migrants sought opportunities for work such as building railways, working in mines and factories, as well as agricultural jobs, including the important soybean industry.[100] Migration to Manchuria was part of a family survival strategy. Most of the time, the family stayed at home, while a young son might go off to work for a few years.[101] Two-thirds of migrants eventually returned home. In some years the numbers returning were greater than the numbers leaving. One study found that most workers could send home between 20–50 yuan per year, and the average yearly remittance was 40 yuan. For rural families in Hebei, whose income averaged 124 yuan a year (88 yuan in Shandong), this was a substantial additional income.[102] Since most migrants came from those counties near the rail lines, one can surmise that the benefits of remittances were concentrated in those counties, as exhibited in the case of Jing County discussed below.

Local Experiences

The introduction of railways, the growth of Tianjin, and the spread of cotton cultivation and weaving, as well as other commercial crops and handicrafts, altered the economic situation for many localities in Hebei. Favorable location near Beijing or Tianjin, or on the rail lines, particularly the Peking-Hankow line, created new economic opportunities for rural districts. Favorable location did not always effect a radical transformation, but it at least alleviated the poverty of many districts. Local gazetteers and other sources of the 1930s give voice to a range of local experiences. Because of the new awareness of social surveys, and perhaps because of government directive, almost every county produced a new edition of its local history in the 1930s, if not in the

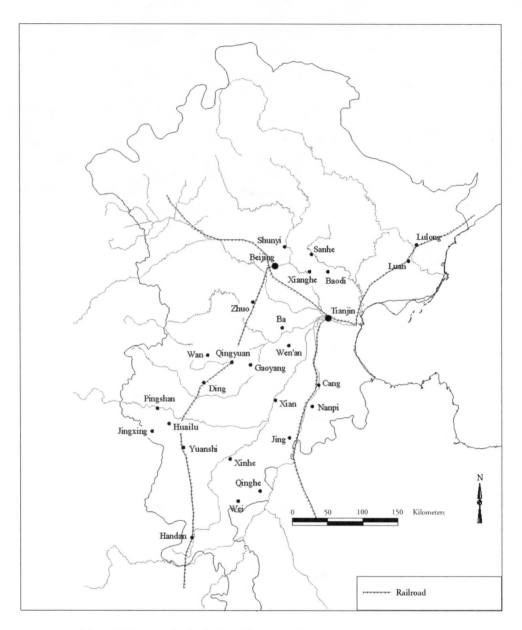

MAP 11.1. Selected Hebei counties in the Republican period

1920s. Compared with earlier editions, they devoted greater attention to issues of agricultural productivity and rural poverty, and they often provided valuable social and economic detail. Although statistics were occasionally provided, these gazetteers were more notable for their observation of trends. Quite noticeable are the number of times the phrase "in recent years" appears in the descriptions, often contrasted with conditions "in the past," as cited in Chapter 3.

IN THE SOUTH, ALONG THE FUYANG RIVER

Handan is an excellent example of a county that prospered from the structural changes to the economy. (See Map 11.1 for locations of counties discussed in this section.) Located in Guangping Prefecture, Handan city was a major stop on the Peking-Hankow rail line, but it also benefited from its location on the Fuyang River, which offered direct transport by junk to Tianjin. The river helped to irrigate the nearby fields, and agriculture in the district prospered. The local leaders subsidized the digging of wells for those farmers whose land could not be irrigated; they also promoted tree planting. Because farming was profitable, some large owners cultivated a thousand mu each with the help of laborers. Cotton was grown here, but also grains, fruits, and nuts. In their spare time, some farmers found work in clay mining, a lucrative local industry.

Handan was a local collection point for agricultural and mineral products from surrounding districts. Grains, coal, fruits, especially peaches, nuts, pepper, melon seeds, and almond kernels were among the well-known commodities. Persimmon cakes, dried persimmons strung together, were a famous product of neighboring Henan. Brought to Handan by mules, they were then transshipped by rail to Beijing, Zhengding, and Baoding. Another product was straw braid produced at Daming, Nanle, and other localities. Although Nanle was 180 li distant from Handan city, transshipping via the railroad vastly expanded the market for this local handicraft. The Fuyang River provided direct water route to Tianjin, but it took fifteen days.

The people who lived near the city enjoyed a better standard of living than the rural folk. Well-to-do city residents usually consumed wheat flour, while the rural population still depended on millet, maize, sorghum, and beans. Villagers often sought side jobs either in farm work or handicrafts, or in mining. A local carpenter could earn 50 qian a day plus food. This was about the amount needed to live in the countryside, while the minimum cost of living for urban folks was about 70 qian a day.[103]

Downstream on the Fuyang River, Xinhe County (in Jizhou) was another humble district that experienced significant change in the 1920s because of its favorable location on both water and rail routes. In 1913, it was a rather impoverished locality: city walls were crumbling; markets and streets were deserted; there were few shops. "The district is very poor; very few places are this poor." Cotton was an important crop, mostly sold to foreign companies. There was an agricultural experiment station to help promote this crop. Native cloth was woven and sold to Shanxi and Zhangjiakou shops. Peanuts, the second most important crop, were sold to Tianjin. The soil was sandy. Fruit trees were planted, but their fruit was not good, and half were cut down.[104] Grain commerce had been small scale, as was typical. "Small peasants sell grain at the local periodic markets. Grain shipments (to other areas) are made only by grain merchants who sell the grain to cities and market towns."[105]

But "in recent years," according to the 1928 gazetteer, commerce had flourished. "Merchants come from Zhangjiakou, Baoding and Tianjin. The biggest exports are peanuts, followed by fruit products and cotton. All are shipped by the Fuyang River to Tianjin. Imports are foreign goods,

shipped by railroad, roads, or water."[106] Yet these changes did not protect against natural disasters; when floods occurred, the villages became isolated.[107] Xinhe was seriously affected both in
the 1917 flood and the 1920 drought. Still, the improvements in trade were reflected in a higher
standard of diet. People ate wheat for their noon meal, but when the price of wheat was high,
they substituted it with beans and legumes. In bad years, they ate sweet potatoes. They also
smoked tobacco and opium![108]

ALONG THE NAN YUNHE AND ZIYA RIVER

In the counties along the southern Grand Canal, structural changes were experienced differently.
In Qinghe County (Guangping Prefecture), the land was quite poor and agriculture did not flourish. Cotton had just been introduced, but it required better soil than this district possessed. There
were no large landlords with more than 200 mu of land, and landlords found that they had to pay
increasingly high wages to laborers, 40 yuan (a year[?]). "In recent years" the population pressure
on the land had led to insufficiency and forced many to seek employment elsewhere, particularly
because the cost of living had risen.[109] Still, the local *mantou* industry was successful, facilitated by
convenient transportation, and must have been an important sideline activity.

Jing County (or Jingzhou) in Hejian Prefecture was an agriculturally poor district that prospered after railroad and steamship; its workers could get employment elsewhere. It was conveniently located on the section of the southern Grand Canal where the Tianjin-Pukou railway paralleled the canal. "In the past" the diet had been a typical combination of millet and corn. Wheat
noodles, meat, and tea were all rare luxuries. But by the 1930s, a marked change had occurred.
Most of the changes benefited the wealthier locals, but even the poor experienced some improvements, however modest, such as the use of boiled rather than unboiled water.

> *Today, it is different.* All farming families, regardless of whether it is a good or bad harvest, have one
> meal a day of millet, corn bread [*wotou*], and pickled vegetables. And at lunch they must have hot
> dishes including some meat. For drinks, they must have tea. There are two or three teahouses in
> each village. And because those who drink wine are gradually increasing, the teahouses also serve
> wine. Children buy snacks to eat. When the workers go out to the fields, they must take boiled wa-
> ter with them [*leng kai shui*]; no one drinks unboiled water [*sheng shui*]. The extravagant habits
> of the rich are increasing daily. *The difference between old and new customs is immense.*[110]

This improvement in the standard of living could not be attributed to agricultural development, but rather to favorable location that allowed local men to find work elsewhere or to consider some innovations in farming or enterprise. The Jing xian gazetteer describes the county as
lacking any famous mountains or rivers, and therefore having few natural resources or big markets
or industry. It was located on a desolate plain, and the people had very old-fashioned views about
agriculture. "In the past," they looked only to the rainfall for a good harvest and did not consider
the advantages of digging wells and using irrigation. The people knew only about minding their
own business and remained very poor and hardworking. Aside from working hard, they had no
other method of preparing for drought or waterlogging. "However, since the establishment of the
Republic, rail and steamship transportation has become convenient, and the number of people
who go elsewhere to seek their living is increasing daily. . . . Inside the city there is a post-office,
and we can see that the income coming in each year is not less than 100,000 yuan. So now people
can actually think of irrigation and industry, and the whole district benefits."[111]

Jing County was on the boundary with Dezhou County in Shandong, close to the Grand

Canal and also to the Tianjin-Pukou rail line to the south. At Jinan, passengers could easily transfer to the Shandong rail line to various points on the peninsula. So the "elsewhere" mentioned in the gazetteer undoubtedly included destinations in Manchuria. In Jing and elsewhere this economic lifeline was reflected in the steadily rising grain prices, especially after the turn of the century.

Elsewhere along this section of the Grand Canal, changes in the standard of living could be observed. In Nanpi County, Tianjin Prefecture, the typical diet and frugal habits of earlier times were improved by certain extravagances that could be enjoyed even by the rural population: "In recent years, the expensive habits have gradually spread to the countryside. In the old days at weddings and funerals you used only 8–10 bowls of wine per table, but now it is much more. And there are other extravagances."[112] In Cang County (Tianjin Prefecture), class differences in diet were more pronounced. Although wheat accounted for about 40 percent of the agricultural output, less than 1 percent of the people ate wheat. Upper-class folks ate more wheat than rice because the cost of rice, which was not produced locally, was double that of wheat flour. In the towns as well as in the villages, there were people who made and sold wheat products like *mantou* on the street, but those below the middle class could not afford to buy them. Ordinary people ate mostly corn noodles, followed by millet and red sorghum noodles. In the winter sweet potatoes, as well as carrots, were important to the peasants. The rural people hardly ever had fish or meat.[113]

In nearby Xian County (Hejian Prefecture), which was on the Ziya River, there had been improvements since the late nineteenth century, but "recent" developments provided risks as well as opportunities. According to the old gazetteer, in former times the people were very poor. The land was inferior and without irrigation, and it was frequently subject to drought and waterlogging. When there was a bad harvest, people just sat around waiting for a handout, "*ao ao dai bu*," or else they fled in four directions. Those who were tenants borrowed millet from their landlords in the spring when they had no food. The landlord expected them to return the grain in the fall at the values of the spring and often left little of the harvest to the tenant, who had to keep quiet and just shed a tear. Many took their hoes and went into the city to find work. If the city was not prospering, they went even farther to seek work.

This situation, described in the old gazetteer, basically remained the same until the mid-Guangxu period, when railroads and factories were built, but there were also military disturbances. Farmers became soldiers or workers. Those who continued to farm the land discovered that after the fall harvest, their [net] income was less than in previous times. Whether the harvests were good or poor, the grain prices keep rising.[114] These last two statements appear to be contradictory. If grain prices kept rising, peasants should have experienced a benefit if they sold any part of their crop on the market. But if they were basically subsistence farmers, or needed to buy part of their own grain from the market, then they would find their costs rising faster than their income.

NEAR BEIJING

Toward the north, the districts close to Beijing enjoyed a new prosperity that was not limited to urban residents. In Xianghe County (Shuntian), when the peasants came into town on a market day, they could indulge in food and drink before returning home. Describing their diet, the local history wrote:

> Millet, corn, and various beans are most important. Wheat flour and rice are luxuries and imported through Tianjin. Rice is eaten only at weddings, funerals and festivals. Vegetables are grown

locally. Formerly, fish, meat, chicken were all luxuries. Restaurant food was only for officials, merchants, etc. But *in recent years*, fish and meat have become plentiful, and filled the markets, and the restaurants hold many banquets so that this has become a practice. When the peasants come to town, they eat and get drunk before they go home.[115]

At nearby Shunyi County (also in Shuntian), just 25 miles north of Beijing, the signs of prosperity were visible to all and described in the local gazetteer. Shunyi residents were not solely dependent on local products for their food, clothing, or other aspects of daily life. "Since the land is near the capital, it is easy to make a living." The standard of living had risen with the tide of change in the region. This could be seen in changes in dress styles. Although local folks did not weave, they bought cloth from Shandong, Gaoyang, Xianghe, Baodi, and other nearby places. Since the turn of the century, people used Western goods (*yanghuo*) or "patriotic" cloth (*aiguo bu*, that is, Chinese cloth woven from machine-spun cotton), and they adopted bright colors and modern styles. Under missionary influence, education had been made widely available.[116]

Improvements in the diet included greater use of wheat and rice, as well as the use of soy sauce and oil.

> People here eat corn in great quantities. Millet, wheat, *gaoliang*, and potatoes are next most important. . . . People purchase rice from the south for leisurely occasions. In winter and spring when days are short, they eat two meals a day. During the fourth lunar month [*maiqiu*] when there is leisure time, [they eat] three or four meals. At breakfast they have *zhou*. At noon, they usually have noodles together with edible wild herbs [*yecai*] in the summer, or Japanese pickles [*wogua*], potatoes, or yams in the winter. In the summer, they have *shuifan* in the morning and evening, taking cooked rice and cooling it in cold water.

Banquets had become commonplace, but the author was disapproving, feeling that social competition had led to excesses that the local economy could not support.

> On holidays (dragon-boat, mid-autumn, or new years), or on big occasions such as weddings or funerals, people prepare feasts with wine and meat for family members and workers. But *in recent years*, the standard of living has gone up, and people value appearances. Whenever guests come, they prepare tea, cakes, dried meats, fresh fruit, wine from the south, chicken, fish, and all sorts of delicacies. Such a meal costs 20 yuan. People buy condiments such as soy sauce, vinegar, sesame oil, peppers, and other spices. But since local economy is not basically abundant, such refined taste in food means that once a bad harvest is encountered—floods, droughts, locust, hail, and military disturbances, and vagrancy occur repeatedly—there is no escape from worries.[117]

The basic facts about Shunyi's population and economy would not by themselves explain this apparent improvement in the standard of living. One of its villages, Shajing, was among those studied by the South Manchurian Railway Company between 1939 and 1943. Known as the Mantetsu surveys, these Japanese investigations have provided rich social and economic data for later historians and economists. Shajing shared many of the characteristics of rural poverty typical of Hebei. Each household held on average only 14 mu of land, and there were 5.6 persons in each household; this was below the standard for self-sufficiency. The soil was poor, yields were low, and the peasants could not remember any improvements for the past fifty years. This observation is confirmed by the local gazetteer, which also noted how peasants were conservative and clung to their old methods. Household division among sons made small holdings even smaller. The survey showed that most households were either deficient in food crops, or had many debts, or both.[118]

In the face of this, how could the improvements in "lifestyle" described in the local gazetteer, be accounted for, and why had the population expanded in the recent decades? Proximity to

Beijing and location on a rail line must have been key factors. Since it was said that there were no suitable sideline occupations, locals found jobs elsewhere, most likely in Beijing, either as long- or short-term laborers. These jobs included "making incense sticks, carving buffalo horns, baking rice cakes, watching crops in other villages, selling old clothes, making rice jelly, candy, and noodles, manufacturing straw mats, hauling goods by cart, and serving as clerks in stores." Some daughters were sent to work as servants in other households.[119] In a small sample of seventeen household budgets, nonfarm income represented 22.5 percent of the average household's total income.[120]

FROM TIANJIN TO BAODING

Traveling from Tianjin westward toward Baoding and beyond, one would first traverse the constantly flooded areas in the region where the several rivers came together. At Ba County, as described above, the population-to-land ratio had become noticeably difficult. In the 1930s the locality was still not particularly prosperous, and 80–90 percent of the economy was dependent on agriculture, which had not experienced any improvements. Corn and cotton had been successfully introduced, but the yield of other grains had declined. Still, the county's standard of living was clearly more secure than elsewhere.

> Farmers eat three meals a day. They eat *zhou*, bread, and vegetables. But during the busy season while working outdoors they might eat cold food in the morning and at noon and drink cold water. . . . The merchants and workers eat three meals a day of wheat, noodles, wine, etc. Corn, wheat, millet, soybeans and mung beans are the principal foods. Barley, buckwheat, *panicum* millet [*moshu*], and red beans are the next most important. The use of rice varies. To the east of the [county] city the ground is depressed [*wadi*]. Whenever it is waterlogged, before the water drains away, much rice is grown here, and its quality and flavor are very fine. Sweet potatoes are grown in great quantity and are eaten in the fall and winter. . . . In the city and towns there are tea houses and restaurants where merchants and travelers can eat and drink.[121]

Wen'an (Shuntian) presented a different case entirely. At the confluence of the Daqing and Ziya rivers, Wen'an was the location of the critical sections of the Thousand-Li Dike. The agricultural situation of the Wen'an *wa*, the Wen'an swamp, had worsened in the nineteenth century because water did not easily drain out. There were only two or three years out of every ten when there was a good harvest. Yet by the 1920s, the district had overcome its disadvantage by emphasizing nonagricultural sources of income. As the gazetteer stated, "Traditionally there was no enterprise. But when the Westerners came in the Daoguang and Xianfeng periods, people began to see the importance of manufacture, and that it could be done together with agriculture."

There were three types of new enterprise: weaving cloth, braiding reed mats, and fishing. Traditional cotton weaving had languished when Western cottons were imported, but when the price of these cottons soared after the 1890s, local weaving was revived and again became a good source of income. The braiding of mats was an industry for which Wen'an was well known and was another important source of income. These mats were marketed widely to the northeast by Shandong merchants, many of whom resided in Wen'an. Locals also made screens and nets out of the same kind of reeds, *wei* or *luwei*, that could be harvested from both the Xi dian and Dong dian, the western and eastern lakes. These reeds, especially those from the Xi dian, were prized for being thin, flexible, and white. The peasants who harvested the reeds also collected arrowroot and water chestnuts, which also fetched a good price. (This domestic industry was an extension of the activities of neighboring Yongqing County.)

The fishing industry in Wen'an was made possible by the constant flooding of the swamp, which dated from the mid-nineteenth century. At first the local residents did not know how to develop the business, but at the end of the century, with the improvement of transportation, the prices rose, and the fishing industry gradually developed. All the *dian* in the region were abundant with fish, and great profits were made. People overfished, but after a while there was a mutual agreement to protect the fish under three inches in length. The fishing households earned even greater incomes, and "what was previously called a water-disaster (*shuihuan*) had been transformed into a water-benefit (*shuili*)."[122]

Toward Baoding, south of the Xi dian, was Gaoyang, the model cotton district, where people said, "Upon entering the district, one can immediately hear the jah-jah of the looms."[123] Ninety percent of the households in the county wove cotton for a living. In the Qing the locality had been quite poor, but since the introduction of the cotton industry, prosperity meant a higher level of education, as well as a better standard of consumption, but people in the countryside still had a simple diet and did not store grain.

> Because of the development of industry, the standard of living has been raised in the city. For food, *mi* and *mian* [rice and noodles] are the chief staples. Meats and vegetables are also plentiful in the cities. But in the rural villages, millet and sorghum are the main diet, with vegetables they grow themselves. People don't eat *mimian* or meat unless it is a holiday. The landlord families, or those who don't farm, buy a whole year's supply of grain after the fall harvest. Except for the desperately poor families, no one purchases grain in small quantities.[124]

In nearby Qingyuan County (Baoding Prefecture), by contrast, there was no industry to alleviate poverty. The gazetteer described it as a rather ordinary place with very few rich people, but it did benefit from being on good roads and was a place where merchants had gathered. After the late nineteenth century, railroads brought changes, and the cultural level improved. Young men no longer had queues and women under the age of thirty or twenty no longer had bound feet. Still, the standard of living was low.

Although some ate three meals a day, most ate only two. The diet of the ordinary people was coarse and plain: millet and corn, with some vegetables. Very few ate rice, wheat flour, or meat. Meat and fish were eaten only at new years or weddings. The diet of the rich was somewhat better and included rice and flour. Peasants ate mostly millet porridge or steamed white potatoes, or else millet as *mi* or in biscuits, *gaoliang* in biscuits, and some other coarse grains and beans. For each day, the proportions (in the whole district[?]) were 40 percent potatoes, 30 percent millet, 20 percent coarse grains, and 10 percent vegetables.[125]

Cooking methods were simple, intended to save fuel and use a minimum of oil or flavoring. Poor families just took the basic ingredients and threw them into a pot of boiling water with some salt. They may have added a few drops of oil. Then everyone put some of this *zhou* (gruel) into his bowl and ate it. It was the same every day. They ate in order to fill their stomachs without consideration of taste or nutrition. Every month each household used on average 4–5 jin of salt and very little oil or vinegar. For the entire year a family might use 10 jin of meat, mostly on the "three holidays." Each family used 40–50 eggs a year, mostly when relatives or friends came to visit.[126]

In Qingyuan, as in so many other places, population density had reduced the average household's landholdings, yields were low, and there was frequent flooding from the Tang River. Cotton planting expanded from 3 percent of the planted acreage to 6.6 percent. Survival depended not only on agriculture but also on nonfarm income. According to the survey conducted by Chen Hansheng and others, 26.8 percent of the average "middle" household income came from sideline occupations, working outside the house, or remittances sent home by locals who had left to work elsewhere. A few sideline occupations included pressing oil (for cooking), making flour, weaving mats, and preparing pig bristles.[127]

At Wan County, also in the vicinity of Baoding city, there were even fewer signs of improvement in the 1930s. The gazetteer described the district as having alkaline soil on a plain to the southeast and barren ground on the northwest. The peasants rarely dug wells for irrigation and relied solely on rainwater. When there was a drought, they lacked a means of relief. Millet was the principal grain, and if the peasants had any surplus they would store it against a bad year. Cotton was recently introduced, but far more important than grains or cotton, were the fruit trees that were grown in the villages to the northwest of the county; persimmons, pears, peaches, almonds, walnuts, and black figs were abundant. They could produce four crops a year and brought a profit four or five times greater than grain.[128]

This county had experienced prosperity in eighteenth and early nineteenth centuries, when there were seven pawnshops, five moneychangers, and tens of large merchant firms, but things had gone downhill in the late nineteenth century. Ever since the Boxer Uprising, said the local history, merchants had stayed away, prices were high, and commerce had never recovered. The district was out of the way and narrow. In addition to the poor soil of the region, there had been endless natural and human disasters since the late Qing, and the people were exhausted. The authors of the gazetteer regretted that the district had not experienced any reform efforts.[129]

TOWARD THE MOUNTAINS IN ZHENGDING PREFECTURE

In Zhengding Prefecture and the mountainous regions bordering Shanxi, conditions were far more bleak than anywhere on the plains, and warlord conflicts had blocked off normal access to Shanxi. Jingxing was a poor and mountainous district, which was not self-sufficient in food in the 1930s and which experienced no benefits from any external changes. Its ground was barren and easily vulnerable to disasters. Ninety percent of the people were peasants; in drought years, they "folded their arms and waited to die"; in abundant harvests, they barely had enough to eat. They looked to neighboring Shanxi and Zhengding for their needs. Although they had animals such as cows and sheep and fruits such as figs, Jingxing was a pitiable place, according to the locals. This was the most desperate, the poorest place in the province. Its gazetteer quoted the Confucian *Analects*, "Those ruling a kingdom or a family do not fear the people being too few; they fear inequality."[130]

Jingxing people ate coarse adulterated foods, such as *kang* (chaff) mixed with other things. They ate vegetables, pulses, and grasses grown wild in the mountains. The custom was to eat three meals a day, but two meals in the winter. In the spring, when the ice on the rivers melted, the flour-milling business flourished. The local people ground the *kang* with the millet grain to form what was colloquially called *shuimomian* (water-ground noodles). "The poor families add vegetables and eat it at lunch, which is called *caibing* (vegetable biscuit). There is also some mixture called *kuailei*. The poor eat only half *kang* and half vegetables. Or else they might eat rotten dates and a *kang* noodle. There are also local foods made out of persimmons." The rich people, by contrast, ate "dry grains" while women mostly ate *caigeng* vegetable stew, *caibing*, or *kuailei*. The slightly better-off could hire servants and eat a little bit better. At breakfast and dinner they ate millet as the main food, noodles, *cai*, and soup as accompanying food. At lunch they had millet noodles, or noodles made out of other grains, and steamed "dry grains." They also took wild vegetables in a thin *zhou*. People—even the rich—did not eat wheat themselves, but saved it for en-

tertaining relatives and friends. Meat was even less frequently eaten. There was a little cotton and
a little rice grown in the locality.[131]

In 1930, the population of the county was 190,000. On the flat ground 2 mu was considered to
be more than enough to support one person. In the mountainous areas the soil was poor, and 2
mu could barely support one person and was not enough for a family to be self-sufficient, so many
turned to animal husbandry. According to local sources, forty years earlier the amount of land devoted to planting carrots was not even one-tenth of what it was in the 1930s. This is clear evidence
of the insufficiency of food supply (because it was a way to use marginal land). Consequently
every year, grain was imported from neighboring areas. However, "*in recent years* for various reasons Shanxi provincial officials have not allowed the export of their grain, so we depend on neighboring Huailu County in Zhengding for grain. This situation has affected the people's subsistence,
and as a result the numbers of unemployed vagrants have increased daily, . . . and the social deterioration has also increased."[132]

Other counties in Zhengding Prefecture also depended on Shanxi imports for food and suffered when trade was disrupted by military activity. In Pingshan County, cotton became a big
crop. Aside from the portion that was retained for local weaving and use, the rest was shipped
mainly to Shijiazhuang and Tianjin, and secondarily to Shanxi. The county also exported rice and
sesame, but because of the mountainous terrain and the extent of cotton cultivation, food grains
were insufficient for local use, and much grain had to be imported from Shanxi. Fruits such as
walnuts, peppers, persimmons, and black figs were produced for sale to Tianjin and other
places.[133] In Yuanshi County the ground was high and dry, and irrigation was not developed, so
agriculture did not flourish. In the northeastern section of the county, 20–30 percent of land was
planted in cotton, with an annual output of 2 million jin, mostly sold to Tianjin, or secondarily
to Shanxi or Henan. In the 1920s ("in recent years"), because of warlords and bandits, trade routes
had been blocked and the price of cotton fell, presenting farmers and merchants with difficulties.
Some fruits were sold to Tianjin, and a small amount of silk was made; there were no modern industries in this region.[134]

TOWARD YONGPING IN THE NORTHEAST

In the northeastern prefecture of Yongping, again good location on transport routes could partially, but only partially, offset poor soil and population density. In Luanzhou, sea transport and
commerce with Manchuria since the mid-nineteenth century had helped to stabilize grain prices.
Twenty to thirty percent of locals went to Guandong (Manchuria) to do business. Of them 60–70
percent went to Shenyang, Jilin, and Heilongjiang. "Although they are far away, every year the
profits earned greatly help this region." Yet, "People here are plain and not ambitious."[135] They
had been so poor that they ate adulterated gruel and drank unboiled water. In the 1930s, a new
edition of the local history noted that there were a million people in the county, of whom 90 percent were peasants. They got by, but the many deaths of infants and others who died of hunger
were simply forgotten or ignored, or taken for granted. This kind of sufficiency was possible because the meager agricultural regimen was supplemented by the planting of trees.[136] The 1938 edition did imply a higher standard of living than 1898. Most of the districts in the county, for example, planted some wheat, which they generally marketed to the towns and neighboring counties.
Their economic self-sufficiency depended on this grain; according to the gazetteer, it was no wonder that the *Shuowen*, China's earliest dictionary, said that wheat was like gold. Millet was the basic food of the common people, but the people's livelihood was fundamentally dependent on corn

production. Corn was used both for human consumption and as feed grain for horses, and some of it was marketed as corn meal.[137]

In nearby Lulong County, also in Yongping, conditions were much bleaker. Local produce accounted for only 60 percent of needed food. People ate three meals in summer and autumn (during farming season) and two meals in winter. Twenty to thirty percent of the diet was potatoes; the rest was millet, sorghum, beans, and corn. Few ate wheat flour. There were no grain shops: grain was marketed by itinerant merchants on donkeys.[138] "The soil is poor, there are no mountains, rivers, or mines, and thus few products to speak of. There are the usual five grains. *In recent years*, people have been planting melons. There isn't enough to sell to other places, but it accounts for about ten percent of the people's diet. They also plant peanuts, make it into oil, and sell this to Tianjin."[139]

The local accounts confirm that rural Hebei was still very poor indeed, but they also reveal distinct improvements in the standard of living in some districts. "Improvement" was judged against a very low baseline (boiled water versus unboiled, not boiled water versus tea). Positive change was almost always related to opportunities for marketing agricultural products, or to sideline occupations, or to opportunities to work elsewhere. Recent studies based on Chinese and Japanese surveys of the 1930s and 1940s have emphasized the extent to which sideline work had contributed to household incomes. Using data collected by the South Manchurian Railway Company, Brandt and Sands found that income inequality in three Hebei villages was not so great when total household income, rather than land ownership, was taken into account. They asserted, "The distribution of landholdings can be a very misleading indicator of the degree of income inequality in the rural economy."[140] All three villages were in the northeastern part of Hebei and responded to the active labor market there and in Manchuria. Hou Jianxin, who used data about Qingyuan County collected by Chen Hansheng, has argued that the extent of its dependency on a wider market meant that North China had actually experienced an epoch-making transformation, and that population "pressure" did not result in "involution," as described by Philip Huang, or "a high-level equilibrium trap," as described by Mark Elvin.[141] In the context of the low standard of living experienced by most of the rural population, the new opportunities for handicrafts, trade, and migration hardly seem epoch making. None of these rural enterprises, except for cotton weaving, was large or lucrative enough to change the fundamental economic outlook for Hebei's peasants. Nevertheless, these were promising developments. The story of rural economy could no longer be reduced to the simple equation of land and population.

Economic Trends

These "snapshots" of localities present impressions at single points in time and must be evaluated in the context of the successive economic trends of the period: first moderate inflation, then depression, and finally rampant inflation. Data from Buck's survey of farm households in "the wheat region"—which included Hebei—shows a steady increase in the prices received by farmers for crops that they sold from 1906 until 1932. Prices in 1906 had been only 37 percent of those of 1926, the base year. Agricultural prices then rose steeply between 1928 and 1932.[142] At Tianjin, the wholesale price of various grains rose gradually until the early 1930s. (See Figure 11.1.) In Hebei, wheat price data collected from individual counties show similar trends. Between 1912 and 1932, grain prices in these counties made steady gains. In a few cases such as Wan County or Xinhe, the prices almost doubled in twenty years, but in the majority of cases, the rate of increase was more moderate. (See Table 11.1.)

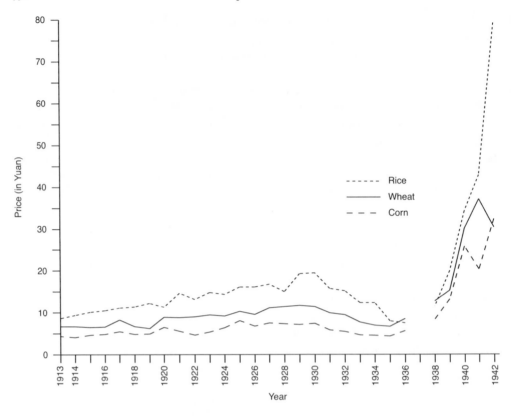

FIGURE 11.1. Tianjin wholesale grain prices (rice, wheat, and corn), 1913–1942

Higher prices should have benefited most farmers, especially to the extent that their agricultural output was not for self-consumption but for the market. The Zhuo County gazetteer, for example, reports that in the 1930s, one-half of the rice produced was sold to Beijing and Baoding; one-third of the wheat was shipped to Tianjin; one-third of the millet was marketed to Zhangjiakou, leaving a local shortage; one-quarter of the corn was sold to Tianjin and Beiping; and half the *gaoliang* was sold elsewhere. This lively commerce left the county very much lacking in grain supplies but presumably with higher income.[143] Jing County, which benefited from remittances from relatives who migrated to work in Shandong or Manchuria, recorded enormous jumps in grain prices between 1882 and 1932. (See Table 11.2.) The increases reported in the local history for 1912–32 seem exaggerated, especially compared with the data given in Table 11.1, but they at least reflect the county's consciousness of economic gains.

Rising income, as measured by grain prices, can benefit farmers only if their costs—for their living and for producer goods—remain lower than their income. Until 1930–32, the "terms of trade," as economists term this relationship, appear to have been generally favorable to agriculture. For China as a whole, Albert Feuerwerker wrote, "While the terms of trade between agriculture and manufactured goods fluctuated in the 1910s, they were increasingly favorable to agriculture in the 1920s, indicating that prices received by the farmer rose even more rapidly than the prices he paid." The terms of trade at Tianjin—between prices received by farmers and either wholesale prices of all manufactured goods, or prices of consumer goods—between 1913 and 1936 followed

TABLE II.I

Wheat Prices in Hebei Counties, 1912–1933

(January 1933 = 100)

County	1912	1931	1932	1933 Jan.	1933 Oct.
Ba	73	113	120	100	76
Cang	91	110	112	100	75
Ding	75	114	118	100	70
Gaoyang	77	104	104	100	60
Jing	69	120	114	100	63
Jingxing	60	79	97	100	43
Luan	85	112	104	100	94
Nanpi	63	73	69	100	115
Shunyi	69	110	107	100	76
Qinghe	87	96	106	100	48
Qingyuan	73	114	111	100	66
Wan	80	—	167	100	113
Xian	67	114	120	100	69
Xianghe	79	106	100	100	69
Xinhe	57	115	117	100	71

SOURCE: "Hebei sheng gexian nongchan wujia zhishu biao" (price indices for agricultural products in Hebei counties). *Nongbao* 1, no. 2 (30 Mar. 1934): 41–45. This source gives data for all Hebei counties; only counties discussed in this chapter are included here.

this national trend.[144] Buck's data for his wheat region revealed that the retail prices of commodities purchased by farmers also showed steady increases, but in most years after 1913 they were lesser than the increases in the prices they received.[145]

Agricultural wages and land prices showed similar increases during the first three decades of the twentieth century. In Buck's "winter wheat–kaoliang region," which included most of Hebei Province, wages increased threefold, that is, 300 percent, between 1900 and 1926, and another 32 percent by 1932.[146] In Jing County, agricultural wages seem to have risen sharply between 1902 and 1912 and continued to rise until 1932. Although the 2,000 percent rise from 1882 to 1932 seems implausible, lesser but substantial gains in income are consistent with the self-description of the county, and from our knowledge that a labor shortage may have developed after many young men sought employment in Manchuria. (See Table 11.2.)

The favorable national trends turned sharply downward from 1931 until 1936, when the world depression caused the foreign market for Chinese goods to decline. The international monetary situation added to China's economic problems. As England, Japan, and the United States abandoned the gold standard, the price of silver rose, causing silver in China to flow outward, which in turn caused prices within China, especially for agricultural products, to decline. Land taxes increased by 8–10 percent between 1931–34 and land values fell.[147] The agricultural sector is more affected by deflation than other sectors in the economy. As Thomas Rawski has written, "In any market economy, low elasticities of supply and demand cause the prices of farm products to display higher volatility than general price indexes. Deflation brings large downswings in the prices received by farmers."[148]

TABLE II.2

Grain Prices and Wages at Jing County, 1882–1932

(prices in wen per dou; wages in wen per day)

	Wheat Prices	*Millet Prices*	*Corn Prices*	*Carpenter Wages*	*Agricultural Wages*[*]
1882	1,200	1,000	500	200	150
1892	1,300	1,100	600	200	150
1902	1,700	1,500	800	250	300
1912	2.760	2,500	1,300	300	1,500
1922	7,000	6,500	4,200	.25 [?]	2,000
1932	14,000	13,000	8,100	.40 [?]	3,000

[*] Agricultural wages are cash wages, not food payments.

SOURCE: *Jing XZ* 1932, 6:4b–6

Whether national and international trends were felt in all regions, all localities, and at all times is quite controversial. Although Western economists, such as Otto or Brandt, have argued that international price trends influenced Chinese prices, Chinese scholars, such as Xia Mingfang, have argued that in isolated and crisis-prone regions, such as Shaanxi, prices were more affected by local harvest conditions and famines than by international trends.[149] Hebei shared most of the resource-poor characteristics of North China, but it was undeniably exposed to national and even international price fluctuations by the twentieth century, and their favorable and unfavorable consequences. In North China the effects of the depression were slightly delayed compared with South China, but as Figure II.I shows, the wholesale prices of wheat and corn at Tianjin began to decline in 1931 and hit bottom in 1935, after which they rose again. In the one year between 1932 and 1933 the price of white wheat, for example, fell from 9.47 to 7.69 yuan. Table II.I shows that in rural Hebei, grain prices at the beginning of 1933 were down from the previous year, but the serious decline was experienced in most counties during the following months. By October 1933, wheat prices were on average 25 to 35 percent down from January, and in some cases even lower. Only Nanpi and Wan counties did not share this experience.

These economic trends explain much of the seeming contradiction between the relatively favorable statistics gathered by Buck and the negative descriptions of North China by so many others. For example, the often-cited examples of rural indebtedness are almost all based on evidence from the 1930s.[150] Agricultural depression caused land values to fall after 1932, even as taxes continued to rise.[151] Falling agricultural prices combined with higher taxes and interest rates created a kind of "scissors effect." Sanhe County (Shuntian) to the west of Beijing had just this experience. According to the gazetteer, at the beginning of the Republic average-quality land was worth 40 yuan per mu, but in 1935 it was worth only 20 yuan. Inferior land previously worth 20 yuan per mu dropped to 10 yuan. According to the local history, while the value of the land kept falling, land taxes kept going up. Eighty to ninety percent of the land was mortgaged, "so the more land you have, the greater is your burden. The life of a well-to-do farmer [*xiao kang zhe*] is generally cruel beyond belief." At the beginning of the Republic, grain prices had been high, but "in recent years" prices had fallen. Fine grains had become so cheap that coarse grains were really pitifully underpriced. Villages were ruined.[152] Although this edition of the gazetteer stressed the poor quality of the land, an earlier edition, cited in Chapter 3, had stressed how much commerce had begun to flourish because of trade in nuts, fruits, and cotton. Like nearby Baodi, this district had also benefited greatly from cotton weaving, which was helpful especially in the sections of the county where land was often flooded. But since 1933, the cotton sales to the main markets beyond the Great Wall had fallen off, probably due to Japanese occupation of Manchuria.[153]

After 1937, inflation became the principal economic trend, particularly affecting large cities like Shanghai and Tianjin. The price of wheat rose from 6.78 yuan per shi in 1935 to 30.57 yuan in 1942, the price of corn from 4.97 to 35.39, and rice from 7.97 to 79.19.[154] At Tianjin, the cost of living for workers was 23 percent higher in 1937 than in 1926, showing slow inflation, but by 1940, it was 250 percent higher, and in 1942, it was 737 percent higher. The greatest portion of workers' expenses was on food, and food costs rose even more steeply in 1942 to 788 percent of the 1926 levels.[155] As is well known, inflation in the cities eventually eroded the middle class's support for the Guomindang and was a factor almost as strong as the rural revolutionary movements in toppling the Nationalist government's rule.

War and politics transformed the economy in several stages. The Mukden incident led to the creation of a Japanese puppet state of Manchukuo in 1932, which despite international diplomatic outrage, remained uncontested and allowed Japan to continue to exert pressure on North China itself by economic, military, and political means. After the Marco Polo Bridge incident in 1937, the Japanese Army overran much of northern, eastern, and central China, forcing the Nationalist government to retreat from Nanjing to Chongqing (Chungking) in Sichuan Province. The Japanese surrender in 1945 restored the Guomindang, but its actual control of northern and eastern China was challenged by the Communists, who had established base areas during the anti-Japanese resistance. After four years of civil war, in 1949 the Guomindang retreated to Taiwan, and the Chinese Communist Party took power.

Japanese Aggression, Communist Insurgency, and Rural Poverty

During the war of resistance against Japan, 1937–45, the Nationalist government, Japanese army, and Communist forces divided the territory of North China into a kind of patchwork quilt. The Nationalists lost practically all control of the north, while the Japanese army extended its power. Soon overextended and overcommitted, the Japanese could hold only the urban centers, including Beijing and Tianjin, while waging a bitter struggle for the rural areas. The Communist border regions and base areas meanwhile expanded their control over Shaanxi, Shanxi, Henan, Hebei, Shandong, and Chahar, and by the end of the war, they controlled the preponderance of the countryside in North China.

The Japanese aggression in North China had three distinct phases. Initially the Japanese forces were in a rather weak position and could barely control the cities they had taken.[156] But by May 1939, Japanese forces occupied the cities along the Peking-Hankow line, as well as most of the county seats in central Hebei and in the piedmont area west of the railway, but they did not extend their control more than a few miles on either side of the railway.[157] In the second phase, from 1940–43, Japanese aggression became much more brutal. Their forces did sweeps of the base areas, burning grain and livestock and killing anyone suspected of collaboration with the guerillas. The Communist-led resistance called these campaigns the "Three Alls"—"Burn All, Kill All, and Loot All." Between 1941 and 1943, there were four major campaigns in Hebei. By creating "points and lines"—roads, ditches, and fortifications—the Japanese army attempted to blockade the villages, and the resistance forces were forced out. What resulted was a great crisis in morale and a resurgence of the landlord elite.[158] After 1943, the tide turned. The Japanese occupation became more of a "holding operation." By the end of the war, the Chinese Communist Party had organized governments that controlled much of North China.

North China was divided by the Communists into border regions. The first and most important was the Shaanxi-Gansu-Ningxia region to the northwest, where Yan'an—the Communist headquarters after the Long March—was located. Hebei was part of two other base regions: the Shanxi-Chahar-Hebei region, usually known as Jin-Cha-Ji, and the Shanxi-Hebei-Shandong-Henan, usually called Jin-Ji-Lu-Yu, region. The latter, not established until July 1941, had four constituent parts, one of which was southern Hebei, but was stronger in Shanxi, just west of the Taihang mountains. The two other border regions in North China were the Shanxi-Suiyuan region and the Shandong base area.[159]

Jin-Cha-Ji was regarded as the second most important region after Shaan-Gan-Ning. It differed from other base regions because of its proximity to large cities and railroads; other bases were more isolated.[160] There were some benefits to its proximity to Beijing; intellectuals and students could join the movement. But at the same time the Japanese occupation of the northern capital meant that there was frequent conflict between the Japanese forces and the guerilla movement. "Base areas were difficult to establish and more difficult to maintain, and much of the region remained contested guerilla territory until the end of the war." Western and mountainous areas of the three provinces were the first developed. Later bases developed on the plains region east and south of Beijing. United Front strategy was stressed. Many of the institutions and practices of Jin-Cha-Ji were later spread to other base areas in North China.[161] The Communist cells in Jin-Cha-Ji had to practice more moderate policies because of repression.[162] Kathleen Hartford has observed that the Communist victory was by no means a foregone conclusion and was achieved despite many setbacks.[163]

Some maintain that the Communists would never have been able to expand their movement into the villages of North China if it had not been for the Japanese, and that it was their leadership of the anti-Japanese resistance that won them followers. In his controversial book, *Peasant Nationalism*, Chalmers Johnson argued that Chinese peasants supported the CCP because it was leading the anti-Japanese resistance in the north, and not because they were attracted to its social radicalism. Mark Selden represented an opposing viewpoint in *The Yenan Way in Revolutionary China*, which described how the party in the northwest won the support of peasants by addressing their economic and social needs. Since then both Johnson and Selden, and their sympathizers, have modified their views, and new scholarship has covered a broader range of the revolutionary experience, with more regional differentiation. Some have emphasized the organizational capabilities of the Communist Party leaders and cadres as a leading factor in eventual victory, but a consensus has formed around the idea that there can be no monocausal explanation for the eventual victory of the CCP, nor was its victory by any means inevitable.[164]

The relationship between rural poverty and revolutionary action in North China during the 1930s and 1940s has been ideologically controversial and will continue to be an arena for historical debate. For the Chinese Communist Party under Mao Zedong's leadership, peasant class consciousness and class struggle were the motive forces of the revolution. Yet, during the anti-Japanese struggle, and at other points in party history, class conflict was played down in favor of United Front strategies and the need to gain wide support against the Japanese. In fact, as is widely recognized, the revolutionary process that led to the Communist victory in 1949 succeeded first in North China, where landlordism and tenancy were relatively limited, rather than in the south where there were greater inequalities in land distribution and landlords were more powerful. Independent, but small-scale, farmers were the rule in North China. Although some farmers may have hired help or rented out some of their land, there were very few large-scale landlords, and absentee landlords were infrequently seen.

If North China did not have many large landlords, peasants certainly had many other grievances and targets of discontent. High rents, large debts, and increasingly heavy taxes had been the enemies of rural survival. Although rent and debt reduction were difficult to implement, in some places significant reductions were achieved, as described by historian Wei Hongyun. Annual interest rates were reduced to 10 percent or less. In the Beiyue base area, near the Taihang mountains, "a total of 320,600 *yuan* of debt was written off and a total of 64,900 *mu* of mortgaged land was returned to borrowers by June 1940. Rent reduction, where it occurred, was more spectacular still. Rent was reduced from 50 percent to 37.5 percent of the harvest."[165] Some of these steps led indirectly to improvements in land distribution. Some landlords sold land voluntarily. In a 1943 survey of twenty-four villages in the Beiyue base area, more land was owned by middle peasants, poor peasants, and others, while less land was owned by landlords. According to Wei, the war years saw the decline of the landlord economy and the rise of the middle peasant economy throughout the Jin-Cha-Ji border region, and in some villages in central and eastern Hebei, landlords simply disappeared.[166]

A process of "state involution" in North China since the early twentieth century helped to create great social discontent at the village level. As described by Prasenjit Duara in *Culture, Power and the State: Rural North China, 1900–1942*, starting from the end of the Qing period, provincial governments began to extract larger tax revenues from the countryside, which produced vast increases in provincial revenues. (In Hebei, unlike the typical provinces, a greater proportion of the tax came from commercial taxes in addition to land taxes.) According to Duara, this was an involutionary process because the state-building efforts were more successful in extracting income from the countryside than in developing new institutions or controlling rural society.[167] Under the Nationalist government the level of formal administration was extended from county level to the township and municipality, while periodic levies, called *tankuan*, were assessed on each village as a unit without regard to what the landholding pattern was and how taxes would be assessed on households within the village.[168] "The tankuan burden that villages had to bear was not only onerous but arbitrary."[169] In this *tankuan* system of collection wealthy local leaders were required to pay the village taxes in advance and then to collect payment from the villagers. For the local leaders, the job of tax collection was thankless and difficult.[170] Many village leaders walked away from their duties, while others developed into what is known as "local bullies" or *tuhao*. It was the local bullies, Duara concludes, who became the object of peasant protest, not the landlords.[171] In Long Bow Village, described in Hinton's *Fanshen*, these thugs were known as "local despots," or *opa (eba)*.[172] As Duara concludes, "It is becoming increasingly clear that there was no single factor—such as landlordism or imperialism—that brought the Communists to power in China; if there was one, it was their ability to mobilize along a range of local grievances: from wife beating to concealed land. A significant set of local grievances in northern villages was the product of state-society relations: heavy taxation, political arbitrariness, and the pursuit of village office for profit."[173]

Under Japanese occupation, North China villages again found themselves exploited for their agricultural produce. Starting in 1939, the Japanese army intensified its effort to gain control over the agricultural produce of North China in order to support diminished supplies at home. After the outbreak of the Pacific War, in 1941 exports of food from North China to Japan increased greatly. In 1941, a bumper harvest eased the pain, but the subsequent two years saw poor harvests. These substantial exports during a period of great hardship for North China "indicated the strength of the Japanese economic control structure," according to one historian, but they were achieved through coercion and deepened the famine conditions already developing. "These conditions sustained the resistance morale of the Chinese peasantry and made them more susceptible to Chinese Communist Party leadership."[174]

This pillaging was combined with the destruction from the four major extermination campaigns in Jin-Cha-Ji between 1941 and 1943. Pingshan County in western Hebei suffered the worst kind of treatment by the Japanese because it was a center of guerilla activity. Up to the end of 1942, it sustained the following damage: 60,000 sections of houses burned, 58.6 million catties of grain destroyed, 50,000 mu (10 percent of total acreage) of crops trampled, 5,000 deaths, and 20,000 people taken away (of a population of 236,000).[175] In Raoyang County in central Hebei, villages that appeared to comply were spared the wrath of the Japanese army, while neighboring villages that harbored resistors were brutalized.[176]

Natural disaster compounded the human devastation wrought by the Japanese army, a dreadful example of *tianzai renhuo*. The famine that ravaged Henan in 1942 and 1943 also affected other parts of North China, including the Taihang mountain region of Shanxi and Hebei, the western and central parts of Hebei. The years 1941 and 1942 witnessed droughts. In some parts of this area only 20–40 percent of the crop was harvested. An estimated 336,000 people needed relief. In 1943, there was no rain in southern Hebei for the first eight months. A total of 8,840,000 mu, in localities such as Daming and Nangong, had no spring harvest and were unable to plant fall crops; they had only 20–30 percent of their normal harvest that year. In addition, starting in June other areas experienced locust infestations; this included a wide area including northern Henan, western Hebei, and Shanxi. Locusts consumed spring grain crops in the field, as well as vegetables; the land was "swept clean." Many districts in southern Hebei were hit by locusts after the drought: Daming, Wei, Yuancheng, Julu, Qinghe, and so on. Then, with cruel fate, thirty districts in the same area were flooded in September after the Zhang, Fuyang, and Wei rivers, as well as the southern Grand Canal, all overflowed their banks. In this flood, 1,260,000 mu were covered, rendering much of southern Hebei like a huge swamp, *zeguo*, and an estimated 1.5 to 1.6 million victims in need of relief.[177] Most of the districts severely affected were part of either the Jin-Ji-Lu-Yu or the Jin-Cha-Ji base areas, but hunger knew no military boundaries. Guomindang-controlled districts liberated by the Eighth Route Army in July 1943 were reported to be full of corpses of those who had starved to death. There was no grain available, and large numbers of people had fled their villages. In the most devastated areas, as many as 40 percent had died, and 90 percent had fled. As a whole, 5–15 percent had died, and 30–50 percent had fled. In sum, in this period in southern Hebei a total of 200–300,000 had perished, and 1 million had fled.[178]

In Wugong village in Raoyang County, tax reforms under Communist leadership began in 1938, even before the Japanese appeared in this area, and had reduced the holdings of the five richest households and helped others survive. "This silent revolution across North China kept countless villagers from dying in the 1943–44 disaster." But still, the 1943 harvest failed and, according to investigations made in the 1980s, 101 of 329 households sold their land and tools to survive; 21 households fled; 29 families sold children; 25 went out to beg, and 15 people died of hunger.[179] The village leader later recalled that he had to eat famine foods such as peanut shells and tree leaves. "In the desperate spring of 1943 he sold his eldest daughter . . . to a household in another village for 45 catties of sorghum, but several months later she returned home. . . . Children for sale huddled in markets with sale placards hung around their necks."[180]

Hunger and famine were pervasive, and together with violence and destruction, were woven into the fabric of the human tragedy of North China in the 1930s and 1940s. Hunger alone does not cause rebellion, or even revolution.[181] Hungry men don't rebel, it has often been said. But hunger and famine tear at the social fabric and create degradation. As one Chinese historian has written, famine lowers the quality of human life, or *suzhi*. It caused people to flee their homes, to sell their daughters, to kill their newborn, to engage in prostitution, and to steal and cheat. Suicide and cannibalism were some extreme outcomes. Malnutrition and disease led to degraded and short lives. Such circumstances influenced people's psychological well-being and their attitudes toward law, morality, and ideology.[182]

The smallest human conflict or social inequality could then be a cause for grievance. The fact that one's neighbor or landlord or local "bully" was also a very poor person hardly made a difference when the competition for scarce resources was so sharp. After the Japanese surrender in August 1945, rural North China was more than ready to accept the social revolutionary message of Chinese Communist cadres and to engage in land revolution. In Long Bow Village in Shanxi Province, just on the other side of the Taihang mountains from Hebei, villagers first settled scores with "traitors" in the Anti-Traitor Movement, and by January 1946, they began to "settle accounts" with the local landlords who were also the "bullies." Although the official policy of the liberated areas was still "double reduction"—reduction of rents and interest rates—since the United Front with the Guomindang was still in force, the villagers soon forced the local landlords to give up their property and to flee. The first target of the villagers was not the richest man, but the one considered the meanest because he had seized and hoarded grain during the last famine and allowed his tenants to starve to death. In the settling of accounts, all kinds of property were included: housing, draft animals, and grain.[183]

By March, when the process was finished, 242 acres of land had been reallocated to the landless and land-poor. Their average holdings had doubled from 0.44 acres to 0.83 acres per capita. About half of the families in the village, 140 families with 517 members, "turned over" [*fanshen*] during this process. William Hinton wrote, "This amount of land did not make them wealthy by any means, but it was sufficient to maintain a minimum standard of living. It meant that they had moved from the ragged edge of starvation into relative security. Peasants who formerly grew only half enough to live on and had to work out or rent land for the remainder of their subsistence suddenly became peasants who could raise enough to live on, on their own land." He added, "The impact of this shift on the outlook and morale of the landless and land poor was tremendous. For the first time in their lives they felt some measure of control over their destiny."[184]

Conclusion

Was China, particularly North China, in the 1920s, 1930s, and 1940s the "land of famine"? In Zhili-Hebei, as in most of North China, the fundamental economic problem of the early twentieth century was the decreasing amount of land per capita, compounded by the poor quality of soil and the dry conditions generally unaided by irrigation. Yet there were also important structural changes in the economy that began to complicate the simple equation of land and people. The development of railroads that crisscrossed this part of North China, together with the growth of the city of Tianjin into a major industrial center as well as port—two interrelated events—stimulated the commercialization of agriculture and the development of rural industry, particularly cotton. Fruits, nuts, and vegetables were marketed to Beijing and Tianjin, as well as points north and south. Cotton weaving was a major income-earner for many districts within the region. Other districts, unable to subsist on agriculture alone, found alternative sources of income through minor handicrafts such as weaving mats and baskets, and so forth. In short, the economic status of some households began to depend on sources of income beyond grain crops, beyond self-sufficiency, and beyond the absolute dependency on each year's weather and harvest.

These developments hardly constituted a fundamental economic "break-through," but had there been political stability and government support, they might have led to further development.[185] In some respects the local initiatives and small-scale projects of the 1920s and 1930s resemble the small-scale rural enterprises of the 1980s. For the relatively short period in which they started in a halting way, they could be considered economic escape-hatches—small ways in which the incomes of rural households could be raised at least to the level of self-sufficiency if not to a better standard of living. Migration to Manchuria provided a similar type of escape from abject poverty by significantly increasing household income. Nationally, the import of wheat not only satisfied a new, mostly urban, demand for wheat flour but also allowed for comparative advantages through international trade to work (although at the time the import of even 5 percent of grain supply was regarded as a national crisis).

Japanese violence and plunder in North China undercut these hopeful new developments. All the disruption and damage caused by warlord rivalries, as well as local bandits and bullies, were trivial compared with Japanese aggression.[186] When interlocked with famine conditions, Japanese aggression followed by Communist insurgency put hunger and poverty back to the front and center of the historical stage. Whereas the economic changes of the 1910s through the early 1930s presented the hope that famine might become secondary in importance, the events of the late 1930s and 1940s guaranteed that famine in one form or another would continue to be a major factor in China's twentieth-century history. The CCP's earlier rent- and interest-reduction policies, and later emphasis on land revolution and class struggle, seemed to address these problems in a radical way unfamiliar to traditional ideologies; yet, ironically, the focus on the conquest of hunger as the basis for political legitimization seemed to keep alive a familiar historical perspective.

The earlier and greater success of the Communist movement in North China has generally been taken as a sign of the correctness of the "Yan'an model"—one forged under Mao's direct guidance in conditions of great austerity and rural backwardness. Having overcome great adversity on the Long March, Mao saw the wartime experience at Yan'an as the model of how Chinese Communism should be spread through the rest of China. He favored the experience of Shaan-Gan-Ning border region over that of the other base areas of the north. Jin-Cha-Ji was arguably as important in the formation of organizational experience and bore the brunt of Japanese depredations, but it was not quite so high in profile. Still, the entire northern experience of the 1937–45 war and the 1945–49 civil war periods shows that Mao favored a "northern model" of revolution over other models, such as that of the New Fourth Army in central China. The idea that poverty and backwardness were advantages in the revolutionary struggle was developed principally in the north and became an essential part of Mao Zedong's ideological vision for China, especially after the Great Leap Forward in 1958.[187]

CHAPTER TWELVE

Food and Famine Under
Socialist Rule, 1949–1990s

IN THE SECOND HALF of the twentieth century the Chinese people experienced five decades of revolutionary change that affected all aspects of life. During the imperial period, the "ordinary people" (in traditional parlance) were largely unaware of the dynastic changes in the capital; except for military disturbances and rebellions, they would not be conscious of shifting historical tides. For them, the phrase "Heaven is high, and the emperor is far away" expressed a profound reality. Under socialist rule, by contrast, no family could be unaware of the party directives, communicated by party cadres and the propaganda organs, that affected their land and housing, their relationships with neighbors and village, their food supply, education, marriage practices, family relations, and even their reproductive options. Mao Zedong and the other top party leaders who came out on the national holiday to review the parades from the Gate of Heavenly Peace may have been as far away as the emperors, but their images were known even in the countryside, and the importance of their pronouncements was not lost on the people.

Although this new rulership provided ordinary people, the "masses" (in Communist parlance), a measure of security that was previously unknown, frequent, abrupt, and violent shifts in the party line affected not only high-level policies but also undermined individual gains and security achieved in each previous period. The period of land reform, 1949–52, witnessed both agricultural recovery and political consolidation. From 1953 onward, agriculture became increasingly collectivized, while the first Five-Year Plan launched a Soviet-style effort to expand heavy industry. Impatient to see even greater industrial and agricultural gains, and perhaps encouraged by the relative ease of collectivization, compared to the Soviet experience, Mao pressed on with the Great Leap Forward in 1958, and within a year or two, all rural life and agricultural production was organized into large-scale communes. The Great Leap had disastrous consequences, resulting in world history's largest famine, which occurred in the years 1959–61. With radicalism temporarily discredited, and Mao sitting on the sidelines, party leaders reverted to a more moderate course between 1961–65. Various ideological campaigns in the 1960s culminated in the Cultural Revolution, 1966–76, which pitted neighbors and family members against each other, students against teachers, and undermined education, research, and culture. Agricultural policy took another radical turn around 1968, with an emphasis on regional self-sufficiency, a return to brigade-level accounting, and extreme measures of austerity and self-reliance as found in the Dazhai model. Starting in the late 1970s, the tide began to shift in favor of more "rational" economic planning and away from the campaign style of leadership. The commune system was disassembled, and under the leadership of Deng Xiaoping, a program of economic modernization was launched. The crackdown on the Tiananmen student uprising in 1989, however, showed indisputably that economic reform would not spill over to liberal political reforms. The 1990s brought continued success in industrial growth and international trade, confirming the uncanny "correctness" of Deng Xiaoping's gamble that economic reform must precede political reform.

The conquest of hunger was the guiding force and the legitimizing principle of the Chinese Communist Party, especially after the defeat of the Japanese and victory over the Guomindang. No goal was more compelling than its commitment to help peasants achieve self-sufficiency and subsistence, and thus human dignity. The tax- and rent-reduction campaigns in the base areas in the north had already demonstrated the sincerity and ability of the party to address the basic needs of farmers. From land reform through the various stages of collectivization, nothing seemed to be a higher priority than feeding the people, and nothing was more persuasive for the people than this commitment. As Mao sought a "Yan'an way" or a Maoist way for China in the 1950s, he reached back to the experience during the war years, and making a virtue out of necessity, he saw richness in poverty. In his 1958 article, "China Is Poor and Blank," Mao said that the poverty of the Chinese peasantry was a virtue, and the Chinese people like a blank sheet of paper upon which one could write beautiful words. "China's 600 million people have two remarkable peculiarities; they are, first of all, poor, and secondly, blank. That may seem like a bad thing, but it is really a good thing. Poor people want change, want to do things, want revolution. A clean sheet of paper has no blotches, and so the newest and most beautiful words can be written on it, the newest and most beautiful pictures can be painted on it."[1] Following this, he stressed the potential of human will to overcome objective circumstances. The Chinese peasants were able to enact through human will a great leap forward in agriculture and industry.

The ideology of Mao was firmly based in a world of scarcity and hunger. Its radicalism was found in its approach to addressing these issues. The root cause of poverty was not overpopulation, land scarcity, or technological backwardness; it was the unequal distribution of wealth in the countryside. The monopoly of wealth by the landlords and rich peasants could only be broken through class struggle; it would never be achieved in a peaceful way. And class struggle could only take place when the oppressed were made aware of their situation and achieved class consciousness. In this way their very poverty became a potent force for achieving social change. This view was both radical and populist. In its most extreme iteration at the time of the Great Leap Forward, the people (not just the poor peasants and workers) could all acquire through struggle and learning the appropriate class perspective even if they were not born into that class. Thus, the objective problem of scarcity of land for the given population size could be overcome by the will of the people. This was a radical approach to the population and land problem that had been recognized since at least the eighteenth century. Rather than seeing people and land in a harmonious balance, and seeking the restoration of the status quo ante after a natural disaster, the Maoist vision saw people expanding the potential of the land through sheer human effort.

Yet Maoism was in other ways deeply traditional in its approach to ordering the world. "Feeding the people" was the most important sign of imperial legitimacy and claim to the Mandate of Heaven. As the cult of Mao developed in the Cultural Revolution, the paternalism of the old imperial mode of leadership became more outwardly visible. This emperor and his successors not only fed the people but also controlled the rivers in the tradition of the sage emperor Yu. In fact, the state's distribution of food by rationing and other means, as well as its river control projects, can be seen as an intensification of past practices of state intervention under the Qing—perhaps not such a radical departure from the past. Mao's emphasis on the peasantry and agriculture can also be seen as traditionalist, some have said nativist, rather than a progressive or modernizing, or indeed classical Marxist, view that emphasized the importance of capitalism and industrial labor. Although heavy industry was recognized as important, the Maoist insistence that agriculture was the basis of the economy could not be more consistent with the traditional Confucian perspective, even to the point of viewing markets, merchants, and trade as being parasitic, not productive. Thus "radicalism" met its "roots" in a deep fundamentalism with respect to agriculture.

During the Mao years there were two basic approaches to addressing the problem of subsistence. The first was to create incentives for increasing agricultural production by equalizing the ownership of land through land reform and then collectivization. The second was to control the allocation of food at the household, village, provincial, and national levels. Both approaches involved a degree of intervention in the economy that was bold and historically unprecedented. A third approach was the control of nature through river conservancy and technical inputs to agriculture such as irrigation, chemical fertilizers, mechanization, and the like, but in Hebei they did not play a major role until the 1960s.

The results of all the twists and turns in policies were mixed although internal stability and strong government measures could be said in most periods to have brought minimal self-sufficiency to most people, but hardly prosperity. Agricultural output did expand rapidly in the 1950s, but it could barely keep ahead of the growing population, and it certainly could not generate enough of a surplus to underwrite industrial growth. The Great Leap Forward held forth the illusory promise of allowing China to "walk on two legs," to provide for both agricultural and industrial expansion, but the "three lean years" of 1959–61 actually resulted in the estimated loss of 30 million lives, the largest famine in world history. In a long century of human tragedies in China, the Great Leap Forward was the most deeply tragic, not only for its magnitude, but because it was almost entirely manmade and avoidable.

Population growth, only briefly arrested by the Great Leap famine, also undercut any gains made in agriculture, and until the 1980s kept large portions of the population at a subsistence standard of living. Although rapid population growth was characteristic of all developing societies in the post–World War II era, in China birth rates, and hence rates of natural increase, were pushed even higher than normal through Maoist pronatalist policies, which had roots in the Yan'an period. After 1949, Mao Zedong continued to regard population growth as a favorable development, particularly after the devastation of the war years, but during the First Five-Year Plan, other leaders, such as Deng Xiaoping, then vice premier, saw the danger of too much population growth. Population planning and control were seen as key components of economic planning, as was the tight control of food supplies through a unified procurement system, but birth control, or birth planning, remained controversial among party leaders and followers. With the Great Leap Forward, Mao Zedong advanced in full force his belief in humanity, the more the better. Although he had previously endorsed birth planning, he now began to see its advocates as rightist enemies. The 1959 attack on Beijing University president and sociologist Ma Yinchu as a neo-Malthusian resulted in the complete silencing of any dissent.[2]

By 1962 Zhou Enlai and other leaders began to speak of measures to curtail the rate of population growth, but the Cultural Revolution and other political forces delayed the implementation

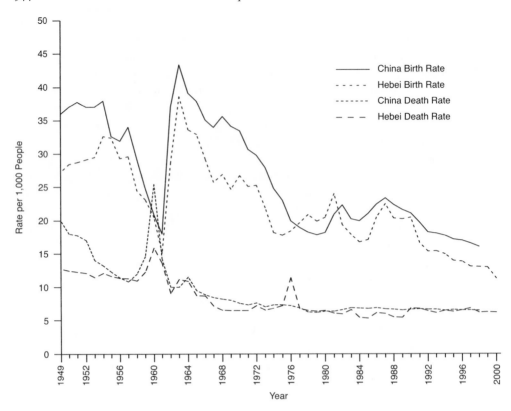

FIGURE 12.1.   China and Hebei birth and death rates, 1949–2000

SOURCE: For Hebei: 1949–51, *Xin Hebei sishinian, 1949–1989*, 321; 1952–2000, *Hebei jingji nianjian*, 224. For China: *Zhongguo tongji nianjian 1999*, 111.

of a new birth-control plan until 1975. As a symbol of the final reversal of policy, the party reha-bilitated Ma Yinchu in 1979.[3] In the previous two decades China's population had increased from 660 million in 1958 to 975 million in 1979; by 1995, it exceeded 1.2 billion. Eventually the crude birth rate was brought down from its high of 43 per thousand in 1963, to about 16 per thousand in 1998. (See Figure 12.1.) The imposition of the new birth-control policy, generally known as the "one-child policy," has brought its own problems and controversies and has had its own tragic short-term social consequences, such as the revival of preference for boy babies and the termina-tion of unwanted girl babies either by abortion or by infanticide.

Critics point out that if there had not been two decades of almost unrestrained population growth, China's food supply would have been adequate, and the economy would have developed sooner. The process of demographic transition is not a uniquely Maoist invention; it has been a fairly universal historic experience, especially in the postwar era. Premodern societies were charac-terized by high birth rates and high death rates that resulted in slow net population growth, or low rates of natural increase. As public health and sanitation measures became widespread, death rates were brought down quickly while birth rates remained high. The result was high rates of natural increase and rapidly expanding populations. In the final stage of transition, birth rates decline and eventually fall closer to the lowered death rates. In China, however, pronatalist policies combined

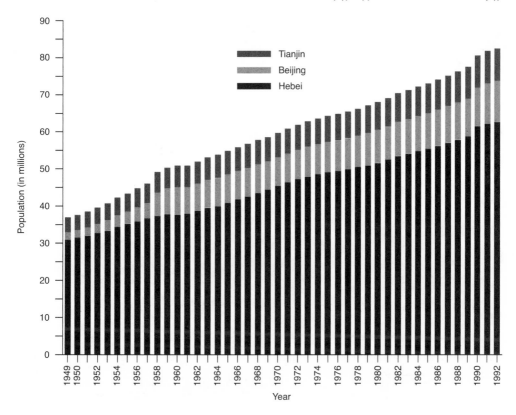

FIGURE 12.2.   Hebei, Beijing, and Tianjin population, 1949–1992

SOURCE: *Zhongguo changyong renkou shujuji*, 12, 14, 16.

with the extreme fluctuations of agricultural policy greatly compounded the population pressure. For China the process of demographic transition is just being completed in the first part of the twenty-first century. The question is whether it could have been accomplished earlier and without the harsh and intrusive measures employed in the last two decades.[4] (Figure 12.1 shows the demographic transition for China and Hebei.)

Population, Agriculture, and Grain in Hebei

In the fifty years since the establishment of the People's Republic of China, the total population of Hebei, Beijing, and Tianjin—which together constituted Republican-period Hebei Province—has more than doubled, from about 36.9 million in 1949, to 40.8 million people in 1953 (the year of the first census), to 82.6 million in 1992, and then to 88.6 million by 1999. Beijing municipality's population by itself grew from 2.03 million in 1949, to 12.6 million in 1999, while Tianjin municipality increased from 4.03 million to 9.67 by the end of the century. (See Figure 12.2.) Hebei Province's demographic transition has followed the national pattern in most respects. As Figure 12.1 shows, its birth and death rates in the 1949–55 period were not so high as the national rates, so the decline in its death rate has not been so pronounced as the national death rate decline. Its birth rates followed the same pattern as China's, but not at such a high level. Like the nation as a

TABLE 12.1

Hebei Grain Output and Procurement, 1949–1988

Year	Total Grain Output (million metric tons)	Tax and Procurement (million metric tons)	Procurement Rate (percent)	Agricultural Purchases (million metric tons)	Retained in Village (million metric tons)	Agricultural Population (10,000 persons)	Grain Per Capita (Agricultural) (kg)
1949	4.70						
1950	6.06	0.96	15.7				
1951	5.80	1.35	23.2				
1952	7.72	1.47	18.9				
1953	6.86	1.59	23.16				
1954	6.78	1.73	25.49				
1955	7.71	1.59	20.58	1.41	7.53	3233.01	233
1956	6.82	1.28	18.77	2.00	7.54	3261.94	231
1957	8.19	1.84	22.41	1.26	7.62	3309.84	230
1958	8.38	2.64	31.53	1.39	7.13	3283.38	217
1959	7.40	3.32	44.93	1.35	5.42	3290.76	165
1960	6.23	2.18	35.03	1.03	5.08	3290.81	154
1961	5.92	1.52	25.59	0.80	5.21	3389.94	154
1962	6.23	1.12	15.95	0.79	6.29	3541.82	178
1963	5.52	0.99	17.89	2.06	6.59	3616.21	182
1964	7.47	1.32	17.67	1.44	7.59	3644.77	208
1965	9.65	1.18	12.26	1.14	9.60	3726.35	258
1966	10.95	1.57	14.36	0.65	10.03	3819.34	262
1967	10.63	1.47	13.83	0.59	9.75	3881.43	251
1968	9.77	1.23	12.6	0.85	9.40	3970.62	237
1969	11.06	1.61	14.58	0.50	9.95	4071.67	244

TABLE 12.1 (continued)

Year	Total Grain Output (million metric tons)	Tax and Procurement (million metric tons)	Procurement Rate (percent)	Agricultural Purchases (million metric tons)	Retained in Village (million metric tons)	Agricultural Population (10,000 persons)	Grain Per Capita (Agricultural) (kg)
1970	12.73	1.87	14.68	0.47	11.32	4163.9	272
1971	12.81	1.71	13.34	0.58	11.69	4239.65	276
1972	11.55	1.44	12.5	0.86	10.96	4281.2	256
1973	13.88	2.03	14.63	0.59	12.44	4346.73	286
1974	15.69	2.16	13.79	0.55	14.07	4393.92	320
1975	15.43	2.16	14.03	0.69	13.96	4431.03	315
1976	14.80	2.13	14.03	0.82	13.49	4452.3	303
1977	13.12	2.01	15.87	1.25	12.37	4485.04	276
1978	16.88	2.28	15.31	0.88	15.48	4516.08	343
1979	17.80	2.61	13.51	0.92	16.11	4525.14	356
1980	15.22	1.82	14.62	1.27	14.68	4565	322
1981	15.22	2.38	11.97	1.36	14.19	4626.13	307
1982	17.52	2.71	15.6	0.84	15.64	4690.7	334
1983	19.00	4.55	15.48	0.68	15.12	4730.35	320
1984	18.65	4.89	23.95	0.87	14.63	4774.27	306
1985	19.67	2.96	26.2	0.49	17.19	4806.4	358
1986	19.66	2.51	15.07	0.64	17.79	4846.44	367
1987	19.20	2.31	12.7	0.94	17.83	4894.57	364
1988	20.23	2.36	12.3	0.75	19.07	4960.97	384

NOTE: Total grain per capita = (total grain output - tax and procurement + agricultural purchases)/agricultural population.
Data converted to million metric tons (10,000 kg = 10 metric tons).

SOURCES: *Hebei sheng liangshi zhi*, tabs. 2.4 and 2.6, 48–49, 54–55. Grain output 1949–54; *Xin Hebei sishinian, 1949–1989*, 327.

whole, Hebei's Great Leap Forward had serious demographic consequences. Births fell sharply from as early as 1956 and 1957, hitting a low in 1961, while deaths rose in the same period, but not so sharply. By 1962 and 1963, there was a huge rebound in births. Deaths, by contrast, remained elevated in 1963 and 1964—due to the extensive floods of those years. (Also visible is the sharp increase in deaths in 1976 due to the earthquake in Tangshan.)

During this half century of rapid population growth, the amount of arable land has suffered a marked decline, due partly to diminished territorial boundaries, but principally to industrial and urban land use. The exact figures are rarely published and always controversial. Provincial statistics published in the early 1990s confirmed a decline in arable land from 88.347 million mu in 1949, to 79.508 million mu in 1959, to only 66.811 million mu in 1988.[5] As a result of these two trends, the ratio of arable land to population experienced a sharp decline. In 1949 there was 3.5 mu per person; in 1970, 2.3 mu, and in 1982, 1.8 mu per person, as reported by *Hebei jingji dili*.[6] Even this detailed source, and other recent compendia, fail to give figures for cultivated acreage. Figures from this source imply that in 1982 there was 96.4 million mu of *cultivated land*.[7] The figures given for 1957 by the same source, 36.7 million population and average landholdings of 3.1 mu per person, imply that even in 1957 total cultivated acreage was only 113.8 million mu, less than the figure of 132 million mu reported for 1953–57 (see Table 3.4 in Chapter 3).[8]

Despite the loss of arable land, there was a great increase in total grain output from 1949 until the end of the century. Official data from Hebei provincial sources show an increase from 4.7 million tons in 1949 to 20.2 million tons in 1988, a gain of more than fourfold. When compared with the population, which "only" doubled over the same period of time, this was undeniably a significant achievement. A look at the long-term trends, however, barely begins to tell the whole story. In terms of grain output per capita, in the 1950s Hebei ranked as the lowest province; only the autonomous cities of Tianjin, Beijing, and Shanghai ranked lower.[9] The national average for 1952–57 was 293 kg per head, but Hebei was the poorest with 223 kg per capita.[10] The other two northern provinces, Henan and Shandong, were also low on the scale of agricultural output. For China as a whole, in 1957 average daily per capita food consumption was "much the same as in the early 1930s."[11]

Grain output in Hebei rose in the initial years from 4.7 million tons in 1949 to 7.7 million in 1952, but for the next four years, from 1953 through 1956, total output fluctuated around this level, even as the population was increasing, as seen in Table 12.1. When the population and grain output trends are compared, as in Figure 12.3, it is apparent per capita grain output did not rise between 1952 and 1959. In 1952, it reached a 155 percent over the base year of 1949, but from then until 1959, per capita grain figures remained in a certain range and did not exceed the 1952 level. After reaching 8.37 million tons in 1958, grain production was sharply reduced because of the Great Leap Forward. Although in most places this crisis lasted from 1959 through 1961, in Hebei production fell again in 1963 after starting to recover in 1962. The massive 1963 flood resulted in widespread damage. Output began to recover after that, but not until 1965 did total output, and per capita grain, exceed that of 1958, as seen in Figure 12.3. This compared favorably with China as a whole, which did not regain the levels of 1956–58 until the mid-1970s.[12]

After 1965 grain output in Hebei began its strong upward growth. But Figure 12.3 also shows that this upward growth was subject to periodic setbacks in cycles of three to five years, perhaps reflecting climatic cycles, until the early 1980s, when the trend became more linear, reflecting the lessening impact of climate.[13] On a per capita basis, grain output followed the same cyclical developments in the same period of time. Per capita grain output reached 229 in 1979 and 233 in 1985

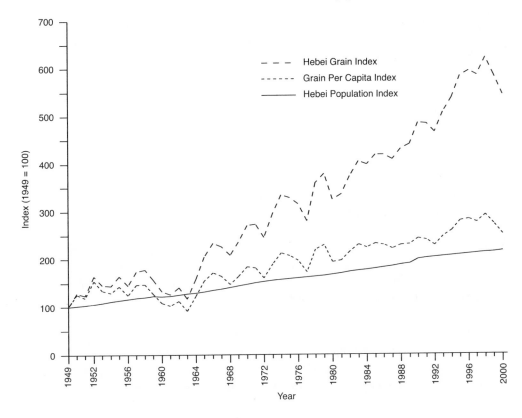

FIGURE 12.3. Hebei grain and population, 1949–2000

SOURCE: *Xin Hebei sishinian, 1949–1989*, 327. 1992–2000 data from *Hebei jingji shudian, 1949–2001*, 97, 111.

over the base year of 1949. In the 1980s and 1990s grain output increased steadily, reaching a high in 1998 of 621, but per capita grain output reached only 292. The sharp drop in production after that probably reflects the encroachment of real estate and industry on arable land. These figures provide only an approximate measure of per capita grain *consumption* since grain figures include feed grain as well as food grain and do not account for any imports to the province from elsewhere.

During the 1950s, Hebei was "a chronic net importer." Each year it imported more than 1 million tons a year, which was equal to 14.9 percent of average annual production, according to Kenneth Walker's estimates. Between 1960 and 1967, 0.7 million tons was imported each year.[14] In terms of grain "potentially available for use" (provincial output plus imports, from which amounts were deducted for seed, livestock feed, and storage), there was on average 242 kg of grain per person for 1953–57 versus 270 kg in 1971—an improvement of 11.6 percent, but still hovering close to subsistence level.[15] Figures in Table 12.1 show the amount of grain per capita available for the agricultural population alone, after accounting for grain procurement (a negative) and agricultural purchases or transfers, including grain imports (a positive). They show that the 1950s levels were not regained until the mid-1960s, and not until 1970 did they begin a steady rise. In 1988, the last year of this series, per capita grain availability was 384 kg per "agricultural-person" (*nongye renkou*)—much higher than the per capita grain availability shown in Figure 12.3, which is calculated simply on the basis of provincial output and total provincial population, both urban and rural.[16]

Hebei did not actually become self-sufficient until 1982, when it became so in a marginal way.[17] Between 1949 and 1981, there were only five years of self-sufficiency, and twenty-four years of insufficiency, according to recent publications. Hebei needed to import on average 0.5 million metric tons of grain a year during that period. During the two big flood years, 1956 and 1963, imports reached a high of 1.4 million tons. Grain imports originated from all provinces except Taiwan and Tibet and included foreign imports. When trade was permitted, Hebei imported fine grains—rice and wheat—from other provinces, while exporting corn, beans, and coarse grains in return.[18] This exchange is reflected in the Table 12.1, which shows the amount of agricultural purchases by Hebei. In 1956, 1963, and 1964, the amounts purchased (imported) exceeded the amounts procured by the state.

The cities of Beijing and Tianjin were largely dependent on grain imports. During the 1953–57 period, Beijing imported an annual average of 887,000 tons of grain and Tianjin 629,000. When added to the estimated 1,114,000 tons imported by Hebei, the dependency of this region on external sources was striking and represented 34.2 percent of all the provincial grain transfers for this period. If the total for Liaoning Province, which was also heavily dependent on imports, is added, the proportion was 55.8 percent.[19] The boundaries of Liaoning Province under the People's Republic of China includes the major part of northeastern Zhili that was part of Qing-dynasty Chengde Prefecture, exclusive of the city of Chengde, as well as most of what was previously Fengtian Province. That Liaoning was so dependent on imports certainly represented a historic change since Fengtian had been a great supplier of grain to Zhili during the Qing.[20] The entire northeast, including Liaoning, Jilin, and Heilongjiang, reversed its Qing-dynasty status as a grain-supplying region; in 1956 it became a grain-deficit area.[21] Instead, the northern provinces and cities generally depended on the southwestern (Sichuan) and central (Hunan, Jiangxi, and Hubei) provinces for their grain imports.

Within Hebei province, cropping patterns changed greatly from the Republican period. Wheat continued to be an important food grain, but millet and sorghum occupied a less important place than traditionally, while corn and potatoes began to play a much larger role. In 1982, millet accounted for only 9.0 percent of total grain output, and sorghum only 4.9 percent. Corn was a whopping 41.4 percent (only 29.9 percent of sown acreage), and wheat 26.3 percent (33.8 percent of sown acreage).[22] Both potatoes and soybeans were now counted as grain crops, their weight converted to a "grain equivalent" for accounting purposes. Although people had a strong preference for "fine grains" (*xiliang*) as opposed to "coarse grains" (*culiang*), the government dictated an emphasis on high-yielding crops.[23] As Figure 12.4 shows, the steady rise in corn production began in the early 1960s, and the steady rise in wheat production began after 1970. Although yields of grain crops as a whole doubled between 1949 and the early 1980s, wheat yields tripled and corn yields increased sixfold.[24] These gains were due to improved varieties, better irrigation, chemical fertilizers, and other technical inputs.

The policy of regional grain self-sufficiency enforced during the Cultural Revolution resulted in severe economic inefficiencies as well as ecological damage in many regions of China. Land that was more suited to cash crops, such as cotton in Hebei, was forced to be planted with grain. There was a virtual cessation of interregional grain transfers, which certainly resulted in much hardship for the poorer regions of China. Mao Zedong himself was directly responsible for this move. He was "profoundly antagonistic to the concept of specialized production based on comparative advantage." In 1966 Mao specifically cited the need to eliminate North China's dependency on South China for grain.[25]

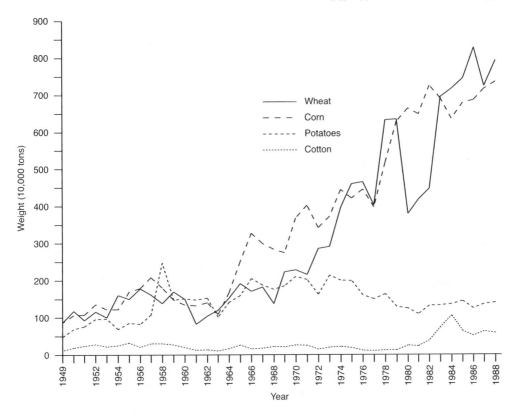

FIGURE 12.4.   Major crops in Hebei, 1949–1988

SOURCE: *Xin Hebei sishinian, 1949–1989,* 327.

The success of the reform policies for agriculture was reflected in the immediate increase in grain output. In the first years of the reforms, from 1977 to 1984, per capita food grain output jumped by 31 percent for all of China.[26] For Hebei, the increase was less dramatic because growth began earlier. Still, the transition from a grain-based agricultural economy to one that emphasized cash crops made a huge difference. Figure 12.4 shows the sharp increase in cotton production in the 1980s. In 1982 cotton output was 386 thousand tons; in 1983 it rose to 740 thousand tons, and in 1984 production peaked at 1.05 million tons before leveling off.[27] Ironically when the policy of grain self-sufficiency was abandoned, economic self-sufficiency was actually achieved. For the first time, Hebei—not including Beijing and Tianjin—became truly self-sufficient in grain, and in addition, its output was able to sustain a much larger nonfarming population. For China as a whole, and Hebei as well, the story has been one of rising rural as well as urban incomes, not just increasing amounts of grain per capita. This rapid transition since 1978 from a grain-deficit economy, to a grain self-sufficient economy, and finally to an income-dependent economy has largely been due to the increased technical inputs to agriculture by the state, as well as the better incentives provided by a market economy.

The transition from agriculture to manufacturing and industry has been Hebei's major economic development over the last two decades. Its major industries have been textiles, chemicals, metals, machinery, and food processing, as well as the more established heavy industries like coal mining and steel production. Industrial growth has expanded far more rapidly than agriculture. In 1949 agriculture accounted for 75.5 percent of the economy; by 1988 it was only 23.4 percent, while heavy industry accounted for 43.6 percent and light industry 33.0 percent. Average annual income rose from 69 yuan per person in 1949 to 986 yuan in 1988. For the farmers, average income rose from 114.1 yuan in 1978 to 546.6 yuan in 1988, but for urban residents "income for living expenses" rose from 276.2 to 1,080.5 yuan per person.[28]

A significant demographic consequence of industrialization has been the shift from a predominantly rural population to one that is almost half nonagricultural. In Hebei the population was less than 10 percent urban before 1954, but by 1989 it was 43.6 percent urban. In Beijing municipality, the trend has been the reverse. Before 1954, the population was about 80 percent nonagricultural; by 1971 it reached a low of 52.5 percent; by 1989, it was 61.7 percent. These changes reflect the changing boundaries of the independent municipality rather than any de-urbanization process. In Tianjin the nonagricultural population has stayed more constant than in Beijing, from about 52 percent in the early 1950s to 55.9 percent in the 1989, with a slight dip in the 1970s. In 1989, 47.3 percent of the population taken together was nonagricultural.[29] Another way of expressing this relationship is to say that in 1953 the ratio of agricultural population (*nongye renkou*) to ration-using population (*dingliang renkou*) was 11.35:1, but in 1988, this ratio was only 5.95:1.[30]

Like the rest of China, Hebei's agriculture has been subject to extreme swings of policy. Summing up the four decades from 1949 to the late 1980s in a masterpiece of understatement, a recent Hebei gazetteer stated:

> The condition of Hebei province's agricultural production has had its special characteristics, having both its beneficial side and its harmful side. Although every level of party and state organization and all the masses of people have energetically grasped agricultural production, in seeking the appropriate methods for the province's conditions, taking the path of grain production as the center of developing the rural village economy *definitely has not been smooth.* There are places where there have been substantial developments, but there are other places where *leftist mistakes have resulted in losses.*[31]

Socialism and Subsistence in Hebei, 1949–1958 and Beyond

For most of rural Hebei, 1949 was not a sharp dividing line.[32] Land reform in North China was a process started during the period of the anti-Japanese resistance movement, and by late 1948, every part of Hebei except Beijing had been "liberated."[33] There are two classic accounts of this process in English, Isabel and David Crook's *Revolution in a Chinese Village: Ten Mile Inn,* and William Hinton's *Fanshen.* A third account is found in *Chinese Village, Socialist State,* a retrospective study by three American scholars who did fieldwork in Wugong Village, Raoyang County, starting in 1978.[34] The two contemporary accounts testify to the enthusiasm with which land reform was welcomed by villagers, while the recent publication presents a more qualified account.

Ten Mile Inn was a village at the center of the Jin-Ji-Lu-Yu border region and was located at the crossroads of its four provinces, Shanxi, Hebei, Shandong, and Henan. The Crooks witnessed the "Adjustment of Landholdings and Educating and Re-organizing the Party Members" campaign in April 1948, having first arrived in the village in November 1947. Based on the interviews they conducted with villagers, they wrote:

> Ten years of struggle had profoundly changed Ten Mile Inn. In 1937 before the beginning of reforms, 70 percent of the people of the village lived in the most dire circumstances. For much of the year they subsisted on husks, wild herbs, and watery gruel 'so thin you could see the reflection

of the moon it it.' In terms of an economically advanced country, there were no wealthy people in Ten Mile Inn. Landlords and peasants alike were pitifully poor. Nevertheless there was a profound difference between them. In time of famine, it was the members of the poor families who died or emigrated, who were forced by poverty to kill or sell children whom they could not feed, who were driven by hunger to join the warlord armies, who were imprisoned for the nonpayment of taxes or lost their meager property by default for nonpayment of debts. But for the landlords and rich peasants, famine was a time for foreclosure on mortgages and for adding to their own landholdings.[35]

The 1942–43 famine had been a formative experience. The Guomindang, according to what the Crooks heard, had ignored the situation. "The Communists, however, urged the peasants to mobilize against the famine and the [Japanese] enemy. It was in the course of combating this bitter disaster that the newly formed peasant union established itself as the villages most powerful mass organization. . . . The peasants began to see their lives and their society with new eyes."[36]

Long Bow Village, Shanxi Province, where Hinton had lived, had about 250 families and about 5,600 mu of farmland; before "liberation" landlords held an average of 17.4 mu per capita, rich peasants 11.2 mu, middle peasants 6.4 mu, and poor peasants 3 mu. After several rounds of land adjustments, after 1948, there was one remaining landlord family that held 6.7 mu per capita; rich peasants held 4.6 mu on average, old middle peasants 6 mu, new middle peasants 5.8, and poor peasants 5.1 mu.[37] By these successive steps, poor peasants had raised their per capita landholdings from 3 mu to 5.1 mu. In Hinton's view, "The new Draft Agrarian Law was destined to play as important a role in China's Civil War of 1946–1950 as the Emancipation Proclamation played in the American Civil War of 1861–1865. . . . With the promulgation of the new Draft Law, a 'thunder and lightening, drum and cymbal' attack was launched on the remnants of traditional exploitation and on the residues of landlord and rich peasant thinking in the revolutionary ranks throughout the Liberated Areas of North China."[38]

In Wugong Village, tax reforms undertaken in the 1930s had begun to close "the gap between the richer and poorer."[39] The 1943 famine took a high toll, but tax reforms had given the poorer households a better chance at survival.[40] In 1946, when land reform was ordered, "the basis for redistribution was how much land each household owned in 1936, prior to wartime economic reforms." Wugong leaders found the class categories difficult to understand. Because all had suffered together, "the notion that class exploitation based on landlord-tenant relations was primarily responsible for the plight of the poor distorted reality. Tenancy and hired labor accounted for a minute fraction of the cultivated area and labor power in the prewar village. By the 1930s all social groups were experiencing vulnerability to general decline related to disorder, market disruption, war, famine, and the worsening land-population ratio." The notion of class struggle seemed strange to those who had worked together against the Japanese, said interviewees in the 1980s. In 1936, two landlord households owned 4.5 percent of the land, and averaged 10.6 mu per capita. Rich peasant households, all three, owned 5.9 percent of the land and had 7.9 mu per capita. Middle peasant households had 4.3 mu per capital, and poor peasants 0.9 mu per person. After land reform, landlord and rich peasant households had 5.8 mu per person, while middle peasants had 3.1 and poor peasants 2.2 mu. Poor peasants had more than doubled their holdings, but they still held pitifully small plots.[41] "In fact, because independent tillers predominated in the region and because tax reform had already wrought its silent revolution, only 7.7 percent of the land in the 764 villages of Raoyang, Hejian, and Shenxian countries had been confiscated and redistributed in the 1947–48 land reform."[42]

When the land reform period, 1949–52, was coming to an end, Wugong's early history of cooperativization reached the attention of provincial party leaders, who were determined to promote it as a model village. In 1951–52, the provincial party officials rewrote Wugong's history to make it appear that grain and cotton had been the source of its success, and not its sideline activities. The actual sources of the village's success—rope making and peanuts—were ignored since the party line now stressed basic agricultural production. This political shift resulted in a serious loss of income; in 1949–50, 45 percent of the co-op's income had come from sideline activities, but in 1952 it had dropped to only 8 percent. The village could not escape these political pressures particularly since its leader, Geng Changsuo, had been selected as a national agricultural model and invited to join a Chinese delegation to tour Soviet collectives.[43] In April 1954, the fourth district in Raoyang County was the first in China to achieve 100 percent cooperativization.[44] Geng had advanced the argument that collectivization could give the village a greater measure of security against the effects of a drought such as they experienced in 1952.[45] Collectivization offered a way to mechanize agriculture, and "provincial planners dreamed that, despite its poor soil and unreliable water, central Hebei could become China's Ukraine, the North China grain bowl."[46]

There were some Hebei officials who opposed aspects of collectivization. In a "secret speech" in April 1957, Mao referred to a former vice governor of Hebei who had opposed the unified purchasing and marketing system and advocated free trade.[47] But Mao had already determined to speed up the pace of collectivization. His sense of urgency was in large part caused by the realization that agricultural output, principally grain output, was barely keeping pace with population growth. Collectivization promised technical efficiency in agriculture, economies of scale that would allow for mechanization. It also was to provide a social incentive toward higher productivity. And underlying this was the advantage it gave the state in being able to plan production and therefore plan the extraction, distribution, and allocation of grain.

The move toward collectivization was paralleled by steps to gain control over the grain market. By at least 1953, the inadequacy of grain supplies was already undeniable, and steps were taken to shift grain marketing from commercial circulation to state control. In 1949–53, grain marketing was done in parallel channels—private grain merchants and peddlers (*shang* and *fan*) on the one hand, and government agencies on the other; both were holdovers from practices of the wartime period.[48] In 1953 grain prices rose by 12 percent due to higher demand from "construction" and from excessive government procurement. In addition, some places experienced natural disaster. Grain merchants and peddlers took advantage and seized grain, causing prices to rise. In July there were actually seizures of grain in various localities across the province, such as Xianghe, Fengrun, Ba xian, Gaoyang, and so on. At Ba and Jinghai counties, thirty merchants actually fought with authorities over the grain stocks. In Tianjin and Beijing, wholesale merchants struggled with unauthorized Hebei merchants, and riots broke out. By September the situation was so bad that in 90 out of Hebei's 131 counties, there was no grain for sale at the county capital.[49]

In October the provincial government convened a meeting on the grain supply problem and decided to apply a unified food grain procurement and purchase (*tonggou tongxiao*) policy starting with the fall harvest. A procurement target of 1.7 million tons of unhusked grain was set. More than 50,000 cadres were deputed to villages to implement this decision. They confiscated 1,450 tons of grain from 12,507 grain dealers, who were prohibited from further trading. In December there was a campaign to encourage households to sell grain to the state. Model counties were designated for a campaign to "love the country and increase grain production and sales." Raoyang was one of them. Within three months the goal of 1.7 million tons was met.[50] But even in 1954 there were outbreaks of violence or near-violence. In March in Gaoyang city, every day 500 or 600 people struggled to purchase grain (*qianggou*). In at least one village "bad elements" incited mobs to beat up the cadres.[51]

PHOTOGRAPH 12.1.   Hebei Province grain ration coupons, 1975

Thus began the grain procurement system that was to last until the mid-1980s, when it was replaced by the contract system. Private trading in grain was totally eliminated, and the state became the sole purchaser of grain and the sole determinant of prices. *Tonggou tongxiao*, literally "unified sales and unified purchase," was the key component in a complex system for dividing the harvest. It provided a guaranteed share, or ration, for individual and family consumption, while allowing the state to procure grain at below-market price levels. The relative proportions of rations and procurement were always determined by the state.

The grain ration was set by the state based on the standards necessary for subsistence. In Hebei in the 1950s the standard was one jin (0.5 kg) per person per day. The popular saying was "Gou bu gou, sanbailiu," or "Enough or not, three hundred sixty." In 1954 the minimum yearly ration in Hebei was set at 160–180 kg per capita, but it was lower in the mountainous and disaster districts (140–165 kg) and higher in the Zhangjiakou mountainous area (180–210 kg).[52] In the 1960s, nine ounces was the standard daily ration, or 328 jin per year (164 kg); there was an upward limit of 420 jin (210 kg). If the ration fell between 8 and 9 ounces per day, the state would neither procure nor sell grain. If the ration dropped below 8 ounces, or 294 jin (147 kg) per year, the state would make up the difference.[53] In fact, actual rations were often much lower.[54] Data that are now available for Hebei Province from 1965 to 1980 show the grain ration (*kouliang*) to have varied annually from a high of 221 kg (1979) to a low of 167 kg (1972).[55] (See Photograph 12.1.)

Grain rationing was not principally directed to the urban population, as is often said. Jean Oi has shown that "rationing had a far more significant impact on the lives of rural rather than urban dwellers." Urban residents purchased grain from state stores (free grain markets were closed after 1957) with cash and ration coupons, which were issued by their work units. Peasants used their work points to purchase grain from their team. If they did not have enough work points, they could pay cash or credit, but they were limited to the amount of the ration. Work points were intended to provide an incentive for harder work, but in reality work points did not determine the amount of grain a person could receive since it could not exceed the basic grain ration. As Oi points out, the ration system—together with household registration—essentially limited the mobility of peasants and kept them in their native villages.[56] Urban rationing included cooking oil, meat, eggs, chicken, bean curd, as well as major consumer items such as bicycles.[57]

On the other side, the state's claim on the harvest had two parts. The first was the state tax, which was levied as a percentage of the grain harvest, but was not very large and declined from an average of about 10.5 percent of the total grain output in the 1950s to 4.5 percent in the late 1970s. This tax was always paid in kind, and fine grains (*xiliang*), usually wheat or rice, were required.[58] The unit of accounting—that is, the unit on which the tax was levied—was the household at first, and in 1956 transferred to the cooperatives.[59] Under the communes, the team became the tax unit.

The second part claimed by the state was more variable and more controversial, the state procurement, or *tonggou*. This was supposed to be claimed only from the portion of the harvest that was considered to be a "surplus" (*yuliang*), that is, the amount that remained after the agricultural tax and the "three retained funds" (amounts for seed, fodder, and grain rations) had been deducted. Oi shows, however, that "the surplus was nothing more than an artifact of state regulations that manipulated the harvest's apportionment to legitimate the notion that the state was procuring only excess grain."[60] The amount of state procurement was not always a function of how much grain had been produced, and the amount of the basic grain ration was not absolutely guaranteed. State procurement amounted to compulsory sales by peasants at a set price that was usually under what a free-market price would have been. Procurement prices were adjusted only three times, in 1961, 1966, and 1979, and provided no incentive for the peasants. The basic procurement, *gouliang*, was a "forced delivery." The over-quota grain, *chaogou*, fetched a higher price. After 1979, there were negotiated-price sales, *yijia*, which provided more incentive.[61]

Although agricultural production and procurement both increased after the introduction of planning in 1953–54, in Hebei there were many problems and "sharp contradictions" in managing the unified procurement system.[62] In March 1955 Hebei Province applied the national policy of "*Sanding*," or "three-fixes": fixed production, purchase, and sales. Its purpose was to encourage the formation of cooperatives through advanced planning. In 1965 the policy shifted to "*Yiding sannian*," or "One fix in three years," that is, there was a commitment to maintaining quotas for at least three years at a time and to reducing procurement. This was followed by an adjustment of quota prices the next year. In 1971 central party policy changed to five years, "*Yiding wunian*," to stabilize agriculture even more and encourage increased production. Prices were raised once again. In 1982, at the start of the reform period, the party line changed to "*Sannian baogan*," or three-year guarantee of a household's contract for land and taxes, as well as procurement prices. This resulted in an unusual situation of overselling to the government because the government price was higher than the market price. In 1984 procurement quotas were lowered, and the Hebei provincial government further loosened the restrictions on planting of secondary farm products. Finally in 1985, the unified procurement system was replaced by the contract purchase system, and later the contract sales were reduced while the market-negotiated amounts were increased.[63]

As Table 12.1 shows, the rate of tax and procurement (*zhenggou lü*) in Hebei was highly volatile, starting at 23 to 26 percent in 1953–54, and rising to a high of 45 percent in 1959—the year of "exaggerated reporting." After the Great Leap debacle, procurement rates dropped to 12 percent in 1965 and generally remained under 16 percent thereafter. From 1962–68, after the Great Leap, the authorities reduced not only the level of procurements but also reserves to encourage production. From 1969 to 1978, there was an emphasis on local grain storage in order to reduce the dependence of localities on the state, but local storage created many problems of its own.[64] In 1983 and 1984, the rate rose to 24 and 26 percent because of the unusual price situation of those years. Because output has expanded in the last two decades, the amount of the procurement has increased even when the rate has been lowered.

The complex system of unified procurement that prevailed for almost thirty years gave peasants little incentive or opportunity to make investments in the land. It is not simply that the socialist organization of production failed to raise agricultural productivity, but that the socialist distribution system undercut it. At the same time that the state exhorted peasants to greater production, it extracted from them the fruits of their labors, leaving what was barely enough for survival. The grain ration was a guarantee of minimum subsistence, but it was also a limit on consumption. Despite the rhetorical support of agriculture, the state invested relatively little in the agricultural sector. When viewed from the village level, the state was a plunderer of local resources, struggling with peasants over the harvest.[65] But the state had other priorities to consider, principally the provisioning of cities and the reallocation of grain to other regions that had suffered disaster or were less well endowed. The details of redistribution of grain in the 1950s–80s are not fully known even now. But favoring urban areas over rural populations is not unique to China, and the reallocation of grain interregionally was undertaken, in more modest form, even in imperial times through the grain tribute and granary systems. The balance of right and wrong will continue to be debated, but there is little debate over the stark reality of grain insufficiency that was already clear in the mid-1950s.

The Great Leap Famine, 1959–1961

In 1958, a few localities in Hebei had collectivized more radically than others and claimed monumental harvests. In August, Mao visited Xushui County, north of Baoding, which became a model commune for the Great Leap Forward.[66] The local cadres said that the wheat harvest had yielded 754 jin per mu, for a total output of 1.1 million tons. Mao asked how the 310,000 people of the county could possibly eat so much grain! The following days he also visited Anguo and Ding counties and then proceeded to Henan and Shandong. He was said to have been greatly impressed and approved of the name *renmin gongshe* or "the people's commune" for these megacollectives.[67]

The Great Leap was motivated by a fundamental optimism—now regarded as a delusion—that China could overcome its essential economic backwardness through a collective will manifested in agriculture, industry, and way of life. (Mao had other reasons for launching the Great Leap; the Sino-Soviet split gave impetus to creating a Chinese form of socialism.) Agriculture was thoroughly collectivized. Households were organized into production teams, similar in size to a neighborhood. Teams were organized into brigades, similar in scale to a village. Brigades were organized into communes, which was a portion of a county (in the most radical phase, communes were county-sized). The commune was an administrative unit as well as a work unit, and organized social services such as clinics, dining halls, sewing centers, schools, nurseries and kindergartens, and so forth, in order to free women to engage in production outside the house.[68] One of the peasant household's central functions was eliminated when families were ordered to stop preparing their own meals and to begin eating in communal dining halls. Local practices varied somewhat, but private plots, previously the source of a family's vegetables, were forbidden.

A great wave of enthusiasm allegedly accompanied these changes. Impossible production targets were set for both agriculture and industry. The Great Leap's premise was that China could progress by "walking on two legs"—both agriculture and industry could develop simultaneously without waiting for gradual development. Peasants would increase steel production by working backyard furnaces. China would overtake Great Britain in "iron, steel and other major industrial products" in fifteen years.[69] Grain output could increase exponentially through the techniques of close planting and deep plowing.[70] When Mao went out to visit the masses in Xushui, children stood on top of the grain in the fields as if it were a closely woven carpet.[71] There was such an abundance that people were told to eat all they wanted free in the dining halls.[72] Mao said that the amount of land devoted to grain could actually be cut back because some land could be planted more intensively. "Plant less, produce more, and harvest the most." As a result, in 1959, cultivated acreage declined in most provinces, including Hebei.[73]

The harvests of 1958 had been particularly abundant all over China. Although good weather was probably the major factor, the bumper harvest was interpreted as a clear triumph of the Great Leap itself.[74] Peasants were enjoined to redouble their efforts, and cadres were reporting higher and higher harvest figures. As a result, procurement levels rose, and the state appropriated more and more grain. The reality, however, was that in 1959 output dropped sharply, so higher procurement levels left little in the countryside for people to eat. Intense political pressure was applied on local cadres by higher-level cadres to volunteer more grain for the state. There was grain in the granaries and some grain was even exported throughout the famine period.

In the initial period, the dining halls were a source of waste in large part because peasants were told to "Eat as much as you can, and do as much as you can." According to Xue Muqiao, leading Chinese economist, in the first year of the Great Leap overconsumption of grain amounted to 17.5 million tons. Some now see a link between the enthusiastic promotion of mess halls and the high excess mortality: the provinces that suffered the most deaths had been among those that had implemented dining halls earliest and most vigorously. Some households also hid grain during the early commune period.[75] Dali Yang's study establishes the correlation between the percentage of participation in "mess halls" in 1959 and famine mortality in 1960. Those provinces having more than 90 percent participation at the end of 1959 were: Yunnan, Hunan, Henan, Sichuan, Gansu, and Anhui. He calls this "the tragedy of the commons."[76] By 1959, people were not getting enough to eat. By 1960 the effects of famine were everywhere. Bad weather also affected output. In Hebei there was severe drought in the early part of 1960 followed by hailstorms and heavy rains.[77] In 1961 some regions had altered their harmful practices, and the state cut back on the procurement levels, but in other areas people continued to suffer greatly.

All told, the total excess mortality from the Great Leap Forward has been estimated at 30 million. Official figures acknowledge a lower figure, but some Chinese scholars believe that the number could have reached 40 million, or even higher.[78] The famine was experienced all over China, but more severely in some provinces than in others. Sichuan, Anhui, Henan, and also Tibet were the most seriously affected provinces, as seen from the demographic record and other evidence.

Sichuan had the highest level of mortality; estimates range from 7 to 9 million from a population of about 70 million. The severity of the famine in Henan and Anhui reflected the fanaticism of their "ultra-leftist" party leaders, which Jasper Becker details convincingly.[79] The horrors of the famine in Anhui have been documented in a remarkable publication from Fengyang County. Most shocking are the details about cannibalism, of which there were 63 reported cases. No doubt there were many more. Apparently the traditional principle, *yizi er shi*, was invoked in some of these cases. In one county in Henan there were 200 cases reported. Guangxi Province also had reported cases of cannibalism.[80] In Anhui the party chairman, a stalwart supporter of Mao, drove the cadres to enforce procurement through terroristic methods. Twelve and a half percent of the rural population were victims of punishment of crimes such as stealing food or refusing to give up food. The man-made nature of the tragedy was underscored by the fact that the granaries in the state were apparently full. The official count of fatalities in Anhui was 2 million, with another

2 million who fled. Others believe that as many as 8 million, or even more, died, representing one-quarter of the population of the province.[81]

In Henan Province, Xinyang County suffered so much abuse from extremist party leaders that reports of the "Xinyang incident" have been suppressed. The party head declared in 1959 after the Lushan Plenum that the peasantry was the enemy in the class struggle, and war must be waged against them. Cadres used violence, terror, and degradation to coerce peasants to hand over their grain and even their domestic possessions. Cannibalism was widespread, but severely punished. As in Anhui, the Henan granaries at this time were well stocked. The begging certificates that were allowed in other provinces were forbidden in Xinyang, so peasants could not even migrate.[82] Finally in early 1961, the People's Liberation Army troops were sent into Xinyang to distribute grain from the granaries and arrest the leaders; even Mao Zedong, who had turned a deaf ear to all news of famine, saw the Xinyang situation as excessive.[83] The death toll in Henan is a matter of dispute. At least 1 million may have died in the province, some say 2 million. Some older residents claimed as many as two-thirds of the population in their villages had perished; others reported at least 20–30 percent. In Xinyang and elsewhere in Henan, "holocaust" is perhaps a better word to describe what happened than "famine."[84]

By comparison with these provinces, Hebei was not one of the worst cases. Still, a recent semi-official publication edited by Deng Lichun gives the figure 1.49 million for excess mortality and reduced or postponed births during 1959–61.[85] Previous estimates had been much lower. Walker estimated that Hebei was among "the least affected" provinces. Although his estimate of total excess mortality of 18.5 million was lower than Banister or Ashton's, his estimate for Hebei for 1959–61 was 330,000. Added to 71,000 for Beijing and 58,000 for Tianjin, the total excess mortality may have been 459,000 for the region we have roughly called the Hai River Basin or Zhili Province.[86] Peng Xizhe, whose estimated national total was 23 million, gave a remarkably similar figure for just Hebei that includes four years, 1958–62: about 296,000.[87] Peng also observes, "Grain availability for the agricultural population in Hebei Province during the crisis was as limited as in Sichuan and Henan, but the extent of deaths in the former was much smaller than in the latter two provinces."[88]

A very revealing account of the "three lean years" in Hebei is provided in the gazetteer of the Hebei Province Grain Bureau, published in 1992, and is translated almost verbatim here with emphasis added.[89]

> In June 1958 the dining halls were set up in Hebei, but due to inadequate advance planning, there was large-scale waste of grain. In the fall there was a bumper harvest, but there was *a shortage of labor to harvest the grain. Serious losses and waste resulted.* For the entire province there was a *loss of 30–40 yi kg* [3–4 million tons].
>
> In the spring of 1959 there were more villages that had serious grain shortages. In Handan District alone, there were 6,650 production brigades, or 83.3 percent, that were short of grain. In order to calm people down, and protect production, the province launched a movement to economize grain, mobilized grain brigades to plant vegetables and look for food substitutes. At 220,000 dining halls, ration coupons were issued. By May the food situation was increasingly critical. The number of people lacking grain and the amount of food grain purchase were daily increasing. *The number of rural village people being supplied by the state reached 20 million, or 60.7 percent.* By the end of June the grain reserves in province dropped to 3 yi kg [0.3 million tons]. In nineteen counties there was less than one month's stock left. In some counties they had to import and sell grain on a daily basis. In not a few places each person could be guaranteed *only half a jin* of rations a day. Because people were eating wild vegetables, they developed edema and "*abnormal deaths*" [*feizhengchang siwang*] followed. That year the entire province had a poor harvest. *Because of overestimates of output and high procurement, too much grain was procured, and the average availability of grain per*

person was 164.5 kg, and peasants' standard of living declined. The provincial committee organized 54,000 cadres "to go down to the grassroots-level units" to manage the dining halls with grain as the focus, and to manage the livelihood of the masses. Ninety thousand dining halls practiced the method of using food grain substitutes and additives. Using dried vegetables of 36.5 yi kg [3.65 million tons], they were able to meet the absolute minimum nutritional needs of the peasants.

In 1960, the national economy reached its most difficult period. In the whole province large numbers of the population blindly left for other places. By mid-February about 110,000 village workers migrated to the northeast, Inner Mongolia, Beijing, and other places. There were about 59,000 people who developed edema and 450 abnormal deaths. In order to prevent further migration and to protect the spring planting, the provincial party authorities convened a conference and ordered shipments of grain; within one month . . . *a total of 13.08 yi kg [1.3 million tons] was delivered for the dining halls. 98.9 percent of the production brigades in the province thus received some form of care [zhaogu]* . . . . According to central guidelines, the rural per capita rations were reduced to 130–140 kg. In the fall most people ate *350–400 grams per day* [0.35–0.4 kg a day], 450 was the absolute top. In the three winter months, some were reduced to *250–300 grams.*

From February to April [1961], people could get *300–350 grams,* but not more than 400. In April, according to the provincial party directives, the standard should have been 350 grams all across the rural population; if it was insufficient, the state would supply the difference. Starting in the summer, at both at the national and local levels there was an adjustment of the policy of "egalitarianism" [*pingjun zhuyi*] in the distribution of rural grain. . . . On May 10 the provincial party committee forwarded to Chairman Mao the provincial governor's report on the dining-hall problem. At the beginning of May, each locality voluntarily disbanded dining halls.

This terse and nonjudgmental official account is remarkably candid and detailed. Several points need to be emphasized.

First is that massive trouble was apparent as early as the fall harvest of 1958. The loss or waste of 30–40 yi kg is monumental and amounts to something like half of the normal grain output for the year. In Table 12.1 the total output for 1958 is listed as 83.7 yi kg (8.3 million tons), and the grain output for 1957 was 81.9 yi kg (8.2 million tons).[90] The loss or waste was attributed to "a shortage of labor to harvest the grain," which almost certainly refers to the diversion of labor to construction of roads, dams, or backyard furnaces during the Great Leap Forward.

Second, in the spring of 1959 grain shortages were already critical. Twenty million people, or 60.7 percent of the rural population, were being subsidized by the state. That provincial grain reserves dropped to 3 yi kg (0.3 million tons) reveals that reserves *were* being used to address the situation. It is not clear what the total reserves had been, but figures given for the 1970s were in the range of 5.3 to 9.2 yi kg (0.53–0.92 million tons).[91] Transfers of grain in 1960 amounted to 13 yi kg (1.3 million tons) and suggest that the state still had some capacity to mobilize grain from externally held reserves.

Third, if rations in some places declined to just half a jin (one-fourth of a kilogram) in late 1959, that was just 250 grams a day, a pitifully small amount. In the fall and winter of 1960 rations were at the level of 250–400 grams per day (= 0.25 to 0.40 kg). By the start of 1961, the rations appeared to increase slightly.

Fourth, desperate measures were imposed: the emergency planting of vegetables instead of grains and the use of food substitutes and additives. People ate wild "vegetables," that is, grasses, weeds, and bark, as well as corncobs and chaff.[92] Other food substitutes that were served in the dining halls included soybean flour, sweet potato stalks, cottonseed cakes, and starches made of leaves and grasses.[93] Peasants would grind the dried food substitutes, such as tree bark or corn cobs, into a powder, and then cook them by boiling or steaming so they could be swallowed. Green herbs, leaves, and grass roots could be boiled without preparation. Feeling their stomachs to be empty, famine victims often resorted to eating nonedible matter that could not be digested and could have adverse consequences. One was called *guanyin tu* (the bodhisattva earth, or Buddha's soil); others were cotton or sawdust. Such famine "foods" provided a temporary feeling of fullness, but they had a disastrous impact on the digestive system. Some survivors recall their families ate such "foods," even knowing that they had no nutritional value, simply to have the sensation of fullness. The village social networks that had in other crises helped sustain famine victims had been destroyed by the communal kitchens and high levels of procurement.[94]

Fifth, as in the Qing and Republican periods, masses of people fled outside the province in search of food. Although the passage states that 110,000 people fled, the actual numbers were likely to have been greater, although not so numerous as in the Republican period, when there were no official constraints on migration.

Sixth, the document acknowledges many cases of edema and some cases of "abnormal" deaths. It is not clear whether the phrase "abnormal deaths" is used for the demographic term "excess mortality," or whether it suggests worse situations such as infanticide or cannibalism. Edema was called *fuzhong bing*, swelling sickness. It is not actually a disease, but rather a condition or outcome of malnutrition. Since malnutrition or starvation was not acknowledged, this euphemism was used. During these years other sources believe that throughout China, 10 percent of the urban population and 10–30 percent of the rural population suffered from edema. In Fengyang, Anhui, the proportion was 38 percent.[95]

Seventh, the document acknowledges, but does not emphasize, that "because of overestimates of output and high procurement, too much grain was procured." This underplays what many have felt was the principal cause of scarcity, the exaggeration by cadres of harvest output that allowed the state to claim an unduly large proportion of the harvest based on false information. This was later described as "*fukua.*" Cadres were under intense political pressure to report high figures; any suggestion that the unusual expectations of the Great Leap were unrealistic could lead to their being branded as rightists.[96]

Lastly, the document says that in 1960, 98.9 percent of production brigades received the "care" (*zhaogu*) of the state, a term reminiscent of the use of the term "comfort" (*fu*) in the late nineteenth-century disasters. Both terms avoided, for different reasons, describing this grain as "relief" (*zhenji*). Use of the term would be an acknowledgment that there was a famine. Befitting an official account, it emphasizes the orderly mobilization of resources to address the problems at hand and does not dwell on the human and social disaster that was at the heart of these years.

Under these circumstances, the extreme individual and social consequences of famine experienced in Hunan and Anhui must have been present to some degree in Hebei also, but they may have been more contained, less widespread. The fact that 1.3 million tons of grain were mobilized to help the communal dining halls suggests that reserves, either held within the province, or imported from other provinces, could still be utilized. This is remarkable, considering the chaotic situation and poor harvest of 1959 and 1960, and suggests why the mortality was not worse than it was even when the food supplies were so low. Of course provincial "exports" were the outcome of high procurement rates, but they also suggest that interprovincial transfers continued to take place, as they had in the mid-1950s. Walker estimates that in 1958–62, Beijing, Hebei, and Tianjin were "consistent grain importing provinces, with average annual amounts of 1,076,000 tons, 216,000 tons, and 777,000 tons respectively."[97] Only after 1961 did state policy change to halt interprovincial transfers because it could no longer sustain them; for the first time since 1949, foreign grain imports were permitted.[98]

The social history of this traumatic period has yet to be written. Some evidence from Wugong and Raoyang illustrates the general pattern. "Some brigades with no food in spring 1959 issued certificates to villagers granting them permission to go begging." By late that year, "Wugong villagers were reduced to eating cornstalks. There was little fuel and no cooking oil. It would be two decades before cooking oil became readily available. That winter, vegetables grown in fields fertilized by excrement had to be eaten uncooked." Raoyang was better off than other areas, but still "a few husbands sold their wives for food and cash. . . . To hide the shame, the wives were called cousins. . . . As in the famine fifteen years earlier, in some of the worst-hit areas children with placards around their necks were left at busy places, in hopes that some better-off family would take in the starving young." Edema was common and famine deaths were known.[99] A later account said that some peasants had been selling the flesh of dead children.[100]

Despite the fact that the food system established in the 1950s—grain procurement, rationing, and household registration—favored China's cities, the urban population was not spared the effects of famine. "Even in Beijing there was nothing to eat, while in the countryside just outside the capital peasants who had survived were too weak to plant the new crops or harvest them. In villages a few miles outside Beijing, most peasants were grotesquely swollen by oedema and were dying in sizeable numbers."[101] In all the cities, grain rations were drastically reduced or stopped entirely, while cooking oil and vegetables were unobtainable. In Beijing, university students' monthly rations fell from 33 to 26 lbs per month for males and from 28 to 22 lbs for women. When rations were 22 lbs, students stretched it to last for twenty-five days and had no grain left for the rest of the month.[102] But students were among the social groups that received special treatment; others included the sick, the young and elderly, leaders and cadre, and so forth. In general the average monthly grain ration was only 1.5 kg.[103] Those caught stealing grain were put to death. It was forbidden to buy or sell any food, even chickens one might have raised at home. By 1960, the party was trying to empty the cities of workers from rural areas and to send as many people to the countryside as possible.[104]

With so little nourishment, people fell ill or became extremely lethargic. Some workers were told to stay home. Within families extremely scarce food supplies had to be divided carefully among the children. People who survived these years can recall such details vividly—a grandmother who gave her share to the grandchildren, the father who managed to find some extra food, people with some privileged connections who got an extra amount of food. One Beijing resident, who was eight or nine years old during the famine, recalls that his parents would divide the family's meager rations into individual daily portions so that the children would not quarrel. One night his older brother was so hungry that he ate his next day's share and had nothing the next morning. Fortunately, his grandmother took pity on him and gave him her portion. At school, however, they were given extra food.[105] In Tianjin schools and universities closed down, and students tried to gather grass or bark.[106] Other people recalled having barely enough energy to walk home. One Tianjin old-timer recalled a saying that the fat got thin (from malnourishment) and the thin got fat (from edema).[107]

In the countryside, why did peasants comply with the orders to give up grain even in the face of certain starvation? Fundamentally they had no choice. Just as cadres were coerced or pressured to comply with unreasonable procurement goals, ordinary peasants were coerced by cadres. There was very little room for social bonds or humane instincts to be played out. In a social situation where everything became public, peasants were almost certainly aware that there were political reasons for their starvation, and that it was not just the weather. Yet some credence must be given to the notion that peasants had a deep trust in the party leaders, and that the leaders were sharing in their suffering as well. Peasants in Quzhou and Wei counties recounted to me that during the crisis, Zhou Enlai had visited their county. Although their resources were depleted, the commune leaders managed to find enough to prepare a banquet for Zhou. But Zhou refused to eat the banquet food, and instead ate the *wotou* that he had brought with him.[108] Although this appeared to be a touching parable repeated for the benefit of the overseas scholar, evidence of such a visit does exist. In May 1961, Zhou visited Hebei and visited some dining halls; in one he refused the meat that had been prepared for him, and in another he allegedly found nothing but thin gruel in the pots and ate a piece of *wotou*. The peasants spoke frankly with him about their suffering and their dislike of communal mess halls. Zhou reported his findings to Mao Zedong.[109] According to Becker, the same or similar incident took place in February 1961, when Zhou had spent three weeks in Hebei and reported to Mao that the peasants were so weak they could not work, and they wanted to dismantle the communes.[110] Perhaps that was the trip that my respondents had heard of.[111]

When asked to describe the natural disasters that they had experienced in their lifetimes, Hebei peasants that I interviewed in 1989 spoke at length of the dreadful experience of the 1943 famine and the relatively better experience of the 1963 flood. Only when asked directly, would they talk about the 1958–61 years. In addition to the Zhou Enlai parable, they spoke also of the bad weather of those years.[112] Sometimes they mentioned low rations. Most often repeated was that China suffered grain shortages in those years because of the need to repay Soviet loans. This was circulated officially as a reason for the suffering.[113] Older peasants compared the 1963 flood experience favorably with their memories of the 1943 famine by saying that they received ample government relief during 1963, whereas in 1943 "no one was in charge." But for 1958–61, no standard of comparison was even mentioned.

The Great Leap Famine of 1959–61 has never been described officially within China as a famine or disaster, using the words *zaihuang* or *jihuang*. The commonly accepted term today, the politically correct one, is "the three difficult years," usually translated "the three lean years." In 1962 Liu Shaoqi acknowledged that the cause of the three difficult years had been 30 percent natural disasters (*tianzai*) and 70 percent human error (*renhuo*), but even after his posthumous rehabilitation in the post-Mao years, and the party's repudiation of the Great Leap Forward, the designation of famine has been avoided. If intellectuals or officials refer to the "three lean years," they may also speak of *fukua*, which refers to the overprocurement that was the direct cause of the hunger. Perhaps the only book published in China on this famine still uses the term "natural disaster," *ziran zaihai*, in its title.[114] Only a book published in Hong Kong by a Chinese scientist residing in the United States uses the title *Renhuo* (human catastrophe).[115] Scholarly compilations of historical famines fail to refer to these years as a famine, although they may refer to bad weather and crop losses of those years.[116] A recent exception lists 1959–61 as "China's Big Famine" (*jihuang*), but also calls it "The Three Years of Natural Disaster."[117]

It is well known that as early as the Lushan plenum in 1959, Peng Dehuai, a founding father of the Chinese Communist movement, wrote to Mao describing the failures of the communes and the suffering of the peasants. Although Mao had been considering some pullback, when he was challenged by Peng, he reacted by insisting on the correctness of his ideas and ordered the continuation of the Great Leap policies. Peng Dehuai was dismissed for his troubles, and others were silenced by the example. In 1961 and 1962 the Great Leap was finally brought to an end because Liu Shaoqi, Deng Xiaoping, and other party leaders finally forced the truth on Mao. Communes were not disbanded, but the most egregious aspects of the procurement process were eliminated. But there was no acknowledgment of any fundamental error, just an admission of overzealousness by local cadres in carrying out directives. Although he was forced to step aside after the Great Leap, and the planners like Deng were in charge, Mao clearly was biding his time and nursing his grudges. In the Cultural Revolution, many "enemies" were persecuted, some to their deaths. Deng Tuo, who had dared to speak about the Great Leap Famine and impute a connection between it and the historical famines that he had studied, was the first victim, probably killed in 1966.[118] Liu Shaoqi and Peng Dehuai were the major political victims. It is abundantly clear that the Cultural Revolution was the outcome not simply of the failure of the Great Leap Forward but Mao's failure to acknowledge his mistake. Scholars have found the evidence of this connection, but Becker has expressed it most bluntly, "In effect, the Cultural Revolution was nothing more than a purge of those who had been responsible for ending the famine."[119]

The Great Leap Famine bears some resemblance to the famine in Soviet Ukraine in 1932–33, which is sometimes referred to as "Stalin's famine." Both came about as the result of cruel and unusually large grain procurements, not as the result of a harvest failure. Both took place in the process of forced collectivization of agriculture. Both were silent famines, unacknowledged by any authorities and ignored by the international press.[120] The human costs were extremely high in both cases; estimates of mortality in the Stalin famine range from 5 to 8 million deaths, which must be added to other deaths resulting from forced collectivization.[121] The differences between the two are also important. Although both famines were the result of forced collectivization, Stalin is well known to have distrusted the peasantry, particularly the *kulaks* or rich peasants, and was in effect waging war on them, a war that can also be interpreted as a war against Ukrainians.[122] "In the Chinese case, there is simply no evidence that the state regarded peasants in this light. . . . There is no evidence that GLF procurements were viewed as a weapon of war . . . designed to force peasants into submission to state goals." Rather, according to Thomas Bernstein's analysis, the famine was the unintended result of a false assumption—that output had increased.[123] Also, in China the famine was not contained in one region, like the Ukraine, but affected all regions to one degree or another.

In Chinese historical perspective, the Mao famine also stands alone, utterly unlike anything that had occurred before. When Chinese referred to natural disaster and human calamity, *tianzai renhuo*, the latter usually referred to a human event such as rebellion or war, not to an "error" of an individual human being. Some Qing emperors were exemplary leaders who genuinely cared for the welfare of the peasants; others were lacking in ability, negligent or overwhelmed by external events. But none could be said to have actually *caused* a famine to occur. When the Mao famine took place, the country was not experiencing political or dynastic decline, foreign invasion, or internal rebellion. The spirit of the country was high, and the leaders enjoyed great legitimacy and popularity. The government was fully functional and enjoyed a greater degree of control than any bureaucracy of the past.[124] In imperial times, when large-scale famines took place, emperors and bureaucrats tried to deliver famine relief to the stricken region. Whether their efforts were efficacious or not, they were *on record* as having done their duty. The Qing official record of famines and famine relief was overwhelming in its volume and detail. For the Mao famine, there is no record, no acknowledgment, no acceptance of imperial responsibility.[125]

Controlling Nature

In addition to the *renhuo* of the Great Leap Famine, North China continued from the 1950s through the 1980s to experience destructive and costly natural disasters, the historically familiar *tianzai.* In Hebei between 1949 and 1988, there were seven years when there were droughts affecting more than 10 million mu: 1962, 1965, 1972, 1975, 1980, 1986, and 1987. There were five years when there were floods or waterlogging affecting 20 million mu or more: 1954, 1956, 1963, 1964, and 1977.[126] The period from 1949 to 1964 was generally a wet period, and the period from 1965 through the 1980s was a dry period.[127]

After 1949 Hebei continued to experience unfavorable climatic conditions, a deteriorating river system, and soil degradation. Its agricultural output was extremely vulnerable to weather fluctuations, and showed great annual variability. Figure 12.3 shows that with the exception of the difficult years from 1959–64 (including both the Great Leap and the 1963 flood), grain output in Hebei showed periodic cycles of three to five years that appear very much like the short-term price cycles seen in the eighteenth century. This pattern continued even from 1963 to the early 1980s, when grain output was consistently improving, but after the early 1980s, these short-term cycles seem to have disappeared. Although weather is still the most important factor in short-run fluctuations in yield, North China has become less vulnerable to fluctuations in the weather compared to the 1930s, according to Y. Y. Kueh. Among other factors, large-scale instability in the amount of sown area due to disasters has been eliminated.[128]

The achievement of agricultural growth and stability has been credited to the post-Mao market reforms and agricultural decollectivization of the 1980s, but as observed in Figure 12.3, agricultural productivity in Hebei began its upward trajectory in the mid-1960s, well before decollectivization took place. Much, if not most, of the improvement in yields were the result of technical improvements in agriculture, sometimes called China's Green Revolution, and the more scientific and rational management of water and soil conservancy.[129] These gains were made in the context of recovery from the Great Leap Famine. The slogan "take grain as the key link" first appeared in the *People's Daily* as early as February 1960 and was generally attributed to Zhou Enlai. In subsequent years it would be repeated in different contexts, but it always stressed the primary importance of agricultural production, particularly grain—a return to fundamentals. Even when the highly political and high-profile campaign "In Agriculture, Learn from Dazhai" was launched in 1964 and became part of the Cultural Revolution, agricultural research and water management were somewhat sheltered from the political storms.[130] The policy of self-reliance has been regarded as harmful to economic development as a whole since it restricted commercial crops, sideline industries, and periodic markets, but the emphasis on grain benefited Hebei's food economy.[131] Agricultural innovations were designed and implemented by hydraulic engineers, agronomists, soil specialists, and other technicians, who were protected from the political pressure applied to most intellectuals, and could remain both "red and expert," applying their technical skills to solving urgent agricultural problems.

Soon after the establishment of the People's Republic in 1949, there was excessive rainfall that caused much damage in the eastern, central, and southern parts of the province—so attention was focused on flood control and prevention. The repair of dikes along the major rivers—including the Daqing River (including the Thousand-Li Dike), the Yongding River, and others, as well as the opening up of outlets that were blocked—were top on the agenda. Each year 100,000 laborers were mobilized to undertake this construction. In addition, several major dams were built in the upper reaches of major rivers.[132] During the Great Leap Forward and afterward, 1958–63, an accelerated program of construction was undertaken. Many reservoirs of different sizes were built to retain water upstream, according to a 1958 plan for the Hai River Basin. This included ten large and twenty medium-size dams.(See Map 12.1.) Under the Great Leap Forward's mass mobilization

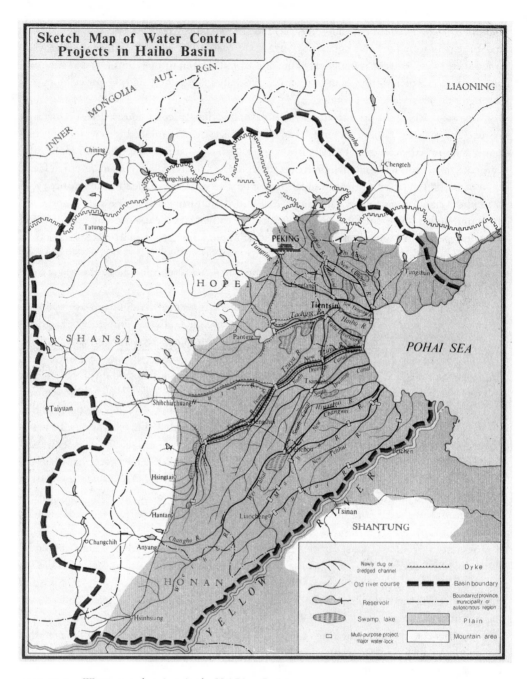

MAP 12.1.   Water control projects in the Hai River Basin, c. 1975

SOURCE: Ho Chin, *Harm into Benefit*, foldout map.

techniques, huge workforces totaling 2 million people were sent out to hard labor. Although these were great achievements, it is now acknowledged that "leftist" mistakes were also made, and that projects were overly large and built too hastily. To guard the plains against flood and to collect and save water was the principal task, *xushui*, without draining out the water, *paishui*.[133]

In 1963, right after the Great Leap Famine, the entire Hai River Basin experienced massive flooding, described as a *hongshui*, which was followed in 1964 by a severe case of waterlogging, *lishui*. In early August 1963, unusually heavy rains fell in the Taihang mountain western portion of the province. This rainfall was torrential, described as a *baoyu*, "explosive rain." In five days, more than 600 mm of rain fell in the area from Handan to Baoding. Handan alone received over 1,000 mm of rainfall, including 500 mm that fell in one day![134] Although the ten big reservoirs in the mountains could retain some of the rainfall, much of it drained into the other rivers in the Hai River system, causing practically all to overflow their banks. This classic *hongshui* affected 101 counties and flooded more than 53 million mu of crop land.[135] A total of 75 million mu of land were under water, and 20 million people were affected.

A massive relief effort was launched: 100,000 cadres and 51,000 soldiers and sailors deployed in boats distributed 1.5 million kg of cooked food to flood victims.[136] It was exceptionally well organized. Relief included rice, potatoes, cabbage, and clothing. Peasants compared it favorably with earlier crises, particularly that of 1943. In 1963 all suffered together, not just the peasants, and there was help from the outside.[137] In the words of one old peasant who had lived through several natural disasters, "Someone was in charge" [*you ren guan*]. Although he was comparing 1963 to 1943, he may also have been thinking of the Great Leap Famine.[138] In another part of the province, a peasant interviewee compared 1963 relief effort to the 1939 flood, when "no one was in charge" [*meiyou ren guan*].[139] Ten years later in 1973, by comparison, a smaller-scale flood (*lau*) yielded less government assistance; no one had any reserves; they purchased grain back from the government.[140]

In this crisis, Mao Zedong made several well-publicized visits to the disaster regions and reportedly knew all the details about crop losses and so forth. Perhaps this was an attempt to regain some of the credibility he lost in the Great Leap Forward. In November Mao heroically declared, "We must control the Hai River," looking very much a serious engineer poring over maps of the region, thus launching another kind of campaign. (See Photograph 12.2.) The strategy was to store water upstream, retain water in midstream, and flush it out in the lower reaches, but the main emphasis was on drainage, or *pai*. After approval from the State Council in 1965, every year a labor force of 300,000 men was mobilized to dig outlets and canals to fulfill the large-scale plan for controlling the Hai River system. When the project was completed in 1979, channels to the ocean were created for the Ziya, Yongding, Chao-Bai, Zhang-Wei, Duliu, Heilonggang, and many other rivers. (See Map 12.1.) Called *xinhe* or "new rivers," these were diversion canals that would relieve the pressure on the Hai River in times of rising waters. The total cost was 1.725 billion yuan.[141]

The expansion of irrigation was the second thrust after 1963. In the 1950s many tube wells were dug, but starting in the 1960s and continuing into the 1980s, there was a rapid expansion of mechanized wells, and by 1988 about 80 percent of irrigation facilities were power-driven.[142] The period of most concentrated development started in 1965. At a conference in October 1966 Premier Zhou Enlai cautioned against overly hasty digging of wells, urging attention to getting it right. At that time there were 75,800 wells that generated 700,000 horsepower and could irrigate 25.20 million mu; by the end of 1988 there were an additional 687,000 electrical wells that could irrigate 39.08 million mu.[143] Altogether, from 1949 to 1985, Hebei's irrigated land expanded from 11.54 million mu to 53.59 million mu, more than a fourfold increase. Grain yields rose from 100

PHOTOGRAPH 12.2. Mao and the Hai River Basin. (Chairman Mao studying map of the Hai River Basin.)

SOURCE: Ho Chin, *Harm into Benefit*, front.

CALLIGRAPHY: "The Hai River must be brought under permanent control! Mao Zedong, November 17, 1963."

jin per mu to 700 jin.[144] Irrigated land was 10.6 percent of cultivated land in 1949: in 1988, it was 55.3 percent.[145]

Irrigation, which included canals and reservoirs in addition to wells, vastly expanded output in Hebei, but such intense use of underground water combined with inadequate drainage contributed to the growing challenge of salinization and alkalinization of the soil, which by the 1970s had become a grave environmental challenge, equal to that of flood or drought. The "salt-affected soils," or *yanjian di*, resulted from poor drainage of the plains area and the dry weather. The old expression that out of every ten years there were nine years of waterlogging was not an exaggeration. Irrigation accelerated the process of salinization because the water table was raised, causing more salts to rise to the surface. Before the 1950s, waterlogging had existed, but more water eventually drained to the ocean. The tenfold increase in irrigation since 1949 had raised productivity in some areas, but in the Heilonggang region, salinization had wiped out these gains. By 1960–62 there was actually a "salt crisis," *yanzai*.[146] Most specialists now consider that there were "errors" in water conservancy in the 1950s stemming from too much storage on the plains in small reservoirs and insufficient drainage. In the late 1950s water was diverted from the Yellow River for irrigation and storage on the North China plain, but secondary salinization developed because the problem of drainage was neglected. The area of saline soil increased from 1.9 million hectares to 3.2 million, and it took more than ten years to correct the mistake.[147]

The problem of salinization had no simple solution. In such a drought-prone climate, water storage and irrigation are necessary for agriculture, while too much water concentrated in one period and not drained causes salinization and low yields. Some experts, including the Hebei provincial authorities, advocated drilling deep wells, 300 meters or more, which would lower the water table and reduce salinization. But other specialists felt that deep wells would reduce the underground water too rapidly—water that could not be restored easily. A new approach was developed at Quzhou (in southern Hebei) under the direction of Beijing Agricultural University (now Chinese Agricultural University) that simultaneously addressed the four problems of drought, waterlogging, salinization, and mineralization of the underground water. This comprehensive method used a complex network of wells and canals. For each deep well dug for irrigation, there were also three to five shallow wells that could be used alternately for irrigation or drainage. A network of major and minor channels permitted the collection of underground water, but also allowed for drainage, depending on the time of the year. The main canals were for irrigation, while trunk and branch ditches were used for the regulation of groundwater and drainage.[148]

In the Quzhou experimental district, there was a dramatic improvement in yields between 1972 and 1982, with two- to fourfold increase in grain yields, and a fourfold increase in cotton production. The per capita income of the peasants increased fivefold.[149] Local cadres considered that Quzhou had achieved self-sufficiency by 1980.[150] Comprehensive soil and water management was extended all over the Heilonggang region with basically positive results. In Shulu County alkalinization, waterlogging, and flooding in 1977 caused output to decline drastically. During 1977–78, a huge labor force was mobilized to dig a series of canals and ditches to improve irrigation. The next year the output more than doubled.[151] These were the results of intense application of scientific and technical skills by agronomists, soil chemists, plant specialists, climatologists, and engineers. They also required a large investment of central and provincial funds and required electrical and other inputs. This modern management of the soil may be compared in its intensity and complexity with the traditional water control—*shuili*—that had transformed land and agriculture in South China in earlier centuries.

Insufficiency of water remains the fundamental environmental constraint. The twenty-nine large reservoirs that retain water in the mountains prevent flooding and also irrigate the regions near the mountains. But the rivers that have traversed the Hai River Basin region have virtually dried up, and none are navigable. One cannot travel from Tianjin to Baoding by water; even in the late Qing this was problematic. The Nan Yunhe is basically dry, except perhaps in the summer months. The historically turbulent Yongding River is also dry most of the time. Most of the riverbeds are used to plant crops. Even the Daqing River, the best river system in the region, was dry during the 1980s drought period. Its several lakes and ponds were completely dry from 1982–87, including the extensive Baiyang Lake (previously the Xi dian). The lake's surface had been shrinking since the early Qing due to encroachment and reclamation. But from the 1960s it became so dry that its ecosystem changed; fish were no longer able to survive.[152] In 1989 some water was released from the reservoirs upstream in anticipation of summer floods, but generally speaking the Water Conservancy Bureau is conservative because it does not want to be blamed for any floods. Local authorities were engaged in a coordinated effort to preserve the lake and exploit its economic potential. In 1989, local industry in the Baiyang Lake region flourished, as the *luwei* reeds were collected and used once again for weaving mats and baskets.[153]

Water-management policies have been caught between the contradictory goals of conserving water (for irrigation and to prepare for drought) and pumping out water (to avoid waterlogging and salinization). In the 1950s, the building of reservoirs stressed the conservation of water, but this emphasis on collecting water, *xushui*, was later criticized for accelerating the process of salinization. During the Great Leap Forward, large-scale dam construction efforts were accompanied by the building of many local dikes and dams that were described as a chain of grapes across the plains region. Later described as a "leftist" mistake, the policy of "each piece of land has its own piece of sky" meant that each locality should store its own rainwater and not allow it to flow downstream. This strange form of the self-reliance policy meant that serious conflicts among localities arose, and water tables were raised, causing further salinization.[154] After the 1963 flood, the emphasis turned from *xushui* to *paishui*, as the drainage canals flushed water out to the ocean. In the 1970s, the comprehensive systems of irrigation and drainage built at Quzhou and all over the Heilonggang region were meant to address the dilemma of too little and too much water. But officials from the water-deficient regions such as the Yongding River and Baiyang Lake still complained about excessive *pai* and not enough *xu*.[155]

It is the cities and industries that have most keenly felt the shortage of water. The rapid expansion of urban population, particularly in Beijing and Tianjin, together with the industrial demands for water have created a serious crisis. Previously the rivers supplied water to Tianjin, but this is hardly possible any more, even in rainy years. In the worst drought years, 1980–82, some urban residents had to line up to get water.[156] In 1981 the State Council decided to launch the construction of a channel to divert water from the Luan River, northeast of Hebei, a distance of 234 km, to supply Tianjin with water. Completed in the 1990s, this water supply has sufficed for Tianjin's needs through the end of the twentieth century. In 2002 an even more ambitious project to divert Yangzi River water to Beijing and Tianjin, debated for decades, was launched. Called Nanshui Beidiao, "Bringing the southern waters to the north," this project is widely accepted as necessary, but its route and implementation have been almost as controversial as the Three Gorges Dam project in the central Yangzi River because of the negative consequences for the regions from and through which the water would be diverted. Three routes will be constructed. The eastern route using the former Grand Canal to bring water toward Tianjin is the first. The central route will divert water from the Yangzi upstream from the Three Gorges Dam and the Han River via a newly constructed canal. It will supply Beijing but displace hundreds of thousands of farmers in Hubei and Hunan. A western route will not be completed until midcentury.[157]

Unleashing the Market

In reflecting on the significant agricultural advances in the 1970s and 1980s, cadres at Quzhou cited three reasons for improvement in the standard of living: land and water conservancy (*gaitu gaishui*), scientific management (*keji*), and the household responsibility system.[158] The Third Plenum of the Eleventh Central Committee in 1978 stands out as a pivotal event in the history of the People's Republic of China. Deng Xiaoping, the new party leader, took a bold step to promote economic modernization, a set of programs that would eventually lead to "market socialism." In agriculture, the process of decollectivization and the household responsibility system, already under way in many localities, was made universal. The commune, brigade, and team system of production and administration was almost completely disbanded. The household became the decision-making and production unit. By the late 1980s, it could be said that "peasants are now allowed to consume as much as their own family harvests can provide. No longer do they depend on the team for their basic food supply. Work points, grain rationing, and state-set limits on consumption are relics of the past."[159] Although land was not privatized, households could contract with the local authorities for the amount of land they were willing to farm, in return for which they would agree to sell to the state a certain amount, not proportion, of the harvest at certain prices. The amount of tax and quota procurement that was compulsory was lowered, and the above-quota procurement price was supposed to be competitive with market prices. By 1985, the unified procurement system was replaced by a contract system. These new arrangements gave farm households incentives to increase production.

With markets revived, farm households were also encouraged to produce commercial crops to engage in sideline productive activities, and no longer forced to "take grain as the key link." In Hebei, the dramatic increase in cotton production, seen in Figure 12.3, was a direct response to the new policies. Other commercial crops in Hebei included oil-producing crops such as peanuts, sesame, huma, and rape seed. The increase in corn production was also related to its commercial use as feed grain, rather than food grain. Fruits and nuts, important commercial crops in the first half of the century, were once again abundantly produced. Livestock production also received a boost.[160] Although much agricultural output was marketed interregionally, grains, vegetables, fruit, and meat were also marketed within rural localities as periodic markets were revived. Between 1980 and 1993 in China as a whole, they increased from 38,000 to 67,000.[161] In North China, this type of market activity constituted in effect a revival of the practices that were highly developed in the Republican period.

Off-farm employment was another way in which farm households could increase their income since people were no longer tightly bound to their home localities because of grain rationing. In all parts of China, starting in the economically advanced regions of eastern and southern China, rural industries flourished. By 1996, there were 23 million rural enterprises that employed 135 million people, or about one-third of the rural workforce.[162] These industries were largely the product of entrepreneurial initiatives taken by county and local governments as well as individual entrepreneurs. The commune-brigade-team structure of administration was replaced by townships and traditional villages. To earn income and to provide employment opportunities for the local

PHOTOGRAPH 12.3.   Three generations of a Hebei farm family and corn harvest, 1989. Photo by author.

population, counties and townships began to operate enterprises along a wide range: from light industry to handicrafts to merchandising. Cadres were transformed into entrepreneurs. This phenomenon has been described as a "local corporate state" with three levels of authority: county, township and village.[163] The result was a kind of corporatism that changed the nature of political authority and blurred the distinction between state and market, public and private. In their study of Shulu County, Blecher and Shue highlight the entrepreneurial role of the county government in economic development, a process that started in the 1970s, even before Mao's death, including promotion of industry, trade, foreign trade, and residential real estate.[164] Although the range of enterprises in North China did not match the variety in South China, their importance in contributing to rising family incomes cannot be overestimated.[165]

In the 1980s, peasant households all over Hebei saw a marked improvement in their standard of living. Previously in many villages in the Heilonggang District, which was most impoverished, people said, "To eat grain, you depend on the state; to farm, you depend on loans; and to live, you depend on relief."[166] After the reforms, peasants' incomes from rising grain yields, sales of commercial crops, and engagement in off-farm labor permitted them to eat better, live more comfortably, and have some measure of security against disaster. In Quzhou, where land had been so waterlogged and later salinized, peasants in the 1980s grew wheat, corn, and cotton, where they had once raised only sorghum. They ate mostly fine grain, *xiliang*, where they once ate coarse grains, *culiang*. Every year they had a surplus, mainly of corn and beans, that they sold. Households claimed to have at least one year's grain reserve. The older generation complained that the younger generation could not understand the suffering they had been through. In some places, the richer peasant families were building spacious brick houses with tile roofs in place of the simpler houses of the past.[167] (See Photograph 12.3.)

In Baodi County, in the northern part of the province not far from Tianjin or Beijing, most households have three years' grain reserve, and they were eating rice. The previous low-lying land *wadi* had been transformed into rice fields (perhaps realizing the dream of Prince Yi). Among the flourishing commercial crops were the "three-hots" for which the county was known: red pepper, garlic, and scallions. Township enterprises included camping tents (a joint enterprise with European firm), clothing, shoes, cotton linings for curtains, furniture, optical equipment, and so on. There was an impressive new housing development, and in general the region exuded an air of confidence.[168]

Regulating the Grain Market

Although market reforms and the household responsibility system provided great incentives for farmers to increase production, the marketing of grain was never entirely "free." The state decollectivized production, reduced procurement quotas, and allowed prices to play an equilibrating role—but from 1978 to the end of the 1990s, the pendulum swung back and forth between more liberalization and more government intervention in the market. "Getting the prices right" has not been easy.

In the initial period 1978–84, the unified procurement system was adjusted so that peasants were allowed to sell excess grain either on the free market, or to the state at the above-quota price. "Whereas it had meant a kind of obligation for the farmers to sell all marketable grain to the state, it was now a kind of obligation for the state to purchase all the grains that the farmers wanted to sell." This was advantageous for the farmers. "When the market price was favourable, they would sell the extra-quota amount of excess grain in the market. When it was not favourable, they would sell the product to the state." The above-quota price "functioned essentially as a protective price (or a price support). The actual procurement was in effect one of 'mandatory procurement at low price plus high price protection for above-quota production.'"[169] Negotiated price sales became much more important, with greater latitude allowed to private traders in the grain market. Nevertheless, throughout the period 1975–91, the state was still the major buyer of grain, accounting for well over 80 percent of all marketed grains, but an increasingly larger share of the state purchase was through negotiated purchase prices.[170]

A grain glut in 1983–85 was the unexpected result. The market price fell to close to the above-quota price in many areas—so farmers preferred to sell to the state. Since the state was obligated to purchase the grain, a glut developed. Granaries could not hold the amount of grain that was purchased. It also created a financial burden for the government.[171] Thus in 1985 the unified procurement was replaced by "contract procurement." The *amount* of grain sold to the government was determined through mutually agreed contracts. The quota and above-quota prices were replaced by a single price. At first the price was so low that farmers were slow to sign contracts. "The implementation of the contract system at the local level was therefore far from voluntary."[172] In times of shortage, however, the government had to adjust the negotiated price to encourage farmers to sell. In 1988 poor harvests resulted in grain shortages that produced a "rice war." Provinces competed to buy grain, while some blocked grain from leaving their provinces, reminiscent of the occasional grain blockages in the Qing period. In 1989–90, by contrast, when there were record-high grain harvests, the state stepped in to purchase more grain from farmers to protect them. A "special grain reserve system" was established for emergencies and also to stabilize grain supplies, similar in principle to the ever-normal granaries of the Qing. But since then, there have been difficulties with grain reserves, mostly with insufficient capacity and deteriorating granaries (many were built before the 1970s).[173]

In the early 1990s, greater market liberalization was permitted as surpluses continued and prices fell. Rationing was discontinued, and procurement prices were raised to market levels.[174] For the first time the majority of grain was traded through private traders. These reforms resulted in market or price integration. By 1993 greater nationwide price integration had been achieved.[175] Urban grain ration coupons were terminated in 1993. Previous subsidies for urban provisioning were huge, 40.8 billion Rmb, or 14 percent of total budgetary revenue.[176] The marketing of grain within cities was commercialized, but shops had to sell grain and oil at market prices. The shops could choose their own suppliers, not necessarily the government.[177] In rural areas, prefectural and county grain bureaus and township grain stations were converted into commercial grain trading companies, which agreed to carry out certain government functions, such as quota procurement and storage of grain reserves.[178]

After 1994, however, price inflation set in and caused officials to reassert control.[179] Grain prices rose 70 percent or more in rice and 60 percent in wheat and maize. No one really knows why. The market reforms were blamed. "Private traders and 'unscrupulous quasi-state traders' were accused of draining surplus areas of local stocks, driving prices even higher. Urban wholesalers were accused of stockpiling inventories in deficit areas, taking advantage of their market power." There was a perception that the government had lost control of the grain market and needed to step in.[180] The 1994 grain-buying panic by grain-deficit coastal provinces ended only when the central government released 2.5 million tons of grain reserves to lower prices and calm the market.[181] Thus began a period of retrenchment and adjustment. The strategy was to "safeguard the quantity while liberalizing the prices," but there were many difficulties.[182] Price controls and rationing of state grain were reintroduced in twenty-nine of the thirty-five largest cities. In rural areas procurement quotas at below market prices were reintroduced.[183]

In 1995 "the governor responsibility system" gave governors the ultimate responsibility for food and grain in the provinces. The new policy was a reaction against the decline in grain output in the southeastern provinces and tilted back toward a greater emphasis on regional self-sufficiency in grain.[184] It called on provincial governors to assume responsibility for "the rice bag," including guarding acreage, grain output, grain supply, and grain reserves. Seventy to eighty percent of marketable grain was to be controlled by province. The central government was to maintain national grain reserves and set policy about imports and exports and coordinate with other provinces.[185] It increased the pressure on provinces to develop agriculture and food production and to reverse the trend of declining crop land. It had some good results, but bad outcomes included regional protectionism, inefficiencies in resource allocation, and overreporting of production.[186] In 1998 the state reversed earlier policies and allowed only state grain stores to purchase grain from peasants. Private traders were still allowed but had to buy grain from state stores (that are the middlemen), not directly from the peasant households, unlike the practice of the 1980s and early 1990s of permitting private grain traders to buy directly from peasant households, competing with state grain stations for grain supply.[187]

Retrenchment policies pursued since the mid-1990s may in part have reflected the Chinese reaction to *Who Will Feed China: Wake-Up Call for a Small Planet* by Lester R. Brown, an American who heads World Watch Institute, an environmental research organization in Washington, DC. Brown argued that declining crop land in China, coupled with increasing consumption of meat, would cause China to import large quantities of grain over the next few decades. In 1994 China had already imported, he claimed, 20 million tons of grain. Following on his earlier work and that of Frances Moore Lappé's classic *Diet for a Small Planet*, Brown emphasized the amount of grain that is diverted from human consumption when grain-costly livestock are raised. China's demand for grain imports would, he claimed, destabilize world markets, raise grain prices, and cause great hardship for poorer countries in Africa and elsewhere in Asia.

The official Chinese reaction to this book was fast and furious. The Ministry of Agriculture denounced it, saying that by 2035, China's grain output would double and there would be no problem.[188] What ensued was a vigorous debate within China's political and technical elite, with most experts publicly criticizing Brown's facts, assumptions, and conclusions. The State Council's Institute for Development Research invited Brown to Beijing to discuss his ideas.[189] In 1996 and 1997 there were many newspaper articles about China's "food grain problem," *liangshi wenti*.[190] Privately, however, agricultural bureaucrats and specialists were glad for the attention drawn to the needs of the agricultural sector, which had been somewhat overshadowed by development in industry and international trade during the recent decade.[191] It increased pressure on the central government to allocate more resources to agriculture and to pay more attention to the neglected rural sector of the economy and the "food grain problem." Intellectuals could safely use this issue to criticize policy. A book with the inflammatory title *A Cry to Awaken the World: Will Famine Again Knock at China's Door?* supported Lester Brown's position.[192] While causing a furor in China, Brown's book received little attention in the West. The few Western analysts who did pay attention were dismissive of its perspective and evidence, observing that he had underestimated the growth potential of Chinese agriculture and at the same overestimated how quickly Chinese would turn to a meat-heavy diet.[193]

The spectacular advances in agricultural output, industrialization, and a higher standard of living in the twenty years from the late 1970s to the late 1990s have largely been credited to "market socialism" and the Deng-era reforms. Economic performance has been judged by higher gross national product and a higher standard of living for most people, and not by grain output or sufficiency. Although economic growth has shifted attention away from grain or food fundamentalism, it is clear that the leadership must readdress the food grain issue periodically, and that it remains highly sensitive to criticism that China cannot feed itself. Even with market liberalization, the state has never relinquished its overall control of the grain market, and large grain bureaucracies exist at every level of government to regulate grain contracts, sales, and reserves.[194] The government never completely liberalized the grain market in the 1980s. "Instead, planners directed a vast network of bureaucratic agents to procure, transport, process, and sell grain in an effort to preserve the government's influence over the economy. . . . Parastatal marketing agencies . . . play a leading role in controlling the scope of market activity and moving goods to key sectors and regions." The strategy puts "pressure on deficit regions to increase investments in agriculture by threatening to deny them grain shipments."[195]

Conclusion

At the end of the century, prosperity for many people in China has allowed them to leave hunger behind. Indeed, it may be a mark of how far the urban population, at least, has improved its standard of living that the food problem for the spoiled only-children, the "little emperors," is not scarcity and hunger, but obesity and indulgence in fast food and snacks. Whereas the older generation remembers the famine years of the Great Leap Forward, the rationing of grain and other key foods, and standing in line at poorly stocked state stores, the younger generation regards such tales of scarcity as irrelevant to their experience.[196]

The vanquishing of famine, and the extension of food security to most of the population, have been heralded as a great achievement of the Chinese Communist Party. When contemplating the travails of the past, Chinese over a certain age will invariably say, "At least in China today, everyone has enough to eat." On this point there is wide agreement, yet at the same time left unspoken is the memory of the great physical hunger endured by so many for so long, as well as the spiritual and psychological scars left by the various leftist campaigns and policies that only increased hunger rather than lessening it. A corollary to food fundamentalism particularly since the failure of the Great Leap has been the birth control policies that have been tantamount to "rationing the children." Only with serious grain shortages and declining per capita grain rations did the state take draconian measures to enforce the one-child policy, the other side of the population-food equation.[197]

While trumpeting the conquest of hunger, state and party leaders are sometimes deeply ambivalent about food security issues. It is, of course, the case that hunger has not been completely eliminated, and there are many poor people, often in the poorest regions of China, who have been untouched by the general prosperity of the 1980s and 1990s. It is also quite evident that "the food grain problem" requires constant vigilance, particularly in the face of China's enormous water shortages and environmental degradation. But equally critical and problematic is that the complete disappearance of the hunger problem, even if possible, would deprive the party of what has been its least controversial basis of political legitimacy. While the Communist Party simultaneously addressed and worsened the problem of food, the problem of food helped to shape the party's ideology and enhance the state's power.

In the late 1990s party leaders resorted to food fundamentalism when pressed on issues such as human rights or democracy. During his 1997 visit to the United States, Jiang Zemin argued that China was still a land-poor country with a large population, and therefore political freedom and democratization had to take second place to the challenge of feeding the people. At that moment in time, the party leadership chose to emphasize China's fundamental food problem. Even the relatively moderate "dissident" philosopher Li Zehou has asserted that food must come before freedom. "The mouth has two functions, first and foremost is to eat, the second is to speak," he said, reminding his American students that many Chinese people are still hungry.[198] Food fundamentalism thus created an ideological bridge between radicalism and traditionalism, and between past and present.

Conclusion

FAMINE HAS BEEN a fundamental part of the Chinese historical experience. It was not only the direct experience of millions who lived and died, but the will to overcome natural disasters and famines was central to the ideological foundation of rulership. Between Yu the Great and Mao Ze-dong were many Chinese rulers of varying degrees of talent, yet the ideals of controlling nature and nourishing the people were not forgotten. The great rulers of the last dynasty faced these challenges with extraordinary commitment and resources. Paradoxically, the outcome was even greater environmental and social challenges. Famine and hunger loomed even larger in the late nine-teenth- and early twentieth-century historical experience. Not only did China experience famines more frequently and extensively than those in other historical eras, but because of the unprece-dented size of the population, more lives were terminated by famine or affected by other forms of hunger than ever before. Even those whose lives were relatively sheltered from hunger were indi-rectly affected because the entire nation's attention was directed toward addressing this issue al-most as much as its fate was threatened by internal warfare, Japanese aggression, and cold war en-mities. This experience further shaped China's self-perception, as well as the image it presented to the outside world. In these ways, China *was* indeed the "Land of Famine."

Chinese civilization had been associated with wealth; the world sought its silks, teas, and porce-lain. Yet memories of scarcity and the fear of dearth always loomed on the imperial horizon. Famine relief administration included the knowledge of exactly how many ounces of grain an adult or a child needed for minimum subsistence. Beautifully illustrated *materia medica* described the wild plants that were suitable as famine foods. The Manchu emperors were known to prefer plain foods, and the Yongzheng emperor praised the Han Chinese for their frugal vegetable-based diet, while admonishing the Manchus for indulging in too much meat! Even in the era when the capital could command grain tribute in quantities far in excess of its needs, every sack of grain leaving the city was scrutinized when there was a lean harvest in the region. In the Republican pe-riod, frequent large-scale famines and difficult economic circumstances compelled an even greater food consciousness. Western-trained famine relief workers continued the practice of counting calories and rations. Under Mao, food consciousness turned into food fundamentalism, which, like all fundamentalist thinking, placed appropriate emphasis on the basics, in this case on food, but did so narrowly and rigidly. Food fundamentalism was not a direct continuity from the past, but an intensification of past ideas. The pressure of population on food, a condition created by Maoist policy, allowed ancient ideas about agriculture-as-foundation to become perverted into a kind of food fundamentalism. It was not inevitable, but large population, large empire, and strong central government led to this result.

Hunger was not only a physical reality but also a metaphor for China's national plight. In his preface to Eileen Chang's *The Rice-Sprout Song*—a novel about hunger during the 1950s—David Der-wei Wang writes that "early Chinese Communist literature abounds in works dealing with hunger. . . . From bodily destitution to political institution, hunger as a spiritual state has been reified, so to speak, in the discourse of the Chinese Communist revolution."[1] Physical hunger has often led to spiritual hunger, hunger as a metaphor for the death of the soul. Lu Xun used cannibalism as a metaphor for China as a whole—where he saw that people were consuming each other. Wang Ruowang's *Hunger Trilogy* focuses on both spiritual and physical hunger during imprisonment. In recent years hunger has increasingly been a motif in Chinese literature.[2] Postmodern writers have also used hunger and cannibalism as themes.[3] Unlike the Cultural Revolution, the human testimony of the Great Leap Famine has yet to find full literary expression, yet both experiences together were the formative experience of the older generation of Chinese—just as the Depression was for a generation of Americans, and the Holocaust for Jews.

As an historical topic, famine provides insight into the relationship between state, society, economy, and environment during the last three centuries. Famine was not simply the outcome of bad weather and natural disasters, nor was it necessarily the result of overpopulation, that is, when population growth outstrips the food supply. The worst famines occurred during times of war or rebellion, when the normal support systems failed to respond, yet we cannot say that famines were caused solely by political events. The ability to withstand a poor harvest, or years of drought and famine, were affected by the extent of household or community preparation, such as grain storage, and also by the overall economic situation. Famine, as well as the ability to survive it, was the result of the complex interplay of various forces; polarities such as food versus population, man versus nature, or state versus market, drastically oversimplify history. The story of famine, and fighting famine, is a story of human choices and human will, and not of historical inevitability or historical determinism. In this story there were sometimes bad decisions and, often, unintended consequences. Food fundamentalism and its authoritarian manifestation were not inevitable, but scarcity of resources, pushing the limits, reinforced these prior tendencies. Ideological preferences shaped responses to concrete situations but were not the direct cause of them.

It may be argued that North China's experience represents only that of the north and cannot be considered all of "China." To be sure the scarcities and hardships of the north were not entirely shared by the south. Yet it is precisely the imperial ambition to rule over a large empire embracing both north and south that is the key to understanding the sweep of Chinese history, and it is what makes the story of North China not simply a regional story. Although abundant in land and water resources in ancient times, the north became over the centuries far less agriculturally productive than the south. Choosing to maintain the traditional northern capital, the emperors of the Yuan, Ming, and Qing sacrificed economic convenience for strategic security along the northern frontier.[4] They reconstructed and maintained the Grand Canal in order to bring the resources of the south to the north. Grain tribute was the principal means for transfer of resources, but again and again, in crises during the Qing period, the court ordered not only the diversion of grain tribute for famine relief but also frequent additional shipments of grain from Henan, Shandong, and especially Fengtian. The importance of the Manchurian "breadbasket" in the economy of the north has not been given due recognition. In addition, the forgiveness of taxes and other benefits were frequently extended to Zhili Province.[5] The north, especially the capital region, was heavily subsidized by the rest of the empire.

Although the capital was located in the north, the cultural, social, and economic center of the empire was, arguably, in the Jiangnan (Lower Yangzi) region. Since the Song period, scholarly and bureaucratic leadership was largely in the hands of southerners. Not only did the south in effect subsidize the north economically, but southerners tended to assume that the superior practices of the south should be exported to the north. The repeated attempts to introduce rice cultivation to the north were based on the premise that the rice economy could flourish everywhere. Similarly, Qing officials hoped that the gentry-led initiatives in famine relief and other charities that were so successful in the Jiangnan region could be emulated in the north. They were almost always disappointed and found gentry leadership in the north to be lacking.

The tension between a northern state-centered model and a southern community model of leadership stems from at least Song times. The statesmen of the Northern Song, especially Wang Anshi and Sima Guang, had faith in a more *dirigiste* model, while the Southern Song model, following Zhu Xi, assumed that local communities could initiate and carry out local activities based on volunteerism. A similar swing of the pendulum from state-centered activism to local leadership occurred in the Ming period.[6] In the Qing period, the model of strong state and weak community prevailed, especially for the north. At the end of the dynasty, state resources were scant, but the state resolve, found in Li Hongzhang's leadership, commanded resources from the south—in the form of both official "contributions" and gentry initiatives, where the gentry were from the south.

During the Qing, imperial ambition played the dominant role in the famine-fighting activities described in this book. The highly interventionist behavior of Kangxi, Yongzheng, and Qianlong bespoke their personal commitment to prevention, regulation, and control. Although handicapped by diminished resources and other problems, their successors Jiaqing and Daoguang were mindful of the high standards set by their forbearers. Similarly the best of the Qing statesmen—Prince Yi, Fang Guancheng, Nayancheng, Li Hongzhang, and others—supported the imperial enterprise in river control, grain storage, and famine relief. The amount of imperial funding given to all river conservancy projects, routine grain storage, special mobilization of grain in emergencies, and tax remissions and cancellations taken together represented a portion of the budget probably second only to military expenditures.

Yet for all the earth dug up, dikes built, and grain transported and distributed, we must ask if Li Hongzhang was not accurate in his sad conclusion that little good had ultimately come from all this effort. Never has the distinction between short-term results and long-term, unintended, consequences been so clear. From Kangxi's determination to control the unruly Yongding River in the late seventeenth century, through the Qianlong repairs of the Thousand-Li Dike in the mid-eighteenth century, there were measurable benefits not only in flood prevention but also in maintaining internal water transportation in a region not blessed by water routes. The Grand Canal itself, with its northern sections in Zhili, allowed grain from the south to reach not only the capital, but indirectly to the entire capital region. Evidence of its benefit is seen in the price integration of the eighteenth century. The silting of the internal routes meant price disintegration, on the one hand, and greater vulnerability to flooding, on the other. The gradual disappearance of critical drainage basins and shallow lakes that once served as a flood plain threatened crops when even a small amount of excess rainfall occurred. As these problems became very difficult in the late Qianlong reign and throughout the Jiaqing reign, even greater expense and effort was required to fix the problem—precisely at a time when the state was unable to meet these demands. The stirring notion of a "once-and-for-all" solution had proved to be wrong in its premise that there could ever be such a solution. Indeed, even the successful engineering projects only caused the needs to escalate. Emperors, engineering, and ecology did not mix well.

Grain storage was the second major form of state intervention into the provisioning process and the prevention of famine. Zhili Province was particularly affected by grain storage because of the centrality of Beijing. Grain tribute that was targeted for the population of the capital formed part of the grain supply of the entire region and helped to offset the fluctuations of the regional harvests. Although the mighty walls and gates of the capital suggested an economic fortress, in fact the provisions of Beijing were more like a faucet that could be turned on and off, and that sometimes leaked. Until the 1850s—when foreign invasion, rebellion, and currency crisis struck—the food security of the capital was well maintained, and not at the expense of the region at large. Keeping the ever-normal and other state granaries stocked was far more problematic and controversial. Despite the costs to the state, and the consequences for other regions, the restocking of the Zhili granaries did provide a measure of price stability and sometimes ample reserves for emergencies. Grain prices reflected the effect of harvest failures, or poor harvests, but, with relatively rare exceptions, they did not rise to the levels of historic crises of medieval or early modern Europe.

It was probably the very presence of large stocks of grain that was responsible for price moderation rather than any of the micromanaged techniques of sales or distribution such as *pingtiao* or famine relief per se. *Pingtiao* was practiced with greater regularity in Beijing than anywhere else in order to counteract seasonal scarcities and price rises. Elsewhere it was used principally as a means of famine relief, particularly in the nineteenth century when even the pretense of grand relief—that targeted households—was abandoned. Although we cannot say that every famine ration reached its intended recipient, it seems that just the public process of distributing grain, operating soup kitchens, or selling grain at below-market prices helped to maintain the public order and social stability, which after all was the state's primary motive for famine prevention and relief.

The price data reveal that major price rises were definitely weather-related and in the eighteenth century even seemed to follow a regular cycle. Yet the most destructive subsistence crises were also related to political disorder such as warfare, rebellion, or invasion, when the state's resources were directed elsewhere. The drought of 1759 resulted in surprisingly large and sustained price rise because the expected sources of relief were being directed toward the northwestern provinces. The 1813 drought coincided with banditry and rebellion especially in the southern part of the province. The capital-centered crisis of the late 1850s was partly due to instability in the copper-silver exchange rate and partly due to the flight of the court to Rehe. The Boxer Uprising and serious drought combined in a lethal way. In the twentieth century, the Henan famine of 1943 was definitely the outcome of wartime rivalries.

Whether the state was antimarket in conducting large-scale grain storage is a matter of some debate. In entering the grain market as a large purchaser was not the state dominating the grain market and making it difficult for merchants to be grain wholesalers? By preventing or even outlawing the holding of large inventories of grain, the state was in effect substituting itself for some of the functions normally performed by the market. Wasn't the demeaning appellation "evil merchants" more than just rhetoric? Yet the state was very much dependent on the market mechanism for the circulation of grain, or *liutong*, which was seen as the best way to keep even, or keep down, the price of grain. So merchants were encouraged to engage in small-scale trade, but no single merchant was able to dominate the market. The Chinese state was willing to grant monopolies or privileges in the salt trade and in foreign trade, but never in the grain trade because it was so central to the state's very existence. It was neither the market, nor the market mechanism, that it feared, but a market dominated by a few large merchants. The contrast with French grain traders in the ancien régime and later is striking; some were powerful and hated for their association with the monarchy, but when there was a grain liberalization policy briefly in the 1760s, prices rose even higher, and the mobs protested.[7] In Tokugawa Japan, rice merchants served as the brokers for the various daimyo, feudal lords, who wished to sell tax-grain on the wholesale market in Osaka. Since rice was a unit of payment, a store of value, and it was the main income of the daimyo, and the samurai at large, they focused on its monetary value and worked toward keeping prices high rather than low.

If the purpose of the market was circulation, *liutong*, then the Qing state's successes were not long lasting. After the eighteenth century, the silting of internal waterways impeded circulation, while the increasing dysfunction of the Grand Canal by the mid-nineteenth century was only partly offset by sea transport from Fengtian. The importance of transportation was shown after the introduction of railways, particularly in the 1920 drought, when famine relief workers all remarked that even worse disaster was avoided by the rapid shipments of grain by the railway from points north and south. The 1870s drought in virtually the same region had led to worse consequences because neither internal canals nor railways were available. Next to canal transport, a few good roads in the interior might have helped a great deal in the late nineteenth century.

The cost of such ambitious and large-scale intervention was high indeed. Not only were there the actual financial costs, but there were also the often unavoidable costs of bureaucratic corruption. From the 1780s onward, the large funds intended for river work in Zhili were known to have been misappropriated. The huge Gansu famine relief scandal of the 1780s was extreme, but it suggests what could happen to large appropriations for famine relief. Even the Jiaqing emperor's reformist zeal failed to make a real difference in the long run; the next emperor, Daoguang, openly described the connivance and scheming of subbureaucrats who merely "divided the fat." It was the need to shake up the bureaucracy that prompted the "campaign" style of Jiaqing's 1801 flood relief effort. By involving himself personally with the work and riding herd on his high officials, he hoped to emulate Kangxi's diligence and to prevent malfeasance. In famine relief and river conservancy, as in other areas of state activity, the vigilance of the emperor was needed to guard against corruption, and even then it was often too little or too late.

Population growth may have been another unintended consequence of state activism in the eighteenth century. Agricultural efficiency, flood prevention, famine relief and prevention, and general peace and prosperity at least promoted, if not caused, population expansion. Although the concern over too large a population pressing on too little land was expressed by Kangxi himself, for the most part large-scale "Malthusian" catastrophes were avoided because of the generally favorable economic conditions and state interventions. The records of harvest shortages and subsistence crises in the eighteenth century do not usually mention high mortality as a result. Of course, it was not the custom to calculate the severity of a crisis by the number of deaths; the shortfall in harvest was the usual standard of measurement. Still, there is every reason to think that many of the subsistence crises (*zaihuang*) did not develop into "famines" defined by high excess mortality (*jihuang*).

In their controversial book *One Quarter of Humanity: Malthusian Mythology and Chinese Realities, 1700–2000*, authors Lee and Wang have asserted, "Famines were relatively few and had a very limited impact. . . . Overall there is no evidence of increases in mortality or in the frequency and intensity of mortality crises during the last 300 years. . . . The threat of overpopulation appears to have been a myth."[8] Readers of this book, however, cannot remain in much doubt that in the period 1850–1950 the "frequency and intensity of mortality crises" certainly did increase. When there are sufficient demographic data, the effects of a large famine can always been seen in the age structure of the affected population. "Excess" mortality, the demographic term for mortality in excess of the normal patterns, is also reflected in abnormally low fertility, that is, the fewer births in a given period because mothers either died or were unable to conceive. There may also be a discernable abnormality in the age structure/pyramid and an echo effect in the next generation. Yet demographic models—as well as historical evidence—have shown that even a major mortality crisis affecting millions of people may have little long-term effect on total population size because societies can recover, demographically speaking, from such crises, and eventually resume their precrisis fertility and mortality rates.[9] Malthus himself recognized this rebound phenomenon. "The effects of the dreadful plague in London in 1666 were not perceptible 15 or 20 years afterwards. The traces of the most destructive famines in China and Indostan are by all accounts very soon obliterated. . . . The most tremendous convulsions of nature, such as volcanic eruptions and earthquakes . . . have but a trifling effect on the average population of any state."[10] Gamble's Ding xian study, shows the clear effect of the 1876–79 famine on the age pyramid, but it also shows the immediate recovery of the birthrate after the crisis.[11] Even the huge Great Leap Forward famine of 1959–61 was followed by a rebound that propelled Chinese population to even greater numbers. Recent studies find that the secular decline in mortality after 1750 in Europe was 90 percent due to "normal" factors, and only 10 percent due to the decline to crisis mortality.[12]

Only in this sense, might the statement that famines had "very limited impact," possibly make any sense. The statement that famines were "relatively few," however, seems impossible to understand. Even if high famine mortality was not necessarily the outcome of subsistence crises, at least in the eighteenth century, other damaging consequences compounded. Hunger and malnutrition were probably more consistent than famine mortality itself. Large population and all the conditions of uncertainty, such as the weather and political activities, meant that there was a thin margin between individual survival and failure to survive. These precarious situations were measured by short life expectancy, high infant and childhood mortality, and infanticide. Female infanticide, which appears to have been widely practiced, was the result of poverty, not prosperity. It may have been "rational," as Lee, Campbell, and Wang have argued, but it is difficult to accept that it was the outcome of anything other than difficult economic circumstances for a family. State activism may have helped to avert major mortality crises, but it did not go beyond to eliminate hunger or a marginal existence. So it was possible for the increasingly large population of Zhili to survive many natural and agricultural crises, but not to improve their standard of living and reduce their vulnerability. Although solid data on birthrates and death rates comes largely from the 1920s and 1930s, it seems unlikely that the same fundamental conditions did not exist earlier. In fact the gazetteers from the 1930s report that the standard of living had actually improved "compared with the past."

By the mid- to late nineteenth century, crises in Zhili assumed a different character than those of the previous century. Floods seemed to increase in frequency and ferocity. In some decades, they were almost annual occurrences and were larger in scale than before. Natural disasters of the previous century had been harvest crises for the most part, and the status quo ante was regained in most cases within a season, a year, or a couple of years. In 1810s, 1870s, 1890s, and through the Republican period, however, flooding seemed almost chronic, and the status quo ante was not regained. Simple remedial patchwork never would last very long. Recovery from a crisis was made less feasible with the decline in central government resources, especially before the advent of foreign assistance. Finally, natural disasters were exacerbated by human disasters from 1813 all the way until 1949. Mortality crises were often the result of rebellion and foreign invasion rather than natural disaster and harvest failure as such. *Renhuo* overshadowed and compounded the effects of *tianzai*.[13] Before the war of resistance against the Japanese, there were some structural changes that held the promise of improving the rural economy, such as the new rail lines, the commercialization of agriculture, and the greater opportunities offered by the growth of Tianjin, but these were overwhelmed by the destruction of war and insurgency.

Famines in the Republican period differed from "traditional" subsistence crises also in the national and international publicity they received. A regional crisis had grave national implications. During the war against the Japanese, hunger and poverty affected every part of the country, including the treaty ports. But it is the base areas in the north where the Communist leadership developed its mobilization skills, including their approach to the issues of land and subsistence. During the 1940s, the "northern" model of revolutionary mobilization was brought to the south by the strategists of the Chinese Communist Party. In eastern and central China, Communist successes "resulted from Mao Tse-tung's determination to transplant the successful experience of base construction from North China to central China."[14] The "northern" model thus became the standard for the extension of Communist rule through the rest of China during the civil war and consolidation period, replacing a model of prosperity with one of scarcity. It was a reversal of the late imperial tendency to import southern models to the north.

The establishment of the People's Republic of China in 1949 meant liberation from foreign imperialism and from the discredited Nationalist government of Chiang Kai-shek. For millions it also promised liberation from hunger and poverty. In land reform and, later, agricultural collectivization, the party put forth truly radical ideas about equal distribution of land to peasants and about collectivizing ownership and coordinating labor and farm tasks. Yet in other respects, Mao's socialism employed techniques that seemed like an intensification of traditional practices. The rationing of grain and other commodities resembles the historical precedents in famine rationing. A bureaucracy that knew exactly how many ounces of grain were needed for basic subsistence was nothing new. The restrictions on mobility, particularly migration to cities, seem to resemble of the old practice of trying to keep peasants in their villages and discourage them from roaming around (although at times migration beyond the Great Wall was tacitly permitted). The propensity to attack environmental problems with human labor organized on a large scale also seems familiar. Only the birth control campaigns, when they took place, were a form of intervention into personal lives that went far beyond traditional practices, as well as contrary to the old ideal of many children.

Population planning when reintroduced in the 1980s was a belated response to China's demographic explosion, when its population more than doubled between 1949 and 1999. Unlike the rapid growth of the eighteenth century, the mechanism of natural increase in the second half of the twentieth century is fairly well understood and follows a pattern that all developing nations have followed to one extent or the other. In the process of "demographic transition," countries start from a traditional pattern of high birth rates and high death rates. In the second phase, lowered death rates combine with continued high birth rates to generate rapid population growth. In China this phase lasted longer than it should have due to failure to enact population control in a timely way. Only in the last two decades has China begun to enter the third phase of demographic transition, when birth and death rates are both low. Birth limitation policy came later than desirable, was harshly implemented, and had many unintended negative social consequences. It is important to note that in both second and third phases of the demographic transition, food, or even high income, are not the key variables. The lowering of the death rate took place in many countries that were very poor; the societies that could least afford it suffered gigantic population increases in the second half of the twentieth century. Population growth was not caused by the greater availability of food but by the availability of basic health care that lowered mortality.

The Great Leap Famine was totally unlike anything that had occurred before in China and was unique in the annals of world history. It was caused neither by natural disaster, nor by a breakdown of the social or political order, nor by Malthusian pressure. China was not engaged in warfare or in internal struggle. In fact popular morale and faith in the political leadership were both unprecedentedly high. The famine occurred not in one region but affected the entire nation; the hardest-hit provinces, Anhui and Sichuan, were in locations distant from each other. The severity of the famine was a function not of the harvest, but the venality of the provincial leaders. Even when famine developed, it was not discussed and its extent beyond one's local area was unknown. Because the crisis was unacknowledged at the time, there were no steps to provide relief until very late in the process. Not only did his policies cause the famine, but also Mao failed to halt the campaign even when confronted with the truth. Instead of "feeding the people," he ended up starving them. Mao has often been compared to an emperor, but in the Great Leap Famine, as in subsequent events, Mao did not live up to the standards set by the Qing emperors.

The Great Leap Famine was the ultimate example of a horrible tragedy made possible through secrecy. Like the Stalin famine, the Great Leap Famine went unreported, even by those who were aware of what was happening. In democracies, Amartya Sen argued, famines can never occur because the bright light of public knowledge and public opinion would make it impossible.[15] The Great Leap Famine certainly is a good example of how dictatorship can suppress information and therefore prevent, perhaps unwittingly, grain supplies and other relief from reaching the disaster area. The famines in Africa, particularly in Ethiopia, in the 1970s–80s, were caused by bad weather, low-level of resources, and warfare, but they received publicity and Ethiopia did receive some international aid. The genocide in Rwanda in the 1990s, however, was known to the world, but Western nations declined to intervene seeing it as a politically caused crisis, and perhaps not so important for international interests. Famine in North Korea can certainly be ascribed to the secretive machinations of the Democratic People's Republic of Korea and its isolation from international trade. Yet the World Food Program and several international nongovernmental agencies have provided substantial amounts of grain over the last few years. International agencies recognize that some of the aid, if not most, may not reach those in need, but rather the army or the party elite—but most are committed to the idea of giving aid in a humanitarian, nonpolitical, way.

If democracies and famines are imperfectly related, markets and famines seem to have a more direct relationship. In the modern world, famines were even less than previously a matter of population outstripping food supply, or the simple outcome of poor harvests. What is critical for Sen is that access to food be unimpeded. In major crises, the absolute volume of food is not the issue, rather it is the *entitlement* to food that counts, particularly *trade entitlements*. Some classic famines, such as the Bengal Famine of 1943, grain had been harvested, but some farmers did not bring their grain to market, and many agricultural laborers, fishermen, and others without land perished because they did not have the money to purchase grain. At the height of the famine, prices rose to 300–500 percent above normal. In Ethiopia in the 1970s, by contrast, prices did not rise in the famine district because the residents were too poor to be able to purchase grain. Markets did not matter because there was no purchasing power.[16] The normal expectation is that if transport routes are unimpeded, and grain can circulate, then prices will come down. People need only to have the money to buy grain at the marketplace. These principles were known in China centuries ago, and practices such as encouraging grain circulation, grain storage, and *pingtiao* were based on them. Those who advocated giving cash relief rather than grain had the same principles in mind. The socialist practices of land reform, work points, grain rationing—in different ways embodied the same understanding that entitlement was as important as harvest levels themselves. Yet in a preindustrial economy, such understandings alone could not triumph over an absolute scarcity of grain and other food.

In the early twenty-first century, the fact is that most parts of the world, including China, have put famines behind them. Mortality crises due to war and genocide will recur, as well as natural disasters such as earthquakes, but mortality crises arising from poor harvests should be "history." This is due more to the process of industrialization and economic development than to democracies or markets per se, although one is often accompanied by the other. Local harvest failure has a small effect on food supply and prices when Australian beef feeds Europe, U.S. soybeans feed Chinese pigs, and asparagus grown in Chile is available year-round in American supermarkets. In China, not only do more people live in cities than in the past, but even in the countryside, farm household incomes are supplemented with income from local industries and wages sent home by family members working in the city. In the cities, a growing middle class has more disposable income and worries more about the price of real estate than the price of rice or vegetables.

Yet the near elimination of famines and even of subsistence crises has not meant the elimination of hunger and poverty. In 1978 the number of rural poor in China was estimated as 250 million people, or about 30 percent of the rural population. In 1998 the number had declined to 42 million (4.6 percent of the rural population), and in 2002 to 28.2 million. The large numbers of migrant worker population—"80 to 100 million people on the move"—form a modern-day version of *liutong*, where people, not grain, circulate. Although the trend shows a decline in rural poverty since the start of economic reforms, the absolute numbers remain large, and the rural poor are increasingly concentrated in the western provinces where reform efforts have not been so successful as elsewhere.[17] Poverty and malnutrition are closely related. In October 2003, Zhang Baowen, vice minister for agriculture, reported that 120 million Chinese people suffer from malnutrition.[18] Malnutrition in turn impacts particularly on infants and children. In 1997 the Chinese Academy of Preventive Medicine estimated that 310,000 infants die annually from malnutrition. In addition more than a quarter of rural children of preschool age suffered from anemia, rickets, or "other illnesses related to vitamin and protein deficiencies." In a joint report with the United Nations Children's Fund (UNICEF), the academy reported that "39 per cent of rural children suffered from below-normal growth rates due to malnutrition."[19] Still, by 2004, the head of the UN's World Food Program praised China for having lifted its people from poverty in less than a generation. "China has had more experience removing people from poverty and hunger than any other country in the world or in the history of mankind."[20]

Environmental crisis now looms as one of the most critical national and international concerns. For China, where once land was considered the limiting factor, water shortages now rank higher as an impending catastrophe. Industrial and urban water needs have placed an impossible demand on diminishing water supplies particularly, but not exclusively, in North China. While the Nanshui Beidiao project tries to bring Yangzi waters to the north, the Three Gorges Dam has hydroelectric power generation as its principal objective, combined with flood control and irrigation as secondary objectives. No undertaking has generated so much debate both within China and internationally. The great expense, the uncertain ecological outcomes, and the social costs of relocating more than a million people have all been controversial. For China in the 1980s, protest against the project tested the limits of political dissent, with some critics being jailed. The idea of such a dam on the Yangzi originated in the early twentieth century—Sun Yat-sen was the first to propose such an idea—but not until the 1990s did the idea come to fruition under the leadership of the Communist Party. Like the projects of the early Qing emperors, the Three Gorges Dam was offered with a "once-and-for-all" promise. And although the technical and scientific and even political opinions were split—one third of the National People's Congress voted against the proposal in 1992—the party heads presented this gigantic project as a sign of their visionary leadership.[21]

Since 1982, the party's top leadership has become increasingly technocratic in its composition. In 1997 eighteen out of twenty-four members of the Fifteenth Politburo, fully three-quarters, were engineers. Others were architects or other kinds of technocrats.[22] They included Jiang Zemin, then secretary-general of the Party, and Li Peng, the former premier. The latter, a hydraulic engineer staked his reputation on the Three Gorges Dam project, especially after the 1989 Tiananmen student movement tarnished his reputation. Today's top leaders, Hu Jintao, the party head, and Wen Jiabao, the prime minister, are also engineers.

What happens when the engineers become the emperors? Neither revolutionary founding fathers, nor ideologues, these men were welcomed as efficient pragmatists, men who would analyze problems and solve them rationally, "seeking truth from the facts." In fact since Mao's death, the top leadership has tended to avoid the cult of personality—although both Deng Xiaoping and Jiang Zemin on occasion resorted to old-style campaign rhetoric and low-grade personal charisma. Their successors seem to have adopted a lower profile for the moment and also a collective style of work. This is consistent with the Tiananmen generation's desire to have "government by law," not "government by persons." It remains to be seen, however, whether this can be accomplished. The operation of a large bureaucracy inevitably seems to lapse into corruption; corruption is arguably the most serious challenge of today's leaders. Can corruption be controlled through legal channels? Or must it take a strong "emperor" to shake up the bureaucracy? Recent news accounts suggest that Hu Jintao and Wen Jiabao's low-profile approach may not be enough. During trips outside Beijing, Hu and Wen like to meet the people, to show the concern with their suffering. But they have found numerous examples of bureaucrats or bosses cheating workers and local residents out of wages or other benefits due to them. "Despite the efforts by China's new leaders to cast themselves as populists, issues like income distribution, labor rights, taxation and land policy tend to divide the Communist Party against itself."[23] Can they overcome bureaucratic and private forms of corruption and shake off the inertia of the state apparatus? And can they do so without resorting to a Jiaqing-like, or Mao-style, ideological campaign? Historians are no better at prediction than anyone else, but one thing seems certain: despite market reforms, legal reforms, and economic gains, the state is not going to wither away.

REFERENCE MATTER

Reign Periods of the Qing Dynasty (1644–1911) and Use of Dates

Use of Dates

In Chinese documents before the twentieth century, dates were expressed by the reign year, lunar month, and day. In the text and notes of this book such dates have not been converted to the solar calendar, but expressed in the following form: KX 54/8/23, meaning the twenty-third day of the eighth lunar month of the fifty-fourth year of the Kangxi reign. The lunar calendar required every few years a thirteenth month so that it could catch up with the solar calendar. Such months have been indicated with a "#" sign. Thus KX 54/#8/23 would refer to an intercalary eighth month. Months of the solar calendar, by contrast, are expressed in words, not numbers, for example: September 5, 1924.

Weights and Measures

Measures Used in Qing

VOLUME OF GRAIN — SHI

10 he (ke) = 1 sheng
10 sheng = 1 dou
5 dou = 1 hu
10 dou = 2 hu = 1 shi

WEIGHT — DAN

16 liang = 1 jin (catty)
100 jin = 1 dan (picul)

WEIGHT OF 1 SHI OF GRAIN

In the eighteenth century, 1 shi of milled rice weighed 175–195 lbs.[1]
In the nineteenth century, 1 shi of unhusked rice weighed 120 jin, or 60 kg.[2]
At Tianjin in the 1920s, "a picul of husked and polished rice weighs 160 catties."[3]

RELATIONSHIP OF HUSKED TO UNHUSKED GRAIN

In the official regulations, 1 shi of *gu* (unhusked grain) yielded 0.5 shi of *mi* (milled rice). The same proportions are given for *sugu* and *sumi*. Millet may have yielded 20 percent more from milling, with 0.6 units of consumable grain for 1.0 unhusked grain, even though the regulations specified a 0.5 ratio.[4] One shi of wheat could be ground to 110 catties (65.6 kg) of flour (*mian*), according to one governor of Hubei in 1754.[5]

LAND AREA

1 mu (mou) = 0.0667 hectare = 0.1647 acre

100 mu = 1 qing

Measures Used in People's Republic of China

1 mu (mou) = 0.0667 hectare = 0.1647 acre

15 mu = 1.0 hectare

1 jin (catty) = 0.5 kg

1 dan (100 jin) = 50 kg

1 dun (ton) = 1,000 kg (1 metric ton) = 2,000 jin

1 yi = 10,000 x 10,000 = 100,000,000

1 yi kg = 100,000,000 kg = 100,000 metric tons

10 yi kg = 1 million metric tons

10 yi jin = 0.5 million metric tons

ERRATA

Stanford University Press has found that the
Glossary, pages 393–398, has some elements
missing from some of the Chinese characters.
To download the corrected glossary, go to the
Stanford University website (www.sup.org),
search on "Fighting Famine," and follow the
"Glossary Correction" link in the list of the
book's online resources. The file can be viewed
and downloaded for printing.

ome personal names are in Bibliography.

aimai 採買
andou 蠶豆
angchang shilang 倉場侍郎
angchu 倉儲
angliang 倉糧
angmi 倉米
Cao Cao 曹操
aoyun 漕運
hangpingcang 常平倉
Chao-Bai he 潮白河
Chen Dashou 陳大受
Chen Dawen 陳大文
Chen Hongmou 陳宏謀
Chen Yi 陳儀
hengse mi 成色米
hengzai 成災
Chouzhenju 籌賑局
huantong zibi 串通滋弊
hunfu 吞撫
hunhan 吞旱
ipin 次貧
isumi 次粟米
uliang 粗糧
ladou 大豆
laizhen 待賑
laji 大飢

daji 大集, xiaoji 小集
  (periodic markets)
Daqing River 大清河
Da Yu zhishui 大禹治水
daomi 稻米
daxiu 大修
dazhen 大賑
di 堤 or 隄
dian 淀
Dian he 淀河
dianpo 淀泊
diedao 壋道
ding 丁
dingliang renkou 定口人口
dizhang 堤長
Dong dian 東淀
dou 斗
douhang 斗行, doudian 斗店
duanjia 短價
duifang 碓房
Emida 鄂彌達
enmi 恩米
fanchang 飯廠
Fang Guancheng 方觀承
Fang Shouchou 方受疇
fanlan 汎濫
fengmi 俸米
Fengtian 奉天
fu 府
fuhan 伏旱
fukua 浮夸
fuqiu daxun 伏秋大汛
fuxu 撫卹
Fuyang he 滏陽河
fuzhong bing 浮肿病
gai zhen wei fu 改賑為撫
Gao Bin 高斌
gaoliang 高粱
gengmi 粳米
gongfen kouliang 工分口糧
gu 穀, 谷
Gubeikouwai 古北口外
Gu Cong 顧琮
guandu shangban 官督商辦

Guangrentang 廣仁堂
Hai he 海河
Han Fuju 韓復榘
hanhun 含混
hanzai 旱災
haofan 浩繁
haoxian 耗羨
Hedong hedao zongdu 河東河道總督
he 河
hegong 河工
Heilonggang 黑龙港
heidou 黑豆, or hei tou 黑豆
heitu 黑土
Heshen miao 河神廟
hesi 餓死
hongmai 紅麥
hongshu 紅薯
hongshui 洪水
hu 斛
huahong 化紅
huahu 花戶
huali wuwen 猾吏舞文
huandai 緩待
huanfan 換飯
huang 荒
  (crop failure disaster)
huang 蝗
  (locust)
huangdou 黄豆
Huang-Huai-Hai 黄淮海
Huang Mao 黄懋
huangtu 黄土
huangzheng 荒政
huangzhuang 皇莊
huatou 花頭
Hu Guangyong 胡光墉
Hu Jitang 胡季堂
Huiji miao, ci 惠濟廟, 祠
Hui Shiqi 惠士奇
hukou 戶口
huma 胡麻
Hun he 混河
huomian 餻免
hutou shewei 虎頭蛇尾

Hutuo he 滹沱河

ji 稷
  (*Panicum miliaceum*, or broomtail millet)

ji 飢, jihuang 飢荒
  (hunger, famine)

jianhe 減河

jiami 申米

Jiang Youxian 蔣攸銛

jianshang 奸商

Jiaqing yitong zhi 嘉慶一統志

jiazhen 加賑

jiben kouliang 基本口糧

jibo 瘠薄

jiecao or jieliu 截漕, 截留

Jifu 畿輔

jijing 机井

jin 斤

Jin Fu 靳輔

jingfei zhi fan 經費之繁

jingji 經濟

Jin Ji Lu Yu 晉冀魯豫

jipin 極貧

jihuang de Zhongguo 飢荒的中國

jiuhuang 救荒

Jiuhuang bencao 救荒本草

Jiyun he 薊運河

jizhen 集鎮
  (market town)

jizhen 急賑
  (emergency relief)

juanhuan 蠲緩

juanmian 蠲免

juekou 決口

Juma he 拒馬河

kang 糠

Kangjilu 康濟錄

kanzai 勘災

kemi 客米

keshui 客水

Koubei Santing 口北三廳

kouke 扣剋

kouliang 口糧

kouwai 口外

kuailei 塊壘

kucai 苦菜

kuikong 虧空

lao 澇, 涝

laomi 老米

li, lilao 沥, 沥涝 灄澇

Li Fu 李紱

Li Guangdi 李光地

Li Hongzhang 李鴻章

Li Jinghan 李景漢

Li Wei 李衛

Li Weijun 李維鈞

liangshi wenti 粮食问题

liaodou 料豆

lijia 例價

Lin Qing 林情

Linzhang 臨漳

liumaidi 留麥地

liumin 流民

liutong 流通

liuyangju 留養局

liuyu 流寓

Liu Yuyi 劉於義

lixia 立夏

Longwang miao 龍王廟

Luan he 灤河

ludou 稑豆, 樚豆

Lugou qiao 盧溝橋

Lu Shiji 魯仕驥

Lushui ketan 潞水客談

luwei 蘆葦

mai 麥

maiqiu 麥秋

Majia he 馬頰河

mi 米
  (husked grain)

mi 糜
  (rice gruel)

miju 米局

Ming'an 明安

minshu gushu zouzhe 民數穀數奏摺

mizi 麋子
  (glutinous *panicum* millet, colloquial)

mobing 饃餅

momo 饃饃 or 饝饝

moshu 穈黍

mu 畝

nanshui beidiao 南水北調

Nan Yunhe 南運河

Nasutu 那蘇圖

Nayanbao 那彥寶

Nayancheng 那彥成

Nei cang 內倉

niangu 黏穀

Oertai 鄂爾泰

nongye weiji 农业危机

nuomi 糯米

paimai 派買

paishui 排水

Pan Jixun 潘季馴

pianzai 偏災

pingjia 平價

pingtiao 平糶

pomi zhou 破米粥

pujitang 普濟堂

pumian jiqian 普免積欠

puzhen 普賑

qian 錢

qianjia 錢價

qianggou 抢购

qiangxiu 搶修

qiaomai 蕎麥

qidi 旗地

qingdou 青豆

qinghuang bujie 青黄不接

qingyu lu 晴雨錄

Qin Yong zhi di 秦雍之地

Qishan 埼善

qu 渠

quannong 勸農

rangtu 壤土

ren xiang shi 人相食

San ding 三定

Sang'gan he 桑乾河

Sanjiao Dian 三角淀

sannian baogan 三年包干

sannian kunnan shiqi 三年困难时期

Sha he 沙河

shantang 善堂

shaoguo 燒鍋

shao zhan yurun 稍沾餘潤

shecang 社倉

Shen Lianfang 沈聯方

sheng 升

shi 石

shijia 時價

   (government-set seasonal price)

shijia 市價

   (market price)

shijia shanggu 世家商賈

shouzai mianji, chengzai mianji 受災面積, 成災面積

shu 秫

   (glutinous *setaria* millet)

shu 黍

   (glutinous *panicum* millet)

shuhuang 熟荒

shuihuan 水患

shuili 水利

shuili yingtian 水利營田

shuimomian 水磨麪

shuizai 水災

shushu 蜀黍

siken 私墾

su, sumi 粟米

sugu 粟谷

suimi 碎米

suixiu 歲修

Sun Jiagan 係嘉淦

suomi 稷米

Tang he 唐河

tankuan 攤款

tianzai renhuo 天災人禍

tonggou tongxiao 统购统销

Tongxing 同興

Tongzhou 通州

Tuhai he 徒駭河

tunji 囤積

tunji huicao 囤積囤漕

wa 窪, wadi 窪地

Wang Fengsheng 王鳳生

Wang Huizu 汪輝祖

Wang Wenshao 王文韶

Wei he 衛河, 沘河

Wei Xi 魏禧

wen 文

Wen Chenghui 溫成惠
wotou 窩頭
Wuding he 無定河
wudou 烏斗, or wu tou 烏豆
Ximen Bao 西門豹
xialao 夏澇
xian 縣
xianmi 秈米
xiaoliu peisi 銷六賠四
xiaomai 小麥
xiaomi 小米
Xi dian 西淀
xifan 稀飯
xiliang 綑糧
xiliutang 棲流堂
ximi 細米
Ximen Bao 西門豹
xinhe 浙河
Xiong Mei 熊枚
Xiong Xiling 熊希齡
Xu Guangqi 許光啟
Xu Yisheng 徐以升
Xu Zhenming 徐貞明
xuanbing 旋餅
xun 汛
　(patrol)
xun 汛
　(flood, high water)
xun 旬
　(ten-day period)
xushui 蓄水
yahang 牙行, yahu 牙戶
yan 鹽, 盐
yanjian di 鹽鹼地, 盐碱地
Yanjian 顏檢
Yang Eryou 楊而酉
Yang Jingren 楊景仁
yanglian 養廉
Yang Xifu 楊錫紱
yangjiyuan 養濟院
yanzai 盐灾
yaodi 遙隄
yaoyi 徭役
yi 疫
yicang 義倉

yiding sannian 一定三年
yifu wei zhen 以撫為賑
yigong daizhen 以工代賑
yikuai di dui yikuai tian 一塊地對一塊天
yilao yongyi 一勞永逸
yimai di sanqiu 一麥抵三秋
yiman yimai 一沒一麥
yimianzhe 藝棉者
yimi ergu 一米二谷
Yinjishan 尹繼善
yinshi dapuhu 殷實大鋪戶
yipian wangyang 一片汪洋
yishui yimai 一水一麥
yizhang 義漿
yizhen 義賑
yizi er shi 易子而食
Yongding he 永定河
Yongji qu 永濟渠
youcai 油菜
Yuan Shoutong 袁守侗
yuban qiangxiu 預辦搶修
yubeicang 預備倉
Yu Chenglong 于成龍
yugong 義公
yumi 玉米
yushushu 玉蜀黍
yusu 玉粟
yuxue fencun 雨雪分寸
yuyingtang 育嬰堂
zai 災
zaihuang 災荒
zaliang 雜糧
zaohu 窯戶
zeguo 澤國
zha 閘
Zhang Boxing 張伯行
Zhang he 漳河
Zhangjiakou 張家口
Zhang Peiyuan 張不遠
Zhang Tingyu 張廷玉
Zhang Xu 章煦
Zhao Hongxie 趙弘燮
zhaoshang 招商
zhen 賑
zhenfu 賑撫

zhenggou lü 征购率

Zheng Guo qu 鄭國渠

zhengzhen 正賑

zhese 折色

zhezhen 摘賑

Zhigu 直沽

zhiqian 制錢

zhou 粥
　(gruel)

zhou 州
　(department)

zhouchang 粥廠

Zhou Dingwang 周定王

Zhou Yuanli 周元理

zhuangtou, zhuangding 莊頭, 莊丁

Zhulong he 豬龍河

Zhu Shi 朱軾

zhuo 濁

zhuzhen 煮賑

zhuzhen yidai fuxu 煮賑以代撫恤

zisong 資送

Ziya he 子牙河

Appendix 1: Prefectures and Counties in Zhile Province in Qing Period

(with Map A.1)

1   Bazhou (Ba xian after 1913) 霸州
2   Baodi 寶坻
3   Baoding 保定 (xian, not fu)
4   Changping 昌平
5   Dacheng 大城
6   Daxing 大興
7   Dong'an 東安 (or Anci 安次）
8   Fangshan 房山
9   Gu'an 固安
10 Huairou 懷柔
11 Jizhou 薊州 (note homonym Jizhou 冀州)
12 Liangxiang 良鄉
13 Miyun 密雲
14 Ninghe 寧河
15 Ping'gu 平谷
16 Sanhe 三河
17 Shunyi 順義
18 Tongzhou 通州
19 Wanping 宛平
20 Wen'an 文安
21 Wuqing 武情
22 Xianghe 香河
23 Yongqing 永情
24 Zhuozhou 涿州

BAODING FU 保定府

25 Anzhou 安州 (also Anxin 安新 or Xin'an 新安)

26 Ansu 安蕭 (later called Xushui xian 徐水縣)

27 Boye 博野

28 Dingxing 定興

29 Gaoyang 高陽

30 Li 蠡

31 Mancheng 滿城

32 Qizhou 祁州 (Anguo安國)

33 Qingyuan 清苑

34 Rongcheng 容城

35 Shulu 束鹿 (listed as part of "zhili Baoding fu," tucked between Dingzhou, Zhengding fu, and Shenzhou, barely touching Baoding fu itself)

36 Tang 唐

37 Xiong 雄

38 Xincheng 新城

39 Wan 完

40 Wangdu 望都

YONGPING FU 永平府

41 Changli 昌黎

42 Dushan 都山

43 Funing 撫寧

44 Leting 樂亭

45 Luanzhou 灤州

46 Lulong 盧龍

47 Qian'an 遷安

47.5 Linyu 臨榆

XUANHUA FU 宣化府

48 Bao'anzhou 保安州

49 Chicheng 赤誠

50 Huai'an 懷安

51 Huailai 懷來

52 Longmen 龍門

53 Wanquan 萬全

54 Weizhou 蔚州

55 Yanqingzhou 延慶州

56 Xining 西寧

57 Xuanhua 宣化

HEJIAN FU 河間府

58 Dong'guang 東光
59 Fucheng 阜城
60 Gucheng 故城
61 Hejian 河間
62 Jiaohe 交河
63 Jingzhou 景州
64 Ningjin 寧津
65 Renqiu 任邱
66 Wuqiao 吳橋
67 Xian 獻
68 Suning 肅寧

TIANJIN FU 天津府

69 Cangzhou 滄州
70 Jinghai 靜海
71 Nanpi 南皮
72 Qing 青
73 Qingyun 慶雲
74 Tianjin 天津
75 Yanshan 鹽山

ZHENGDING FU 正定府

76 Fuping 阜平
77 Gaocheng 藁城
78 Huailu 獲鹿
79 Jinzhou 晉州
80 Jingxing 井陘
81 Lingshou 靈壽
82 Luancheng 欒城
83 Pingshan 平山
84 Wuji 無極
85 Hangtang 行唐
86 Xinle 新樂
87 Yuanshi 元氏
88 Zanhuang 贊皇
89 Zhengding 正定

SHUNDE FU 順德府

90 Guangzong 廣宗
91 Julu 鉅鹿
92 Nanhe 南和

93 Neiqiu 内邱
94 Pingxiang 平鄉
95 Ren 任
96 Shahe 沙河
97 Tangshan 唐山
98 Xingtai 邢臺

GUANGPING FU 廣平府

99   Cheng'an 成安
100 Cizhou 磁州
101 Feixiang 肥鄉
102 Guangping 廣平
103 Handan 邯鄲
104 Jize 雞澤
105 Qinghe 清河
106 Quzhou 曲周
107 Wei 威
108 Yongnian 永年

DAMING FU 大名府

109 Changyuan 長垣
110 Daming 大名
111 Dongming 東明
112 Kaizhou 開州
113 Nanle 南樂
114 Qingfeng 情豐
115 Yuancheng 元城

CHENGDE FU 承德府 (prefectural status after 1778)

*116 Chaoyang潮陽
*117 Chifeng赤峰
118   Fengning 豐寧
*119 Jianchang 建昌
120   Luanping 灤平
*121 Pingquan 平泉

*Counties not on map A.1, but included in *Hebei
sheng yange tugao*, and in *Zhongguo lishi dituji* 8:7–8.

ZUNHUA ZHOU 遵化州

122   Fengrun 豐潤
122.5 Zunhua 遵化(州治)
123   Yutian 玉田

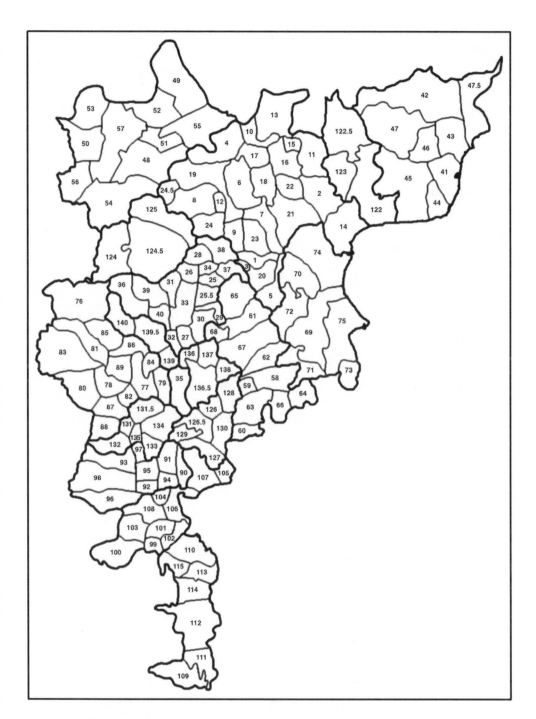

MAP A.1.   Prefectures and counties in Zhili Province (excluding Chengde Prefecture)

YIZHOU 易州

124   Guangchang 廣昌 (north of the Great Wall)
124.5 Yi 易(州治)
125   Laishui 淶水

JIZHOU 冀州 (note homonym Jizhou 薊州)

126   Hengshui 衡水
126.5 Ji 冀(州治)
127   Nangong 南宮
128   Wuyi 武邑
129   Xinhe 新河
130   Zaoqiang 棗強

ZHAOZHOU 趙州

131   Gaoyi 高邑
131.5 Zhao 趙 （州治）
132   Lincheng 臨城
133   Longping 隆平
134   Ningjin 寧晉
135   Baixiang 柏鄉

SHENZHOU 深州

136   Anping 安平
136.5 Shen 深 (州治)
137   Raoyang 饒陽
138   Wuqiang 武強

DINGZHOU 定州

139   Shenze 深澤
139.5 Ding 定 （州治）
140   Quyang 曲陽

NOTE: Prefectural-level units, *fu* (prefectures) and *zhilizhou* (autonomous departments), are called "prefectures" in this study. County-level units, *xian* (county) and *zhou* (ordinary or dependent departments), are called "counties." The prefectural-level *zhilizhou* usually directly administered one county that had the same name. For example, Yizhou Prefecture had an Yizhou County. In the Republican period, some county names changed from *zhou* to *xian*; for example, Dingzhou became Ding xian, and Bazhou became Ba xian. This book follows the practice of retaining *zhou* as part of the county or prefectural name, but *xian* is rendered "county." For example, Dingzhou, but later Ding County.[1]

Appendix 2: Data

Zhili Grain Price Data

During the Qing dynasty each provincial governor was required to submit to the throne a monthly report of grain prices in his province. This became a regular bureaucratic practice by the beginning of the Qianlong period in 1736 and was continued to the end of the dynasty in 1911. The First Historical Archives in Beijing and the National Palace Museum in Taipei together have preserved a rather complete set of reports from Zhili for this entire period. I collected data from Taipei in the summer of 1982, and data from Beijing in 1985 and again in 1989. I am indebted to the staffs of both archives for allowing me access to these materials.

In the first phase of this project, up to 1988, I collected approximately 609 of these monthly lists. These include 233 lists for 1738–64, 171 for 1765–95, and 205 for 1796–1910. Articles I published in 1989 and 1992 were based on this set of data, which emphasized the eighteenth century. In the second phase, I completed the collection of all the available Zhili grain price lists held in Beijing. The data set that is used in the analyses done for this study includes a total of 1,668 monthly lists covering the period 1738–1911, or 77.5 percent of the 2,152 lunar months falling in this period. (There were 64 intercalary months in this period of 174 years, of which I have 48. In other words, there were 64 years in which there were 13 lunar months.)

After this work was completed, Susan Naquin found among materials she had previously collected in Taipei six additional monthly price reports for the crisis period of 1801–2. The data from these lists have been used in the case study of the 1801–2 flood crisis in Chapter 9, but they have not been incorporated into the larger data set. (These were JQ 5/1, 7/4, 7/6, 7/7, 7/9, and 7/10.)

In general, there are relatively few lists extant for the early 1790s and the first decade of the 1800s. There are almost no lists for 1821–26, the first six years of the Daoguang period. Lists are sparse for the period between the fourth lunar month of 1900 and the sixth lunar month of 1903.

In the first subperiod, 1738–64, the lists give the low and high prices of seven types of grain from each prefecture (*fu*) or independent department (*zhilizhou*) in the province: *daomi* (rice), *shang sumi* (high-grade millet), *cisumi* or *zhongsumi* (ordinary millet), *baimai* (white wheat), *hong-mai* (red wheat), *heidou* (black beans), and *gaoliang* (sorghum). After 1765, only five grains were reported: *sumi* (millet), *gaoliang* (sorghum), *nimi* (probably a type of glutinous millet), *mai* (wheat), and *heidou* (black beans). In this book, three major grains are studied: wheat, millet, and sorghum. For the 1738–64 period, white wheat is taken to be the equivalent of the "wheat" reported in the subsequent periods; the prices of high-grade millet and ordinary millet are averaged and made comparable to that of "millet" in the later period.[1]

There were seventeen prefectures or independent departments reported by the governor-general of Zhili, although not all were represented in every period. Shuntian fu (where Beijing was located) was not included until 1771. Chengde fu was not included in the reports until 1778. From 1736–68, the prices for Baoding fu, the location of the provincial capital, were reported a month in advance of the other provinces. For example, the Zhili Province grain price report for the fourth month was submitted in the fifth month; it would record the fourth-month prices of all the prefectures, but the fifth-month prices for Baoding.

Although Beijing was technically under the administrative purview of Shuntian Prefecture by virtue of its being situated in two counties, or xian—Daxing and Wanping—in fact the imperial city was governed separately. Its grain prices were reported on the same basis, but they were not included in the monthly report of the Zhili governor-general. The prices reported for Shuntian prefecture each month are preceded by a note explicitly stating that they exclude Daxing and Wanping. Price reports for these two prefectures were reported to the Neiwu fu, the Imperial Household Administration, and have not yet been cataloged by the First Historical Archives.

The Zhili Province grain price reports were submitted monthly, according to the Chinese lunar calendar—with intercalary months ("leap-months") added from time to time to make the lunar year catch up to the solar year. Any lunar month might lag behind its corresponding solar month as much as two months. Solar months are a more appropriate way to study the agricultural cycle. In this study, lunar-month prices have been used where aggregated data for year or multiyear periods would cancel out the variations in the months, but where seasonality is an important concern, data converted to correspond with the solar months has been used. I am grateful to Peter C. Perdue for sharing with me a method by which lunar data can be converted to solar data. This involves a calculation based on the number of days of each lunar month that falls in each solar month, and a weighting of the prices based on the relevant proportions.

The provincial grain price reports were compiled monthly by each provincial government from prefectural reports that had been compiled from ten-day reports from each xian (county or department), within the fu or zhilizhou (prefecture or autonomous department). In the provincial governor's summary of these local reports, the high and low price of each grain in each prefecture therefore represents the highest and lowest price reported in the prefecture during that month. Thus, there is some ambiguity about the exact meaning of high and low as they may represent either a temporal or a spatial dimension, or both. The highest price reported might always be from a particular xian, in which case a spatial dimension would be represented. On the other hand, the highest price might have come from a different xian each month. Since there is no way of knowing the source of each high and low price, throughout this price study I have used the mean of the high and low prices reported for each month. Fortunately, it seems unlikely that this has resulted in any significant distortion. The section below shows that the high and low prices of each prefecture usually followed the same trend. Only in the final years of the Qing, the 1890s through 1911, do we see that high and low prices diverged greatly.

Grain prices were reported in silver taels per cangshi, "granary shi." Taels (liang) were the official unit of accounting. Shi was a measure of volume of grain, roughly equivalent to the weight of 175–95 pounds of milled rice.[2] The character for shi is also pronounced dan when it referred to a measure of weight. Cangshi was the standard granary measure. The reports also specified how each price differed from that of the previous month, for example, "this is 5 fen lower than the previous month." A general summary of conditions was also given: whether prices were higher, lower, or about the same as the previous month.

The exact way in which the grain prices were collected every ten days in each xian is unclear. Yeh-chien Wang believes that in the more central areas, the reported prices were wholesale prices, which would have been negotiated in silver taels, as opposed to the copper cash prices in which retail transactions were made. Wang believes that in all likelihood, the wholesale prices were provided by brokers and shops.[3] Endymion Wilkinson in his study of county-level Shaanxi grain prices 1900–10, finds that the grain prices were retail prices originally reported in (copper) coin or cash together with the prevailing local exchange rate. These cash prices were then converted to taels in the governor's summary report.[4]

RELIABILITY OF THE DATA

Given the ambitious scope of this reporting system, questions about the reliability of the reports are inevitable. Did the local officials or yamen functionaries actually go to the markets personally every ten days? Did they record the information accurately? Was it copied and transmitted accurately? Opportunities for scribal errors presented themselves at several levels of the hierarchy: the xian, the prefecture, the province, and at the central government, where copies were made. In my work, there have been further opportunities for errors when the data have been transcribed for me from the Chinese characters in the original palace memorials (both in Beijing and Taipei), into Arabic numerals, and again when student assistants entered the data from these tables into the computer. To the greatest extent possible, the data entry has been checked, but aside from correcting obvious transcription errors (for example, high and low prices reversed), we have no way of discerning errors made in earlier stages.

Of these, the possibility that the numbers were simply fabricated poses the greatest cause for concern. In working with these data for several years I have become convinced of their essential integrity. They reflect the long-term trends, seasonal patterns, regional differences, secular shocks, and other forms of behavior that seem not only internally consistent but also credible in historical context. Moreover, the essential long- and medium-term correspondence of prices across the prefectures, despite their having been collected separately, shows the probable veracity of the data. Such patterns could not have been discerned by scribes or clerks without the benefit of computers that we have today. Moreover, neither officials or scribes would have any motive for fabricating a long-term trend.

The credibility of Qing population reports has often been called into question. Recently, G. William Skinner has shown that the population and household data reported for Sichuan province in the nineteenth century reflects systematic fabrication by local scribes. This custom was so consistent that it resulted in a serious overestimation of Sichuan's population in the nineteenth century, and it calls into question the provincial population figures usually given for 1850.[5]

These revelations about the population data raise serious questions about the veracity of any statistical reporting in the Qing. However, grain price reporting and population statistics differed in several important respects. Population and household information was generated from the *baojia* system of mutual responsibility, which was in itself a moribund institution in the mid-Qing period. Such reporting required a household registration system that was kept up to date. Since tax rates after the early eighteenth century were only theoretically connected to population size, there was relatively little pressure from higher-level officials to keep the *baojia* records current. Knowledge of grain prices, however, did not require house-to-house surveys, but reporting from the county market level—a bit less strenuous an exercise for local functionaries. Moreover grossly inaccurate reporting of prices could more easily be discovered since prices were a matter of public knowledge. Inaccurate reporting or falsification in Zhili Province, in the immediate vicinity of the imperial court, was presumably riskier than elsewhere in the empire. Most important, however, was that for most of the Qing period, with the exception of the mid-nineteenth century, grain price reporting was not an empty exercise, but had a real function and real consequences. Tax remissions and other forms of famine relief continued to be administered on the basis of such reports until the end of the dynasty.

Bureaucratic inefficiency or laziness, and perhaps unstable local conditions, are the major reasons one can imagine why prices may not have been collected regularly and accurately in short- and medium-run periods. Repetition of the same price over several months would certainly suggest bureaucratic inattention. In a procedure first suggested by Yeh-chien Wang, and later by Robert Marks, the number of repetitions in the data (number of times in a row the same price is repeated) were counted. In my tabulation of prices in each prefecture, I then calculated the percentage of times the price was repeated three times or fewer (assuming that the repetition of a price two or three times might be seen as harmless, affecting neither the overall trends nor seasonal patterns in a serious way). Then I compared the percentage of three-repeats-or-less over time in order to see if there was a deterioration in the quality of record-keeping that was commensurate with dynastic decline.

The results, shown in Table A.1, reveal that in general, during 1738–64, the quality of record keeping seems to have been uniformly high, with most prefectures showing that in more than 90 percent of the cases, the same value was repeated no more than three times. In the second period, 1765–95, the quality also seems to have been high, with an average of 82 percent of the cases showing three repeats or fewer. Roughly the same level was maintained in the 1796–1820 period. After 1821, however, standards seem to have declined in all prefectures, with the worst prefectures showing that only 60 percent of cases with three repeats or fewer. In the last period, 1851–1911, some improvement was shown by some prefectures, while in other prefectures the quality of reporting remained low or even declined: Xuanhua, Zunhua, Jizhou, Zhaozhou, and Shenzhou (Prefectures 4, 12, 14, 15, 16).

Comparing the prefectures, we see that some prefectures continually maintained a high standard, the best being: Baoding, Hejian, Tianjin, and Shunde (2, 5, 6, 8), and possibly Yongping, Guangping, and Daming (3, 9, 10). Some prefectures showed steady deterioration of reporting: Xuanhua, Chengde, Zunhua, Jizhou, Zhaozhou, Shenzhou, and Dingzhou (4, 11, 12, 14, 15, 16, 17). The rest fell in between: Shuntian, Zhengding, and Yizhou (1, 7, 13).

HIGH AND LOW PRICES COMPARED

Various procedures performed on high and low price series failed to find any consistent pattern. For the most part high and low prices followed the same trends. The exceptional years differed for each prefecture and followed no consistent pattern. When the ratio of the high price to the low price in each prefecture was regressed over time, it showed that the ratio did increase over time in all prefectures, but the rate of growth was very slow—in the range of .003–.005 per year. (At those rates, it would have taken approximately 500 years for the ratio of high and low prices to double.)

TABLE A.I

Percentage of Cases When Price Is Repeated
Three Times in Sequence or Less

Prefecture	1738–1764	1764–1795	1796–1820	1821–1850	1851–1911
1 Shuntian	—	80.9	79.6	71.4	80.2
2 Baoding	93.9	82.5	81.9	75.9	81.1
3 Yongping	94.3	81.6	83.0	71.4	87.6
4 Xuanhua	88.1	77.5	74.6	71.9	58.4
5 Hejian	90.4	83.9	81.0	78.0	82.3
6 Tianjin	94.1	87.6	82.1	80.4	88.1
7 Zhengding	87.2	75.6	85.4	74.4	71.0
8 Shunde	94.5	88.4	86.1	81.1	78.3
9 Guangping	90.9	84.3	84.2	81.8	76.4
10 Daming	94.6	90.0	86.0	75.8	85.0
11 Chengde	—	78.1	72.9	—	—
12 Zunhua	95.9	81.0	78.9	59.8	63.3
13 Yizhou	87.6	81.3	85.2	72.4	83.6
14 Jizhou	84.1	73.7	81.9	62.5	60.2
15 Zhaozhou	92.1	80.3	75.9	63.1	61.6
16 Shenzhou	93.5	89.1	84.3	74.2	62.7
17 Dingzhou	95.1	81.3	78.9	63.6	75.7
Average	91.8	82.2	81.3	72.4	74.7

When crisis years were coded as dummy variables (see Appendix 3, section on regression analysis), results were inconclusive and varied by prefecture.

Analysis of prices from Tianjin Prefecture, which appears to have had the most accurate reports (see Table A.I), reveal that high and low monthly wheat prices tended to follow the same trends. Only after about 1894, however, did the gap between high and low prices seriously diverge. Similar trends are found for millet prices, except that the magnitude of the gap between high and low prices is smaller. From the mid-nineteenth century, there were years in which the ratio between high and low prices dramatically increased, but they were not always the same years for wheat and millet until the 1890s. The regression of the ratio on the year also showed the slow rate of growth. Finally, the ratio did not necessarily increase during flood and drought crises.

Other Grain Price Data

FENGTIAN

Grain price data for Fengtian Prefecture, Liaoning Province, was collected by James Z. Lee from the First Historical Archives in Beijing, and by Yeh-chien Wang from the National Palace Museum in Taipei. James Lee has graciously made these data available to me for the purpose of seeing how closely Fengtian grain prices were related to the Zhili prices.

The Fengtian data include more than 1,500 monthly lists covering 1765–1910. Six grains were reported: rice, wheat, unhusked millet, husked millet, sorghum, and beans. James Lee converted lunar data to solar in the same way that I did. He also filled in missing data by "splining," that is, weighted averaging according to seasonal patterns.[6]

LOWER YANGZI

Yeh-chien Wang has been the pioneer in the collection of Qing price data. For this study, I have employed the lower Yangzi rice price data from the series he compiled from various archival and nonarchival sources, as published in Table 1.1 of his "Secular Trends of Rice Prices in the Yangzi Delta, 1638–1935."[7]

Rainfall and Harvest Data

In addition to grain prices, local officials were also obliged to report on the weather and the harvests. The *qingyu lu* (records of clear and rainy days) were daily weather records, including qualitative observations of sky conditions, wind direction, and precipitation. The earliest known imperial edict ordering such reports dates from KX 24 (1685). Records from about forty locations have been found, with Beijing having the longest record. Each month, local officials reported the inches of precipitation (rain and snow, *yuxue fencun*) that fell at the county seat, supplemented with other observations. Such reporting began in the first year of Qianlong (1736) and continued to the end of the Qing period. Finally each summer and autumn local officials presented reports on the harvest rated on a scale of 1 to 10, 10 being a bumper harvest. One report was presented as a forecast of the harvest and another after the harvest was completed.[8]

For a number of years, scientists in China have been collecting such historical data from the First Historical Archives. Zhang Peiyuan, Deputy Director of the Institute of Geography, Chinese Academy of Sciences, who has been engaged in the study of historical climate for many years, has generously shared with me data from areas relevant to this study.

The data series that he has provided me measures millimeters of monthly rainfall in Beijing during the Qing period. Beijing has the best preserved and most numerous *yuxue fencun* and *qingyu lu* records for the empire. For the late nineteenth century these data also include instrument readings from the Meteorological Station in Beijing. For the earlier parts of the eighteenth and nineteenth centuries, Zhang Peiyuan has constructed a rainfall series by modeling available rainfall information to the seasonal patterns known from the later period. About two-thirds of the data comes directly from the bureaucratic weather reports; gazetteers and other sources helped to fill in the rest.[9]

The summer and autumn harvest ratings that Professor Zhang has shared with me include five localities in Zhili: Tianjin, Tangshan, Cangzhou, and Shijiazhuang counties, and Baoding Prefecture. These ratings cover the years 1730–1910 and 1730–1915, respectively. About two-thirds of these data came from actual reports found in the First Historical Archives, about one-tenth were estimated from gazetteer references, and the rest were filled by interpolation, according to Professor Zhang. In this study only the Baoding harvest ratings were employed because they seemed to provide consistent and meaningful results.

How accurate were the harvest ratings (and grain price reports)? One metropolitan censor said that inflation of ratings was a common practice by magistrates who wished to gain favor with their superiors.

> Except when their jurisdictions are visited with actual calamities which they do not dare conceal, it
> has long been the practice of county-level magistrates to report 50 to 60 per cent successful harvests

as 70 to 80 per cent successful ones, and 70 to 80 percent successful harvests as 90 to 100 percent successful ones. In their grain-price reports, they represent a price of 0.8 to 0.9 tl./bushel as only 0.6 to 0.7 tl./bushel. The purpose is to suggest that all has gone well with the jurisdiction's crops, and there is no need to disturb the peace of mind of their superiors. This is an entrenched habit.[10]

Copper-Silver Exchange Rate

The data, all annual rates, are drawn from three sources.

1723–1806. These exchange rates for Beijing and vicinity are from Chen Chau-nan, *Fluctuations of Bimetallic Exchange Rates in China, 1700–1850: A Preliminary Survey*, 14. These do not come from a single series, but rather are derived from official documents or "estimated from descriptions of monetary conditions in available documents." Consequently these figures indicate "the long-run trend rather than the actual fluctuations."

1800–1835, 1836, 1843, 1844, 1845, 1850. From Chen Chau-nan, *Fluctuations of Bimetallic Exchange Rates in China, 1700–1850: A Preliminary Survey*, 30. Chen Chau-nan adapted these data from Yen Chung-ping, *Zhongguo jindai jingjishi tongji ziliao xuanji*, 37. They were based on observations from shops at Hebei, Ningjin xian, Daliao zhen. Prices are indexed to 1821 as base year.

1857–1911 (–1931). From Sidney D. Gamble, *Ting Hsien: A North China Rural Community*, 272. These data were taken by Gamble from county yamen accounts and are expressed in cash per dollar rates. These have been converted back to silver taels at the rate of 0.72 taels per dollar. Although, as Gamble notes on 251, Ting Hsien exchange rates were sometimes quite different from Beijing's, this is the longest continuous series for this region and is thus a unique source.

Appendix 3:
Quantitative Methods

(Scott Hodges, coauthor)

Ordinary least square linear regression analysis has been used to study the long-term movement of grain prices. The technique attempts to measure the effect of other variables, including dummy variables, on changes in the price. R^2 is the measure of the amount of price variation that is explained by all the variables used in the regression analysis. The *t*-value for each variable shows the statistical significance of that variable alone. If the true value of a coefficient is zero, indicating no effect on the dependent variable, then the probability that the *t*-value will be between -1.96 and +1.96 is 95 percent. Thus *t*-values *not* between plus and minus two are considered to be statistically significant. The F statistic is another measure of significance.

Regression with Seasonal and Climate Variables, 1738–1911
(Tables 4.1a–b, Figures 4.4, 4.5a–b)

This regression analysis attempts to measure the effects of variables that can be considered "internal," close to the local agricultural process, on the provincial average prices of wheat and millet within Zhili (excluding Xuanhua and Chengde) from 1738 to 1911: monthly seasonal influences, drought and flood crises, and the harvest size. Lunar-month prices were first converted to solar-month prices in order to capture seasonal effects, and then detrended in order to remove the possibly larger and distorting effect of long-term secular trends. The multiple regression of prices was based on the following equation:

$$P = a + b_1Y + b_2M_2 + b_3M_3 + \ldots + b_{12}M_{12} + b_{13}\text{Crifld} + b_{14}\text{Cridrt} + b_{15}\text{BDharv}$$

This model states that the price in a given month is the sum of a constant term (a), the product of the year (Y) and the coefficient for the year (b_1), the coefficient of the dummy variable for the appropriate month (b_2–b_{12}), the coefficient of the dummy variable for presence of flood (b_{13}) or the dummy for the presence of drought (b_{14}), if appropriate, and the product of the harvest coefficient (b_{15}) and the Baoding harvest rating for the current season.

Because this long-term series shows such a strong time trend, in order to measure the effects of variables on the behavior of prices, it is advisable first to remove the trend from the data. Using the log of prices is inappropriate for this task since the trend is not linear. In this analysis, the solar monthly price data were detrended in six subperiods chosen according to an analysis of the long-term price trends, with the exact end points for each grain picked so that they represented the absolute high and low points of the cycle. The specific dates and types of cycles were (based on solar-month data):

Type	Wheat Dates	Millet Dates
Stable	6/1738 to 7/1805	6/1738 to 7/1805
Inflation	7/1805 to 4/1814	7/1805 to 6/1814
Deflation	4/1814 to 8/1856	6/1814 to 3/1856
Inflation	8/1856 to 3/1858	3/1856 to 7/1858
Stable	3/1858 to 8/1893	7/1858 to 9/1893
Inflation	8/1893 to 7/1911	9/1893 to 7/1911

The data were detrended by taking all the observations on a specific grain for a given subperiod and regressing on a time trend, which was subtracted or added from the data. (These results and others below indicated by * are available from the author.)

The same regression was run on the detrended price data from Yongping, Tianjin, and Daming prefectures individually. The principal purpose was to see if the seasonal patterns varied from prefecture to prefecture, and by how much.

The procedure for detrending was the same, but with slight adjustments in the end-points of each period to account for missing data and small variations in timing for peaks and troughs.*

A number representing the calendar year (1738–1911). This variable is included despite our focus on short-term trends because the detrending procedure does not guarantee elimination of an overall drift in the average price values. In other words the variable "year" represents the residual trend *across* the time periods that is left after detrending *within* the time periods.

A dummy variable for the months February–December (thus implying a January base). The coefficient for each month represents the amount (in taels) that should be added to the base price to represent the expected price change for that month. These coefficients have been graphed in Figure 4.4, which shows the monthly difference in price from the January base.

A dummy variable for flood. The variable is coded on a crop-year basis because most of the relevant rainfall in a calendar year fell in the summer and early fall. If a given year is included in the flood list, then the months of July–December in that year and January–June of the next year are coded as 1; if it is not on the list, then it is coded as 0. The flood list was derived from a combination of rainfall data and documentary evidence and includes 40 flood years. All years above 850 mm, as seen in the rainfall data, are listed, plus 4 additional years of 800–850 mm where documents tell of serious flooding (more than 20 counties declared "disaster"). Only one year, 1747, is less than 800 mm, but it was included because of evidence of wide flood damage. N.b. there are eleven years with 800–850 mm *not* listed as "flood" The rainfall data are from Beijing only. (See Appendix 2.) The forty years were:

1738	1739	1747	1749	1750	1751	1761	1762	1770	1771
1779	1780	1781	1789	1790	1794	1797	1800	1801	1806
1807	1808	1816	1819	1822	1823	1834	1840	1853	1871
1873	1883	1886	1889	1890	1891	1892	1893	1894	1901

CRIDRT

A dummy variable for drought. This variable is coded in the same manner as CriFld. The drought list includes all years when rainfall was under 400 mm, according to data provided by Zhang Peiyuan, as well as a few additional years when drought was acknowledged in documentary sources to have been extensive. These twenty-two years were:

1743	1744	1745	1752	1758	1759	1792	1802	1813	1817
1825	1832	1854	1857	1862	1869	1877	1878	1880	1895
1899	1900								

BDHARVEST

The harvest rating from Baoding for the appropriate crop. The summer harvest rating (wheat) codes June of the year in which the rating is made with the number of the rating. The same number is also coded for the *previous* July–June. (For example, the harvest rating for 1750 is coded for each month from July 1749 through June 1750.) The autumn (millet) harvest rating is back-coded for the period October–September. (For example, the fall harvest rating for 1750 is coded for each month from October 1749 through September 1750.)[1] The decision to code the previous year reflects an assumption that the price effect of a harvest takes place while that crop is growing and does not wait until the grain reaches the market. This is related to the assumption of classical economists that prices fully and completely reflect all available information. In the case of rural China, this assumption is controversial. However, experimentation with different timing of the price response suggested that it fits the data better (in terms of higher *t*-values and a higher explanatory power as measured by R^2) than the alternative assumption that prices react in the year following the harvest rating. The Baoding harvest rating was chosen as a representative because experimentation showed that of the five ratings provided by Zhang Peiyuan, it tended to have the most effect on prices elsewhere.

STATISTICAL SIGNIFICANCE

The R^2 is .375 and .221 for wheat and millet, respectively. These values indicate that the internal factors explain 37.5 and 22.1 percent of the variability remaining after detrending. In regressions done on nondetrended data, with external variables included with internal ones (see below), R^2 have proven to be in the as high as .618 and .723 for wheat and millet, with the time variable (year) making the largest contribution, that is, accounting for the largest amount of the variation in price.

The *t*-values for the monthly dummy variables are mostly under 2. The small coefficients show that monthly changes did not account for very much of the price variation. However, there was still a pattern of monthly variation even though the *t*-values show that the estimation of this pattern is subject to error.

The *t*-values for flood crises were under 2 for both wheat and millet, showing that the effect of floods on the price was marginal. The coefficient for wheat was negative, -.015, but the standard error is such that it is statistically insignificant, that is, indistinguishable from zero. Although it seems counterintuitive that floods could have lowered prices instead of raising them, it must be remembered that the provincial average (except Xuanhua and Chengde) price obscures intraregional differences, and that floods tended to be more localized in effect than droughts. (See Chapter 4 for further discussion of this result.) When the same regression was run only on data from individual prefectures of Yongping, Tianjin, and Daming, the coefficients for flood were positive except for Yongping, and the *t*-values were significant in some of the cases. (Tables 4.1a–b.)

Regression on Two Time Periods*

In order to see if there was any change in the seasonal pattern during the two centuries under consideration, the data were split into two periods, 1738–1820 and 1821–1911, and a Chow test[2] on the stability of seasonal coefficients was performed separately for each grain and each prefecture. The results were generally negative, implying that there was no statistically significant difference in the seasonal cycles between the early and later periods. The *F*-statistics were nearly always less than 1 and in all cases failed to be high enough for even a 10 percent significance level.

Regression on Provincial Average Price with Rainfall Alone*

In order to evaluate the impact of rainfall itself on the price, we created a variable called "Dry," which measures the impact on the price of every 100 mm less than 900 mm of rainfall. A coefficient of 0.03 means, for example, that in a year when 500 mm of rain fell, then 0.12 taels of the price (0.03*4) could be attributed to the lack of rain. (See next section for an explanation of how this variable was created.)

In a regression on detrended prices with months as dummy variables and Dry as the single other variable, the dry coefficient was .032 ($t = 8.430$) for wheat and .011 for millet ($t = 4.135$).

Because the variables Dry, CriFld, and CriDrt are all constructed from a common source, the rainfall data, it was not advisable to use them in the same regression. When these variables are used together, multicolinearity takes effect, with one variable diminishing the strength of the other.

Regression on the Effect of Multiyear Rainfall
(Figure 4.7)

In order to capture, in a linear regression format, the effect on the price in a given year of "dryness" over the same and previous years, a technique was developed to regress the price information on dryness measures taken at different points in time. The variables employed were:

PRICE

The dependent variable used is the first difference of the price of wheat or millet. These prices are annual averages of the prices for solar months July–June (Wheat) or October–September (Millet).

DRYNESS

In order to calculate the dryness variable, the first step was to sum the rainfall during a given crop year. The crop years were the same as those used for the price data. Thus there were two different sets of calculations. July–June was the crop year for wheat, while October–September was considered the crop year for millet. Once the rainfall for the crop year was computed, it was converted into the Dry variable (defined as [900 – Crop Year Rainfall]/100), which measures the amount by which rain in the period fell short of 900 mm.

Once these proxies for dryness in a given period were calculated, they were used with different lags as explanatory variables in the regression. This means that the price for a given crop year was regressed simultaneously on the dryness during the concurrent crop year, dryness during the previous crop year, and dryness two, three, and four years ago. The annual price for wheat (from July to June), for example, was regressed on the Dry variable for the exact same period as well as those from each of the preceding four years. Each year's price will be affected by the rainfall in the previous four years. Conversely, each year's "dryness" will affect prices in each of next four years. From this perspective, the coefficients represent the isolated effect of a single year's dryness on the prices for successive years.

In Figure 4.7, each of these annual coefficients is isolated and viewed in this way. The y-axis measures the amount of price change from the previous year per 100 mm under 900 mm. For example if 700 mm of rain fell in a given year (Dry = 2), its effect on the wheat price in the year *prior* to the harvest, would be .04 taels.

Regression of Grain Prices on Cash-Silver Exchange Rate, 1765–1895
(Tables 4.2a–b)

The variable Year measures the long-term trend of the prices (year 1738 = 1,738). The copper-silver exchange rate is the copper price of silver divided by 1000. See Appendix 2 on Data for the source of the annual exchange rates.

Regression of Zhili Grain Prices on Fengtian
and Lower Yangzi Grain Prices, 1765–1895
(Tables 7.5a–b)

This set of regressions attempts to measure the influence of Fengtian grain prices (wheat and millet), and Lower Yangzi rice prices on grain prices in Zhili Province excluding Xuanhua and Chengde. Prices are not detrended because the purpose is to look at the long-term trends themselves. The Lower Yangzi rice prices are annual averages (the same price is entered for each month), while the Fengtian grain prices are monthly. For an explanation of the sources of these data, see Appendix 2 on Data.

Case Studies: Predicted Price
(Figures 8.1a–b, 8.3a–b, 9.1a–b, 9.3a–b)

The price prediction is intended to represent what the price would be in the absence of crises. In order to generate this prediction, information on seasonal patterns is used as well as a time trend. A base prediction is generated by using the constant term and time trend from a linear regression, as described below. The seasonal data is then incorporated by adding the value of the appropriate monthly dummy to each observation. These monthly dummy coefficients were generated by regressing the province average price on eleven monthly dummy variables, a time trend, and a constant for the 1738–1911 time period.

The generation of a time trend is potentially more controversial. There is a necessary trade-off between using a fixed procedure for each case study and using a procedure that allows a reasonable fit to the data. In most cases the price level before and after the crises is fairly flat and thus relatively insensitive to the choice of method. The procedure is to generate a time trend via regression using the years before and after the crisis. This procedure is implemented differently in each case in order to accommodate multiple crises in the period of study, as well as to avoid contamination by crises immediately before or after the period studied. The years used to generate each time trend are as follows:

> Figures for 1738–50: Years 1738–42 are used.
> Figures for 1754–70: Years 1754–59, 1760–61, and 1764–70 are used.
> Figures for 1799–1816: Years 1799–1801 and 1803–12 are used.
> Figures for 1865–85: Years 1860–65 and 1882–90 are used.

A regression of the monthly data for these years on a constant and a time trend was performed to generate the base prediction to which the seasonal dummies were added to form the final predicted price. For all but the last study, there is a clear "norm" for the price level, which is reestablished after the flood or drought. In the final study, a linear trend fits the price rise for the period quite well. Alterations in the years chosen will not significantly affect the location of the time line, unless they accidentally incorporate crisis years which would impart an upward bias to the data.

In comparing predicted and actual prices, we also took the log of the price, but found that the difference was imperceptible. Because a graph of plain prices is easier to understand, we have preferred this version.

Case Studies: Normal Rainfall
(Figures 8.2a–b, 8.4a–b, 9.2a–b, 9.4a–b)

For each month, rainfall is cumulated over the previous year. For example, April 1750 uses the sum of monthly rainfall observations from May 1749 through April 1750. May 1750 then uses the sum of monthly data from June 1749 through May 1750, and so forth. This sum is then converted into a percentage index using the "normal" rainfall for the period. For case studies prior to 1851, normal rainfall is taken to be 712 mm, which is the average annual rainfall from 1738–1850. For case studies after 1850, average annual rainfall for 1851–1911 of 653 mm is used. The actual rainfall is divided by the appropriate average to generate the index. For example, if the sum for April 1750 was 1,424 mm, the index would be 1,424/712 = 2.0.

Abbreviations Used in Notes

ABCFM	American Board of Commissioners for Foreign Missions
BCSX	*Bachao shengxun*
CYQS	*Caoyun quanshu*
FZ	*fuzhi* (prefectural gazetteer)
GZD	*Gongzhongdang*
GZDKXC	*Gongzhongdang Kangxichao zouzhe*
GZDQLC	*Gongzhongdang Qianlongchao zouzhe*
GZDYZC	*Gongzhongdang Yongzhengchao zouzhe*
HBZL	*(Qinding) Hubu zeli*
HCJSWB	*Huangchao jingshi wenbian*
HDSL	*Da Qing huidian shili*
HHLY	*Haihe liuyu lidai ziran zaihai shiliao*
JFSLSA	*Jifu shuili si'an*
JFTZ	*Jifu tongzhi*
JJD	*Junjidang*
JJSZ	*Jingji shuizai shanhou jishi*
JWSL	*Jinwu shili*
NCDN	*North China Daily News*
QDHH	*Qingdai Haihe Luanhe honglao dang'an shiliao*
XYGZJS	*(Qinding) Xinyou gongzhen jishi*
USDS	U.S. Department of State
XZ	*xianzhi* (county gazetteer)
YDHZ	*Yongding he zhi*
ZPZZ	Gongzhongdang zhupizouzhe
ZPZZ, CZCC	Caizheng cangchu
ZPZZ, CZDD	Caizheng diding
ZPZZ, CZTF	Caizheng tianfu
ZPZZ, NZZJ	Neizheng zhenji
ZPZZ, SL	Shuili

NOTES

Introduction

1. Mallory, *China: Land of Famine*. Deng Tuo's *Zhongguo jiuhuangshi*, the most influential twentieth-century work on famines, was a response to the challenge posed by Mallory's book.

2. Whether Marco Polo ever reached China is irrelevant; his *Travels* contributed to the European view of China as a land of riches. Frances Wood's *Did Marco Polo Go to China?* discusses the evidence for and against Marco Polo's veracity.

3. Needham 4:3, 247–49.

4. Yates, 155.

5. *Hsun-tzu* (Xunzi), chap. 17 on nature, translated in W. Chan, *Sourcebook*, 117 and 122. For Xunzi, the Chinese word *tian* could mean either Nature or Heaven, depending on the context. John Knoblock, *Xunzi: A Translation and Study of the Complete Works*, 3:3–12. Deng Tuo, 7–11, has other classical references.

6. The *Guanzi*, a work attributed to the seventh or sixth century B.C. statesman Guan Zhong, also speaks of ever-normal granaries. W. Chan, *Sourcebook*, 192.

7. Yates, 164–65.

8. The two earliest histories, the *Shiji* and *Han shu*, had sections on "rivers and canals," but not until the Song period did this topic become a regular part of the standard dynastic histories. Wilkinson, *Chinese History*, tab. 31, p. 512.

9. Brook, *Confusions of Pleasure*, 104–7, 190–92, describes some famines of the sixteenth century.

10. These are the estimates by Ping-ti Ho, *Studies on the Population of China, 1368–1953*, 281, which have been widely accepted, but recently challenged by Martin Heijdra, who believes there was a much greater population expansion in the Ming dynasty than Ho and others have estimated. Heijdra's "guesstimates" of late Ming population range from 230 to 290 million. Such figures challenge the notion that the eighteenth century experienced a population explosion. Heijdra, 436–40.

11. "In 40 years, the 170 yi yuan and 2000 yi gongjin have been spent on disaster relief." Headline in overseas edition of *People's Daily*, Sept. 7, 1989. This article points to China's long history as the land of famine, *jihuang zhi Zhongguo*, but says it no longer is.

12. Interview with Jim Lehrer on PBS, Oct. 30, 1997. Charges of human rights abuses in China had been used by congressional opponents in the debate about China's entry into the World Trade Organization.

13. Jordan, 15–16, 21–22.

14. Gottfried, 80–89, describes the profound changes in religious attitude and practice that resulted from the Black Death.

15. Walter and Schofield, *Famine, Disease and the Social Order*, esp. 41. Other essays in this important

collection question the link between high grain prices and mortality. Dupâquier is especially skeptical of this link. Others have suggested that poor nutrition lowers resistance to infectious disease, thus causing higher mortality. See McKeown and other essays in Rotberg and Rabb, *Hunger and History.*

16. Wrigley and Schofield, 354–55, conclude that disease, rather than harvests or economic factors, was the major factor explaining mortality in early modern England. See also Appleby, "Disappearance of the Plague."

17. Walter and Schofield, 41.

18. Post, esp. xiii.

19. Ibid., 54–60.

20. Walter and Schofield, 49.

21. Mokyr, *Why Ireland Starved*, employs a quantitative approach to the different theories.

22. C. Tilly, esp. 385, 396.

23. R. Bin Wong has drawn attention to the apparent similarity between grain blockages in China and those in Europe, but argues that the different historical contexts give different meanings to them. Wong, *China Transformed*, chap. 9, 209–29. In an earlier article, "Food Riots," esp. 785, Wong describes the food riot as a "a common type of conflict in Qing China," but "the riot event was a small-scale conflict with the limited purpose of gaining food," not linked to any "large social upheavals."

24. Su Xiaokang, producer of the six-part television documentary "Heshang" of 1988, was subject to sharp political criticism and eventually sought exile in the United States. "Heshang" has also been translated "Deathsong of the River." See Su Xiaokang and Wang Luxiang, *Deathsong.*

25. Similar to Jordan, 7, who adds that the 1315 famine was both extensive and prolonged.

26. Post, xiii.

27. M. K. Bennett, "Famine," in *International Encyclopedia of the Social Sciences*, vol. 5, ed. David L. Sills (New York, 1968), 322–26, quoted in McAlpin, 6.

28. Ibid.

29. As in Shapiro, *Mao's War Against Nature.*

30. Malthus, 56. Even Malthus, 46, did not assume such an outcome was inevitable, but he assumed that "misery and vice" were the main checks to population growth. This appears only in the first edition.

31. Lee and Wang, *One Quarter of Humanity*, 35–37.

32. Myers, *Chinese Peasant Economy*, 276.

33. Brook, *Confusions of Pleasure*; Perdue, *Exhausting the Earth*; Perkins, *Agricultural Development in China*; Rowe, *Hankow: Commerce and Society*; Will, *Bureaucracy and Famine*; Will and Wong, *Nourish the People.*

34. Wong, *China Transformed*; Lee and Wang, *One Quarter of Humanity*; Pomeranz, *Great Divergence.*

35. Frank, *ReORIENT.*

36. Bu Fengxian, "Zhongguo nongye zaihaishi yanjiu zonglun," gives a comprehensive account of recent scholarly work in China on the history of agricultural disasters. Most of these articles were published after the main research for this book was completed.

37. Li Wenhai, the president of People's University and a member of the Central Committee, received a large grant to organize teams of scholars and support work on the history of famines.

38. One compilation particularly important for this book is *Qingdai Hai he Luan he honglao dang'an shiliao.* Several other publications are cited below in the Bibliography.

Chapter One

1. Yates, 150–51.

2. Zuo and Zhang, 473.

3. Will, "Clear Waters."

4. Perdue describes the process of encroachment in the Dongting Lake region of central China in the Qing period and later. Schoppa documents the resistance to encroachment on the Xiang Lake in Zhejiang, a reservoir, over the centuries. Chapters in Elvin and Liu treat environmental transformations in other regions of China.

5. Hebei, Beijing, and Tianjin in 1989 produced about 6.07 percent of the national output of grain. Together with other North China provinces, excluding the northeast, they produced 25.18 percent of the

national total of grain and 58.18 percent of cotton. Calculated from *China Statistical Abstract 1990*, tab. T3.13, p. 30.

6. McNeill, "China's Environmental History," 34–35.

7. Summarized from *Zhongguo ziran dili, Lidai ziran dili fence*, 152–54.

8. Needham, 4:3, 271.

9. *Hebei fengwu zhi*, 221–23; originally from the *Shiji* (Book of History).

10. *Haihe shi jianbian*, 25–29, esp. map on 26. This volume gives an accurate history of Hai River Basin until Yuan period, when it starts to impose a heavy ideological interpretation on events. *Zhongguo ziran dili*, 155–57, gives a more nuanced account of the formation of the Hai River Basin but acknowledges the formative influence of Cao Cao, 180. *Jifu hedao shuili congshu* is the standard source for the history of the rivers and their name changes. Mainly juan 1, and also juan 10.

11. *Haihe shi jianbian*, 37–46. *Huang Huai Hai pingyuan*, 149–50, sees the Sui as the period when the Hai River system really became independent of the Yellow River.

12. Van Slyke, 68–73.

13. *Haihe shi jianbian*, 75.

14. *Zhongguo ziran dili*, 159–61, describes the evolution. Also *Huang Huai Hai pingyuan*, 154–55, gives the ancient history.

15. Summarized from *Huang Huai Hai pingyuan*, 156–57. Also *Zhongguo ziran dili*, 161–62. *Jifu hedao shuili congshu* I:24–35, gives a brief history of the river through the mid-Qing period.

16. *Huang Huai Hai pingyuan*, 157–58, and *Zhongguo ziran dili*, 164–66.

17. *Huang Huai Hai pingyuan*, 159, and *Zhongguo ziran dili*, 166–70.

18. Summarized from *Huang Huai Hai pingyuan*, 162. See also *Zhongguo ziran dili*.

19. *Huang Huai Hai pingyuan*, 131–32; also stressed elsewhere.

20. Summarized from *Zhongguo ziran dili*, 175–79. Leonard, 171, recounts the difficulties during the Grand Canal crisis of 1824–36.

21. *Haihe shi jianbian*, 43–44.

22. See Chapter 10 in this book.

23. This is the view of *Haihe shi jianbian*, 70–75ff., although the book acknowledges that the Ming officials also took measures to construct diversionary channels and other water control projects, and that the Grand Canal conferred other economic benefits to North China, such as providing a north-south transport link, 77–79.

24. The editors of *Haihe shi jianbian* want to rewrite it. Briefing at Ministry of Water Conservancy and Hydroelectric Power's Research Institute, May 4, 1985.

25. *The Haihe River Basin and . . . Water Resources in the Basin*, official pamphlet, 1989. Also draft papers 1989 by same, *Zhongguo jianghe*. See Chapter 12 below for further discussion of conservancy projects, including the Baiyang Lake.

26. Zuo and Zhang, 476.

27. *The Haihe River Basin*. Compare this to Ho Chin, *Harm into Benefit*, 1–2, where the region is described as having only 265,000 sq. kilometers, but more cultivated land, 180 million mu. The discrepancy in these figures reflects the loss of land to industrial and urban use in the years between these two publications.

28. Skinner, "Regional Urbanization," 212–13. Skinner designates Manchuria as a ninth region of China, but excludes it from his analysis because "the settlement of the region by Han Chinese got under way on a large scale only in the last decade of the Ch'ing period . . . [and] its urban system was embryonic or at best emergent."

29. The description of districts below roughly follows a briefing at Beijing Agricultural University on June 3, 1989, on the Huang-Huai-Hai region, as well as the descriptions in *Hebei sheng jingji dili*, 114–21, and *Hebei sheng zonghe nongye quhua*, esp. 124–26. These publications define these zones somewhat differently, and they both omit the independent municipalities of Beijing and Tianjin. The northwestern section of Shandong Province is also a part of the Huang-Huai-Hai region. The numbering of the zones in Map 1.3 follows the agricultural maps in *Hebei sheng jingji dili*, 120, and *Hebei sheng zonghe nongye qukua*, facing p. 124.

30. *Huang Huai Hai diqu*, 21.

31. Its exact geographical definition varies somewhat from the description here. See *Zhongguo baike nianjian* 1983, 71, where only forty-six counties are included.

32. A recent Hebei gazetteer identified three special characteristics of Hebei's agriculture: its varied and uneven natural and economic conditions, including the presence of Beijing and Tianjin; its marked intraregional differences; and the instability of its agricultural production. *Dangdai Zhongguo de Hebei*, 1:569–76.

33. The first is the range cited at briefings by the Hai River Commission; the second figure is from its publication, *The Haihe River Basin*.

34. *Population Atlas of China*, 5. This source gives 571 mm for the Hai River basin.

35. Han Xiangling, 1.

36. "Huabei zhi ganhan ji qianyin houguo," reprint of 1934 article in *Zhu Kezhen wenji*, 181.

37. Han Xiangling, "Drought Characteristic." Huang Rangtang, "Hebei pingyuan," 73–80, surveys the same points.

38. Gong Gaofa et al., tab. 1, p. 446.

39. *Huang Huai Hai diqu*, 13. Note that this source uses data from 1960–80 generally.

40. Ibid., 13–15; Han Xiangling, 8.

41. *Huang Huai Hai diqu*, 21.

42. Ibid., 13–14; Han Xiangling, 8–9.

43. Duan Yunhuai and Zhang Qingchen make the same points about seasonality.

44. *Nongye qihou*, 51.

45. Ibid., 55.

46. In addition to Map 1.4 in this book, see also *Hebei shengzhi*, vol. 8, and *Qixiang zhi*, 44–45, where the figures given for the range of precipitation in each subregion are lower by 50 mm each.

47. Han Xiangling, 3.

48. *Hebei jingji dili*, 69, 71, 83, respectively.

49. *Huang Huai Hai diqu*, 15.

50. Chu Ko-chen, "Preliminary Study," 230–38.

51. Ibid., 244. Western historians differ on which years constituted the Little Ice Age, or whether there really was a Little Ice Age. See Rotberg and Rabb, *Climate and History*.

52. Chu Coching, "Climatic Change," 38; Chu Ko-chen, "Preliminary," 245.

53. Ibid.

54. "Beijing shi jin wubainian hanlao fenxi," esp. fig. 2, 127.

55. Feng Liwen, tab. 6, p. 204. She also finds that the number of no-rain days has decreased over the period of 256 years, and that there have been cycles of about 100 years each. The years 1944–79 witnessed a particularly dry period.

56. Duan and Zhang, 49. They used unspecified records from Central Meteorological Bureau.

57. Wang Shao-wu et al., "Reconstruction," fig. 3, 120, and 119–22.

58. Gong Gaofa, 447.

59. *Beijing shuihan zaihai*, 7.

60. *Dangdai Zhongguo de Hebei* 1:681.

61. *Beijing shuihan zaihai*, 7.

62. These form our definitions of "normal" rainfall in the case studies in Chapters 8 and 9. See Appendix 3 on Quantitative Methods. The rainfall data for Beijing is discussed in Appendix 2.

63. 1884/1934, juan 108–10.

64. See Chapter 2 in this book.

65. Observed in *Tianjin FZ* 1898, 6:1a.

66. Wang Shouchun, "Yongding he," 111–13.

67. Dong Kaichen, 78.

68. Yin Junke, 90ff.

69. "Zhili dili he huanjing he shuizai," reprint of 1927 article in *Zhu Kezhen wenji*, 114–15.

70. *Wen'an XZ* 1922, final juan, 10b–11a, as discussed in Chapter 2 in this book.

71. See discussion in Chapter 8 in this book. *Haihe liuyu*, 585–91, is the source for the nonquantitative generalizations.

72. For example *China Agricultural Development Report '96*, tab. 8, p. 117, shows "disastrous areas" as a percentage of "the whole area hit by disasters." In 1995 this was 49 percent.

73. *HCJSWB* 43:11a. Discussed in Chapter 4 below.

74. *Huangzheng beilan* (1824), 1:11ab, cited and translated by Will, *Bureaucracy*, 25. Wang served in Zhejiang Province, central China, not in the north.

75. Buck, *Chinese Farm Economy*, 179. Also in Chapter 3, below.

76. *Xincheng XZ* 1935, 22:7b–15.

77. *Xingtai XZ* 1905, 3:17–21.

78. *Pingxiang XZ* 1886, 1:36–38.

79. *Xinhe XZ* 1928, ce 1, 17b–21b.

80. *HHLY* 441–59, provides excerpts from local gazetteers.

81. In addition to gazetteer references, see Dunstan, "Late Ming Epidemics"; and Brook, *Confusions of Pleasure*, 163–67, 239.

82. Ibid., 104–7, 190–91.

83. Dated from the early fifteenth century, this guide was in the class of *materia medica*, listings of medicinal plants. In 1940 it was translated by Bernard E. Read as *Famine Foods listed in the Chiu Huang Pen Ts'ao*.

84. Juan 49–59. About a third of this massive work (1639) is devoted to famine relief. Vol. 3 of annotated version (1980).

85. Pictures from Yang Dongming, *Jimin tushuo*, 1688, are reproduced and discussed in Des Forges, 34–55.

86. *Xianghe XZ* 1639, 10:3b–4b.

87. See Chapters 3 and 11 in this book for discussion of demographic trends.

88. See Chapter 11 below for a discussion of infanticide.

89. *Jingxing XZ* 1934, 10:26ab, 4:1.

90. See Chapter 12 below.

91. Historians contributing to *Climate and History*, edited by Rotberg and Rabb, represent different sides of this issue. De Vries, "Measuring the Impact of Climate on History," presents the most balanced but skeptical view. Appleby, "Epidemics and Famine in the Little Ice Age," 80–82, asks why during the mid-seventeenth century, "England managed to prevent harvest failures from turning into famine at the same time that France was becoming especially vulnerable to famines" when they had the same climate pattern. His answer is that England had the advantages of a more developed grain trade, a better system of parish relief, a more favorable tax structure, and an "agricultural revolution." The recent work of David C. Smith and William R. Baron on climate in the New England colonies prompted a headline in the *New York Times*, "Don't Blame King George III. It Was the Weather!" (Nov. 29, 1996).

Chapter Two

1. This term was coined by Pierre-Étienne Will, "Un cycle hydraulique."

2. The terminology is variable. According to Needham, *ba* is usually translated dam, dike, or embankment, but was often a "flying dike"—"a very long shallow U-shaped spillway . . . running along a bund of a canal or lake." Needham, IV:3, 362.

3. Schoppa, 18–24, on Xiang Lake in Zhejiang during the Song dynasty. Perdue, 219–33, on the Dongting Lake region in Hunan during the Qing period.

4. *Oriental Despotism: A Comparative Study of Total Power.*

5. *Haihe shi jianbian*, chap. 5. Also see above, Chapter 1.

6. In sharp contrast to previous publications, Wang Shouchun, 117, praises the Qing official management of the Yongding and other Zhili rivers, which he sees as more efficient and advanced than anything before it. Also Ding Jinjun.

7. For example, *Beijing lishi jinian*, 202. Edict KX 37/2, *JFTZ* 1:24.

8. *HHLY* 499–504; Table 1.2 above.

9. *HHLY* 528–29; Table 1.2 above.

10. Edicts of SZ 12/8, 13/8, and 14/12, *JFTZ* 1:3–4.

11. Edict KX 8/6, *JFTZ* 1:5.

12. KX 10/12, *JFTZ* 1:5, and KX 23/12, *JFTZ* 1:9, on bandits. On the epidemic, probably malaria, KX 19/2, and 19/4, *JFTZ* 1:7.

13. KX 28/9, *JFTZ* 1:13. See also 1695, KX 34/9, *JFTZ* 1:21–22.

14. Shang Hongkui, 124–41.

15. Wang Yongqian, passim; Hummel, 161–63, 938–39. On Jin Fu (Chin Fu), see also Needham, IV:3, 325–26.

16. Ding Jinjun, "Kangxi yu Yongdinghe," 33: the bed of the river had risen to 30–40 meters above the ground level of the district around the capital.

17. Ibid., 34.

18. KX 37/2, *YDHZ* 1:6, and *JFTZ* 1:23.

19. Ding, 34.

20. *YDHZ* 1:539–40; see map on 384–85, and slightly different figures on 387.

21. KX 37/3, *JFTZ* 1:24.

22. Ding, 34.

23. Ibid., and KX 38/10, *JFTZ* 1:26.

24. Ding, 35. *YDHZ* 1:390–92.

25. KX 38/10, *JFTZ* 1:25–26.

26. KX 39/2, *JFTZ* 1:26–27.

27. Rescript by Kangxi on memorial of KX 51/4/3 by Zhao Hongxie, *GZDKXC* 3:566–68.

28. KX 39/no month, *YDHZ* 1:7.

29. Ding, 34. *YDHZ*, 2:896ff. gives all the changes in river administration.

30. *YDHZ* 2:729.

31. Ding, 35, from *YDHZ* juan 15.

32. Ding, 36.

33. Ibid.

34. KX 45/12/17, *GZDKXC* 1:387–92.

35. KX 49/7/25, *GZDKXC* 2:636–41; KX 54/8/13, *GZDKXC* 5:648–50.

36. In an exceptional case, in 1719 officials were asked to raise contributions from "rich households" to support dike repairs. Memorials in *YDHZ* 1:1138–45.

37. In the previous year, Governor-general Li Weijun had noted that the official roads in Zhili, *guanlu*, were all lower than the ground, and during heavy rains, they formed rivers and traffic was impeded. YZ 2/2/25, *GZDYZC* 3:888–89.

38. *HHLY* 562–64. The report of thirty-two dikes toppled comes from the memorial of head of the Board of War, Cai Ting, *JFSLSA* 1:1b. Additional details about the flooding and famine relief can be found in memorials by Li Weijun, *GZDYZC* 4:732–33, and 760. See Chapter 8 in this book.

39. YZ 4/3, *JFTZ* 1:66.

40. *HHLY* 563, for Xincheng, Dingxing, and Lingshou counties.

41. *JFSLSA* 1:1ab.

42. *JFSLSA* 1:9a. On the important relationship between the emperor and this brother, see Bartlett, 68–79.

43. *JFSLSA*, 1:1–2a.

44. The Bai River on Map 2.1 flows south to Tongzhou where it connects with Bei Yunhe; today this is the Chao-Bai he.

45. According to Chen Yi's "Zhili hequ zhi," the Dian River was five li north of Tianjin County, where the Yongding, Ziya, and Qing rivers converged. From the head of this river until it joined the Bei Yunhe, it flowed for 40 li; the rush of water was rapid. Because the banks got steep at this point, this was also called the "head" of the river. *Jifu hedao shuili congshu*, 58:23. In *JFTZ* 10:493–99 the Dian he is defined as one of the main tributaries feeding into the Hai River; it connected the Yongding, Qing, and Ziya rivers with the Hai River five li north of Tianjin County. It ran for a 110 li before it merged with the Bei Yunhe. The historians of the Chinese Water Conservancy Research Institute identify the Dian he as river(s) connecting the Xi dian, Western Lake with the Dong dian, Eastern Lake. Communication with author, Mar. 1999.

46. "Yi xian Qinwang shu," in *Jifu hedao shuili congshu* 58:322, 324–25, 338. This same description is found in Zhu Shi's essay dated 1725, *HCJSWB* 108:30a. Zhu Shi, the grand secretary who was assigned

to assist Prince Yi in the rice irrigation scheme, and who carried on with it after the latter's death, was probably the ghost-writer of the essays attributed to the prince. Hummel, 188–89.

47. *JFSLSA* 1:29a.

48. *JFSLSA* 1:6b; also *Jifu hedao shuili congshu* 58:332.

49. Ibid., 58:321.

50. Calculated from *JFSLSA* 1:55–83. "Shuili yingtian ceshuo" in *Jifu hedao shuili congshu* 58:415–577 gives a description and a map of each county involved in the project. Brook, "Spread of Rice Cultivation," provides a comprehensive discussion of this entire project. In note 41 he cites the figure 6,000–7,000 qing.

51. *JFSLSA* 1:32b. For more on rice cultivation as a part of Zhili's agriculture, see Chapter 3 in this book. For definition of shi, see Appendix on Measures.

52. Found in *Jifu hedao shuili congshu* 58:231–93, and elsewhere.

53. YZ 13/11, *JFTZ* 1:113.

54. "Zhili hequ zhi," by Chen Yi, a native of Wen'an, gives a river-by-river description for the Yongzheng period. *Jifu hedao shuili congshu* 58:9–95; see also his essays, 58:97–229.

55. *JFSLSA* 1:29–33. Other repairs on this dike included a big repair in QL 3–17 and again in QL 33, and another big repair in JQ 11. Also described in "Chen Xueshi wen chao," *Jifu hedao shuili congshu* 58:119–21.

56. *YDHZ* 1:393–97, 542–43. Map 2.1 identifies the Sanjiao dian and shows the dike completed in 1727.

57. Ibid. This was sometimes divided into two posts, sometimes combined into one. See *YDHZ* 2:897–99.

58. "Chen Xueshi wen chao," *Jifu hedao shuili congshu* 58:190.

59. Ibid., 58:122–24.

60. *YDHZ* 2:895–96; *Yongding he zhiben jihua*, 80; and also *Gong Bu Zeli* 1815, 40:6ab.

61. *Qinding Da Qing Huidian* 1899, 60:1a. Compare Brunnert and Hagelstrom, entry 820D.

62. Chang-tu Hu, "Yellow River Administration," 508–9. See also Dodgen, "Hydraulic Evolution," 45.

63. *YDHZ*, 2:895–1092 traces the history and provides a table of incumbents through JQ 20.

64. *Yongding he zhiben jihua*, 79–80.

65. *Gong Bu Zeli* 1815, 41:1ab. See also *YDHZ* 2:900–18.

66. *YDHZ* 2:715–18. Also *Gong Bu Zeli* 1884, 31:1ab, on the governor-general's duties.

67. Ibid., 31:3ab.

68. *YDHZ* 2:729–30, lists expenditures by year for Yongding River. An example of haggling over details is in YZ 10/3/10, *GZDYZC* 19:519–20.

69. YZ 9/10/22, *GZDYZC* 19:62.

70. YZ 12/11/15, *GZDYZC* 23:750.

71. YZ 9/7/1, *GZDYZC* 17:510.

72. YZ 4/6/11, *JFSLSA* 1:27a.

73. YZ 8/3/18, *JFSLSA* 1:49.

74. Spence, *Treason by the Book*, 26, 91–92.

75. YZ 12/8, *JFTZ* 1:110. Elvin, "Who Was Responsible for the Weather," 227, discusses the same edict as well as other examples of what he terms "moral meteorology."

76. *QDHH* 66–77.

77. *QDHH* 77–89. esp. 1738-Doc. 3 and 4.

78. *QDHH* 79, 1738-Doc. 12.

79. *QDHH* 83–87, 1738-Doc. 38.

80. *QDHH* 88, 1738-Doc. 40.

81. *QDHH* 88, 1738-Doc. 39.

82. See estimates in Chapter 3 below.

83. QL 2/6/6, 3/2/12, ZPZZ CZDD, archive microfilm 1:440–42, 588–90.

84. *QDHH* 88, 1738-Doc. 42.

85. QL 4/5/4, ZPZZ CZDD, archive microfilm 1:804–10.

86. QL 3/9 in *BCSX*, Gaozong, 126:12ab. Also QL 3/9/10, ZPZZ, Shuili, 4. In the rhetoric of the early Qianlong years, especially it seems around 3/9, the term *yilao yongyi* was frequently invoked. For example, documents QL 3/9/26, also Gu Cong, 3/9/22 in ZPZZ, Shuili, 4.

87. In 1737, several of the officials asked to deal with the Zhili rivers—Gao Bin, Zhang Tingyu, Oertai, Li Wei—were also heavily engaged with bureaucratic controversies over the Yellow River, and this might account for their lack of focus in Zhili. The emperor was also frustrated with their disputes over the Yellow River. M. Chang, 69–71.

88. For a table of Zhili provincial officials, see *JFTZ* 4:602–58. On Sun Jiagan, see Hummel, 672–73.

89. QL 4/4/9. This constitutes the second of four cases in *Jifu shuili si'an*, *JFSLSA*, juan 2. On Chen Hongmou, see Hummel, 86–87, and Rowe, *Saving*.

90. *JFSLSA* 2:1a–3b.

91. *JFSLSA* 2:7a.

92. QL 3/10 edict, *BCSX*, Gaozong, 126:13ab.

93. *JFSLSA* 2:10a–38b.

94. *JFSLSA* 2:10a. Received rescript 1740/2.

95. *JFSLSA* 2:10a–11a.

96. QL 4/10/23, *JFSLSA* 2:39a–40a.

97. QL 5/7/5, *JFSLSA* 2:42b.

98. *JFSLSA* 2:43a.

99. *JFSLSA* 2:40ab.

100. QL 5/9, 6/1, and 6/3 in *BCSX*, Gaozong, 126:15b–17b. In later years Gu Cong was made to pay back monies that he had apparently misappropriated. When he was unable to completely restore the funds amounting to 27,000 taels, he was ordered to use the *yanglian* (nourishing money) portion of his salary to pay off his obligations by installments. QL 17/11/27 Fang Guancheng memorial in *GZDQLC* 4:435; also QL 19/12/11, in *GZDQLC* 10:275–76, indicates that two years later these accounts had not yet been settled.

101. *JFSLSA* 2:43b.

102. *BCSX*, Gaozong, 126:18ab. The final decision for centralization was made in 1749.

103. *JFSLSA* 3:8b.

104. This constitutes the third case in *JFSLSA*, juan 3. The 1743–44 drought is discussed in Chapter 8 below.

105. *JFSLSA* 3:9b–29a lists projects and costs.

106. *JFSLSA* 3:29b–31b.

107. *JFSLSA* 3:31b–32a.

108. *JFSLSA* 3:33–83.

109. QL 12/4/28, in *JFSLSA* 3:83ab.

110. *QDHH* 152–171.

111. See Chapter 8 below.

112. This was the fourth case discussed in *JFSLSA*, juan 4.

113. See Chapter 8 in this book.

114. Hummel, 234.

115. *JFSLSA* 4:6a–8a.

116. *JFSLSA* 4:8a–9b.

117. QL 27/10, also in *BCSX*, Gaozong, 137:15ab. This was not the first time in the Qianlong reign that a proposal to revive rice cultivation had been decisively rejected. In 1744, Oertai and the grand secretaries had rejected such proposal in favor of a more comprehensive approach. *JFSLSA* 3:2b–8a.

118. *JFSLSA* 4:9a–10a.

119. See Chapters 3 and 4, below, and Appendix 2 on Data.

120. *JFSLSA* 4:1a–2a.

121. Note that the source probably contains an error; the standard was 1 sheng of *mi*, 10 wen of cash and 5 wen of vegetables, as we can see from the totals below.

122. *JFSLSA* 4:3ab.

123. QL 28/2/26 and 10/4, *JFSLSA* 4:22a, 39b–40a.

124. QL 29/3/5, *GZDQLC* 20:734.

125. *JFSLSA* 4:10b–11b.

126. *JFSLSA* 4:12b–13a.

127. *JFSLSA* 4:13a–15a.

128. QL 18/2, *BCSX*, Gaozong, 128:11ab.

129. QL 18/5/24 and 26, *GZDQLC* 5:452–53, 477–78.

130. QL 19/6/9 and 7/28, *GZDQLC* 8:721–22, and 9:259–60.

131. QL 31/8/17, in Fang Guancheng, *Fang Kemin*, 2:1201–7.

132. QL 32/#7/19, GZD 022578. For regulations for taxation of swamps and wetlands, see *Gongbu zeli* 1884, 31:6ab. For other material about river labor, see juan 31–33.

133. QL 37/6, *JFTZ* 1:163. Other relevant edicts follow. Also *Gongbu zeli* 1884, 31:10ab.

134. QL 47/1, *BCSX*, Gaozong, 134:23b–24b.

135. QL 28/3/3 and 3/5, *JFSLSA* 4:25b–27b. Also edict of QL 28/4 in *JFTZ* 1:134.

136. QL 28/6/23, *JFSLSA* 4:35b. Also *JFTZ* 1:135.

137. QL 28/7/6, *JFSLSA* 4:37a.

138. QL 28/6/23, *JFSLSA* 4:36ab. Also QL 28/6, *JFTZ* 1:135.

139. QL 43/8/24, GZD 036090. See also QL 47/12/22, GZD 043648.

140. QL 47/12/25, GZD 043673.

141. Hummel, 965–66. Jones and Kuhn, 116–19.

142. This is a general summary from *Xinyou gongzhen jishi*, hereafter cited as *XYGZJS*. Memorials on salt are found in 25:10–12. Detailed description can also be found in *QDHH* 255–84.

143. *XYGZJS* 16:11a, 34:23–25, 38:18–21.

144. JQ 25/1/11, ZPZZ Shuili hedao, juan 38. JQ 25/9/19 describes its long-term effects.

145. Famine relief and flood control from JQ 6/6/2 to JQ 7/8/13 are detailed.

146. For the famine relief effort, see Chapter 9 below.

147. For example, he instructed Chen Dawen to consult the maps of villages in Fang Guancheng's work on charity granaries. *XYGZJS* 24:6a–7a; Fang's river conservancy work and other work from the Qianlong period were cited in 31:4ff.

148. *XYGZJS* 2:9a–12b, 4:10–13, 9:21b.

149. *XYGZJS* 5:25–27, 9:29a–23b.

150. *XYGZJS*, juan 1–4 passim.

151. *XYGZJS* 23:21–23, and juan 23–24 passim.

152. *XYGZJS*, juan 25–26 passim, e.g., 25:23b–25b.

153. *XYGZJS* 21:8a–10b.

154. *XYGZJS* 26:4a.

155. *XYGZJS* 29:24ab, also 13a–14a.

156. *XYGZJS* 1:7–10, 2:9–12. Also juan 3–4 passim.

157. *XYGZJS* 10:1–5. This occurred at the end of the sixth month of 1801.

158. See Chapter 9, for examples of cases involving famine relief that the emperor personally dealt with.

159. *XYGZJS* 19:5–6. The emperor thought this excessive and asked for only one year's salary.

160. *XYGZJS* 14:5b–10a; also 38:7–11. Copies of these memorials are found in JJD, JQ 7, Shuili, boxes 35–36.

161. *XYGZJS* 16:1a–3b. According to Dodgen, "Hydraulic Evolution," 53, the concept of restitution, *peixiu*, originated in the Kangxi period, and by the nineteenth century officials could be held responsible for 40 percent of the cost of repairs if a dike broke. In order to protect themselves, some river officials began to overestimate costs to guard against possible failure. If no failure occurred, the official could profit. The result, as Dodgen points out, was the opposite of the intention; costs rose and opportunities for cheating multiplied. The principle of personal bureaucratic responsibility for flood prevention had ancient precedents. In the Tang law code, *Tang lu shuyi*, IV:414–15, officials whose neglect of repairs had led to flood damage were subject to various sanctions.

162. *XYGZJS*, juan 13–14 and 17–18 have details about engineering.

163. *XYGZJS* 23:26ff.

164. *XYGZJS* 25:6a.

165. *XYGZJS* 30:8a, 35:1ab.

166. *XYGZJS* 38:24–28.

167. *XYGZJS* 31:12a–15 on relief; 37:1–6 on river expenses.

168. JQ 13/8/22, GZD 011823, and JQ 14/1/2, GZD 013167. *QDHH* 248–366 gives a documentary record of floods in digest form. The number of counties refers to the entire Hai River Basin, not just Zhili Province.

169. *Lidai ciran zaihai*, 660–79, has excerpts from local gazetteers.

170. JQ 6/6/7, GZD 006004.

171. JQ 6/7/11, GZD 005561.

172. *XYGZJS* 18:17b; this was targeted for Beijing relief. Five hundred thousand taels arrived in ninth month, juan 25–26. Also *JFTZ* 1:221–22.

173. A long memorial detailing the ranks and expected contributions is found in JJD, JQ 11, Shuili, 37(2). The memorial refers to Quan Chu (Hubei) project and the Heng gong project, the large-scale construction on the Yellow River after 1803–4 flood in the area where Shandong, Zhili, and Henan converge. This project is documented in a collection found in the archives in Taipei, Heng gong dang.

174. JQ 11/3/22, in JJD, Shuili JQ 11, 39(2).

175. JQ 11/11/24, in JJD, Shuili, JQ 11, 37(1).

176. JQ 13/3, *JFTZ* 1:254.

177. *Gongbu zeli* 1815, 135:1–3, cites precedents from 1751 and later. Elsewhere, 41:1ab, is stated the rule that Yongding River laborers recruited locally should be given 1 sheng of *mi per day*, converted to cash of 10 wen, plus salted vegetables worth 5 wen. There is no mention of additional cash payments. The same rules are printed in the 1884 edition, 32:12. Compare QL section above. See another example from JQ 7 below. The labor relief wages cited in both places were 1 sheng of *mi*, 10 wen cash, plus vegetables *per fang* of earth dug. It is not clear whether a worker was expected to dig only 1 fang of earth per day.

178. *XYGZJS* 23:27b–28a.

179. JQ 7/2/23, JJD, JQ 7, Shuili, box 35–36.

180. *XYGZJS* 32:19a.

181. JQ 7/3/26, GZD 007710, also JQ 7/7/1, GZD 008442. Compare note 177 above.

182. JQ 13/11/10, GZD 012416. The Thousand-Li Dike was a thread running 700 li through the seven counties of Gaoyang, Renqiu, Xiong, Baoding, Bazhou, Wen'an, and Dacheng.

183. JQ 13/11/29, GZD 012583. There is no record of what resulted, probably nothing.

184. Perdue, 178–96.

185. Schoppa, 71–72.

186. Schoppa, 130.

187. *Gongbu zeli* 1815, 39:6a–7a. Also 1884 ed. 33:8ab.

188. Edict of JQ 15, *Gongbu zeli* 1815, 63:6ab.

189. JQ 12/2, *JFTZ* 1:248–49. *Gongbu zeli* 1815, 40:6ab.

190. JQ 10/6, *JFTZ* 1:237–39; also JQ 4/6, *JFTZ* 1:205. Yanjian's career survived this severe imperial reprimand; in the 1825 Grand Canal crisis, the Daoguang emperor appointed him grain transport director, one of the chief officials in charge. Leonard 123, 148, 190.

191. *JFTZ* 1:244–48, 252, 256. See Chapter 9 in this book.

192. JQ 13/#5, *JFTZ* 1:254–55.

193. JQ 15/5[?], *JFTZ* 1:261–62.

194. JQ 25/1/11, ZPZZ, Shuili hedao, juan 38.

195. Early in the reign, Governor-general Hu Jitang had invoked the now-familiar arguments about *shuili*, but he was soon replaced. JQ 3/8/9, GZD 004168.

196. See above. The copy of Chen Yi's essay was presented as an enclosure for the emperor and is found in JJD, JQ7, box 35–36. It is also referred to in *XYGZJS* 30:3–4. The full version is reproduced in *Jifu shuili congshu*, cited above. Excerpts are found in *JFTZ* 10:427–37.

197. See Chapter 9 in this book.

198. *QDHH* 378–79.

199. DG 3/8, *JFTZ* 1:320.

200. DG 2/5, *JFTZ* 1:312.

201. DG 3/10, *BCSX*, ce 374, 47:25a. The relief effort will be discussed in Chapter 9 below, but the documentary records for 1821–23, including grain price reports, are conspicuously absent from the Qing archives in both Beijing and Taipei. Possibly they were extracted for the purpose of commemorating the

relief effort, as the 1801 relief campaign had been documented, but the only published documents are found in collections cited here.

202. DG 4/4, *JFTZ* 1:328.
203. DG 4/3, *JFTZ* 1:326.
204. DG 4/4, *JFTZ* 1:327.
205. DG 3/6, *JFTZ* 1:315.
206. DG 4/6, *JFTZ* 1:329.
207. DG 4/#7, *JFTZ* 1:329–30.
208. DG 4/#7, *JFTZ* 1:330.
209. DG 4/#7, *JFTZ* 1:331–32.
210. DG 4/9, *JFTZ* 1:332.
211. DG 4/10, *JFTZ* 1:335.
212. DG 2/#3, *JFTZ* 1:310–11. On forced labor practices and proposal to commute corvée obligation to silver, see DG 8/10 and 11/2, *JFTZ* 1:349, 353–54.
213. For example, DG 3/12, *JFTZ* 1:323.
214. DG 6/11/23, JJD 057542. This is one of many documents on river conservancy for the Daoguang period that can be found in the Junjidang archive in Taipei.
215. Huang Jianhua, "Daoguang shidai de zaihuang," surveys Daoguang-period famines all over China.
216. Leonard, chaps. 5, 6, and 9 and esp. 150, 172, 252.
217. Dodgen, "Hydraulic," 36, 59.
218. QL 24/5/8, CZCC cangchu, 56:3479–81.
219. Leonard, 38–39.
220. DG 1/2 and 1/3, case of extortion from rice-field owners by functionaries shows that there were some rice fields in Tianjin County. *JFTZ* 1:305–6. In DG 2/5 Yanjian proposed to extend rice cultivation. *JFTZ* 1:311.
221. DG 3/7, *JFTZ* 1:317.
222. *Jifu hedao shuili congshu* 58:226–27.
223. Wu Postface to "Shuili yingtian tu shuo," *Jifu hedao shuili congshu*, 58:579–82.
224. Preface, 1b–2b.
225. Pomeranz, *Making of a Hinterland*, 132, 162.
226. Villages in this region were surrounded by water and experienced floods in nine out of ten years. *Jinmen baojia tushuo*, esp. preface.
227. Liu, "Li Hung-chang in Chihli," 52.
228. Li Hongzhang's memorial in response to edict, GX 7/2/30, *JFTZ* 10:606–11.
229. GX 7/11/12, *JFTZ* 10:604–6. The Dong dian has not quite disappeared; it can be seen on present-day maps of the region.
230. GX 7/2/30, *JFTZ* 10:606–11. Li's low expectations about river conservancy may have reflected more than realism; for him foreign relations, maritime defense, and "self-strengthening" projects had higher priority than provincial administration.
231. GX 16/6/9, ZPZZ, NZZJ, 0090.
232. GX 16/6/15, ZPZZ, NZZJ, 0090.
233. Aug. 6, 1890, ABCFM, 21/111.
234. Aug. 12, 1890, ABCFM, 21/291.
235. Apr. 30, 1891, ABCFM, 14/44.
236. *Wen'an XZ* 1922, 1:8ab. Part of this section follows Chen Yi's description of Wen'an in the Yongzheng period, "Chen Xueshi wenchao," in *Jifu hedao shuili congshu* 58:151–56.
237. See the definition of *yaodi* in HHLH 641.
238. *Wen'an XZ* 1922, 1:13b–14a.
239. Ibid., final juan, 10b–11a.
240. Ibid., 1:14a–15b.
241. Ibid., 1:16b–17a.
242. Ibid., 1:17ab.
243. Ibid., 1:17b.

244. Ibid., 1:18a.

245. Ibid., 1:19a.

246. Ibid., 1:19a–23a.

247. Ibid., 1:24a.

248. Ibid., 1:17b, gives some examples of this.

249. *Xincheng XZ* 1935, 2:1b.

250. [*Xu*] *Yongqing XZ* 1875, 5ab, 6a–7b, 10a–11a.

251. *Wangdu XZ* 1934, 1:17–26.

252. Ibid., 1:17b–21b.

253. Ibid., 1:18b.

254. Ibid., 1:21b–22a.

255. Ibid., 1:23a.

256. Will, "State Intervention . . . Hubei," analyzes the "fluctuating and ambiguous" role of the state in hydraulics in Hubei Province in the Qing period.

257. *Jifu shuili anlanzhi*, fanli, 2ab. By contrast to the rain shrine in Handan sought relief from drought through divine intervention. Pomeranz, "Water into Iron."

258. *Jifu shuili anlanzhi*, Yongding he, 10:1a–2a.

259. Ibid., 10:2b–4a. See also *YDHZ* 2:875–87.

260. Ibid., Hutuo he, 4:43a–48b.

261. Enclosures in memorials of Nayancheng, JQ 10/4/9 and 11/4/9 in JJD LFZZ, JQ, Caizheng, 37/2. Also JQ 8/8/21, in JJD LFZZ, Shuili 36.

262. M. Chang argues persuasively that river control was the central objective of Qianlong's tours.

263. Hummel, 412–13.

264. See Dodgen, "Hydraulic," 40–44; Leonard, 11, 34–35; and Needham, IV:3, 237, and 325–26, on the Yellow River controversies.

265. Dodgen, 46–51.

266. Philip Kuhn, in *Soulstealers*, 221, 228, writes that the Qianlong emperor used his witch hunt for queue-clippers to shake the bureaucracy out of its routines in a way similar to Mao's campaigns.

267. *North China Daily News*, Nov. 22, 1917. See Chapter 10 below.

Chapter Three

1. Malthus, 56, 53.

2. *The Conditions of Agricultural Growth*.

3. Perkins, 78. However, he believes that yields did increase in the north, a conclusion not supported by evidence in this chapter.

4. Perkins, esp. chap. 2.

5. Although Table 3.1 in this book does not show it, other evidence tells us of great population losses during the wartime period of the 1940s. See *Zhongguo renkou: Hebei fence*, fig. 3.2, 68.

6. Heijdra, 428–39.

7. Ho, 37–39; translation of imperial edict.

8. However, Ho, 31–33, considers the data for Zhili *ding*—the unit for an adult male—to be more reliable than those from other provinces. Cao, 51–68, has an updated discussion of the *ding*, including a discussion of its special characteristics in Zhili.

9. Perkins, 202, discusses how others have disagreed.

10. Skinner, "Sichuan's Population," esp. 61–74.

11. Ho, 56–57.

12. Cao, 10–11. Cao credits Jiang Shou's 1993 publication for the discovery of the inconsistencies and errors in the *Jiaqing yitong zhi*.

13. Cao, 6.

14. Skinner raises a similar question about the 1812 and 1820 figures for Sichuan, observing the *Jiaqing yitong zhi* was not actually published until Daoguang period, and so the figures may actually represent some year later than what is purported. Skinner, "Sichuan's Population," 61, n. 21.

15. Cao, 327–51.

16. Guomin zhengfu zhuji chu tongji ju, ed., *Gesheng nongye gaishu guji zong baogao* (1932).

17. The population data is given by households, *hu*, only and not by individuals, or *kou*. In the summary table 1, on p. 1, the average number of mouths per household in Zhili is given as 5.71. If the household figures in the Hebei table, 15–16, are multiplied by this factor, they seem implausibly large; probably 5.71 is too large a multiplier.

18. Huang, *North China*, append. C.

19. Wang, *Land Taxation*, 26–32.

20. *Hubu zeli*, as cited in Li Hongyi, 6347–49.

21. Wan Weihan, *Muxue juyao*, 20a, discussed in Will, *Bureaucracy*, 253 n. 72.

22. See Perkins, 231–37, tab. B.12. Shi mu was the Republican-period measure.

23. Perkins, 236, tab. B.14.

24. Huang, *North China*, append. C. We might also consider the fact that the Qing mu was smaller than that of the Republican-period mu by about 8 percent. See Table 3.4 in this chapter.

25. Private communication with author, Nov. 25, 1989.

26. Wang, *Land Taxation*, 87, tab. 5.1, shows a 60 percent increase in population between 1787 and 1933, from 23.0 to 34.6 million, with no increase in cultivated acreage. The figure in col. 6 seems to be a misprint for 36.4 million.

27. Heijdra, 535–36.

28. Li Wenhai, 151–52.

29. Chao, *Man and Land*, 119, tab. 6.5.

30. Liang Fangzhong, 401.

31. *Shina nōgyō* 1, 15–16.

32. Gamble, *Ting Hsien*, 4, 209.

33. Ibid., 84.

34. Myers, 41.

35. Ibid., 67.

36. QL 4/5/4, ZPZZ/Caizheng. Archive microfilm 1:804–20. See below for more from this document.

37. Myers, 158.

38. Although the subject of managerial landlordism occupies a central place in Philip Huang's work on North China, he is clear to point out that "a small-family-farm economy" was predominant in this region from at least the late eighteenth century onward (103–5).

39. In the Qing they were administered mostly by the Imperial Household Department [Neiwufu], but a few were administered by the Board of Rites, or by temples. Liu Jiaju, 69. Torbert, 84–87.

40. Yang Xuechen, 177–79. Muramatsu, 1–2. Ju Zhendong, 39549–50.

41. Ju, 39605–7. Muramatsu, 1–2.

42. Ju, 39558–62.

43. *Qingdai de qidi* 1:4.

44. Chen Jiahua, 69.

45. Liu Jiaju, 1–3 of English summary.

46. Muramatsu, 4–9.

47. This occurred notwithstanding the attempts of the Yongzheng and Qianlong courts to buy back the land at its original price. Ju, 39575–84.

48. According to Ju, 39621–22, in 1657 there was 674,385 qing of taxable land, of which 175,539 qing was banner land. The difference should be 498,846 qing, not 426,483, which is an error that leads to the result of 29 percent instead of 35 percent banner land. Huang, *North China*, 87, follows Ju's mistake. In 1906, Ju reports that there was only 50,000 qing of banner land of a total of 945,298 qing, or 5 percent, not his misprint of 15 percent. Chen Jiahua, 69, estimates modestly that there were at least 140,000 qing of banner lands. The Board of Revenue reported 688,410 qing of regular fields and 38,755 qing of banner land for the mid-nineteenth century. *Hubu zeli* (1874) 5:2a–3a. See Elliott, 192–93, for a general discussion of banner land. One qing = 100 mu, or about 15 acres.

49. Liu Jiaju, 65–66, has a table by county. Liu also shows that in twenty-nine counties around the capital, banner lands accounted for 61.7 percent of land (the date is not clear), but he cautions that this figure does not include regular land bought by Manchus, or land later appropriated, 85–87.

50. *Yutian XZ* 1884, 13:1ab.

51. KX8/6 edict in *JFTZ* 1:5.

52. Quotation from *Tingxun geyan*, Yongzheng emperor's preface 1730, 62b–63a, translated by Marta Hansen. Also in Spence, *Emperor*, 98.

53. YZ 2/#4/6, *GZDYZC* 2:557; also 457–58.

54. YZ 2/9/18, *GZDYZC* 3:244–45.

55. QL 21/11/11, *Fang Kemin*, 2: 753–56.

56. QL 29/10/1, *Fang Kemin*, 2: 1129–32.

57. YZ 2/4/6, *GZDYZC* 2:457–58.

58. QL 4/5/4, ZPZZ/Caizheng. Archive microfilm 1:804–820.

59. *JFSLSA* 3:2b–4a, 6b.

60. QL 2/6/24, Yifudang 1609, 377–80.

61. QL 28/7/17, *Fang Kemin*, 2:1083–88.

62. Brook, "Rice," 659; and Chapter 2 in this book.

63. KX 46/6/3, *GZDKXC* 1:453–57. Other memorials follow.

64. KX 48/3/3, Zhao Hongxie. *GZDKXC* 2:85–92.

65. Brook, "Rice," 674.

66. See Chapter 2 in this book.

67. Quoted by Brook, "Rice," 660.

68. Spence, *Emperor*, 57.

69. *Zhongguo gudai gengzhitu*, 77–186.

70. Ibid., 149–58. QL 30/4/11, and 7/16. *Fang Kemin*, 2:1149–51.

71. Preface by Shi Shenghan, *Nongzheng quanshu*, shang, 3. Bray, 64–70, provides an evaluation of the significance of Xu Guangqi's agricultural work.

72. Lin Zexu, 1877, 8a. Brook, 689, estimates that "at no time, with the possible exception of the Yongzheng era, did rice production exceed 5 percent of the total grain output of Zhili." Probably it was more like 2 percent at most in the Ming, 678–79.

73. *Xiong xian xiangtu zhi* 1905, 14:6b, and *Xiong xian xinzhi* 1930, 8:9b.

74. *Xingtai XZ* 1905, 1:55a, 57a.

75. *Zunhua tongzhi* 1886, 15:2.

76. Xu Qixian, 10.

77. Edkins, 22–23.

78. *Wanping xian shiqing diaocha* 1939, 152.

79. *HCJSWB* 108:28.

80. HCSHZ 5/cangchu, juan 1. *Pingshan XZ* 1898, 2:4b–5.

81. Based on an estimated grain output of 100 million shi in the Republican period. See Chapter 6, note 161, below.

82. *Shina shōbetsu zenshi* 18:535–40.

83. Bray, 464, says the spring-sown type of barley was a later development in China and was not grown widely.

84. *Jiaohe XZ* 1916, 1:63–64. This passage appears in many gazetteers.

85. *Sanhe xian xinzhi* 1935, 7:1b.

86. "Cereal Trade in Tientsin," 107.

87. QL 24/5/8, ZPZZ, CZCC 56: 3479–81.

88. "Cereal Trade in Tientsin," 107.

89. Bray, 464.

90. Ibid., 465, from Xu Guangqi, *Nongzheng quanshu* 25:15b, trans. Ping-ti Ho, 179.

91. Fang Guancheng memorial, n.d., printed in *Jiaqing Shulu XZ*, 10:59ab.

92. Fang also uses this term in a memorial about river labor in Henan, QL 27/12/1. ZPZZ/Shuili 32, Microfilm #71. The term *yishui yimai* is also found in memorials around QL 3/9/-, e.g., Gu Zong, QL 3/9/22. ZPZZ/Shuili, 4.

93. *Xiong XZ* 1905, 6ab; also *Xiong xin xianzhi* 1930, 8:9a.

94. Buck, *Farm Economy*, 179, as cited in Chapter 1 in this book.

95. *Zhaozhou zhi* 1897, 2:22a.

96. Bray, 474–76.

97. 1/13b, cited in Bray, 459; Sun translation, 13.

98. Fang Guancheng, *Zhenji*, 2:9b. This report is repeated in *Baoding FZ* 1881, 25:5a.

99. This information from Fang memorial proposing a ban on sheep grazing on wheat fields. See also QL 29/10/1. *Fang Kemin*, 2:1129–32. Will, *Bureaucracy*, 253, cautions that "the bureaucracy had no precise notion of local cropping patterns, only the very general figure that 30 percent of the arable land in Zhili was supposed to be in wheat (compared with 60–70 percent in Shandong and Henan)." *Baoding FZ* 1881, 25:5a, repeats almost verbatim the same information as Fang's *Zhenji*, giving insight into cropping patterns, but not at all updated.

100. Fang, *Zhenji*, 6:10a; emphasis added. This comes from an edict on guidelines for lending wheat seeds during famine relief. See Chapter 8 in this book. In a routine memorial concerning famine relief in 1762, Fang suggested that farmers should be encouraged to plant wheat in the fall that would be harvested next spring. Those with thirty mu or less should be particularly encouraged to do this with loans of seeds. This may imply that normally wheat was grown by those with larger holdings. QL 27/7/26. ZPZZ NZZJ 0051.

101. Huang, *North China*, 110, gives examples from Shandong.

102. Buck, *Land Utilization*, 1:416.

103. *Gaozong Shilu*, juan 214, 1058, as cited by Wu Jianyong, "Qingdai Beijing," 171.

104. *Xingtai XZ* 1905, 1:57a.

105. QL 43/6/4, 6/8, and 7/2, GZD 035137, 035185, and 035680.

106. *Baoding FZ* 1881, 27:1–3.

107. Bray, 622, terms it a "thesaurus of botany." See *Guangping FZ* 1894, 18:2b, for another reference to it.

108. In *Jiaohe XZ* 1916, 1:63–64, *gu* is called *xiaomi*.

109. *Gaoyi XZ* 1933, 2:10–11.

110. Bray, 437–41, says that homophonous characters were often confused, so sometimes *ji* was inaccurately used for *setaria* millet. See Bray, 440, for a useful glossary of the Chinese terms for millets.

111. Bray, 440.

112. *Shulu hekan* 1935, reprint of JQ3 ed., 10:61–62, traces the confusion of terms back to ancient times. Also, *Baoding FZ* 1886, 17:1b–2a.

113. For example, *Zhuo ZZ* 1765, 8:1b, states that *ji* is popularly called *mi* (*hemp radical*); if it is sweet, it is called *shu* (*glutinous panicum*); if it is not sweet, it is called *ji*.

114. *Xiong XZ* 1905, 14:5b–6a; also *Xiong xian xinzhi* 1930, 8:8b–9a.

115. *Baoding FZ* 1886, 27:1. Also in *Guangping FZ* 1894, 18:2b.

116. In nearby Wan County in Baoding Prefecture: the soil was thin and not fertile, so millets of various types were grown in abundance. *Wan XZ* 1934, 7:1ab. Also, for example, *Zhengding XZ* 1874, 19:1ab.

117. Bray, 443–47.

118. Professor Song Zhanqian, Nanjing University, provided this insight. Simoons, 73, calls this "common" millet and describes it as "well adapted to dry, continental conditions."

119. Bray, 434.

120. *North China Famine*, 130–32.

121. The date of introduction is unclear, perhaps as early as prehistoric times, but perhaps not until the tenth century A.D., but in any case sorghum existed in India and the Arab world before it was known in China. Bray, 449–51.

122. Bray, 451–52.

123. "Experiments with Drought-Resisting Crops."

124. QL32/#7/19, GZD 022578.

125. "Experiments with Drought-Resisting Crops."

126. *North China Famine*, 130–32.

127. QL 12/1/2, ZPZZ, CZCC, 56:128–33.

128. JQ 20/11/11, ZPZZ, NZZJ, 58:1936–38.

129. QL 24/10/22, ZPZZ, CZCC, 57:85–86. The same memorial suggested that Xuanhua peasants

should exchange their *gaoliang* for *sugu*, or unhusked millet, to repay loans to the granaries in the fall. The *sugu* price was 0.70–1.16 taels per shi, while *gaoliang* was 0.60–1.20, but this was unusual. In most years, the price of sorghum was substantially lower than that of millet. See Chapter 4 below.

130. QL 17/7/27, *GZDQLC* 3:476–77.

131. JQ 17/11/16, ZPZZ, NZZJ 0077, Cat. 359-4-75.

132. JQ 23/1/26, ZPZZ, NZZJ 0080, cat. 359-4-75.

133. "Cereal Trade," 108.

134. These empirewide discussions included rice wine in the south. Rowe, *Saving*, 161. Dunstan, *Conflicting*, 203–45, discusses and translates documents from the debate over liquor prohibition in the early Qing.

135. KX 55/11/30, *GZDKXC* 6:700–4.

136. KX 56/8/19, *GZDKXC* 7:196–200.

137. Dunstan, *Conflicting*, 227.

138. QL 16/7/29, *GZDQLC* 1:296–99; and QL 18/4/4, *GZDQLC* 5:22–23.

139. Rowe, *Saving*, 161.

140. R. Lee, 97.

141. *Xuanhua XZ* 1922, in "Fangzhi wenchao," 37:177. According to this source, each household can make wine from 1 shi of grain a day.

142. Bray, 514.

143. "Soya Beans . . . in Manchuria," 794. Listed are the eight types of yellow, green, and black beans; 500 subvarieties exist.

144. *Yuanshi XZ* 1884, 1:49ab.

145. *Gu'an XZ*, GX and XT eds., in "Fangzhi wenchao," 40:60. Black beans were sometimes used in medicine. *Baoding FZ* 1881, 27:3.

146. *Xinle XZ* 1885/1968, 369–71.

147. *Guangping XZ* 1939, 5:1.

148. *Handan XZ* 1933, 6:2–3.

149. "Soya Beans . . . in Manchuria," 794.

150. Interview with Song Zhanqing, Professor of Agricultural History at Nanjing University, May 1989.

151. QL 2/11/26, Huke tiben Tianfu Box 31.

152. QL 16/7/18, *Fang Kemin*, 1:505–15. But in 1759 he proposed that shipments be halted because a surplus had developed. QL 24/12/5, ZPZZ, CZCC, 57:129–32.

153. YZ 6/7/24, *GZDYZC* 10:911–12. Fang Guancheng memorial, QL 16/5/22, ZPZZ, CZCC, 56:2457–58, also states that beans do not store very long.

154. QL 26/4/10, *Fang Kemin*, 2:981–87.

155. JQ 6/10, *CYQS* 61:18ab.

156. *Shina shōbetsu* 18:541–51.

157. Tsao Lien-en, 942, 948.

158. Ibid., 944.

159. This date was somewhat controversial, but now seems to be widely accepted. Bray, 456–58. Tong Pingya, 60.

160. This is the view of Ping-ti Ho in his classic work. It is also the view of Tong Pingya, "Yumi."

161. Chen Shuping, 189, 192; original source not clear.

162. *Xianghe XZ* 1675, 2:20a.

163. Zhang Gang, 99, but he does not cite sources.

164. *Qianlong Dong'an XZ* 1749, 8:5b. Corn is not mentioned in the 1673 edition of this gazetteer.

165. Chen Shuping, 192.

166. *Tang XZ* 1878, 2:57. *Qingyun XZ* 1855, 3:12. *Xinle XZ* 1885/1968, 369–71.

167. *Jiaohe XZ* 1916, 1:63b.

168. Ping-ti Ho, 187–89; Bray, 434. Originally it was grown mainly in hilly areas, but later it was extended to plains areas. Zhang Kai and Li Genpan, 95.

169. *Shunyi XZ* 1933, 10:2b.

170. Zhang Kai and Li Genpan, 97.

171. Bretschneider, 55.

172. *Ba xian xinzhi* 1934, 4:9.

173. Ibid., 3:9. See below and Chapter 11.

174. *Sanhe xian xinzhi* 1935, 7:3. See Chapter 11 for other examples from the 1930s.

175. Bray, 457.

176. Chen Shuping, 195, 199.

177. Will, *Bureaucracy*, 15. Chen Hongmou also began to promote sweet potato planting in the 1740s after studying the imperially commissioned agricultural guide, *Shoushi tongkao*. Rowe, *Saving*, 234–35.

178. In the Jiaqing period, there were records of its being grown in Anxiu and Qizhou, both in Baoding fu. Chen Shuping, 199.

179. Chen Shuping, 201.

180. *Guangping XZ* 1939, 5:3.

181. *Tangshan XZ* 1881, 2:24a.

182. *Shenzhou fengtu ji* 1900, 21:1b–2.

183. *Sanhe XZ* 1928, 4:16b.

184. *Sanhe xian xinzhi* 1935, 7:3.

185. *Guangzong XZ* 1933, 3:2b.

186. Figs were grown in large quantity in Xianghe xian. *Xianghe XZ* 1936, 3:19b.

187. "Fangzhi wenchao."

188. *Xinhe XZ* 1928, ce 1:17b.

189. *Ningjin XZ* 1679, 1:22.

190. *Mianhuatu*, ce 2. The last section is translated in Huang, *North China*, 112–14. See also QL 30/4/11, and 7/16, in Fang Kemin, 2:1149–51, 1165–68.

191. *JFTZ* 1:256–57.

192. Qianlong *Dong'an XZ* 1749, 8:5b.

193. *Yanshan XZ* 1868, 5:22ab.

194. *Xinle XZ* 1757, 3:10.

195. *Boxiang XZ* 1766, 10:13.

196. *Nangong XZ* 1830, 6:2ab.

197. *Yongqing XZ* 1779/1813, hushu 2:74b.

198. *Luancheng XZ* 1846, 2:7ab.

199. *Jinghai XZ* 1873, 3:8–9.

200. Philip Huang asserts that cotton cultivation was widespread in Zhili by the late Ming period and cites the above passages from Fang Guancheng, but Loren Brandt has questioned whether cotton played such a large role in the Qing period. See Brandt's review of Huang's book.

201. Huang, *North China*, 128, estimates 2–3 percent. Brandt, 674, estimates 1 percent.

202. Pomeranz, *Great Divergence*, 140–41.

203. *Wei XZ* 1925, 8:15b.

204. *Land Utilization in China*, 1:211–12. Because there was some double-cropping, the percentages exceed 100.

205. Bray, 429–33.

206. Buck, *Chinese Farm Economy*, 177–79. Huang, *North China*, 111, gives other examples.

207. Huang, *North China*, 58. The index of double-cropping measures the sown area to the cultivated area.

208. *Sanhe XXZ* 1935, 15:2b.

209. Buck, *Chinese Farm Economy*, 191–93, including tab. 6.

210. *Jifu hedao shuili congshu* 2:618, in an essay on opening up military tuntian.

211. In Baoding, the price of millet (*sumi*) was 1.05 taels, the best price in ten years. QL 19/9/12, *GZDQLC* 9:548.

212. *Hejian XZ* 1759, 3:4.

213. *Yongping FZ* 1774, 3:21.

214. *Changli XZ* 1865, 10:3a. The next passage, 10:3b, says that this is not a big commercial center, but they do get grain from beyond the pass and silks from Hangzhou.

215. Even Buck's wider range of estimated yields for the early twentieth century of 400–1,200 kg/ha cannot compare with late twentieth-century yields in China that were in the range of 2,200–4,500 kg/ha thanks to modern inputs. Bray, 448.

216. Chao, *Man and Land,* 234–38.

217. Ibid., 209–13.

218. Mai Shudu, 75–76. They were similar to those of Shaanxi and Jilin.

219. "Experiment with Drought-resisting Crops," 957–62.

220. *Shunyi XZ* 1933, 10:2b. See above for corn, and Chapter 11 for prosperity.

221. *Ba xian xinzhi* 1934, 3:9.

222. *Wangdu XZ* 1934, 1:35a.

223. Ibid., 1:19a.

224. *Jing XZ* 1932, 6:2b–3. This description was intended to show how much conditions had improved by the 1930s. See Chapter 11 below.

225. *Nanpi XZ* 1932, 3:9–10. But in the Republican period, extravagant new habits developed. See Chapter 11 below. *Jing XZ,* cited just above, also alludes to giving workers the wheat to eat.

226. *Nanpi XZ* 1932, 3:9–10.

227. *Luanzhou zhi* 1898, 16b–18b.

228. "This is all recorded in the old gazetteer of 30 yrs ago," no date given. Recorded in *Luan XZ* 1938, 4:8b. See Chapter 11 for description of some improvements by the 1930s.

229. 1673 ed., reproduced in *Nangong XZ* 1830, 6:2ab.

230. *Nangong XZ* 1673, 1:16.

231. *Nangong XZ* 1830, 6:2ab.

232. This section is based on *Yongqing XZ* 1779/1813, hushu 2:74b–77b. This local history has unusually rich detail on social and economic life. One *she* was about 30 li in distance; 1 li was about one-third of a mile; thus the distance from Tianjin was less than 20 miles.

233. The *luwei* industry is still important in this region. See Chapter 12 in this book.

234. Macartney, 106.

235. Fortune, 350.

236. Freeman-Mitford, 137.

237. Fortune, 347–48.

238. Freeman-Mitford, 134.

239. Fortune, 361–63; Rennie 1:52–53, 189, 206–7; Freeman-Mitford, 180, 282.

240. *Hebei jingji dili,* 43. In 1949 Hebei produced 93.9 yi jin of grain, giving an average of 300 jin of grain per person. One yi = 100 million. See Figure 12.4 in Chapter 12 of this book.

241. Huang, *North China,* emphasizes "involution" in North China farming: "applying more labor than was optimally necessary, at the cost of sharply diminished marginal returns," 155ff., and also 15 and elsewhere.

242. Elvin was evaluating the nondevelopment of technological innovation in China after the fourteenth century. *Pattern,* 312–13.

Chapter Four

1. Wilkinson describes the historical background for price reporting, in "Studies in Chinese Price History," 97–108.

2. QL 3/5, *JFTZ* 1:116. The emperor castigated Li Wei, Zhili governor-general, for his report. The year 1738 was the first year the reports were fully implemented in Zhili.

3. QL 8/4/1, *Shilu* 189:1–3, translated by Rowe, *Saving,* 158.

4. Will and Wong, *Nourish,* 157–58.

5. See, for example, articles by Wang Yeh-chien on the Lower Yangzi provinces, Perdue on Gansu, Wong and Perdue on Hunan, all in Rawski and Li, *Chinese History in Economic Perspective.* Marks, *Tigers,* has made effective use of price data from Guangdong and Guangxi.

6. Wilkinson, "Studies," 108–16ff.

7. See Braudel and Spooner, "Prices in Europe from 1450–1750," esp. fig. 35, 486. Also Abel *Agricultural*

Fluctuations, passim. D. H. Fisher, *Great Wave*, has a comprehensive bibliography and discussion of price history and sources.

8. Some key examples of earlier price history based on more scattered sources are Chuan Han-sheng, "Qianlong"; Chuan and Wang Yeh-chien, "Qing Yongzheng"; Nakayama Mio, "Fluctuation"; Kishimoto-Nakayama Mio, "Kangxi Depression," and "Shindai bukkashi"; and Wang Yeh-chien, "Secular Trend of Prices." Recent studies are noted above.

9. These figures were calculated from the annual solar data using the provincial average excluding the prefectures of Xuanhua and Chengde.

10. "Secular Trends of Rice Prices" (1992). In " Secular Trend of Prices During the Ch'ing Period" (1972; 351, 354), he estimates a 50 percent increase from 1750–1800, and 125 percent growth from 1700–1800. In 1992, he relates these trends to population growth, money supply, and velocity.

11. Abel, 197–99.

12. Rowe, *Saving*, 158–59.

13. Edict of QL 12/12 [Jan. 1748], quoted in memorial of Yang Xifu, Hunan governor. Translated by Dunstan, *Conflicting*, 279–80.

14. Ibid.

15. Yang Xifu in ibid., and also Will and Wong, *Nourish*, 141–47. See Chapter 6 in this book for further discussion.

16. Marks, "Price Inflation," 116; emphasis in original. Taking the entirety of China into account, Yeh-chien Wang, on the contrary, finds a rough correspondence between population and price trends. "Secular Trends of Rice Prices" (1992), 55–58. He also considers the roles of money supply and velocity in price determination.

17. Rowe, *Saving*, 158–59.

18. Will and Wong, 152–54.

19. Kishimoto-Nakayama Mio, "Kangxi Depression"; and Marks, *Tigers*, 153–56.

20. In Nakayama, "Fluctuation," 82.

21. From the *Hanshu* in ibid., 75. "*Shengui shangmin, shenjian shangnong.*" Another version of this expression used in the Qing was "*Gujian shangnong.*" Also see Will and Wong, 143.

22. Nakayama, "Fluctuation," 75–79.

23. Fisher delineates price revolutions, or inflationary periods, in the thirteenth, sixteenth, eighteenth, and twentieth centuries, which he calls the four "Great Waves."

24. See Goldstone, "Monetary Versus Velocity Interpretations."

25. Abel, 188–93, 292–94.

26. Fisher, 241–46, provides an excellent overview of the key theories about causes of price revolutions.

27. Abel, 9–12. The impact of good or poor harvests depends on the scale of a farmer's production and surplus. Fisher, 409.

28. *Agrarian History*, 123, 127.

29. In European price history, the observation of short-term cycles has in the past generated a considerable amount of interest. Braudel and Spooner, 430–42, have a full description of this work, in which cycles have been named for the economists who have observed them—the Kondratieff cycle, the Juglar cycle, the Kitchin cycle, and so forth—in the manner of astronomical observation. Abel, 165–69, describes a ten-year "harvest cycle." Since no clear explanations have resulted from any of these observations, it would seem prudent to leave the matter as an unexplained observation. Slicher Van Bath, 99–100, notes that "these theories are more or less discounted today."

30. Appleby, "Grain Prices," 882. This hypothesis has been questioned by David Weir, "Markets and Mortality," 231, who finds that while the availability of cheap substitutes may have increased the elasticity of demand for wheat, it did not necessarily result in weaker correlations between the prices of different crops.

31. According to *Zhenji* by Fang Guancheng, 2:2b, wheat was planted in the eighth or ninth lunar month, which would have been September to October.

32. The fourth lunar month, according to memorial of JQ 6/12/2, GZD 006858.

33. According to a Republican-period source. Mai Shudu, 82, wheat came onto the market in the

eighth, ninth, or tenth months. He was probably referring to lunar months, since it appears that even in the 1930s city markets and exchange shops still followed the lunar calendar. If so, this would have corresponded roughly to September to November.

34. *HBZL* 16:9ab; *CYQS* 65:3b–4. Other sources say the granary sales took place in the tenth lunar month in Tongzhou and third and fourth lunar months in Beijing. Tribute deliveries began in the third month but continued into the sixth month and later. See Chapter 5 in this book.

35. These results are roughly comparable to findings from the 1930s. The seasonal variations found in Buck, *Land Utilization*, 333–39, are quite similar to my results except wheat's high price for Buck was in February. Buck also remarked that the amplitude of fluctuation was not great. "These data do not show as excessive variation as one is often led to believe," 339. See also with Mai Shudu, 105, on wheat, which shows prices not falling until autumn. See note 33 above.

36. According to the *Da Qing huidian*, the collected statutes of the Qing code, 1899, 21:17a, as translated by Marks, "Climate and Harvests," 423: "Harvest ratings: 80 percent (eight *fen*) and above are plentiful (*feng*); 60 percent (six *fen*) and above are average (*ping*); 50 percent (five *fen*) and below are deficient (*qian*). The reality [of the harvest size] is to be investigated thoroughly and reported."

37. QL 19/9/12, *GZDQLC* 9:548. Also cited in Chapter 3 in this book.

38. Work on price correlations among prefectures, Table 7.3, in Chapter 7, shows strong to medium ties between Baoding and other key prefectures.

39. There is evidence that temperatures in the northern hemisphere declined in the first half of the nineteenth century. Gordon C. Jacoby and Rosanne D'Arrigo, "Reconstructed Northern Hemisphere Annual Temperature since 1671," *Climatic Change* 14 (1989): 39–59, as cited in Marks, *Tigers*, 199, fig. 6.2. Marks finds an intriguing apparent correlation between the northern hemisphere temperatures and grain prices in Guangdong, but he is unable to test this relationship statistically. Zhili grain prices did not fall in the same decades of the nineteenth century as the northern hemisphere temperatures, and in any case, the fall in grain prices was largely caused by the monetary factors described in this chapter.

40. King's Law is discussed in Abel, 9–13; and Slicher Van Bath, 118–20.

41. Wrigley, "Some Reflections on Corn Yields," presents a sophisticated analysis of the King model, suggesting that factors such as amounts set aside for seed, extent of home consumption, risk-spreading practices, and so on must be taken into account. The French grain yield and price data from 1815–1914, for example, "show unambiguously that it is dangerous to argue from the behaviour of a wheat price series to the pattern of annual fluctuations in the wheat harvest," 244–45, 256.

42. Marks, "It Never Used to Snow," 437–42.

43. Ibid., 426.

44. It should not be surprising that prices changed in anticipation of the next harvest, which people could predict by observing the weather in the growing season. In the winter of 1817, the governor-general reported, "In Zhili, 105 zhou and xian were affected by drought, hail, or frost, of which 53 were *chengzai* [declared disasters], 29 of which were relatively heavy. They all planted wheat, and because of winter snow there is hope of harvest. The price is stable, and the people are calm. Wait until next spring to see what relief will be required." JQ 22/12/19, ZPZZ, NZZJ 0079.

45. Our coding of flood or drought years is based in part on Beijing rainfall data, and in part on documentary evidence that shows widespread rainfall. See Appendix 3. Even so, it is only a rough measure.

46. *Xincheng XZ* 1935, 2:1b–2a.

47. Jordan, 51, 135.

48. Summarized in Appleby, "Grain Prices," 865–66, 870–71. Abel, 38–39, discusses famine in Western Europe during 1309–19 when prices rose three to nine times their normal levels. In the Netherlands in the fifteenth century a poor harvest was resulted in a 200 percent price rise, 60.

49. Post, 37.

50. According to Jordan, 7, and Post, xiii, a famine should also be described as prolonged and extensive. The Irish Potato Famine of 1845–47, which was more severe than that of 1816–17, was geographically more limited and may not strictly fit this definition.

51. Sen, *Poverty and Famines*, 54, 66, 69.

52. Ibid., 132, 149.

53. Excellent discussions in English of the currency system can be found by Chen Chau-nan, Lin Man-

houng, Wang Yeh-chien, King, and Von Glahn. The standard source in Chinese is Peng Xinwei. See below for distinction between bimetallic and duometallic systems.

54. Technically, the term "brass" would be more accurate and is employed by Dunstan, *Conflicting*, but copper was the principal component of this money. See Von Glahn, *Fountain of Fortune*, 146–47, 189–90, and 208, for information about the changing metallic composition of coins in Chinese history. The government controlled the minting of copper coins, but did not mint silver. In North China in the nineteenth century, cash notes were also widely used and functioned in the same way as cash coins. Wang Yeh-chien, "Evolution of the Chinese Monetary System," 483–90; Lin Man-houng, "Currency and Society," 180.

55. Dunstan, "Emergence," 7.

56. Chen Chau-nan, 2, 20–21, and 29–30.

57. Dennys, 492.

58. Ibid.

59. Gamble, *Ting Hsien*, 250–51. King, 58, cites Gamble.

60. Other evidence indicates that this was exceeded. Hsin-pao Chang, 39–40, n. 84, gives 2,500 for 1828; 4,600 for 1846. Peng Xinwei, *Monetary History*, 740, gives other examples.

61. See Chapter 9 for further discussion. Millet harvests were fairly good in 1839 (6 fen), 1848 (8), 1861 (9)—so without further investigation these could not be considered natural crises. The 1871 millet harvest, by contrast was only a 5.

62. Vogel, 6–7. This article presents a useful series of copper-silver rates for Beijing, 1567–1855, and for Ningjin, Zhili, 1798–1850.

63. Von Glahn, 253–54, introduces the work of the Japanese scholars Adachi Keiji and Kuroda Akinobu.

64. Peng Xinwei, 831–32.

65. King, 142–43, 147–48.

66. Lin Man-houng, "Currency and Society," pt. 2, esp. 213. She and others also point to the increased value of silver in the West. Louis Dermigny as discussed in Von Glahn, 256.

67. Peng Xinwei, 861.

68. "In general, silver ingots were more widely used in the South, while copper coins were more widely used in the North." Chen Chau-nan, 17.

69. In the 1744–45 crisis, the latter view gained the day. Dunstan, "Orders Go Forth," esp. 105–16. Lin Man-houng, "Currency and Society," treats in detail the ideological debates during the monetary crisis of the Daoguang period.

70. Dunstan, "Orders Go Forth," 79ff., and 112ff.

71. QL 17/9/6, *Fang Kemin* 1:557–64; emphasis added.

72. QL 17/9/12, *Fang Kemin* 1:567–74. More of same, in QL 17/10/5, *GZDQLC* 4:74–75, 274–75. The rich households were given incentives to comply.

73. QL 17/12/20, *GZDQLC* 4:644. QL 18/1/9. *GZDQLC* 4:709, shows that prices did fall because of good winter wheat harvest and spring wheat could be planted early; emphasis added.

74. QL 18/3/27, *GZDQLC* 4:911–12; emphasis added.

75. QL 18/12/23, *GZDQLC* 7:245–46; emphasis added.

76. Contrary to what is generally thought, and what Fang said, Wang Qingyun, 215, says that in the Qianlong period in Zhili taxes were paid in coin. Wang Yeh-chien *Land Taxation*, 60, says that from the mid-eighteenth century, taxes everywhere were paid principally in coin.

77. Wang Yeh-chien, "Evolution," 489–90. "The massive silver drain at the time hit particularly hard the south because it relied heavily upon silver and silver-based notes as circulating media. Ironically, owing to illegal debasement of coin by government mints and wide-spread counterfeiting, the supply of coin was rather steady despite a drastic decrease in copper output and copper import in the early 19th century. Prices in terms of coin remained therefore relatively stable. Primarily dependent upon coin and coin notes for business transactions, the north suffered much less severely from the monetary crisis than the south," 490. Lin Man-houng's work disputes this; she feels that the impact of foreign silver was nationwide, chap. 3, esp. 73–83. Nakayama Mio, "Fluctuations," 62–63, cites mid-eighteenth-century sources from Jiangnan saying that "the use of coin even for large transactions of a thousand taels or more had become commonplace."

78. *Xu Tianjin XZ* 1870, 16:65–67b.

79. "Big coin" minted in the Xianfeng period was debased coinage. King, 147, writes, "The incentive for big-coin came from the provinces and was, in effect, an official debasement. *De jure* the big-coin were token coins in that they were intended to be exchangeable for standard coin at the ratio implied by the denomination of the coin; *de facto* they were full-bodied coins since they passed current at less than the face value and since they were not, except in usual circumstances, exchangeable at par with standard coin." See also Chapter 9 in this book.

80. King, chap. 6, 144–63, discusses the monetary crisis of the Xianfeng period, with the last section devoted to Beijing in 1861.

81. Rennie, 1:209–10.

82. Ibid., 1:268. Entry for July 3, 1861. See Chapter 9 below, for more on this midcentury crisis.

83. Chen Chau-nan, 1; Peng Xinwei, 819.

84. Rockoff, 187.

85. Chen Chau-nan, 19–20. In a case study of agricultural prices in Hebei (Zhili) during 1814–29, Chen concludes that grain prices affected the exchange rate rather than the reverse, 29.

86. Ibid., 2–3. Wang Yeh-chien, "Evolution," 472–77, also does not consider the Chinese system a strictly parallel bimetallic system.

87. Chen Chau-nan, 3–16.

88. Wang Yeh-chien, "Evolution," 487–88.

89. Lin Man-houng, 202–6. She uses a series constructed by Yen Chung-p'ing in 1955. Wang Yeh-chien, "Secular Trend," 355–57, also uses this series.

90. There is evidence that in Beijing even large-scale transactions were made in coin. Dunstan, "Orders Go Forth," 102, 117, 123–24.

91. Chen Chau-nan, 21.

92. Crossley, 147.

93. Peng Xinwei, 843–47, 859–63. Peng says that even if workers were paid in coin, they suffered because of the debasement of the coin, 863. Kaplan transl., 1:764.

94. Qing-dynasty North China does not seem to have presented a situation similar to that of the Ethiopian famine of 1973, where, in the province of Wollo, grain prices remained low despite widespread starvation. According to Amartya Sen's analysis, grain prices did not rise because so many peasants were too poor to be involved in the market. Harvest failure was directly translated into hunger and deprivation. Sen, *Poverty and Famines*, 93–96.

Chapter Five

1. The reader is referred to Li and Dray-Novey, "Guarding Beijing's Food Security in the Qing Dynasty: State, Market, and Police," for further details about Beijing's population, food supply, and police.

2. Ibid., tab. 1, which is based on Han Guanghui, *Beijing lishi renkou dili*.

3. Ibid., 126, 129; and tab. 2 in Li and Dray-Novey.

4. H. Hinton, 7, 9a.

5. The emperor and the court actually ate rice that was produced locally, the excellent rice that was grown west of the capital. Xu Qixian, 10. See also E. Rawski, 47.

6. According to Bray, 490–94, *gengmi* was japonica rice, which was higher priced, while *xianmi* was indica or Champa rice, associated with early growing types. Both came from Zhejiang Province.

7. For example: "Tongzhou each year is allowed to store *suomi* 130,000 shi. In QL 4 there was insufficient *daomi*, so it was decided to substitute *suomi* for *daomi* 20,000 shi." *CYQS* 55:18b–19. Playfair, 356, defines *suomi* as "upland rice" from the Jiang-Zhe region. Will, *Bureaucracy*, 153 n. 7, and 352, describes *suomi* as an inferior grade of rice, but he gives an alternate writing for the character.

8. *HDSL* 102:7a, SZ 1.

9. *HDSL* 185:4a, QL 18.

10. Oblique reference in *CYQS* 61:22ab, DG 4; this passage also appears in *HDSL* 1139:16b–17a.

11. *HBZL* 18:1–2. The 1791 ed., 24: front, has the same information with printing errors. Both editions report thirteen Beijing granaries. *HDSL* 1143:15b–16a says ten; *JWSL* 7:47ab says fourteen. Li and Jiang, 170, has a table showing names and locations of thirteen granaries in Beijing and two in Tongzhou, with a total capacity of 1,206 buildings. *Shuntian FZ* 1885, juan 10, lists sixteen granaries in Beijing.

12. In 1754, however, twenty-eight of forty-eight buildings at the Bei cang were unfit for use. *Tianjin FZ* 1898, 29:24–34, records grain diverted to storage in the Bei cang.

13. *HDSL* 184:26a.

14. Will, *Bureaucracy*, 154; Will and Wong, 118, 133.

15. *HDSL* 186 passim lists types of grains, uses, and storage. The original principle was "*Bailiang* is exclusively stored at the Tongzhou granaries. Wheat, black beans, and barley are at the Beijing granaries. All the *geng, suo, and sumi (san se)* are allocated equally among the granaries." *Huangchao shihuo zhi* 5/cangchu, 1. *Bailiang* was sent to the Nei cang (in Beijing) as well. *HDSL* 184:26ab, 185:13b.

16. Wu Jianyong, "Qingdai Beijing," 172.

17. *Huangchao shihuo zhi* 5/cangchu 1.

18. *Qing Shilu*, cited in Wu Jianyong, "Qingdai Beijing," 172.

19. H. Hinton, 7, 9ab.

20. Will, *Bureaucracy*, 284 n. 26.

21. Will and Wong, 134.

22. Li and Jiang, 54–58, contains a comprehensive table based on registers held at the Qing archives. See also 405–6, and Chapters 9–10 below, on mid-nineteenth-century problems. Commercial purchases in late Qianlong and Jiaqing periods were targeted principally for famine relief in Beijing and Zhili, 93–99.

23. This would be true using several possible standards of measurement. For example, in the eighteenth century the adult ration for famine relief was half a sheng (= 5 he) or 0.005 shi of *mi* (husked rice or grain) per day. Will, *Bureaucracy*, 130–35, and see Chapter 8 below. Thus each person would require 1.83 shi per year, and 3.5 million shi could have fed approximately 2 million adults a year at subsistence standards. This is very similar to another subsistence standard: the average per capita yearly grain consumption in Beijing in 1979, under the People's Republic of China, was 300 jin. Croll, 131, or about 333 lbs (1 jin = 1.1 lb), or in Qing terms, 1.9 shi (1 shi = 185 lbs). By this low standard, 3.5 million shi could have fed 1.94 million people a year. Using a much higher standard, Li and Jiang, 85, state that in the Qianlong period, about 4 million shi arrived in Beijing and Tongzhou each year, and they calculate that if each person consumed 0.3 shi of grain per month, or 3.6 shi a year, then the grain tribute would have been enough to feed 1.1 million people for a year. Crossley, 52, cites the standard of 0.25 shi of grain per individual per month, which amounts to 3 shi per person per year. Using that standard, 3.5 million shi would feed slightly fewer than 1.2 million adults a year. According to H. Hinton, 97, 3.5 million shi would be equivalent to 280,000 tons.

24. Li and Jiang, 59 n. 1, also 72 citing *CYQS*, juan 17.

25. Will, *Bureaucracy*, 283, has estimated that about half a million shi of grain was the difference between the needs of the capital and the "maximum yield" of grain tribute, and this amount could be considered available for discretionary use.

26. *CYQS* 56; cited in Wu Jianyong, "Qingdai Beijing," 170. Also, Li and Jiang, 72, 83.

27. Will, *Bureaucracy*, 285–87.

28. Dunstan, *Conflicting*, 90. Translated from Shangyudang, QL 9/2/23 and *Qing shilu*, QL, 213:10a–12b.

29. *Qingchao wenxian tongkao*, 37/5198, cited in Dunstan, *State or Merchant?* chap. 2. Wu Jianyong, "Qingdai Beijing," 177, cites Wang Qingyun, juan 4.

30. See Chapter 6 in this book.

31. Wu Jianyong "Qingdai Beijing"; and Han Guanghui, "Jin Yuan Ming Qing," and *Beijing lishi renkou dili*.

32. QL 16/7/20, *GZDQLC* 1:192.

33. The Zhili Province monthly grain reports give the prices for Shuntian Prefecture exclusive of the Daxing and Wanping districts where Beijing was located. Some undetermined number of price reports for Daxing and Wanping are housed at the First Historical Archives in Beijing, but they have not been systematically located and cataloged. I obtained a few Daxing and Wanping price reports in Taipei in 1982 and Beijing in 1992, but they were not numerous enough to be analyzed. Table 5.1 is a sample of such a report.

34. *JWSL* 4:59ab [1822]; 4:60ab [1817]; 4:63a [1807]; 4:64a–66b [1806, 1808, 1810]; 4:67a–68a [1804].

35. The term "hoarding," *tunji*, was a stock phrase in official discourse about grain trade and storage, almost as common as the stock phrase "mean merchants," *jianshang*. To the officials, it was illegitimate for merchants to purchase and then withhold grain from the market until the prices became very high. The

officials wanted to see a constant and rapid circulation of grain so that prices would remain low and stable. To this end, if merchants retained a large inventory, this could lead to "hoarding."

36. *HBZL* 73:1.

37. This description follows Crossley, 51–53. In reality a bannerman rarely had more than one horse.

38. Chen Jiahua, 63–66.

39. *HDSL* 186:4a, YZ 9.

40. *CYQS* 60:6.

41. *HDSL* 186:8a.

42. *CYQS* 61:5b–6.

43. *CYQS* 62:9.

44. He used the phrase *qianbaiwan shengmin*. KX 48/12/4 in *GZDKXC* 2:402–4. See also Chapter 6 below.

45. *CYQS* 60:2b–5.

46. *CYQS* 60:14.

47. In 1723, *HDSL* 1143:15b. In 1737 or 1738, *CYQS* 60:6b. In 1761, *HDSL* 606:20ab. In 1768, *CYQS* 60.

48. *HDSL* 186:11b.

49. *CYQS* 61:22ab; *HDSL* 1139:17ab.

50. Wu Jianyong, "Qingdai Beijing," 179; *CYQS* 63.

51. *HDSL* 1146:14a–15b, YZ 5. Elliott, 287, cites a similar edict from the same year, 1727.

52. *Gaozong Shilu* 214, 1058; cited in Wu Jianyong, "Qingdai Beijing," 171. Wu writes that before the mid-Qing period Beijing residents ate mostly rice, but after the decline of grain tribute in the Daoguang period, their preferences changed. By 1911, rice constituted only 30 percent of the diet. Wu et al., *Beijing chengshi shi*, 345 n. 11. A sharp nineteenth-century shift of preference from rice to wheat and coarse grains is difficult to document, but the estimate of preferences in the twentieth century is probably reliable.

53. JQ 17/11/16, ZPZZ, NZZJ 0077.

54. Freeman-Mitford, 138; Fortune, 338, 347–48, 362–63.

55. *Laomi* was often reddish in color, had a bland taste, and was deficient in starch. *Qingmo Beijing zhi ziliao*, 530. Regulations of the Board of Punishments for the treatment of prisoners in Beijing said that they should be fed one large bowl (half jin) of rice made of *laomi* in the morning and one medium-sized bowl of *laomi zhou* (gruel) each for lunch and dinner. 147. Jailed criminals at the gendarmerie headquarters ate *laomi*, some of which had been confiscated by police at the city gates. *JWSL* 12:38a.

56. *Qingchao wenxian tongkao*, 37/5197. Identified but differently translated in Dunstan, *State or Merchant?* chap. 2. This passage is also in Wang Qingyun, 390.

57. *Shizong Shilu* 66, cited in Wu Jianyong, "Qingdai Beijing," 179–80. See Dunstan, "Anthology," sec. 31; and Dunstan, *State or Merchant?*, chap. 2, for a discussion of reasons for creating and later disbanding the rice bureaus.

58. Hosoya Yoshio, 190.

59. Wu Jianyong, "Qingdai Beijing," 180.

60. Dunstan, *Conflicting*, refrains from categorically identifying this shift as "sprouts of liberalism," as she did earlier. She writes, "The paradox is thus that belief in free circulation is not the same thing as economic liberalism," 257, 330–31.

61. *HBZL* 17:35a; also *HDSL* 191:30ab, QL 34.

62. QL 17/[?]/14, *GZDQLC* 4:597.

63. Shangyudang 199–901, QL 40/5/10, courtesy of Susan Naquin.

64. *HDSL* 1026:12b–14a.

65. Ibid.

66. *JWSL* 4:61a–62a, JQ 13/# 5/13.

67. *HDSL* 186, passim.

68. *Huangchao shihuo zhi* 2, cangchu 2; also in *HDSL* 186, QL 1.

69. *HDSL* 185:5b, QL 59.

70. *HDSL* 186:15b, QL 57.

71. *HDSL* 1038:20–24.

72. *CYQS* 61:19.

73. *HDSL* 1161:10b–11, JQ 15.

74. *CYQS* 63:6b–7.

75. An edict in the sixth month observed that such abuses by granary personnel had started in 1798. The documents for this case are reproduced in "Jiaqing shisinian." The sentence that refers to corruption since 1798 is found at the bottom of page 53. A similar case occurred in 1825. *CYQS* 61:22ab.

76. The term *michang* usually referred to these *pingtiao* stations, which sold reduced-price grain from the tribute granaries, while the term *miju* referred to the Eight-banner grain bureaus, which bought grain from bannermen and later resold the grain at reduced prices. The terms are sometimes used interchangeably even in the original documents. What they had in common was that both were government-run institutions. Wang Qingyun, 386–90, uses the term *miju* in this generic sense to include both types of institutions. The private *miju*, discussed above, add additional confusion to the terminology.

77. Li and Jiang, 77.

78. *Gaozong Shilu* 216; cited in Wu Jianyong, "Qingdai Beijing," 182; and Wu Jianyong, "Jingshi de liangshi," 386.

79. *HDSL* 275:8a–9b.

80. *HDSL* 275:23b–24a; *Shuntian FZ* 1885, 66:29ab.

81. Censors and police attached to the Five Districts focused on the nonbanner population and therefore on the Outer City and on suburbs around the capital. Although the term "Wucheng" referring to the entire capital went back to the Ming period, in the Qing dynasty the same term also was used to refer to five sections of the Outer City. Only context reveals which definition is intended in particular references during the Qing.

82. *HDSL* 275:7b–9, QL 16.

83. *CYQS* 65:1a.

84. *CYQS* 65:6a. The year 1759 was a crisis year when little relief was provided for the region as a whole. See Chapter 8 in this book. Li and Jiang, 78–79, gives the market and *pingtiao* price schedule from YZ 11–DG 4.

85. One dou = 1/10 shi. *HBZL* 16:8a; also appears in 1791 edition.

86. *CYQS* 65:3b–4.

87. *HBZL* 16:9ab; also appears in 1791 edition.

88. *HBZL* 16:10ab; also appears in 1791 edition.

89. *CYQS* 65:10 refers to a case in 1770.

90. *CYQS* 65:7b.

91. *HDSL* 1160:7b–8.

92. *CYQS* 65:6ab.

93. *HDSL* 1034:12b–13.

94. *HDSL* 1034:7–8, 1038:20–24, QL 52.

95. *CYQS* 65:13b–14a.

96. Ten sheng = 1 dou = 1/10 shi. *CYQS* 64:41a–42a.

97. *CYQS* 64:42ab.

98. *CYQS* 64:41–53, documents dated Jiaqing through Xianfeng reigns.

99. *HBZL* 84:18–19.

100. *JWSL* 4:58ab; Naquin, *Peking,* 641–45. Before 1780, soup kitchens did not start operations until the eleventh month, 642.

101. For an unspecified year. *JWSL* 9:58ab.

102. JQ 6/6/25, ZPZZ, NZZJ 0069.

103. *HDSL* 273:1b.

104. *BCSX* 274, Renzong, 57:19ab.

105. *CYQS* 65:23b–24.

106. *BCSX* 274, Renzong, 57:23a.

107. *CYQS* 65:26b–27, 28ab.

108. This was a smaller famine ration than the 5 he standard of the eighteenth century; see note 23 above.

109. *BCSX* 374, Xuanzong, 47:21–22.

110. *JFTZ* 5:14ab.

111. *BCSX* 374, Xuanzong, 47:28ab. The chaotic conditions in the region are described in Chapter 9 in this book.

112. *JWSL* 5:42a–43a [1838]; 5:60a–61a [1813]; 6:1a–5b [1829]; 6:6a–14b [1845]; 8:8ab [nd]; 8:14ab [1851]; 8:15a–21b [nd]; 8:22a–48a [nd]; 8:51a [nd].

113. *JWSL* 11:19a.

114. Han Guanghui, "Qingdai Beijing zhenxu," 23–26, has a list of soup kitchens in Beijing throughout the Qing period, as well as an informative discussion.

115. Naquin, *Peking*, 643. Han Guanghui, "Qingdai Beijing zhenxu," 25, entries also indicate this.

116. This was part of the overall tendency toward charitable activities involving elite participation from all over the empire, not just the immediate locality. This trend is discussed in Rankin, 142–47; Naquin, *Peking*, 662–64. See also Chapter 9 in this book.

117. Gamble and Burgess, 267–68, 277, 304.

118. Ibid., facing p. 270, 278.

119. Strand, 204–5.

120. *HDSL* 1160:10ab, QL 51.

121. *HDSL* 191: 27b–28a; also cited by Will, *Bureaucracy*, 181.

122. *HDSL* 1038:20–24.

123. *BCSX* 273, Renzong, 56:18a–19a; emphasis added.

124. *JWSL* 4:61a–62a [1808], 64a–66b [1810].

125. *JWSL* 4:64a–66b [1810].

126. *HDSL* 191:31b–32a.

127. *JWSL* 4.59ab [1822], 4.63a [1807].

128. *JWSL* 4:45a–46a [1801].

129. *JWSL* 4:67a–68a [1804].

130. Deposition of Cao Fuchang, JQ 18/10/21, in *Gugong zhoukan* 227:3, 228:1.

131. *JWSL* 9:58ab [nd].

132. *JWSL* 4:63a [1807].

133. *JWSL* 4:59ab [1822], 64a–66b [1810].

134. The references to "wealthy large grain shops" in 1787 and to "rich shops" in 1813 cited above are the only such descriptions that we have seen, and the concept of "large" is not quantified. Wu Jianyong, *Beijing chengshi shi*, 280 n. 10, mentions one large grain merchant family, located just outside the Chongwen gate, that was prominent from the Ming to the end of the Qing.

135. Wang Qingyun, 387; Hosoya, 186; Elliot, 221.

136. Fortune, 362, 370; other sources in Li and Dray-Novey, 1022.

137. *Qingmo Beijing*, 343–45.

138. QL 43/6/8, GZD 035185.

139. Translated and summarized by Dunstan, "Emergence," 533–534 n. 26, from *Tongzhou zhi* 1879, 10:23a–27a.

140. There is mention of three large grain dealers in Tianjin starting from the Xianfeng period. See *Tianjin wenshi ziliao xuanji*, 20, 1982/8, 40–41.

141. The writings of Wu Jianyong, cited above in the section on sale of stipends, are most noteworthy in this regard. Outside of China, Dunstan, *Conflicting*, and *State or Merchant?*; Rowe, *Hankow: Conflict and Community*; and Will, "Discussions on the Market Place," have focused on the relationship between state and market in the Qing.

142. DG 4/3, *JFTZ* 1:325.

143. Chen Jinling says that Beijing grain prices were stable in the eighteenth century, but that in the nineteenth century prices rose faster than in other places in China. His conclusions are based on anecdotal evidence, not a price series.

144. Ormrod, 88–91.

145. Tilly, 416.

146. Wong 1982, 767–88. See also Introduction above. This is contradicted by one Western observer. See Li and Dray-Novey, 1025 n. 42.

147. There are instances of bannermen engaged in public protests over the inadequacy of the silver

portion of their stipends. In Beijing 1692 and 1725 there were two demonstrations in the Imperial City. Crossley, 56. These could not be called food riots.

148. Crossley, 52–54, 147–48.

149. Elliott, 221.

150. Han Guanghui, *Beijing lishi renkou dili*, 318–19.

151. McClain and Ugawa, 461.

152. Hayashi, 228–33. In commodities other than rice, the authorities followed an "Edo-first" policy and encouraged commerce from other areas. "Because it was in the daimyo's interest to have rice sell at as high a price as possible, most daimyo governments enacted laws that, in effect, gave special protection to the rice dealers . . . [and] strictly prohibited the importation of rice from outside [their] home domain[s], except during times of famine," Nakai and McClain, 547.

153. Walthall, 407, 410, 413, 428.

154. Kaplan, *Bread, Politics*, xvi, xxxvi; Kaplan, *Provisioning Paris*, 23–29.

155. Kaplan, *Bread, Politics*, 1:8–9.

156. Ikegami and Tilly, 454.

Chapter Six

1. *Bureaucracy and Famine* by Pierre-Étienne Will was the first major study of grain storage and deployment; it focused on Zhili Province. Will and R. Bin Wong wrote the definitive and comprehensive work on the state civilian granary system during the Qing period, *Nourish the People*. Together with coauthors James Lee, Peter Perdue, and Jean Oi, they have provided not only a compendium of statistical data collected from the archival records but also a detailed study of the technical aspects of granary operation and management and an overall interpretation of the granary system. Much of the survey in the first section of this chapter is based on their book. Rowe's *Saving the World* provides an excellent discussion of the theory and practice of grain storage, as seen through the eyes of the Qing statesman Chen Hongmou.

2. Tribute rice was husked in contrast to the unhusked grain stored in the state granary system; so its volume was reduced by a half. Will and Wong, 338; also see tab. 8.1, pp. 236–50. But some tribute grain diverted to North China destinations, such as Zhili or Shandong, was wheat or millet, not rice, and it is not clear whether it was husked or not.

3. Ibid., 494–95.

4. Will and Wong, 8.

5. Ibid., 6.

6. Von Glahn, "Community and Welfare," 221, 234–35, 253.

7. Brook, *Confusions*, 70–71.

8. Will and Wong, 10–11.

9. Ibid., 19.

10. Rowe, *Saving*, 253–54.

11. Will and Wong, 7, 9.

12. Ibid., 37; but without much success.

13. Ibid., 69.

14. Ibid., 69–70.

15. Ibid., 25–33.

16. *HDSL*, juan 190.

17. See n. 2 above.

18. KX 58/5/7, *GZDKXC* 7:511–13.

19. The general regulations for *shecang* are found in *HBZL* 17:25–29.

20. Will and Wong, 37; Rowe, *Saving*, 274.

21. KX 47/1/18, *GZDKXC* 1:567–70.

22. KX 50/5/22, *GZDKXC* 3:118.

23. KX 53/10/27, *GZDKXC* 5:197–201.

24. YZ 4/12/24, *GZDYZC* 17:191–92. But the next year, possible errors in Li Fu's *shecang* accounting were reported to the throne. YZ 5/1/28, *GZDYZC* 17:384.

25. Will and Wong, 185–89.

26. Ibid., tab. 1.1, p. 22.

27. Ibid., 40.

28. YZ 1/12/16, *GZDYZC* 2:170.

29. YZ 2/2/26, *GZDYZC* 3:574.

30. YZ 4/11/2, *GZDYZC* 4:800.

31. YZ 7/6/4, *GZDYZC* 13:332–33.

32. Will and Wong, 296–97. Guangdong may actually have stopped storing grain in the 1760s. See n. 182 below. Research on other provinces may reveal similar cases of overrepresentation of stocks.

33. Seen also in Will and Wong, tab. 9.5, p. 308.

34. Ibid., 53–54.

35. *HBZL* 16:14a–16b.

36. *HBZL* 17:20ab.

37. Quotas for each county in Zhili are given in the 1791 edition of the *HBZL* 27:1–5.

38. As seen in Will and Wong, tab. 6.1, p. 180.

39. Will and Wong, 371–79.

40. Ibid., 385.

41. QL 11/2/23, ZPZZ, NZZJ 0040.

42. As seen in Will and Wong, tab. 6.1, p. 180. They point out that this difference between theoretical and actual reserves was not a sign of inefficiency, 60.

43. YZ 13/# 4/10, *GZDYZC* 24:513–14; emphasis added.

44. Will and Wong have excellent general discussion, 142–78.

45. See Chapter 4 above.

46. QL 14/8/25, ZPZZ, CZCC 56:1957–86.

47. Ibid.

48. QL 13/8/25, JJD 002881.

49. In that year Fang Guancheng proposed establishing granaries in these two key counties with holdings from the Bei cang in Tianjin or from Fengtian grain. QL 25/10/16. *Fang Kemin* 2:941–45. Nasutu's figures were received with skepticism at court. QL 13/9/9, ZPZZ, CZCC 56:1399–1401.

50. *HDSL*, juan 190.

51. Will and Wong, tab. 8.7, Provincial Targets and "Quotas," 278–84.

52. Rowe, *Saving*, 265.

53. QL 14/10/22, ZPZZ, CZCC 56:2015–17.

54. QL 15/6/1, ZPZZ, CZCC 56:2244–46; emphasis added.

55. QL 27/5/14, ZPZZ, CZCC 57:652–54.

56. QL 29/4/11, *GZDQLC* 21:178–79; emphasis added. This memorial is also discussed in Will and Wong, 57, 154, 191–92.

57. Ibid.

58. This follows the translation of Will and Wong, 45, 168. See also Rowe, *Saving*, 263.

59. QL 38/10/9, ZPZZ, CZCC 57:1992–94.

60. QL 44/3ff., *JFTZ* 1:177–81.

61. Will and Wong, 45. Also, Will, *Bureaucracy*, 189.

62. Li and Jiang, 93–99.

63. Dunstan, *Conflicting*, 271–73.

64. QL 40/6/23, ZPZZ, CZCC 57:2133–34.

65. QL 40/10/9, ZPZZ, CZCC 57:2167–68.

66. QL 45/4/23, ZPZZ, CZCC 57:2601–3.

67. JQ 1/1, *BCSX* 273, Renzong, 56:1–2.

68. JQ 4/8, *BCSX* 273, Renzong, 56:9a–10a.

69. JQ 4/8, *BCSX* 273, Renzong, 56:10b–12a.

70. JQ 5/3, *BCSX* 273, Renzong, 56:12a–13a.

71. Ibid.

72. See Chapter 7 in this book.

73. JQ 7/11/5, GZD 009398.

74. JQ 11/6, *BCSX* 273, Renzong, 56:35a–37a.

75. JQ 12/5/18, ZPZZ, CZCC 58:1239–40.

76. JQ 20/11/11, ZPZZ, CZCC 58:1936–38. However some questioned Nayancheng's report of a deficit of up to 1.5 million shi in ever-normal granary stocks. From Jiaqing 3–12, it had been reported that 570,000 had been restocked, and that was eight years ago. The emperor chastised the governor-general, telling him not to mix up old and new reports, and ordered an investigation. JQ 20/11, *BCSX* 274, Renzong, 57:35a–36b.

77. YZ 4/7 and 4/8, *JFTZ* 1:69–71.

78. *HBZL* 17:37–38.

79. JQ 17/5, *BCSX* 274, Renzong, 57:20a–21a.

80. QL 57, *HDSL*, juan 189.

81. Will and Wong, 203–4, discussing this same edict.

82. Memorial of JQ 7/5/30, quoted by Will and Wong, 215 n. 50.

83. DG 11, *HDSL*, juan 189. These were general observations, not from Zhili specifically.

84. DG 13/3/15, JJD 063339 and enclosure.

85. DG 13/4/21, JJD 063344. *Huangchao shihuozhi*, cangchu, 24, reproduces memorials from 1832 that stated that ever-normal granaries had inventories of 480,000 shi, but a later memorial revealed that actual stocks were only about 40 percent of that figure, and some counties had no grain at all. See Will and Wong, 271.

86. DG 13/11/19, JJD 065811; emphasis added.

87. *HBZL* 17:19–24.

88. *Daming FZ* 1853, 7:28ab.

89. On Chen, see Rowe, *Saving*, 276–84.

90. QL 12/1/2, ZPZZ, CZCC, cited in Will and Wong, 70.

91. QL 18/2/19. *Fang Kemin* 2:587–93. Also in Fang's *Jifu yicang tu*, 1ab.

92. *Jifu yicang tu*, 10a–12a. The guidelines of Nasutu, QL 12/1/2, ZPZZ, CZCC 56:128–33. Nasutu said that the *yicang* in Zhili would emphasize the collection of unhusked grain. The general rules are found in *Jifu yicang tu*, preface, and also *Fang Kemin* 2:519–615. They are reproduced also in *HBZL* 17:30–32.

93. Fang, *Jifu yicang tu*, 11b.

94. *Yongqing XZ* 1779/1813, Hushu 2:73ab.

95. *Jifu yicang tu*, 11a–12b. Rules on loans are also found in *Fang Kemin* 2:607–10.

96. *Jifu yicang tu*, 2b–3a.

97. *Tianjin FZ* 1898, 31:2a.

98. *Jifu tongzhi* 1884, juan 103–4.

99. Ibid., juan 104; rept. 1934, 4145.

100. Fang's work was widely reprinted in local gazetteers, for example *Baoding FZ* 1886, 38:11–15, and *Xiaoning XZ* 1756, 2:4b–7.

101. Many maps showing the locations of charity granaries appear in the gazetteers. For example, *Zaoqiang XZ* 1803, *Changyuan XZ* 1810, *Huailu XZ* 1881.

102. Also seen in Will and Wong, tab. 9.5, p. 308.

103. Available reports on charity grain (*yigu*) contributions are found for 1755, *GZDQLC* 10:836–37; 1756, ZPZZ CZCC 56: 2882–83; 1767, GZD 024694; 1773, GZD 027607; 1777, GZD 033468; 1778, GZD 037069; 1779, JJD 025480; 1781, GZD 040271; 1782, GZD 043458; and 1789, GZD 059048.

104. JQ 20/10/23, NZZJ, CZCC 58:1927–29.

105. This information is revealed in Nayancheng's memorial of 1826 described below. Nayancheng memorial of DG 6/12/12 is reprinted in *Qingyuan XZ* 1873, 15:6a–8b.

106. Ibid.

107. DG 7/10/14, JJD 057124.

108. See above, DG 13/4/21, JJD 063344.

109. DG 13/3/15, JJD 063339 and enclosure.

110. *Baoding FZ* 1886, 38:6b.

111. *Xingtai XZ* 1905, 2:52–56.

112. *Huailu XZ* 1881, 7:2b.

113. *Shuntian FZ* 1885, 55:2ab. Other examples are found in Xiong County, *Xiong XZ* 1930, 2:34b–35b; Jizhou, *Shuntian FZ* 1885, 55:11a; and Cangzhou, *Tianjin FZ* 1898, 31:5ab.

114. For example, *Shuntian FZ* 1885, 55:2a.

115. DG 13/2, *BCSX* 375, Xuanzong, 48:24b, 30a.

116. See, for example, *Shuntian FZ* 1885, 55:1–13, esp. 11a. Also *Ding XZ* 1934. 3:11b–12a. Xu Zuoting's, *Zhongjian Fengjicang tu'an* (Records and maps of the reconstruction of the abundant relief granary), 1902, describes the reconstruction of a granary in Qinghe County in Zhili between 1870–80. Source described in Wong and Perdue, "Famine's Foes," 328.

117. *Ding XZ* 1934, 3:11b–12a.

118. *Wangdu XZ* 1934, 5:52ab. Other examples of merchant involvement: *Guangping FZ* 1894, 23:1ab. Also at Cangzhou, in *Tianjin FZ* 1898, 31:5ab.

119. *Shuntian FZ* 1885, 55:3b–4a.

120. For example in Yongqing xian and Dong'an xian, discussed in *Shuntian FZ* 1885, 55:2b–3b.

121. Ibid. *Shuntian FZ* 1885, 55:2b–3b. A similar situation was described for Sanhe xian, ibid., 55:4b–5b. Also in *Xianghe XZ* 1936, 4:28a–29b. *Liangxiang XZ* 1924, 2:43b–44a.

122. *Yuanshi XZ* 1931, ce 3:43a–45a.

123. *Xinhe XZ* 1928, 2:70ab.

124. *Xiong XZ* 1930, 2:34b–35b with a table.

125. *Shuntian FZ* 1885, 55:1a.

126. Will, *Bureaucracy*, 202–4. The discussion pertains to China in general, not just Zhili. Where they existed, community granaries were seen to be vulnerable to abuse and dishonesty by granary managers, thus requiring bureaucratic intervention, a kind of vicious cycle.

127. KX 56/4/18, *GZDKXC* 6: 908–12.

128. Will, *Bureaucracy*, 170–71, esp. tabs. 9 and 10.

129. QL 11/2/23 memorial of Nasutu cited above.

130. Cited by Will, *Bureaucracy*, 287, but he notes in n. 33, that this is not a verifiable figure.

131. Cited by Will, *Bureaucracy*, 287 n. 34 and 35. See also Chapter 8 in this book.

132. QL 21/12/19, *Fang Kemin* 2:767–70.

133. QL 24/4/14, *Fang Kemin* 2:889–96.

134. See Chapter 9 in this book. Thus the assertion by Will, *Bureaucracy*, 289, that practically no grain tribute was used in famine relief after 1801 needs to be modified, but his statement that "by the end of Jiaqing reign (1820), aid in kind taken from the tribute had ceased to play a major role in the history of famine administration" is largely correct.

135. In the Ming period, commerce along the Grand Canal brought luxuries from Jiangnan to Zhili; Hejian Prefecture was a major beneficiary. Brook, *Confusions*, 117–18.

136. Xu Tan, 311–16, 325.

137. KX 48/11/19, *GZDKXC* 2:402–4. In referring to *qianbaiwan shengmin*, Zhao most likely meant the capital region, not Beijing alone.

138. KX 55/7/12, *GZDKXC* 6:495–98.

139. KX 56/2/25, *GZDKXC* 6:829–32.

140. Imperial rescript, ibid.

141. QL 24/4/6, ZPZZ, CZCC 56:3444–47.

142. QL 28/4/21, *GZDQLC* 17:516–17.

143. R. Lee, 4.

144. KX 48/11/24, (*Da Qing*) *Shilu* 240:10.

145. Yang Jingren, "Tong shang," in *HCJSWB* 41:43a.

146. Will, *Bureaucracy*, 224. Wu Hui and Ge Xianhui, 134. QL 50/10/19, ZPZZ, CZCC 57:3104–7.

147. From Will, *Bureaucracy*, 218; his source is Kato Shigeshi, "Manshū to Shina hondo to no tsūshū."

148. QL 16/1/19, JJD 006353. The average price of millet in Zhili was 1.65 taels in the first lunar month of 1751, and 1.72 in the second. See Figure 4.1 in Chapter 4 in this book.

149. QL 17/7/27, *GZDQLC* 3:476–77; emphasis added.

150. QL 17/11/15, *GZDQLC* 4:321–23, also in *Fang Kemin* 2:577–85; emphasis added.

151. JQ 6/6/8, GZD 005925. But there were rumors that Fengtian completely banned the commercial shipment of grain to protect the local supply. This was protested because "each province's harvest is different and we rely on the merchants to circulate the grain." JQ 6/12, *BCSX* 273, Renzong, 56:19ab.

152. JQ 12/2/27, ZPZZ, NZZJ 0075.

153. JQ 17/2/9, ZPZZ, NZZJ, juan 5.

154. JQ 17/11/16, ZPZZ, NZZJ 0077.

155. DG 2/1/29, ZPZZ, CZCC 4, Box 505.

156. JQ 15/11/14, ZPZZ, NZZJ 0075.

157. *CYQS* 75:17b.

158. TZ 6/7/1, *HBZL* 16:7. Jiangsu and Zhejiang governors were also ordered, if their harvest was good, to purchase rice to ship by sea to Tianjin for reduced-price sale.

159. JQ 15/6/9, ZPZZ, CZCC 58:1351–53; emphasis added. This passage is quoted fully in Chapter 7 in this book.

160. Hsiao, 144–83. For others, see Will and Wong, 20 n. 3.

161. Wu Chengming estimated that Zhili's output in 1873 was probably about the same as its known output of 100 million shi in 1933. A private communication with author, Nov. 25, 1989. See Chapter 3 above.

162. Will, *Bureaucracy*, 183–84, also doubts the impact on seasonal fluctuations, as well as price stabilization in general.

163. Dunstan, *Conflicting*, 276–78. Dunstan's translations and discussions of the *Huangchao jingshi wenbian*, especially in chaps. 6 and 7, provide an excellent introduction to these issues.

164. *HCJSWB* 41:43a–45a.

165. *HCJSWB* 41:7a–9b.

166. Translated by Dunstan, *Conflicting*, 279–89. Yang argued that water control, by contrast, was far more important task for officials, and they should be held responsible for any floods or droughts that occurred due to their negligence of water works.

167. Ibid., 87; and her discussion, 67–69.

168. Rowe, *Saving*, 255, 260-61. Dunstan, *Conflicting*, 264–67.

169. Rowe, *Saving*, 169, and chap. 8, "Accumulation," which is entirely on grain storage.

170. Ibid., 210.

171. Wu Jianyong, "Qingdai qianqi de shangpinliang."

172. Will and Wong, 278–84.

173. Ibid., append. A–1.

174. Ibid., 296–98.

175. QL 31/8 and QL 31/9 in *JFTZ* 1:139–40.

176. In the private communication mentioned above, Wu Chengming estimated that Zhili's external supply of grain, including grain tribute, was about 6–7 million—less than what I have estimated here—and that the rate of commercialization of agriculture was about 16 percent, including the external sources. If the total consumption of grain in Zhili was about 100 million shi, then the logic of Wu's calculation suggests that 16 million shi was commercial; of this 6–7 million came from external sources, and the remaining 9–10 million was from internal commerce. This is consistent with the assumption that the extent of commercialization in North China's agriculture was relatively limited.

177. McCloskey and Nash.

178. Komlos and Landes, 36–37.

179. Ibid., 43. Huang and others have discussed the applicability of Chayanov's model to the Chinese rural economy. P. Huang, *Peasant Economy*, 5–8, based on A. V. Chayanov, *The Theory of Peasant Economy* ([1925] 1986).

180. *The Moral Economy of the Peasant*, 1976; *The Rational Peasant*, 1979.

181. *Jifu yicang tu*, 11b, cited above.

182. Marks, *Tigers*, 234–38.

183. Ibid., 239–45. Very little seems to be known about private storage in other parts of China. Will and Wong, 496.

184. Ibid.

185. Ibid., 189–90, reaches a similar conclusion.

Chapter Seven

1. Will, "Discussions," 324–25, points out that in English or French, the "market" refers both to "market-places" and "market-principle." Chinese statesmen were focused on the "market" in the first sense.

2. In the 1766 edict cited in Chapter 6, above, the emperor approved Fang Guancheng's decision to move against merchants reported to have been cornering the market. "We have found that merchants in Hejian and Tianjin often trade by water routes with Dezhou and Linqing, and we have not prohibited this because it benefits both sides. But recently we hear that evil brokers who hoard [*jianya tunhu*] have been raising prices when they hear of a shortage in the neighboring province, and making an illicit profit from this," QL 31/9, *JFTZ* 1:140.

3. Kwan, *Salt Merchants of Tianjin*, is the most recent study of salt merchants. The Canton merchants are best known through studies of the opium trade at that port.

4. The exact way in which the northern grain trade was organized is not well documented, but the wholesale trade at Tianjin in the early nineteenth century has been studied. The rice trade in Guangdong Province was probably less restricted than in the north. Will, "Discussions," 358–59ff., finds evidence of "super-brokers" in the eighteenth century, authorized by the provincial authorities and enjoying a "*de facto* monopoly." Yet authorities at Foshan, a regional market for Guangdong and Guangxi, limited grain shop inventories to 100 and later 200 shi each. Marks, *Tigers*, 244–45. The rice trade at Wuhu, Anhui, 1877–1937, is described by Fan I-chun. And the rice trade at Hankow is discussed briefly in Rowe, *Hankow: Commerce and Society*, 54–55, 268, but does not figure as a major subject although it was the first or second most important commodity at this centrally located market.

5. Wu Chengming took a lead in this development. See below. Other scholars are too numerous to cite, but Wu Jianyong's work on Beijing, and Li Bozhong's work on the Lower Yangzi region are notable. The shift in historical interpretation followed the 1980s economic reforms in China.

6. This scholarship includes that of Yeh-chien Wang, Pierre-Étienne Will, R. Bin Wong, Peter C. Perdue, Timothy Brook, William Rowe, and Helen Dunstan—all of whose works have been previously discussed. In addition the work of James Lee and his associates on demographic history has stressed the rational aspects of family size limitation, especially in Fengtian Province. See Lee and Campbell, *Fate and Fortune*. Pomeranz, *Great Divergence*, and Wong, *China Transformed*, have emphasized that the high level of the Chinese economy in the Qing period compares favorably with that of Western Europe.

7. Skinner, "Marketing," 214–15.

8. Persson gives a succinct overview of these developments.

9. *Zhongguo zibenzhuyi yu guonei shichang.*

10. Y. C. Wang, "Food Supply and Grain Prices"; and Brandt, *Commercialization*.

11. Skinner, "Regional Urbanization," 217.

12. Ibid., 219; and Skinner, "Cities," 344.

13. Skinner, *City in Late Imperial China*, 13; and Skinner, "Cities," 298.

14. Skinner, "Regional Urbanization," 228, 233. In criticizing the concept of macroregions, Sands and Myers have argued that urbanization is an inappropriate standard to apply to an economy that was overwhelmingly rural.

15. Wong and Perdue, "Grain Markets," is one exception.

16. Wu Chengming, 265.

17. Rowe, *Hankow: Commerce and Society*, 68.

18. "Treaty Ports and China's Modernization."

19. This perspective resembles Philip Huang's view that markets in North China were not so important in the lives of peasants as villages, and that, even in the 1930s, villages were isolated from each other and relatively uncommercialized. He proposes that "instead of conceiving of an all-intrusive state, we need to think in terms of a two-tiered structure in which the state wielded power in the upper tier alone," Huang, *Peasant Economy . . . in North China*, 219–24. The results in this chapter suggest, on the contrary, that while villages may have been physically isolated, they were not impervious to either market or state influences.

20. Skinner's North China macroregion omits part of Chengde, considering it part of Manchuria, which he did not include within the eight macroregions.

21. Skinner, "Cities," 343, points out that Daming's inclusion in Zhili, rather than Henan and

Shandong, was an example of "high level gerrymandering" that broke the natural ties that Daming would have with the trading systems of Kaifeng or Dongchang-fu.

22. This model was developed and executed by Scott Hodges.

23. The price data were broken up into six periods based on a qualitative assessment of inflationary/ deflationary trends and were then detrended by removing the slope of a time trend regression line. The six periods used for detrending (and computing average harvest and price data) are: 1736–1804, 1805–13, 1814–55, 1856–77, 1878–95, and 1896–1910.

The same procedure was also applied to data from the concurrent year (before and after the harvest) and the following year (twelve months after the harvest), neither of which yielded results as strong as those obtained by using the preceding year. The logic of this seems clear. Prices of a particular grain anticipated the upcoming harvest based on known information about weather conditions visible to all. If drought conditions prevailed during the growing season, prices started to rise in anticipation of a poor harvest.

24. The first period represented the "golden age" for the granaries, *perhaps* accompanied by relatively weak commercialization. The second period witnessed the relative decline in the granary system and *perhaps* some increase in commercialization. The third period marked the opening of the treaty ports and *perhaps* greater commercialization. Data from a fourth period, 1896–1910, was omitted partly because of the political instability of the period, and in part because of the small size of the data pool, including only fourteen data points, thus making the estimates relatively imprecise.

25. QL 15/6/1, ZPZZ, CZCC 56:2244–46. Cited in Chapter 6 in this book.

26. QL 52/5/18, GZD 050965.

27. *Douhang jingji* at Tongzhou are discussed in a memorial concerning a case during the 1801 flood. JQ 6/10/11, GZD 006374. In another document from the same period, quoting the confession of Tongzhou merchant arrested for cheating on a government purchase, there is reference to five markets in Tongzhou that had five *douhang jingji*, who seemed to act as purchasing agents for the Tongzhou magistrate. JQ 6/9/29, *XYGZJS* 25:16b–18b.

28. Hamaguchi Nobuko, 137–39. Most of this very informative article describes the transformation of the late Qing *doudian* from a traditional institution to a modern company in the Republican period. In contrast to the sources cited by Hamaguchi, the Japanese gazetteer of Chinese provinces, *Shina shōbetsu zenshi* 18:973–76, traces the institution of *doudian* to Li Hongzhang, governor-general in the Guangxu period, not the Daoguang and Xianfeng periods, but it would appear to be wrong on the dates.

29. From the same memorial of Liu E, QL 52/5/18, GZD 050965.

30. *Qing XZ* 1931, 11:3b. This passage seems to refer to the previous decades, as well as to the present-day. It is very similar to a gazetteer entry from Cang County, cited below. Cang and Qing counties, both in Tianjin Prefecture, were adjacent to each other.

31. A rare exception is found in *Jingxing XZ* 1934, 11:34–35, which gives the rags-to-riches biography of a local grain merchant. He was not only successful but also virtuous and lenient to his debtors especially during famines. This example, however, is from the Republican period.

32. *Yongqing XZ* 1779/1813, 2:77b–78a. This county was extensively described in Chapter 3 in this book. The *yahang* were local merchants who purchased a license from local officials and served as tax-collecting agents and middlemen. According to Susan Mann's study of this institution, the Qing state used *yahang* as instruments of regulation rather than revenue. Because of complaints of abuse, in 1758 an imperial order limited the number of commodities requiring brokerage in Shuntian Prefecture. The purpose of brokerage was to keep prices stable and avoid undue competition. Mann, 41–49. On the functions of *yahang* in North China, see Xu Tan, 257–66.

33. *Xiong XZ* 1905, 9:1.

34. Ibid., 15:1–2.

35. In Luancheng xian, only 40 percent of the land was planted to grain crops, the rest to cotton; so there was dependence on outside grain merchants from Henan and Shanxi. Zhang Gang, 101.

36. *Xingtang XZ* 1763, 13:5. *Wuji xuzhi* 1893, 1:6. *Jinzhou zhi* 1925, 6:80–82, *Jin XZ liao* 1935, juan shang, jinrong zhi 2–3b.

37. *Lingshou XZ* 1686, 1:11; *Huailu XZ* 1881, 2:58b.

38. *Lingshou XZ* 1873, 2:11.

39. *Jingxing XZ* 1730, 2:22ab.

40. *Zunhua zhilizhou tongzhi* 1886, 15:2b–3a.

41. Zhang Gang, 101.

42. *Gaoyi XZ* 1799, 2:17a.

43. *Changli XZ* 1865, 10:3b. See Chapter 3 for descriptions of the passivity of the local people.

44. For example, *Hejian XZ* 1759, 3:4b; *Pingshan XZ* 1854, 1:38b; *Yongqing XZ* 1875, 13:8b.

45. "The custom of marketing and gathering results from the willingness of the merchants to travel around," *Tongzhou zhi*, quoted in *Jifu tongzhi*, 1884/1934, juan 71, 3015.

46. Many examples, including, *Hejian XZ* 1759, 1:36.

47. Skinner, "Marketing"; Rozman, *Population*; Yamane Yukio; Ishihara Jun.

48. For example, *Zaoqiang XZ* 1876, 1:15b–16.

49. *Nanpi XZ* 1888, juan 2, n.p.

50. *Shunyi XZ* 1719/1915, 1:10ab.

51. *Zaoqiang XZ* 1876, 1:15b–16.

52. *Yutian XZ* 1884, 5:1.

53. Jiang Shoupeng, 126–30.

54. *Xu Tianjin XZ* 1870, 16:59–60.

55. Ishihara Jun, table on 252, and maps on 253. Rozman, *Population*, tab. 5.2, pp. 105–6, also shows the increase in periodic markets, but he sharply disputes Ishihara's finding that population increased more than the number of markets, 122, while acknowledging the uncertainties in his own method of estimation, 104–10.

56. Skinner, "Marketing," 216.

57. A good description of routes is found in Kwan, "Merchant World," chap. 4. These, however, were not passable during the winter months. From Tianjin to Baoding, water transport was possible only in summer months. He Hanwei, 96, cites Li Hongzhang and others.

58. QL 27/6/27, ZPZZ, CZCC, 57:691–92.

59. This was observed by Li Hongzhang whose essay is found in *JFTZ* 10:555. The process of deterioration echoes the neglect of the Grand Canal and Yellow River conservancy in the same period, which had a depressing effect on the region at the juncture of Zhili, Shandong, and Henan. This process is described in detail by Pomeranz, *Making of a Hinterland*, chaps. 4 and 5.

60. Skinner, "Social Ecology," 9, has a good summary description. Also Rozman, *Urban Networks*, 151. *Shina shōbetsu zenshi,* vol. 18, has pull-out map showing these routes and actual and projected railroad lines as of that date.

61. Mayers, Dennys, and King, 484.

62. Ibid., 487. The authors recommended ponies or mules if they could be found.

63. A. Smith, *Village Life*, 36–38.

64. *Cang XZ* 1933, 12:4a.

65. *Tianjin FZ* 1898, 29:28a, gives this information, among other places.

66. QL 18/10/24, *Fang Kemin*, juan 5, in 2:633–40.

67. JQ 22/10/17, ZPZZ, NZZJ 0079 gives the rate by land as 1 qian per shi per 100 li, while water costs 1 fen 5 li, as does Tianjin *FZ*, cited above.

68. QL 19/11/19, *GZDQLC* 10:111.

69. QL 19/9/12, *GZDQLC* 9:546–48.

70. JQ 5/3, *BCSX* 273, Renzong, 56:12a–13a, cited in Chapter 6 in this book.

71. Within a few years of the opening of the first railway, from Beijing to Hankou, in 1905, rail transport quickly displaced water transport. In 1912, 53 percent of the value of goods transported between Tianjin and the hinterland was carried by rail and 44 percent by river; in 1921, the figures were 70.5 percent and 25.5 percent, respectively. "The various inland waterways converging at Tientsin are small and narrow, and the carriage of goods to and from Tientsin and the hinterland by water has entailed slow and uncertain transit, and frequently numerous transshipments," Arnold, 530.

72. See Chapter 6 in this book.

73. Guo Songyi, 97. He stresses the importance of Fengtian grain for Zhili, 103.

74. QL 50/10/19, ZPZZ, CZCC 57:3104–7.

75. JQ 15/6/9, ZPZZ, CZCC 58:1351–53. This memorial is also cited in Chapter 6, above. The figures presumably referred to unhusked grain (*gu*).

76. "Cereal Trade in Tientsin," 106.

77. During 1863–65 the severe rice shortage in South China was exacerbated by poor harvests in Siam, which had been exporting significant quantities of rice to China. Supplies from Burma were substituted. Latham and Neal, 261.

78. JQ 10/7/9, ZPZZ, NZZJ 0072, Cat. 359–4–75.

79. Xu Tan, 312–16. As cited in the previous chapter, this historian estimates that Shandong exported 1–2 million shi of grain annually to Zhili and an additional 1–2 million shi of beans. In turn Shandong imported 2–3 million shi from the Jiangnan region, Henan, and Liaodong, Xu Tan, 325.

80. Brandt, *Commercialization*, esp. chap. 3.

81. Latham and Neal; Coclanis.

82. Murphey, 60–61.

83. Kwan's work has shown the extent to which trade between Zhili and Manchuria and Mongolia flourished even as internal transport in Zhili was sometimes blocked. Kwan, "Merchant World," chap. 4. Kwan, "Mapping," argues that both Skinner and Murphey assume a neoclassical model with no obstacles to trade, while in fact Tianjin's marketing network was highly asymmetrical. This quotation is from 193. Historians of South China have identified three different forms of marketing: "plate," "dendritic," and "necklace." Marks, *Tigers*, 190–93.

Chapter Eight

1. The rules and supporting regulations were reprinted verbatim in *Baoding FZ* 1881, 25:1–10.

2. Will, *Bureaucracy*, 188–89. First published in French in 1980, *Bureaucracy and Famine* was the first to draw attention to the Qing famine relief efforts and the state granary system. It took Fang's *Zhenji* as its principal source, but it also drew on the entire range of famine relief literature. My debt to this book and Will's other work, already clear in previous chapters, is especially great in this chapter.

3. The corpus of famine relief literature is quite extensive. Will, *Bureaucracy*, 7–17, and elsewhere, provides another overview. Wong and Perdue have a useful discussion and an annotated bibliography.

4. Will, *Bureaucracy*, 10.

5. Ibid., 9. Wang Zhiyi's *Huangzheng jiyao* invokes the precedents and texts of earlier times.

6. J. Smith, "Chinese Philanthropy," 136–37.

7. Ibid., 142–43.

8. Will, *Bureaucracy*, 141–42.

9. *HCJSWB* 41:57ab. See Dunstan, *Conflicting*, 109ff., 128–33. She finds that Yang's positive view of private wealth was rather unusual.

10. *HCJSWB* 41:1a–3b.

11. Will, *Bureaucracy*, 9ff.

12. This process is described extensively in Will, chap. 6.

13. *HBZL* 84:10–12.

14. These terms are not used in the *HBZL*, but are frequently employed in the memorials concerning famine investigation.

15. *Zhenji* 2:18a. The text says *niu*, or oxen, but in North China donkeys or mules were more numerous for farm work. See Buck, *Chinese Farm Economy*, 218.

16. Will, *Bureaucracy*, 97–102.

17. For example, households classified as "less poor" received relief only for children and elderly, but not for adults. Ibid., 121.

18. Will, *Bureaucracy*, 89–90.

19. *Zhenji*, juan 8, preface 1a.

20. KX 54/11/20, *GZDKXC* 5:853–56.

21. KX 55/2/13, *GZDKXC* 6:91–93.

22. YZ 3/7/29, *GZDYZC* 4:760.

23. YZ 10/5/20, *GZDYZC* 19:749–51.

24. Will, *Bureaucracy*, 92, 125.

25. Ibid., 108.

26. Ibid., 122.

27. Ibid., 129–30, translates *dazhen*, literally, as "grand relief." *Zhenji* 2:5.

28. Will, *Bureaucracy*, 127–30.

29. *HBZL* 90:10–12.

30. *HBZL* 84:10–22. *Zhenji* 3:1a.

31. According to statutes of QL 3, the rate for commutation to silver was 0.155 qian for each *dou* of *mi*; thus each 5 he of *mi* was commuted to 7 li 5 hao, equivalent to 6.5 wen cash, zhiqian. *Zhenji* 2:5b.

32. *Zhenji* 2:8b–9a. *HBZL* 84:15a states that in Zhili Province the conversion rate for the poor people, *pinmin*, was 1 shi = 1.2 taels, and for poor "students," *pinsheng*, 1 shi = 1 tael. *Pinsheng* refers to poor holders of the *shengyuan* degree who were busy studying for higher-level exams.

33. The rations for relief in *Huangzheng jiyao*, 8:5a, compiled by Wang Zhiyi (1806), who had served as Jiangsu governor, were: in giving out *mi* and *dou* (rice and beans), each adult should get 1 sheng, each child under thirteen should get 5 he, and children under three are not on the schedule. Everything should be calculated clearly on the tally; it is not permitted to calculate it on the spot.

34. *HBZL* 84:10–22. The date of these regulations is not clear. The term *dazhen* is not used. Will, *Bureaucracy*, 128, cites from the *HDSL* the same regulations except that in the localities with a 50 percent loss, the very poor households were not required to pay back their loans, while the less poor needed to repay their loans.

35. *Zhenji* 2:18a.

36. *Zhenji* 2:18ab.

37. *Zhenji* 2:9–10; Will, *Bureaucracy*, 250–53.

38. JQ 14/11/24, ZPZZ, NZZJ 0076.

39. *Zhenji* 2:8ab.

40. These limits were needed because "poor students," *pinsheng*, sometimes misrepresented their household size in order to get more rations. *Zhenji* 2:60a–63a. Will, *Bureaucracy*, 136.

41. Early examples date from the Han period. Deng Yunte 1978, 290–92.

42. QL 22/5/13, ZPZZ, NZZJ 0045. The rate of 0.60 taels per shi of *gu* would be equivalent to the 1.20 taels per shi of *mi*, cited above.

43. JQ 4/12/14, ZPZZ, NZZJ, Box 67.

44. *XYGZJS* 15:25–26a.

45. JQ 6/8/22, GZD 005924.

46. *BCSX*, Renzong, 54:42b–43a.

47. JQ 25/1/10, and JQ 25/7/28, both in ZPZZ, NZZJ, juan 5.

48. XF 7/8, *Shichao shengxun*, Wenzong, 105:5ab.

49. JQ 17/11/16, ZPZZ, NZZJ 0077; emphasis added. 10 dou = 1 shi.

50. JQ 23/1/26, and JQ 24/11/12, ZPZZ, NZZJ 0081.

51. On the not very clear distinction between charity and philanthropy as applied to Chinese society, see J. Smith, "Social Hierarchy," 419–20. On the equally unclear distinction between Buddhist and Confucian motives, see J. Smith, "Chinese Philanthropy," 148–51: "The tradition of famine relief cannot . . . be reduced to a particular system of belief."

52. *HBZL* 84:18–19.

53. Will, *Bureaucracy*, 139–43.

54. KX 45/10/29, *GZDKXC* 1:343.

55. QL 18/2/19, *Fang Kemin*, 2:595–615. These recommendations were the same as those for grain distributions.

56. JQ 24/8/6, and JQ 24/9/22, in ZPZZ, NZZJ 0081. See also Chapters 5 and 9 in this book.

57. *HCJSWB* 41:19b.

58. *HCJSWB* 41:22b.

59. *HCJSWB* 41:7a–9b. The other three evil practices were persuading people to share grain, suppressing prices, and prohibiting sales.

60. *HCJSWB* 42:16–17.

61. *HBZL* 16:16–17.

62. Fang Guancheng citing the regulations of QL 7 [1742]. QL 25/3/17, ZPZZ, CZCC 57:253–54. He invoked the same regulations in 1763. QL 28/2/8, *GZDQLC* 16:784–85.

63. JQ 16/2/4, ZPZZ, NZZJ 0076.

64. JQ 19/5/7, ZPZZ, NZZJ, juan 5; emphasis added.

65. No date, but Xu was dismissed from office in QL 16. ZPZZ, NZZJ 0065.

66. Tang Menglai, *HCJSWB* 42:11–14.

67. *HBZL* 16:16–17.

68. Examples above, and QL 25/3/17, ZPZZ, CZCC 57:253–54.

69. Will, *Bureaucracy*, 182–89.

70. *HBZL*, juan 83–84.

71. *HBZL* 84:3a.

72. *HBZL* 83:1–12. Jing Junjian, 67–68.

73. *HBZL* 83:38a.

74. *HBZL* 83:40ab.

75. See Chapter 2 in this book for discussion of Wen'an's peculiar characteristics.

76. *HBZL* 84:1.

77. *HBZL* 83:49–51. These totals seem to be different from the general amnesty declared a year later, as described above.

78. *HBZL* 83:53ab.

79. *HBZL* 83:55b–58.

80. *HBZL* 83:58b.

81. *HBZL* 83:60

82. *HBZL* 83:63.

83. *HBZL* 84:4–9. Will, *Bureaucracy*, 245, tab. 18, indicates these rules were the same in 1728.

84. *BCSX*, Renzong, 54:5ab.

85. JQ 21/8/17, ZPZZ, NZZJ 0081.

86. *(Xu) Yongqing XZ* 1874, 1:5a–13a. *Sanhe xian xinzhi* 1935:11–14 has a full record of tax remissions for that county.

87. *HBZL* 84:3b–4a.

88. *HBZL* 84:4–9.

89. QL 4/5/4, ZPZZ/Caizheng. Archive microfilm 1:804–820. Also discussed in Chapter 3 in this book. The tax remission was discussed in QL 4/4/5, ibid., 1:730–31.

90. *HCJSWB* 44:2a–3b. Also discussed in Will, *Bureaucracy*, 242.

91. Jing Junjian, 69.

92. QL 13/8/24, JJD 002873.

93. Jing Junjian, 76–79.

94. Will, *Bureaucracy*, 38.

95. Perdue, "Liu-min," 19–26.

96. Will, *Bureaucracy*, 230–32.

97. QL 19/12/11, *GZDQLC* 10:274–75. Assuming a normal exchange rate, then 20 wen cash might be equivalent to 2 fen of silver, but in this period cash was more expensive than the normal rate. See Chapter 4 in this book.

98. QL 24/#6/29, Fang Guancheng memorial, reprinted in *Baoding FZ* 1886, 38:14b–15a. Zhou Yuanli said Fang started the tradition. Ibid., 38:3ab.

99. *Baoding FZ* 1886, 38:1–15, lists charitable institutions in every county in Baoding Prefecture, including *liuyangju* or *liuyangyuan*.

100. *Zhengding FZ* 1762, 14:29b–36.

101. *Wangdu XZ* 1934, 5:58–60. Also found in 1904 ed., 3:71ab.

102. Liang Qizi, 103.

103. *HBZL* 90:1–7a.

104. *HBZL* 90:8–12.

105. Liang Qizi, 259–84.

106. Discussed in *BCSX*, Renzong, 52:21b.

107. *HDSL*, juan 1018.

108. *Jifu tongzhi* 1884/1934, 109:1–15a has list of shelters in each county and how many were aided in 1808.

109. See *Yongqing XZ* 1874, for illustration of *yangjiyuan*, divided into men's and women's quarters, and offices.

110. *HBZL* 90:17–22 gives information for different counties in Zhili.

111. *HBZL* 90:15–16.

112. The term she uses is *guanliaohua*. Liang Qizi, chap. 4. Also discussed in Rowe, *Saving*, 368–69.

113. Liang Qizi, 129.

114. Will, *Bureaucracy*, 25–27.

115. Ibid., 229–30.

116. Ibid., 103–8.

117. *Zhenji* 2:6a. A sample is presented at 2:52ab.

118. Will, *Bureaucracy*, 118, tab. 2. These procedures are summarized in *Baoding FZ* 1881, 25:1–10.

119. *Zhenji* 2:5b, 4:1b.

120. Will, *Bureaucracy*, 153–75, documents and maps these distributions; also see append. A.

121. Will, *Bureaucracy*, 170, tab. 9.

122. *Zhenji* 2:2b.

123. *Zhenji* 3:16a.

124. Final reports submitted by each county are in *Zhenji*, juan 8.

125. These principles had been enunciated as early as QL 2. *Zhenji* 2:6, 3:1a–6.

126. Will, *Bureaucracy*, 41.

127. *Zhenji* 5:22b–23a. At the outset of the crisis in the sixth month, an imperial edict ordered all governors-general to take steps to shelter or aid famine refugees from neighboring provinces and to be vigilant against bandits who might take advantage of the situation. *Zhenji* 1:2a–3a.

128. *Zhenji* 5:43, 5:54a.

129. Will, *Bureaucracy*, 234–35.

130. *Zhenji* 5:40–43b.

131. *Zhenji* 3:16b.

132. *Zhenji* 6:7ab, 6:10a–11b.

133. Will, *Bureaucracy*, 117–18, calculates that each investigator would have had to visit 50–150 households per day, a pace that could not possibly have been met.

134. *Zhenji*, juan 8, preface 1a.

135. Will, *Bureaucracy*, 171, tab. 10.

136. *Zhenji* 1:5a, 2:2b.

137. *Baoding FZ* 1881, 25:1–10.

138. *Zhenji* 3:16a.

139. *HHLY* 585–87, has found at least thirty-six different local gazetteers mentioning this phenomenon.

140. *HHLY* 587–90.

141. Data available on request.

142. *HHLY* 591–93, records good harvests in some localities; one or two counties at most recorded hunger or disease.

143. QL 12/8/22, in *QDHH* 108.

144. Harvest ratings for Baoding and four other localities.

145. *HHLY* 604–8.

146. QL 24/6/4, ZPZZ, NZZJ 0048.

147. *Dingxing XZ* 1779, 12:6ab.

148. QL 24/#6/17, ZPZZ, NZZJ 0048.

149. QL 24/9/7, ZPZZ, NZZJ 0048.

150. Ample documentation for the various rivers that flooded in 1759 is found in the archive section ZPZZ SL, various memorials by Fang Guancheng. Also *QDHH* 144–51.

151. Perdue, "Qing State and Gansu Grain Market," 114, fig. 3.2.

152. *Zhongguo jin wubainian*, 150.

153. Perdue, "Qing State," 103, 111–13. Relief to Gansu and Shaanxi in 1759 included tax remissions, grain, and silver. *Shichao shengxun*, Gaozong, 144:7a–10a.

154. There is no extant record of granary holdings between 1757–62. See Table 6.1 in this book.

155. QL 33/2/21, GZD 024298. Fang Guancheng's 1768 memorial reviews the famine relief measures taken since QL 27.

156. *Jifu tongzhi* 1884/1934, juan 108, 4301.

157. *Dingxing XZ* 1779, 12:6b.

158. *HHLY* 608–13.

159. QL 27/12/1 and 27/12/7, ZPZZ, NZZJ 0051.

160. QL 33/2/21, GZD 024298.

161. QL 27/2/1, ZPZZ, NZZJ 0051.

162. QL 27/11/11, ZPZZ, NZZJ 0051.

163. See n. 62 above.

164. See Chapter 2 in this book. Many references to labor relief include QL 27/4/6, ZPZZ, NZZJ 0051.

165. QL 28/3 in *JFTZ* 1:133. QL 28/4, *GZDQLC* 17:345–50. Earlier, in a memorial of the second month, he reported 800,000 taels authorized by the Board of Revenue, including Guangping and Daming. QL 28/2/24, ibid., 49–50.

166. QL 28/2, in *JFTZ* 1:130. Also QL 28/1/16, *Fang Kemin*, 2:1025–29.

167. QL 28/4/21, *GZDQLC* 17:516–17. Also *Fang Kemin*, 2:1057–61, QL 28/2/24. Fang Guancheng encouraged the regular commerce of Fengtian grain in Zhili, seeing clearly that it was plentiful and cheap and would therefore help Zhili's food supply. In a memorial of the eleventh month of 1763, he said that millet and sorghum in particular should be shipped since they were staple food products, whereas sesame, hemp seed, and other products were merely luxuries. QL 28/11/2, *GZDQLC* 19:476–78.

168. QL 28/12/11, *GZDQLC* 20:6–8. These figures represent the actual holdings. The total theoretical holdings of the ever-normal granaries were 4.5 million shi.

169. QL 32/12/12, GZD 023616.

170. QL 28/1/16, *Fang Kemin*, 2:1025.

171. QL 28/2/24, *GZDQLC* 17:49–50.

172. QL 28/4/n.d., *GZDQLC* 17:348–50.

173. QL 28/5/27, *GZDQLC* 17:830.

174. QL 28/5/4, *GZDQLC* 17:623.

175. QL 39/7/17, GZD 029339.

176. QL 39/9/5, GZD 029770. QL 39/9/11, GZD 029850. QL 39/10/16, GZD 030307.

177. QL 40/10, *JFTZ* 1:171.

178. *Jifu tongzhi* 1884, juan 108, 4304.

179. L. M. Li, "Using Grain Prices," 491.

180. Chapter 4 in this book; Appleby, "Grain Prices," 882.

181. Will, *Bureaucracy*, 152.

182. These are totals calculated from *Jifu tongzhi, Da Qing huidian*, and other standards sources by Wang Shulin, 213–15.

183. Will, *Bureaucracy*, 292–301, esp. tab. 20.

184. Li Xiangjun, 79.

185. Ibid., 76–79. There are many assumptions made in this estimate, and the author admits they may be on the high side because he assumes the 12 percent rate of 1766 was the norm, whereas it is more likely that it represented a high point in spending on relief.

186. QL 28/3, *JFTZ* 1:131–32. See also Chapter 2.

187. Usiar and Yang.

188. In 1790 the governor-general's year-end report stated that fifty-three counties should be relieved, but did not indicate that they received relief. QL 55/12/8, in *QDHH* 233. Other references for QL 59, *QDHH* 247–48.

Chapter Nine

1. *Tangshan XZ* 1881, 3:5a.

2. Enclosure in memorial of JQ 6/6/19, *QDHH* 268–71.

3. See Chapter 2 in this book. The Jiaqing emperor was generally strict toward even high officials, including the grand councilors. Bartlett, 242–45. This forms the context for his extreme watchfulness

in the 1801 relief campaign, for example, holding officials personally and financially responsible for past negligence in river work.

4. *XYGZJS* 18:11–12, 29:7–8, and 36:17–18.

5. JQ 7/2/27, *XYGZJS* 31:11a–15b. See Chapter 2 in this book for river expenditures.

6. See Chapter 8 in this book.

7. JQ 6/6/8, GZD 005925.

8. JQ 6/6/17, ZPZZ, NZZJ 0069.

9. *XYGZJS* 6:14b–15a, and 18:11a–12b.

10. JQ 6/8/6, *XYGZJS* 18:11a–16b. See also juan 35–36, JQ 7/4/12.

11. JQ 6/8/24, *XYGZJS* 21:4ab.

12. JQ 6/9/24, *QDHH* 277–83.

13. JQ 6/11/21, *XYGZJS* 28:21–24.

14. JQ 6/12/2, GZD 006858. Map 9.1 in this book is based on this memorial.

15. JQ 6/12/11, GZD 006964. Also JQ 6/11/26, GZD 006770. This incident was also reported in the tenth and eleventh months in *XYGZJS*, juan 27–28.

16. See Chapter 5 in this book.

17. *XYGZJS* 12:15ff. and 15:8ff.

18. JQ 7/2/14, *XYGZJS* 30:15a–16a.

19. JQ 7/2/29, *XYGZJS* 31:12a–15.

20. JQ 7/4/17, *XYGZJS* 36:6a–7b, 36:4ab.

21. *XYGZJS* 10:8b–14a, 14:10b–11a, and 15:3aff. Also 27:11b. See also *QDHH* 258.

22. *XYGZJS* 34:15–16. Also juan 15–16.

23. *XYGZJS*, juan 29–32, tabulated from various memorials.

24. JQ 7/2/25, GZD 007485.

25. *XYGZJS* 34:19–20, 35:5ab.

26. JQ 7/4/2, *XYGZJS* 35:3ab.

27. JQ 7/5/2, *XYGZJS* 37:1.

28. *XYGZJS* 26:9–10.

29. *XYGZJS*, juan 5–6 [6/19], 15–16 [7/20], and 34:23–25.

30. JQ 7/7/26, GZD 008581.

31. *Jifu tongzhi* 1884/1934, juan 108, has a complete record.

32. JQ 8/3/5, ZPZZ, NZZJ 0070. Emphasis added.

33. *XYGZJS* 27:17b and 28:18a.

34. *XYGZJS*, juan 19–20.

35. *XYGZJS* 28:7a–20b.

36. JQ 6/11/26, GZD 006770.

37. JQ 6/7/16, GZD 005593.

38. JQ 6/7/7, GZD 005529.

39. JQ 6/7/20, GZD 005630.

40. JQ 6/8/6, GZD 006004–1.

41. *XYGZJS* 26:16–17, 28:13ff., and 37:15–27, for examples.

42. *XYGZJS*, juan 19–20.

43. *XYGZJS* 28:19a–20b.

44. JQ 6/10/11, GZD 006374.

45. *XYGZJS* 21:10–12, 23:21a–23a.

46. JQ 8/9/4, ZPZZ, CZTF 2:2412–14.

47. JQ 8/n.d., ZPZZ, NZZJ 0070.

48. JQ 8/10/16, ZPZZ, NZZJ 0070.

49. JQ 10/7/9, ZPZZ, NZZJ 0072.

50. JQ 11/3/25, ZPZZ, CZTF 2:2843–46.

51. *HHLY* 649–55.

52. JQ 18/9/1, and JQ 18/n.d., ZPZZ, NZZJ 0077.

53. Ibid.

54. JQ 18/9/1, ZPZZ, NZZJ 0077.

55. JQ 18/n.d., *CYQS* 71:44b–45.

56. JQ 18/12/n.d., ZPZZ, NZZJ, juan 5.

57. In another memorial, 200,000 shi of *fengmi* had been set aside for soup kitchens. JQ 18/n.d., ZPZZ, NZZJ 0077.

58. JQ 18/12/12, ZPZZ, NZZJ 0077.

59. JQ 18/12/n.d., ZPZZ, NZZJ, juan 5.

60. JQ 19/11/23, GZD 016996. Map 9.2 in this book is based on this memorial.

61. Naquin, *Millenarian Rebellion*, 243–45.

62. Ibid., 203, 208. Nayancheng, appointed Zhili governor-general in 1814, had previously been active in suppression of the White Lotus rebels in the northwest. He had just successfully overseen a major famine relief campaign in Gansu Province; his account of that experience bears the same title as Fang Guancheng's model *Zhenji*. His career is described in Hummel, 584–87.

63. JQ 19/5/7, ZPZZ, NZZJ, juan 5.

64. See Chapter 5 in this book.

65. JQ 19/3/10 to 4/15, Nayancheng, 45:1–8.

66. JQ 19/1/5, ZPZZ, NZZJ, juan 5.

67. JQ 19/2/12, ZPZZ, NZZJ 0078.

68. JQ 17/1/25, ZPZZ, NZZJ 0075.

69. JQ 17/4, *BCSX*, Renzong, 54:13b–14b.

70. JQ 18/n.d., ZPZZ, NZZJ 0077. Another undated memorial from the same place speaks of the landless and jobless poor, as well as the homeless and orphans, and so forth.

71. In the 1810s high quality land in a good year was worth 10,000 cash per mu, but only 1,000 cash in bad years. Low quality land in a good year was worth 3,000–4,000 cash per mu, but only 300–400 in a bad year. Naquin, *Millenarian Rebellion*, append. 3, 281, based on Nayancheng's memorials.

72. JQ 19/9/8, ZPZZ, NZZJ 0078. Another edict stated land should be sold back to peasants at its original price, that is, no one should make a profit. This seems to contradict the first statement. JQ 19/n.d., *JFTZ* 1:296.

73. *HHLY* 666–70.

74. *Jingxing XZ*, in *HHLY* 669.

75. *HHLY* 669. Nayancheng reported pestilence, *yi*, around Baoding and in the southern part of the province. He requested and received medicines from the court, documented by the ounce in his memorial. JQ 19/5/26, Nayancheng, 44:41b–43b.

76. *HHLY* 672–74.

77. JQ 22/12/19, ZPZZ, NZZJ 0079.

78. JQ 19/8, *BCSX*, Renzong, 54:23ab. JQ 19/12/17, GZD 017266.

79. JQ 19/5/7, ZPZZ, NZZJ, juan 5.

80. JQ 19/11/23, GZD 016996.

81. JQ 19/4/1, Nayancheng, 44:8b–10b.

82. JQ 22/10/17, ZPZZ, NZZJ 0079. In this period, increasing pressure was placed on local leaders, salt merchants, as well as officials to contribute funds for relief. In Zhili officials had contributed more than 60,000 taels from the *yanglian* part of their income.

83. JQ 24/8/6, and JQ 24/9/22, ZPZZ, NZZJ 0081.

84. JQ 24/8/11, ZPZZ, NZZJ 0081.

85. JQ 24/8/17, ZPZZ, NZZJ 0081. It is not clear whether this was intended to be a one-time dispensation, or per month.

86. DG 2/10/4, ZPZZ, CZTF 3:2701–7. *QDHH* 369–93.

87. *QDHH* 380.

88. *QDHH* 391–92.

89. DG 3/7, *BCSX*, Xuanzong, 47:19ab.

90. DG 3/2, *BCSX*, Xuanzong, 47:10b–11a.

91. DG 4/#7 and DG 6/5, *BCSX*, Xuanzong, 47:32ab and 34a–35a. Another case is found in DG 4/1, *BCSX*, Xuanzong, 50:6b–7.

92. DG 2/1/29, ZPZZ, CZCC, Box 505.

93. DG 3/8/8, ZPZZ, NZZJ 0082.

94. DG 3/8, *JFTZ* 1:318–19.

95. DG 4/3, *JFTZ* 1:325.

96. DG 3/8, *JFTZ* 1:320. See also Chapter 2 above.

97. DG 4/2, *BCSX*, Xuanzong, 47:28ab.

98. DG 3/7, *BCSX*, Xuanzong, 47:16a.

99. DG 3/7, *BCSX*, Xuanzong, 47:17a–18a.

100. DG 3/2, *BCSX*, Xuanzong, 47:10b–11a.

101. DG 3/8, *BCSX*, Xuanzong, 47:20–23. At the same time Jiangnan had a flood and was instructed to get grain from Hubei and Hankou where the price was stable.

102. DG 4/2, *BCSX*, Xuanzong, 47:28ab.

103. DG 3/8, *JFTZ* 1:310.

104. These gazetteer citations are collected in *HHLY* 680–82.

105. *HHLY* 682–88.

106. Huang Jianhua documents the natural disasters of the Daoguang period.

107. DG 3/10, *BCSX*, Xuanzong, 47:25a.

108. *HHLY* 700–6. *QDHH* 414–29.

109. Will, "Problem of Official Corruption."

110. JQ 14/7, *JFTZ* 1:260–61.

111. JQ 14/9/22, GZD 015452.

112. JQ 19/8, *BCSX*, Renzong, 54:23a–24a

113. DG 6/10, *BCSX*, Xuanzong, 47:36.

114. JQ 17/1/25, ZPZZ, Falu tanwu, juan 53.

115. DG 2/1, *BCSX*, Xuanzong, 47:4b–5b, and also DG 2/7, ibid., 6b–7b. The Jiaqing emperor even suspected falsification in giving rewards to famine relief contributors. JQ 19/5/29, ZPZZ, NZZJ 0078.

116. JQ 24/#4/1, ZPZZ, Falu tanwu, juan 49. Also JQ 24/#4/10, ibid.

117. DG 1/4, *BCSX*, Xuanzong, 47:3.

118. DG 3/8, *BCSX*, Xuanzong, 47:21ab.

119. DG 2/10/4, ZPZZ, CZTF 3:2701–7.

120. JQ 15/11/14, ZPZZ, NZZJ 0075.

121. DG 2/11, *BCSX*, Xuanzong, 47:7b–8b.

122. DG 3/8/20, ZPZZ, NZZJ 0082.

123. Wang Jiange, 106. Prices in cash were likely very high, but exchange rate data is missing for this period. See Figure 4.9a in this book.

124. Naquin, *Peking*, 656–59.

125. King, 144–51.

126. Peng Xinwei, 744. See Chapter 4 in this book.

127. *Beijing tongshi* 8:35–36. King, 152. Peng Xinwei, 743–44.

128. *Cang XZ* 1933, 12:4a gives an interesting account.

129. Peng Xinwei, 743.

130. H. Hinton, 31–33. A picul was 1 dan, a measure of weight, but here probably means shi, a measure of volume.

131. Rennie, 1:268–69. See also Chapter 4 above.

132. Rennie, 1:319, 329, 337.

133. "During the last five years of the reign of Hsien Feng, 1857–1861, there was a 20 percent increase in the exchange rate. It is rather surprising that the Ting Hsien rate was not more seriously affected, for there was serious inflation in Peking," Gamble, *Ting Hsien*, 247–49.

134. See discussion in Chapter 4 in this book.

135. *HHLY* 707–13; and Figure 4.6 in this book.

136. *Zhongguo jinwubainian*, 195. See also the data for Figure 7.4 in this book.

137. Peng Xinwei, 741, 744–45.

138. TZ 9/11/4, JJD 104527.

139. TZ 10/9/7, JJD 109345.

140. TZ 10/11/26, JJD 110267 and 110271.

141. TZ 11/12/19, *QDHH* 469–70.

142. TZ 12/10/12, *QDHH* 474–75.

143. TZ 12/8/3, ZPZZ, NZZJ 0085.

144. TZ 9/10/29, JJD 103821. See also memorials of TZ 9/12/19, JJD 105275, and TZ 10/11/26, JJD 110271. The term *fuxu* was not new; it had been used by the Jiaqing emperor in a rescript in 1801, JQ 6/7/10, GZD 005554, and see above.

145. TZ 10/11/1, ZPZZ, NZZJ 0085.

146. TZ 9/9/26, JJD 109679.

147. TZ 12/9/16, JJD 111585.

148. TZ 10/9/24, JJD 109678. On Hu, see Rankin, 153.

149. TZ 10/10/19, JJD 110006.

150. TZ 12/7/21, ZPZZ, NZZJ 0085. Also found in JJD 110842.

151. Davis, *Late Victorian Holocausts*, shows that the late nineteenth century saw devastating droughts also in India, Egypt, Brazil, and many other places in Asia and Africa, which he attributes to El Niño-Southern Oscillation (ENSO), a phenomenon that has attracted scientific attention in the late twentieth century. "After the cycle of seasons itself, ENSO is the most important source of global climate variability," 239.

152. *Report of Committee of the China Famine Relief Fund*, 9; Bohr, 113. The figure 9.5 million was the estimate of the *Report*; other estimates by Western observers were as high as 17 million. *Zhongguo jindai shi da zaihuang*, 98. He Hanwei, 121. The 2.5 million figure for Zhili may be too high; the drought was felt mainly in the southern part of the province, and relief did reach this area. Compare Cao Shuji, 5:688.

153. *Report*, 3.

154. Ibid., 3, 10.

155. He Hanwei, 35.

156. Edgerton-Tarpley, "Family and Gender," traces the gender differences in the social consequences of famine.

157. *Report*, 7–9.

158. He Hanwei, 33.

159. Gazetteers cited in *HHLY* 764–72.

160. *Great Famine*, 6–7.

161. Ibid., 46–47. He Hanwei, 15–30, gives scattered examples of prices.

162. No cannibalism was reported in Hejian-fu, Tianjin, or Tongzhou. *Great Famine*, 105–7.

163. Ibid., 66.

164. Ibid., 101.

165. *Tangshan XZ* 1881, 5:2b.

166. Ten dou = 1 shi. This may be a stock phrase.

167. *Tangshan XZ* 1881, 3:8ab.

168. He Hanwei, 33.

169. *Report*, 4.

170. He Hanwei, 48, 74–75, 53–54, 67.

171. Edgerton-Tarpley, "Narratives of Blame"; Janku, "Integrating."

172. He Hanwei, 45–46.

173. Ibid., 49–52, tab. 13, shows the expenses for Beijing *pingtiao* during the first eight months of 1878. Eighty-seven thousand shi of grain were sold, costing 300,000 taels and selling for 225,000, with net subsidized cost of 75,000 taels.

174. *Report*, 3.

175. He Hanwei, 51–52.

176. Bohr, 65–70.

177. He Hanwei, 87–110.
178. *Lingyu XZ* 1929, 8:22b–23.
179. *Report*, 3.
180. *Great Famine*, 21.
181. Ibid., 25.
182. He Hanwei, 69.
183. Ibid., 76, and chap. 4, which gives an overview of the fund-raising effort.
184. Bohr, 56.
185. Ibid., 94–98.
186. Preface, *Famine in China.*
187. Bohr, 94–113.
188. Ibid., 114.
189. Ibid., 119.
190. GX 16/6/9, ZPZZ, NZZJ 0090.
191. GX 16/6/15, ZPZZ, NZZJ 0090.
192. GX 16/7/2, ZPZZ, NZZJ 0090.
193. GX 16/12/19, ZPZZ, NZZJ 0090.
194. List of contributions, GX 16/12/19, ZPZZ, NZZJ 0090.
195. GX 17/2/7, ZPZZ, NZZJ 0091.
196. GX 18/#6/6, and GX 18/#6/20, ZPZZ, NZZJ 0091.
197. GX 18/12/12, ZPZZ, NZZJ 0091. The same information is excerpted in *QDHH* 564ff.
198. GX 19/6/19, ZPZZ, NZZJ 0092.
199. GX 19/9/12, in ZPZZ, NZZJ 0092
200. GX 20/9/3, ZPZZ, NZZJ 0093.
201. GX 20/12/11, ZPZZ, NZZJ 0093.
202. GX 21/12/23, ZPZZ, NZZJ 0094.
203. GX 21/9/14, ZPZZ, NZZJ 0094.
204. GX 23/8/28, JJD 141505 plus enclosure.
205. For example, reports in GX 29/2/25, JJD 154426, and GX 34/12/16, JJD 169090.
206. Rankin, 142–47.
207. Bohr, 40, based in part on an unpublished paper by Ts'ui-jung Liu, "Private Famine Relief Efforts from South China, 1876–1879."
208. *Jifu tongzhi* 1884, 109:15b.
209. Rogaski, "Beyond Benevolence," 54–55. On the origins of *shantang*, see J. Smith, "Benevolent Societies." On benevolent societies at Hankow, see Rowe, *Hankow: Community and Conflict*, 105–8.
210. Rogaski, "Beyond Benevolence," 68.
211. Naquin, *Peking*, 662–64.
212. Ibid., 667–70.
213. *Yongnian XZ* 1877, 5:6–7b.
214. [*Xu*] *Yongqing XZ* 1874, 19ab, with illustrations.
215. *Luanzhou zhi*, 1898, 10:55–59. The most interesting rules of management are appended. *Luancheng XZ* 1872, 5:6b–8, also has rules for operation of *liuyangju*. *Kaizhou zhi* 1882, 2:6b–7, shows similar initiatives in the Daoguang, Xianfeng, and Tongzhi periods.
216. *Tianjin FZ* 1898, 7:20b–21b. Also *Wangdu XZ* 1934, 5:58–60.
217. *Dong'guang XZ* 1888, 5:2ab.
218. *Wen'an XZ* 1922, 6:1–3.
219. C. A. Stanley, Tientsin, Nov. 29, 1890, ABCFM, 21/295.
220. E. E. Aiken, Tientsin, Feb. 16–Mar. 4, 1893, ABCFM 17/46.
221. Chi Zihua and Li Hongying provide quantitative and qualitative documentation.
222. Chi and Li, 77–82.
223. Report of Peking station for the year ending Apr. 30, 1900. ABCFM, 16/36.
224. P. Cohen, 34–38, and chap. 2.
225. A. Smith, *China in Convulsion* [1901], 1:219, quoted in P. Cohen, 81.

Chapter Ten

1. Naquin, *Peking*, 679–86.

2. Mallory.

3. See *Zhongguo jindai shi da zaihuang*, for descriptions of each of these events.

4. Xia Mingfang, *Minguo*, tab. 2.2, p. 78, shows that for the period 1912–49, 88.3 percent of drought victims and 57.2 percent of flood victims, came from the Yellow River basin region. As many as 79.2 percent of victims of all different categories of famines came from the north.

5. Turner, 8. Also, China International Famine Relief Commission, Chihli Committee, "Report of the Distribution Board on Famine Conditions and Plans to Meet Them" (Nov. 1924), enclosure in dispatch of Jan. 12, 1925, in USDS, M-329, Roll 132.

6. "History of the Chihli River Commission," 634.

7. *Jindai Tianjin tuzhi*, 209.

8. Sept. 25, 1917. Enclosed in a dispatch of the same date in USDS, M-329, Roll 128.

9. *NCDN*, Sept. 25, 1917.

10. Articles in the *NCDN*, from Sept. 29 through Oct. 12, 1917.

11. *JJSZ* 2:2a.

12. "Caring for the Tientsin Sufferers," 765–66. Letter from Ambassador Reinsch, Oct. 29, 1917, in USDS, M-329, Roll 128.

13. *Jindai Tianjin tuzhi*, 209.

14. *JJSZ* 3:4a.

15. *NCDN*, Feb. 19, 1918.

16. U.S. Consul General's letter of Sept. 3, 1912, in USDS, M-329, Roll 128.

17. Monthly Rainfall at Tientsin, 1891–1922, enclosed in Chihli River Commission, *Reports*.

18. *JJSZ* 3:3a; Chapter 9 in this book.

19. *Ershi shiji Zhongguo zaibian tushi* 1:310.

20. Tuan-sheng Ch'ien, 65–66.

21. Boorman, 2:108–10.

22. *JJSZ*, see 1:1a–4a for regulations of the Directorate, and also 16:15b on the role of private charity.

23. *JJSZ* juan 3, includes the questionnaire that was sent out.

24. *JJSZ* 3:3a.

25. *Peking Daily News*, Oct. 16, 1917, in USDS, M-329, Roll 128.

26. *NCDN*, Nov. 7 and 8, 1917. *JJSZ* 22:2b–3a has a list of organizations contributing money.

27. Materials documenting the role of the Chamber of Commerce in famine relief in other years can be found in *Tianjin shanghui dang'an huibian (1912–1928)*, vol. 2 pts. 2 and 3.

28. Greene's subsequent career is related in W. Cohen.

29. *Peking Daily News*, Oct. 16 and 18, 1917, enclosures in dispatches of the same dates, USDS, M-329, Roll 128.

30. Dispatch of Oct. 15, 1917, in USDS, M-329, Roll 128.

31. "North China Christian Flood Relief Committee: Work and Plans," enclosed in dispatch of Apr. 2, 1918, in USDS, M-329, Roll 128. See also "Caring for the Tientsin Flood Sufferers," 765–66.

32. Dispatch from Ambassador Reinsch, Oct. 29, 1917, in USDS, M-329, Roll 128.

33. Dispatches of Oct. 2–6, 1917, in USDS, M-329, Roll 128.

34. Dispatches of June 1918, in USDS, M-329, Roll 128.

35. *JJSZ* 2:2ab, 3:3a.

36. *JJSZ*, juan 4.

37. *JJSZ* 9:11a–12a.

38. This roughly corresponded to the average cost of these grains as reported on Dec. 21, 1917: 2.7 yuan per shi of red sorghum and 2.9 yuan per shi of corn. See *JJSZ* 9:5b.

39. *JJSZ* 9:7a.

40. "Cereal Trade in Tientsin," 108.

41. *JJSZ* 9:11a–12a. These figures are not consistent with the known grain prices. See above.

42. *Tianjin shanghui dang'an huibian (1912–1928)*, vol. 2, pt. 2, 1697–1707.

43. *JJSZ*, juan 9.

44. *JJSZ* 16:46a–53a gives a table, 22:4a gives costs.

45. *JJSZ* 22:1b; *JJSZ* 16:27a–39a gives a table, 22:4a gives costs.

46. *JJSZ* 2:33b, 35a–39a.

47. *JJSZ* 6:10b–11a. These numbers do not add up correctly.

48. *JJSZ* 6:2a–3b gives the regulations, also 6:5b.

49. *JJSZ* 1:1a, 7:4a.

50. *JJSZ* 7:18ab, 7:19–24 shows that 615,700 yuan were distributed to 101 counties.

51. *JJSZ* 7:6b–7a.

52. *JJSZ* 9:5ab.

53. *JJSZ* 3:6a–7a.

54. *JJSZ* 3:4ab, 15:14a–15b, table on 15:25b–41b.

55. *JJSZ* 22:3b.

56. *JJSZ* 5:42–46b.

57. *JJSZ* 15:15b–16a.

58. *JJSZ* 14:7a, 8a–11b. Juan 14 has various documents.

59. *JJSZ* 15:9b–10b.

60. *JJSZ* 15:1a–13b, 22:3a.

61. *JJSZ* 22:2b–3a has a list.

62. Tang Zongyu. *Zhenzai shudu wuliu heji.*

63. North China Christian Flood Relief Committee, "Flood Conditions," Apr. 2, 1918, enclosure in USDS, M-329, Roll 128.

64. *Wen'an XZ* 1922, 6:1b–2a. The rate cited for cash relief corresponds with the bureau's general guidelines.

65. *Xinhe XZ* 1928, 1:21ab.

66. Ibid., 4:11–12.

67. Gamble, *Ting Hsien,* 444–46.

68. Description from *Zhili shangpin* 3/15–16.

69. *HHLY* 824–28.

70. *JJSZ* 16:9b–39a. Another place in this source gives the figures 181 at the cost of 251,628 yuan. *JJSZ* 16:27a–39a has a table, 22:4a gives costs. See also above.

71. Letter to police, 1917/11/3, *JJSZ* 16:53ab.

72. Rogaski, "Beyond Benevolence," 63.

73. *JJSZ* 16:1bff.

74. Data in my article, "Life and Death in a Chinese Famine" about women during the 1935 flood in Shandong, shows the likelihood of high rates of female infanticide even by those mothers who were being publicly sheltered during the crisis. See Chapter 11 below.

75. Hershatter, 98–99.

76. Rogaski, "Beyond Benevolence," 62. See Chapter 9 in this book.

77. *JJSZ* 6:17b.

78. "Caring for the Tientsin Sufferers," 765.

79. Report enclosed in dispatch of June 17, 1918, in USDS, M-329, Roll 128.

80. "North China Christian Flood Relief Committee: Work and Plans," enclosed in dispatch of Apr. 2, 1918, in USDS, M-329, Roll 128. Such constructive activities were also emphasized in famine shelters in Shandong during the winter of 1935 discussed below.

81. *NCDN,* Oct. 18, 1917.

82. *NCDN,* Nov. 9, 1917.

83. Description of the flood and the relief program is found in *Tianjin shuizai ji Hebei ge zaiqu zhenjiu zong baogao.* Also *Ershi shiji Zhongguo zaibian tushi,* vol. 1, chap. 17.

84. *Tianjin Yizujie shuizai nanmin jiuji.*

85. *Tianjin tebie shi shuiizai jiuji shilu,* esp. 227–30 on sanitation. Rogaski, *Hygienic Modernity,* examines the concepts of public sanitation, *weisheng,* in Tianjin. See also 70–72, 205, 218.

86. *JJSZ* 3:4ab.

87. F. C. Jones, 132–33.

88. Haiho Conservancy Commission, "Report on Floods, 1912," enclosure in consul general's letter, Sept. 3, 1912, in USDS, M-329, Roll 128.

89. Enclosure not identified, in consul general's letter, Sept. 28, 1917, in USDS, M-329, Roll 128.

90. "Floods of North China," 755–56.

91. Bouillard, *North China Floods in 1917.*

92. *Hegong taolun*, English sec., 5.

93. "History of the Chihli River Commission," 634–44.

94. Todd, 411, has more information on this.

95. "Famine Relief in 1926." See also, "Engineering Accomplishments: Famine Prevention and Relief Projects," CIFRC A21 [1919], enclosure in USDS, M-329, Roll 129.

96. Turner, 8.

97. "Chihli River Commission: Final Report and Grand Scheme, 1918–1925," enclosure in dispatch of Oct. 17, 1927, in USDS, M-329, Roll 219.

98. "The Hai Ho Conservancy Commission Report for 1926," enclosure in dispatch of Oct. 6, 1927, in USDS, M-329, Roll 219.

99. A 1924 article reprinted in Todd, 23.

100. Turner, 8. Also, China International Famine Relief Commission, Chihli Committee, "Report of the Distribution Board on Famine Conditions and Plans to Meet Them" (Nov. 1924), enclosure in dispatch of Jan. 12, 1925, in USDS, M-329, Roll 132.

101. *North China Famine*, 10–11.

102. Bergère, 1365–72, based on North China International Society for Famine Relief, Tientsin, *The Report on Famine Conditions, November 15, 1920.*

103. *North China Famine*, 2–4.

104. Ibid., 19, 26.

105. Nathan, *History*, 6. A total of 17 million dollars was collected for this effort in China and abroad. *North China Famine*, vii.

106. Presbyterian Historical Society, 82/20/11, contains the records of the China Famine Fund.

107. Baker, 71, 81–82.

108. *North China Famine*, 25–26.

109. Ibid., 51–53.

110. Ibid., 85.

111. Ibid., 15.

112. Ibid., 10.

113. Ibid., 53–55.

114. Ibid., 48–49.

115. Ibid., 53.

116. Ibid.

117. Ibid., 53–57.

118. Ibid., 128–29. Pages 124–29 give interesting guidelines to workers in the Shunde and Daming districts on how to conduct investigations and distribute grain tickets.

119. Ibid., 57–60.

120. See Chapter 3 in this book on the nutritional value of these grains; also *North China Famine*, 130–32.

121. Each direct recipient probably shared his portion with others. *North China Famine*, 63–64.

122. Ibid., 20.

123. Ibid., 26.

124. Ibid., 12–13.

125. See entries in *HHLY* 830–33.

126. *North China Famine*, 13.

127. Ibid., 14.

128. A 1930s survey of mostly Shandong migrants, ibid., 5.

129. Ibid., 47. See Chapter 11 below.

130. Gottschang and Lary, tab. A–2, p. 171.

131. *North China Famine*, 87.

132. Ibid., 14, but on 87, there were 10,000 sold.

133. Ibid., 87.

134. Ibid., 90.

135. Bergère, 1370.

136. *Xinhe XZ* 1928, ce 1:21b–22a. One sheng = 10 ke.

137. Ibid., 4:11–12.

138. Gamble, *Ting Hsien*, 446–47.

139. *Wan XZ* 1935, 4:25ab.

140. Portions of this section appeared in my article, L. M. Li, "Famine and Famine Relief: Viewing Africa in the 1980s from China in the 1920s."

141. Baker, 81, 157–66.

142. Nathan, *History*, 13–16.

143. Baker, 99.

144. China International Famine Relief Commission, 9–12.

145. Edwards, 695.

146. Blom, 696–99.

147. Baker, 189.

148. Ibid., 80.

149. Related by John K. Fairbank, Cambridge, MA, Mar. 1985.

150. *Famine Commission Bulletin* V, no. 1 (Oct. 1927).

151. *Famine Commission Bulletin* V, no. 2 (Dec. 1927): 1.

152. Ibid., with map. Also *Zhongguo jindai shi da zaihuang*, 187.

153. Ibid., 183–84.

154. *Famine Commission Bulletin* V, no. 4 (Apr. 1928): 23–24.

155. Ibid., 24.

156. *Famine Commission Bulletin* VI, no. 4 (Apr. 1929): 43.

157. Ibid., 34–35.

158. *Famine Commission Bulletin* VII, no. 1 (Oct. 29): 4–5. Hebei also experienced locusts and floods in these same years. *Zhongguo jindai shi da zaihuang*, 184–85; also *Ershi shiji Zhongguo zaibian tushi*, vol. 1, chap. 9.

159. *Zhongguo jindai shi da zaihuang*, 176.

160. Ibid., 174.

161. Ibid., 169–76.

162. *Ershi shiji Zhongguo zaibian tushi*, 1:140–46.

163. Ibid., 146–48. Jerlian Tsao, 2–4.

164. *Zhongguo jindai shi da zaihuang*, 195–201.

165. *Jindai Zhongguo zaihuang jinian xubian*, 208.

166. Godement, 17–18.

167. *Famine Commission Bulletin* VI, no. 3 (Feb. 1929), 23.

168. *Famine Commission Bulletin* VI, no. 4 (Apr. 1929): 33. *Zhongguo jingji nianjian*, vol. 11, 80, in J. Tsao, 5.

169. This is the view of Godement, 12–13.

170. Godement, 15, reproduces the list of groups aiding refugees along the railway line from Fengtai, Zhili, to Manchuria, probably from Chen Hansheng, "Nanmin de dongbei liuwang" (1930), 23.

171. J. Tsao, pt. 2.

172. Ibid., 9–10. *Zhongguo jindai shi da zaihuang*, 169.

173. *Far Eastern Times*, Sept. 29, 1925, enclosure in USDS, M-329, Roll 219.

174. *Peking and Tientsin Times*, Sept. 29, 1925, enclosure in USDS, M-329, Roll 219.

175. *New York Times*, Feb. 22, 1929[?]; enclosure in USDS, M-329, Roll 128.

176. Enclosure of May 17, 1928, in USDS, M-329, Roll 128.

177. Nathan, *History*, 16–22; American National Red Cross, 30.

178. For more on CIFRC policies, see *Famine Commission Bulletin* VI, no. 3 (Feb. 1929).

179. Johnson papers, Jan. 18, 1930, 27/11.

180. Johnson papers, Mar. 1930, 14/235.

181. These estimates are from *Zhongguo jindai shi da zaihuang*, 230–31.

182. China, National Flood Relief Commission, 7–13; Stroebe, 676.

183. Stroebe, 678; Baker, 371.

184. China, National Flood Relief Commission.

185. L. M. Li, "Life and Death," esp. 470–74.

186. White and Jacoby, 166–78.

187. The lower figure was the government's. *Zhongguo jindai shi da zaihuang*, 272–78.

188. Ibid., 269–70, 283–85.

189. Ibid., 204.

190. Xia Mingfang, *Minguo*, tab. 2.3, p. 79. Deng Yunte had estimated mortality from famines from 1810 to 1888 at 62.8 million; from 1920 and 1936 at 18.4 million. The basis for his nineteenth-century estimate is not clear. *Zhongguo jiuhuangshi*, 1998 reprint, 142–43.

191. Xia Mingfang, *Minguo*, 80–81, including tab. 2.4.

192. *Zhongguo jindai shi da zaihuang*, 202.

193. Lydia Liu shows that Lu Xun's "Ah Q" was based in part on Arthur Smith's book, *Translingual Practice*, chap. 2.

194. Deng Tuo, *Zhongguo jiuhuang shi*, reprint 1998. Mallory is invoked on 5, 7, and 43.

195. Cheek, 49–50. Deng Tuo was a major Chinese intellectual; he later became editor of the *People's Daily* but committed suicide during the Cultural Revolution.

196. Deng Tuo, 196–97.

Chapter Eleven

1. Such an approach has been the underlying premise of international assistance programs in the late twentieth century and probably originated in China relief work of the early twentieth century. OXFAM and other international agencies have generally stressed the importance of giving poor people the tools for subsistence rather than food itself; the fishnet and not the fish.

2. Tawney, 176–77.

3. *North China Famine*, 11–12.

4. Buck's data have been criticized by some economists for presenting too optimistic a view of rural life. Because his students tended to conduct the surveys in their home villages and towns, the sample may have overrepresented better endowed localities.

5. Buck, *Land Utilization*, 20–22. Stross discusses Buck and other American agricultural reformers, esp. chap. 7.

6. Hayford, 92–97.

7. Hayford, esp. chap. 5.

8. Alitto, chap. 12. Yenching, Nankai, and Cheeloo universities, all in North China, all had smaller rural projects. Hayford, 159.

9. Alitto, chap. 12.

10. Tawney, 63.

11. Stross, 166, 173.

12. Myers, 14–15, terms Chen's approach as the "distribution theory," as opposed to the "eclectic theory" of others.

13. The mutual attraction, and later repulsion, between Mao and Liang is a major theme of Alitto's book, esp. 283–92.

14. Alitto, 272.

15. Mao Tse-tung, 1:23–59.

16. The compendium *Zhongguo jindai nongyeshi ziliao*, vol. 3, employs the term *nongye weiji* (agricultural crisis). The "world capitalist economic crisis deepened the Chinese agricultural crisis."

17. Huang, esp. 185, 216, 222–23, 299.

18. Myers, esp. 205, 276, 292–95.

19. T. Rawski presents the fullest case for this point of view.

20. Brandt and Sands.

21. This was the dominant view at the International Workshop on Urban Modernization of North China sponsored by the Institute of History, Tianjin Academy of Social Sciences, in August 2001. The proceedings were published in *Ershi shiji Huabei chengshi jindaihua* 21 (July 2002).

22. Zhang Xinyi survey cited in Chapter 3 in this book.

23. See Table 3.3 in this book.

24. *Ba xian xinzhi* 1934, 4:4. There was a total of 1,687 square li, with 139,139 people, which meant an average of 6 mu per person. In a good year, peasants could get 5 dou per mu, or 150 jin. At 6 mu per person, there was an equivalent of 900 jin per person. Each person needed 18 liang (16 liang = 1 jin) per day, more or less, but since there were also landlords, landless folks, and animals to feed, the agricultural output was inadequate for the needs of the county. At 18 liang per day, a person would consume 1 shi 3 dou 7 sheng of grain per year, leaving 1 shi 6 dou 3 sheng surplus, which the gazetteer regarded as inadequate to cover other needs.

25. See Table 3.7 in this book, and related discussion.

26. Huang, *North China*, 54–56, and map. Xu Xiuli, "Guan'gai," 53. Xu, 41, explains that irrigated land improved cotton yields by 50 percent, corn yields at least 100 percent, and wheat yields also over 100 percent.

27. Gamble, *North China Villages*, 160.

28. Gamble, *Ting Hsien*, 111–12.

29. *Ba xian xinzhi* 1934, 4:9. Chapter 3 in this book.

30. *Ba xian xinzhi* 1934, 3:9. Also cited in Chapter 3 in this book.

31. Mallory, 7–10.

32. Cited in Gottschang and Lary, 93.

33. Gamble, *Ting Hsien*, 81, 89.

34. Ibid., 95, 108.

35. Gamble and Burgess, 268–69, also cited in Mallory, 11. Other surveys of Beijing corroborate the large portion of the family income spent on food. See summary in Campbell, "Public Health," 184.

36. Gamble, *How Chinese Families in Peiping Live*, 52–57, and tab. 12, p. 321. Gamble observed that the results conformed to Engel's law, which states, "As the income of a family increases, a smaller percentage is spent on food."

37. Gamble attributed this discrepancy to the characteristics of the sample. Ibid., 56.

38. Ibid., 83–84, 88–89. Gamble cites Buck, *Chinese Farm Economy*, but I cannot find the exact reference. Compare this with famine rations of half a sheng, less than a pound, in the Qing period, or half a catty in the 1920–21 famine. See also Chapters 5 and 10 in this book.

39. Gamble, *Ting Hsien*, 252, 258–59.

40. Li Jinzheng, 16.

41. Gamble, *Ting Hsien*, chap. 8, gives a rundown of taxes of all sorts imposed on farmers. Hebei in particular had great increases in provincial revenue. Duara, 67.

42. Those surviving until age 5 could expect to live 47–48 more years, 47.58 for males and 46.95 for females. Notestein and Chiao, 391.

43. At age 5, men in the north could expect to live 40 more years, women 36.9 more years. Barclay, 620–21. This reconstruction has been challenged by others who find that life expectancy at birth in 1930 was more like 32 years. See Lavely and Wong, 724.

44. Lee and Campbell, 60.

45. Notestein and Chiao, 389–93.

46. Barclay, 618.

47. Notestein and Chiao, 389.

48. In 2004, China's infant mortality rate was 32 per thousand; the U.S. rate was 6.7, and Mozambique's was 127. The 2004 World Population Data Sheet, published by the Population Reference Bureau.

49. Notestein and Chiao, 393.

50. L. M. Li, "Life and Death," 487–95. This record also reveals high rates of childhood mortality up to age ten.

51. Ibid., 471.

52. Lee and Wang, 49–51.

53. Lee and Campbell, 65–70, 95–101; Lee and Wang, 47–51. This idea has been severely criticized by other scholars. See especially Wolf, "Is There Evidence of Birth Control in Late Imperial China?" and also Lee et al.'s rebuttal, "Positive Checks or Chinese Checks?," Lavely and Wong, 733–38, have also acknowledged the role of infanticide in regulating fertility and consider the possibility that it may have contributed to the slowing of population growth.

54. Lee and Wang, 60–61.

55. Lee and Campbell, 56.

56. Wolf, 142.

57. Liu Haiyan, 35-41.

58. Arnold, 311.

59. Liu Haiyan, 35-41.

60. Ibid.

61. Gottschang and Lary, tab. 2.2, p. 50, using Buck's data.

62. Huang, 125–28, based on various sources. Excellent map on 127. Table 3.6 in this book uses the overall figure of 7 percent. Also maps and figures in Wang Youmin, prior to page 1.

63. For example, Wang Youmin, discussion of Renqiu, Ding, and other counties, 46, 54. Cotton could be grown in various types of soil: "light sandy soil, loams, heavy clays, and sandy bottom lands." Chao, *Cotton*, 14.

64. Estimates by Wang Youmin, 100.

65. Wang Youmin, 8–9.

66. Some of the Indian cotton was transhipped via Japan. Fong, 303–4.

67. Wang Youmin, 8–9.

68. Fong, 290.

69. Ibid., 305.

70. Grove, "International Trade," 110; Fong, 242.

71. Fong, 233–34, 241.

72. Chao, *Cotton*, 195.

73. Fong, 242.

74. Chao, *Cotton*, 193.

75. Ibid., 191–92. Wang Youmin, 92.

76. Arnold, 537.

77. Hershatter, chap. 2.

78. Arnold, 530.

79. Grove, "International Trade," 97–101.

80. Liu Haiyan. Other papers in *Ershi shiji Huabei chengshi jindaihua* also argue for the increasing connection between Tianjin and its hinterland, for example, Wang Shousong.

81. Fortune, 362–63.

82. "China Flour Industry," 106.

83. *Zhongguo jindai mianfen gongyeshi*, 278–81.

84. Ibid., 280. Arnold, 539. Detailed information on Tianjin's flour mills can be found in *Tianjin shanghui dang'an huibian (1912–1928)*, vol. 2, pt. 3, 2806–22.

85. Gamble, *How Chinese Families Live*, 78–80. Another study estimated more conservatively that Beijing had a population of 1,400,000, one-fourth of whom depended on wheat flour. If each person consumed 12 ounces per day, then 210,000 jin per day were consumed. Of this one-third was machine-made, or 70,000 jin. Mai Shudu, 88.

86. *Wei XZ* 1925, 13:8.

87. *Qinghe XZ* 1933, 9:1b–2b.

88. Ibid., 9:11b–12.

89. Friedrich Otto, 400.

90. Chen Kung-po, 118–22.

91. Ibid., and C. C. Chang (Chang Hsin-I or Zhang Xinyi), 1931 and 1932.

92. Liu Ts'ui-jung, "Problem of Food Supply," has argued that there really was no national food

shortage problem before 1930s, although there were local shortages when natural calamities occurred. The impression of food shortage had been created by the gradual increase in grain imports after 1912.

93. Arthur G. Coons cites C. C. Chang, "China's Food Problem."

94. Wallace, 824, 817.

95. Coons.

96. Otto, 390, 400.

97. Gottschang and Lary, figs. 1.1 and 1.2, 38–39, based on their append., tab. A.2, p. 171.

98. Ibid., tab. A.4, p. 174.

99. Ibid., tab. 1.1, p. 5; and 59.

100. Ibid., 3, 50.

101. Ninety percent stayed two years or longer. Ibid., 116.

102. Ibid., 93.

103. Summarized from "Hantan, An Agricultural Center of Chihli," 464–72.

104. *Zhili shangpin* 6/26–27. *Xinhe XZ* 1928, 4:16b.

105. *Xinhe XZ* 1928, 2:39b.

106. Ibid.

107. Ibid., 1:21, 4:11–12.

108. Ibid., 4:5a.

109. *Qinghe XZ* 1933, 5:16ab.

110. *Jing XZ* 1932, 6:2b–3; emphasis added. See Chapter 3 in this book.

111. Ibid., 6:1b–2.

112. *Nanpi XZ* 1932, 3:9–10.

113. *Cang XZ* 1933, 11:14–15.

114. *Xian XZ* 1925, 17:34b–35a.

115. *Xianghe XZ* 1936, 5:2ab.

116. *Shunyi XZ* 1933, 12:2ab.

117. Ibid., 12:2b–3a.

118. Myers, 40–59.

119. Ibid., 50.

120. Ibid., 56–57.

121. *Ba xian xinzhi* 1934, 4:7a. This section gives many other interesting details about consumption habits and costs.

122. *Wen'an XZ* 1922, 6:2a–3b; 12:32–35.

123. Wang Youmin, 45.

124. *Gaoyang XZ* 1933, 2:20–21.

125. *Hebei sheng Qingyuan xian shiqing diaocha*, 2:26–28.

126. Ibid.

127. Hou Jianxin, 57–65.

128. *Wan XZ* 1934, 7:26b–27b.

129. Ibid., 7:37, 39b.

130. *Jingxing XZ* 1934, 5:1b. Of course in the 1930s, the concern was too many people, not too few. The rest of the passage is more relevant: "I have heard that those who administer a state or a family do not worry about there being too few people, but about the unequal distribution of wealth. They do not worry about poverty, but worry about the lack of security and peace on the part of the people. For when wealth is equally distributed, there will not be poverty," translated by W. Chan, 44–45.

131. *Jingxing XZ* 1934, 10:3–4.

132. Ibid.

133. *Pingshan XZ* 1931, 5:38b.

134. *Yuanshi XZ* 1931, ce 1:48.

135. *Luanzhou zhi* 1898, 16b–18b.

136. *Luan XZ* 1938, 15:1a.

137. *Luan XZ* 1938, 15:1b–3b. Yields are included in Table 3.7 in this book.

138. *Lulong XZ* 1931, 10:1b–2b.

139. *Lulong XZ* 1931, 9:1b–2b.

140. Brandt and Sands, esp. 201.

141. Hou Jianxin, 65–66.

142. Buck, 316, tab. 3, "Farm Price Relationships in the Wheat Region, 1906–1933."

143. *Zhuo ZZ* 1936, 3.1:6a.

144. Feuerwerker, 68–71, including tab. 14. Also Brandt, *Commercialization*, 80–82. Brandt argues that international grain prices strongly influenced the gradual increases in Shanghai and Yangzi valley rice prices starting from the 1880s. See his chap. 3

145. Buck, 316, tab. 3.

146. The index numbers were 33 for 1900, 100 for 1926, and 132 for 1932. Buck, 321, tab. 6. This trend is also shown more generally in Buck's data for farm wages for the "wheat region," a steady rise from 1906 to 1932. Buck, 316, tab. 3.

147. Feuerwerker, 71; T. Rawski, 172–79.

148. Ibid., 178.

149. Xia Mingfang, *Minguo*, 179–93.

150. Li Jinzheng, 16, 28, and see above.

151. Li Jinzheng, 43.

152. *Sanhe xian xinzhi* 1935, 15:4b, 15:1ab.

153. Ibid., 15:9b, 15:6b. See Chapter 3 in this book.

154. *Nankai jingji zhishu ziliao*, 59–60, tab. 1.

155. Ibid., 241, tab. 1.

156. Hartford, "Repression," 97–107.

157. Lincoln Li, 164.

158. This description is from Hartford, "Repression," 107–11.

159. Feng and Goodman give a clear description and clarify the definitions of border region, border area, and base area, ix–xiv, 12–18. Also Goodman, "JinJiLuYu in the Sino-Japanese War," 1010, points out that this border region had "little cohesion and consequently little clear identity before 1945."

160. Wei Hongyun, 93–95.

161. Feng and Goodman, Introduction, 14–15.

162. Hartford, "Repression," 124.

163. Hartford, "Fits and Starts," esp. 169; Hartford, "Repression," esp. 94.

164. Hartford and Goldstein provide an excellent historiographical review. *Single Sparks*, chap. 1, 3–33.

165. Wei, 102.

166. Wei, 103–6.

167. Duara, chap. 3, "Building the Modern State," and 73. Duara, 214–15, believes the village became more important a "locus of coordination in local society" in the twentieth century, but deep bonds of community solidarity did not develop.

168. Ibid., 195–98.

169. Ibid., 195. In Shunyi, villagers told investigators that the land tax itself had not been so onerous, but these *tankuan* periodic levies were. Myers, 63–64.

170. Ibid., 218–24.

171. Ibid., 251–52.

172. W. Hinton, 53. Hinton refers to them as "gentry," a term which probably confers too much status on this class of person.

173. Duara, 252–53.

174. Lincoln Li, 178–80. Zeng Yeying, "Riwei," describes in some detail the attempts of the Japanese army to exploit agricultural production in North China; in his view, they failed because there was so little to be siphoned off.

175. Hartford, "Repression," 108.

176. Friedman et al., 40.

177. Li Wenhai, 278–80.

178. Ibid., 281. In southern Hebei, more than 230,000 people may have died of starvation between 1942–44. *Hebei sheng liangshi*, 56.

179. Friedman et al., 52.

180. Ibid., 60.

181. Elizabeth J. Perry's important study of the ecologically troubled Huaibei area, *Rebels and Revolutionaries in North China, 1845–1945,* incisively shows that traditions of rebellion or banditry do not necessarily lead to revolution.

182. Xia Mingfang, *Minguo,* 119–38, esp. 123–28.

183. W. Hinton, chaps. 13 and 14, 128–46.

184. Ibid., 154–55. Subsequent steps in the land-equalization process are described in chap. 21, 198–209. Also see summary table, "Changes in Landholding by Classes (1944–1948)," 592.

185. In his review of recent scholarship on this topic, Xia Mingfang, "Jindai Huabei," reaches a similar conclusion; he cautions against reading too much into the economic changes of this period.

186. All forms of warfare in the early twentieth century probably did more damage to agricultural production than natural disasters, according to some Chinese interpretations. Liu Yanwei, "Zhongguo jindai zhanzheng."

187. Benton has developed these comparisons in his work on the New Fourth Army. See Benton, 192, 214–15. "Northern backwardness" is also discussed in Selden, 32–35.

Chapter Twelve

1. Article dated Apr. 15, 1958, published in *Hongqi* (Red Flag), extracted in Schram, 351–52.

2. Summarized from T. White, "Origins," 250–74, but White also shows that the simple periodization of birth control policy, as given here, obscures the struggles within the party leadership, and the nuances of policy in each period.

3. Ibid., 274–77.

4. The 1999 figures are from *Zhonguo renkou tongji nianjian 1999.*

5. *Hebei sheng liangshi,* 48. Working without official sources, Kenneth Walker estimated that the three northern provinces of Hebei, Henan, and Shandong lost about 17 percent of arable land between the 1950s and 1970s; Hebei itself lost 13 percent in those years, not counting the two independent municipalities. "Grain Self-Sufficiency in North China, 1953–75," 560–62.

6. *Hebei jingji dili,* 334.

7. If we take the 1982 total population figure of 53.56 million offered on table 8.2, page 336, as the base, at 1.8 mu per person, the result is 96.4 million mu. On page 370 this publication contradicts itself by stating that there were 2.1 mu per person in Hebei, presumably in the mid-1980s; in that case the total cultivated land might have been to 112–115 million mu.

8. That figure is based on Perkins, 236–37, which in turn was based on estimates from 1953 and probably includes Beijing and Tianjin. The *Hebei jingji dili* figures do not necessarily confirm the loss of arable land estimated by Walker, but they do confirm the increasing population density.

9. Walker, *Food Grain Procurement,* 26–27.

10. Ibid., 165.

11. Lardy, 148.

12. Riskin, 419, says that China's pre–Great Leap standard was not reached until 1973. Lardy, 149, shows that by the standard of food grain output per capita, China did not regain its 1957–58 levels until 1975.

13. Cycles of five years were found in grain prices of the eighteenth century. See Figure 4.1a in this book.

14. Walker, "Grain Self-Sufficiency," 571–72, 581. See also Walker, *Food Grain Procurement,*" tab. 24, p. 71, for an annual estimates. These imports allowed Hebei to raise its annual per capita grain from 217 to 241 kg in the 1950s. Ibid., tab. 25, pp. 75–76.

15. Walker observes that the government seemed to consider 240–50 kg the standard for self-sufficiency. "Grain Self-Sufficiency," 573–75.

16. The last column in Table 12.1, "average grain per peasant population" reflects not the grain produced within the province, but that amount less the state procurement plus the imports, divided by the peasant population. Neither these figures, nor the 1965–1980 grain ration figures in *Hebei sheng liangshi,* 54, represent the actual amounts consumed by individuals. The difference between the rations and the grain availability is accounted for by seed, fodder, team utilization, and so on. These recent figures confirm to a remarkable degree the estimates made by Walker before official statistics were published.

17. Earlier Chinese claims said that North China had achieved grain self-sufficiency in the early 1970s. In Walker's view, only by recognizing the extent of imports and the strict grain rationing could that claim be substantiated. "Grain Self-Sufficiency," 583.

18. *Dangdai Zhongguo de Hebei*, 2:68–69. Converted from 10 "yi jin" (50,000 tons). *Hebei sheng liangshi*, 56, also says that in 1963 a total of 14.2 yi kg of grain was deployed from other provinces.

19. Calculated from Walker, *Food Grain Procurement*, tab. 28, p. 87. If Shanghai's grain imports are added to those of Tianjin and Beijing, the three cities together accounted for 45.4 percent of the total provincial imports.

20. Walker, 72–75, explains the special circumstances that accounted for Liaoning's grain-deficit status—its large urban population and the fact that its large output of corn was not counted as "real grain."

21. Walker, *Food Grain Procurement*, 89.

22. *Hebei jingji dili*, 371.

23. Walker, "Grain Self-Sufficiency," 564.

24. *Hebei jingji dili*, 371.

25. Lardy, 48–51, citing Mao, "Speech to an Enlarged Politburo Meeting," in *Long Live the Thought of Mao Tse-tung* (Taipei, 1969), 634–40.

26. Riskin, 420.

27. *Xin Hebei*, 327.

28. *Xin Hebei*, diagrams section, n.p., and 336–37.

29. Figures based on *Zhongguo changyong renkou shuju ji*, 12–16.

30. *Hebei sheng liangshi zhi*, 84.

31. *Dangdai Zhongguo de Hebei*, 1:563; emphasis added.

32. Said in Friedman, xxiii.

33. See 1948 map in W. Hinton, 612; other maps on 88 and 245.

34. Friedman.

35. Crook, *Ten Mile Inn*, 8

36. Ibid., 10–11; details in Crook, *Revolution*, chap. 5.

37. W. Hinton, 592; also 209.

38. W. Hinton, 8–9.

39. Friedman, 42, and chap. 2 generally.

40. Ibid., 52. See Chapter 11 above.

41. Ibid., 81–86. Between 1936 and 1946 the population had expanded, and average per capita landholding had dropped from 3.3 to 2.8 mu per person.

42. Ibid., 104–5.

43. Ibid., 127–34.

44. Ibid., 172, 175.

45. Ibid., 143.

46. Ibid., 169.

47. *Secret Speeches of Chairman Mao*, 370.

48. *Dangdai Zhongguo de Hebei*, 2:63.

49. *Hebei sheng liangshi*, 44.

50. Ibid., 44.

51. Ibid., 59.

52. Ibid., 44.

53. *Dangdai Zhongguo de Hebei*, 2:67.

54. The theoretical baseline was 26 jin per person per month, but 18 jin was the actual rate. If rations fell below this, the team was entitled to apply for tax relief. Oi, *State and Peasant*, 22.

55. *Hebei sheng liangshi*, 54. It is not clear why this source does not publish *kouliang* figures for the 1950s; it may be that they were too low to publish, even in the 1990s.

56. Oi, *State and Peasant*, 29–42.

57. A good description of urban rationing in the 1970s can be found in Whyte and Parish, 86–90, 96–97. Most of these other food items were in short supply, except in Beijing, Shanghai, and Tianjin, where sometimes they were unrationed.

58. Oi, *State and Peasant*, 17, 24

59. *Hebei sheng liangshi*, 45.

60. Oi, *State and Peasant*, 15–16, 26–29.

61. Ibid., 49. Even in the 1960s, before the reform period, there were precedents for over-quota purchases and negotiated price sales, but the amounts were limited and the practice varied by time and place. Cheng and Tsang, 1084–86.

62. *Dangdai Zhongguo de Hebei*, 2:64.

63. This follows the periodization in *Hebei sheng liangshi*, 45–47.

64. Oi, *State and Peasant*, 73–74, dates this from 1969–78, but *Dangdai Zhongguo de liangshi gongzuo*, 127–31, states that from 1961 onward, local reserves were required and were drawn upon first in times of crisis. Emphasis on regional self-sufficiency may also have been related to Mao's fears of war with the Soviet Union.

65. This is the perspective of much writing on the subject, including Oi's book.

66. Mentioned in Mao's speech of November 1958, *Secret Speeches*, 464–67. Friedman, 215–19.

67. *Renmin Ribao* and *Hebei Ribao*, Aug. 11 and 12, 1958.

68. Crook, *Yangyi Commune*, chap. 14–15, 151–81. The Crooks' book describes the formation of this commune in She County in the southwestern corner of Hebei, near the Shanxi border; Yangyi Commune included Ten Mile Inn, which was the subject of their earlier books, and where they lived during the war of resistance.

69. First said by Mao in Moscow in 1957 and repeated publicly by Liu Shaoqi in December. MacFarquhar, 17.

70. MacFarquhar, 124.

71. Later these demonstrations were revealed to have been Potemkin-village setups; the children were standing on benches hidden under the grain. Becker photos.

72. MacFarquhar, 103–4.

73. Ibid., 125–26.

74. Kueh points out that a shift in North China cropping from soybeans to high-yielding potatoes helped to increase the grain output in 1958. Kueh, 157.

75. Peng Xizhe, 664.

76. Dali Yang, 54–64.

77. In Yangyi Commune, the rains caused the dam to collapse and ruined the crops. Crook, *Yangyi Commune*, chap. 8, 87–94, stresses weather as a cause of agricultural instability.

78. Becker, 270–74. Becker gives some good reasons why the real numbers will never really be known. The more widely accepted 30 million figure is the result of Judith Banister's computer reconstruction of the official data and can be found in *China's Changing Population*, 85, 116–19. Ashton et al. "Famine in China," arrived at the same conclusion; in addition to an excess famine mortality of 30 million, they estimate that there were 33 million "lost or postponed births," 614. Peng Xizhe, 649, estimates the total to have been 23 million.

79. Becker, 100, and chaps. 8–9.

80. Ibid., 137, 212, 218, and chap. 14 generally. Also, *Xiangcun sanshinian*.

81. Becker, chap. 9, esp. 137–39, 143–44, 149.

82. Ibid., 118–20.

83. Ibid., 126–27.

84. Becker uses the term on 128.

85. *Dangdai Hebei jianshi*, 127.

86. Taking the average death rate for 1954–57 as the base of 100, Walker calculates that Hebei's death rate was 106 in 1959, 137 in 1960, and 118 in 1961. Walker, "Food and Mortality," 115, 118.

87. Peng Xizhe, 646, tab. 2 shows an excess CDR for four years of 7.8; using Hebei's 1961 population figure, roughly 38 million, from Figure 12.2 in this chapter, the result is 296,000.

88. Ibid., 663.

89. *Hebei sheng liangshi*, 59–60.

90. Ibid., 55.

91. Ibid., 54, tab. 2.5.

92. Becker, 206–10, 228–29. Becker records that the central government introduced food substitutes in 1960, but in Hebei this was started in 1959, according to the official account given above.

93. From interviews in Quzhou and other places, Oct. 1989.

94. Yunxiang Yan.

95. Becker, 199.

96. Thomas Bernstein's 1984 article was the first to identify this pattern.

97. Walker, "Food and Mortality," 127–30. This represents a decline from Walker's 1953–57 estimates above.

98. Ibid., 128.

99. Friedman, 240–42.

100. Told to Becker, 151.

101. Ibid., 96.

102. Ibid., 223.

103. *Dangdai Beijing jianshi*, 183.

104. Summarized from Becker, 220–31.

105. Related to author in Nov. 1989.

106. Becker, 229.

107. Related to author in Nov. 1989.

108. Related to author in Quzhou and Wei counties, Oct. 1989.

109. *Hebei shengzhi* 16:103–4. The communes were in Wu'an and She counties in the southwestern corner of Hebei Province near Linzhang and Wei counties, which the author visited in 1989.

110. Becker, 236.

111. There were also parables about Mao, who was said to be sharing the peasants' suffering by giving up meat and not wasting one kernel of grain. Friedman, 240.

112. Outside of China it is now generally accepted that overprocurement was the principal cause of the famine, but Kueh, 152–55, without evaluating the counterevidence, maintains that "weather disturbance" played a larger role than bad policy.

113. Friedman et al. found out years after they began their study of Raoyang County that the villagers had been told that they could speak to the foreign scholars about any topic except the Great Leap Forward and the Cultural Revolution.

114. Chu Han. The Liu Shaoqi reference is on 20. The author reviews the 1958–61 weather situation in China on 20–27.

115. Ding Shu.

116. For example, *Zhongguo zaihuang shiji*, ed. by Meng Shaohua, has a long chapter on the post-1949 period that has no specific reference to the Great Leap Forward famine. *Zaihai lishi xue*, edited by Zhang Jianmin et al., has a section on serious human-caused disasters that refers to fires, ecological damage, and so forth, but not to the Great Leap.

117. *Ershi shiji Zhongguo zaibian tushi*, vol. 2.

118. Becker, 241, 266, 313.

119. Becker, 253. Two scholarly books that trace the connection between the Great Leap Forward and the Cultural Revolution are Roderick MacFarquhar, *Origins of the Cultural Revolution*, and Dali L. Yang, *Calamity and Reform in China*.

120. One notorious aspect of the Ukraine famine was that American and other foreign journalists were fooled into reporting that there was no famine. Conquest, chap. 17. Becker takes to task Western journalists and scholars who failed to report the Mao famine, or take seriously the reports and rumors of a great hunger. Becker, chap. 20.

121. Becker, 45–46. Conquest accepts the figure of 7 million. Conquest, 304–5.

122. Conquest, chap. 2, focuses on the Ukrainian aspect.

123. Bernstein, 370, and generally.

124. Becker also stresses these latter points.

125. In its "Resolution on Party History," presented at the Sixth Plenum of the 11th Central Committee in 1981, the Chinese Communist Party acknowledged Mao's responsibility for the Cultural Revolution, but did not level the same charge against him for the Great Leap Forward, citing only "Left" errors. This was

because the decision for rapid collectivization and the Great Leap had been fully endorsed by the Eighth Party Congress of 1956 and could not be blamed on Mao alone. Goodman, "Sixth Plenum," 523–24. The text of the resolution is found in *Beijing Review*, no. 27 (July 6, 1981).

126. *Hebei shengzhi* 8:88. There is a description of each year on 8:79–87.

127. *Dangdai Zhongguo de Hebei*, 1:681.See Chapter 1 above.

128. Kueh, 78-86, 163.

129. Putterman, 343, attributes only 15–20 percent of improvements in Hebei to the household responsibility system.

130. Dazhai was a model brigade in a commune of the same name in Shanxi Province where model workers created terraced fields from rock with their manual labor. It was the epitome of self-reliance that was the economic premise of the Cultural Revolution.

131. *Hebei shengzhi* 16:105–7. Dali Yang, 109–14, has been critical of the view that "the grain first policy" was responsible for agricultural stagnation during the Cultural Revolution period. He feels that the reaction to the Great Leap Forward caused a lowering of extraction from agriculture, which in turn led to a need for great regional self-sufficiency. Another view is that the regional self-sufficiency policy was partially the result of the leadership's fear of attack by the Soviet Union, and the need to develop industry in the interior of China in case a third front was opened up. Naughton.

132. This chronology and follows *Hebei shengzhi* 20:2–5. *Beijing shuihan zaihai*, 23, uses a slightly different periodization for the Beijing municipal region. *Dangdai Zhongguo de Hebei*, 1:669–86, gives an overview of water conservancy but has a more chauvinistic tone.

133. *Hebei shengzhi* 20:2.

134. Ibid., 8:47, 81. Aug. 4 was the memorable date.

135. Ibid., 20: 2–3.

136. *Hebei sheng liangshi zhi*, 56, 60. As mentioned above, 1.4 million tons of grain were transferred from other provinces to Hebei.

137. Quzhou, Oct. 6, 1989.

138. Wei xian, Oct. 9, 1989.

139. Wen'an xian, Nov. 4, 1989.

140. Quzhou, Oct. 7, 1989. Details about the flood can be found in *Dangdai Hebei jianshi*, 164–81, and *Zhongguo zaiqing baogao 1949–1995*, 37–39.

141. *Hebei shengzhi* 20:3.

142. Ibid., 20:277.

143. Ibid., 20:3.

144. *Dangdai Zhongguo de Hebei*, 1:689.

145. *Xin Hebei*, 324.

146. Shi Yuanchun interview, Nov. 26, 1989.

147. Zhang Shixian, 26.

148. Shi Yuanchun interview; "Characteristics," 191–210. Also "The Comprehensive Control of Drought, Waterlogging, and Salinization in the HuangHuaiHai Plain of China," publication of the Quzhou Experimental Station, ca. 1989

149. Ibid. The Quzhou project is also described in *Dangdai Zhongguo de Hebei*, 1:689–90, and *Hebei shengzhi* 20:207.

150. Quzhou, Oct. 6, 1989.

151. Blecher and Shue, 174–79. However, the lowering of the water table and the heavy demands for water from fruit growers caused serious concerns about water shortage in the 1980s.

152. *Baiyang dian zonghe zhili*, 7.

153. Wu Zhongjian interview. Also site visit, Nov. 2, 1989. *Hebei shengzhi* 20:130–34 gives information about this area.

154. Wu Zhongjian.

155. Ibid., and interviews by author at Anxin County, Nov. 2, 1989, and Lanfang city, Nov. 7, 1989.

156. In Handan, according to Wu Zhongjian, Nov. 2, 1989.

157. "Chinese Will Move Waters to Quench Thirst of Cities," New York *Times*, Aug. 27, 2002.

158. Quzhou, Oct. 6, 1989.

159. Oi, *State and Peasant*, 155.

160. *Dangdai Zhongguo de Hebei*, vol. 1, chaps. 20–21, 593–653.

161. Sicular, "Redefining," 1027.

162. Oi, "Two Decades," 620.

163. Oi, *Rural China*, 99–102ff.

164. Blecher and Shue, 210–11, and in general.

165. Putterman, 120, on the comparison with South China.

166. *Zhongguo baike nianjian*, 71.

167. Quzhou, Oct. 7, 1989.

168. Baodi visit, Nov. 9, 1989.

169. Cheng and Tsang, 1087–88.

170. Ibid., tab. 2, p. 1089.

171. Ibid., 1090.

172. Ibid., 1093.

173. Ibid., 1094–1100.

174. Rozelle, 228.

175. Liaoning corn and Guangxi livestock, for example, were closely correlated. Rozelle, 236–43.

176. Cheng and Tsang, 1100–01.

177. Rozelle, 232–34.

178. Ibid., 234–35.

179. Ibid., 228.

180. Ibid., 246.

181. Cheng and Tsang, 1103.

182. Ibid., 1101–2.

183. Rozelle, 247. Sicular, "Redefining State," 1025. The need to reassert control of prices was a major theme of Li Peng's report of March 1995 to the National People's Congress.

184. *China Agricultural Yearbook 1996*, 52–53.

185. *China Agricultural Development Report*, 61–63.

186. Ke Bingsheng, "Policy."

187. Oi, "Two Decades," 623.

188. Brown, 15.

189. Li and Nie, 2.

190. For example, *Guangming ribao*, Oct. 25, 1989.

191. Shi Yuanchun, June 1997.

192. Li and Nie. Brown's photograph and endorsement grace the opening pages of the book.

193. See reviews by Vaclav Smil and Robert Paarlberg.

194. For Hebei's grain bureaucracy, see *Hebei sheng liangshi*, 18–20, 245–328, and more generally *Dangdai Zhongguo de liangshi gongzuo*.

195. Rozelle, 227.

196. Guo Yuhua, "Food and Family Relations," describes this situation. Other essays in the book, *Feeding China's Little Emperors*, describe other aspects of the changing food habits of children in the market economy.

197. This is the view expressed by T. White, *China's Longest Campaign*, chap. 3.

198. Li Zehou in *The Swarthmore Phoenix*, May 1, 1996. Li considers that Marx also asserted that to eat is most important. However, he acknowledges that his "food philosophy," *chifan zhexue*, has been ridiculed by other intellectuals. Li and Liu, 367.

Conclusion

1. Preface in E. Chang, *Rice-Sprout Song*, xix.

2. David Wang, chap. 4, analyzes this literature, especially with regard to women.

3. Gang Yue.

4. Farmer, 136–37, 191–92.

5. The tax surcharge, *huohao*, funds from Shandong, Shanxi, and Henan, were ordered by Qianlong to

be sent regularly to Zhili and other deficit provinces. "Thus, instead of trying to broaden the fiscal base in provinces with chronic shortages, the central government chose to manipulate the levels of funding already available." Zelin, 284.

6. I thank Paul Smith for these insights.

7. Kaplan, *Provisioning Paris*, 598.

8. Lee and Wang, 35–37. Quoted more fully in Introduction in this book.

9. Bongaarts and Cain, and Charbonneau, as cited in L. M. Li, "Introduction: Food, Famine, and the Chinese State."

10. Malthus, 47. Rich local data from early modern European history has permitted numerous studies of the impact of mortality crises on overall mortality rates.

11. Gamble, *Ting Hsien*, 36.

12. Summarized in Fogel, 5–8.

13. Others have estimated that the mortality from famine was much greater than mortality from rebellions and internal disturbance, but it is impossible to separate *tianzai* and *renhuo*. See Chapter 10 in this book.

14. Yung-fa Chen, 9. Under Liu Shao-chi's guidance, "Party cadres in central and eastern China learned much from their comrades in both North and northwestern China, and many of them surely acquired their first revolutionary experience there."

15. Sen particularly had in mind the contrast with India, equally poor in the 1960s, but with no famine. The Nobel Prize-winning economist has written about the relationship between democracy and famine in several places, including "Democracy as a Universal Value," 7–8: "In the terrible history of famines in the world, no substantial famine has ever occurred in any independent and democratic country with a relatively free press."

16. Sen, *Poverty and Famines*, chaps. 6–7. Drèze and Sen is devoted to the policy implications of such insights.

17. UNDP report, *http://www.unchina.org/about_china/html/poverty.shtmal*. The 2002 figure is from *People's Daily* online at http://english.peopledaily.com.cn/200310/16/eng20031016_126204.shtml#

18. *People's Daily*.

19. Dec. 17, 1997, in http://vikingphoenix.com/news/archives/1997/asai/as970021.htm.

20. Business Daily Update, *Financial Times Information*, Dec. 15, 2004.

21. Barber and Ryder, chap. 1.

22. Li Cheng and White, 252.

23. "Beijing Leaders' Populist Touch Is not Felt by Most Rural Poor," *New York Times*, Jan. 10, 2004.

Weights and Measures

1. Chuan and Kraus, 98.

2. Peng Xinwei, 1:xl.

3. "Cereal Trade in Tientsin," 105.

4. Will and Wong, 236–50.

5. Ibid., 242.

Appendix 1

1. *Hebei sheng yange tugao* (1933); and "(CHGIS) Chinese Historical Geographic Information Service, Version 1.0. 1820 Qing Dynasty," Cambridge, MA: Harvard Yenching Institute, Apr. 2002. On administrative ranks, see Skinner, "Cities," 301–4.

Appendix 2

1. *Baimai* was the superior grade of wheat; *hongmai* was inferior. The difference between the two was usually about 1 qian. See Chapter 3 in this book.

2. Chuan and Kraus, 92–98. At Tianjin in the 1920s "a picul of husked and polished rice weighs 160 catties." "Cereal Trade in Tientsin," 105.

3. Yeh-chien Wang, "Qingdai de liangjia chenbao zhidu," 57.

4. Wilkinson, "Studies in Chinese Price History," chap. 4, and 167–70.

5. Skinner, "Sichuan's Population." Also discussed in Chapter 3 in this book.

6. For a discussion of Fengtian grain prices, see James Lee et al., "Infanticide."

7. In Rawski and Li, 40–47.

8. This description is based on a draft manuscript "Documentary Evidences for Reconstruction of Historical Climate in China," which was provided to the author by Zhang Peiyuan in 1997.

9. In conversations in 1992 and 1997, Professor Zhang expressed his confidence in this rainfall data, but acknowledged that the simulation techniques used to fill in missing data may tend to undercount the number of flood years. He and his colleagues have also found that winter precipitation declined after the mid-nineteenth century, as did the harvest ratings, but they were uncertain whether this was a fundamental shift in climate or a change in the reporting system. We have also found this result in our analysis of the price and rain data. See Appendix 3, section on case studies in this book.

10. Yang Eryou memorial, 1742, trans. in Dunstan, *Conflicting*, 86.

Appendix 3

*These results are available from the author.

1. See Chapter 3 in this book for discussion of crop cycles. Recent publications also describe the seasonal patterns in this way, for example, *Hebei sheng liangshi*, 55.

2. The Chow text was developed by Gregory C. Chow, "Tests of Equality Between Sets of Coefficients in Two Linear Regressions," *Econometrica* 28, no. 3 (July 1960): 591–605.

BIBLIOGRAPHY

Abbreviations that were used in the Notes are also indicated here, in bold after the entry. See List of Gazetteers for prefectural and county gazetteers.

Abel, Wilhelm. *Agricultural Fluctuations in Europe from the Thirteenth to the Twentieth Centuries.* Trans. Olive Ordish. New York: St. Martin's Press, 1980.

Alitto, Guy S. *The Last Confucian: Liang Shu-ming and the Chinese Dilemma of Modernity.* 2d ed. Berkeley: University of California Press, 1986.

American Board of Commissioners for Foreign Missions. North China Mission. 1860–1950. 88 vols. Houghton Library, Harvard University. **ABCFM.**

American National Red Cross. *The Report of the American Red Cross Commission to China.* Washington, DC: American Red Cross, 1929.

Appleby, Andrew B. "The Disappearance of the Plague: A Continuing Puzzle." *Economic History Review,* 2d series, XXXIII, no. 2 (May 1980): 161–73.

———. "Epidemics and Famine in the Little Ice Age." In *Climate and History,* ed. Rotberg and Rabb, 63–83.

———. *Famine in Tudor and Stuart England.* Stanford, CA: Stanford University Press, 1978.

———. "Grain Prices and Subsistence Crises in England and France, 1590–1740." *Journal of Economic History* 39, no. 4 (Dec. 1979): 865–87.

Arnold, Julean, et al. *China: A Commercial and Industrial Handbook.* Washington, DC: Government Printing Office, 1926.

Ashton, Basil, Kenneth Hill, Alan Piazza, and Robin Zeitz. "Famine in China, 1958–61." *Population and Development Review* 10, no. 4 (Dec. 1984): 613–45.

Bachao shengxun 八朝聖訓 [Sacred edicts of the eight reigns]. Guangxu ed. Gaozong (QL), Renzong (JQ), Xuanzong (DG). **BCSX.**

Baiyang dian zonghe zhili yu kaifa yanjiu 白洋淀综合治理与开发研究 [Research on the comprehensive management and development of the Baiyang dian]. Comp. Baiyang dian guotu jingji yanjiu hui et al. 白洋淀国土经济研究会. Shijiazhuang: Hebei renmin chubanshe, 1987.

Baker, John Earle. "Fighting China's Famines." Unpublished manuscript, 1943. Burke Library, Union Theological Seminary, New York.

Banister, Judith. *China's Changing Population.* Stanford, CA: Stanford University Press, 1987.

Barber, Margaret, and Gráinne Ryder. *Damming the Three Gorges.* 2d ed. Toronto: Earthscan, 1993.

Barclay, George W., Ansley J. Coale, et al. "A Reassessment of the Demography of Traditional Rural China." *Population Index* 42, no. 4 (Oct. 1976): 606–35.

Bartlett, Beatrice S. *Monarchs and Ministers: The Grand Council in Mid-Ch'ing China, 1723–1820.* Berkeley: University of California Press, 1991.

Becker, Jasper. *Hungry Ghosts: Mao's Secret Famine.* New York: Free Press, 1996.

Beijing lishi jinian 北京历史纪年 [Annual record of Beijing's history]. Comp. Beijing shi shehui kexue yanjiusuo. Beijing: Beijing chubanshe, 1984.

"Beijing shi jin wubainian han lao fenxi" 北京市近五百年旱涝分析 [Analysis of 500 years of drought and flood in Beijing city]. By Beijing shi qixiang tai 北京市气象台 [Beijing meteorological station]. In *Qihou bianqian he chaochangqi yubao wenji*, 126–28.

Beijing shuihan zaihai 北京水旱灾害 [Flood and drought crises in Beijing]. Comp. Beijing shi shuili ju 北京水利局. Beijing: Zhongguo shuili shuidian chubanshe, 1999.

Beijing tongshi 北京通史 [History of Beijing]. Ed. Cao zixi 曹子西. 10 vols. Beijing: Zhongguo shudian, 1994.

Benton, Gregor. "Comparative Perspectives: North and Central China in the Anti-Japanese Resistance." In *North China at War*, ed. Feng and Goodman, 189–223.

Bergère, Marie-Claire. "Une Crise de subsistance en Chine, 1920–1922." *Annales: Économies, Societés, Civilisations* 28, no. 6 (Nov.–Dec. 1973): 1361–1402.

Bernstein, Thomas P. "Stalinism, Famine, and Chinese Peasants: Grain Procurements During the Great Leap Forward." *Theory and Society* 13, no. 3 (1984): 339–77.

Blecher, Marc, and Vivienne Shue. *Tethered Deer: Government and Economy in a Chinese County.* Stanford, CA: Stanford University Press, 1996.

Blom, C. F. "The Values of Famine Relief Work." *The Chinese Recorder* 63, no. 11 (1984): 696–99.

Bohr, Paul Richard. *Famine in China and the Missionary: Timothy Richard as Relief Administrator and Advocate of National Reform, 1876–1884.* Cambridge, MA: Harvard University, East Asian Research Center, 1972.

Boorman, Howard, ed. *Biographical Dictionary of Republican China.* 4 vols. New York: Columbia University Press, 1967–71.

Boserup, Ester. *The Conditions of Agricultural Growth: The Economics of Agrarian Change Under Population Pressure.* Chicago: Aldine, 1965.

Bouillard, G. *The North China Floods in 1917: Their Consequences and Proposed Methods for Dealing with Them.* Tianjin: n.p., 1918.

Brandt, Loren. *Commercialization and Agricultural Development: Central and Eastern China, 1870–1937.* Cambridge: Cambridge University Press, 1989.

———. Review of Philip C. C. Huang, *The Peasant Economy and Social Change in North China.* In *Economic Development and Cultural Change* 35, no. 4 (July 1987): 670–82.

Brandt, Loren, and Barbara Sands. "Land Concentration and Income Distribution in Republican China." In *Chinese History*, ed. Rawski and Li, 179–206.

Braudel, F. P., and F. Spooner. "Prices in Europe from 1450 to 1750." In *The Cambridge Economic History of Europe*, vol. 4 (The Economy of Expanding Europe in the Sixteenth and Seventeenth Centuries), ed. E. E. Rich and C. H. Wilson, chap. 4, 374–486. Cambridge: Cambridge University Press, 1967.

Bray, Francesca. *Agriculture.* Vol. 6, pt. 2 of *Science and Civilization in China*. Ed. Joseph Needham. Cambridge: Cambridge University Press, 1984.

Bretschneider, E(mil). *The Plain of Peking and the Neighboring Hill Country.* Simla: Government Central Branch Press, 1876.

Brook, Timothy. *The Confusions of Pleasure: Commerce and Culture in Ming China.* Berkeley: University of California Press, 1998.

———. "The Spread of Rice Cultivation and Rice Technology into the Hebei Region in the Ming and

Qing." In *Exploration in the History of Science and Technology in China* (Festschrift volume in honor of Dr. Joseph Needham), 659–89. Shanghai: Shangguji, 1982.

Brown, Lester R. *Who Will Feed China: Wake-Up Call for a Small Planet*. New York: W. W. Norton, 1995.

Brunnert, H. S., and V. V. Hagelstrom. *Present Day Political Organization of China*. Shanghai: Kelly and Walsh, 1912; reprint, Taipei: Book World, 1960.

Bu Fengxian 卜风贤. "Zhongguo nongye zaihaishi yanjiu zonglun" 中国农业灾害史研究综论 [Introduction to research on the history of Chinese agricultural disasters]. *Zhongguoshi yanjiu dongtai* 2001, no. 2: 2–9.

Buck, John Lossing. *Chinese Farm Economy*. Nanking: University of Nanking, 1930.

———. *Land Utilization in China*. Nanking: University of Nanking, 1937; reprint, New York: The Council on Economic and Cultural Affairs, 1956.

Campbell, Cameron. "Public Health Efforts in China Before 1949 and Their Effects on Mortality: The Case of Beijing." *Social Science History* 21, no. 2 (summer 1997): 179–218.

Cao Shuji 曹树基. *Zhongguo renkou shi* 中國人口史. Vol. 5. *Qing* shiji 清時期. Shanghai: Fudan daxue chubanshe, 2001.

Caoyun quanshu 漕運全書 [Complete documents of the grain tribute]. 1875 ed. **CYQS**.

"Caring for the Tientsin Flood Sufferers." *The Far Eastern Review* XIII, no. 19 (Dec. 1917): 765–66.

"Cereal Trade in Tientsin." *Chinese Economic Journal* 2, no. 2 (Feb. 1928): 104–8.

Chan, Wing-tsit, trans. and comp. *A Source Book in Chinese Philosophy*. Princeton, NJ: Princeton University Press, 1963.

Chang, C. C. (Chang Hsin-i). *China's Food Supply Problem*. Institute of Pacific Relations, 1931. Also Zhang Xinyi 張心一. *Zhongguo liangshi wenti* 中國糧食問題 [China's food supply problem]. Shanghai: Zhongguo taipingyang guoji xuehui, 1932.

Chang, Eileen. *The Rice-Sprout Song*. Foreword by David Der-wei Wang. New York: Scribner, 1955; reprint, Berkeley: University of California Press, 1998.

Chang, Hsin-pao. *Commissioner Lin and the Opium War*. Cambridge, MA: Harvard University Press, 1964.

Chang, Michael G. "Fathoming Qianlong: Imperial Activism, The Southern Tours, and the Politics of Water Control, 1736–1765." *Late Imperial China* 24, no. 2 (Dec. 2003): 51–108.

Chao, Kang. *The Development of Cotton Textile Production in China*. Cambridge, MA: East Asian Research Center, Harvard University, 1977.

———. *Man and Land in Chinese History: An Economic Analysis*. Stanford, CA: Stanford University Press, 1986.

Cheek, Timothy. *Propaganda and Culture in Mao's China: Deng Tuo and the Intelligentsia*. Oxford: Clarendon Press, 1997.

Chen Chau-nan. *Fluctuations of Bimetallic Exchange Rates in China, 1700–1850—A Preliminary Survey*. Nankang, Taiwan: Institute of Economics, Academia Sinica, Economic Papers, Selected Series, no. 3, Dec. 1968.

Chen Jiahua 陳佳華. "Baqi bingxiang shixi" 八旗兵餉試析 [Preliminary analysis of the banner stipends]. *Minzu yanjiu* 1985, no. 5: 63–71.

Chen Jinling 陳金陵. "Qingdai Jingshi liangjia ji qita" 清代京師糧價及其他 [Grain prices in Qing-dynasty Beijing]. In *Qingshi yanjiu ji* [Collected research on Qing history], ed. Zhongguo Renmin Daxue Qingshi So, 3:228–64. Guangming ribao chubanshe, 1988.

Chen Kung-po. "Self-Sufficiency in Food Supply." *Chinese Economic Journal* XVII, no. 2 (Aug. 1935): 97–135.

Chen Shuping 陳樹平 "Yumi he fanshu zai Zhongguo chuanbo qingkuang yanjiu" 玉米和番薯 在中國傳播情況研究 [Research on the spread of corn and sweet potato in China]. *Zhongguo shehui kexue* 1980, no. 3: 187–204.

Chen, Yung-fa. *Making Revolution: The Communist Movement in Eastern and Central China, 1937–1945.* Berkeley: University of California Press, 1986.

Cheng, Li, and Lynn White. "The Fifteenth Central Committee of the Chinese Communist Party: Full-Fledged Technocratic Leadership with Partial Control by Jiang Zemin." *Asian Survey* 38, no. 3 (Mar. 1998): 231–64.

Cheng, Yuk-shing, and Shu-ki Tsang. "The Changing Grain Marketing System in China." *China Quarterly* 139 (Sept. 1994): 1080–1104.

Chi Zihua 池子華, and Li Hongying 李紅英. "Wan Qing Zhili zaihuang ji jianzai zuoshi de tantao" 晚清直隸災荒及減災作施的探討 [Investigation of famine and famine relief in late Qing Zhili]. *Qingshi yanjiu* 2001, no. 2 (May): 72–92.

Ch'ien, Tuan-sheng. *The Government and Politics of China, 1912–1949.* Stanford, CA: Stanford University Press, 1970.

Chihli River Commission. *Reports of the Works Department, 1919–1925.*

China Agricultural Development Report '96. Ministry of Agriculture, People's Republic of China. Beijing: China Agriculture Press, 1996.

China Agricultural Yearbook 1996 (Eng. ed.). Comp. The Committee for. . . . Beijing: China Agricultural Press, 1997.

China Famine Fund Records. Presbyterian Historical Society, Philadelphia. 82/20/11.

China International Famine Relief Commission. *The CIFRC Fifteenth Anniversary Book, 1921–1936.* Peiping: CIFRC, 1936.

China, National Flood Relief Commission. *The Work of the National Flood Relief Commission of the National Government of China, August 1931–June 1932.* Shanghai: National Government of China, 1932.

China Statistical Abstract 1990. Comp. The State Statistical Bureau of the People's Republic of China. New York: Praeger, 1991.

"Chinese Flour Industry, 1930." *Chinese Economic Journal* 8, no. 2 (Feb. 1931): 106–12.

Chu, Coching (see also Chu Ko-chen, Zhu Kezhen). "Climatic Changes During Historic Time in China." *Journal of the North China Branch of the Royal Asiatic Society* 62 (1931): 32–40.

Chu Han 楚汉. *Zhongguo, 1959–1961—sannian ziran zaihai changpian jishi* 中国, 1959–1961—三年自然灾害长篇纪实 [China, 1959–1961—the long record of three years of natural disaster]. Chengdu: Sichuan renmin chubanshe, 1996.

Chu, Ko-chen. "A Preliminary Study on the Climatic Fluctuations During the Last 5,000 Years in China." *Scientia Sinica* XVI, no. 2 (1973): 226–49. (Eng. trans. of 1972 article in Chinese.)

Chuan, Han-sheng, and Richard A. Kraus. *Mid-Ch'ing Rice Markets and Trade: An Essay in Price History.* Cambridge, MA: Harvard University, East Asia Research Center, 1975.

Ch'uan Han-sheng 全漢昇. "Qianlong shisan nian de migui wenti" 乾隆十三年的米貴問題 [The question of high rice prices in Qianlong 13]. In his *Zhongguo jingjishi luncong*, 547–66. 1964; reprint, Hong Kong: Zhongwen shudian, 1972.

Ch'uan Han-sheng 全漢昇 and Wang Yeh-chien 王業鍵. "Qing Yongzheng nianjian (1723–35) de mijia" 清雍正年間的米價 [Rice prices in the Yongzheng period]. *Zhongyang yanjiuyuan, Lishi yanjiusuo jikan* 30 (Oct. 1959): 157–85.

Coclanis, Peter A. "Distant Thunder: The Creation of a World Market in Rice and the Transformation it Wrought." *American Historical Review* 98, no. 4 (Oct. 1993): 1050–78.

Cohen, Paul A. *History in Three Keys: The Boxers as Event, Experience, and Myth.* New York: Columbia University Press, 1997.

Cohen, Warren I. *The Chinese Connection.* New York: Columbia University Press, 1978.

Conquest, Robert. *The Harvest of Sorrow: Soviet Collectivization and the Terror Famine.* New York and Oxford: Oxford University Press, 1986.

Coons, Arthur G. "China's Imports and Exports of Foodstuffs." *Chinese Economic Journal* 14, no. 5 (May 1934): 564–20.

Croll, Elisabeth. *The Family Rice Bowl: Food and Domestic Economy in China*. Geneva and London: United Nations Research Institute for Social Development and Zed Press, 1983.

Crook, Isabel, and David Crook. *The First Years of Yangyi Commune*. London: Routledge and Kegan Paul, 1966.

———. *Revolution in a Chinese Village: Ten Mile Inn*. London: Routledge and Kegan Paul, 1959.

———. *Ten Mile Inn: Mass Movement in a Chinese Village*. New York: Pantheon Books, 1979.

Crossley, Pamela Kyle. *Orphan Warriors: Three Manchu Generations and the End of the Qing World*. Princeton, NJ: Princeton University Press, 1990.

Da Qing huidian 大清會典 [Collected statutes of the Qing dynasty]. 1899 ed.

Da Qing huidian shili. 大清會典事例 [Collected statutes and precedents of the Qing dynasty]. 1899 ed. HDSL.

Dai Yi 戴逸, ed. *Jianming Qingshi* 簡明情史 [A simplified history of the Qing]. 2 vols. Beijing: Renmin, 1980.

Dangdai Beijing jianshi 当代北京的简史 [Short history of contemporary Beijing]. Zhou Yixing 周一兴, ed. Beijing: Dangdai Zhongguo chubanshe, 1999.

Dangdai Hebei jianshi 当代河北简史 [Short history of contemporary Hebei]. Ed. Han Licheng 韩立成 et al. Beijing: Dangdai Zhongguo chubanshe, 1997.

Dangdai Zhongguo de Hebei 当代中国的河北 [Contemporary China's Hebei]. Comp. Deng Liqqun 邓力群 et al. 2 vols. Beijing: Zhongguo shehui kexue chubanshe, 1990.

Dangdai Zhongguo de liangshi gongzuo 当代中国的粮食工作 [Contemporary China's food grain]. Ed. The Committee for the Contemporary China Series. Beijing: Zhongguo shehui kexue chubanshe, 1988.

Dangdai Zhongguo de Tianjin 当代中国的天津 [Contemporary China's Tianjin]. Comp. Deng Liqqun 邓力群 et al. 2 vols. Beijing: Zhongguo shehui kexue chubanshe, 1989.

Davis, Mike. *Late Victorian Holocausts: El Niño Famines and the Making of the Third World*. London: Verso, 2001.

De Vries, Jan. "Measuring the Impact of Climate on History: Search for Appropriate Methodologies." In *Climate and History*, ed. Rotberg and Rabb, 19–50.

Deng Tuo 鄧拓 [Deng Yunte 鄧雲特]. *Zhongguo jiuhuangshi* 中國救荒史. Reprint of 1937 and 1957 eds. Beijing: Beijing chubanshe, 1998; Taipei: Shangwu, 1978.

Dennys, Nicholas Belfield, ed. *The Treaty Ports of China and Japan*. London: Trubner, 1867.

Des Forges, Roger V. *Cultural Centrality and Political Change in Chinese History: Northeast Henan in the Fall of the Ming*. Stanford, CA: Stanford University Press, 2003.

Ding Jinjun 丁进军. "Kangxi yu Yongdinghe." 康熙与永定河 [Kangxi and the Yongding River]. *Shixue yuekan* 1987, no. 6: 33–36.

Ding Shu 丁抒. *Renhuo: Da Yuejin yu da jihuang* 人祸: "大躍進" 與大飢荒 [Human calamity: The Great Leap Forward and big famine]. 2d ed. Hong Kong: The Nineties Monthly Going Fine Ltd., 1996.

Dodgen, Randall A. *Controlling the Dragon: Confucian Engineers and the Yellow River in Late Imperial China*. Honolulu: University of Hawaii Press, 2001.

———. "Hydraulic Evolution and Dynastic Decline: The Yellow River Conservancy, 1796–1855." *Late Imperial China* 12, no. 2 (Dec. 1991): 36–63.

Dong Kaichen 董恺忱. "Ming-Qing liangdai de 'Jifu shuili'" 明清两代的"畿辅水利 ["Water conservancy in the capital region" during the Ming and Qing periods]. *Beijing nongye daxue xuebao* 1980, no. 3: 77–87.

Dong Wei 董煟. *Jiuhuang huomin shu* 救荒活命書 [Handbook on sustaining famine victims]. Reprint, Shanghai, 1936.

Drèze, Jean, and Amartya Sen. *Hunger and Political Action.* Oxford: Clarendon Press, 1989.

Duan Yunhuai 段运怀, and Zhang Qingchen 章庆辰. "Huabei pingyuan de jiangshui yu nongye shengchang" 华北平原的降水与农业生产 [Precipitation in the North China plain and agricultural production]. *Ziran ziyuan* 1986: 39–50.

Duara, Prasenjit. *Culture, Power, and the State: Rural North China, 1900–1942.* Stanford, CA: Stanford University Press, 1988.

Dunstan, Helen. "An Anthology of Chinese Economic Statecraft, or the Sprouts of Liberalism." Unpublished manuscript, 1988.

———. *Conflicting Counsels to Confuse the Age: A Documentary Study of Political Economy in Qing China, 1644–1840.* Ann Arbor: Center for Chinese Studies, University of Michigan, 1996.

———. "The Emergence of Economic Liberalism in Eighteenth Century China." Unpublished paper, 1993.

———. "The Late Ming Epidemics: A Preliminary Survey." *Ch'ing-shih wen-t'i* 3, no. 3 (Nov. 1975): 1–59.

———. "'Orders Go Forth in the Morning and Are Changed by Nightfall': A Monetary Policy Cycle in Qing China, November 1744–June 1745." *T'oung Pao* LXXXII (1996): 66–136.

———. "Safely Supping with the Devil: The Qing State and its Merchant Suppliers of Copper." *Late Imperial China* 13, no. 2 (Dec. 1992): 42–81.

———. *State or Merchant? Political Economy and Political Process in 1740s China.* Cambridge, MA: Harvard University Asian Center, forthcoming.

Edgerton-Tarpley, Kathryn. "Family and Gender in Famine: Cultural Responses to Disaster in North China, 1876–1879." *Journal of Women's History* 16, no. 4 (2004): 119–47.

———. "Narratives of Blame: Contested Heroes and Villains of the North China Famine, 1876–2001." Paper presented at the Annual Meeting of the Association for Asian Studies, Mar. 2004.

Edkins, Joseph. *Modern China: Thirty-one Short Essays on Subjects Which Illustrate the Present Condition of the Country.* Shanghai: Kelly and Walsh, 1891.

Edwards, Dwight W. "The Missionary and Famine Relief." *The Chinese Recorder* 63, no. 11 (1932): 689–96.

Elliott, Mark C. *The Manchu Way: The Eight Banners and Ethnic Identity in Late Imperial China.* Stanford, CA: Stanford University Press, 2001.

Elvin, Mark. *The Pattern of the Chinese Past.* Stanford, CA: Stanford University Press, 1973.

———. "Who Was Responsible for the Weather? Moral Meteorology in Late Imperial China." *Osiris* 13 (1998): 213–37.

Elvin, Mark, and Liu Ts'ui-jung, eds. *Sediments of Time: Environment and Society in Chinese History.* Cambridge: Cambridge University Press, 1998.

Ershi shiji Huabei chengshi jindaihua 二十世纪华北城市近代化 [Urban modernization of North China in the 20th century]. Special issue of *Chengshi shi yanjiu* 21 (July 2002).

Ershi shiji Zhongguo zaibian tushi 二十世纪中国灾变图史 [Pictorial history of disasters in twentieth-century China]. 2 vols. Ed. Xia Ming fang 夏明方, Kang Peizhu 康沛竹. Fuzhou: Fujian jiaoyu chubanshe, 2001.

"Experiment with Drought-resisting Crops." *Chinese Economic Journal* 9, no. 3 (Sept. 1931): 957–62.

Famine Commission Bulletin. Monthly publication of the China International Famine Relief Commission. Peking.

The Famine in China: Illustrations by a Native Artist with a Translation of the Chinese Text. Issue by the Committee of the China Famine Relief Fund. Trans. James Legge. London: C. Kegan Paul, 1878.

"Famine Relief in 1926." *Chinese Economic Journal* I, no. 8 (Aug. 1927): 762–65.

Fan I-chun. "The Rice Trade of Modern China—A Case Study of Anhwei and its Entrepôt Wuhu, 1877–1937." In *The Second Conference on Modern Chinese Economic History* (Proceedings), 687–739. Taipei: Institute of Economics, Academia Sinica, 1989.

Fang Guancheng 方觀承. *Jifu yicang tu* 畿輔義倉圖 [Maps of charity granaries in the capital region]. 1753.

———. *Zhenji* 賑紀 [Record of relief]. 1754.

Fang Kemin (Guancheng) gong zouyi 方恪敏公奏議 [Collected memorials of Fang Guancheng 方觀承]. 1851 ed.; reprint, 2 vols. *Jindai Zhongguo shiliao congkan* 11:103; Taipei: Wenhai, 1967.

"Fangzhi wenchao" 方志文抄 [Handcopied notes from gazetteers]. Nanjing Agricultural University, History Department.

Farmer, Edward L. *Early Ming Government: The Evolution of Dual Capitals.* Cambridge, MA: East Asian Research Center, Harvard University, 1976.

Feng, Chongyi, and David S. G. Goodman, eds. *North China at War: The Social Ecology of Revolution, 1937–1945.* Lanham, MD: Rowman and Littlefield, 2000.

Feng Liwen 冯丽文. "Beijing 1724–1979 nian shengzhangji ganhan tezheng ji qi duonian bianhua" 北京 1724–1979 年生长季干旱特征及其多年变化 [The characteristics of drought and its variation during the growing period from 1724–1979 in Beijing]. *Dili xuebao* 37, no. 2 (June 1982): 194–205.

Feuerwerker, Albert. "Economic Trends, 1912–49." In *The Cambridge History of China*, vol. 12, pt. 1, ed. John K. Fairbank, 28–127. Cambridge: Cambridge University Press, 1983.

Fisher, David Hackett. *The Great Wave: Price Revolutions and the Rhythm of History.* New York: Oxford University Press, 1996.

"The Floods of North China." *Far Eastern Review* XIII, no. 18 (Nov. 1917): 755–57.

Fogel, Robert William. *The Escape from Hunger and Premature Death, 1700–2100: Europe, America, and the Third World.* Cambridge: Cambridge University Press, 2004.

Fong, H. D. *Cotton Industry and Trade in China.* Vol. 1. Tientsin: Chihli Press, 1932.

Fortune, Robert. *Yedo and Peking.* London: J. Murray, 1863.

Frank, Andre Gunder. *ReORIENT: Global Economy in the Asian Age.* Berkeley: University of California Press, 1998.

Freeman-Mitford, A. B. (Baron Redesdale). *The Attaché at Peking.* London: Macmillan, 1900.

Friedman, Edward, Paul G. Pickowicz, and Mark Selden. *Chinese Village, Socialist State.* New Haven, CT: Yale University Press, 1991.

Gamble, Sidney D. *How Chinese Families Live in Peiping: A Study of Income and Expenditure of 283 Chinese Families Receiving from $8 to $550 Silver per Month.* New York: Funk and Wagnalls, 1933.

———. *North China Villages: Social, Political, and Economic Activities Before 1933.* Berkeley: University of California Press, 1963.

———. *Ting Hsien: A North China Rural Community.* Institute of Pacific Relations, 1954; reprint, Stanford, CA: Stanford University Press, 1968.

Gamble, Sidney D., and John Stewart Burgess. *Peking: A Social Survey.* New York: George H. Doran, 1921.

Gang, Yue. *The Mouth that Begs: Hunger, Cannibalism, and the Politics of Eating in Modern China.* Durham, NC: Duke University Press, 1999.

Godement, Francois. "Famine in the Warlord Age: The 1928–30 Crisis in North China." Paper presented at the Workshop on Food and Famine in Chinese History, Harvard University, Aug. 1980.

Goldstone, Jack A. "Monetary Versus Velocity Interpretations of the 'Price Revolution': A Comment." *Journal of Economic History* 51, no. 1 (Mar. 1991): 176–80.

Gong Gaofa 龚高法, Zhang Jinrong 张瑾瑢, and Zhang Piyuan 张丕远 [Peiyuan]. "Yingyong shiliao fengqian jizai yanjiu Beijing diqu jiangshuiliang dui dong xiaomai shoucheng de yingxiang" 应用史料奉歉记载研究北京地区降水量对冬小麦收成的影响 [A study of the impacts of precipitation on harvest of winter wheat by historical harvest records]. *Qixiang xuebao (Acta meteorological sinica)* 41, no. 4 (Nov. 1983): 444–51.

(Qinding) Gongbu zeli. 工部则例 [Regulations and precedents of the Board of Works]. 1815 ed.; 1884 ed. reprint, Taipei: Chengwen, 1966.

Gongzhongdang 宮中檔. [Palace memorial archives]. National Palace Museum, Taipei. **GZD.**

Gongzhongdang Kangxichao zouzhe 宮中檔康熙朝奏摺 [Memorials from the Palace Museum Archives, Kangxi reign]. 9 vols. Taipei: National Palace Museum, 1977. **GZDKXC.**

Gongzhongdang Qianlongchao zouzhe 宮中檔乾隆朝奏摺 [Memorials from the Palace Memorial Archives, Qianlong reign]. 75 vols. Taipei: National Palace Museum, 1979–89. **GZDQLC.**

Gongzhongdang Yongzhengchao zouzhe 宮中檔雍正朝奏摺 [Memorials from the Palace Memorial Archives: Yongzheng reign]. 32 vols. Taipei: National Palace Museum, 1977–80. **GZDYZC.**

Gongzhongdang zhupizouzhe 宮中檔硃批奏摺 [Palace Memorial Archives]. First Historical Archives, Beijing. **ZPZZ.**

    Caizheng cangchu 財政倉儲 [Financial affairs, granaries] **ZPZZ, CZCC.**

    Caizheng diding 財政地丁 [Financial affairs, land-poll tax]. **ZPZZ, CZDD.**

    Caizheng tianfu 財政田賦 [Financial affairs, land tax] **ZPZZ, CZTF.**

    Neizheng zhenji 內政賑濟 [Internal affairs, relief]. **ZPZZ, NZZJ.**

    Shuili 水利 [Water control]. **ZPZZ, SL.**

Goodman, David S. G. "JinJiLuYu in the Sino-Japanese War: The Border Region and the Border Region Government." *China Quarterly* 140 (Dec. 1994): 1007–24.

———. "The Sixth Plenum of the 11th Central Committee of the CCP: Look Back in Anger?" *China Quarterly* 87 (Sept. 1981): 518–27.

Gottfried, Robert S. *The Black Death: Natural and Human Disaster in Medieval Europe.* New York: Free Press, 1983.

Gottschang, Thomas R., and Diana Lary. *Swallows and Settlers: The Great Migration from North China to Manchuria.* Ann Arbor: Center for Chinese Studies, University of Michigan, 2000.

The Great Famine. China Famine Relief Committee. Shanghai: American Presbyterian Mission Press, 1879.

Greenough, Paul R. *Prosperity and Misery in Modern Bengal: The Famine of 1943–1944.* New York and Oxford: Oxford University Press, 1982.

Grove, Linda. "International Trade and the Creation of Domestic Marketing Networks in North China, 1860–1930." In *Commercial Networks in Modern Asia*, ed. S. Sugiyama and Linda Grove, 96–115. Richmond, Surrey: Curzon, 2001.

Guan Weilan 官蔚藍. *Zhonghua minguo xingzheng quhua ji tudi renkou tongji biao* 中華民國行政區劃 及土地人口統計表 [Administrative districts and statistical tables on the land and population of the Republic of China]. Taipei: Beikai, 1956.

Guo Songyi 郭松义. "Qingdai guonei de haiyun maoyi" 清代国内的海运贸易 [The coastal trade among the Chinese in the early Qing]. *Qingshi luncong* 1982, no. 4: 92–110.

Guo Yuhua. "Food and Family Relations: The Generation Gap at the Table." In *Feeding China's Little Emperors*, ed. Jun Jing, 94–113. Stanford, CA: Stanford University Press, 2000.

Haihe liuyu lidai ziran zaihai shiliao 海河流域历代自然灾害史料 [Historical materials on natural disasters in the Hai River Basin]. Comp. Hebei sheng hanlau yubao keti zu. Beijing: Qixiang chuban she, 1985. **HHLY.**

The Haihe River Basin and the Development and Utilization of Water Resources in the Basin. Pamphlet of the Hai River Conservancy Commission, Ministry of Water Resources. Tianjin, 1989[?].

Haihe shi jianbian 海河史简编 [Short history of the Hai River]. Comp. Committee to edit the Hai he shi jianbian. Beijing: Shuili dianli chubanshe, 1977.

Hamaguchi Nobuko 濱口允子. "Huabei chengshi de liangshi gongji jiegou—yi Tianjin doudian wei zhongxin" 华北城市的粮食供给结构—以天津斗店为中心 [The grain supply of North China cities—Tianjin's grain warehouses]. In *Ershi shiji Huabei chengshi jindaihua*, 135–51.

Han Guanghui 韓光輝. *Beijing lishi renkou dili* 北京歷史人口地理 [The historical population and geography of Beijing]. Beijing: Beijing daxue chubanshe, 1996.

———. "Jin Yuan Ming Qing Beijing liangshi gongxu yu xiaofei yanjiu" 金元明清北京糧食供需與消費

研究 [Study of the supply and consumption of grain in Beijing during the Jin, Yuan, Ming, and Qing]. *Zhongguo nongshi* 13, no. 3 (1993): 11–21.

———. "Qingdai Beijing zhenxu jigou shikong fenbu yanjiu" 清代北京賑恤機構時空分布研究 [Study of the temporal and spatial distribution of relief organizations in Qing dynasty Beijing]. *Qingshi yanjiu* 96, no. 4 (1996): 20–31.

Han Xiangling. "Drought Characteristic and Agriculture in the North China Plain." English-language draft for *Huang Huai Hai diqu nongye qihou ziyuan kaifa liyong*, ca. 1987.

"Hantan, An Agricultural Center of Chihli." *Chinese Economic Journal* 1, no. 5 (May 1927): 464–72.

Hartford, Kathleen. "Fits and Starts: The Communist Party in Rural Hebei, 1921–1936." In *New Perspectives on the Chinese Communist Revolution*, ed. Tony Saich and Hans van de Ven, 144–74. Armonk, NY: M. E. Sharpe, 1995.

———. "Repression and Communist Success: The Case of Jin-Cha-Ji, 1938–1943." In *Single Sparks*, ed. Hartford and Goldstein, 92–127.

Hartford, Kathleen, and Steven M. Goldstein, eds. *Single Sparks: China's Rural Revolutions*. Armonk, NY: M. E. Sharpe, 1989.

Hayashi Reiko. "Provisioning Edo in the Early Eighteenth Century: The Pricing Policies of the Shogunate and the Crisis of 1733." In *Edo and Paris*, ed. McClain et al., 211–33.

Hayford, Charles W. *To the People: James Yen and Village China*. New York: Columbia University Press, 1990.

He Hanwei 何漢威. *Guangxu chunian (1876–1879) Huabei de da hanzai* 光緒初年 [1876–1879] 華北的大旱災 [The great North China drought of the early Guangxu reign]. Hong Kong: Chinese University Press, 1980.

Hebei fengwu zhi 河北风物志 [Hebei's scenic places]. Ed. Zhang Huiyi 張惠艺. Shijiazhuang: Hebei renmin, 1985.

Hebei jingji dili 河北省經濟地理 [Economic geography of Hebei Province]. Ed. Li Qingze 李庆泽. Beijing: Xinhua, 1987.

Hebei jingji nianjian 2001 河北经济年鉴 [Hebei economic yearbook]. Ed. Hebei sheng renmin zhengfu. Beijing: Zhongguo tongji, 2001.

Hebei jingji shudian, 1949–2001 河北经济数典 [Hebei economic statistics]. Shijiazhuang: Hebei renmin, 2001.

Hebei ribao 河北日報 [Hebei daily].

Hebei sheng gexian gaikuang yilan 河北省各縣概況一覽 [A look at the general conditions in counties in Hebei Province]. 1934.

Hebei sheng liangshi zhi 河北省糧食志 [Gazetteer of Hebei Province grain supply]. Comp. Hebei sheng liangshi zhi bianzuan weiyuan hui 河北省糧食志編纂委員會. Beijing: Zhongguo chengshi, 1994.

Hebei sheng Qingyuan xian shiqing diaocha 河北省清苑縣事情 [Affairs of Hebei Province's Qingyuan County]. Ed. Bian Qiansun 卞乾孫. N.p.: Xinminhui zhongyang zhidaobu, 1938.

Hebei sheng yange tugao 河北省沿革圖稿 [Draft maps of Hebei Province's evolution]. By Chen Tieqing 陳鐵卿. N.p. 1933.

Hebei sheng zonghe nongye quhua 河北省综合农业区划 [Hebei Province agricultural districts]. Ed. Hebei sheng zonghe nongye quhua committee. Shijiajuang: Hebei renmin chuban she, 1985.

Hebei shengzhi 河北省志 [Gazetteer of Hebei Province]. Ed. Hebei sheng difangzhi bianzuan weiyuan hui 河北省地方志编纂委员会. Vol. 8: *Qixiang zhi*. Beijing: Fangzhi chubanshe, 1996. Vol. 16: *Nongye zhi*. Beijing: Zhongguo nongye chubanshe, 1995. Vol. 20: *Shuili zhi*. Shijiazhung: Hebei renmin chubanshe, 1995.

Hegong taolun huiyi shilu. 河工討論會議實錄 [Veritable record of discussion group on river conservancy discussion group]. ca. 1918. 1 ce. English addendum.

Heijdra, Martin. "The Socio-economic Development of Rural China During the Ming." In *The Cambridge*

History of China. Vol. 8. *The Ming Dynasty, 1368–1644, Part 2,* ed. Denis Twitchett and Frederick W. Mote, 417–578. Cambridge: Cambridge University Press, 1998.

Hershatter, Gail. *The Workers of Tianjin, 1900–1949.* Stanford, CA: Stanford University Press, 1986.

Hinton, Harold C. *The Grain Tribute System of China (1845–1911).* Cambridge, MA: East Asian Research Center, Harvard University, 1956.

Hinton, William. *Fanshen: Documentary of Revolution in a Chinese Village.* Berkeley: University of California Press, 1966.

"History of the Chihli River Commission." *Chinese Economic Journal* I, no. 7 (July 1927): 634–44.

Ho Chin. *Harm into Benefit—Taming the Haiho River.* Peking: Foreign Languages Press, 1975.

Ho, Ping-ti. *Studies on the Population of China, 1368–1953.* Cambridge, MA: Harvard University Press, 1959.

Hosoya Yoshio 細谷良夫. "Hakki beiyokuko—Shinchō chūki no hakki keizai o megutte 八旗米局考—清朝中期の八旗經濟おめぐって [Investigation of the Eight Banners grain bureaus: Looking at the economy of the Eight Banners in the mid-Qing period]. *Shūkan tōyōgaku* 31 (June 1974): 181–208.

Hou Jianxin 侯建新. "Minguo nianjian Jizhong nonghu laodong shengchanlü yanjiu" 民國年間冀中農業勞動生產率研究 [Research on the productivity of agricultural labor in central Hebei during the Republican period]. *Zhongguo nongshi* 20, no. 1 (2001): 57–67.

Hsiao, Kung-chuan. *Rural China: Imperial Control in the Nineteenth Century.* Seattle and London: University of Washington Press, 1960.

Hu, Ch'ang-tu. "The Yellow River Administration in the Ch'ing Dynasty." *Far Eastern Quarterly* 14, no. 4 (Aug. 1955): 505–13.

(Qinding) Hubu zeli (欽定) 戶部則例 [Regulations and precedents of the Board of Revenue]. 1791 ed.

(Qinding) Hubu zeli (欽定) 戶部則例 [Regulations and precedents of the Board of Revenue]. 1874 ed. **HBZL**.

Huang Jianhua 黃建華. "Daoguang shidai de zaihuang dui shehui jingji de yingxiang (1821–1850)" 道光時代的災荒對社會經濟的影響. [The social and economic influence of the famines of the Daoguang era]. *Shihuo yuekan* 史貨月刊 4, no. 4 (July 1974): 127–40.

Huang Huai Hai diqu nongye qihou ziyuan kaifa liyong 黃淮海地区农业气候资源开发利用 [The exploitation and utilization of agroclimatic resources in Huang-Huai-Hai region]. Ed. Han Xiangling 韩湘玲 and Qu Manli 曲曼丽. Beijing: Beijing Nongye Daxue, 1987.

Huang Huai Hai pingyuan lishi dili 黃淮海平原历史地理 [Historical geography of the Huang-Huai-Hai plain]. Ed. Zou Yilin 邹逸麟. Anhui Press, 1993.

Huang, Philip C. C. *The Peasant Economy and Social Change in North China.* Stanford, CA: Stanford University Press, 1985.

———. *The Peasant Family and Rural Development in the Yangzi Delta, 1350–1988.* Stanford, CA: Stanford University Press, 1990.

Huang Rangtang 黄让堂, et al. "Hebei pingyuan shui ziyuan tedian he queshui zhuangkuang" 河北平原水资源特点和缺水状况 [Water resources and water shortage on the Hebei plain]. *Ziran ziyuan* 1987, no. 3: 73–80.

Huangchao jingshi wenbian 皇朝經世文編 [Anthology of statecraft writings of the Qing dynasty]. Comp. Wei Yuan 魏源 and He Changling 賀長齡. 1827. **HCJSWB**.

Huangchao shihuo zhi. 皇朝食貨志 [Essays on food and commodities of the Qing period]. Unpublished manuscript held at Ming-Qing Archives, National Palace Museum, Taipei.

Huke tiben 戶科題本 [Routine memorials of the Board of Revenue]. First Historical Archives, Beijing.

Hummel, Arthur W., ed. *Eminent Chinese of the Ch'ing Period (1644–1912).* Washington, DC: U.S. Government Printing Office, 1943.

Hymes, Robert P. "Moral Duty and Self-Regulating Process in Southern Sung Views of Famine Relief." In *Ordering the World: Approaches to State and Society in Sung Dynasty China,* ed. Robert P. Hymes and Conrad Schirokauer, 280–309. Berkeley: University of California Press, 1993.

Ikegami, Eiko, and Charles Tilly. "State Formation and Contention in Japan and France." In *Edo and Paris*, ed. McClain et al., 429–54.

Ishihara Jun 石原潤. "Kakokushō ni okeru Min, Shin, Minkoku jidai no teikiichi-bunpu, kaisō, oyobi chūshin shūraku no kankei ni tsuite" 河北省 に おける 明清民國時代の 定期史分佈階層 お よ び 中心集落 の 關係 に つ い て [Periodic markets in Hebei province during the Ming, Qing, and Republican periods—their distribution and relation with the social strata and central villages]. *Chirigaku hyōron* 46, no. 4 (Apr. 1973): 245–63.

Janku, Andrea. "Integrating the Body Politic: Official Perspectives on the Administration of Relief during the "Great North China Famine." Paper presented at the Annual Meeting of the Association for Asian Studies, Mar. 2004.

Jiang Shoupeng 姜守鹏. *Ming Qing beifang shichang yanjiu* 明清北方市场研究 [Research on North China markets during the Ming and Qing]. Changchun: Dongbei shifan daxue, 1996.

"Jiaqing shisinian Tongzhou liangcang lixu wubi an" 嘉慶十三年通州糧倉吏胥舞弊案 [Cases of malfeasance by Tongzhou granary clerks in Jiaqing 14]. *Lishi dang'an* 1990, no. 1: 44–55.

Jifu hedao shuili congshu 畿輔河道水利叢書 [Collection of works on rivers and water conservancy in the capital region]. Comp. Wu Bangqing 吳邦慶. 1824; reprint, 2 vols., Taipei: Wenhai, 1970.

Jifu shuili anlanzhi 畿輔水利安瀾志 [Gazetteer of water conservancy and control in the capital region]. Comp. Wang Lütai 王履泰. 1808.

Jifu shuili si'an 畿輔水利四案 [Four plans for water conservancy in the capital region]. Comp. Pan Xi'en 潘錫恩. 1823. **JFSLSA**.

Jifu shuili yi 畿輔水利議 [Proposals on water conservancy in the capital region]. Comp. Lin Zexu 林則徐 (1785–1850). 1877.

Jifu tongzhi 畿輔通志 [Gazetteer of capital region]. 1884; reprint, Shijiazhuang: Hebei renmin chubanshe, 1984– . 37 vols. **JFTZ**.

Jifu yicang tu. See Fang Guancheng.

Jindai Ji Lu Yu xiangcun 近代冀魯豫乡村 [Rural society in modern Hebei, Shandong, and Henan]. Ed. Cong Hanxiang 从翰香. Beijing: Zhongguo shehui kexue, 1995.

Jindai Tianjin tuzhi 近代天津图志 [Pictures of modern Tianjin]. Ed. Tianjin shi lishi bowuguan et al. 天津市历史博物馆等合编。 Tianjin guji chuban she. 1992.

Jindai Zhongguo zaihuang jinian 近代中国灾荒纪年 [Record of famines in modern China]. ———*xubian* 续编 [Continued]. Ed. Li Wenhai 李文海 et al. Changsha: Hunan jiaoyu chubanshe, 1990, 1993.

Jing, Jun, ed. *Feeding China's Little Emperors: Food, Children, and Social Change*. Stanford, CA: Stanford University Press, 2000.

Jing Junjian 经君健. "Lun Qingdai juanmian zhengce zhong jianzu guiding de bianhua" 论清代蠲免政策中减租规定的变化 [Changes in the regulations for rent reduction in the tax remission policy of the Qing period]. *Zhongguo jingjishi yanjiu* 1986, no. 1: 67–80.

Jingji shuizai shanhou jishi 京畿水災善後紀實 [Record of reconstruction after the (1917) flood in the capital region]. Comp. Xiong Xiling 熊希齡. 1918. **JJSZ**.

Jinmen baojia tushuo 津門保甲圖説 [Plan and description of Tianjin region's defense]. Tianjin, 1846.

Jinwu shili 金吾事例 [Gendarmerie regulations and cases]. 1851. **JWSL**

Johnson, William R. Papers. Deposited at Day Missions Library, Yale Divinity School, China Records Project, Record Group 6.

Jones, F. C. *Shanghai and Tientsin*. Oxford: Oxford University Press, 1940.

Jones, Susan Mann, and Philip A. Kuhn. "Dynastic Decline and the Roots of Rebellion." In *The Cambridge History of China*, vol. 10, pt. 1, ed. John K. Fairbank, chap. 3, 107–62. Cambridge: Cambridge University Press, 1978.

Jordan, William Chester. *The Great Famine: Northern Europe in the Early Fourteenth Century*. Princeton, NJ: Princeton University Press, 1996.

Ju Zhendong 鞠鎮東. *Hebei qidi zhi yanjiu* 河北旗地的研究 [A study of bannerland in Hebei].
    Taipei: Chengwen reprint, 1977.

Junjidang 軍機檔. [Grand Council copies of palace memorials]. National Palace Museum, Taipei. **JJD**.

Kaplan, Steven L. *Bread, Politics and Political Economy in the Reign of Louis XV.* 2 vols. The Hague:
    Martinus Nijhoff, 1976.

———. *Provisioning Paris: Merchants and Millers in the Grain and Flour Trade during the Eighteenth
    Century.* Ithaca, NY: Cornell University Press, 1984.

Ke Bingsheng. "Policy and Institutional Change for Agriculture in China: Production, Consumption,
    and Trade Implications." Unpublished paper. 1997.

King, Frank H. H. *Money and Monetary Policy in China, 1845–1895.* Cambridge, MA: Harvard University
    Press, 1965.

Kishimoto Mio 岸本美緒. "Shindai bukkashi kenkyū no genjō" 清代物価史研究史の現状 [The present
    situation regarding research into Qing-dynasty price history]. *Chūgoku kindaishi kenkyu* 5 (1987):
    79–104.

Kishimoto-Nakayama Mio. "The Kangxi Depression and Early Qing Local Markets." *Modern China* 10,
    no. 2 (Apr. 1984): 227–56.

Kueh, Y. Y. *Agricultural Instability in China, 1931–1991: Weather, Technology and Institutions.* Oxford:
    Clarendon Press, 1995.

Kuhn, Philip A. *Soulstealers: The Chinese Sorcery Scare of 1768.* Cambridge, MA: Harvard University Press,
    1990.

Knoblock, John. *Xunzi: A Translation and Study of the Complete Works.* Vol. 3. Stanford, CA: Stanford
    University Press, 1994.

Komlos, John, and Richard Landes. "Anachronistic Economics: Grain Storage in Medieval England."
    Economic History Review XLIV, no. 1 (1991): 36–45.

Kwan, Man Bun. "Mapping the Hinterland: Treaty Ports and Regional Analysis in Modern China." In
    Remapping China, ed. Gail Hershatter et al., 181–93. Stanford, CA: Stanford University Press, 1996.

———. "The Merchant World of Tianjin: Society and Economy of a Chinese City." PhD diss., Stanford
    University, 1990.

———. *The Salt Merchants of Tianjin: State Making and Civil Society in Late Imperial China.* Honolulu:
    University of Hawaii Press, 2001.

Lardy, Nicholas R. *Agriculture in China's Modern Economic Development.* Cambridge: Cambridge
    University Press, 1983.

Latham, A. J. H., and Larry Neal. "The International Market in Rice and Wheat, 1868–1914." *Economic
    History Review,* Second Series, 36, no. 2 (May 1983): 260–80.

Lavely, William, and R. Bin Wong. "Revising the Malthusian Narrative: The Comparative Study of
    Population Dynamics in Late Imperial China." *Journal of Asian Studies* 57, no. 3 (Aug. 1998): 714–48.

Lee, James Z., and Cameron D. Campbell. *Fate and Fortune in Rural China: Social Organization and
    Population Behavior in Liaoning, 1774–1873.* Cambridge: Cambridge University Press, 1997.

Lee, James Z., Cameron D. Campbell, and Feng Wang. "Positive Check or Chinese Checks?" *Journal of
    Asian Studies* 61, no. 2 (May 2002): 591–607.

Lee, James Z., Cameron D. Campbell, and Guofu Tan. "Infanticide and Family Planning in Late Imperial
    China: The Price and Population History of Rural Liaoning, 1774–1873." In *Chinese History,* ed. Rawski
    and Li, 145–76.

Lee, James Z., and Feng Wang. *One Quarter of Humanity: Malthusian Mythology and Chinese Realities,
    1700–2000.* Cambridge, MA, and London: Harvard University Press, 1999.

Lee, James Z., and Feng Wang, with Bozhong Li. "Population, Poverty, and Subsistence in China, 1700–
    2000." In *Population and Economy: From Hunger to Modern Economic Growth,* ed. T. Bengtsson and
    O. Saito, 73–109. New York: Oxford University Press, 2000.

Lee, Robert H. G. *The Manchurian Frontier in Ch'ing History.* Cambridge, MA: Harvard University Press, 1970.

Leonard, Jane Kate. *Controlling from Afar: The Daoguang Emperor's Management of the Grand Canal Crisis, 1824–1826.* Ann Arbor: Center for Chinese Studies, University of Michigan, 1996.

Li Hongyi 李鴻毅. *Hebei tianfu zhi yanjiu* 河北田賦之研究 [Research on Hebei's land tax]. 1934; reprint, Taipei: Chengwen, 1977.

Li Jinzheng 李金錚. *Jiedai guanxi yu xiangcun biandong: Minguo shiqi Huabei xiangcun jiedai zhi yanjiu* 借貸關係與鄉村變動：民國時期華北鄉村借貸之研究 [The debit-credit relationship and rural changes—the studies of the debit-credit relationships in rural North China of the Republican era]. Baoding: Hebei daxue, 2000.

Li, Lillian M. "Famine and Famine Relief: Viewing Africa in the 1980s from China in the 1920s." In *Drought and Hunger in Africa: Denying Famine a Future*, ed. Michael H. Glantz, 415–34. Cambridge: Cambridge University Press, 1987.

———. "Integration and Disintegration in North China's Grain Markets, 1738–1911." *Journal of Economic History* 60, no. 3 (Sept. 2000): 665–700.

———. "Introduction: Food, Famine, and the Chinese State." *Journal of Asian Studies* XLI, no. 4 (Aug. 1982): 687–707.

———. "Life and Death in a Chinese Famine: Infanticide as a Demographic Consequence of the 1935 Yellow River Flood." *Comparative Studies in Society and History* 33, no. 3 (July 1991): 466–510.

———. "Using Grain Prices to Measure Food Crises: Chihli Province in the Mid-Ch'ing Period." In *The Second Conference on Modern Chinese Economic History*, vol. 2, 467–509. Taipei: Institute of Economics, Academia Sinica, 1989.

———. 李明珠. "1917 nian de da shuizai: Tianjin yu ta de fudi" 1917 年的大水災: 天津与它的腹地 [The great 1917 flood: Tianjin and its hinterland]. In *Ershi shiji Huabei chengshi jindaihua*, 395–418.

Li, Lillian M., and Alison Dray-Novey. "Guarding Beijing's Food Security in the Qing Dynasty: State, Market, and Police." *Journal of Asian Studies* 58, no. 4 (Nov. 1999): 992–1032.

Li, Lincoln. *The Japanese Army in North China, 1937–1941: Problems of Political and Economic Control.* Oxford: Oxford University Press, 1975.

Li Wenzhi 李文治, and Jiang Taixin 江太新. *Qingdai caoyun* 清代漕運 [Grain tribute of the Qing period]. Beijing: Zhonghua shuju, 1995.

Li Xiangjun 李向军. "Qingdai jiuzai de zhidu jianshe yu shehui xiaoguo" 清代救灾的制度建设与社会效果 [The establishment of the famine relief system of the Qing period and its social effects]. *Lishi yanjiu* 1995, no. 5 (Oct. 15): 71–87.

Li Zehou 李澤厚, and Liu Zaifu 留再復. *Gaobie geming* 告別革命 [Farewell to revolution]. Hong Kong: Tiandi tushu yuxian, 1997.

Liang Fangzhong 梁方中, ed. *Zhongguo lidai hukou tiandi tianfu tongji* 中國歷代戶口田地天賦統計 [Statistics on China's historical population, cultivated land, and land taxes]. Shanghai: Shanghai renmin, 1980.

Liang Qizi 梁其姿 [Angela Leung]. *Shishan yu jiaohua: Ming-Qing cishan zuzhi* 施善與教化: 明清的慈善組織 [Dispensing charity and culture: Philanthropic organization in the Ming and Qing]. Taipei: Lianjing, 1997.

Lin Man-houng. "Currency and Society: The Monetary Crisis and Political-Economic Ideology of Early Nineteenth-Century China." PhD diss., Harvard University, 1989.

Lin Zexu. See *Jifu shuili yi.*

Liu Haiyan 刘海岩. "Jindai Huabei jiaotong de yanbian yu quyu chengshi chonggou [1860–1937]" 近代华北交通演变与区域城市重构近 [Modern transportation and the restructuring of regional cities in North China]. In *Ershi shiji Huabei chengshi jindaihua*, 24–48.

Liu Jiaju (Liu Chia-chü) 劉家駒. *Qingchao chuqi de Baqi quandi* 清朝初期的八旗圈地 [The allotted land policy for the Eight Banners in the early Ch'ing dynasty]. Taipei: Taiwan University, 1964.

Liu, Kwang-ching. "Li Hung-chang in Chihli: The Emergence of a Policy, 1870–1875." In *Li Hung-chang and China's Early Modernization*, ed. Samuel C. Chu and Kwang-ching Liu, 49–75. Armonk, NY, and London: M. E. Sharpe, 1994.

Liu, Lydia H. *Translingual Practice: Literature, National Culture, and Translated Modernity—China, 1900–1937.* Stanford, CA: Stanford University Press, 1995.

Liu, Ta-chung, and Kung-chia Yeh. *The Economy of the Chinese Mainland: National Income and Economic Development, 1933–1959.* Princeton, NJ: Princeton University Press, 1965.

Liu, Ts'ui-jung. "The Problem of Food Supply in China, 1912–1927." In *Zhonghua minguo chuji lishi yanjiu taohui lunwenji*, ed. Zhongyang yanjiuyuan jindaishi yanjiu so, 657–74. Taipei, 1984.

Liu Yanwei 留彥威. "Zhongguo jindai de zhanzheng yu ziran zaihai dui nongye shengchan de pohuai" 中国近代的战争与自然灾害对农业生产的破坏 [The damage to agricultural production by war and natural disasters in modern China]. *Gujin nongye* 2001, no. 1: 17–29.

Lyons, Thomas P. "Feeding Fujian: Grain Production and Trade, 1986–1996." *China Quarterly* 155 (Sept. 1998): 514–45.

Macartney, George (Earl of Macartney). *An Embassy to China; being the Journal kept by Lord Macartney during his embassy to the Emperor Ch'ien-lung, 1793–1794.* Ed. J. L. Cranmer Byng. Hamden, CT: Archon, 1963.

MacFarquhar, Roderick. *The Origins of the Cultural Revolution, 2: The Great Leap Forward 1958–1960.* Published for the Royal Institute of International Affairs. New York: Columbia University, 1983.

Mai Shudu 麥叔度. "Hebei sheng xiaomai zhi fanyun" 河北省小麥的販運 [The marketing of wheat in Hebei]. *Shehui kexue zazhi* 1, no. 1 (1930): 73–107.

Mallory, Walter H. *China: Land of Famine.* New York: American Geographical Society, 1926.

Malthus, Thomas Robert. *An Essay on the Principle of Population.* Norton Critical Edition of 1798 edition. New York: W. W. Norton, 1976.

Mann, Susan. *Local Merchants and the Chinese Bureaucracy, 1750–1950.* Stanford, CA: Stanford University Press, 1987.

Mao Tse-tung. *Selected Works of Mao Tse-tung.* 4 vols. Peking: Foreign Languages Press, 1965.

Marks, Robert B. "'It Never Used to Snow': Climatic Variability and Harvest Yields in Late Imperial South China, 1650–1850." In *Sediments of Time*, ed. Elvin and Liu, 411–46.

———. *Tigers, Rice, Silk, and Silt: Environment and Economy in Late Imperial South China.* Cambridge: Cambridge University Press, 1998.

Marks, Robert B., and Chunsheng Chen. "Price Inflation and Its Social, Economic, and Climatic Context in Guangdong Province, 1707–1800." *T'oung Pao* LXXXI, nos. 1–3 (1995): 109–52.

Mayers, William F., Nicholas B. Dennys, and Charles King, eds. *Treaty Ports of China and Japan.* London: Trübner, 1867.

McAlpin, Michelle Burge. *Subject to Famine: Food Crises and Economic Change in Western India, 1860–1920.* Princeton, NJ: Princeton University Press, 1983.

McClain, James L., John M. Merriam, and Ugawa Kaoru. *Edo and Paris: Urban Life and the State in the Early Modern Era.* Ithaca, NY: Cornell University Press, 1994.

McClain, James L., and Ugawa Kaoru. "Visions of the City." In *Edo and Paris*, ed. McClain et al. 455–64.

McCloskey, Donald N., and John Nash. "Corn at Interest: The Extent and Cost of Grain Storage in Medieval England." *American Economic Review* 74, no. 1 (Mar. 1984): 174–87.

McKeown, Thomas. "Food, Infection, and Population." In *Hunger and History*, ed. Rotberg and Rabb, 29–49.

McNeill, J. R. "China's Environmental History in World Perspective." In *Sediments of Time*, ed. Elvin and Liu, 31–49.

———. *Something New Under the Sun: An Environmental History of the Twentieth-Century World.* New York and London: W. W. Norton, 2000.

Meng Shaohua 孟昭华. *Zhongguo zaihuang shiji* 中国灾荒史纪 [Historical chronicle of Chinese famines]. Beijing: Zhongguo shehui, 1999.

Mianhuatu 棉花圖 [Illustrations of cotton cultivation]. With colophon by Fang Guancheng. 1765; reprint ed. Zhili zongdushu bowuguan 直隸總督署博物館 [Zhili governor-general yamen museum]. Baoding: Zhili zongdushu bowuguan, 1999.

Mokyr, Joel. *Why Ireland Starved: A Quantitative and Analytical History of the Irish Economy, 1800–1850.* London: George Allen and Unwin, 1983.

Munro, Donald J. *The Concept of Man in Early China.* Stanford, CA: Stanford University Press, 1969.

Muramatsu, Yuji. "Banner Estates and Banner Lands in 18th Century China—Evidence from Two New Sources." *Hitotsubashi Journal of Economics* 12, no. 2 (1972): 1–13.

Murphey, Rhoads. "The Treaty Ports and China's Modernization." In *The Chinese City between Two Worlds*, ed. Mark Elvin and G. William Skinner, 17–71. Stanford, CA: Stanford University Press, 1974.

Myers, Ramon H. *The Chinese Peasant Economy: Agricultural Development in Hopei and Shantung, 1890–1949.* Cambridge, MA: Harvard University Press, 1970.

Myers, Ramon H., and Yeh-chien Wang. "Economic Developments, 1644–1800." In *The Cambridge History of China*, vol. 9, pt. 1, ed. Willard J. Peterson, 563–645. Cambridge: Cambridge University Press, 2002.

Nakai Nobuhiko, and James McClain. "Commercial Change and Urban Growth in Early Modern Japan." In *Cambridge History of Japan*, vol. 4, 519–95. Cambridge: Cambridge University Press, 1991.

Nakayama Mio [later Kishimoto Mio]. "On the Fluctuation of the Price of Rice in the Chiang-nan Region during the First Half of the Ch'ing Period." *Memoirs of the Research Department of the Toyo Bunko*, no. 37 (1979): 55–90. (English version of "Shindai Kōnan no beika dōkō," *Shigaku zasshi* 87, no. 9 [1978]: 1–33.)

Nankai jingji zhishu ziliao huibian 南開經濟指數資料彙會 [Nankai compilation of economic indices]. Ed. Kong Min 孔敏 et al. Beijing: Zhongguo shehui kexue chubanshe, 1988.

Naquin, Susan. *Millenarian Rebellion in China: The Eight Trigrams Uprising of 1813.* New Haven, CT: Yale University Press, 1976.

———. *Peking: Temples and City Life, 1400–1900.* Berkeley: University of California Press, 2000.

Nathan, Andrew James. *A History of the China International Famine Relief Commission.* Cambridge, MA: East Asian Research Center, Harvard University, 1965.

Naughton, Barry. "Industrial Policy during the Cultural Revolution: Military Preparation, Decentralization, and Leaps Forward." In *New Perspectives on the Cultural Revolution*, ed. William A. Joseph, Christine P. W. Wong, and David Zweig, 153–81. Cambridge, MA: Council on East Asian Studies, Harvard University.

Nayancheng 那彥成. *Na Wenyi Gong churen Zhili zongdu zouyi* 那文毅公出任直隸總督奏議 [Collected memorials of Nayancheng during the initial period of his tenure as Zhili governor-general]. 1834; reprint, 4 vol. *Jindai Zhongguo shiliao congkan* 21, no. 207. Taipei: Wenhai, 1968.

Needham, Joseph. *Physics and Physical Technology, Civil Engineering and Nautics.* Vol. 4, pt. 3 of *Science and Civilization in China*, ed. Joseph Needham. Cambridge: Cambridge University Press, 1971.

North China Daily News. Shanghai. **NCDN**

The North China Famine of 1920–21, with Special Reference to the West Chihli Area, being the Report of the Peking United International Famine Relief Committee. Peking: Peking United International Famine Relief Committee, 1922.

Notestein, Frank W., and Chi-ming Chiao. "Population." In *Land Utilization in China*, ed. John Lossing Buck, chap. 13, 1:358–99. Nanking: University of Nanking, 1937.

Oi, Jean C. *Rural China Takes Off: Institutional Foundations of Economic Reform.* Berkeley: University of California Press, 1999.

———. *State and Peasant in Contemporary China: The Political Economy of Village Government.* Berkeley: University of California Press, 1989.

———. "Two Decades of Rural Reform in China: An Overview and Assessment." *China Quarterly* 159 (Sept. 1999): 616–28.

Ormrod, David. *English Grain Exports and the Structure of Agrarian Capitalism, 1700–1760.* Hull, England: Hull University Press, 1985.

Otto, Friedrich. "Correlation of Harvests with Importation of Cereals in China." *Chinese Economic Journal* 15, no. 4 (Oct. 1934): 388–414.

Paarlberg, Robert L. "Rice Bowls and Dust Bowls: Africa, Not China, Faces a Food Crisis." Review of *Who Will Feed China?* by Lester R. Brown. *Foreign Affairs* 75, no. 3 (May–June 1996): 127–32.

Peng Xinwei. *A Monetary History of China (Zhongguo Huobi Shi).* Trans by Edward H. Kaplan. 2 vols. Bellingham: Center for East Asian Studies, Western Washington University, 1994.

Peng Xizhe. "Demographic Consequences of the Great Leap Forward in China's Provinces." *Population and Development Review* 13, no. 4 (Dec. 1987): 639–70.

Perdue, Peter C. *Exhausting the Earth: State and Peasant in Hunan, 1500–1850.* Cambridge, MA: Council on East Asian Studies, Harvard University, 1987.

———. "Insiders and Outsiders: The Xiangtan Riot of 1819 and Collective Action in Hunan." *Modern China* 12, no. 2 (Apr. 1986): 166–201.

———. "Liu-min and Famine Relief in Eighteenth-Century China." Unpublished paper, 1974.

———. "The Qing State and the Gansu Grain Market, 1739–1864." In *Chinese History*, ed. Rawski and Li, 100–25.

Perkins, Dwight H. *Agricultural Development in China, 1368–1968.* Chicago: Aldine, 1969.

Perry, Elizabeth J. *Rebels and Revolutionaries in North China, 1845–1945.* Stanford, CA: Stanford University Press, 1980.

Persson, Karl Gunnar. *Grain Markets in Europe, 1500–1900: Integration and Disintegration, 1500–1900.* Cambridge: Cambridge University Press, 1999.

Playfair, George. "The Grain Transport System of China: Notes and Statistics taken from the Ta Ch'ing Hui tien." *China Review* 3, no. 6 (May–June 1975): 354–64.

Pomeranz, Kenneth. *The Great Divergence: Europe, China, and the Making of the Modern World Economy.* Princeton, NJ: Princeton University Press, 2000.

———. *The Making of a Hinterland: State, Society, and Economy in Inland North China, 1853–1937.* Berkeley: University of California Press, 1993.

———. "Water into Iron, Widows to Warlords: The Handan Rain Shrine in Modern Chinese History." *Late Imperial China* 12, no. 1 (June 1991): 62–99.

Popkin, Samuel. *The Rational Peasant: The Political Economy of Rural Society in Vietnam.* Berkeley: University of California Press, 1979.

Population Atlas of China. Compiled and edited by the Population Census Office of the State Council of the People's Republic of China and the Institute of Geography of the Chinese Academy of Sciences. Hong Kong: Oxford University Press, 1987.

Post, John D. *The Last Great Subsistence Crisis in the Western World.* Baltimore, MD: Johns Hopkins University Press, 1977.

Putterman, Louis. *Continuity and Change in China's Rural Development: Collective and Reform Eras in Perspective.* New York: Oxford University Press, 1993.

Qihou bianqian he chaochangqi yubao wenji 气候变迁和超长期预报文集 [Collected articles on climate change and ultra-long-term forecasting]. Ed. Zhongyang qixiangju yanjiu so. Beijing: Kexue chubanshe, 1977.

Qing shilu 清實錄 [Veritable records of the Qing dynasty]. Reprint, Beijing: Zhonghua shuju, 1986.

Qingdai de qidi 清代的旗地 [Banner lands of the Qing dynasty]. Comp. Zhongguo renmin daxue Qingshi yanjiu so 中国人民大学清史研究所 et al. 3 vols. Beijing: Zhonghua shuju, 1989.

Qingdai Haihe Luanhe honglao dang'an shiliao 清代海河滦河洪涝档案史料. Comp. Shuili shuidian kexue yanjiuyuan 水利水电科学研究院 [Research institute for water and electrical power]. Beijing: Zhonghua shuju, 1981. **QDHH.**

Qingmo Beijing zhi ziliao 清末北京之資料 [Historical materials from late Qing Beijing]. Trans. Zhang Zongping 張宗平 and Lü Yonghe 呂永和 . Beijing: Yanshan, 1994. Translated selections from Yamamoto Chūsei, *Pekin shi* (1904).

Quanguo hukou tongji 全國戶口統計 [National population statistics]. Comp. Neizhengbu, Renkou ju. 1948.

Rankin, Mary Backus. *Elite Activism and Political Transformation in China: Zhejiang Province, 1865–1911.* Stanford, CA: Stanford University Press, 1986.

Rawski, Evelyn S. *The Last Emperors: A Social History of Qing Imperial Institutions.* Berkeley: University of California Press, 1998.

Rawski, Thomas G. *Economic Growth in Prewar China.* Berkeley: University of California Press, 1989.

Rawski, Thomas G., and Lillian M. Li, eds. *Chinese History in Economic Perspective.* Berkeley: University of California Press, 1992.

Rawski, Thomas G., et al. *Economics and the Historian.* Berkeley: University of California Press, 1996.

Read, Bernard E. *Famine Foods Listed in the Chiu Huang Pen Tsao* 救荒本草. Shanghai: Henry Lester Institute of Medical Research, 1946. (Trans. of fifteenth-century work by Zhou Dingwang 周定王.)

Renmin ribao [People's daily] 人民日報.

Rennie, David F. *Peking and the Pekingese During the First Year of the British Embassy at Peking.* 2 vols. London: J. Murray, 1865.

Report of the Committee of the China Famine Relief Fund. Shanghai: American Presbyterian Mission Press, 1879.

Rockoff, Hugh. "Money, Banking, and Inflation: An Introduction for Historians." In *Economics and the Historian,* ed. Rawski et al., 177–208.

Rogaski, Ruth. "Beyond Benevolence: A Confucian Women's Shelter in Treaty-Port China." *Journal of Women's History* 8, no. 4 (winter 1997): 52–90.

———. *Hygienic Modernity: Meanings of Health and Disease in Treaty-Port China.* Berkeley: University of California Press, 2004.

Rotberg, Robert I., and Theodore K. Rabb, eds. *Climate and History: Studies in Interdisciplinary History.* Princeton, NJ: Princeton University Press, 1981.

———. *Hunger and History: The Impact of Changing Food Production and Consumption Patterns on Society.* Cambridge: Cambridge University Press, 1985.

Rowe, William T. *Hankow: Commerce and Society in a Chinese City, 1796–1889.* Stanford, CA: Stanford University Press, 1984.

———. *Hankow: Conflict and Community in a Chinese City, 1796–1895.* Stanford, CA: Stanford University Press, 1989.

———. *Saving the World: Chen Hongmou and Elite Consciousness in Eighteenth-Century China.* Stanford, CA: Stanford University Press, 2001.

Rozelle, Scott, Albert Park, Jikun Huang, and Hehui Jin. "Bureaucrat to Entrepreneur: The Changing Role of the State in China's Grain Economy." *Economic Development and Cultural Change* 48, no. 2 (Jan. 2000): 227–52.

Rozman, Gilbert. *Population and Marketing Settlements in Ch'ing China.* Cambridge: Cambridge University Press, 1982.

———. *Urban Networks in Ch'ing China and Tokugawa Japan.* Princeton, NJ: Princeton University Press, 1973.

Sands, Barbara, and Ramon H. Myers. "The Spatial Approach to Chinese History: A Test." *Journal of Asian Studies* XLV, no. 4 (Aug. 1986): 721–43.

Schoppa, R. Keith. *Xiang Lake—Nine Centuries of Chinese Life.* New Haven, CT: Yale University Press, 1989.

Schram, Stuart R. *The Political Thought of Mao Tse-tung*. Rev. ed. Hammondsworth, England: Penguin Books, 1969.

Scott, James C. *The Moral Economy of the Peasant: Rebellion and Subsistence in Southeast Asia*. New Haven, CT: Yale University Press, 1976.

The Secret Speeches of Chairman Mao: From the Hundred Flowers to the Great Leap Forward. Ed. Roderick MacFarquhar, Timothy Cheek, and Eugene Wu. Cambridge, MA: Council on East Asian Studies, Harvard University, 1989.

Selden, Mark. *China in Revolution: The Yenan Way Revisited*. Armonk, NY: M. E. Sharpe, 1995.

Sen, Amartya. "Democracy as a Universal Value." *Journal of Democracy* 10, no. 3 (1999): 3–17.

———. *Development as Freedom*. New York: Alfred A. Knopf, 1999.

———. *Poverty and Famines: An Essay on Entitlement and Deprivation*. Oxford: Clarendon Press, 1982.

Shang Hongkui 商鸿逵. "Kangxi nanxun yu zhili Huanghe" 康熙南巡与治理黄河 [Kangxi's southern tours and controlling the Yellow River]. In *Kang Yong Qian sandi pingyi* 康雍乾三帝评议 [Evaluation of three emperors Kangxi, Yongzheng, and Qianlong], 124–41. Comp. Zuo Buqing 左步青. Beijing: Zijincheng, 1986.

Shapiro, Judith. *Mao's War Against Nature: Politics and the Environment in Revolutionary China*. Cambridge: Cambridge University Press, 2001.

Shi Yuanchun. "The Characteristics of Water and Salt Movement and the Regulation of Salt-Affected Soils in Semi-Humid Monsoon Climate Regions." *Proceedings of the International Symposium on the Reclamation of Salt-Affected Soils*, pt. I. Jinan, May 1985.

Shichao shengxun 十朝聖訓 [Sacred edicts of the ten reigns]. 1880 ed.; reprint, Taipei: Wenhai, 1965.

Shina nōgyō kiso tōkei shiryō 支那農業基礎統計資料 [Basic statistical materials on Chinese agriculture]. Comp. Tōa kenkyūjo 東亞研究所. Vol. 1. Tokyo: Tōa kenkyūjo, 1940; Shanghai: Tōa kenkyūjo, 1941.

Shina shōbetsu zenshi [Complete gazetteer of China's provinces]. Vol. 18 (Zhili Province). Tokyo: Tōa dobunkai, 1920.

Sicular, Terry. "Redefining State, Plan, and Market: China's Reforms in Agricultural Commerce." *China Quarterly* 144 (Dec. 1995): 1020–46.

Simoons, Frederick J. *Food in China: A Cultural and Historical Inquiry*. Boca Raton, Ann Arbor, Boston: CRC Press, 1991.

Skinner, G. William. "Cities and the Hierarchy of Local Systems." In *The City in Late Imperial China*, ed. Skinner, 275–351.

———, ed. *The City in Late Imperial China*. Stanford, CA: Stanford University Press, 1977.

———. "Marketing and Social Structure in Rural China." Reprinted from the *Journal of Asian Studies* by the Association for Asian Studies (1964–65).

———. "Regional Urbanization in Nineteenth-Century China." In *The City in Late Imperial China*, ed. Skinner, 211–49.

———. "Sichuan's Population in the Nineteenth Century: Lessons from Disaggregated Data." *Late Imperial China* 8, no. 1 (June 1987): 1–79.

———. "Social Ecology and the Forces of Repression in North China: A Regional-Systems Framework for Analysis." Paper prepared for the ACLS Workshop on Rebellion and Revolution in North China, Harvard University, July–Aug. 1979.

Slicher Van Bath, B. H. *The Agrarian History of Western Europe, A.D. 500–1850*. Trans. Olive Ordish. London: Edward Arnold, 1963.

Smil, Vaclav. "Who Will Feed China." *China Quarterly* 143 (Sept. 1995): 801–13.

Smith, Arthur H. *Chinese Characteristics*. New York: Fleming H. Revell, 1894.

———. *Village Life in China: A Study in Sociology*. Edinburgh: Oliphant, Anderson, and Ferrier, 1900.

Smith, Joanna F. Handlin. "Benevolent Societies: The Reshaping of Charity during the Late Ming and Early Ch'ing." *Journal of Asian Studies* 46, no. 2 (1987): 309–34.

———. "Chinese Philanthropy as Seen Through a Case of Famine Relief in the 1640s." In *Philanthropy in the World's Traditions*, ed. Warren F. Ilchman, Stanley N. Katz, and Edward L. Queen II, 133–68. Bloomington: Indiana University Press, 1998.

———. "Social Hierarchy and Merchant Philanthropy as Perceived in Several Late Ming and Early-Qing Texts." *Journal of Economic and Social History of the Orient* 41, no. 3 (1998): 417–51.

"Soya Beans and Bean Oil Industry in Manchuria." *Chinese Economic Journal* 5, no. 3 (Sept. 1929): 793–805.

Spence, Jonathan D. *Emperor of China: Self-Portrait of K'ang-hsi*. New York: Alfred A. Knopf, 1974.

———. *Treason by the Book*. New York: Penguin Books, 2002.

Strand, David. *Rickshaw Beijing: City People and Politics in the 1920s*. Berkeley: University of California Press, 1989.

Stroebe, G. G. "The Great Central China Flood of 1931." *The Chinese Recorder* 63, no. 11 (1932): 669–80.

Stross, Randall E. *The Stubborn Earth: American Agriculturalists on Chinese Soil, 1898–1937*. Berkeley: University of California Press, 1986.

Su Xiaokang, and Wang Luxiang. *Deathsong of the River: A Reader's Guide to the Chinese TV Series Heshang*. Intro. and trans. Richard W. Bodman and Pin P. Wan. Ithaca, NY: East Asia Program, Cornell University, 1991.

Sung Ying-hsing 宋應星. *T'ien-kung k'ai-wu* [天工開物]: *Chinese Technology in the Seventeenth Century*. Trans. E-tu Zen Sun and Shiou-chuan Sun. University Park: Pennsylvania State University Press, 1966.

Tang Zongyu 唐宗愈. *Zhenzai shudu wuliu heji* 振災書牘五六合輯 [Collection of letters on relieving disasters]. Wuxi[?], 1918.

Tawney, R. H. *Land and Labor in China*. London: George Allen and Unwin, 1932; reprint, Boston: Beacon Press, 1966.

Tianjin shanghui dang'an huibian (1903–1911) 天津商会档案汇编 (1903–1911). Comp. Tianjinshi dang'an guan, Tianjin shehui kexue yuan lishi yanjiusuo. 2 vols. Tianjin: Tianjin renmin, 1989.

Tianjin shanghui dang'an huibian (1912–1928) 天津商会档案汇编 (1912–1928). Comp. Tianjinshi dang'an guan, Tianjin shehui kexue yuan lishi yanjiusuo. 4 vols. Tianjin: Tianjin renmin, 1992.

Tianjin shuizai ji Hebei ge zaiqu zhenjiu zong baogao 天津水災暨河北各災區賑救總報告 [Comprehensive report on emergency relief for Tianjin flood and Hebei disaster districts]. Tianjin, 1940.

Tianjin tebie shi shuiizai jiuji shilu 天津特別市水災救濟實錄 [Chronological record of flood relief in Tianjin special municipality]. Tianjin, 1940[?].

Tianjin Yizujie shuizai nanmin jiuji weiyuanhui zhengxin lu 天津義租界水災難民救濟委員會政綠 [Financial report of the Tianjin Italian Concession Committee for the Relief of Flood Refugees]. Tianjin, 1939 or 1940[?].

Tilly, Charles. "Food Supply and Public Order in Modern Europe." In *The Formation of National States in Western Europe*, ed. Charles Tilly, 380–455. Princeton, NJ: Princeton University Press, 1975.

Todd, O. J. *Two Decades in China*. Peking: The Association of Chinese and American Engineers, 1938.

Tong Pingya 佟屏亚. "Yumi chuanru dui Zhongguo jindai nongye shengchan de yingxiang" 玉米传入对中国近代农业生产的影响 [The impact of the introduction of corn on modern China's agricultural production]. *Gujin nongye* 2001, no. 2: 60–65.

Torbert, Preston M. *The Ch'ing Imperial Household Department: A Study of its Organization and Principal Functions, 1662–1796*. Cambridge, MA: Harvard University Press, 1977.

Tsao, Jerlian. "The 1928–1930 Famine and Urban Conscience." Unpublished paper. 1987.

Tsao Lien-en. "The Marketing of Soya Beans and Bean Oil." *Chinese Economic Journal* VII, no. 3 (Sept. 1930): 941–71.

Turner, F. B. "Flood and Famine in North China." *Journal of the North China Branch of the Royal Asiatic Society* LVII (1926): 1–18.

Uchida Kusuo. "Protest and the Tactics of Direct Remonstration: Osaka's Merchants Make Their Voices Heard." Trans. James L. McClain. In *Osaka: The Merchants' Capital of Early Modern Japan*, ed. James L. McClain and Wakita Osamu, 81–103. Ithaca, NY: Cornell University Press, 1999.

U.S. Department of State. *Records of the U.S. Department of State Relating to the Internal Affairs of China, 1910–1929*. National Archives and Records Service, General Service Administration, Washington, DC, Microcopy 329, Rolls 128, 132. **USDS.**

Usiar, Muhammad, and Yang Huaizhong. "The Eighteenth Century Gansu Relief Fraud Scandal." Eng. trans. of "Shiba shiji de Gansu maozhen an" 十八世纪的甘肃冒赈案. Paper delivered at Conference on Chinese Islamic Tradition, Harvard University, Apr. 1989.

Vanderveen, H. "Chihli Province River Conservance." *Far Eastern Review* XIII, no. 19 (Dec. 1917): 770–72.

Vogel, Hans Ulrich. "Chinese Central Monetary Policy, 1644–1800." *Late Imperial China* 8, no. 2 (Dec. 1987): 1–52.

von Glahn, Richard. "Community and Welfare: Chu Hsi's Community Granary in Theory and Practice." In *Ordering the World: Approaches to State and Society in Sung Dynasty China*, ed. Robert P. Hymes and Conrad Schirokauer, 221–54. Berkeley: University of California Press, 1993.

————. *Fountain of Fortune: Money and Monetary Policy in China, 1000–1700*. Berkeley: University of California Press, 1996.

Walder, Andrew, ed. *Zouping in Transition: The Process of Reform in Rural North China*. Cambridge MA, and London: Harvard University Press, 1998.

Walker, Kenneth R. "Food and Mortality in China during the Great Leap Forward, 1958–1961." In *Agricultural Development in China, 1949–1989: The Collected Papers of Kenneth R. Walker (1931–1989)*, collected and ed. Robert F. Ash, 106–47. Oxford: Oxford University Press, 1998.

————. *Food Grain Procurement and Consumption in China*. Cambridge: Cambridge University Press, 1984.

————. "Grain Self-Sufficiency in North China, 1953–75." *China Quarterly* 71 (Sept. 1977): 555–90.

Wallace, B. B. "China's Imports and Exports of Foodstuffs." *Chinese Economic Journal* 9, no. 2 (Aug. 1931): 815–25.

Walter, John, and Roger Schofield, eds. *Famine, Disease and the Social Order in Early Modern Society*. Cambridge: Cambridge University Press, 1989.

Walthall, Anne. "Edo Riots." In *Edo and Paris*, ed. McClain et al., 407–28.

Wang, David Der-wei. *The Monster that Is History: History, Violence, and Fictional Writing in Twentieth-Century China*. Berkeley: University of California Press, 2004.

Wang Jiange 王建革. "Qingdai Huabei de huangzai yu shehui kongzhi" 清代华北的蝗灾与社会控制 [Locust plagues and social control in North China in the Qing]. *Qingshi yanjiu* 2000, no. 2: 100–7.

Wang Qingyun 王慶雲. *Shiqu yuji* 石渠餘紀 [Surplus notes from Stone Canal] 1890, 6 ce; reprint, Taipei: Wenhai, 1967.

Wang Ruowang. *Hunger Trilogy*. Trans. Kyna Rubin. Armonk, NY: M. E. Sharpe, 1991.

Wang Shao-wu, Zhao Zong-ci, and Chen Zhen-hua. "Reconstruction of the Summer Rainfall Regime for the last 500 Years in China." *GeoJournal* 5, no. 2 (1981): 117–22.

Wang Shouchun 王守春. "Yongding he qianzai weixian de lishi fazhan ji qi dui Beijing chengshi yu quyu jingji fazhan de yingxiang" 永定河潜在危险的历史发展及其对北京城市与区域经济发展的响 [The historical development of the inherent dangers of the Yongding River and its influence on the economic development of Beijing city and region]. *Huanjing bianqian yanjiu* 5 (1996): 111–21.

Wang Shousong 汪寿松. "Duiwai maoyi yu jindai Tianjin shichang" 对外贸易与近代天津市场 [Foreign trade and modern Tianjin's market]. In *Ershi shiji Huabei chengshi jindaihua*, 152–62.

Wang Shulin 王樹林. "Qingdai zaihuang: yige tongji de yanjiu" 清代灾荒：一個統計的研究 [Famines in the Qing period: A statistical investigation]. *Shehui xuejie* VI (1932): 168–76, 213–15.

Wang, Yeh-chien (Wang Yejian) 王業鍵. "Evolution of the Chinese Monetary System, 1644–1850." In

Conference on Modern Chinese Economic History, 469–96. Taipei: Institute of Economics, Academia Sinica, 1979.

———. "Food Supply and Grain Prices in the Yangtze Delta in the Eighteenth Century." In *Proceedings of the Second Conference on Modern Chinese Economic History,* 423–59. Taipei: Institute of Economics, Academia Sinica, 1989.

———. *Land Taxation in Imperial China, 1750–1911.* Cambridge, MA: Harvard University Press, 1973.

———. "Qingdai de liangjia chenbao zhidu" 清代的糧價陳報制度 [The grain price reporting system of the Qing dynasty]. *Gugong jikan* 13, no. 1 (fall 1978): 53–66.

———. "The Secular Trend of Prices During the Ch'ing Period (1644–1911)." *Journal of the Institute of Chinese Studies of the Chinese University of Hong Kong* V, no. 2 (1972): 347–71.

———. "Secular Trends of Rice Prices in the Yangzi Delta, 1638–1935." In *Chinese History,* ed. Rawski and Li, 35–68.

Wang Yongqian 王永謙. "Jin Fu zhihe shulun" 靳辅治河述论 [On the ways of the Yellow River conservancy by Jin Fu]. *Qingshi luncong* 青史论丛 1985, no. 6: 192–210.

Wang Youmin 王又民, ed. *Minguo ershisan nian Hebei sheng mianchan gaikuang* 民國二十三年河北省棉產概況 [General survey of Hebei Province's cotton production in 1934]. Tianjin: Shiye bu Zhengding mianye shiyan so, 1935.

Wang Zhiyi 汪志伊, comp. *Huangzheng jiyao* 荒政輯要 [Essentials of famine relief]. 9 juan. 1806 preface, 1869 pub.

Wanshou shengdian 萬壽盛典 [The imperial birthday celebration]. 1713, 1717.

Wei Hongyun. "Social Reform and Value Change in the Jin Cha Ji Anti-Japanese Border Region." In *North China at War: The Social Ecology of Revolution, 1937–1945,* ed. Feng Chongyi and David S. G. Goodman, 93–114. Lanham, MD: Rowman and Littlefield, 2000.

Weir, David R. "Markets and Mortality in France, 1600–1789." In *Famine, Disease,* ed. Walter and Schofield, 201–34.

White, Theodore H., and Annalee Jacoby. *Thunder Out of China.* New York: William Sloane, 1946.

White, Tyrene. "The Origins of China's Birth Planning Policy." In *Engendering China: Women, Culture, and the State,* ed. Christina K. Gilmartin, Gail Hershatter, Lisa Rofel, and Tyrene White, 250–78. Cambridge, MA: Harvard University Press, 1994.

———. *China's Longest Campaign: Birth Planning in the People's Republic, 1949–2005.* Ithaca, NY: Cornell University Press, 2006.

Whyte, Martin King, and William L. Parish. *Urban Life in Contemporary China.* Chicago and London: University of Chicago Press, 1984.

Wilkinson, Endymion Porter. *Chinese History: A Manual.* Rev. and enlarged ed. Cambridge, MA: Harvard University Asia Center, 2000.

———. "Studies in Chinese Price History." PhD diss., Princeton University, 1970 (University Microfilms); reprint, New York: Garland, 1980.

Will, Pierre-Étienne. *Bureaucracy and Famine in Eighteenth-Century China.* Trans. Elborg Forster. Stanford, CA: Stanford University Press, 1990.

———. "Clear Waters Versus Muddy Waters: The Zheng-Bai Irrigation System of Shaanxi Province in the Late-Imperial Period." In *Sediments of Time: Environment and Society in Chinese History,* ed. Mark Elvin and Liu Ts'ui-jung, 283–343. Cambridge: Cambridge University Press, 1998.

———. "Un cycle hydraulique en Chine: La province du Hubei du XVIe au XIXe Siècles." *Bulletin de l'École Française d'Extrême-Orient* LXVIII (1980): 261–87.

———. "Discussions on the Market-Place and the Market Principle in Eighteenth-Century Guangdong." *Zhongguo haiyang fazhan shi lunwenji.* 中國海洋發展史論文集 [Essays on China's maritime development]. Vol. 7, 323–89. Taipei: Academia Sinica, Sun Yat-sen Institute of Social Sciences and Philosophy, 1999.

———. "The Problem of Official Corruption in Late Imperial China: Tentative Definitions and a Few Anecdotes." Paper presented at the New School for Social Research, New York City, Apr. 30, 1990.

———. "State Intervention in the Administration of a Hydraulic Infrastructure: The Example of Hubei Province in Late Imperial Times." In *The Scope of State Power in China*, ed. Stuart Schram, 295–343. London and Hong Kong: SOAS and Chinese University, 1985.

Will, Pierre-Étienne, and R. Bin Wong, with James Lee. *Nourish the People: The State Civilian Granary System in China, 1650–1850*. Ann Arbor: University of Michigan, Center for Chinese Studies, 1991.

Wittfogel, Karl A. *Oriental Despotism: A Comparative Study of Total Power*. New Haven, CT: Yale University Press, 1957.

Wolf, Arthur P. "Is There Evidence of Birth Control in Late Imperial China?" *Population and Development Review* 27, no. 1 (2001): 133–54.

Wong, R. Bin. *China Transformed: Historical Change and the Limits of European Experience*. Ithaca, NY: Cornell University Press, 1997.

———. "Food Riots in the Qing Dynasty." *Journal of Asian Studies* 41, no. 4 (1982): 767–88.

Wong, R. Bin, and Peter C. Perdue. "Famine's Foes in Ch'ing China." *Harvard Journal of Asiatic Studies* 43, no. 1 (June 1983): 291–332.

———. "Grain Markets and Food Supplies in Eighteenth-Century Hunan." In *Chinese History*, ed. Rawski and Li, 126–44.

Wood, Frances. *Did Marco Polo Go to China?* Boulder, CO: Westview Press, 1996.

Wrigley, E. A. "Some Reflections on Corn Yields and Prices in Pre-industrial Economies." In *Famine, Disease*, ed. Walter and Schofield, 235–78.

Wrigley, E. A., and R. S. Schofield. *The Population History of England, 1541–1871: A Reconstruction*. Cambridge, MA: Harvard University Press, 1981.

Wu Chengming 吳承明. *Zhongguo zibenzhuyi yu guonei shichang* 中国资本主义与国内市场 [Chinese capitalism and domestic markets]. Beijing: Zhongguo shehui kexue chubanshe, 1985.

Wu Hui 吳慧 and Ge Xianhui 葛贤惠. "Qing qianqi de liangshi diaoji" [The allocation of grain in the early Qing dynasty]. *Lishi yanjiu* 1988, no. 4: 122–35.

Wu Jianyong 吳建雍. "Jingshi de liangshi gongying" 京師的糧食供應 [Grain supply of the capital]. In *Beijing tongshi* 北京通史 [History of Beijing], 10 vols., vol. 7, ed. Cao zixi 曹子西, chap. 3, 372–89. Beijing: Zhongguo shudian, 1994.

———. "Qing qianqi de shangpinliang zhengce" 清前期的商品粮政策 [The policy toward commercial grain in the early Qing]. *Lishi dang'an* 1983, no. 6: 87–92.

———. "Qingdai Beijing de liangshi gongying" 清代北京的糧食供應 [Grain supply of Qing-dynasty Beijing]. In *Beijing lishi yu xianshi yanjiu* 北京歷史與現實研究 [Research on Beijing's past and present], 167–86. Beijing: Yanshan, 1989.

Wu Jianyong 吳建雍, et al. *Beijing chengshi shenghuo shi* 北京城市生活史 [History of urban life in Beijing]. Beijing: Kaiming, 1997.

Xia Mingfang 夏明方. "Jindai Huabei nongcun nonghu shouru zhuangkuang yu nongmin shenghuo shuiping bianxi" 近代华北农村农户收入状况与农民生活水平辨析 [Distinguishing between the income of modern North China villages and households and the standard of living of farmers]. *Jindaishi yanjiu* 2002, no. 2: 211–50.

———. *Minguo shiqi ziran zaihai yu xiangcun shehui* 民國時期自然災害與鄉村社會 [Natural disasters and village society in the Republican period]. Beijing: Zhonghua shuju, 2000.

Xiangcun sanshinian—Fengyang nongcun shehui jingji. 乡村三十年—风阳农村社会经济发展实录 [Thirty years in the village: The society and economy of Fengyang's rural villages]. Ed. Wang Gengling 王耕令 et al. Beijing: Nongcun xu wu chubanshe, 1989.

Xin Hebei sishinian, 1949–1989 新河北四十年, 1949–1989 [Forty years of the new Hebei, 1949–1989].

Comp. Hebei sheng renmin zhengfu bangongting and Hebei sheng tongji ju. Shijiazhuang: Zhongguo tongji chubanshe, 1989.

(Qinding) Xinyou gongzhen jishi 欽定辛酉工賑紀事 [Imperially commissioned record of riverwork and famine relief in 1801]. 1802. **XYGZJS.**

Xu Dong 徐棟. *Muling shu* 牧令書 [Handbook of local administration]. 23 juan. 1848.

Xu Guangqi 徐光啟. *Nongzheng quanshu jiaozhu* 農政全書校注 [Complete book of agriculture collated and annotated]. Ed. Shi Shenghan 石聲漢. 3 vols. Taipei: Mingwen shuju, 1980.

Xu Qixian 徐啟憲. "Qingdai huangdi de yongshan" 清代皇帝的用膳 [Provisions for the Qing emperors]. *Zijincheng* 1980, no. 4: 10–14.

Xu Tan 許檀. *Ming Qing shiqi Shandong shangpin jingji de fazhan* 明清时期山东商品经济的发展 [The development of commodity economy in Shandong Province during the Ming and Qing dynasties]. Beijing: Zhongguo shehui kexue chubanshe, 1998.

Xu Xiuli 徐秀麗. "Jindai Hebei sheng nongdi guan'gai de fazhan" 近代河北省農地灌溉的發展 [The development of irrigation of farmland in Hebei Province in the modern period]. *Jindaishi yanjiu* 1993, no. 2: 37–54.

Yamane Yukio 山根幸夫. "Min Shin jidai Kahoku ni okeru teikishi" 明清時代華北における定期市 [Periodic markets in North China during the Ming and Qing periods]. *Shiron* 8 (1960): 493–504.

Yan, Yunxiang. "A Family Meal Without Food: Food Consumption During the 1959–61 Famine in a Chinese Village." Paper presented at the workshop, "Commensality and the Family Meal in China," Hong Kong, June 28–July 1, 1999.

Yang, Dali L. *Calamity and Reform in China: State, Rural Society, and Institutional Change since the Great Leap Forward*. Stanford, CA: Stanford University Press, 1996.

Yang Jingren 楊景仁. *Chouji bian* 籌濟編 [On planning relief]. 1823. Reprint, 1883 (1878 preface).

Yang Xuechen 杨学琛. "Qingdai qidi de xingzhi ji bianhua" 清代旗地的性质及变化 [The nature of bannerland in Qing times and its change]. *Lishi yanjiu* 1963, no. 3: 175–95.

Yates, Robin D. S. "War, Food Shortages, and Relief Measures in Early China." In *Hunger in History: Food Shortage, Poverty, and Deprivation*, ed. Lucille F. Newman, 147–77. Cambridge, MA: Basil Blackwell, 1990.

Yifudang 議覆檔 [Grand Council record book of discussion memorials]. First Historical Archives, Beijing.

Yin Junke 尹均科. "Qingdai Beijing de ziran zaihai" 清代北京的自然灾害 [Natural disasters in Qing-era Beijing]. *Huanjing bianqian yanjiu* 5 (1996): 89–110.

Yongding he xuzhi 永定河續志 [Supplement to the gazetteer of the Yongding River]. Comp. Zhu Qizhao 朱奇詔. 1882. 16 juan. Reprint, 3 vols., Taipei: Wenhai, 1970.

Yongding he zhi 永定河志 [Gazetteer of the Yongding River]. Comp. Li Fengheng 李逢亨. 1816. 32 juan. Reprint, 4 vols., Taipei: Wenhai, 1970. **YDHZ.**

Yongding he zhiben jihua 永定河治本計劃 [Basic plan for the Yongding River]. Ed. Huabei shuili weiyuanhui. 1933. 4 ce.

Zelin, Madeleine. *The Magistrate's Tael: Rationalizing Fiscal Reform in Eighteenth-Century Ch'ing China*. Berkeley: University of California Press, 1984.

Zeng Yeying 曾业英. "Riwei tongzhixia de Huabei nongcun jingji" 日伪统治下的华北农村经济 [North China rural economy under the Japanese occupation]. *Jindaishi yanjiu* 1998, no. 3: 84–144.

Zhang Gang 张岗, "Qingdai Zhili shangpin jingji fenxi" 清代直隶商品经济分析 [Analysis of the commercial economy of Qing-dynasty Zhili]. *Hebei shiyuan xuebao* 1985, no. 3: 99–104.

Zhang Kai 章楷, and Li Genpan 李根蟠. "Yumi zai woguo liangshi zuowuzhong diwei de bianhua" 玉米在我國糧食作物中地位的變化 [The changing role of corn in our national food supply]. *Nongye kaogu* 1983, no. 2: 94–99.

Zheng Yi. *Scarlet Memorial: Tales of Cannibalism in Modern China*. Ed. and trans. T. P. Sym. Boulder, CO: Westview Press, 1996.

Zhenji. See Fang Guancheng.

Zhili shangpin chenliesuo diyici shiye diaocha ji 直隸商品陳列所第一次實業調查計. Comp. Tianjin Zhili sheng shangpin chenliesuo 天津直隸省商品陳列所. 3 ce. Tianjin, 1917.

Zhongguo baike nianjian 1983 中国白科年鉴 [Annual encyclopedia of China]. Beijing: Zhongguo da baike quan shu, 1983.

Zhongguo changyong renkou shuju ji 中国常用人口数据集 [Basic data of China's population]. Comp. Yao Xinwu 姚新武 and Yin Hua 尹华. Beijing: Zhongguo renkou chubanshe, 1994.

Zhongguo gudai gengzhi tu 中国古代耕識圖 [Farming and weaving pictures in ancient China]. Ed. Wang Chaosheng 王潮生. Beijing: Zhongguo nongye chuban she, 1995.

Zhongguo jin wubainian hanlao fenbu tuji 中國近五百年旱澇分布圖集 [Maps of droughts and floods in China over the last five hundred years]. Ed. Zhongyang qixiangju, Qixiang kexue yanjiuyuan. Beijing: Ditu chubanshe, 1981.

Zhongguo jindai mianfen gongyeshi 中國近代麵粉工業史 [History of China's modern flour industry]. Ed. Shanghai shi liangshi ju 上海市糧食局 et al. Shanghai: Zhonghua shuju, 1987.

Zhongguo jindai nongyeshi ziliao 中国近代农业史资料 [Sources for modern China's agricultural history]. Vol. 1, 1840–1911, ed. Li Wenzhi 李文治. Vol. 2, 1912–27, and Vol. 3, 1927–37, ed. Zhang Youyi 章有义. Beijing: Sanlian shudian, 1957.

Zhongguo jindai shi da zaihuang 中國近代十大災荒 [The ten big famines of modern China]. Ed. Li Wenhai 李文海 et al. Shanghai: Shanghai renmin, 1994.

Zhongguo lishi dituji 中國歷史地圖集 [The historical atlas of China]. Ed. Tan Qixiang 譚其驤. Vol. 8. The Qing Dynasty Period. Shanghai: Ditu chubanshe, 1987.

Zhongguo renkou: Beijing fence 中國人口: 河北分冊 [China's population: Beijing]. Ed. Li Muzhen et al. Beijing: Zhongguo caizheng jingji chubanshe, 1987.

Zhongguo renkou: Hebei fence 中國人口: 河北分冊 [China's population: Hebei Province]. Ed. Wang Mingyuan et al. Beijing: Zhongguo caizheng jingji chubanshe, 1987.

Zhongguo renkou: Tianjin fence 中國人口: 天津分冊 [China's population: Tianjin]. Ed. Li Jingneng et al. Beijing: Zhongguo caizheng jingji chubanshe, 1987.

Zhongguo renkou tongji nianjian 1992 中国人口統計年鑒 1992 [Almanac of China's population statistics 1992]. Beijing: Zhongguo tongji chubanshe, 1992.

Zhongguo renkou tongji nianjian 1999 中国人口統計年鑒 1999 [Almanac of China's population statistics 1999]. Beijing: Zhongguo tongji chubanshe, 1999.

Zhongguo tongji nianjian 1999 中国統計年鑒 [Statistical yearbook of China 1999]. Beijing: Zhongguo tongji chubanshe, 1999.

Zhongguo zaiqing baogao 中国灾情报告 [Report on China's disasters]. Comp. Zhonghua renmin gongheguo minzheng bu 中华人民共和国民政部. Beijing: Zhongguo tongji chubanshe, 1996.

Zhongguo ziran dili 中國自然地理 [China's physical geography]. Ed. "Zhongguo ziran dili" section of Zhongguo kexueyuan. Beijing: Kexue chubanshe. 1982. Vol. 10, *Lishi ziran dili fence*, 152–82. Section on Hai he drafted by Huang Shengci 黄盛辞.

Zhu Kezhen 竺可楨 (also Chu Kochen, Coching Chu). *Zhu Kezhen wenji* 竺可楨文集 [Collected works of Zhu Kezhen]. Beijing: Kexue chubanshe, 1979.

Zweig, David. *Agrarian Radicalism in China, 1968–1981*. Cambridge, MA: Harvard University Press, 1989.

Gazetteers

This list includes only gazetteeers cited, not all those consulted. Characters can be found in Appendix 1. *FZ = fuzhi; XZ = xianzhi*

Baoding FZ. 1881/1886.

Ba xian xinzhi. 1934.

Cang XZ. 1933.

Changli XZ. 1865.

Changyuan XZ. 1810.

Cheng'an XZ. 1931.

Daming FZ. 1853.

Ding XZ. 1934.

Dingxing XZ. 1779.

Dingxing XZ. 1890.

(Qianlong) *Dong'an zhi.* 1749.
   Reprint in *Anci xian jiuzhi sizhong hekan.* 1936

Dong'guang XZ. 1888.

Gaocheng XZ. 1933.

Gaoyang XZ. 1933.

Gaoyi XZ. 1799.

Gaoyi XZ. 1933.
   Reprint, Taipei: Chengwen, 1968.

Guangping FZ. 1894.

Guangping XZ. 1939.
   Reprint, Taipei: Chengwen, 1968.

Guangzong XZ. 1933.

Handan XZ. 1933.

Hejian XZ. 1759.

Huailu XZ. 1881.

Huailu XZ. 1931.

Jiaohe XZ. 1916.

Jifu tongzhi. 1884.
   Reprint. Shijiazhuang: Hebei renmin chubanshe, 1984– . 37 vols. JFTZ.

Jifu tongzhi. 1884.
   Reprint. Shanghai: Shangwu, 1934. 8 vols.

Jinzhou zhi. 1925.

Jin Xianzhi liao. 1935.

Jing XZ. 1932.

Jinghai XZ. 1873.

Jingxing XZ. 1730.

Jingxing XZ liao. 1934.

Kaizhou zhi. 1882.

Liangxiang XZ. 1881/1889.

Liangxiang XZ. 1924.

Liangxiang xian shiqing. 1939.

Lingshou XZ. 1686.

Lingshou XZ. 1873.

Lingyu XZ. 1929

Luan XZ. 1938.

Luancheng XZ. 1846.

Luancheng XZ. 1872.

Luanzhou zhi. 1898.

Lulong XZ. 1931.

Nangong XZ. 1673.

Nangong XZ. 1830.

Nanpi XZ. 1932.

Ping'gu XZ. 1934.

Pingshan XZ. 1854.

Pingshan XZ. 1898.

Pingshan XZ liaoji. 1931.

Pingxiang XZ. 1886.

Qinghe XZ. 1933.

Qingyuan XZ. 1873.

Qingyun XZ. 1854.

Sanhe XZ. 1928.

Sanhe xian xinzhi. 1935.

Shenzhou fengtu ji. 1900.

Shulu wuzhi hekan. 1937.
  Includes 1671, 1762, 1798, *Jiaqing Shulu
  XZ* 1862–74, and 1906.

Shuntian FZ. 1885.

Shunyi XZ. 1933.

Tang XZ. 1878.

Tangshan XZ. 1881.

Tianjin FZ. 1898.

(Xu) Tianjin XZ. 1870.

Wan XZ. 1934.

Wangdu XZ. 1904.

Wangdu XZ. 1934.

[Hebei] *Wanping xian shiqing diaocha.* 1939.

Wei XZ. 1925.

Wen'an XZ. 1922.

Wuji (Xu) XZ. 1893.

Xian XZ. 1925.

Xianghe XZ. 1675.

Xianghe XZ. 1936.

Xiaoning XZ. 1756.

Xincheng XZ. 1935.

Xingtai XZ. 1905.

Xingtang xian xin zhi. 1763.

Xinhe XZ. 1928.

Xinle XZ. (Chongxiu Xinle XZ). 1885.
  Reprint 1939, and Taipei: Chengwen,
  1968.

Xiong xian xiangtuzhi. 1905.

Xiong xian xinzhi. 1930.

Xuanhua XZ. 1922.

Yanshan XZ. 1868.

Yongnian XZ. 1877.

Yongping FZ. 1774.

Yongqing XZ. 1779/1813.

(Xu) Yongqing XZ. 1874.

Yuanshi XZ. 1884.

Yuanshi XZ. 1931.

Yutian XZ. 1884.

Zaoqiang XZ. 1803.

Zaoqiang XZ. 1876.

Zaoqiang XZ liao. 1931.

Zhaozhou zhi. 1897.

Zhengding FZ. 1762.

Zhengding XZ. 1874.

Zhuozhou zhi. 1765.

Zhuozhou zhi. 1936.

Zunhua zhilizhou tongzhi. 1886.

Index

509

Beijing, 7, 98, 144–65, 238, 362; rainfall and climate, 24f, 27f, 33; diet, 90f, 93,108–9; history, 144–46; population, 146; gendarmerie, 147, 161–62; *pingtiao*, 148, 155–59, 230; grain prices, 149–50; soup kitchens, 158–61, 228, 238, 253, 266, 272; refugees in, 252, 263, 266, 275; private charitable efforts, 279–80; standard of living in 1920s, 314. *See also* Monetary crisis; *Pingtiao*; Retail shops; Soup kitchens

Beijing Agricultural University, 369
Bei River, 16
Bei Yunhe, 44, 56, 59
Bengal famine, 8, 133, 384
Bernstein, Thomas, 364
"Big cash," 266
Biodiversity, 102
Birth control policy, *see* One-child policy; Population policy
Black beans, 96–97
Black Death, 5
Black soil, 104
Board of Revenue, 59, 64, 78f, 97, 147; on *pingtiao* at Beijing, 153–58 *passim*; on granary regulations, 167, 176, 178, 183, 186, 192; on famine relief regulations, 221–29 *passim*; on tax remissions, 230–32; on shelters, 235; on extra funding, 263, 269, 271, 278

Board of Works, 54, 56, 64
Boserup, Ester, 75
Bouillard, G., 293
Boxer Uprising, 31, 282
Boxiang County, 100
Brandt, Loren, 197, 219, 331
Braudel, Ferdinand, 37
Bray, Francesca, 94, 103
British and French attack on Beijing, 266
Brown, Lester R., 374f
Buck, John Lossing, 34, 86, 92f, 101f, 310–11, 315
Buckwheat, 91, 93, 107, 109
Buddha's soil (*guanyin tu*), 361

Cadres, 362, 372
Campaigns, *see under* River conservancy
Cang County, 325
Cannibalism, 34ff, 273–74, 300, 358–59, 361; as metaphor, 378
Cao Cao, 15, 18
Carrots, 325, 330
Cash crops, 93, 99, 100. *See also* Commercialized agriculture
"Cathedral Cutting," 294
Chaff, see *Kang*
Chamber of Commerce, Tianjin, 287

Chang, Eileen, 377
Changhuan County, 258, 260
Changli County, 103
Changlu salt district, 79
Changlu salt merchants, 63, 64, 269
Chao-Bai River, 16
Charity granary, 168, 180–85; Fang Guancheng's charity granary plan, 180–82; revival in Jiaqing and Daoguang periods, 182–83; revival in Guangxu period, 184–85
Chayanov, 194
Chen Chau-nan, 141
Chen Dashou, 192
Chen Dawen, 57, 59, 251–52
Chengde Prefecture (and City), 20, 79; relief, 227
Cheng Hanzhang, 63
Chen Hongmou, 51, 65, 95, 180, 192, 221, 248
Chen Yi, 62, 65
Chi Zihua, 282
Chiang Kai-shek, 283, 304, 306
Chihli River Commission, 294
Children, *see* Women and children
China Famine Relief Fund, 276
China International Famine Relief Commission (CIFRC), 285, 294, 302–6, 308; dispute with American Red Cross, 305–6
Chinese Communist Party and hunger, 4, 342; strategy in North China, 336–39 *passim*
Chinese Red Cross Society, 287, 290
Cholera, 31, 62, 159, 264
Chouzhenju (Bureau for Raising Famine Relief Contributions), 276, 279
CIFRC, *see* China International Famine Relief Commission
"Civil society," 287
Civil war, 308
Class struggle, concept of, 311
Climate: in Hai River Basin, 24–27; and history, 37. *See also* Historical climate; Rainfall
Coefficient of variation, 198–200
Cohen, Paul, 282
Collectivization, 341f, 354
"Comfort" (*fu*), instead of relief, 252, 254, 272, 278, 361
Commercialized agriculture, 312f, 321–32 *passim*, 340, 354
Communes, 357
Community granary, 167f, 181–82
Contract system, *see* Household responsibility system
Contributions: for river conservancy, 58f, 62f; from south, 66; to famine relief, by merchants, 251, 260; by local gentry, 261; from the south, 269,